Class C or D

Unspecified Bit Rate (UBR)

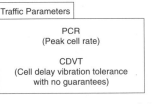

Traffic Parameters
PCR (Peak cell rate)
CDVT (Cell delay vibration tolerance with no guarantees)

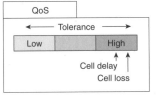

QoS — Tolerance (Low / High) — Cell delay / Cell loss

Data:
E-mail
File transfer
Library browsing
Remote terminal access

Class C or D

Available Bit Rate (ABR)

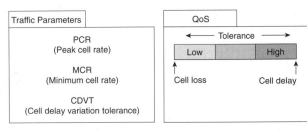

Traffic Parameters
PCR (Peak cell rate)
MCR (Minimum cell rate)
CDVT (Cell delay variation tolerance)

QoS — Tolerance (Low / High) — Cell loss / Cell delay

Data:
Critical data transfer (defense information)
NFS

Class C

Guaranteed Frame Rate (GFR)

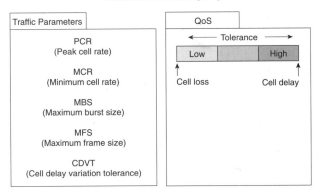

Traffic Parameters
PCR (Peak cell rate)
MCR (Minimum cell rate)
MBS (Maximum burst size)
MFS (Maximum frame size)
CDVT (Cell delay variation tolerance)

QoS — Tolerance (Low / High) — Cell loss / Cell delay

Data:
File transfer

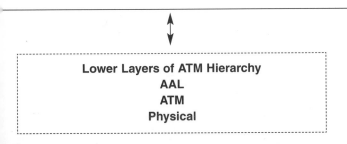

Lower Layers of ATM Hierarchy
AAL
ATM
Physical

Cisco ATM Solutions

Galina Diker Pildush, CCIE #3176, CCSI

Cisco Press

Cisco Press
201 West 103rd Street
Indianapolis, IN 46290 USA

Cisco ATM Solutions

Galina Diker Pildush

Copyright© 2000 Cisco Systems, Inc.

Published by:
Cisco Press
201 West 103rd Street
Indianapolis, IN 46290 USA

Printed in the United States of America 3 4 5 6 7 8 9 0

Third Printing June 2002

Library of Congress Cataloging-in-Publication Number: 99-67925

ISBN: 1-57870-213-5

Warning and Disclaimer

This book is designed to provide information about ATM Solutions for Cisco product-based networks. Every effort has been made to make this book as complete and as accurate as possible, but no warranty or fitness is implied.

The information is provided on an "as is" basis. The author, Cisco Press, and Cisco Systems, Inc., shall have neither liability nor responsibility to any person or entity with respect to any loss or damages arising from the information contained in this book or from the use of the discs or programs that may accompany it.

The opinions expressed in this book belong to the author and are not necessarily those of Cisco Systems, Inc.

Feedback Information

At Cisco Press, our goal is to create in-depth technical books of the highest quality and value. Each book is crafted with care and precision, undergoing rigorous development that involves the unique expertise of members from the professional technical community.

Readers' feedback is a natural continuation of this process. If you have any comments regarding how we could improve the quality of this book, or otherwise alter it to better suit your needs, you can contact us through e-mail at feedback@ciscopress.com. Please make sure to include the book title and ISBN in your message.

We greatly appreciate your assistance.

Trademark Acknowledgments

All terms mentioned in this book that are known to be trademarks or service marks have been appropriately capitalized. Cisco Press or Cisco Systems, Inc., cannot attest to the accuracy of this information. Use of a term in this book should not be regarded as affecting the validity of any trademark or service mark.

Publisher	John Wait
Editor-In-Chief	John Kane
Cisco Systems Program Management	Michael Hakkert
	Tom Geitner
Managing Editor	Patrick Kanouse
Acquisitions Editor	Brett Bartow
Development Editor	Christopher Cleveland
Copy Editor	Theresa Wehrle
Technical Editors	Don Forbes, Don Sheppard, Preston White
Team Coordinator	Amy Lewis
Book Designer	Gina Rexrode
Cover Designer	Louisa Klucznik
Compositor	Steve Gifford
Indexer	Brad Herriman

CISCO SYSTEMS

Corporate Headquarters
Cisco Systems, Inc.
170 West Tasman Drive
San Jose, CA 95134-1706
USA
http://www.cisco.com
Tel: 408 526-4000
     800 553-NETS (6387)
Fax: 408 526-4100

European Headquarters
Cisco Systems Europe s.a.r.l.
Parc Evolic, Batiment L1/L2
16 Avenue du Quebec
Villebon, BP 706
91961 Courtaboeuf Cedex
France
http://www-europe.cisco.com
Tel: 33 1 69 18 61 00
Fax: 33 1 69 28 83 26

**Americas
Headquarters**
Cisco Systems, Inc.
170 West Tasman Drive
San Jose, CA 95134-1706
USA
http://www.cisco.com
Tel: 408 526-7660
Fax: 408 527-0883

Asia Headquarters
Nihon Cisco Systems K.K.
Fuji Building, 9th Floor
3-2-3 Marunouchi
Chiyoda-ku, Tokyo 100
Japan
http://www.cisco.com
Tel: 81 3 5219 6250
Fax: 81 3 5219 6001

Cisco Systems has more than 200 offices in the following countries. Addresses, phone numbers, and fax numbers are listed on the Cisco Connection Online Web site at http://www.cisco.com/offices.

Argentina • Australia • Austria • Belgium • Brazil • Canada • Chile • China • Colombia • Costa Rica • Croatia • Czech Republic • Denmark • Dubai, UAE Finland • France • Germany • Greece • Hong Kong • Hungary • India • Indonesia • Ireland • Israel • Italy • Japan • Korea • Luxembourg • Malaysia Mexico • The Netherlands • New Zealand • Norway • Peru • Philippines • Poland • Portugal • Puerto Rico • Romania • Russia • Saudi Arabia • Singapore Slovakia • Slovenia • South Africa • Spain • Sweden • Switzerland • Taiwan • Thailand • Turkey • Ukraine • United Kingdom • United States • Venezuela

About the Author

Galina Diker Pildush, CCIE #3176, CCSI, is the President and a Senior Consultant at Advanced Communications Experts (ACE), Inc. She provides training and course development for Global Knowledge Network, Inc., a leading Cisco Training partner in the world. After earning her M.Sc. in Computer Science, she worked for 18 years for major worldwide corporations in the areas of internetwork design, architecture, network optimization, implementation, and project management. She has been an academic teacher at York University, teaching Computer Science, Data Communications, and Computer Network courses. Gaining extensive technical experience in internetworking and the Cisco-line of products, she reached her Routing and Switching CCIE certification in 1997. Currently, Galina holds a CCIE in ATM and LAN Switching. Deploying her passion for teaching, Galina teaches a variety of Cisco courses. Upon achieving her CCIE, Galina decided to dedicate the majority of her professional carrier to training and mentoring CCIE candidates by taking on a role of a technical director for the two very successful CCIE preparation programs—NetGun Academy and CCIE BootCamp at Global Knowledge Network, Inc. Areas of interest and specialization are ATM, internetwork design and optimization, and Voice over IP. Besides the demanding professional work, Galina, her husband, their two children, and their dog, who is a Canadian Champion, enjoy spending those rare moments together in travels, skiing, and cycling.

About the Technical Reviewers

Donald Forbes, CCIE #2191, is a Network Support Specialist with Compaq and holds a Computer Science Certificate from Université Laval in Québec City. Don has worked in the planning, installing, and debugging of multivendor computer LAN and WAN networks for the last 20 years.

Donald Sheppard, P.Eng., is a Principal Consultant for Consensus Consulting Services in Toronto. He earned a Bachelor of Engineering at McGill University and a Masters in Applied Science at the University of Toronto. Don has more than 25 years experience as a telecommunications user and consultant. He was involved in the development of ISO/OSI standards and has developed and taught several networking courses. His current areas of interest include QoS and optical networking.

Preston White is President of Quality & Technology, Inc., a communications and networking consulting company based in Marietta, GA. Preston has more than 30 years of experience in datacom and telecom networks, infrastructure, and implementation. Preston is a retired Professor of Electrical and Computer Engineering and has experience as an author and an editor of textbooks and articles in various areas of electrical engineering, networking, and communications.

Dedication

To my loving and very special parents, who taught me that nothing is impossible; to my dear and best friend, my husband Arkady, who is always there for me with his precious beliefs and encouragements; to my bright and handsome sons, the angels of my life, David and Joseph, for their love, understanding, and patience.

Acknowledgments

This book would not have been possible without the help, advice, and encouragements from many people. First, I want to express my sincere thanks to the technical reviewers of the book: Christopher Cleveland, Donald Sheppard, Preston White, and Donald Forbes. Your thorough comments, suggestions, critics and complements helped tremendously. Special thanks to Harold Nott, Technical Analyst of Information Services for London (Canada) Health Sciences Centre for sharing the deployment of ATM technology at the Centre, the diagram of which is in the book. My sincere thanks to Brett Bartow and Chris Cleveland for continuous encouragement, keeping me on track for completing this book and getting it published. Many thanks to Richard Gordon, Vice President and Managing Director at Global Knowledge Network (Canada), Inc., who always persistently believes in me. Special thanks to all my students, who continuously challenge me and remind me that the more you know, the more you know that you do not know. Thanks to all my colleagues and associates, especially Eric Dragowski and Tracy Conforti, for being there when I needed you most. Thanks to GeoTrain Corporation (now Global Knowledge Network [Canada], Inc.) for allowing me to share the wonderful ATM laboratory exercises in the book. Also, my very special thanks to my husband Arkady, my sons, David and Joseph, and my parents. Their support, encouragement, and understanding gave me strength in completing the book.

Contents at a Glance

Contents

Introduction

"There can be no knowledge without emotion. We may be aware of a truth, yet until we have felt its force, it is not ours. To the cognition of the brain must be added the experience of the soul."—Arnold Bennett (1867–1931)

"If you aren't going all the way, why go at all?"—Joe Namath (1943–)

"Good humor and enthusiasm should be the sunshine ahead that will keep that shadow behind."—Charles Field (1836–1912)

"I learned that if you want to make it bad enough, no matter how bad it is, you can make it."—Gale Sayers (1943–)

"Success, achievement of some sort, is a series of steps consisting of failures so long as one does not look back and learns from mistakes."—Galina Diker Pildush

Asynchronous Transfer Mode (ATM) is a subject that is well spread out and yet not completely understood. As with anything, it can be very simple and yet complex. ATM has been talked about and written about for the last several years. The good and bad or "pros" and "cons" of the technology, have been pointed out to me time and time again, and yet, it still fascinates me. So often, when teaching Cisco ATM classes, I meet people who hear little concepts here and there and make up an opinion about the subject without being fully "armed." The interesting part is that, after the five days of training, the light bulbs flash, which is extremely gratifying to see.

Cisco introduced the ATM component into their Cisco Certified Internetwork Expert (CCIE) certification, the most prestigious and difficult networking designation to achieve of all certifications that I've seen. This book helps you prepare for the exam.

Who Should Read This Book?

The audience for this book is any network designer, administrator, or engineer who needs to fully understand the ATM technology and is in a position to design and apply the ATM technology in the networks. The fact that the first part of the book focuses on the overall ATM technology, makes the book applicable to any ATM platform.

The book is targeted not only at engineers trying to obtain their CCIE statuses, but also at engineers who need to advance their current knowledge of ATM. You could be a beginner, an intermediate, or an advanced level professional and still benefit from advancing your ATM knowledge or from a structured review of the material and the practical exercises.

If you are "a beginner" who has some basic networking knowledge, you can learn the basic ATM concepts and internetworking methods applicable to ATM.

If you are an intermediate-level networking professional who has experience with switching and routing, you can broaden your horizons with ATM technology to enhance your overall scope within the networking world and allow you to evaluate ATM and other technologies in full independence.

If you are an experienced networking expert who has extensive internetworking background, you can re-affirm the position of ATM in the networking world and review the previously and newly approved ATM specifications that enable ATM to achieve previously unachievable goals.

Objectives

The ultimate goal of the book is to fully "arm" you with the principles and "know how" of the ATM technology and its internetworking methods. Beyond obtaining enough knowledge for the CCIE lab itself, the book provides you with enough foundation on the ATM subject that enables you to apply it to any vendor.

Each chapter has a series of questions that allow you to reinforce the main ideas and goals. The book takes you from a review and an in-depth discussion of ATM theory into the implementation of ATM internetworking methods and the ATM network itself. The laboratory exercises in Chapters 9, 10, 11, and 13 reinforce your theoretical knowledge gained from the book and allow you to put it into practice.

Approach

The main approach of the book is to lay out a solid ATM theory foundation first. After you lay the solid foundation, you can build a pyramid of any height. Next, the book takes you into various implementation methods of ATM internetworking from the edge device perspective. Then you walk into various methods of implementing the cloud itself, reinforced by a series of extensive laboratory exercises that reinforce all the theory and the practices laid out in the book.

Part I, "ATM Technology," reviews and walks through the basics of ATM, ATM switching, cell structure, the ATM Adaptation layer (AAL), various types of AALs, ATM signaling (when it is used), differences between different types of ATM virtual connections, and internetworking methods over ATM. Part I can benefit any reader who is curious enough to ask such questions as, "What is ATM?", "When should you consider implementing it?", and "What are the layers of the ATM model and what do they do for a living?" You can see an examination of the model from the bottom layer up. Then you dive into the methods of interacting with ATM. How does IP do it? What about other protocols, such as IPX and AppleTalk, for example? What about other services, such as Frame Relay, voice, and video? The book also elaborates on ATM specifications that have been approved recently .

Part II, "Cisco ATM Edge Device Interfaces and Implementations," concentrates on Cisco's implementation of ATM networks. The approach here is to provide implementation examples of various interconnections via ATM networks. These include implementations of multiprotocol encapsulations over ATM, Classical IP, LANE, and MPOA.

Part III, "ATM Cloud: LightStream 1010 ATM Switch," brings you inside the ATM cloud implementation using LightStream 1010 as an example. You encounter implementation examples of various virtual connection types of the ATM network itself.

Organization

The main principle of the flow of the material is to build a solid foundation of the ATM technology prior to introducing any "implementation" components. Then the book approaches Cisco's methods of implementing ATM at the edges of the ATM networks. Finally, the book reaches Cisco's implementation of the ATM cloud itself using LightStream 1010 switches as examples.

The book is divided into three major parts, each of which consists of multiple chapters:

- Part I provides an in-depth discussion of the ATM technology, starting with an introduction into ATM and finishing with MPOA. This part of the book consists of six chapters:

  — Chapter 1, "ATM Introduction," discusses what ATM is, how it compares to other technologies, and when to deploy it.

— Chapter 2, "ATM Reference Model: Lower Layers," discusses physical, ATM, and ATM Adaptation layers. It presents various physical-layer framing formats; ATM cell structure and the purpose of its every field; and the meaning of a variety of AALs and why they are there, including AAL2, which was recently approved.

— Chapter 3, "ATM Reference Model: Higher Layers," brings you to the higher layers of the stack. This chapter discusses various virtual circuit connections and what the differences and the similarities are. This chapter also covers ATM signaling; ATM interworking methods, such as Frame Relay and SMDS; and ATM internetworking methods of other protocols, such as RFC 2684, RFC 2225, LANE, and MPOA.

— Chapter 4, "ATM Traffic and Network Management," discusses the heart of ATM—traffic management and congestion control. How can and does ATM provide its well-known QoS? What are the methods and the techniques behind it? This chapter answers these questions and more. The chapter discusses the ATM dynamic routing protocol, PNNI1, in great detail as well.

— Chapter 5, "LAN Emulation (LANE)," discusses not only LANEv1, but also LANEv2, the differences and similarities between them.

— Chapter 6, "Multiprotocol over ATM (MPOA)," unbundles the intricacies of the MPOA architecture and its components.

• Part II elaborates on the functionality and the implementation of ATM-associated features by Cisco ATM edge devices. It consists of five chapters:

— Chapter 7, "ATM Interface Processor (AIP), Port Adapter (PA), and Network Port Module (NPM) Features and Functions," discusses the types of interfaces used by the Cisco product line to interface ATM networks. The chapter also addresses the methods and the techniques that these devices utilize to enable such vital functions as traffic shaping and traffic management.

— Chapter 8, "Circuit Emulation Service ATM Connectivity and Summary of Cisco ATM Edge Devices," elaborates on other Cisco ATM connectivity, such as CES and Cisco's capability to interconnect voice to the ATM networks.

— Chapter 9, "Multiprotocol Encapsulation (RFC 2684), Classical IP and ARP over ATM (RFC 2225), and NHRP Implementation," provides techniques and methods of ATM internetworking using Cisco IOS Software. Examples are provided for multiprotocol implementation, Classical IP, and multiple LISs implementation with cut-through routing utilizing NHRP.

— Chapter 10, "LANE Implementation," elaborates on LANE implementation in depth. This chapter provides implementation examples of LANE, redundancy, using Cisco's SSRP, and LANE design considerations.

— Chapter 11, "MPOA Implementation," provides MPOA implementation, elaborating on MPOA and LANE interdependency, MPC and MPS operation review and implementation.

• Part III elaborates on the implementation of the ATM cloud itself. It consists of two chapters that provide an overview of Cisco's campus ATM switch, the LightStream 1010, which is being migrated into Cisco's 8500 platform:

— Chapter 12, "LightStream 1010 Features and Functions," discusses the hardware features of the platform and presents its functionality and software features, including traffic management and congestion control during the connection setup and during the data flow phases.

— Chapter 13, "LightStream 1010 Configuration," presents various examples of PVC, PVP, SVC, and Soft VC creations. It elaborates on IISP and PNNI implementations, providing examples of single and multiple layers of ATM network hierarchy.

The book has four appendixes and a Glossary of ATM terms. Appendix A presents a table of all ATM Forum–approved specifications and date of their approval. Appendix B lists and defines the ATM Forum pending approval specifications. Appendix C provides the solutions to the 16 laboratory exercises of ATM implementation presented in Chapters 9, 10, 11, and 13. The labs start off with something simple, like a PVC method of ATM internetworking using RFC 2684, and go into much more complex implementation exercises, such as VP tunneling, Soft VCs, LANE, and MPOA. The exercises include an implementation of the ATM edge devices and the ATM cloud itself. Appendix D presents the answers to the Review Questions sections presented at the end of each chapter, which are designed to test your accumulated knowledge after reading the chapters in question.

Figure Icons Used in This Book

Throughout the book, you will see the following icons used for networking devices:

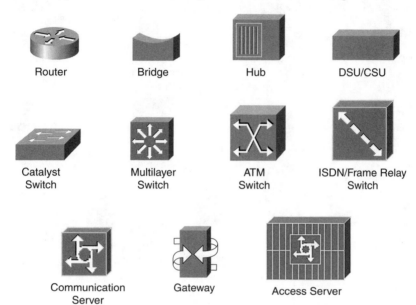

Router Bridge Hub DSU/CSU

Catalyst Switch Multilayer Switch ATM Switch ISDN/Frame Relay Switch

Communication Server Gateway Access Server

Throughout the book, you will see the following icons used for peripherals and other devices.

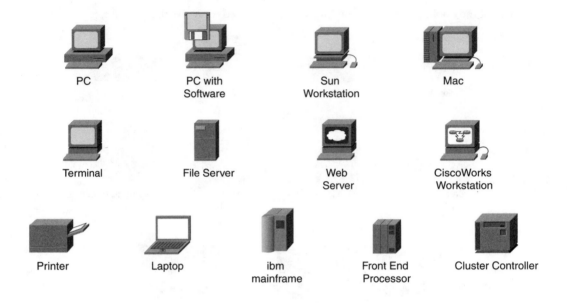

PC   PC with Software   Sun Workstation   Mac

Terminal   File Server   Web Server   CiscoWorks Workstation

Printer   Laptop   ibm mainframe   Front End Processor   Cluster Controller

Throughout the book, you will see the following icons used for networks and network connections.

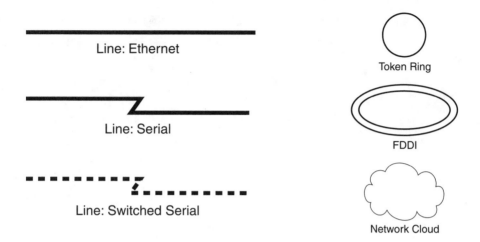

Command Syntax Conventions

The conventions used to present command syntax in this book are the same conventions used in the IOS Command Reference. The Command Reference describes these conventions as follows:

- Vertical bars, I, separate alternative, mutually exclusive elements.
- Square brackets, [ ], indicate optional elements.
- Braces, { }, indicate a required choice.
- Braces within brackets, [{ }], indicate a required choice within an optional element.
- **Boldface** indicates commands and keywords that you enter literally as shown. In actual configuration examples and output (not general command syntax), boldface indicates commands that the user manually inputs (such as the **show** command).
- *Italics* indicate arguments for which you supply actual values.

"Any sufficiently advanced technology is indistinguishable from magic."—Arthur C.Clarke (1917–)

"Excellence is never an accident."—Jerold Panas (1928–)

"Your dream might change our planet."—Edward Lindaman (1920–1982)

"The future belongs to those who believe in the beauty of their dreams."—Eleanor Roosevelt (1884–1962)

ATM Technology

This part defines the Asynchronous Transfer Mode (ATM) technology and concepts. What is ATM? Why would you deploy ATM? What is ATM's role in internetworking? How does it compare with the Open System Interconnection (OSI) reference model? Usually, comparison with the OSI reference model is a very helpful exercise; it allows you to understand the functionality of the technology better. Although ATM is tricky to align with the OSI model, it is still a helpful exercise to do.

This part takes you from the physical layer to the higher layers of the ATM reference model, creating a clear comprehension of the ATM technology. The chapters in this part of the book include

- Chapter 1, "ATM Introduction," introduces you to ATM technology, compares it with technologies/solutions, pushing you to truly evaluate your requirements and traffic types.

- Chapter 2, "ATM Reference Model: Lower Layers," opens your journey into ATM technology with the introduction to the lower layers of the protocol stack—Physical, ATM, and ATM Adaptation layers.

- Chapter 3, "ATM Reference Model: Higher Layers," continues your journey into ATM technology with a close look at upper ATM layers, such as ATM signaling, ILMI, and various ATM interworking and internetworking methods with existing technologies and protocols.

- Chapter 4, "ATM Traffic and Network Management," takes you into the heart of ATM networks, elaborating on preventive measurements of ATM traffic management and control, QoS signaling, and PNNI routing.

- Chapter 5, "LAN Emulation (LANE)," elaborates on LAN emulation across ATM clouds.

- Chapter 6, "Multiprotocol over ATM (MPOA)," elaborates on ATM's ability to handle multiple Layer 3 protocols natively over ATM.

"Our beliefs as well as our actions must come from the heart, for in our hearts the true wisdom that frees us and the path of compassion are inseparable"—Bstan'dzin-rgya-mtsho (1935–)

"Too low they build who build beneath the stars"—Edward Young (1683–1765)

This chapter addresses the following topics:

- What Is ATM?
- Why ATM?
- Role of ATM in Internetworks
- ATM, POS, DWDM, and Gigabit Ethernet
- TDM Network Migration
- ATM Switch Types
- ATM Network Interfaces
- ATM Standards

After reading this chapter, you will be able to understand the role of ATM in internetworks; define the various types of ATM switches and the roles they play in an ATM network; compare POS, ATM, and Gigabit Ethernet technologies; and identify the two major bodies driving ATM standardization.

CHAPTER 1

ATM Introduction

For many years, Asynchronous Transfer Mode (ATM) has been generally regarded as the ultimate technology for integrating voice, data, and video services. Companies have deployed ATM in both LANs and WANs. There have been a lot of promises with ATM—such as Quality of Service (QoS) and dynamic operation with virtual circuits (VCs). Earlier deployments of ATM were based on static ATM configurations, without any use of QoS. Today, ATM is more than ready. The User-Network Interface (UNI) 4.0 specification, which includes dynamic QoS, and the PNNI1 specification, which allows dynamic switched virtual circuit (SVC) setup, have been available since 1996. You will have the pleasure of learning about PNNI1 and its functionality later in Chapter 4, "ATM Traffic and Network Management." Furthermore, recent specification releases of AAL2 allow ATM to handle compressed voice, resulting in the most efficient bandwidth utilization.

NOTE	Bandwidth is like candy given to a small child—you give the child one piece of candy and he wants a pound. You provide 10 Mbps of bandwidth today, tomorrow people will ask for 1 Gbps.

What Is ATM?

ATM is based on the Broadband Integrated Services Digital Network (BISDN) standards, which were designed to provide integrated services to the user at high speeds. Its predecessor—Narrowband ISDN—was the basis for the Frame Relay services. The unique aspect of ATM is that it handles all forms of traffic (regardless of its origin—a human voice, a video CODEC, or a computer), as illustrated in Figure 1-1.

Figure 1-1   *ATM Basics Overview*

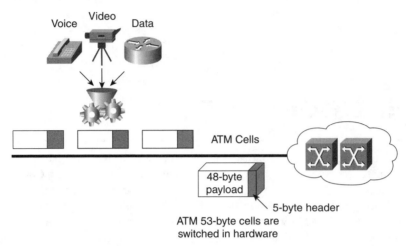

A transmission unit, called a *cell,* is a fixed format consisting of 53 bytes (comprised of a 48-byte payload and a 5-byte header). The cell header, despite being only 5 bytes, contains enough information to allow cells to be forwarded to the right destinations or simply to throw them away and to identify the cell as part of the "management type" cell or as another piece of information such as signaling, the payload itself, or a routing keepalive to be sent. Amazing, isn't it?

Another key aspect of ATM is that it supports QoS. This means that time-sensitive information (I'll call it interchangeable payload) can be sent ahead of something that can wait. Imagine talking on the phone from New York to Tokyo. You expect to have a non-disruptive, clear phone call, right? Well, when you integrate voice with data communications, which might include long file transfers, it is important to send voice first—file transfer can wait! Using cell-based ATM technology, which guarantees to never overpower any link with long packets, you can achieve this and more. Additionally, ATM allows a consistent jitter performance over time, resulting in minimized jitter. *Jitter* is a variable, interpacket timing caused by the network that a packet traverses.

What is more interesting is that ATM is connection-oriented. This implies that before the actual information can be sent, the connection from the source to the destination must be established. While the connection is getting established, a request for a specific QoS can be sent. Using a routing protocol, signaling information is routed through the ATM cloud, establishing an SVC with guaranteed QoS.

NOTE   Since its conception, ATM has been capable of setting up various types of VCs—permanent virtual circuits (PVCs), switched virtual circuits (SVCs), and a variation of both (Soft PVCs). This is a very interesting phenomenon. Until recently, Frame Relay technology, which has been in use longer than ATM, for example, offered only one type of VC connection—PVC. A PVC is defined statically by the network administrator. An SVC, on the other hand, is dynamically established and is torn down upon the completion of transmission or shortly thereafter. SVCs allow the network to dynamically change paths within itself if there are changes to the network topology, while PVCs do not have such flexibility. Soft PVCs provide you with the flexibility of the SVC-based ATM network and a perception of PVC-based connectivity to the ATM network.

You are here for a journey of discovering how all these wonders do happen and to fully appreciate the effectiveness and brilliance of the algorithms and technology involved.

Why ATM?

Many IS department personnel, network architects, and designers have asked this question over the last few years. ATM has been a dream come true since its conception. The idea of handling any type of payload—interactive, real-time, batch, text, video, data, or voice—using the same devices and media has been in people's minds for years. ATM makes it possible. ATM, being truly a layer and a quarter (1.25, as referred to in Figure 1-2) of the OSI reference model, allows this integration to occur. An added advantage is that ATM is a worldwide recognized standard.

Figure 1-2   *ATM Model Versus OSI Reference Model*

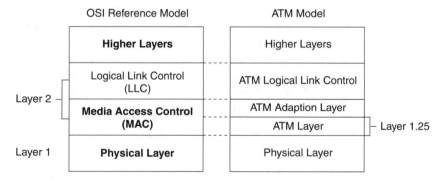

Some companies install ATM because it provides the fastest method of sending data, just data and nothing more, from one location to another. Other companies mold the ATM solution to integrate voice and data networks, including video, and yet other companies use

ATM to extend their LANs. The question is not only "Why ATM?", but also "Where to apply ATM?" Does it belong to the LANs or to the WANs, or metropolitan-area networks (MANs), or all of them? Let's recall that a LAN is a collection of computers and other related devices, such as printers, connected together on the premises within a limited geographic area, like a building or a campus. MANs are quite similar to LANs, with the exception of larger distances within a network. WANs, on the other hand, are the interconnectivity of various networks across large distances using long distance carrier services, such as Frame Relay, ISDN, and so on.

Some people shy away from ATM, thinking it is too complex, while others deploy it with great success. The fact is that you can apply ATM in both WANs and LANs. And this can provide for interconnectivity of networks around the globe.

Case Studies: ATM Implementation

One of the great success stories of ATM implementation is its deployment at a Canadian hospital in London, Ontario. ATM connects several buildings together, carrying voice and data. Any emergency case is helped within a matter of seconds. Figure 1-3 illustrates the hospital's topology. The core backbone of the network consists of five LightStream 1010 ATM switches spanning via 622 Mbps. Three additional switches extend the network further via 155 Mbps. Voice PBXs are attached directly to the LightStream 1010, allowing the complete integration of voice and data for the hospital. Understanding voice natively, ATM guarantees its QoS without any problems.

Another example of a successful ATM implementation is the Moscow (Russia) Metro. More than 50 LightStream 1010 (L1010) switches have been used to automate the entire metro system in Moscow, one of the oldest and most beautiful metro systems in the world. This system is an example of ATM deployment just for data.

Other examples of ATM deployment in Russia include the current creation of the MICEX interbanking networking system and Kostroma-energo multiservice network. The MICEX system stretches the LightStream 1010 deployment within a Moscow complex of three buildings. The buildings accommodate trading facilities and other office positions. The MICEX networking infrastructure carries data between the buildings of the complex. The Kostroma-energo multiservice network stretches for 370 km carrying voice and data services at 155 Mbps and 622 Mbps.

Figure 1-3 *London (Ontario) Hospital Core Network Topology*

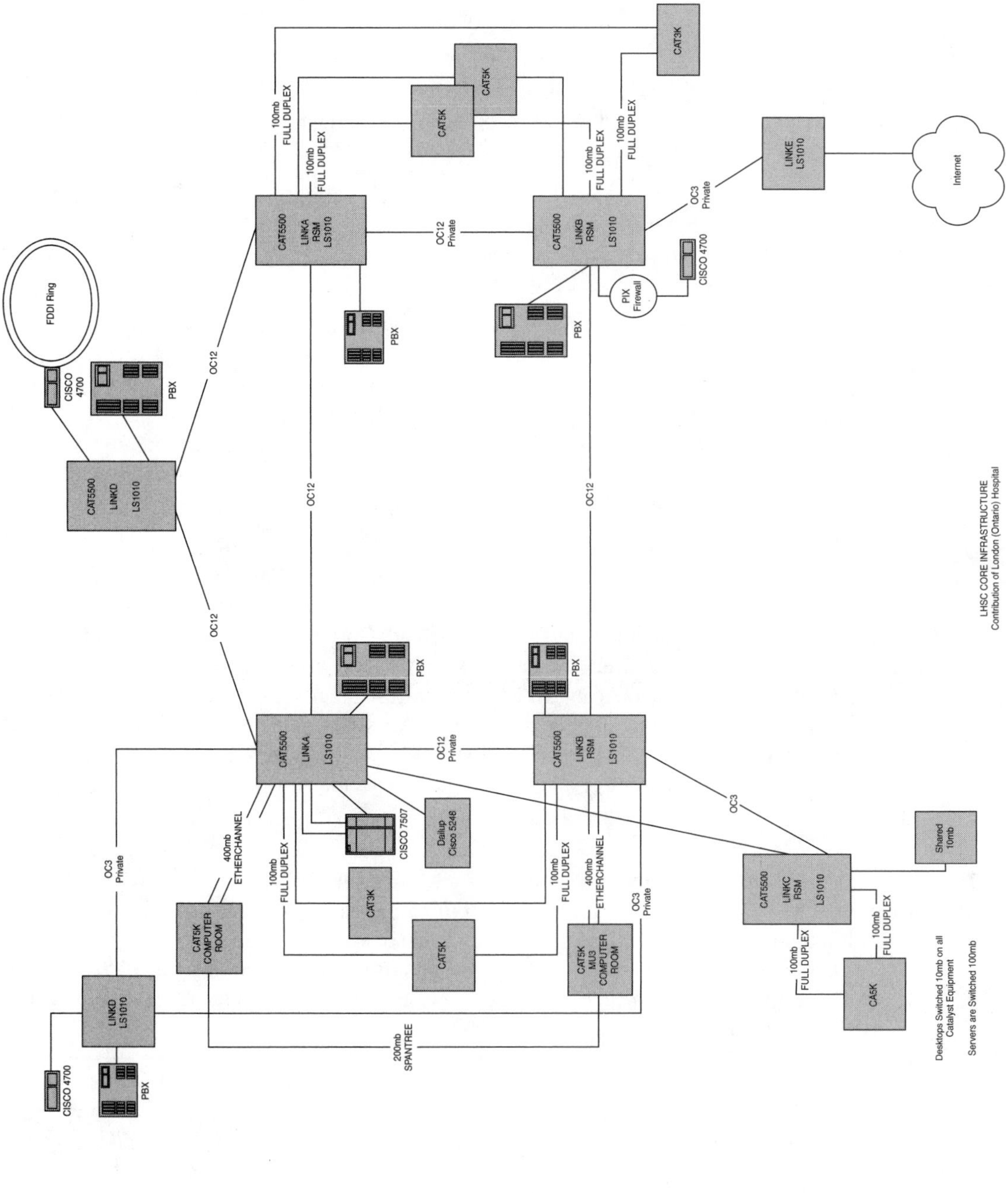

The Beijing Telecommunications Administration (BTA) selected Stratacom ATM switches for the city's first MAN. This network carries Beijing's Internet, corporate, and governmental data.

Swiss Reinsurance (Swiss Re), one of the world leaders in the reinsurance industry, deploys an ATM solution with guaranteed QoS for its voice and data systems. The company's ATM infrastructure includes approximately 4000 nodes on a local campus using LightStream 1010s.

Illinois State University deploys an ATM solution utilizing Catalyst 8540 MSR switches and an OC-12 (622 Mbps) backbone. The infrastructure handles voice and data, integrating current and legacy technologies.

About three years ago, in one of my design classes, a student asked for my opinion about future internetworking architectures that large-scale corporations will deploy. My reply was: "ATM backbone, carrying every potential piece of information from one part of the world to another: voice, data, image, video. Major long distance carrier systems or communication providers will carry out this deployment. Then, at the major hub nodes, for example, Toronto, New York, and so on, voice will terminate at the local central office's telephone switch, and data will be carried out using data switching gear."

One of the students in my class asked: "Have you seen our three-year plan?" Well, I had not. It just made sense. In fact, this had already happened in Canada, the USA, and other parts of the world. Carriers deploy ATM technology as a major high bandwidth pipe, where all kinds of payloads are integrated and intertwined. Corporations should take advantage of that and some already do. Bell Canada, for example, can provide the Ethernet extensions of 100 Mbps to its customers, using ATM as the infrastructure to extend the bandwidth over distances. Another option might be to extend ATM into private networks, into LANs. With deployment of SVCs (see Chapter 3, "ATM Reference Model: Higher Layers"), you can carry QoS across the carrier system to another side of the world.

NOTE   Although a majority of the carrier systems are based on PVC-type ATM networks at present, the SVC implementations are becoming increasingly available. One example is BellSouth in the metropolitan Atlanta area, which offers SVC-based ATM to its customers. You can interconnect your private SVC ATM clouds by implementing a tunnel through the PVC or SVC clouds of the carrier system. This is covered in Chapter 13, "LightStream 1010 Configuration."

The Role of ATM in Internetworks

What is the role of ATM in internetworks and where is it going? Will ATM extend to the desktop? Will ATM and IP co-exist? There are a lot of questions that lack definitive answers.

I think ATM will coexist with IP. Major carrier providers currently deploy, and will continue to deploy in the future, ATM as the backbone. Some companies requiring QoS and voice, data, and video applications will deploy ATM within their own networks, consequently extending the carrier's ATM into their private clouds. Major Internet service providers (ISPs) will continue deploying IP that could be using ATM at lower layers or could be residing over SONET or Synchronous Digital Hierarchy (SDH), the ITU-T equivalent of SONET that is deployed in Europe, Latin America, and the Pacific Rim. Packet over SONET/SDH is called POS and it utilizes PPP at Layer 2. SONET/SDH is a Layer 1 architecture of the OSI reference model capable of bandwidth capacity of up to 36 Gpbs (OC-384) so far. Chapter 2, "ATM Reference Model: Lower Layers," covers SONET in greater detail.

The interesting thing is that the LANs traditionally carried data only. The Internet, which extends traffic between LANs across WANs, adds voice and real-time video. This implies that the LANs have to carry voice and video to the desktop. I am sure that nobody will object to a single desktop device that fully integrates your voice, data, and video applications. One of the engines to achieve this is ATM; another is Gigabit Ethernet.

ATM, POS, DWDM, and Gigabit Ethernet

Most internetwork specialists can be subdivided into one of two categories: cell-lovers and cell-haters.

Why do some people love cells and some people hate them? This is a very tough question. There could be various driving forces behind agreeing to or deploying one type of the technology verses another. When it comes to love, I can speak from my own experience; however, when it comes to hate, I can theorize only. Typically, you love the technology because it meets your expectations, because it has no limitations (or close to it—as you know, any limitation is only a limitation of your own imagination). Well, in my eyes, ATM is that. I think about the brilliance of a cell—something very simple, and yet very powerful, with the complexities and flexibilities of dynamic call setup.

Sometimes, if the promises do not materialize, you have to give up on the promises. Maybe cell-haters became cell-haters for that reason. For example, if they were promised QoS four years ago and the expectations were not met, they would get discouraged—wouldn't you? This is all in spite of the fact that the ATM clouds have been understanding QoS for a couple of years now and yet only some edge devices are just beginning to understand the concept of QoS. You see, typically new technologies are marching 20 years ahead of the industry. Although this gap is decreasing rapidly, the technology is still ahead of us.

Will ATM survive POS across WANs? Will Gigabit Ethernet take over LANs? What is DWDM and how will it affect our networks? These questions are asked often.

The Cyclical Evolution of Technology

n of a technology and its deployment, like life itself, is cyclical. Remember the
he only solution for data network architecture was centralization: one host
,,,..... un kinds of applications, and everyone had to talk to the host for anything? Then
distributed processing arrived and the slogan for new internetworking designs was "the
client/server architecture has become a new solution." And now? Let's have a server of
servers—we're back to centralized processing, or sort of.

What Is Packet over SONET?

Packet over SONET (POS) is promoted by some organizations as an alternative to ATM for
carrying data. The concept is quite simple—position Layer 3 protocols (for example, IP)
over SONET/SDH. SONET/SDH is a physical layer, Layer 1, when compared to the OSI
reference model. POS is the serial transmission of data over SONET/SDH frames through
the use of PPP. RFC 2615, which you can find in its entirety at http://info.internet.isi.edu/
in-notes/rfc/files/, describes a method for running PPP over SONET/SDH (see Chapter 2
for more details on SONET). The POS approach avoids the ATM overhead only if it is used
solely for data transfer and does not include real-time voice and video traffic. Also, the POS
approach loses the flexibility of the ATM's switching capability.

Your network requires Gigabit switch routers to handle switching at higher speeds
comparable to the ATM switching throughput and to allow for flexibility at Layer 3 of the
OSI reference model. Why? Simply because of the throughput requirements of the device
that needs to perform Layer 3 switching/routing between Gigabit networks.

What Is Dense Wavelength Division Multiplexing?

DWDM is a more recent technology than deployment of IP over SONET/SDH. DWDM
enables carriers to send multiple wavelengths across a single strand of optical fiber. With
the growing need for bandwidth, T3 circuits at 44.736 Mbps are no longer sufficient. There
are requirements for SONET OC-3 (155 Mbps) and OC-12 (622 Mbps). With the dramatic
data and multimedia growth, there also are requirements for bandwidth beyond 2.5 Gbps.

Wave Division Multiplexing (WDM), the predecessor to DWDM technology, could double the
capacity by providing two wavelengths. The wavelengths are two different non-overlapping
frequency bands (or colors), one in the forward direction and another in the reverse direction that
could be transmitted simultaneously over a single optical fiber. For long term, WDM does not
solve the problem of literally limitless bandwidth availability. Consequently, in the mid-1990s,
researchers came up with 4-, 8-, and 16-wavelength channels through a single fiber. The 16-
wavelength fiber is known as DWDM.

DWDM is based on one basic principle of fiber—optical fiber can potentially transmit trillions of bits of information per second. This transmission speed is achieved by sending 16 or more wavelengths (or *colors*) over a single fiber pair. This results in 40 Gbps in each direction. Currently, the technology allows up to 100 colors at 9.6 Gbps each, resulting in a whopping 1 Terabits per second (Tbps) over a single pair. Some vendors have even introduced higher fiber density of 128 colors, resulting in the bandwidth of more than 1.2 Tbps.

What Is Gigabit Ethernet?

Gigabit Ethernet is a standard for high speed LANs, IEEE 802.3z. It expands the bandwidth by an order of magnitude over Fast Ethernet and by two orders of magnitude over the original 10 Mbps Ethernet. The popular misconception is that Gigabit Ethernet technology is just an upgraded version of Ethernet or Fast Ethernet. Well, this is not quite the case. It does comply with the 802.3 standard for frame format, minimum and maximum frame sizes containing from 46 to 1500 bytes of data. The differences are at the physical layer. Gigabit Ethernet, which extends to distances greater than 100 m, uses a modified version of the ANSI X3T11 Fibre Channel standard. This standard is the only technology that supports Gigabit speeds at distances greater than 100 m. The original Fibre Channel technology, operating at 1063 Mbps, has been enhanced to run at 1250 Mbps, thus providing the full 1000 Mbps data rate. There are two types of Gigabit transmissions that are based on Fibre Channel: multimode fiber (1000Base-SX) and single-mode fiber (1000Base-LX).

Two standards for Gigabit Ethernet over copper cabling also exist: 1000Base-CX and 1000Base-T. 1000Base-CX uses the Fibre Channel–based 8B/10B coding at the serial line rate of 1250 Mbps and runs over 150-ohm balanced, shielded cable, known as *twinax cable*. The 1000Base-T physical layer standard provides 1000 Mbps Ethernet signal transmission over four pairs of Category 5 UTP cable.

Table 1-1 lists a summary of media types and distance limitations for Gigabit Ethernet.

Table 1-1   *Gigabit Ethernet Media Types and Distance Limitations*

Media Type	Distance Limit
Category 5 UTP (1000Base-T)	100 m
150-O STP (1000Base-CX)	25 m
62.5-μm multimode fiber with shortwave lasers (1000Base-SX)	260 m
50-μm multimode fiber with shortwave lasers (1000Base-SX)	525 m
62.5-μm multimode fiber with longwave lasers (1000Base-LX)	550 m
50-μm multimode fiber with longwave lasers (1000Base-LX)	550 m
10-μm single-mode fiber with longwave lasers (1000Base-LX)	3000 m

Gigabit Ethernet operates either in half- or full-duplex mode. In full-duplex mode, packets travel in both directions at the same time, thus literally doubling the available bandwidth to 2 Gbps. This can occur only in point-to-point designs. Half-duplex mode is problematic for Gigabit Ethernet. This is due to the fact that for a station to detect the collision and to do something about it, the round-trip propagation time must be less than the frame transmission time. With Gigabit Ethernet, this is not the case—the frame transmission time supersedes the round-trip time. This problem is alleviated by increasing the frame transmission time or by "frame bursting," which is useful for short frames. This, of course, results in less efficient use of bandwidth, lowering its promise of 1 Gbps.

ATM Versus POS

My view on the subject of ATM versus POS is quite simple—a room exists for everyone in the family. The Internet is here to stay, which implies that IP is here to stay. Will all data applications reside on top of IP? Maybe, one day. The solution of POS definitely has room for pure data applications. One example of it is the SprintLink Backbone Architecture. The design deploys Cisco 12000 routers.

Well, what about voice and video? There are products on the market today that can compress voice to 8 kbps (or even less) and carry it directly on top of IP. This co-exists with uncompressed voice. Now, can you take IP, with voice and video in it, and carry it directly on top of SONET? Yes, you can! There are issues, however. QoS is one issue. ATM took care of QoS very effectively. Another issue is overhead. Please do not get misled by the fact that POS results in 25 to 30 percent higher throughput than ATM-based networks. This is true in *pure data* networks. Voice over IP requires data fragmentation or chopping, which results in the creation of *subpackets*, each requiring its own header. Hence, multimedia over POS results in the same issue as ATM—overhead. Why must chopping be done? So data does not overpower the bandwidth! You wouldn't want part of your speech to be delayed, would you?

As an underlying architecture, SONET/SDH co-exists with DWDM, which both ATM and IP can deploy. Furthermore, in July 1999, a new ATM Forum specification, af-phy-0128.000, was created that puts ATM cells directly on top of fiber, bypassing SONET/SDH framing. You can find this specification in its entirety at www.atmforum.com. So far, only 622 and 2488 Mpbs have been specified. This means that ATM cells do not occupy extra bandwidth by being encapsulated into SONET/SDH frames.

As far as the future is concerned, I do foresee that ATM will continue its existence as one of a number of WAN technologies, in the deployment of Digital Subscriber Line (DSL) technology, in campus networks, and in MANs.

DSL Technology

There are various types of DSL technology. This is because different applications require different data rates, and the various DSL technologies deliver those speed variations. For example, High-Bit-Rate Digital Subscriber Line (HDSL) and Symmetrical Digital Subscriber Line (SDSL) deliver services at T1/E1 speeds. Rate Adaptive Digital Subscriber Line (R-ADSL) can adjust the speed of the line automatically. Asymmetric Digital Subscriber Line (ADSL) can achieve speeds between 1.5 Mbps and 8 Mbps downstream. ISDN Digital Subscriber Line (IDSL) delivers services at 128 kbps, and Multirate Symmetrical Digital Subsriber Line (M-SDSL) can support eight distinct rates between 64 Kbps and 128 Kbps. Generally, the different variations of DSL technology have been implemented to meet the specific needs of home users; small- and medium-sized businesses; schools and colleges; and corporate sectors.

You can obtain a copy of the DSL standards from the ANSI at www.ansi.org or from the European Telecommunications Standards Institute at www.etsi.org.

Table 1-2 summarizes ATM versus POS characteristics.

Table 1-2   *ATM Versus POS*

ATM	POS
Supports any payload.	Payload must be packetized.
Supports QoS.	No imbedded QoS is available.
Has overhead.	Similar overhead is created when used to carry multimedia.
Switching is performed at Layer 1.25 of the OSI reference model.	Switching mechanism is Layer 3 of the OSI reference model. Modifications could be made with the use of various caching mechanisms.
Handles compressed voice.	Handles compressed voice.

ATM Versus Gigabit Ethernet

The question of ATM versus Gigabit Ethernet has concerned network architects since the conception of Gigabit Ethernet. Will Gigabit Ethernet replace the use of ATM within LAN environments? What will it do to LANE and MPOA (see Chapter 5, "LAN Emulation (LANE)," and Chapter 6, "Multiprotocol over ATM (MPOA)," for details of these architectures)?

I can say only that, like POS versus ATM, Gigabit Ethernet and ATM both have their places in internetworks. ATM does offer QoS within a LAN, within a MAN, and across a WAN.

ATM allows you to stretch your private ATM networks across great distances and to carry your required QoS from one part of the world to another. Gigabit Ethernet, on another hand, is just beginning to realize the meaning of QoS in its own way. IEEE 802.1p tagging is a form of QoS for Layer 2 frames. IEEE 802.1p adds 16 bits to the Layer 2 header, which includes three bits that can be used to classify priority or tagging. The standard specifies six different priorities, which still do not offer extensive policy-based service levels. You have to be careful with IEEE 802.1p implementation because older switches could misinterpret the unexpected 16 bits. Furthermore, Layer 2 prioritization must be mapped to a Layer 3 prioritization to prevent bottlenecks at the boundaries of your networks. If the ATM networks can stretch the required QoS across WANs, the IEEE 802.1p prioritization is lost at the LAN/WAN boundary routers, leaving Gigabit Ethernet prioritization less flexible.

I am sure all of you have heard the question "Why do I need QoS if I have enough bandwidth?" Well, I answer that question with another question. What is enough bandwidth and how much bandwidth is enough? Networks are application driven. Today, you could have applications that are "happy campers" with just 1 Gbps. Before you know it, new applications will be created that will require much more bandwidth. Should you have multimedia-type applications, you do require QoS, which ATM provides to ensure that your real-time voice and video have better QoS than data. Should you have time-sensitive data applications that require some form of bandwidth guarantee, again, ATM provides that through its QoS.

So, any consensus? Just as I mentioned previously, a room exists for everybody in the family. ATM has and will continue to have its place within LANs and MANs and so does and will Gigabit Ethernet.

Table 1-3 summarizes ATM versus Gigabit Ethernet characteristics.

Table 1-3   *ATM Versus Gigabit Ethernet*

ATM	Gigabit Ethernet
Supports QoS across WANs and LANs. Allows LAN QoS to be interrelated across WANs.	Priority-based QoS up to six levels. Layer 2 only. Does not extend through WANs.
Is based on VCs, thus resiliency.	Bus-type topology, which can be built as switched dedicated or partially dedicated segments.
Can be 10 Gbps and more.	Limit of 1 Gbps (unless full-duplex).

TDM Network Migration

The multiplexing principle takes several independent streams of data, interleaves them into one and sends them over the same physical medium. Various types of multiplexing technologies exist. Frequency-division multiplexing (FDM), which the telephone companies deploy, interleaves different frequencies together by applying modulation/demodulation techniques. Time-division multiplexing (TDM) is a second type. TDM can be divided into synchronous time-division multiplexing (STDM) and asynchronous time-division multiplexing (ATDM). STDM allows two or more channels of information to share a common transmission medium, providing each channel with a fixed length time slot when it is its turn to send the information. In ATDM, the data streams are converted into either fixed- or variable-length time slots and are transferred asynchronously. If the data stream is of variable length, it is called *packet/frame switching*. If the data is of fixed length, it is called *cell switching*. So you can refer to ATM as being *cell switching based on ATDM*.

ATM takes the data, potentially being a packet or a frame, and chops it into fixed-size cells, each individually labeled with a VC identifier. Cells then are switched in hardware, as illustrated in Figure 1-4.

Figure 1-4   *Creating Cells from Packets/Frames*

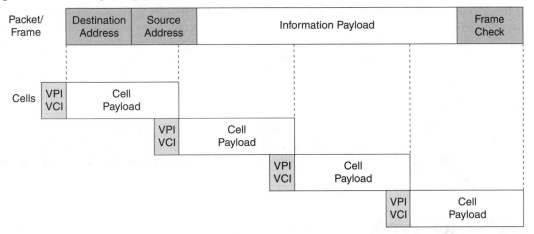

There are several motivating factors to move from STDM technology to ATM. As detailed in the sections that follow, they are

- Reduced WAN bandwidth cost
- Improved performance
- Reduced downtime

Reduced WAN Bandwidth Cost

Consider voice, data, and video applications utilizing different types of WAN technologies. Using different types of technologies results in a lot of wasted bandwidth, which increases the cost per unit of transfer. Some people might argue that the integration does not buy much if you have a high bandwidth pipe. My reply to that is—what is a high bandwidth pipe? How much bandwidth is enough to the desktop? I do not know. When I look at the bandwidth, it reminds me of giving candy to a kid: When you give one piece of candy to a child, he/she wants two. Today, there could be enough bandwidth for specific applications; tomorrow there won't be—that is guaranteed.

The deployment of ATM results in increased bandwidth efficiency, which is a very important factor in lowering WAN costs, especially when you are transferring multimedia. Remember, the efficiency of ATM lies at its core: It is there to handle multimedia—voice, data, video. The so-called *cell tax* does not become so much of an issue when your ATM carries multimedia. Why? Simply because other methods introduce similar taxes, if not more! The initial cost of the ATM platform and interfaces might be high, but it is offset by on-going monthly lower costs.

Improved Performance

Higher throughput based on higher bandwidth is the major factor in improved performance. When you top it off with QoS, you end up with even higher performance. ATM, using its QoS, guarantees that time-sensitive applications can have the least delay possible while still forwarding bursty LAN data traffic.

Reduced Downtime

With SVC use, ATM networks are capable of rapid and dynamic re-routing of payloads, should there be a circuit failure in the ATM cloud. Typically, ATM switching gear is provisioned with redundant processors, power supplies, and trunk interfaces to reduce any unforeseen network downtime.

ATM Switch Types

When providing an integrated ATM solution for your networks, be aware that ATM switches can be divided into two major categories: LAN switches and WAN switches. The major differences lie in the number and the types of interfaces supported, the redundancy level, the sophistication of the traffic management mechanism, and the amount of bandwidth supported.

Just as you can do a hierarchical network design using routing technology, you can apply the same design principles to ATM switches. Based on the hierarchical nature of your network, the ATM switches can be further categorized as follows:

- Workgroup
- Campus
- Enterprise
- Multiservice access

Figure 1-5 illustrates this categorization.

Figure 1-5   *The Role of ATM Switches in an Internetwork*

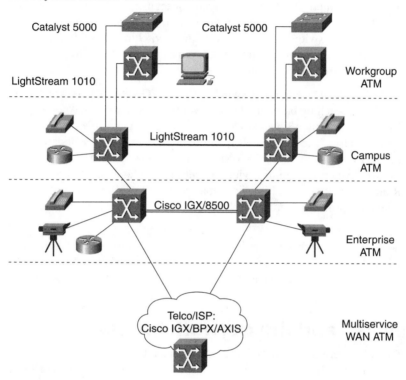

Workgroup ATM Switches

Workgroup ATM switches are categorized by their capability to interconnect ATM to other types of LAN infrastructure, such as Ethernet. An example of the workgroup switch is the Cisco Catalyst 5000. Furthermore, you can claim that a router also functions as a workgroup switch when it is interconnecting an ATM cloud to your Ethernet.

Campus ATM Switches

Generally, you can use campus ATM switches for small-scale ATM backbones to alleviate backbone congestion while carrying various types of traffic. Various ATM interconnection methods exist (see Chapter 3). Campus ATM switches must support a variety of LAN/WAN interconnection methods, have traffic management and congestion control mechanisms in place, and be competitively priced to be deployed in a campus situation. The Cisco LightStream 1010 (LS1010) is a good example of a campus ATM switch.

Enterprise and Multiservice Access ATM Switches

Enterprise ATM switches are designed to form the core backbones of the large enterprise networks. Campus ATM switches interconnect using enterprise-level switching. Enterprise switches also can integrate all technologies and services within a corporation. This implies that enterprise switches must support LAN switching, WAN interfaces (such as Frame Relay), and circuit emulation for PBX trunking. This allows for complete integration of the infrastructure and uniform management of the networks.

One example of an enterprise switch is Cisco's IGX 8400. This switch provides a redundant 1.2 Gbps switching bus and integrates voice, video, and data. Another powerful example of an enterprise switch is Cisco's StrataCom BPX/AXIS. BPX has a redundant 9.6 Gbps switch matrix. The AXIS shelf is an important part of a consolidation platform that takes Frame Relay, T1 to your PBX systems, and so on and integrates them all. Another addition to Cisco's family of multiservice switches is the Catalyst 8500 series Multiservice Switch Router. It integrates multiservice, non-blocking OC-48 (2488.32 Gbps) ATM switching with multiprotocol routing and Layer 2 switching onto a single platform.

Service providers deploy ATM as part of the public network offering. Some providers offer network services that are applications of an ATM infrastructure (Frame Relay is a good example). Often, providers use enterprise switches for multiservice access. This is because of redundancy, scalability, and the capability to support a variety of interfaces.

ATM Devices and the Network Interfaces

Cisco has various products that are ATM-capable. On the ATM switching side, as I mentioned earlier in the chapter, IGX and BPX are good candidates for large-size companies and ISPs. The Catalyst 8500 can serve both as an enterprise and a campus solution. The Lightstream 1010 is a campus switch; the Catalyst 5500 is the workgroup switch.

Regarding connectivity to ATM, Cisco has both routing and LAN switching type products that are ATM-ready, as listed in Table 1-4.

Table 1-4 *ATM-ready Cisco Routers and Switches*

Router Series	Switch Series	Multilayer Switching Series
12000	5000/5500	6000
7xxx	3xxx	8500
4xxx	28xx	
38xx		
36xx		
26xx		

Interface speeds between the edge devices and the ATM cloud varies from T1/E1 to OC-48, which is either within the ATM cloud or at the access layer to the ATM cloud.

Cisco and associated ATM companies are working to provide ATM network interface cards (NICs) to connect high performance servers and workstations directly to ATM clouds. These companies include the following:

- Efficient Networks (ATM NICs for PCI-, EISA-, and Sbus-based systems)
- Adaptec (ATM NICs for PCI- and Sbus-based systems)
- Interphase (ATM NICs for PCI-, Sbus-, VME-, EISA-,and GIO-based systems)
- Olicom (ATM NICs for PCI-based systems)

You can use ATM NICs to connect high-performance servers and workstations directly to ATM networks. These are very useful in providing high-speed, multiple ATM access to shared data, applications, and resources from the LAN level.

ATM Standards

Standardization usually is perceived as being good for a product or a technology. It allows multiple vendors equipment interoperability and helps to promote an open market, which ultimately results in lower costs. On the other hand, it can take months, if not years, for a specific standard to be finalized and approved. In fact, no successful company would wait for standards to be fully approved before starting product development.

The two bodies responsible for the ATM standards are the International Telecommunication Union-Telecommunication (ITU-T) and the ATM Forum. The ITU-T, a truly international organization, has been responsible for telecommunications standards since 1932. (Initially, the name was CCITT—International Telegraph and Telephone Consultative Committee; it was renamed to ITU-T on March 1, 1993.)

One of the major contributions of ITU-T was Recommendation I.320 (the ISDN Protocol Reference Model), which is shown in Figure 1-6. Figure 1-6 illustrates how the model is three-dimensional, slicing the responsibilities of all layers into two major planes: User and Control.

The User Plane has the important task of managing the transfer of the actual data (often called the *payload*), including tasks of flow control and error recovery. The Control Plane is responsible for generating and managing signaling requests, including call control, connection control, management functions related to the whole system, and coordination between all planes. Plane Management is responsible for the management and the coordination of the complete system, and Layer Management is responsible for layer-specific functions. Higher layer protocols include signaling, LANE, IP, and other internetwork protocols. Chapter 3 addresses the ATM-related higher layer protocols. Chapter 2 addresses the ATM Adaptation, ATM, and Physical layers.

Figure 1-6 *ISDN Protocol Reference Model*

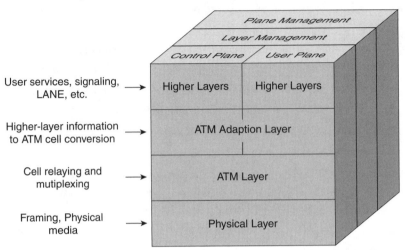

To deploy the ATM standards-based technology faster, an organization was needed that would be responsible strictly for ATM, similar to how the IETF functions in the IP internetworking world. Following this need, the ATM Forum was set up in September 1991 by Cisco Systems, NET/Adaptive, Northern Telecom, and US Sprint. Now there are approximately 1000 voting members within the Forum. The main purpose for creating the ATM Forum was to form "an international non-profit organization whose objective is to accelerate the use of ATM products and services through a rapid convergence of interoperability specifications" [ATM Forum]. The ATM Forum speeds up the process of standardization instead of waiting for the long procedure from ITU-T.

The ATM Forum's goals are to ensure interoperability and early availability of the ATM standards to vendors. The ATM Forum consists of Technical, Marketing, and Awareness Committees. At present, the Technical Committee is divided into 18 separate Sub-Working Groups (SWGs), which are listed in Table 1-5.

Table 1-5 *ATM Forum Sub-working Groups*

Sub-working Group Acronym	Definition and Responsibility
B-ICI	Responsible for Broadband Inter-Carrier Interface specifications.
CS	Responsible for UNI, PNNI, and other ATM control signaling.
DANS	Responsible for Directory and Naming Services.
DEI	Responsible for Data Exchange Interface specification.
FATM	Responsible for frame-based ATM transport.

Table 1-5   *ATM Forum Sub-working Groups (Continued)*

Sub-working Group Acronym	Definition and Responsibility
ILMI	Responsible for Integrated Local Management Interface specification.
LANE/MPOA	Responsible for LANE and MPOA specification.
NM	Responsible for Network Management specification.
PHY	Responsible for Physical Layer specification.
PNNI	Responsible for Private Network to Network Interface specification.
RA	Responsible for Routing and Addressing specifications, including ATM Addressing.
RBB	Responsible for Residential Broadband specification.
SAA	Responsible for Service Aspects and Applications specification.
SEC	Responsible for ATM Security Aspects specification.
SIG	Responsible for User Interface Signaling specification.
TEST	Responsible for ATM Test definitions specification.
TM	Responsible for Traffic Management for specification.
VTOA	Responsible for Voice and Telephone over ATM specification.
WATM	Responsible for Wireless ATM specification.
UNI	Responsible for User-Network Interface specification.

These SWGs are responsible for solving the technical issues and concerns that impact the implementation of ATM. The SWGs are subdivided according to the area of concern and according to the ITU-T's ISDN Protocol Reference Model (refer to Figure 1-6). A list of all SWGs, including the approved specifications and the specifications pending approval (at the time of writing this book), appears in Appendixes A and B.

NOTE   You can obtain your own copy of any approved ATM Forum specification from www.atmforum.com. If you are a member of the ATM Forum, the address is www-mo.atmforum.com.

Summary

This chapter introduces ATM as a Layer 1.25 technology of the OSI reference model. Before truly navigating into ATM, it is important to understand the reasons for choosing ATM.

ATM provides you with the flexibility of carrying multiple types of payloads across great distances at high speeds. Because ATM understands QoS natively, it provides the proper QoS for real-time voice and video applications. ATM's role in internetworks is quite versatile—you can deploy them in LANs, MANs, or WANs. You can extend the QoS request for a specific application from one part of the world to another.

When compared to other technologies, such as POS, DWDM, and Gigabit Ethernet, it is clear that each technology has its own advantages and disadvantages. It is our responsibility to ensure that we closely examine all the technological aspects, applications, and requirements prior to making a commitment to any technological solution.

ATM, like any other networking technology, allows you to build a hierarchical infrastructure using various types of ATM switches and network interfaces.

Two ATM international bodies are responsible for standards—ITU-T and ATM Forum. The ATM Forum is a fairly recent organization. It focuses on accelerating the use of ATM interoperable specifications and their deployment in the products from different vendors.

Review Questions

1 What is ATM?

2 Why would you choose ATM?

3 What is POS?

4 Are there advantages to using POS or Gigabit Ethernet versus ATM?

5 How can you categorize various ATM switches?

6 What is DWDM?

7 What standard bodies are responsible for ATM standardization?

"Everything should be made as simple as possible…but not simpler."—Albert Einstein (1879–1955)

"Where the willingness is great, the difficulties cannot be great"—Niccolo Machiavelli (1469–1527)

After reading this chapter, you should be able to understand the lower layers of the ATM reference model, which includes the ATM physical layer, the ATM layer, and the ATM adaptation layer. Specifically, the chapter elaborates on the following:

- **ATM Physical Layer**—Consists of transmission convergence and physical media dependent sublayers and their functionality. This includes SONET/SDH framing, structure, and signaling hierarchy.

- **ATM Layer**—Includes ATM cell structure, various types of ATM Forum–defined network interfaces, and ATM switching operation.

- **ATM Adaptation Layers for Different Traffic Classifications**—Includes an explanation of various traffic classes, traffic parameters, and Quality of Service for each.

CHAPTER 2

ATM Reference Model: Lower Layers

Your journey into ATM technology begins with the lower layers of the ATM reference model: physical, ATM, and ATM adaptation layers. These lower layers are responsible for converting the packets or the frames into ATM cells, and then possibly into Layer 1 frames, and sending them to the destination.

This chapter explores the responsibilities of these lower layers, how the Layer 1 frames are formed, how the cells are formed, and the functions of the ATM adaptation layer.

The ATM Physical Layer

The ATM physical layer very much coincides with Layer 1 of the OSI reference model. It controls the transmission and the receipt of bits on the physical medium.

In Figure 2-1, you can see that the ATM physical layer is divided into the two sublayers: transmission convergence (TC) and physical medium dependent (PMD). The input into the TC sublayer are 53-byte cells, and the output of the PMD sublayer are the Layer 1 frames, containing ATM cells.

The ATM physical layer has many responsibilities. Figure 2-2 illustrates that the TC sublayer is responsible for the following tasks:

- Cell header error check (HEC) generation, verification, and fixing one bit error
- Cell delineation and rate decoupling
- Transmission frame adaptation
- Transmission frame generation and recovery

The PMD sublayer's functions include

- Bit timing/time recovery
- Line coding
- Physical medium

Figure 2-1 *ATM Physical Layer Positioning Within the ATM Stack*

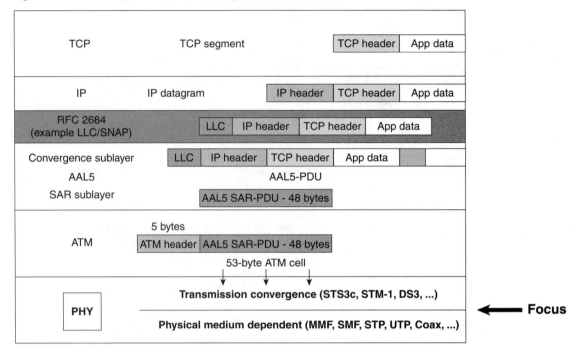

Figure 2-2 *ATM Physical Layer Responsibilities*

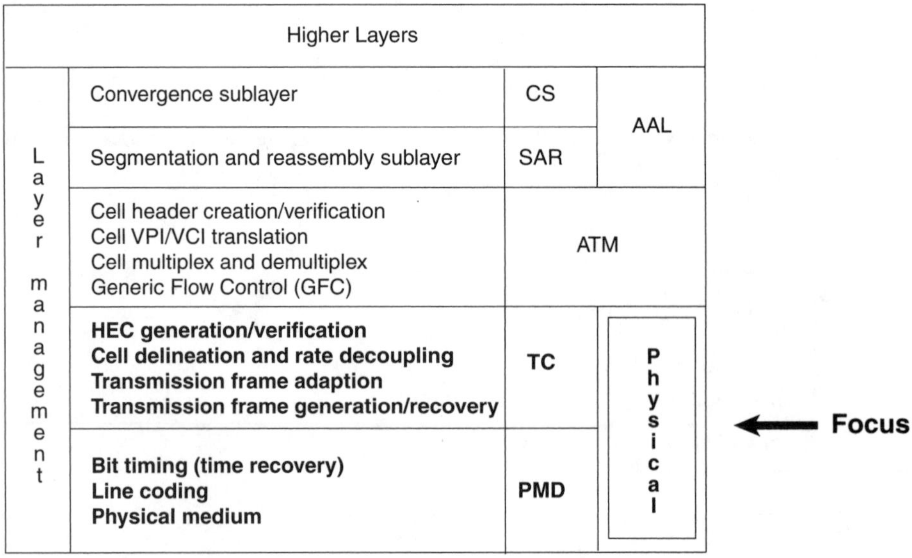

Figures 2-1 and 2-2 are your compass to all the responsibilities of the lower layers within the ATM stack.

Transmission Convergence Sublayer

Now look more closely at what happens between the ATM layer, where there are asynchronous cells, and the ATM physical layer, where synchronous Layer 1 frames are converted into bit streams. Figure 2-3 illustrates the relationship between the two layers.

Figure 2-3   *The Relationship Between the ATM Layer and the ATM Physical Layer*

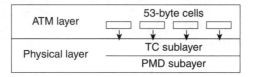

At the top of the physical layer, the TC sublayer looks at the cell header and uses the 8-bit HEC to check for errors in the cell header. If an error exists, an ATM switch has the capability to fix a 1-bit error. In addition, the ATM switch is capable of detecting multiple-bit errors. Should the switch detect multiple-bit errors, it discards all cells with detected errors.

Upon the initial startup of the ATM device interface connected to the ATM cloud, the switch performs cell delineation. The purpose behind the cell delineation is to maintain cell boundaries. The switch waits to see the flag of the beginning of a cell by performing a hunting function (looking for the first legitimate cell). The principle behind which the Cisco LightStream 1010 operates is by counting the first seven cells and ignoring them. The idea is that if the switch sees seven legal 53-byte cells with recognition of 5 header bytes and 48 payload bytes, then the next cell is where the switch begins to worry about sending them. The fact that the first seven cells get dropped is not a concern considering that the throughput of an OC-3 (155 Mbps) link is approximately 2.5 million cells per second.

ATM is asynchronous in nature, meaning that payloads are sent whenever there is information to be sent. ATM simply does not care when you send the data. SONET and digital signal level 3 (DS-3), on the other hand, are synchronous in nature. Cell rate decoupling handles asynchronous data by a synchronous mechanism. The cell rate decoupling function inserts or supresses idle (or empty) cells into synchronous media, such as DS-3 or SONET.

NOTE   An ATM switch recognizes empty cells by checking the virtual path identifier (VPI) and the virtual channel identifier (VCI). If VPI equals 0 and VCI equals 0, then it is an empty cell. Table 2-1 summarizes the VPI/VCI reserved values for idle cells.

Table 2-1   *VPI/VCI Reserved Values for Empty Cells*

VPI	VCI	Meaning
0	0	Empty cell

The transmission frame adaptation function packages ATM cells into frames acceptable to the particular physical layer implementation. Transmission frame generation and recovery generates and maintains the appropriate physical layer frame structure.

Physical Medium Dependent Sublayer

The physical medium dependent sublayer is responsible for sending and receiving a continuous flow of bits with associated timing information to synchronize transmission and reception. Because it includes only physical-medium–dependent functions, its specification depends on the physical medium used. Physical-wired medium systems can be either optical or copper. Fiber cabling is divided further into single-mode (SMF) and multimode fiber (MMF); copper cable is divided into coaxial and twisted-pair types. Figure 2-4 summarizes this cabling structure.

Figure 2-4   *Cabling Structure*

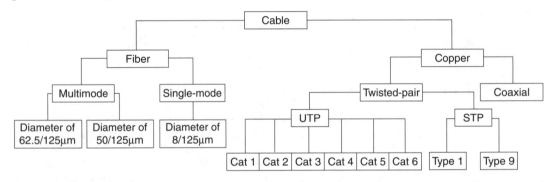

ATM cells can be transported over many different physical media—fiber and copper—using a variety of framing infrastructures, one of which is SONET.

Table 2-2 lists the various Layer 1 framing types, the corresponding data rates, and the types of media that ATM deploys.

Table 2-2   *ATM Physical Interface Rates and Framing*

Framing	Data Rate (Mbps)	Specification	Media Supported					
			MMF	SMF	Coaxial Cable	UTP-5	UTP-3	STP
DS1	1.544	Af-phy-0064.000			✓			
E1	2.048	Af-phy-0064.000			✓			

Table 2-2   *ATM Physical Interface Rates and Framing (Continued)*

Framing	Data Rate (Mbps)	Specification	Media Supported					
			MMF	**SMF**	**Coaxial Cable**	**UTP-5**	**UTP-3**	**STP**
J2	6.312	Af-phy-0029.000			✓			
Fractional DS-1/E1	From 0.064 to 1.544/2.048	Af-phy-0130.000			✓			
DS-3	44.736	Af-phy-0054.000			✓			
E3	34.368	Af-phy-0034.000			✓			
E4	139							
ATM 25 (subset of 4B/5B)	25.6	Af-phy-0040.000				✓	✓	✓
4B/5B_ (TAXI)	100		✓					
SONET (STS-1)	51.84	Af-phy-0018.000					✓	
SONET (STS-1)	25.92	Af-phy-0018.000					✓	
SONET (STS-1)	12.96	Af-phy-0018.000					✓	
SONET (STS-3C) /SDH (STM-1)	155.52	Af-phy-0015.000 Af-phy-0053.000 Af-phy-0047.000 Af-phy-0062.000	✓			✓	✓	✓

continues

Table 2-2 *ATM Physical Interface Rates and Framing (Continued)*

Framing	Data Rate (Mbps)	Specification	Media Supported					
			MMF	**SMF**	**Coaxial Cable**	**UTP-5**	**UTP-3**	**STP**
SONET (STS-12C) / SDH (STM-4)	622.08	Af-phy-0046.000	✓	✓				
8B/10B (Fibre channel)	155.52	IBM's patented Escon 8B/10B coding	✓	✓				
SONET (STS-48C) / SDH (STM-16)	2488	Af-phy-0133.000		✓				
Cell-based	2488 / 622	Af-phy-0128.000	✓	✓ / ✓				

Table 2-2 illustrates that ATM can transmit cells via twisted-pair cable, coaxial cable, and fiber-optic cable, utilizing various framings, such as SONET/SDH, DS-3/E3, DS-1/E1, and even without any framing.

---

622 Mbps and 2488 Mbps Cell-based Physical Layer

One ATM Forum specification, AF-PHY-0128.000, of July 1999, specifies the positioning of cells directly over SMF and MMF using speeds of 622 Mpbs and 2488 Mpbs. Another specification of 1000 Mbps of cell-based physical layer is under way. In case of direct cell transmission over physical fiber, the Physical Layer is still divided into the TC and PMD sublayers. With the new specification, you can achieve transmission speeds of 620.620 and 2482.560 Mbps. Furthermore, the specification results in more efficient bandwidth utilization with lower overhead—after all, cells no longer are required to be packaged cells into Layer 1 frames. The

"Cell-Based Physical Layer specification provides the necessary functions to transport ATM cells directly on the physical media without using any frame structure. The intent of this specification is to provide a simple ATM physical interface with robust transmission properties, maximum bandwidth, and only the minimum set of functionalities for ATM transport"

[ATM Forum Specification—AF-PHY-0128.000]

Using a hierarchical approach to the design of the physical media, you deploy SMF across long distances, MMF between wiring closets or buildings, and UTP Category 5 cable to the desktop.

ATM Transmission Over Fiber

Although the basic differences between these types of media should be obvious intuitively, many people get confused between SMF and MMF.

SMF uses lasers, which means that only one mode of light is allowed to propagate through the fiber. The core diameter of SMF is very small—about 8 microns. MMF uses multiple rays of light (modes) that can enter the fiber from different angles. Because the rays of light for each mode enter the fiber at different angles, the path length through the fiber for each mode is different. Light emitting diodes (LEDs) inject light into MMF. LEDs are not sufficient to inject light into SMF because SMF transmits light over a wide area. MMF core ranges from 50 to 125 microns. SMF's intermediate reach is 15 km and its long reach is up to 80 km at a transmission speed of 2488 Mbps. MMF can reach up to 2.4 km.

Both types of fiber, SMF and MMF, are deployed in ATM using SONET, Transparent Asynchronous Transmitter/Receiver Interface (TAXI) and Fibre Channel framings. SONET framing is discussed further in this chapter.

TAXI 4B/5B was readily available because of the FDDI chipset standard. Initially, the ATM Forum encouraged the ATM development efforts by endorsing TAXI 4B/5B as one of the first ATM media encoding standards to reduce the expense of FDDI to ATM migration. Today, however, the most common framing ATM interface using fiber is STS-3c/STM and STS-12c/STM-4 (SONET framing).

8B/10B (Fibre Channel) is another form of frame encoding, where eight data bits are translated to a 10-bit group, with the two extra bits being used for error detection and timing recovery. The Fibre Channel provides connection speeds of 155.52 Mbps.

ATM Transmission Over Copper

Copper wiring includes coaxial and twisted-pair cabling (refer to Figure 2-4). Due to fiber cost and the existing copper infrastructures, ATM connectivity is being extended to shielded twisted-pair (STP), unshielded twisted-pair (UTP), and coaxial cabling.

Copper has its own limitations, which include loss of signaling and increased crosstalk, when communicating via long hauls. Still, when applied to short distances, connectivity of 155 Mbps can be achieved.

The STP cable consists of two pair, with each pair being individually foil-shielded. Then there is an overall braid shield that is applied to the cable. It is a higher cost cable than the UTP cable, which does not have any shielding. STP runs are quite limited—up to 100m.

UTP cable is divided into six categories. The most recent one is Category 6, also called *screened twisted-pair*. It has four twisted pairs, as other UTPs do, but has a foil shield, which results in its capability to extend high-speed communication, such as 1000 Mbps, across distances longer than 100m.

The ATM Forum specified the deployment of UTP Categories 3 and 5 cabling for speeds of up to 155 Mbps (see Appendixes A, "Approved ATM Forum Specifications," and B, "Pending Approval ATM Forum Specifications").

SONET/SDH Framing

SONET technologies were developed in the early 1980s and were standardized by the joint efforts of the American National Standards Institute (ANSI), the Exchange Carriers Standards Association (ECSA), and Bellcore. The initial specification allowed a transfer rate of 50.688 Mbps (the frame format consisted of 3 rows by 265 columns with signaling at 125 microseconds—264 octets × 3 rows × 8000 × 8 bits/octet = 50,688,000). The real market interest in SONET began after AT&T Bell Labs utilized it in its Metrobus project. Later, the SONET designers modified the SONET frame size to allow for T1 mapping into the frame and to the rate of and the multiples of 51.84 Mbps. This resulted also in compatibility between North American and European standards. ANSI's international counterpart, ITU-T, was responsible for the European specification based on optical signaling—Synchronous Digital Hierarchy (SDH).

SONET/SDH is an optical-based transport network, utilizing synchronous clocking. The terminal/service adapter (or *multiplexer*) maps the user signal, such as T1, E1, and ATM, into a Synchronous Transport Signal (STS). STS is an electrical signal and the basic building block of SONET. Synchronous Transport Module (STM) is an electrical signal and the basic building block of the SDH transmission hierarchy. The base rate in North America is 51.84 Mbps (STS-1). The basic rate in the rest of the world is 155.52 Mbps (STM-1), which is three times faster than in North America.

SONET Layers

SONET, categorized as a physical layer technology according to the OSI reference model, consists of multiple sublayers, as illustrated in Figure 2-5. The principles of the hierarchical OSI reference model are the basis for this design.

The user layers run on top of the SONET physical layer. The physical layer is divided into three major sublayer entities:

- Transmission *path*
- Digital *line*
- Regeneration *section*

Figure 2-5   *SONET Layers Configuration*

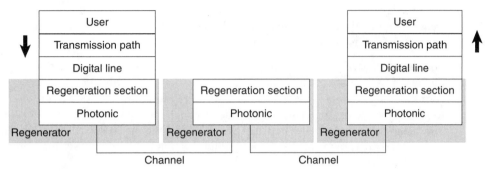

It is important to realize that the path layer might not be accessible within the network by the intermediate switches, because the path layer takes care of an end-to-end operation. Traffic is passed from the user layer to the path layer, where the path header or overhead is attached. Some of the responsibilities of the path layer include

- Performance monitoring
- Path status
- Path trace
- Assembly and disassembly of cells into STS signals

From the path layer, the traffic is passed to the line layer. The line layer attaches its header (overhead) and performs some operations, such as multiplexing the signals. The line overhead functions include

- Multiplexing (or concatenating) signals
- Performance monitoring
- Switching protection
- Line maintenance

Upon completing its functions, the line layer passes the traffic to the regeneration section.

The regeneration section consists of section and photonic layers. The section layer attaches the section header and performs the following functions:

- Performance monitoring
- Framing
- Local orderwire
- Form message-based channel for Operations, Administration, Maintenance, and Provisioning (OAM&P)

Upon completing its functions, the section layer sends the traffic to the photonic layer. The photonic layer is responsible for converting the electrical signals to the optical signals and for regenerating the optical signals. The photonic layer does not add the header. It encodes the traffic into bits and transmits them.

You can see that SONET framing constitutes three levels of overhead, as illustrated in Figure 2-6. Above the photonic layer, the section, line, and path layers add their corresponding headers to the payload, consequently forming a SONET frame or envelope. Repeaters or regenerators, which are needed when the signal through the fiber becomes too low due to the long distances between SONET/SDH multiplexers, join sections. The multiplexers are responsible for mapping, aligning, multiplexing, and stuffing various input rates from asynchronous signals.

Figure 2-6 *Three Levels of SONET Overhead*

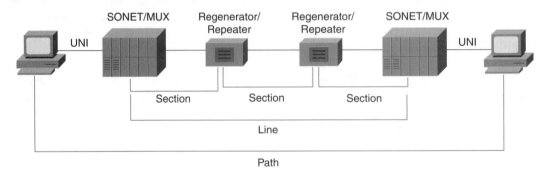

SONET/SDH Signaling Hierarchy

Table 2-3 shows the SONET and SDH multiplexing signaling hierarchy and both the Optical Signaling (OS) and Electrical Signaling (ES) levels. STS-1 forms the basis for the Optical Carrier–1 (OC-1) signal. OC-1 is the foundation for the synchronous optical signal hierarchy; STS-1 forms the basis for the synchronous electrical signal hierarchy in North America, and STM-1 forms the basis for the synchronous electrical signal hierarchy in the rest of the world. The electrical rate is used primarily for transport within a specific piece of hardware. When lower level signals are multiplexed, you can achieve higher level signals, such as OC-192, for example. The common notation of reference to any level of SONET signaling hierarchy is STS-n or OC-n, where n is an integer number, corresponding to the level of multiplexing or concatenation in North America. The common notation reference in the rest of the world is STM-n, where n also signifies the concatenation level.

The SONET/SDH signaling hierarchy does not stop at OC-192. It carries on up to OC-768 with link speeds of 39 Gbps and more. With new technology developments and the growing bandwidth demands, these higher levels of SONET hierarchy no doubt will be deployed to a greater extent than can be imagined today.

Table 2-3   *SONET and SDH Signaling Hierarchy*

SONET/SDH OS	SONET ES	SDH ES	Link Rate Mbps
OC-1	STS-1		51.84
OC-3	STS-3	STM-1	155.52
OC-9	STS-9	STM-3	466.56
OC-12	STS-12	STM-4	622.08
OC-18	STS-18	STM-6	933.12
OC-24	STS-24	STM-8	1244.16
OC-36	STS-36	STM-12	1866.24
OC-48	STS-48	STM-16	2488.32
OC-96	STS-96	STM-20	4876.64
OC-192	STS-192	STM-24	9953.28

SONET Envelope

The SONET Envelope, also called Synchronous Payload Envelope (SPE or frame) consists of the STS-1 basic transmission unit. SDH, on the other hand, differs, because it starts at the STS-3 level, which is the equivalent of STM-1. When you say STS-3c or OC-3c, it means "Synchronous Transport Signal-3 concatenated" or "Optical Carrier-3 concatenated." The concatenation process is actually a byte interleaving technique. All levels of the SONET/SDH hierarchy consist of bytes (each is 8 bits) that are transmitted serially along the optical fiber.

For ease of documentation, the SONET payload typically is illustrated as a two-dimensional map, consisting of m columns and 9 rows. Figure 2-7 illustrates how each entry in this map can be represented as an individual byte (B) of the frame. The transmission of the frame starts with the flag (F) that denotes the beginning of the frame. The flag is positioned within the section header of the frame. The frame bytes are transmitted in the sequential order starting with the first byte, B(1,1), B(1,2), and so on. A row at a time gets transmitted until the last byte, B(9,m), is sent.

The frames are sent continuously and the payload is inserted into the envelope under strict timing rules. However, there could be instances when the user payload might be inserted into more than one envelope. This creates the flexibility of the exact positioning of the payload, which can be inserted anywhere within the boundaries of the envelope. So how do you know where the beginning of the payload is? Simply by using the pointer, which indicates the beginning of the payload. This flexible nature of SONET framing allows it to accept synchronous and asynchronous (which is ATM) types of traffic. The pointer is positioned within the Line header.

Figure 2-7   *Illustration of SONET Payload as a Two-dimensional Map*

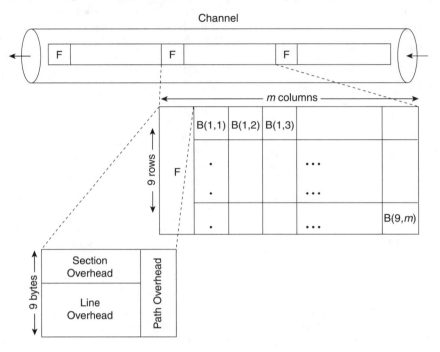

In Figure 2-6, you saw that the SONET frame or envelope contains three types of overhead: Path, Line, and Section. Line Overhead and Section Overhead are called *transport overhead*, that is, TO = LO + SO. SONET achieves its *n*th levels of hierarchy by interleaving *n* frames in such a way that the Path Overhead does not get duplicated. It is strictly one column, consisting of 9 bytes, regardless of the level of hierarchy. For example, Figure 2-8 illustrates the STS-3c/STM-1 SONET frame format. You can see that the transport overhead is nine columns, resulting in 81 bytes, and the Path Overhead remains at 9 bytes.

Utilizing the frame length of 125 microseconds (8000 frames per second), the total number of bytes in the STS-3c frame is

90 bytes/frame × 9 rows × 3 frames × 8 bits/byte × 8000 frames/second = 155.52 Mbps

To calculate the STS-*nc* efficiency, you need to compare the amounts of payload bytes and the total number of bytes. The following example illustrates the STS-3c efficiency calculation:

Total number of bytes: 90 bytes × 3 frames × 9 rows = 2430 bytes

Total number of payload bytes:
(87 bytes – 1 byte path overhead) × 3 frames × 9 rows = 2322 bytes

The STS-3c efficiency is:
2322 ÷ 2430 × 100% = 96%.

Figure 2-8   *Example of STS-3c SONET Frame Format*

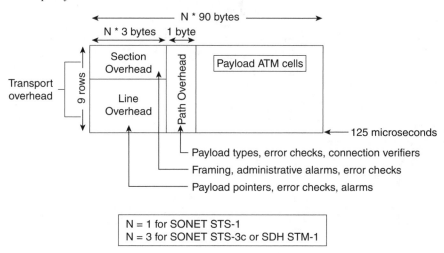

N = 1 for SONET STS-1
N = 3 for SONET STS-3c or SDH STM-1

DS-3/E3 Framing

In addition to SONET/SDH framing, there is also DS-3/E3 framing for high-speed dedicated circuits. DS-3 is a North American transmission standard that runs at 44.736 Mbps; the E3 is the European transmission standard that runs at 34.368 Mbps.

Now that you know how the ATM cells are mapped into SONET/SDH frames, let's look at the DS-3/E3 framing.

DS-3 Framing

There are two techniques to map ATM cells to a DS-3 frame:

- Using a Physical Layer Convergence Protocol (PLCP)
- Direct mapping to a DS-3 frame

PLCP is a subset of the PLCP defined in IEEE P802.6 (SMDS principles). Mapping ATM cells (PLCP payload) into the DS-3 frame is accomplished by inserting the 53-byte ATM cells into the DS-3 PLCP frame. Figure 2-9 illustrates the ATM cell mapping for the PLCP frame format over DS-3 transmission.

At the network destination, the extraction of ATM cells from the DS-3 frame operates in the reverse procedure (that is, by framing on the PLCP and then simply extracting the ATM cells directly). The PLCP mapping is defined in the ATM Forum's UNI 3.0/3.1 specification. Because of the overhead, the available bit rate with PLCP mapping is 40.704 Mbps. The DS-3 PLCP consists of a 125-microsecond frame within a DS-3 payload. Note, that the DS-3 PLCP frame might begin anywhere inside the DS-3 payload. Because the DS-3 PLCP is not aligned to the DS-3 framing bits, the alignment of the DS-3 PLCP frame to the DS-3 payload envelope is accomplished by using the trailer bytes, which are between

6.5 and 7 bytes in length. The trailer bytes are stuffed after the twelfth cell to provide the synchronization, which is required by the DS-3.

Figure 2-9 *ATM Cell in DS-3 Frame Using the PLCP Frame and the Direct Mapping Formats*

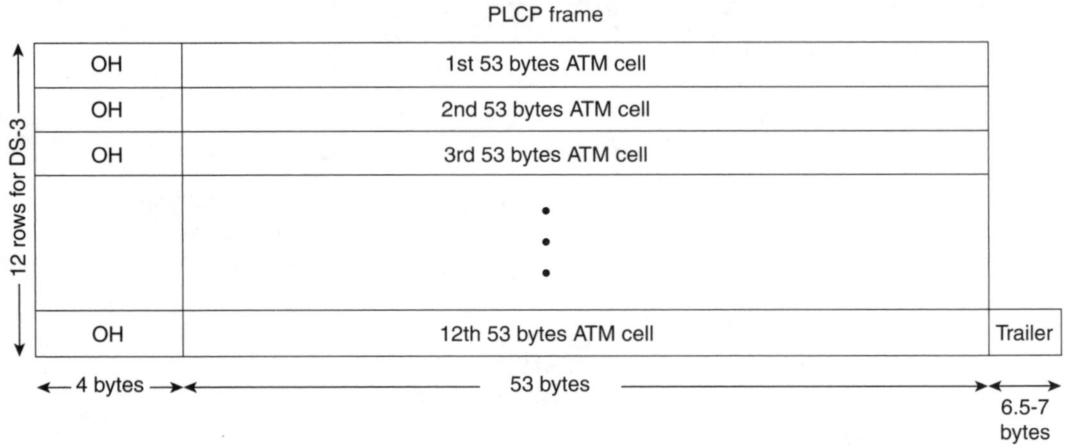

PLCP frame

OH	1st 53 bytes ATM cell
OH	2nd 53 bytes ATM cell
OH	3rd 53 bytes ATM cell
	• • •
OH	12th 53 bytes ATM cell	Trailer

← 4 bytes →←————— 53 bytes —————→←→ 6.5-7 bytes

12 rows for DS-3

Direct mapping of ATM cells to DS-3 frame

←———————————— 680 bits ————————————→

M frame	1 bit	84 bits	1 bit	84 bits	1 bit	84 bits	1 bit	84 bits	1 bit	84 bits	1 bit	84 bits	1 bit	84 bits	1 bit	84 bits
1	OH	84 bits	OH	84 bits	OH	84 bits	OH	84 bits	OH	84 bits	OH	84 bits	OH	84 bits	OH	84 bits
2	OH	84 bits	OH	84 bits	OH	84 bits	OH	84 bits	OH	84 bits	OH	84 bits	OH	84 bits	OH	84 bits
3	OH	84 bits	OH	84 bits	OH	84 bits	OH	84 bits	OH	84 bits	OH	84 bits	OH	84 bits	OH	84 bits
4	OH	84 bits	OH	84 bits	OH	84 bits	OH	84 bits	OH	84 bits	OH	84 bits	OH	84 bits	OH	84 bits
5	OH	84 bits	OH	84 bits	OH	84 bits	OH	84 bits	OH	84 bits	OH	84 bits	OH	84 bits	OH	84 bits
6	OH	84 bits	OH	84 bits	OH	84 bits	OH	84 bits	OH	84 bits	OH	84 bits	OH	84 bits	OH	84 bits
7	OH	84 bits	OH	84 bits	OH	84 bits	OH	84 bits	OH	84 bits	OH	84 bits	OH	84 bits	OH	84 bits

Note: OH = Overhead   ATM cells

Direct mapping to a DS-3 frame was the later technique to map ATM cells to a DS-3 frame that is based on the ANSI T1.646 standard and is referred to in the ATM Forum "DS3 Physical Layer Interface Specification," AF-PHY-0054.000, standard. Direct mapping, illustrated in Figure 2-9, is a more efficient method—the available bit rate with direct mapping is 44.21 Mbps.

E3 Framing

Europe employs two techniques to map ATM cells to E3 frames:

- PLCP
- Direct mapping to an E3 frame

Figure 2-10 shows the PLCP frame format for E3 transmission, which is quite analogous to DS-3 PLCP format. The PLCP frame format uses the G.751 standard and is a 125-microsecond frame within the standard E3 information payload. The trailer length is 18 to 20 bytes, which is used for stuffing to provide synchronization with the E3 frame.

The direct mapping of ATM cells to E3 frames uses the G.832 standard (ITU-T, 1994). The ATM Forum refers to the direct mapping of ATM cells to E3 frames in the "E3 Public UNI" specification, AF-PHY-0034.000. Essentially, the ATM cells are mapped to the 530 bytes of payload directly. The overhead consists of 7 bytes, as illustrated in Figure 2-10.

Inverse Multiplexing Over ATM

When it comes to network designs, you always are faced with a question of bandwidth demand. ATM access speeds range from the T1/E1 level up to several gigabits per second. When you gradually migrate to an ATM cloud, you might begin with a T1/E1 access level progressing into DS-3/E3, and then OC-3, and so on. Well, what if you require only, say, 5 Mbps speed? Do you need to get four T1s, because T3 is just an overkill for now? By getting four T1s, you create four parallel links.

Inverse Multiplexing over ATM (IMA) offers a solution to this dilemma. IMA is a breakthrough standard (ATM Forum AF-PHY-0086.001) that enables *right-sizing* and *right-pricing* of access solutions for organizations with low- and mid-range traffic requirements. IMA simplifies and reduces WAN costs by traffic consolidation.

IMA divides an aggregate stream of ATM cells across multiple T1/E1 ATM access links on a cell-by-cell basis. IMA specifies a transmission scheme by which several T1/E1 lines transmit the source ATM cells in a round-robin fashion. For example, the first cell is sent on the first T1/E1 circuit, the second on the second circuit, and so on, as illustrated in Figure 2-11. Control information is added so that the status of each link can be determined and the link can be corrected, if needed. As a result of this transmission scheme, cells are reassembled at the receiving end without loss of the original ATM cell order or QoS.

An important feature of IMA is the capability to add or delete T1/E1 circuits on demand. With IMA, the ATM switch sees one access link (that is, one ATM trunk) to the ATM network. Another interesting aspect of IMA is the fact that IMA reduces bandwidth consumption by removing idle cells (remember, those cells with VPI equals 0 and VCI equals 0?) from the original stream and reinserting them at the receiving end. IMA is totally transparent to the application and to the rest of the ATM network.

Figure 2-10 *ATM Cell in an E3 Frame Using the PLCP Frame and Direct Mapping Formats*

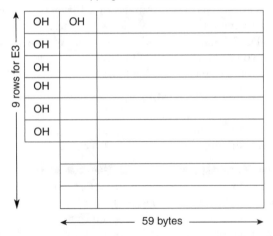

Note: OH = Overhead

How does an IMA access device know which order to put the cells back in? Putting cells in order is absolutely imperative, because there is no sequence number that is located in the original cell header (as discussed in the section on the ATM layer). The ATM edge device that performs frame/packet re-assembly reconstructs the frame/packet based on the order of the cells' arrival. The order of the cell flow, however, is altered with the introduction of IMA. The solution to the alteration of cell flow order introduced by IMA lies in the IMA Control Protocol (ICP). The ATM Forum (AF-PHY-0086.001) defines how ICP works. The transmit IMA periodically sends special cells, ICP cells, containing information that help the flow reconstruction at the receiving IMA side. These cells provide the definition of an

IMA frame. The information includes the IMA Frame Sequence Number (IFSN) that indicates the location of the ICP cell within the IMA frame. The complete structure of an ICP cell is in the ATM Forum specification, AF-PHY-0086.001.

Figure 2-11 *Inverse Multiplexing and Demultiplexing of ATM Cells*

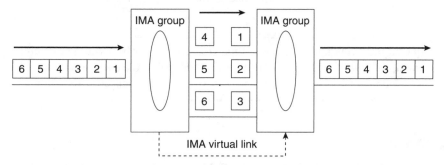

Figure 2-12 positions IMA into the ATM stack. IMA is located at the top of the physical layer, between the traditional TC sublayer and the ATM layer.

Figure 2-12 *IMA Sublayer in the ATM Reference Model*

	Higher Layers		
L a y e r m a n a g e m e n t	Convergence sublayer	CS	AAL
	Segmentation and reassembly sublayer	SAR	
	Cell header creation/verification Cell VPI/VCI translation Cell multiplex and demultiplex Generic Flow Control (GFC)	ATM	
	ATM cell stream splitting and reconstruction **ICP cells insertion/removal** **Cell rate decoupling** **IMA frame synchronization** **Stuffing**	**IMA**	Physical
	HEC generation/verification Cell delineation and rate decoupling Transmission frame adaption Transmission frame generation/recovery	TC	
	Bit timing (time recovery) Line coding Physical medium	PMD	

IMA has many advantages, including

- Sub-T3/E3 rates are utilized efficiently
- Failed T1/E1 links are added/restored transparently
- Cell order and ATM traffic management are preserved

NOTE   In October 1999, the ATM Forum finalized even lower bandwidth utilization to the ATM end users. Specification AF-PHY-0130.000 describes the use of fractional T1/E1 for ATM, which constitutes 24×64 kbps and 32×64 kbps channels correspondingly.

ATM Layer

Above the physical layer resides the ATM layer, which is the bottom quarter of Layer 2 of the OSI reference model (illustrated in Chapter 1, "ATM Introduction," in Figure 1-2). The ATM layer is responsible for cell switching and multiplexing through the ATM network. The ATM layer is the highest layer within the ATM cloud that the switches deploy when switching payload traffic. Figure 2-13 traces the payload cells from the edge device Router1 to the edge device Router2.

Figure 2-13 *ATM Switches Switch Payload Cells at Layer 1.25 of the OSI Reference Model*

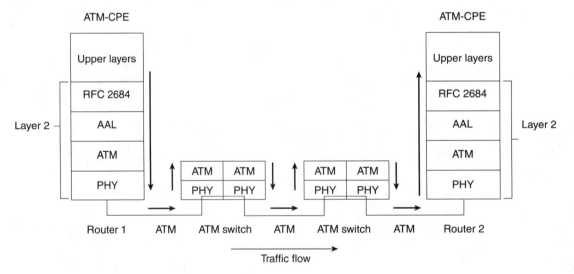

ATM differs from synchronous transfer methods, such as with TDM techniques that pre-assign users to timeslots. ATM is an asynchronous multiplexing mechanism and, hence, makes use of bandwidth on demand.

Based on Figure 2-1, one of the compass figures, Figure 2-14 shows that the input into the ATM layer is a 48-byte payload, called be segmentation and reassembly-protocol data unit (SAR-PDU), and the output of the ATM layer is a 53-byte cell that is passed to the physical layer for transmission. The SAR-PDU size is the 48-byte payload of the ATM cell.

The ATM layer is responsible for producing the 5-byte ATM cell header for attachment to the payload.

Figure 2-14 *ATM Layer Positioning Within the ATM Stack*

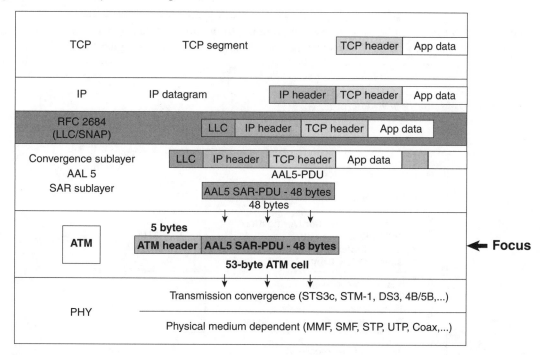

Other responsibilities of the ATM layer are VPI/VCI translation, cell multiplexing/demultiplexing, and Generic Flow Control (GFC). Based on Figure 2-2, the second compass figure, Figure 2-15 illustrates all ATM layer responsibilities.

ATM Switching Operations

Answering the question, "How does an ATM switch know where to send the cell?" can help you better understand the ATM layer. Any kind of switching device, be it a router, an Ethernet switch, an ATM switch, or a telephone switch, makes its switching decisions based on some forwarding tables. The content of a forwarding table must include some sort of addressing. In the case of an IP router, addressing involves an IP logical network number;

in the case of an Ethernet switch, addressing involves a MAC physical address; in the case of a telephone switch, addressing involves a set of digits that are part of a telephone number; and, in the case of an ATM switch, addressing involves a combination of the VPI/VCI numbers. The VPI/VCI numbers could be defined either by ATM network administrators or dynamically by the ATM switch. Regardless of who assigns the VPI/VCI, for the ATM switch to forward (or switch) cells, it must have a forwarding table that identifies which VPI/VCI is to be forwarded to which interface.

NOTE   Always remember that VCI values, ranging from 0 to 31 inclusive, are reserved by ATM Forum and ITU-T. This means that you should use VCI values higher than 31.

Figure 2-15 *ATM Layer Responsibilities*

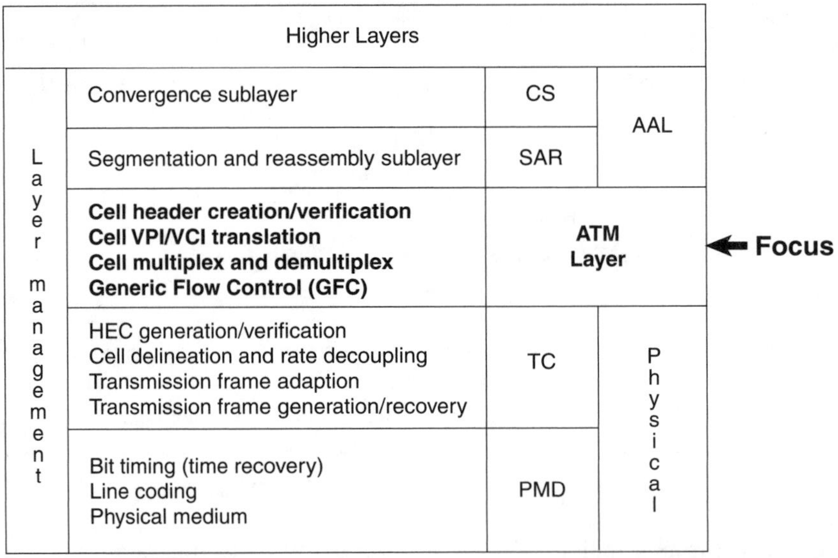

Looking closer at one of the responsibilities of an ATM switch (cell VPI/VCI translation), it is clear that the switch expects to see a form of an address within the incoming cell header. Then, based on that address, it checks its forwarding tables to identify the new address that the old one must be translated into for the next network leg as well as which interface this particular cell must be sent through. Figure 2-16 illustrates the VPI/VCI address translation within an ATM switch.

Figure 2-16 *VPI/VCI Address Translation*

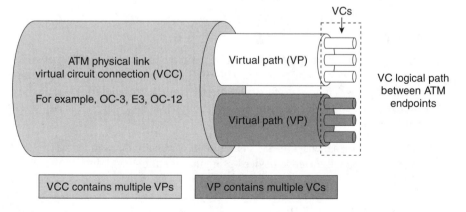

Forwarding Table

Input		Output	
Port	VPI/VCI	Port	VPI/VCI
1	2/39	2	4/55
2	4/55	1	2/39
1	6/64	3	2/89
3	2/89	1	6/64

The VPI/VCI values are locally significant at the interface level. This is very similar to the Frame Relay addressing of the Data Link Connection Identifier (DLCI). Each switch along the way either changes the VPI/VCI value or leaves it unchanged—it truly does not matter. An ATM switch analyzes the information in the header to switch the cell to the output interface that connects the switch to the next appropriate switch as the cell works its way to its destination.

When you refer to the VPI/VCI combination, the idea is that you are referring to the VCI within a VPI number. For example, a reference to 3/40 means VCI number 40 within a VPI number 3. A combination of VPI/VCI comprises the connection identifier. As illustrated in Figure 2-17, a virtual path (VP) contains multiple virtual circuits (VCs), and a virtual circuit connection (VCC) contains multiple VPs.

Figure 2-17 *Virtual Path and Virtual Circuit*

A good logical analogy between VPs and VCs is the PBX connectivity to a telephone company's Central Office (CO). On the user side of the PBX, there could be hundreds of telephones, each of which has a dedicated line to the PBX. The PBX, however, could be interconnected to the CO via several local CO trunks (much fewer than the number of telephones). So, ATM's VCs are the lines going from the ATM end point to the ATM switch (logically, a line going from the user to the PBX), and VPs are the trunks extending from one ATM switch to another (logically, a local CO trunk going from a PBX to the local CO). A single VP is a bundle of several VCs, as a single PBX trunk can carry a bundle of lines. Figure 2-18 shows this. VCC, logically similar to trunks between COs, is a transmission path, like OC-3, E3, OC-12, and so on.

Figure 2-18 *The Relationship Between VPs and VCs Is Analogous to the Trunk and Line Relationship*

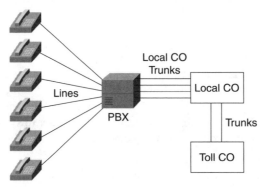

Although the VPI/VCI addressing idea theoretically is quite simple, the question is who assigns the VPI/VCI numbers? Before answering this question, let's address the various types of VCs that exist in ATM. The types of VCs are

- Permanent virtual circuit (PVC)
- Switched virtual circuit (SVC)
- Soft VC

PVCs are preset within the ATM cloud by people administering ATM networks. A PVC is a permanently defined collection of VPIs/VCIs that enables the cell switching using the predefined paths. There is no flexibility for dynamic path generation within the PVC cloud, should there be a link failure. Consequently, duplicate PVCs are necessary should you need redundancy in the PVC-type networks.

SVCs are not permanent. The SVC is set up dynamically through the ATM cloud upon the demand from one of the edge devices using the signaling PVC. In an SVC environment, the VPI/VCI numbers are assigned dynamically by ATM switches, and forwarding tables are generated dynamically. You can think of the phenomenon of SVC setup as the SVC "drilling through the ATM cloud." How does the signaling PVC know which direction to go and how does the ATM source device refer to the destination? The idea is quite simple—the ATM source refers to the destination using globally significant addresses (NSAP or E.164) and the ATM signaling PVC is routed through the ATM cloud by the ATM switches. The routing protocols responsible for the routing of the signaling could be either Interim Interswitch Signaling Protocol (IISP) or Private Network-to-Network Interface (PNNI). Chapter 3, "ATM Reference Model: Higher Layers," discusses SVCs, signaling, and call setup in greater detail.

The Soft PVC means that the ATM cloud is SVC-based, whereas the edge device(s) access to the cloud is via a PVC. Figure 2-19 illustrates the Soft VC idea. Chapter 3 discusses the various VC types in greater detail.

Figure 2-19 *Soft PVCs*

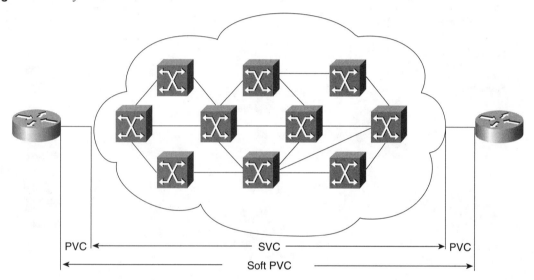

As you deploy ATM PVC networks, you can design the VPI/VCI numbering scheme with a strategy in mind. The idea is quite simple: Deploy a two-layer addressing hierarchy with a simple idea, without complications of variable-length subnet masks (VLSMs) that are used in IP addressing. Let's look at the following example.

You have to design an ATM PVC addressing scheme for the sites located in the three major states across the United States: California, Texas, and New York, as illustrated in the Figure 2-20. Within each of the states, you have three cities to be connected to the ATM cloud. In California, the cities are San Francisco, Los Angeles, and San Jose. In Texas, you have Houston, Dallas, and Austin. In New York, the cities are Buffalo, New York City, and Albany.

Upon the analysis of the traffic patterns, you come to the conclusion that it is cost effective to have a fully meshed topology. To ease your ATM network manageability, you decide to use a hierarchical approach by referring to a specific state by a single number only—VPI.

When the connectivity is made to a switch within a state, you need to refer to the city within the state by adding another unique address identifier—VCI. Looking closer, when switches see VPI equals 9 in the cells coming in from the backbone cloud, they know that this traffic is destined to go to the California switch. If VPI equals 11, the traffic is destined to go to New York; if VPI equals 5, the traffic has to go to Texas. Then the second layer of switching takes place, where the state switch examines both VPI and VCI values to direct the traffic into the appropriate city. For example, the California switch directs cells with VPI equals 9, VCI equals 181 to San Francisco. Your entries into each state can happen from any direction with identical or different VPI numbers. Remember, the VPI numbers (as well as the VCI numbers) are locally significant to every interface of a switch.

Figure 2-20   *Example of VPI/VCI Hierarchical Addressing Assignment Within ATM PVC Clouds*

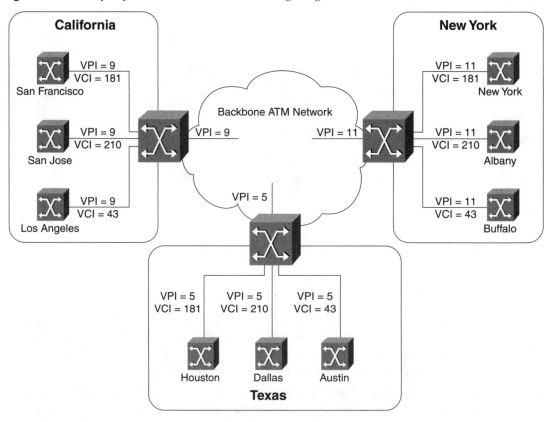

It is important to note that when you see the reference to the VCC, the ATM switch is performing cell forwarding based on the VPI/VCI combination. If you see a reference to the VPC, the ATM switch is performing cell switching based on VPI only. Figure 2-21 illustrates the ATM switch acting as a VP switch. It establishes VPCs based on VPs only. Note that the VCI values within a VPC must be the same at both ends.

Figure 2-21 *ATM VP Switch Establishing VPC*

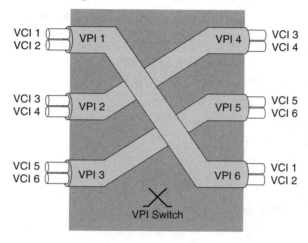

Figure 2-22 shows the ATM switch acting as both a VP switch and a VC switch, which establishes both VPCs and VCCs.

Figure 2-22 *ATM VP and VC Switch Establishing VPC and VCC*

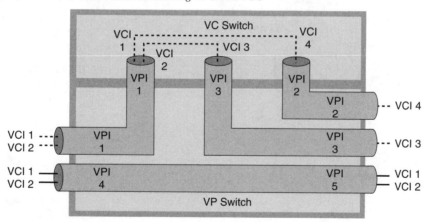

Now, that we established the fact that the VPI/VCI numbers are part of the ATM cell header, the question is how many bits are used for the VPI and the VCI? Knowing the number of bits used for VPI and VCI will identify the scalability of the ATM networks. Prior to answering the question, it is important to differentiate between various types of ATM network interfaces, as defined by the ATM Forum. Why? Well, simply because the VPI/VCI scalability is different for various types of ATM logical interfaces.

ATM Forum–defined Network Interfaces

The ATM Forum defines a number of different types of interfaces in a network. The interfaces are actually the functions that are performed between two adjacent entities, such as between a router and an ATM switch or between two ATM switches. Figure 2-23 positions the various standardized ATM network interfaces:

- Private User-Network Interface (UNI)
- Private NNI (PNNI)
- Public UNI
- Public NNI
- BISDN Inter Carrier Interface (B-ICI)
- ATM Internetwork Interface (AINI)

Figure 2-23 *ATM Network Interfaces*

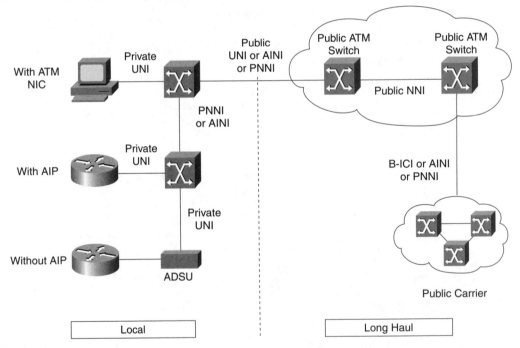

User-Network Interfaces

The UNI defines the logical procedures and protocols that enable an edge device to interface an ATM switch. An edge device could be a host, a router, an Ethernet switch, or a private ATM switch talking to the public ATM switch. The ATM Forum comprehensively defined the UNI functions (UNI 3.0/3.1/4.0), the most recent being UNI 4.0. Table 2-4 identifies all functions provided in the UNI Signaling 4.0 and whether the functions are Mandatory (M) or Optional (O) on the ATM edge device and the ATM switch.

Table 2-4   *UNI 4.0 Signaling Features*

Feature	ATM Edge Device	ATM Switch
Point-to-point calls	M	M
Point-to-multipoint calls	O	M
Signaling of individual QoS parameters	M	M
Leaf initiated join	O	O
ATM anycast	O	O,M[1]
ABR signaling for point-to-point calls	O	O
Generic Identifier Transport	O	O
Virtual UNIs	O	O
Switched VP service	O	O
Proxy signaling	O	O
Frame discard	O	M[2]
Traffic parameter negotiation	O	O
Supplementary services:		
Direct Dialing In (DDI)	O	O
Multiple Subscriber Number (MSN)	O	O
Calling Line Identification Presentation (CLIP)	O	O
Calling Line Identification Restriction (CLIR)	O	O
Connected Line Identification Presentation (COLP)	O	O
Connected Line Identification Restriction (COLR)	O	O
Subaddressing (SUB)	O	M[3]
User-User Signaling (UUS)	O	O

Source: ATM User-Network Interface (UNI) Signaling Specification, Version 4.0 (AF-SIG-0061.000), July 1996.

[1]This feature is optional for public networks/switching systems and is mandatory for private network/switching systems.

[2]The transport of the frame discard indication is mandatory.

[3]This feature is mandatory for networks/switching systems (public and private) that support only native E.164 address formats.

There are two types of UNIs: Private and Public. The basic difference between the two UNIs is that the Private UNI specifies the protocols of the edge device connectivity to the private ATM switch, and the Public UNI specifies the protocols of the edge device connectivity to the public ATM switch. Table 2-5 provides a complete comparison between the functions of the two types of UNIs and whether the functions are Mandatory (M) or Optional (O) on the ATM edge device and the ATM switch. The most significant difference between the Public UNI and the Private UNI is the SVC addressing.

Table 2-5 *Public and Private UNI Responsibilities*

ATM Attribute	Private UNI	Public UNI
Global addressing format for SVC	NSAP[1]	E.164
Support for point-to-point VPCs	O	O
Support for point-to-point VCCs	M	M
Support for point-to-multipoint VPCs	O	O
Support for point-to-multipoint VCCs, SVC	M	M
Support for point-to-multipoint VCCs, PVC	O	O
Support of PVC	M	M
Support of SVC	M	M
Support of specified QoS classes	M	M
Support of unspecified QoS class	O	O
Multiple bandwidth granularities for ATM connections	O	M
Peak rate traffic enforcement via UPC	O	M
Sustainable cell rate traffic enforcement via UPC	O	O
Traffic shaping	O	O
ATM layer fault management	O	M
ATM anycast	M	O
Subaddressing (SUB)	O	M
Interim Local Management Interface (ILMI)	M	M

Source: ATM User-Network Interface Specification, Version 3.1 (AF-UNI-0010.002), September 1994.

[1]NSAP (Network Service Access Point) is the OSI generic standard for network addressing.

Network-to-Network Interfaces

It is interesting to note that both Private and Public NNIs specify switch-to-switch interconnection, including routing and signaling aspects. PNNI is used in private ATM clouds and Public NNI is used within a single ATM service provider. NNI signaling is based on a subset of UNI 4.0 signaling. It does not support some UNI 4.0 signaling features, such as proxy signaling, leaf-initiated join capability, or user-to-user supplementary service. NNI signaling does add new features, however, such as PNNI routing for dynamic call setup.

BISDN Inter Carrier Interfaces

The B-ICI is responsible for interconnectivity between multiple ATM service providers. B-ICI is tightly interrelated with NNI. Whereas the NNI specification includes the SONET/SDH physical layer and the ATM layer, the B-ICI specification includes layers above ATM, such as AAL and other intercarrier service specific layers, as illustrated in Figure 2-24.

Figure 2-24 *Relation of B-ICI to NNI*

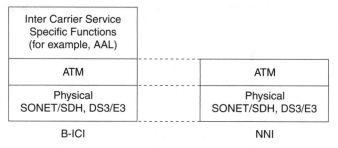

Specification of support for other intercarrier services is absolutely imperative for B-ICI because it enables ATM to interconnect to a variety of various existing services, such as Frame Relay, voice, and SMDS.

ATM Internetwork Interfaces

In July 1999, the ATM Forum approved the AINI for interconnection of private and public networks. AINI is another method for private-to-public and public-to-public ATM network interconnectivity.

AINI is based on PNNI signaling. The goal in defining the AINI protocol is to facilitate interworking of one network running PNNI internally with another network running Broadband ISDN User Part (B-ISUP) protocol or two networks running PNNI internally, as depicted in Figure 2-25. AINI does not support the following features that PNNI supports:

- PNNI Designated Transit List (DTL)
- ATM Anycast

Figure 2-25 *AINI Interworking Scenarious*

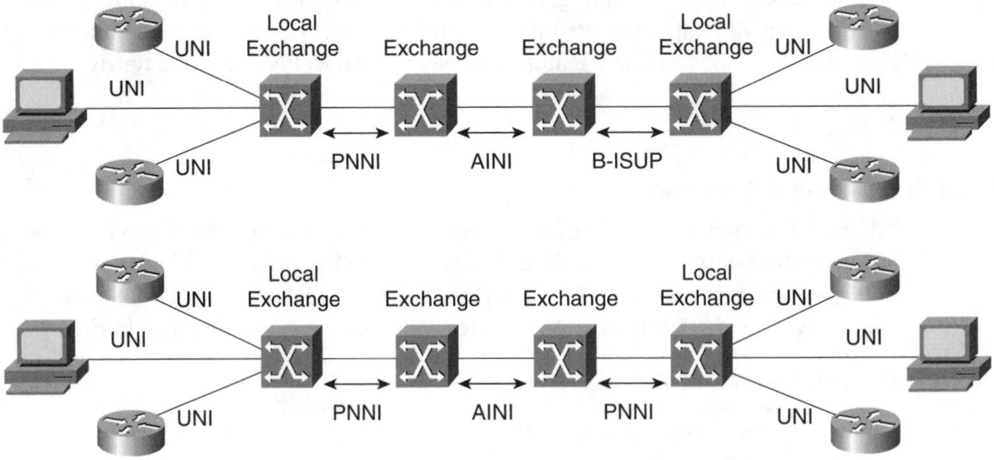

ATM Interface Summary

Table 2-6 summarizes types of ATM interfaces and their applicability.

Table 2-6   *ATM Interfaces Summary*

To→ From↓	Private ATM Networks	Public ATM Networks	Edge Devices
Private ATM networks	IISP, PNNI	Public UNI, AINI	Private UNI
Public ATM networks	Public UNI, AINI	PNNI, B-ICI, AINI	Public UNI
Edge devices	Private UNI	Public UNI	N/A

ATM Cell Header: UNI and NNI Formats

The ATM cell header is only 5 bytes long, containing only pertinent information, and yet the 5 bytes are enough for switching cells, identifying "who" is important, identifying the end of the frame, marking the network management cells, and so on.

ATM cell headers can be used for either UNIs or NNIs. Both are 5 bytes in length. The only difference is that the UNI header has a GFC field of 4 bits; whereas, the NNI header does not. Figures 2-26 and 2-27 illustrate the UNI and NNI cell headers, respectively.

Figure 2-26 *UNI Cell Format*

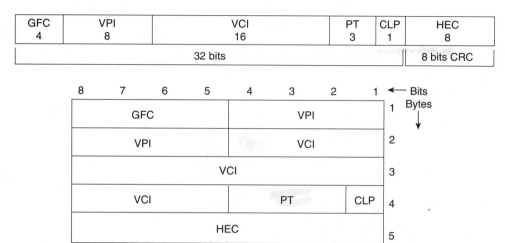

Figure 2-27 *NNI Cell Format*

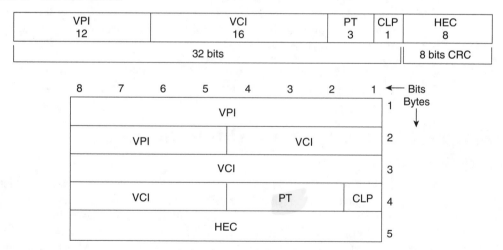

GFC has been specified only at the UNI side. Because it is not carried through the ATM network, it has local significance only, from the edge device to the first ATM switch. At this point, nobody uses this field, although some vendors have proposed a proprietary use of it.

The VPI and VCI are unique only for a particular interface and might change as they travel through each ATM switch. At the UNI side, the VPI field is 8 bits long; thus, it can identify

s. At the NNI side, the VPI is 12 bits long and has the flexibility to expand to more
)0 VPs. This is very useful for trunking between ATM switches. In both cases, the
identify up to 65536 VCs.

The 3-bit Payload Type (PT) field indicates the payload type, the end of the frame, and the
congestion. Table 2-7 illustrates the details of the bit structure of the PT field.

Table 2-7 *PT Values*

Bit #	1		2		3	
Bit Value	0	1	1	0	1	0
Meaning	Data cell	OAM cell[1]	Congested (EFCI is on)[2]	Not Congested	End Of Message (EOM)[3]	Not End of Message

[1]Operation and Maintenance (OAM) cells are used for ATM cloud management.

[2]Explicit Forward Congestion Indication (EFCI) indicates whether a cell has experienced congestion.

[3]End of Message (EOM) identifies the final cell of the higher layer frame/packet.

The cell loss priority (CLP) bit indicates whether a cell can be discarded by the network
should there be congestion. When the bit is turned on (equals 1) and if there is congestion,
the cell is discarded; otherwise, the cell must go through, unless something drastic happens.
It is very similar to the discard eligible (DE) bit of the Frame Relay clouds. Chapter 4,
"ATM Traffic and Network Management."

The HEC field, using the other fields of the cell header, is calculated at the TC layer. Each
ATM switch can fix a 1-bit error in the header.

ATM Adaptation Layers for Different Traffic Classifications

The AAL resides above the ATM layer. When compared to the OSI reference model, it is
part of Layer 2, the data link layer, which IEEE divides into two sublayers: Media Access
Control (MAC) and logical link control (LLC). Well, the functionality of the top part of the
MAC sublayer reminds me of AAL. AAL converts higher-layer information, such as data
packets, into ATM 48-byte payloads for transmission across the ATM network. At the
receiving end, the AAL converts the payloads back into the higher-layer information.

NOTE   The similarity between AAL and the top part of the MAC layer is obvious based on the following responsibility of the MAC sublayer. The MAC sublayer is responsible for carrying out all the operations concerned with the transmission and reception of frames according to the rules of the protocol for accessing the physical channel. As a sender, the MAC calculates check values used by the receiver to detect transmit errors, assembles, and sends frames of data. As a receiver, it assembles the data frame from the physical layer, checks for transmit errors, discards bad frames, checks addresses, and discards frames intended for other devices.

The job of AAL is not that simple. It has to adapt the higher layers of information, whatever they might be—voice, video, data—into a stream of equal size cells.

Let's go back to the compass figures (refer to Figures 2-1 and 2-2), which are very useful in navigation through the ATM stack.

Figure 2-28 illustrates the AAL in comparison to other layers of the ATM model using a TCP data application. You can see that the Layer 2 frames are the input into the AAL, and segmented 48-byte payloads are the output from the AAL.

Figure 2-28 *ATM Adaptation Layer Within the ATM Stack*

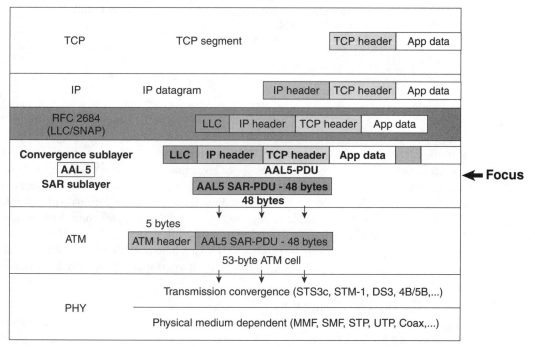

Based on the second compass figure (refer to Figure 2-2), Figure 2-29 lists the responsibilities of AAL. As you can see, the AAL is divided into two sublayers for the majority of traffic types:

- Convergence sublayer (CS)
  - — Service specific convergence sublayer (SSCS)
  - — Common part convergence sublayer (CPCS)
- Segmentation and reassembly (SAR) sublayer

Figure 2-29 *AAL Responsibilities*

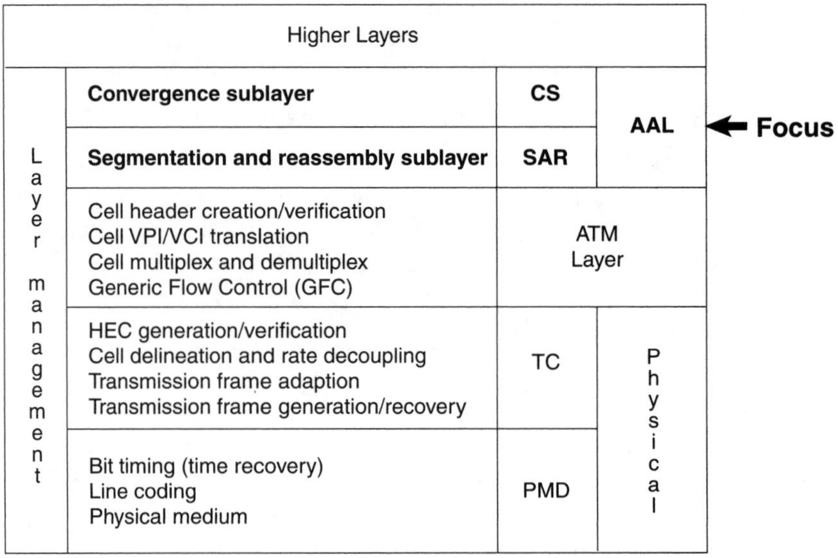
Higher Layers
Layer management
Convergence sublayer
CS
Segmentation and reassembly sublayer
SAR
AAL
Focus
Cell header creation/verification
Cell VPI/VCI translation
Cell multiplex and demultiplex
Generic Flow Control (GFC)
ATM Layer
HEC generation/verification
Cell delineation and rate decoupling
Transmission frame adaption
Transmission frame generation/recovery
TC
Bit timing (time recovery)
Line coding
Physical medium
PMD
Physical

Referring to Figure 2-28, where the TCP/IP application is to be converted into ATM cells, the CS is responsible for converting the upper layer information into a form suitable for segmentation into equal size ATM payloads. The CS is divided further into two parts: the SSCS and the CPCS. The SSCS part is related to characteristics of various types of traffic; whereas, the CPCS is responsible for framing and error checking by appending the input frame with the variable-length pad characters and a trailer. The padding exercise is necessary so that the frame can be subdivided into a whole number of equal size payloads, 48 bytes each. The trailer includes such information as error checking, which is discussed later in this chapter.

The SAR sublayer is responsible for segmenting the *converged* frame into equal sizes of 48-byte payloads at the sending edge device and for reassembling the 48-byte payloads into the converged frame at the receiving edge device.

Traffic Classifications

AAL commonly is associated with different service categories (commonly called *service classes*), such as Service Class A, B, C, or D. These classes are associated with various types of traffic/applications, requiring different bandwidth and network throughput guarantees. Some applications require constant bandwidth and very little network delay (constant bit rate [CBR] service category). Others can adapt to the available bandwidth, maybe with some lower QoS (variable bit rate [VBR] service category). Still others can make use of whatever bandwidth is available and use dramatically different amounts from one instant to the next (unspecified bit rate [UBR] service category). Yet others, although capable of using whatever bandwidth is available, still want some guarantee on bandwidth availability (available bit rate [ABR] service category). These service classes are identified in the ATM Forum Traffic Management Specification 4.0 with guidelines for implementation.

In March 1999, the ATM Forum released Traffic Management Specification 4.1. This version of Traffic Management defines a new service category—Guaranteed Frame Rate (GFR). GFR is a frame-aware service that applies only to VCCs.

Table 2-8 illustrates the types of applications associated with the various types of traffic.

Table 2-8   *Application Examples for ATM Service Categories*

ATM Service Category	Service Class	Service Type	Application Example
CBR	Class A	Voice	Telephone conversation(s)
			Audio distribution (for example, radio)
			Audio library
			Voice mail
		Video	Videoconferencing
			Video distribution (for example, television)
			Video on demand
rt-VBR	Class B	Voice	Voice mail
			Telephone conversation(s) using packetized voice
		Video	Videotex
			NTSC-quality TV
			HDTV-quality TV
nrt-VBR	Class C	Data	Airline reservations
			Banking transactions
			Frame Relay internetworking

continues

Table 2-8   *Application Examples for ATM Service Categories (Continued)*

ATM Service Category	Service Class	Service Type	Application Example
UBR	Class C or Class D	Data	E-mail File transfer Library browsing Remote terminal access
ABR	Class C or Class D	Data	Critical data transfer (defense information) NFS
GFR	Class C	Data	File transfer

The following list defines the service categories in Table 2-8.

- **CBR**—CBR service category is used by connections that require a constant amount of bandwidth that is continuously available during the connection. This amount of bandwidth is characterized by a peak cell rate (PCR) value. CBR is intended to support real-time applications requiring very tight constraints with cell delay or cell loss.

- **rt-VBR**—rt-VBR service category is intended for real-time applications, requiring tight constraints on cell delay and delay variation but do not need constant bandwidth. Sources of this service category transmit at a rate that varies in time, implying that it can be bursty. rt-VBR connections are characterized by PCR, sustainable cell rate (SCR), and maximum burst size (MBS). SCR is really an average cell rate; whereas, MBS is measured in number of cells.

- **nrt-VBR**—nrt-VBR service category is used by non–real-time applications with bursty behavior. It can be characterized by PCR, SCR, and MBS. The applications of the service category do not like losing cells; however, cell delay should not be a problem.

- **UBR**—UBR service category is intended for non–real-time applications, meaning that any cell delay is not an issue. UBR service does not provide any guarantees, but is instead a best effort service.

- **ABR**—ABR service category is not intended to support real-time applications. Its goal is to provide rapid access to unused network bandwidth at up to PCR, whenever the bandwidth is available. In addition, there is a minimum bandwidth commitment from the network measured by the minimum cell rate (MCR). This is similar to the committed information rate (CIR) of the Frame Relay network. The ABR service allows end systems to adapt their traffic in accordance with the feedback that they receive from the network. Therefore, the amount of lost cells should be minimum.

- **GFR**—GFR rate service category is intended to support non–real-time applications. Its goal is to provide the minimum guaranteed rate for applications as well as additional bandwidth dynamically, should it be available. The GFR service requires the end system to specify PCR, MCR (which could be zero), MBS, and maximum frame size (MFS). The GFR service category requires that the user data cells be organized in the form of frames that can be delineated at the ATM layer, which positions ATM to be able to discard the entire frame should there be any network congestion.

Justifying the Need for Traffic Categorization in ATM

I often wonder about the need for the categorization of traffic. Why have different types of traffic and consequently various ATM adaptation layers? You will see later that the various AALs might be robbing the 48-byte payloads for extra information, such as sequence numbers and cell error checking. Realistically, one type of AAL should be sufficient, provided that it supports QoS and that all the applications understand the QoS that was selected. Well, as you know, technology always marches ahead of business, although this gap gets shorter every day. At the time of the specification developments, ATM clouds did not support QoS. Furthermore, at present the link between data application QoS and ATM QoS is missing. Hence, the only method to guarantee preference of voice over data, for example, was treating it with a different service class that can be statically embedded into ATM clouds.

Traffic Contracts

Each service class requires a different traffic contract. The traffic contract is signed between the edge device and the ATM cloud from end to end during the connection establishment, as illustrated in the Figure 2-30.

Figure 2-30 *Traffic Contract*

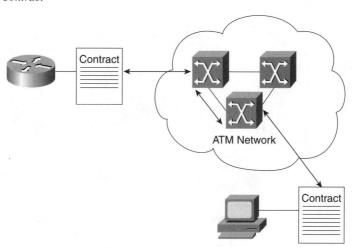

Figure 2-31 illustrates the traffic contract parameters associated with various ATM service categories.

Figure 2-31 *Traffic Contract Parameters for CBR, rt-VBR, nrt-VBR, UBR, ABR, and GFR Service Categories*

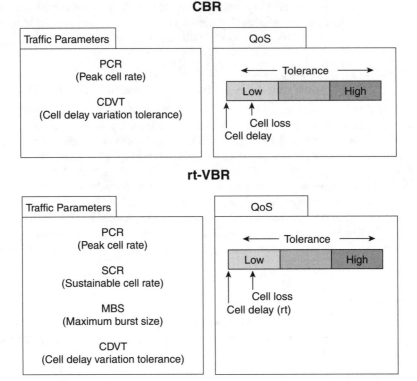

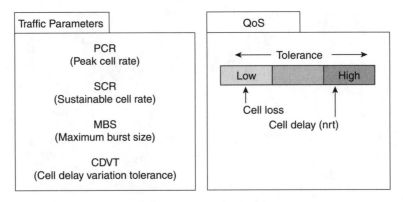

continues

Figure 2-31 *Traffic Contract Parameters for CBR, rt-VBR, nrt-VBR, UBR, ABR, and GFR Service Categories (Cont.)*

UBR

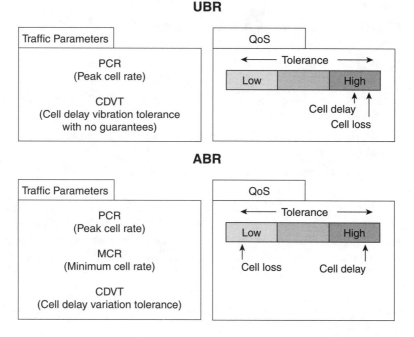

ABR

GFR

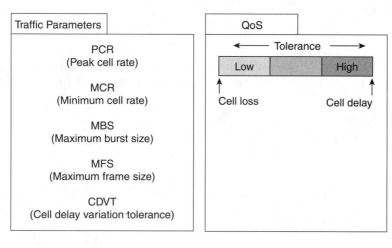

Traffic contract consists of traffic parameters and QoS parameters. The traffic parameters are as follows:

- **PCR**—Specifies the upper bound on the traffic that can be submitted on the ATM connection. It is measured in cells per second.

- **SCR**—Specifies the upper bound on the conforming average rate of the ATM connection. It is measured in cells per second.

- **MBS**—Specifies the maximum number of cells at the PCR that might traverse a specific ATM connection.

- **MCR**—Specifies the rate at which the source is allowed to send. It is measured in cells per second.

- **CDVT**—Represents the maximum acceptable cell delay variation.

NOTE   Contrary to the common belief that CDVT is associated with QoS, it is not. CDVT is not signaled. As per ATM Forum Traffic Management Specification 4.0, CDVT is part of the traffic parameter value that "need not have a unique value for a connection."

There are two types of QoS parameters—negotiated, while the connection is getting established, and not negotiated.

The negotiated QoS parameters are as follows:

- **QoS**—Delay

  — **Maximum cell transfer delay (MCTD)**—Refers to the maximum length of time it takes the network to transmit a cell from one endpoint to another.

  — **Peak-to-peak cell delay variation (peak-to-peak CDV)**—Refers to the best and the worst case of Cell Transfer Delay. It is the line distortion caused by change in interarrival times between cells also known as *jitter*.

- **QoS**—Cell loss

  — **Cell loss ratio (CLR)**—Refers to the acceptable percentage of cells that the network can discard due to congestion.

  CLR = Lost Cells ÷ Total Transmitted Cells.

The not negotiated QoS parameters are as follows:

- **Cell error ratio (CER)**—Errored Cells ÷ (Successfully Transferred Cells + Errored Cells)

- **Severely errored cell block ratio (SECBR)**—Severely Errored Cell Blocks ÷ Total Transmitted Cell Blocks

- **Cell misinsertion rate (CMR)**—Misinserted Cells ÷ TimeInterval, where the TimeInterval is the time period within which the misinserted cells were collected.

AAL Categories

There are different types of AALs, dependent on the service class. Table 2-9 categorizes various service classes, AALs, and the corresponding ATM service category.

Table 2-9   *Categories of AAL and Service Classes*

ATM Service Category	Service Class	AAL Type
CBR	Class A	AAL1
		AAL5[1]
rt-VBR	Class B	AAL2
nrt-VBR	Class C	AAL5
UBR	Class C	AAL5
	Class D	AAL3/4
ABR	Class C	AAL5
	Class D	AAL3/4

[1]ATM Forum Specification – Voice and Telephony Over ATM to the Desktop (AF-VTOA-0083.001 came out in February 1999) specifies AAL5 enhancements to carry 64 kbit PCM voice with 40 bytes used for payload. UNI4.0 and PNNI1.0 are required to allow AAL5 format.

Now let's examine each individual AAL in details.

AAL1

AAL1 has been standardized by ITU-T since 1993 and is incorporated in the ATM Forum specifications. Until AAL2 came out, AAL1 was the only method to handle voice traffic.

AAL1 is used for CBR type of traffic that is sent at regular intervals. The AAL1 uses parts of the 48-byte payload for additional information, such as Sequence Number (SN) and Sequence Number Protection (SNP). This leaves 47 bytes of the actual payload for the traffic information. The question is whether the entire 47 bytes are filled with the traffic information. This depends on the type of encoding used for DS-1/E1/J2 as well as whether clear channel or fractional DS-1 is used.

When you examine the process of cell coding involved in AAL1, as specified in ITU-T document I.363.1, you find that the coding is divided into handling structured (fractional) DS-1/E1/J2/nx64-kbps and unstructured (clear channel) DS-1/E1/J2.

The cell coding for the structured DS-1/nx64-kbps with Channel Associated Signaling (CAS) uses a special AAL1 format. In this format, AAL1 is divided into two parts:

- Payload substructure
- Signaling substructure

The Payload substructure carries the nx64 payload and the Signaling substructure carries the signal bits that are associated with the payload.

NOTE   CAS is a form of circuit state signaling in which the circuit state is indicated by one or more bits of signaling. This allows for dynamic detection of on-hook and off-hook states of voice calls and thus allows for very efficient bandwidth utilization.

A significant source of the delay in AAL1 is the cell payload assembly delay, which is the amount of time it takes to collect enough data to form an ATM cell payload. The AAL1 structure is $n \times 24$ bytes in length for the nx64-kbps DS-1 with ESF framing. This results in 3 ms time delay (delay = 24 bytes × 125 ms).

In the case of the structured data mode, one byte out of the 47-byte payload, called a *pointer*, is used to indicate the first byte of the payload substructure. The pointer is not required in every cell of the sequence. Figure 2-32 illustrates the example of the AAL1 structure for 3x64 kbps with CAS. In this example, each AAL1 block contains payload from three timeslots.

Figure 2-32 *Example of AAL1 Structure for 3x64 kbps with CAS*

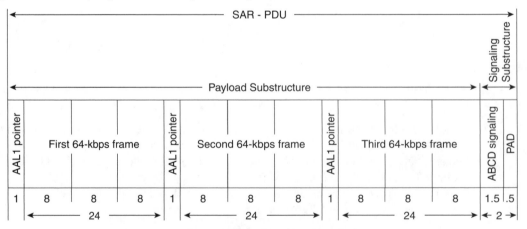

Unless otherwise specified, all numbers are expressed in bytes

In case of the unstructured data mode, bits received from the service interface are packed into cells in such a way that the entire 47-byte cell payload is filled with DS-1/E1/J2 data.

In both the structured and unstructured modes, the SN and the SNP fields, illustrated in Figure 2-33, provide the information that the receiving AAL1 needs to know in order to

- Verify that it has received all the cells in the correct order
- Recognize the missing payloads so that error-concealment routings can be executed

Figure 2-33 *Resulting AAL1 Cell Structure*

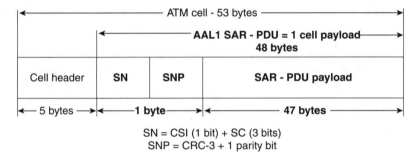

The SN consists of 1-bit Convergence Sublayer Indication (CSI) and 3-bit Sequence Count (SC). CSI is used not only for CSI but also for timing. CSI transfers the Recovery Time Stamp (RTS) in successive PDU headers with the odd-numbered SC field. RTS provides information about the difference between the local and remote clocks.

Voice Error Corrections

Another method for error checking and assurance of proper cell order (besides the CRC-3 error checking and sequence number) could have been simple reliance on the application layer. As an analogy, consider the human ear. If you do not hear a word properly when talking to someone, what do you do? Simply ask to have the information repeated.

AAL2

AAL1 is not the optimum solution for compressed voice over ATM because it handles voice in bundles of only 64 kbps without the capability to handle voice compression, silence detection/suppression, and Common Channel Signaling (CCS) deployed in ISDN.

The ATM Forum specification "ATM Trunking Using AAL2 for Narrowband Services" of February 1999, and ITU-T 363.2 specification provide the details of AAL2. AAL2 handles compressed voice up to 5.3 kbps, silence detection/suppression/removal, CCS, and echo cancellation, thus providing greater bandwidth efficiency. AAL2 also provides the functionality of packaging small packets into one or more ATM cells. This results in much higher bandwidth utilization.

Like any other AAL, AAL2's convergence sublayer is divided into the CPCS (called the common part sublayer [CPS]) and the SSCS. SSCS, the purpose of which is to provide a link between AAL2 and the higher layer applications of the individual users of AAL2, resides above CPS. CPS provides the basic structure for identifying users of AAL2, error correction, and assembling and disassembling various payloads.

The uniqueness of AAL2 is that it allows the existence of variable-length payloads within an ATM cell and across multiple cells. The service specific convergence sublayer-protocol data unit (SSCS-PDU) is formed by the SSCS with specified trunking. CPS forms a CPS packet, which becomes a payload for the common part sublayer-protocol data unit (CPS-PDU). Figure 2-34 demonstrates the relationship between the AAL2 sublayers and all the fields of the SSCS and CPS.

Figure 2-34 *ATM AAL2 Encapsulation and Functionality*

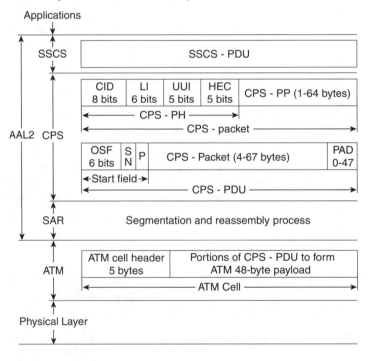

The SSCS and CPS fields are defined as follows:

- **CID field**—Channel Identifier (8 bits). It uniquely identifies the user channels within AAL2. It can identify up to 248 users, not 255, because CID values 1 through 7 are reserved by ITU-T.

- **LI field**—Length Indicator (6 bits). It identifies the length of the packet for each user.

- **UUI field**—User-to-User Indicator (5 bits). It is a link between CPS and SSCS.

- **HEC field**—Header Error Control (5 bits). It is used to check the CPS packet header.

- **CPS-PH**—Common Part Sublayer Packet Header (3 bytes or 24 bits). CPS-PH = CID + LI + UUI + HEC.

- **CPS-PP**—Common Part Sublayer Packet Payload (1–64 bytes).

- **OSF field**—OffSet Field (6 bits). It points at the location of the start of the next CPS packet within CPS-PDU.

- **SN field**—Sequence Number field (1 bit). Used to protect data integrity.

- **P field**—Parity bit field (1 bit). Used to protect the Start field.

- **Start field**—The header of the CPS-PDU (1 byte or 8 bits). Start field = OSF + SN + P.

- **PAD field**—Padding bits used to complete the ATM cell payload.

The size of the CPS-PP depends on the packet fill delay (PFD) and the bandwidth provided for each voice conversation. PFD is the time during which AAL2 PDUs are assembled and segmented into cells. The setting of PFD allows you to alter the delay characteristics of voice into the ATM adaptation phase of AAL2. Different voice circuits might have different minimum delay requirements. Typically, there is a trade-off between the delay and the bandwidth utilization efficiency factors within voice over ATM environments. Table 2-9 lists the relationship between PDF and the AAL2 payload required to support a single voice channel.

Table 2-10   *Packet Fill Delay (PFD) Relationship to the AAL2 Payload*

PDF (ms)	CPS-PH (bytes)	32 kbps ADPCM[1]		64 kbps PCM[2]	
		Payload (bytes)	Efficiency (%)	Payload (bytes)	Efficiency (%)
2	3	8	73	16	84
4	3	16	84	32	91
6	3	24	89	48	94
8	3	32	91	64	96

[1] Adaptive differential pulse code modulation (ADPCM) is a voice compression algorithm that encodes the difference between an actual audio sample amplitude and a predicted amplitude and adapts the resolution based on recent differential values.

[2] Pulse code modulation (PCM) is used for voice traffic at 64 Kbps.

For example, a 32-kbps ADPCM channel with a PFD of 6 ms uses a 24-byte payload, meaning that the CPS-PP is 24 bytes. Figure 2-35 demonstrates the example of AAL2 use for six channels of 32 kbps with a PFD value of 6 ms.

Figure 2-35 *Example of AAL2 Use for Six 32-kbps ADPCM Channels with PFD = 6 ms*

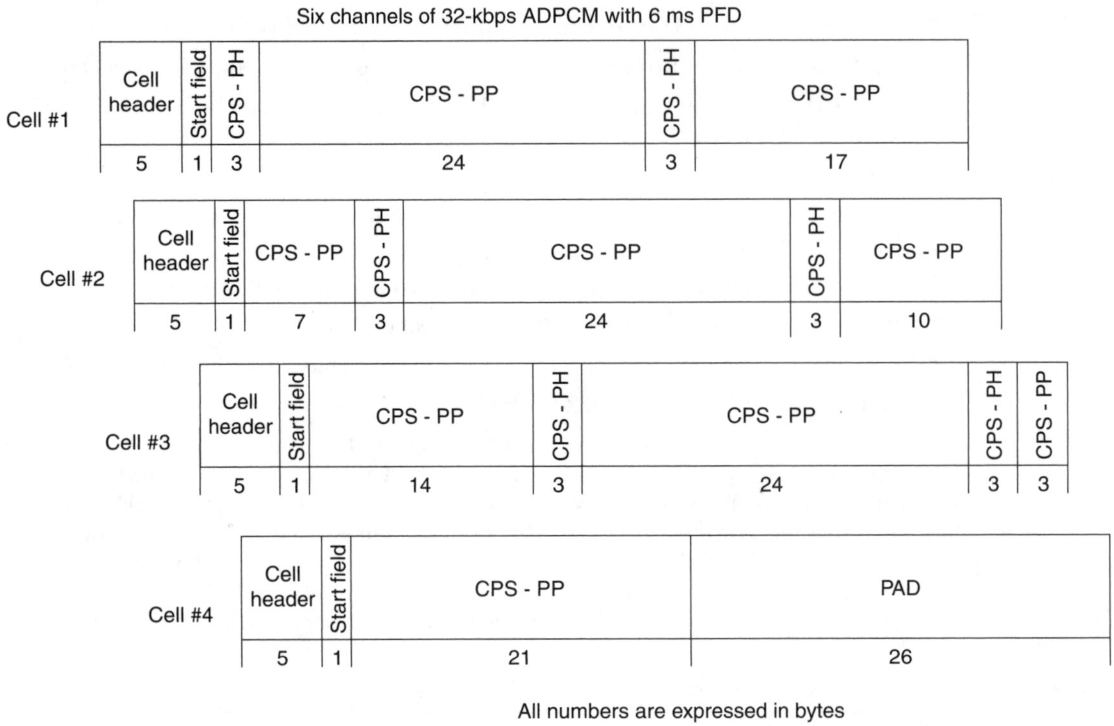

Six channels of 32-kbps ADPCM with 6 ms PFD

All numbers are expressed in bytes

You can see that six 32-kbps ADPCM channels fit into four ATM cells. The 1-byte Start field, indicating the beginning of the CPS-PDU, follows the cell header. Each 24-byte CPS-PP is prepended with the 3-byte CPH-PH.

For comparison, Figure 2-36 illustrates a 32-kbps ADPCM channel with a PFD of 4 ms, which uses 16-byte payload.

AAL3/4

The initial specifications of AAL type 3 and type 4 were very similar with respect to functionality and PDU format. Hence, ITU-T decided to combine the two specifications into a single one and call it type 3/4.

Figure 2-36 *Example of AAL2 Use for Six 32-kbps ADPCM Channels with PDF = 4 ms*

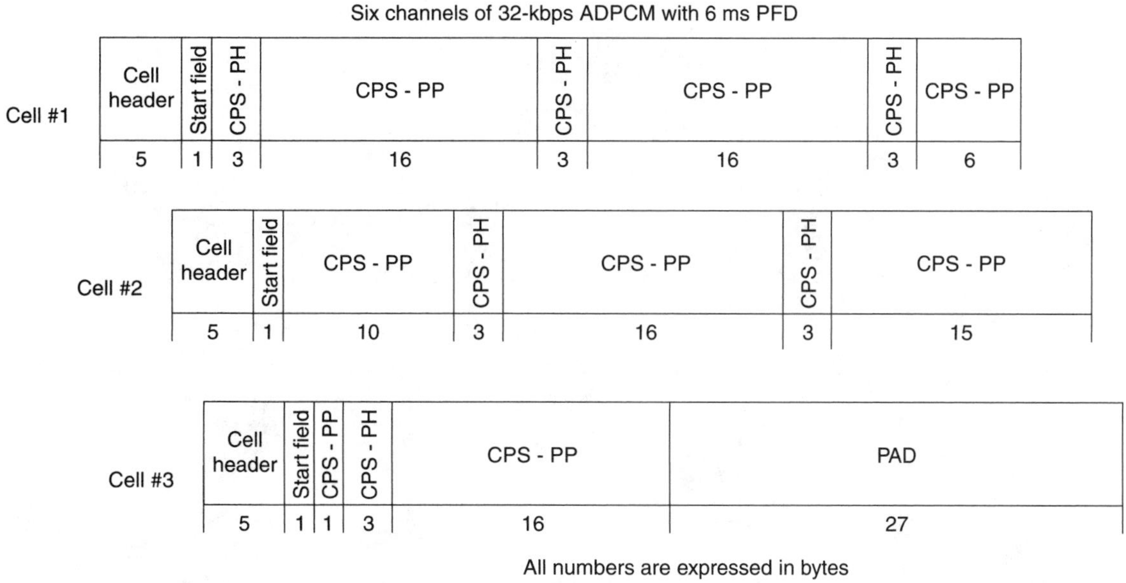

Six channels of 32-kbps ADPCM with 6 ms PFD

		Start field	CPS - PH	CPS - PP	CPS - PH	CPS - PP	CPS - PH	CPS - PP

Cell #1

Cell header	Start field	CPS - PH	CPS - PP	CPS - PH	CPS - PP	CPS - PH	CPS - PP
5	1	3	16	3	16	3	6

Cell #2

Cell header	Start field	CPS - PP	CPS - PH	CPS - PP	CPS - PH	CPS - PP
5	1	10	3	16	3	15

Cell #3

Cell header	Start field	CPS - PP	CPS - PH	CPS - PP	PAD
5	1	1	3	16	27

All numbers are expressed in bytes

AAL3/4 specifies the connection and connectionless data transfer. This makes AAL3/4 suitable for the deployment of connectionless services, such as Switched Multimegabit Data Services (SMDS).

Service Classes C and D can use AAL3/4. Class D (connectionless) type protocols do not require SSCS; whereas, Class C protocols do require SSCS.

Below the SSCS resides the CPCS with responsibilities of error detection and handling, identifying the CPCS-SDU to be transmitted and determining the length of CPCS-PDU.

The job of the SAR is the segmentation and reassembly of the SAR-PDU. Each SAR-PDU holds a maximum of 48 bytes, four of which are used for additional header and trailer information, including SN, error checking, and so on. Figure 2-37 illustrates the details of the AAL3/4 structure. These additional headers provide for message multiplexing from multiple users connected over the same VC between the ATM end systems.

Figure 2-37 *Details of AAL3/4 Structure*

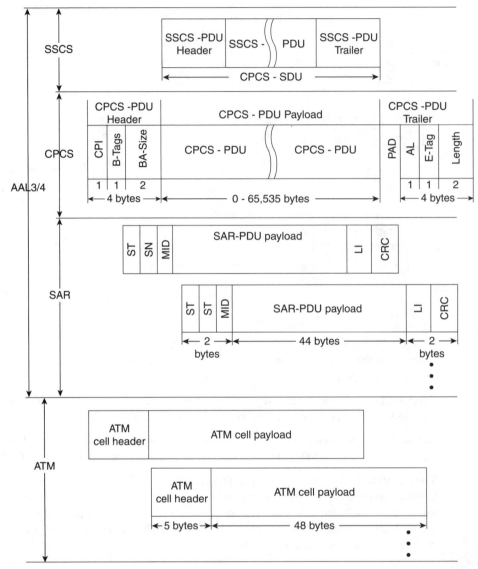

The AAL3/4 fields depicted in Figure 2-37 are defined as follows:

- **SSCS-PDU field**—Service specific convergence sublayer-protocol data unit. Protocol data unit to be delivered to the destination CPCS sublayer.

- **CPCS-PDU field**—Common part convergence sublayer-protocol data unit. Protocol data unit to be delivered to the destination SAR sublayer.

- **CPI field**—Common part indicator indicates the unit (bytes, KB, MB) used for the buffer reservation values (BA-Size) and Length fields.

- **B-Tag field**—Beginning-Tag signifies the end of the CPCS-PDU header.

- **BA-Size field**—Buffer allocation-size indicator tells the receiving station the amount of buffer space that needs to be provided to accommodate the incoming CPCS-SDU.

- **AL field**—Alignment field (separator) comprises the length of the CPCS trailer to 32 bits.

- **E-Tag field**—Ending-Tag signifies the start of the CPCS-PDU trailer.

- **Length field**—CPCS-PDU length provides the length of the PDU information field.

- **ST field**—Segment type identification indicates whether the SAR-PDU contains the beginning of a SAR-SDI (BOM—beginning of message), one of the parts from the middle (COM—continuation of message), the end (EOM—end of message), or that can be transmitted using only one SAR-PDU (SSM—single-segment message).

- **SN field**—Sequence number identifies the order in which cells should be reassembled.

- **MID field**—Multiplex identification identifies cells from different traffic sources interleaved on the same VCC so that the correct cells are reassembled at the destination.

- **LI field**—Length information holds the number of SAR-SDU bytes.

- **CRC field**—Cyclic redundancy check detects errors in the SAR-PDU using CRC-10 checksum calculations.

AAL5

AAL3/4 was the first attempt for a cell-relay technology. The next one, much more efficient and simplified, is AAL5. Like AAL3/4, AAL5 is applicable to both connection-oriented and connectionless types of data.

NOTE   AAL5 is known as the Simple and Efficient Adaptation Layer (SEAL), and rightfully so. It uses the entire 48 bytes of the cell payload for the payload information, without stealing the bits for information, such as sequence numbers, cell error checking, and so on. After all, who needs to know the sequence numbers in a connection-oriented world, which is exactly what ATM is? And who needs to check the errors in every little cell? Let the edge devices worry about data integrity, keeping in mind the basic integrity of Layer 1 infrastructure in place for ATM.

As in AAL3/4, the AAL5 convergence sublayer has application-specific SSCS and a CPCS that is shared by all higher application layers. The CPSC provides error detection and handling, padding of bytes to complete the 48-byte payloads, and discarding incompletely transferred CPCS-SDUs.

Figure 2-38 illustrates the AAL5 transfer from SSCS sublayer to ATM layer.

Figure 2-38 *AAL5 Frame and Cell Formats*

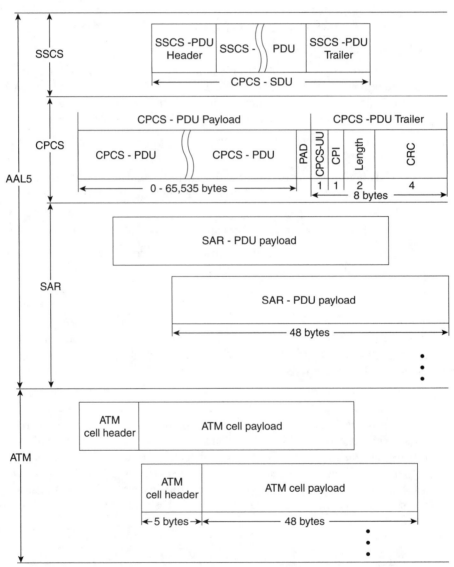

The AAL5 fields depicted in Figure 2-38 are defined as follows:

- **PAD field**—Padding bits. The number of bytes involved could be 0 to 47. It is used to extend the CPCS-PDU to multiples of 48 bytes.

- **CPCS-UU field**—Common Part Convergence Sublayer–User-to-User field is used to transparently transfer user-to-user information.

- **CPI**—Common part indicator field indicates the interpretation of the remaining fields in the CPCS PDU header.

- **Length field**—Indicates the length of the CPCS-PDU field.

- **CRC field**—Cyclic redundancy check detects errors in the CPCS-PDU using CRC-32 checksum calculations.

Summary

This chapter introduced the lower layers of the ATM model, including the following:

- Physical
- ATM
- ATM adaptation layer (AAL)

The physical layer consists of two sublayers—transmission convergence (TC) and physical media dependant (PMD)—that are responsible for

- TC sublayer:
  - HEC generation/verification
  - Cell delineation and rate decoupling
  - Transmission frame adaptation
  - Transmission frame generation/recovery
- PMD sublayer:
  - Bit timing (time recovery)
  - Line coding
  - Physical medium

The ATM layer is responsible for the following:

- Generic Flow Control
- Cell header creation/verification
- Cell VPI/VCI translation
- Cell multiplex and demultiplex

The AAL layer consists of two sublayers—convergence sublayer and segmentation and reassembly sublayer. The convergence sublayer is responsible for converting the upper layer information into a form suitable for segmentation into equal size ATM payloads, including framing and error checking. It also prepares the payloads for segmentation by padding the payloads. The segmentation and reassembly sublayer is responsible for segmenting the converged frame into equal size of 48-byte payloads at the sending edge device and reassembling the 48-byte payloads into the converged frame at the receiving edge device.

Review Questions

1 What are the sublayers of the Physical Layer of ATM?

2 What is cell delineation?

3 What is rate decoupling?

4 What is the difference between SONET and STS?

5 At what layer is the HEC performed?

6 What is the purpose of the ATM Layer?

7 What is the purpose of PTI and CLP bits?

8 How many bits are used for VPI and VCI at UNI and NNI?

9 How many sublayers does AAL consist of, and what are they?

10 What is the purpose of AAL2?

11 What AAL is more bandwidth-efficient, AAL3/4 or AAL5? Why?

12 What is the purpose of the PAD field?

13 How can you categorize various types of traffic?

"Don't be afraid to take a big step. You can't cross a chasm in two small jumps."
—David Lloyd George (1863–1945)

"Iron rusts from disuse, stagnant water loses its purity, and in cold weather water becomes frozen; even so does inaction sap the vigors of the mind."—Leonardo da Vinci (1452–1519)

After reading this chapter, you should be able to understand the following:

- **ATM Virtual Circuit Types**—ATM is a connection-oriented protocol that can provide connectivity using permanent virtual circuits (PVCs), switched virtual circuits (SVCs), Soft PVCs, and permanent virtual path (PVP) tunneling. PVCs must be predefined manually, involving an intense setup. SVCs are connections that are established dynamically within the ATM network with the help of the signaling PVC. Soft PVCs are permanent connections of the edge ATM-attached devices to an SVC-based ATM network. PVP tunneling is an interconnection method of two SVC networks across a PVC-based network.

- **ATM Global Addressing**—In contrast to PVC-based networks that use a locally significant VPI/VCI addressing scheme, SVC-based networks use globally significant addressing. ATM global addresses, consisting of 160 bits, can be either private or public. ATM standards provision for ATM-attached edge devices to obtain the global addresses dynamically.

- **ATM Connections**—ATM networks support three types of connections: point-to-point, point-to-multipoint, and anycast.

- **WAN Interworking**—ATM, being a technology that is widely deployed in WAN environments, has the capability to interwork with legacy WAN technologies, such as Frame Relay and Switched Multimegabit Data Services (SMDSs). Frame Relay services are deployed around the world. Although not spread as widely as Frame Relay, you can find SMDS services within public networks in Europe and the United States.

- **Voice Interworking**—One of the major advantages of ATM over any other method of transport is its capability to handle multiple types of services simultaneously, one of which is voice. AAL1 handles your uncompressed voice traffic, whereas AAL2 handles the compressed voice traffic. The three methods for voice handling are

  — Circuit emulation service (CES), which carries full- or fractional-rate T1/E1 circuits between endpoints.

  — Dynamic bandwidth circuit emulation service (DBCES)

  — Voice solutions using variable bit rate (VBR) and AAL2

- **ATM Internetworking with Existing Protocols**—ATM, being a high-speed technology, provides the capability of seamless internetworking for the existing applications that reside on IP, IPX, AppleTalk, and other Layer 3 protocols. You can run Layer 3 protocols over ATM in several ways, which include Classical IP and Multiprotocol over ATM (MPOA). Also, you can use ATM to extend your Ethernet and Token Ring LANs across distances without changing the currently used technologies or applications. This method is called LAN Emulation (LANE).

- **MPLS and Tag Switching**—Multiprotocol label switching (MPLS) is a method of Layer 3 routing/switching with deployment of meaningful, fixed-length labels. If the ATM network is used as the transport for the MPLS networks, the labels could provide the ATM VPI/VCI values.

CHAPTER 3

ATM Reference Model: Higher Layers

This chapter takes you into the higher layers of the ATM infrastructure and addresses the following aspects of ATM:

- ATM signaling
- ATM addressing and when it is required
- ATM internetworking methods and when to deploy which method
- ATM management

Having a solid knowledge of the ATM lower layers can help you complete the ATM puzzle and understand the ATM's tiered architecture, which Figure 3-1 illustrates.

Figure 3-1 *ATM Higher Layers*

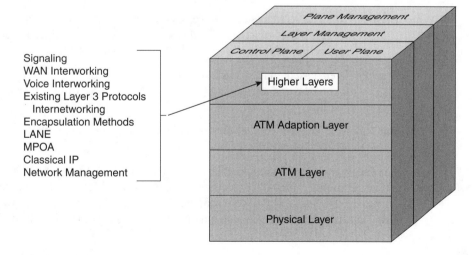

ATM Virtual Circuit Types

As mentioned in Chapter 1, "ATM Introduction," ATM is connection-oriented technology, meaning that a VC needs to be set up across the ATM network prior to any data transfer. You can break down the whole process of ATM communication into three parts:

Step 1 Establish a connection.

Step 2 Communicate.

Step 3 Tear down the connection.

In an ATM network, you can establish a connection in three different ways:

- You can preconfigure the ATM cloud manually for every possible connection that could exist (PVC).

- You can let the ATM cloud set up the connection dynamically when it receives a request, based on various parameters (SVC)

- You can combine the two methods (Soft PVC).

The Mechanics of Establishing ATM Connections

The basic objective of the connection establishment process is to obtain a translation or forwarding table within every ATM switch along the way:

Step 1 When an ATM switch receives a cell across a link on either a predetermined or a dynamically established VPI/VCI value, it checks the connection value in the local VPI/VCI translation table.

Step 2 Then, based on the translation table, the switch determines the outgoing port of the connection and the new VPI/VCI value of the connection on that link.

Step 3 Next, the cell gets retransmitted on that outgoing link with the appropriate VPI/VCI values.

It is very interesting to compare the connection-oriented nature of the ATM technology with a connectionless protocol (IP, for example). Part (a) of Figure 3-2 illustrates an IP routing network that consists of five core routers, R1, R2, R3, R4, and R5, and two routers, Ra and Rb, that are the source and the destination for the packets to be transmitted.

Figure 3-2   *ATM and IP Traffic Flow Comparison*

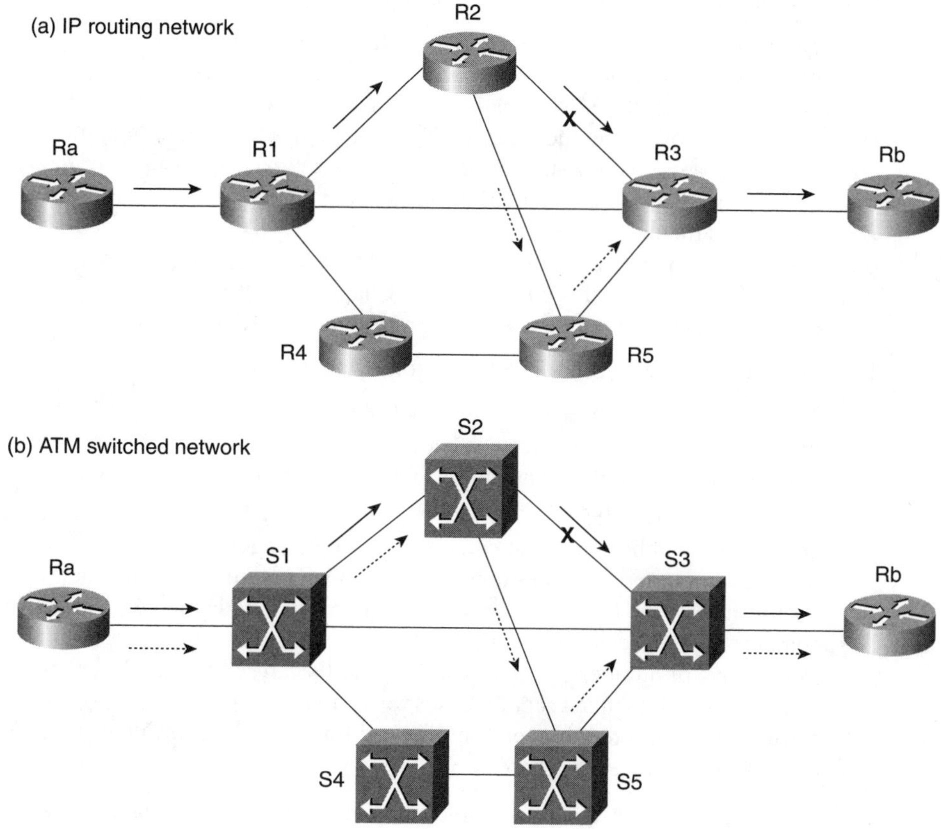

(a) IP routing network

(b) ATM switched network

Let's assume that the IP routing protocol is Enhanced Interior Gateway Routing Protocol (EIGRP), which, using the EIGRP formula, calculates the optimal path from the Ra network to the Rb network. Assume that the optimal path is {Ra,R1,R2,R3,Rb}. When link R2,R3 disappears, routers reconverge and provide an alternate path, if it is available, from Ra to Rb. Assume that the new path becomes {Ra,R1,R2,R5,R3,Rb}. When the R2,R3 link becomes available, the old path becomes available again and R2's routing protocol selects it again. R2 and R3 announce the change to all their neighboring routers. As a result, all the routers reconverge, and Ra sets up a previous path {Ra,R1,R2,R3,Rb}, which has the better metric.

Now, let's examine the events in the ATM environment illustrated in part (b) of Figure 3-2. Assume that the backbone consists of ATM switches and you have Ra and Rb as two edge devices. In the SVC environment, when Ra initiates a call, the signaling protocol establishes a connection based on QoS requirements. Assume that the switches along the path {Ra,S1,S2,S3,Rb} meet that QoS and the VC gets set up. Upon completion of the setup, the cell transmission resumes. Now the link S2,S3 disappears. The entire VC gets torn down and a new one must be established.

Assume that the new VC is set up along the {Ra,S1,S2,S5,S3,Rb} path, provided that this path meets the required QoS. Now the cells can "walk" along this new path. The interesting part is that even when the S2,S3 link becomes available, it does not affect this path—the cells continue to flow along the {Ra,S1,S2,S5,S3,Rb} route, even though the first path could have been a more optimal one. ATM SVC call setup is performed to comply with the originator's requested QoS, who really does not care what paths are taken inside the cloud itself, as long as the cloud meets the required QoS. ATM SVCs are set up using a routing protocol, whose job is to set up a connection that meets the QoS parameters. The section, "ATM Signaling," later in this chapter and in Chapter 4, "ATM Traffic and Network Management," elaborate on the call setup process and the routing protocols in use.

Based on the examples, you can make the following conclusions:

In IP routing environments, if a best metric connection between a source edge device and a destination edge device goes down, the routers must reconverge to set up a new connection. If the failed connection comes back up, the routers must reconverge to re-establish the better metric connection.

In an ATM switched environment, if a link in a VC connection between a source router and a destination router goes down, the entire VC is torn down and a new one must be established. If the failed link becomes available again, the new VC connection remains in place, even if the original VC was a more optimal route from the perspective of number of hops; however, ATM's call setup is not based on hop count, nor is it based on a fixed set of metrics for various destinations. A single source might have various QoS requirements at different times for different VCs, which is exactly what ATM's call setup is based on—QoS.

Whereas IP routing is based on the hop-by-hop paradigm, ATM signal routing is based on source route, where the signaling frame knows the entire path (meeting the QoS request).

Permanent Virtual Circuits

PVCs are based on the simplicity of the basic ATM operation. An ATM network administrator assigns VPI/VCI values statically, "walking" from switch to switch. This has been the only method available for Frame Relay clouds until a couple of years ago.

The "Fun" of PVC-based Cloud Creation

One of the labs in my ATM class involves establishing a PVC cloud among three ATM switches. Upon the completion of the lab, students have a total appreciation of how labor-intensive and error-prone this exercise is. You need to plan out your VPI/VCI values ahead of time, carefully map out all the connections, and then very carefully input the data into the switches.

A PVC is a logical, rather than a physical, connection between endpoints. When the connection is set up, it remains up permanently until it is torn down manually, which results in increased requirements for network resources.

Figure 3-3 illustrates the PVC setup, where VPI/VCI values are preset manually by the network administrator. Starting with VPI/VCI equal to 0/100 between Ra and S1, continuing with VPI/VCI equal to 0/110 between S1 and S2, and ending with VPI/VCI equal to 0/120 between S2 and Rb.

Figure 3-3   *PVC*

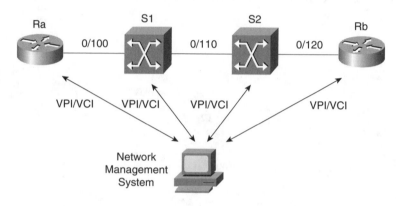

PVCs are a good choice for connections that are always in use and are in frequent, high demand. However, they are not very scalable and are not a good solution for short-lived connections or for large ATM networks.

Switched Virtual Circuits

SVCs are the solution for the on-demand connections. They are set up as needed and are torn down when no longer needed. To achieve this behavior, SVCs use a "drilling" mechanism—signaling. The reason I call it "drilling" is because, based on the edge device's request, the signaling VC sets up ("drills") a circuit based on the requirements of the requestor. These connections are then dynamically torn down if they are no longer being used. This behavior results in freeing up the network and achieving much better bandwidth utilization.

The signaling protocol makes the connection establishment process dynamic. No longer do administrators need to program every switch along the way with static forwarding tables. The signaling protocol takes care of it in a very efficient way, as discussed in Chapter 4.

The ATM signaling protocol varies by the type of ATM network interface. As illustrated in Figure 3-4, ATM signaling uses three types of ATM network interface:

- **User-Network Interface (UNI)**—UNI signaling is used between an ATM end-system and an ATM switch across UNI links or between two ATM switches (when connecting a private ATM network to a public one).

- **Network-to-Network Interface (NNI)**—NNI signaling is used between ATM switches across NNI links.

- **BISDN Inter Carrier Interface (B-ICI)**—B-ICI signaling is used between different ATM domains (for example, two ATM service providers).

Figure 3-4   *SVCs: Signaling Protocols Based on ATM Interface Type*

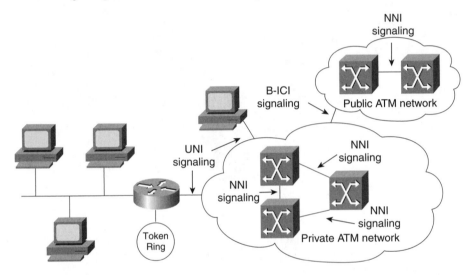

UNI signaling in ATM defines the "drilling" mechanism, that is, the protocol by which the ATM devices in the network dynamically set up the SVCs. NNI signaling, being part of the Private Network-to-Network Interface (PNNI) specification, includes both signaling and routing. The signaling part is the continuation of the UNI signaling through the ATM cloud, and the routing part is the dynamic routing of the signaling request through the ATM cloud based on the required QoS for that specific request. Chapter 4 elaborates on the PNNI algorithm and routing.

The ATM Forum UNI specifications are based on the Q.2931 public network signaling protocol developed by the ITU-T. Chapter 4 addresses the signaling in detail.

If a network administrator created the PVC's forwarding table with the pre-assigned VPI/VCI values, the ATM switches generate the SVC's forwarding table dynamically, with dynamically created VPI/VCI values, using VCI values greater than 31. (Recall that VCI values 0 to 31, inclusive, are reserved by the ATM Forum and the ITU-T.) The question is: How does the signaling protocol "know" where to go? It must have a destination address.

Furthermore, how does an SVC refer to that destination? Even if the SVC could use VPI/VCI values, those only are significant locally. The SVC needs a form of an address with global significance, such as a network service access point (NSAP) address, for example, or an X.121 address that is used for X.25 networks.

Well, SVCs do use a global form of addressing in which the addresses are 160 bits long. You can use different forms of ATM addressing, as you see later in this chapter in the section, "ATM Global Addressing." For now, I'll just refer to this form of addressing as *global*. Also, for any SVC setup, you need one PVC. This PVC, called the *signaling PVC*, uses VCI equal to 5. You need only one *signaling PVC* for any number of SVCs. Table 3-1 summarizes the VPI/VCI assignments that I've talked about so far.

Table 3-1   *Reserved VPI/VCI Assignments*

VPI	VCI	Meaning
0	0	Empty cell
x^1	0–31	Reserved by the ATM Forum and the ITU-T
x	5	Signaling

[1]x refers to any value. If tunneling is involved, the value of x must equal the VPI of the tunnel.

Watch the Scalability of ATM Global Addressing

One hundred-sixty bits! This is quite an achievement! If the IP world is struggling today to *convert* to 128 bits with the IPv6, claiming enormous scalability, can you imagine the massiveness of ATM scalability! You have the flexibility to extend your ATM networks to 2^{148} number of ATM end points, considering the fact that only the domain-specific part of the addresses are available for end-system identifications.

SVC Connection Establishment

Figure 3-5 demonstrates how a basic SVC is set up from Router A to Router B using signaling.

Figure 3-5 *Establishing an SVC Call*

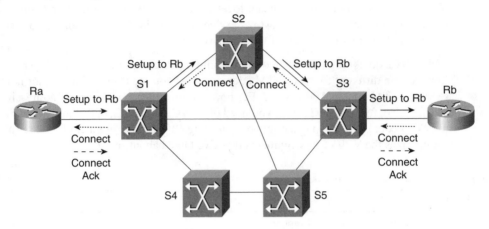

The steps in the process are as follows:

Step 1 Ra sends a signaling request to its directly connected switch—S1. This request, called a *setup message*, contains the ATM address of both the calling party (Ra) and the called party (Rb), as well as the basic traffic contract requested for the connection. Ra converts the signaling request into the signaling packet and then converts the signaling packet into cells for transmission over the signaling PVC, which has been defined for this link.

Step 2 S1 reassembles the signaling cells into the signaling packet and examines them.

Step 3 If S1 has an entry for Rb's ATM global address in its routing table and it can accommodate the QoS requested for the connection, it reserves resources for the virtual connection, creates dynamic VPI/VCI values for that connection, and forwards the request to the next ATM switch (S2) along the path. It also sends a *connect* message back to the calling party.

Step 4 Every switch along the path to Rb reassembles and examines the signaling packet, and then forwards it to the next switch if the traffic parameters can be supported on the ingress and egress interfaces. Each switch also sets up the virtual connection with the dynamically generated VPI/VCI values as the signaling packet is forwarded. If any switch along the path cannot accommodate the requested traffic contract, the request is rejected and a rejection message is sent back to Ra along the same route.

Step 5 When the signaling packet arrives at Rb, Rb reassembles it and evaluates the packet. If Rb can support the requested traffic contract, it responds with a *connect* message. The *connect* message is propagated back to Ra to indicate that the user accepted the call.

Step 6 S3 sends a *connect acknowledge* message to Rb to indicate that Rb has been awarded the call. Also, Ra sends a *connect acknowledge* message to S1 to complete all symmetrical call control procedures.

NOTE This is a simplified view of call establishment. PNNI1, covered in Chapter 4, introduces more variables into the signal routing.

Now that the path has been "drilled" through the ATM cloud and the VPI/VCIs have been generated, the data can start to flow from Ra to Rb.

SVC Connection Release

To free up the SVC, there must be an initiator of the call release or *clearing*. Either party involved in the connection/call (sending or receiving) can initiate its removal from the already established connection/call. If the connection is between the two parties only, then the whole connection/call is removed. The call release happens in stages exactly in the same fashion as the establishment stages. Figure 3-6 illustrates the stages of call release as defined in the steps that follow.

Figure 3-6 *Releasing an SVC Call*

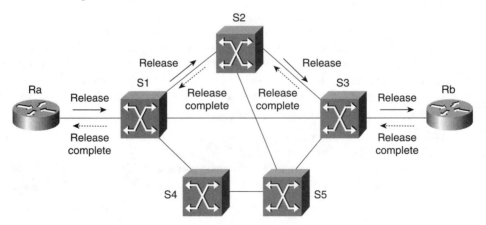

Step 1   Ra issues a call *release* request to its directly attached ATM switch, S1.

Step 2   The switch must acknowledge the receipt of the release request by sending a *release complete* (a form of an OK) to the requestor.

Step 3   Each ATM switch sends the *release* message to other switches along the dynamically preset VC until it reaches the destination. Each ATM switch must receive a *release complete* message from the switch, to which the release message was sent.

Step 4   The destination sends the *release complete* message, which must reach the requestor of the release message.

Soft PVCs

In addition to the PVC and SVC connections, there is a third, hybrid type, called Soft PVC and Soft PVP. These connections appear permanent to the end user, because the end user's connectivity to the ATM cloud is PVC based. However, because the cloud itself is SVC based, the end user achieves the flexibility if a link fails. Figure 3-7 illustrates the Soft PVC example, where the connections from Ra and Rb to the ATM cloud are PVCs, whereas the cloud is SVC.

NOTE   Soft PVCs are very similar to Soft PVPs. Both use the permanent virtual identifiers from the edge devices to the ATM SVC-based cloud. The only difference is that a Soft PVC uses VPI/VCI values for the VC from the edge to the ingress/egress switch, whereas a Soft PVP uses only the VPI value for the addressing.

The steps involved in the Soft PVC/PVP setup are very similar to the SVC connection setup. The only exception is that the edge devices and the ingress/egress ATM switches must be configured manually to be attached to each other via PVCs/PVPs. The ingress switches provide the translation between the attached PVCs/PVPs and the globally significant ATM addresses of the egress switches, where the similar sort of translation is provided but in the opposite direction.

Using Figure 3-7 as an example, S1 provides the translation between VPI/VCI equal to 0/100 and the *global* ATM address 22.2222000000000000000000.000000000000.00 of Rb. S3, on the other hand, provides the translation between VPI/VCI equal to 0/200 and the *global* ATM address 11.1111000000000000000000.000000000000.00 of Ra.

Figure 3-7   *Soft PVCs*

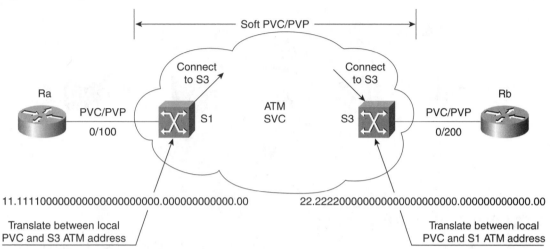

Some of the advantages of this kind of setup are as follows:

- The Soft PVC provides the appearance of a PVC connection to the end user, thus a perception of a fast call setup.

- The SVC cloud guarantees dynamic call setup in the event of failed link.

Permanent Virtual Path (PVP) Tunneling

Imagine a situation in which you have several private SVC ATM networks in different parts of the country, say in California, New York, and Texas. You need to interconnect these networks using the public ATM network, which, unfortunately for you, does not support SVCs yet. You can obtain only a PVC-based ATM WAN connectivity. Yet, you need your SVC networks to be seamlessly interconnected so you can take advantage of such features as QoS. What can you do? Well, PVP tunneling provides the solution for you. You can create tunnels through the public ATM WAN cloud in such a way that the SVC clouds in California, New York, and Texas can exchange signaling as if they all are interconnected together using the SVCs. Figure 3-8 illustrates the PVP tunneling concept. The reason they are called PVP tunnels is because only VPIs are used in the PVC cloud. The signaling between the SVC clouds is carried using VPI/VCI equal to $x/5$, where x is the VPI number of the PVP.

Figure 3-8 *PVP Tunneling*

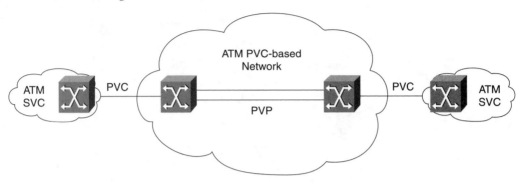

ATM Global Addressing

ATM global addresses are required for purposes of establishing SVCs. Consequently, signaling uses the ATM addresses when setting up a switched connection. ATM addresses also are used by the Integrated Local Management Interface (ILMI) to learn the addresses of neighboring switches. The term *address* implies some logical association between a physical entity and the method of locating it in a unique way. The ATM Forum Addressing User Guide (AF-RA-0105.000, January 1999) explains it as follows:

> An address may have two functions: location and identification. To ensure a manageable routing system, an address should have significance within the network topology, that is, it should be a *locator* that indicates *where* in the network topology (not geography) the interface can be found. As such, addresses should not be portable from one ATM Service Provider to another, or from one network to another, or even necessarily from one part of a network to another, as this defeats their ability to function as locators. There are, of course, exceptions, but every exception causes the routing system to have to deal with routes that cannot be aggregated and so increases routing table sizes throughout the ATM network... The term "address" may sometimes be used as an *identifier* that indicates *what* the function is (rather than *where* the interface is). For example, Ethernets have addresses that are identifiers, but that are not locators... A telephone number has traditionally been a locator and an identifier... The ATM Forum uses the term *locator* only.

Categorization of Addresses by Structure

The ATM Forum specifications define the use of two main categories of addresses: E.164 and the ATM End System Addresses (AESAs). The history behind these separate categories is quite interesting. The ITU-T long ago settled on telephone number–like addresses, which are E.164 numbers, for use in public ATM networks (that is, B-ISDN). Because telephone numbers are a public resource, the ATM Forum considered another model for private ATM addresses—AESAs, which are based on the semantics of an OSI NSAP address. This led to the separation in use of E.164 and NSAP addresses. Public ATM domains use only E.164 addresses; whereas, private ATM networks use only NSAP addresses.

E.164 Numbering

ITU-T uses the E.164 *number* term because an E.164 number can be used for purposes other than a specific telephone number. E.164 numbers also are used for purposes of service identification. An example of this is the use of 800 numbers, which the telephone network uses to identify the caller toll-free service. In ATM Forum specifications, only E.164 numbers that are addresses (which are sometimes referred to as *native* E.164 addresses) are recognized. These are not to be confused with the embedded E.164 AESA addresses, which are formed by encapsulating the E.164 number within an NSAP structure. The native E.164 addresses consist of a maximum of 15 digits and are denoted as E.164N. One example of an E.164N address is 70952519890, where '7' is the code for Russia, '095' is the code for Moscow, and '2819890' is the telephone number in Moscow.

AESA Numbering

The ATM Forum defines the AESA format to consist of 20 octets and to be available in four different types, as illustrated in Figure 3-9.

Figure 3-9 *AESA Formats*

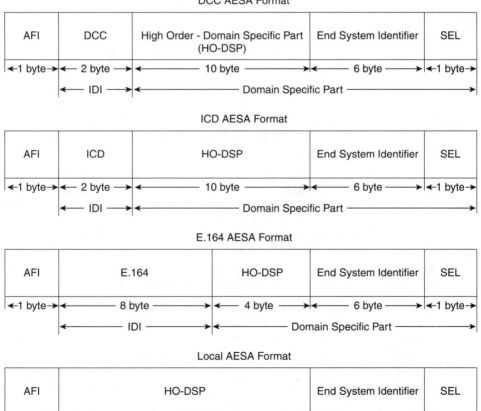

ATM Forum specifications UNI3.1, UNI Signaling 4.0, ILMI 4.0, and PNNI version 1.0 discuss the use of the top three types: Data Country Code (DCC), International Code Designator (ICD), and E.164. Voice and Telephony Over ATM (VTOA) to the desktop uses the Local AESA. The DCC, ICD, and E.164 AESA formats differ by which authority assigns them. Table 3-2 lists the AESA address fields.

Table 3-2   *Address Fields of AESA Format*

Address Field	Meaning
IDP (Initial Domain Part)	Consists of two elements: AFI and IDI.
AFI (Authority and Format Identifier)	The value of this field determines the type of AESA—DCC, ICD, E.164, or Local. AFI AESA Type 0x39 DCC 0x47 ICD 0x45 E.164 0x49 Local Also, the value of the AFI indicates what authority can assign codes in the rest of the addressing space and the encoding (binary or decimal) used in DSP. The ATM Forum uses only binary encoding.
IDI (Initial Domain Identifier)	The content depends on the values of AFI. It actually refers to the values of DCC, ICD, or E.164. Local AESA has an IDI of Null.
DCC	This type of AESA is assigned by ISO 3166 and it specifies the country in which the address is registered.
ICD	This type of AESA is intended for use in the construction of internationally recognized codes. Each ICD code assignee is free to decide the structure and the rules used for DSP. The value of the ICD field indicates to which code set or organization that particular ICD is assigned. For example, an ICD value of 0x0091 indicates Cisco as the organization responsible for that specific code.
DSP (Domain Specific Part)	The DSP is subdivided into High Order Domain Specific Part (HO-DSP) and low order part, which consists of ESI and SEL.
HO-DSP (High Order Domain Specific Part)	The contents of this field describe the hierarchy of the addressing authority and the topological significance. The coding is specified by the authority that is identified in IDP.
ESI (End Station Identifier)	This field identifies the end system. It must be unique within a particular value of IDP + HO-DSP. The ESI value is usually an IEEE 802.2 MAC address.
SEL (Selector)	SEL is not used for ATM routing but can be used by end systems to differentiate multiple addresses associated with the same interface.

Table 3-2 *Address Fields of AESA Format*

Address Field	Meaning
E.164 AESA	E.164 AESA generally is used between private and public ATM domains. There are two types of E.164 AESAs:
	1. The embedded E.164 AESA does not use HO-DSP, ESI, and SEL components, which all are set to zeros. It is called E.164e.
	2. The non-embedded E.164 AESA, HO-DSP, ESI, and SEL can be administered by the private organizations for use within the private ATM network. It is called E.164A.

Categorization of Addresses by Ownership

ATM address assignment is somewhat similar to IP address assignment. In fact, I can say that the ATM Forum learned from IP addressing mistakes and took some precautions to prevent a massive surge of sporadic address assignments, which consequently reduces network scalability.

The ATM Forum divides the registered class of addresses into three categories, based on the ownership of the associated prefix:

- ATM Service Provider (ASP) addresses
- Customer Owned (CO) addresses
- Unregistered ATM prefix addresses

Each ASP can support CO addresses within its own network. An ASP address is an address from a block of addresses allocated to the service provider by the national or world registration authority. This registration authority is identified in the left-most part of the address. A CO ATM address also is allocated by the national or world registration authority, but directly to the customer. An Unregistered ATM prefix is not obtained from a registration authority. These can be used only in private networks. In fact, to prevent any future complications, it is recommended to use the local AFI (49) for the unregistered addresses.

Addressing Assignment Tactics

Some of you remember the days when nobody thought of the global internetworking idea using IP. During those times, anyone could choose any IP address and assign it within his network. Who needed Internet access? The answer to that question was shortsighted. Consequently, those organizations found themselves having to renumber their networks or perform address translations when talking to other organizations through the Internet.

In the IP world, the Internet Assigned Numbers Authority (IANA) assigns the IP addresses. In addition, the IANA assigns address space to IP network service providers (NSPs) who assign some part of that space to ISPs, who, in turn, assign part of that to customers attached to them.

In the ATM world, the ISO and the ITU-T jointly assign the AFIs, the DCC country codes, and the ICD values. Furthermore, a particular country, organization, or region handles requests within its scope of authority. For example, the ANSI handles the assignment of codes within USA DCC address space; whereas, the Federation of the Electronics Industry (FEI) handles requests within the UK, and so on. You can see that there is a hierarchy of registration authorities that is involved in assigning AESAs. Still, the root of the hierarchy is the ISO/ITU-T registrar. You can find a complete list of standard body representatives for various countries at www.iso.ch/addresse/membodies.html.

Figure 3-10 illustrates a hierarchical tree of ATM address assignment standard bodies.

Figure 3-10 *Hierarchical Tree of ATM Address Assignment*

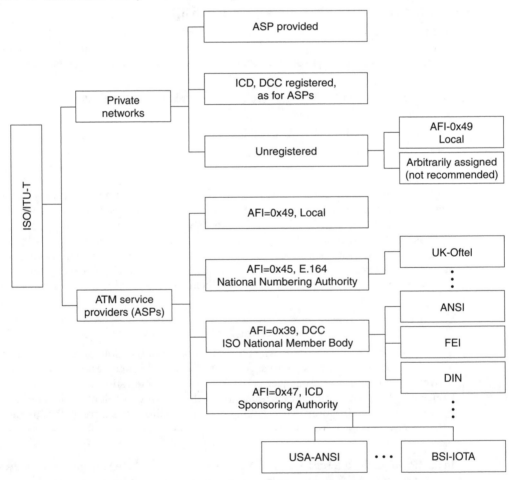

ATM Addressing Tools

How often have you typed a wrong IP address, thinking it was right? Well, IPv4 addressing consists of only 4 bytes. Can you imagine typing a 20-byte long ATM address?

To simplify matters, to reduce the human errors in addressing specifications, the ATM Forum came up with a similar idea as Domain Name System (DNS) in IP. ATM Name System (ANS) is a protocol that translates ATM system names to ATM addresses (as defined in ATM Name System Specification Version 1.0—AF-SAA-0069.000). ANS supports both types of ATM addresses: NSAP and E.164.

Furthermore, ATM's ILMI protocol includes dynamic mechanisms for ATM address assignments at the UNI.

ANS Address Resolution

ANS is an extension of the Internet Engineering Task Force's (IETF) DNS (RFC 1034 and RFC 1035). The difference is that ANS is a native ATM application and does not run on top of the TCP/IP or the UDP/IP as DNS does. ATM-attached devices that use ANS communicate with ANS servers dynamically with the help of SVCs. ATM address lookup is analogous to IP address lookup; the requestor sends a query requesting the ATM address for the provided domain name.

ILMI Address Registration

The ATM switch uses the ILMI address registration protocol to provide one or more of 13 octet prefixes to the ATM edge device. The ILMI uses the VPI/VCI assignments provided in Table 3-3.

Table 3-3   *Reserved VPI/VCI Assignments*

VPI	VCI	Meaning
0	0	Empty cell
x^1	0–31	Reserved by ATM Forum and ITU-T
x	5	Signaling
x	16	ILMI

[1]x means any value

The ATM edge device constructs an NSAP address by appending its ESI and a Selector to the prefix provided by the switch. The resulting 20-byte address then is returned to the switch. The edge device can register multiple addresses using different network prefixes or different ESIs. Upon receipt of the 20-byte address, the switch validates the prefix of the returned address and then identifies the UNI for call delivery. Figure 3-11 illustrates the dynamic address registration using ILMI.

Figure 3-11 *ILMI Dynamic Address Registration*

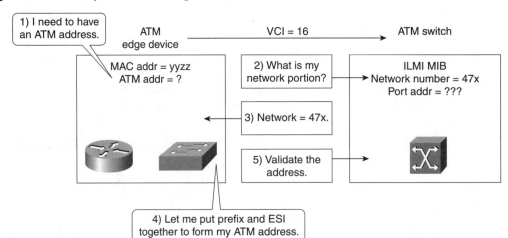

It is interesting to note that the ILMI protocol also is used to inform the end systems of E.164N addresses that are assigned to the Public UNI by the ATM service provider. If E.164N addresses are deployed, then the ATM switch provides the entire E.164N address, which is treated as a "normal" prefix that is concatenated with the null user part.

ATM Address Translation

When you have private ATM networks interconnected through the public domain or simply a private ATM network interconnected to the public one, your ATM addresses must be translated. This characteristic is very similar to the Network Address Translation (NAT) of the IP networks.

In Figure 3-12, a call from private network A must traverse the public ATM network to reach private network B. When the call leaves the switch at the end of the private network or egress, the NSAP source and destination addresses are translated into E.164 format, while preserving the NSAP source and destination addresses. At the ingress switch, the address is translated back into the NSAP format used on private network B.

Figure 3-12 *Address Remapping Across a Public ATM Network*

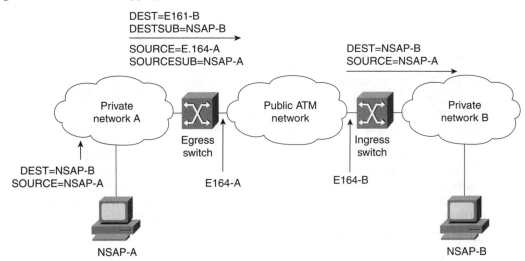

The ATM switch provides three options for performing the address translation needed between private and public addresses, as documented in Table 3-4. The option you choose depends solely on the address format that you deploy for your ATM network.

Table 3-4   *Address Translation options*

Option	Description
E.164 gateway	Private addresses are in ICD or DCC format and a call must traverse an E.164 network.
E.164 autoconversion	Private addresses are in E.164e or E.164A formats and a call must traverse through an E.164 network.
E.164 one-to-one	This is a manual E.164-to-NSAP address translation.

The E.164 gateway option allows calls with AESAs to be forwarded (based on the prefix matching) to the interfaces that are statically mapped to the E.164 addresses. The E.164 address autoconversion uses the embedded E.164e or E.164A address to perform the address conversion. The E.164 address one-to-one translation uses a static translation table, the creation and maintenance of which is very time-consuming and error-prone.

ATM Connections

ATM is a connection-oriented protocol that requires a connection to be established before user traffic can start flowing. The ATM signaling protocol is responsible for call establishment, or for "drilling the tunnel" through the ATM cloud, as mentioned earlier in the chapter.

ATM Signaling

Signaling is the procedure that helps with establishing and releasing connections. The B-ISDN network signaling protocol has a lot of responsibilities, including dealing with cell loss rates, cell delays, AAL types, bit rates, and so on. To cope with all of that, the Q.931 signaling recommendation, deployed in N-ISDN, has been considerably expanded into Q.2931.

UNI signaling is based on Q.2931 ITU-T specification. Q.2931 specifies the procedures used to establish, maintain, and clear connections at the UNI. ATM Forum UNI signaling specifications versions 3.0 (UNI 3.0) and 3.1 (UNI 3.1) bundle up traffic management, ILMI, and UNI signaling into one document, while UNI 4.0 separates the specifications into three separate documents:

- UNI 4.0 Signaling Specification
- Traffic Management 4.0
- ILMI 4.0

Signaling uses the services of the Signaling ATM Adaptation Layer (SAAL), which combines all the AAL functions necessary for the responsibility of signaling, including the reliable transfer of the signaling message. As illustrated in Figure 3-13, SAAL uses AAL5 and consists of the following sublayers:

- **Common Part Convergence Sublayer (CPCS)**—Responsible for error detection, bit padding, and other functions, as mentioned in Chapter 2, "ATM Reference Model: Lower Layers."

- **Service Specific Convergence Sublayer (SSCS)**—Breaks down further into two sublayers:

  — **Service Specific Coordination Function (SSCF) - UNI**—Specified in Q.2130, this sublayer is responsible for mapping the particular requirements of the signaling layer to the requirements of the ATM layer at the UNI side (between the ATM edge device and the ingress/egress ATM switch).

  — **Service Specific Coordination Function (SSCF) - NNI**—Specified in Q.2130, this sublayer is responsible for mapping the particular requirements of the signaling layer to the requirements of the ATM layer at the NNI side (between the ATM switches).

  — **Service Specific Connection Oriented Protocol (SSCOP)**—Specified in Q.2110, this sublayer is responsible for providing the mechanisms for call establishment, call release, and call monitoring.

— **Common Part AAL Peer-to-Peer Protocol (CP-AAL)**—Provides unassured information transfer and a mechanism for detecting the corruption of SDUs.

Figure 3-13 *ATM SAAL Structure*

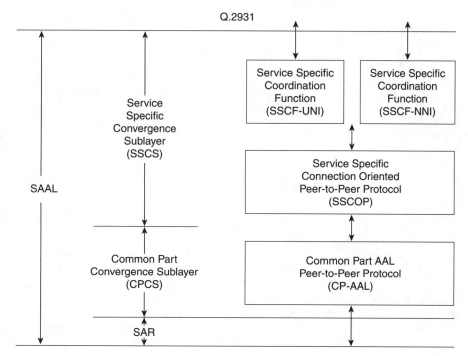

ATM signaling protocols vary by type of the ATM network interface. You can have UNI signaling, used between ATM edge devices and ATM switches across UNI links, or between two ATM switches. Also, you can have NNI signaling, strictly used between ATM switches. Consequently, SSCF is subdivided into two categories: SSCF-UNI and SSCF-NNI (as illustrated in Figure 3-13). UNI signaling in ATM defines the protocol that dynamically sets up SVCs by the ATM devices. NNI signaling is a part of the PNNI protocol, which is discussed in Chapter 4.

NOTE   The Q.2931 signaling protocol could be associated with Layer 3 of the OSI reference model, if not higher. The protocol gets *routed* based on logical addressing (a characteristic of Layer 3 functionality) and carries information pertinent to the ATM switch, which is a form of an application destined for specific network hosts.

Tracing ATM Call Setup

Now, let's "trace" an ATM call setup in a very generic way, based on the illustration in Figure 3-14.

Figure 3-14 *Overall Scenario of ATM Signaling*

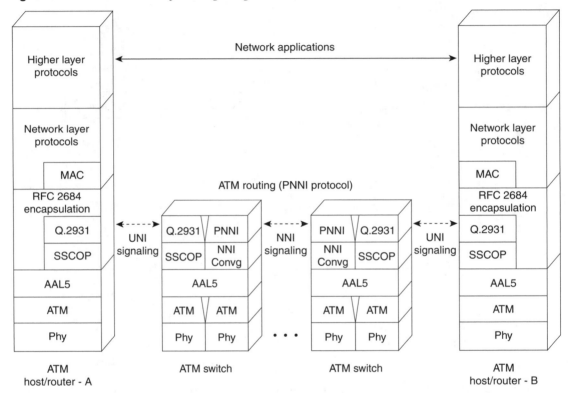

Assume you need to set up a connection between the ATM edge devices A and B. During the connection establishment phase, the calling ATM edge device, depicted in Figure 3-14, invokes the Q.2931 protocol. Q.2931 "gathers" the necessary information, such as QoS, the destination address, the type of a message, and so on. Then the Q.2931 message is introduced to the SAAL, which uses AAL5, the bottom sublayer of which takes care of the segmentation and reassembly (SAR) function. Fourty-eight–byte payloads are introduced to the ATM layer, which adds on a header with VPI equals x, VCI equals 5 to the Q.2931 message cells. Now these cells are either forming a Layer 1 frame or are going directly on top of fiber, as discussed in Chapter 1. When these cells arrive at the first switch, the switch "knows" that these are special cells (because they came in on a VCI equals 5). The switch behaves as an ATM edge device would by eliminating the cell headers, reassembling the 48-byte payloads, checking the errors at AAL5 level, and introducing the Q.2931 message to the ATM switch itself. This process continues from switch to switch along the path that meets the QoS requirements. Chapter 4 provides more detailed information on the connection establishment process and the algorithms involved at the UNI and NNI levels.

About ATM Routing and Switching

It is interesting to note that the Q.2931 protocol is one of those rare instances where the ATM switch is operating at a higher layer. Maybe this is the reason why some people associate ATM switches with routers and confuse other people by saying that. Notice that ATM switches route the signal but switch the payload. When payload information is shipped across the ATM cloud, the ATM switches do NOT reassemble the payload cells. Only the ATM edge devices reassemble the payload cells.

As far as the discussion on routing versus switching, I will comment only that routing consists of two functions—path determination and Layer 3 switching. Yes, ATM switches follow the logic of path determination for connection establishment signaling requests. The payload cells, however, are switched at the cell level, which is Layer 1.25.

Signaling Differences within UNI *x.x*

The UNI specifications are grouped as follows:

> **UNI 3.x**—Consists of two sets of interoperable specifications, UNI 3.0 and UNI 3.1.
> **UNI 4.0**—Includes UNI 3.x specifications and adds new features that are not supported in UNI 3.x.

The UNI 3.0 specification provided the signaling for point-to-point and point-to-multipoint connections. UNI 3.1 includes the provisions of UNI 3.0 and provides closer conformance with the ITU-T standards. UNI 4.0 replaces the explicit specification of the signaling protocol and provides a superset of UNI 3.1, including mandatory and optional features as identified in Table 3-5.

Table 3-5   *UNI 4.0 Signaling Capabilities*

Capability	ATM Edge Device	ATM Switch
Point-to-point calls	Mandatory	Mandatory
Point-to-multipoint calls	Optional	Mandatory
Signaling of individual QoS parameters	Mandatory	Mandatory
Leaf Initiated Join (LIJ)	Optional	Optional
ATM anycast	Optional	[1]
ABR signaling for point-to-point calls	Optional	Optional
Generic Identifier Transport	Optional	Optional

continues

Table 3-5   *UNI 4.0 Signaling Capabilities (Continued)*

Capability	ATM Edge Device	ATM Switch
Virtual UNIs	Optional	Optional
Switched Virtual Path (VP) service	Optional	Optional
Proxy signaling	Optional	Optional
Frame discard	Optional	Optional[2]
Traffic parameter negotiation	Optional	Optional
Supplementary services	—	—
Direct Dialing In (DDI)	Optional	Optional
Multiple Subscriber Number (MSN)	Optional	Optional
Calling Line Identification Presentation (CLIP)	Optional	Optional
Calling Line Identification Restriction (CLIR)	Optional	Optional
Connected Line Identification Presentation (COLP)	Optional	Optional
Connected Line Identification Restriction (COLR)	Optional	Optional
Subaddressing (SUB)	Optional	[3]
User-User Signaling (UUS)	Optional	Optional

[1]This feature is optional for public networks and mandatory for private.

[2]Transport of the frame discard indication is mandatory.

[3]This capability is mandatory for public and private networks that support only E.164N (native) address formats.

Signaling of individual QoS parameters allows the creation of ABR SVCs. Before UNI 4.0, there was no way to signal an ABR SVC.

The proxy signaling capability allows a device (called the *proxy signaling agent*) to signal on behalf of devices that are not capable of supporting signaling. For example, a router might signal for devices behind it that do not support signaling.

Virtual UNI supports a bunch of "little" UNIs on an interface. For example, several end stations can connect through a multiplexor; the multiplexor connects via UNI to an ATM switch. In this case, the end stations use multiple signaling channels, but only one UNI.

ATM Connection Types

ATM can support several types of connections, as illustrated in Figure 3-15:

- Point-to-point
- Point-to-multipoint
- Anycast

Figure 3-15 *ATM Forum UNI Signaling—Connection Types*

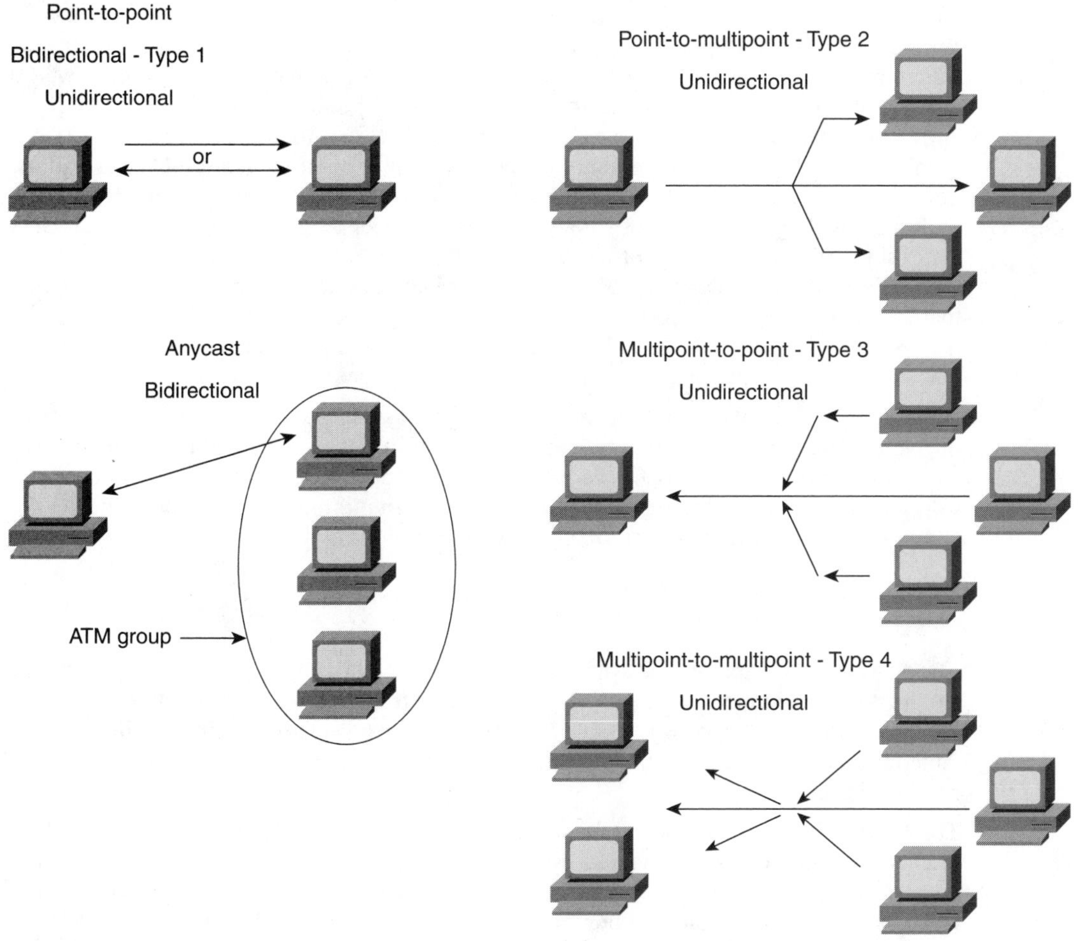

Point-to-point

Bidirectional - Type 1

Unidirectional

or

Point-to-multipoint - Type 2

Unidirectional

Anycast

Bidirectional

ATM group

Multipoint-to-point - Type 3

Unidirectional

Multipoint-to-multipoint - Type 4

Unidirectional

Point-to-point Connections

It is important to understand that ATM VCs consist of two unidirectional connections, one in each direction. Although a separate QoS can be provided in each direction, typically the requirements are symmetrical. The most basic connection type is the point-to-point bidirectional type, as illustrated in Figure 3-15. ITU-T refers to it as Type 1 and specifies that both directions of the VC travel along the same physical path. Please see Chapter 4 for more information on point-to-point VC signaling.

Point-to-multipoint/Multipoint-to-point/Multipoint-to-Multipoint Connections

Another connection type is point-to-multipoint, which is much more complex in behavior. Within a point-to-multipoint connection, you must have the initiator of a call, which is called the root. The destinations are called leaves. These destinations, driven fully by demand, can be dynamically added or deleted. UNI 3.1 point-to-multipoint signaling allows only the root (one end device) to add or delete leaves to a connection. The LIJ capability of UNI 4.0 allows users to independently join point-to-multipoint calls without intervention from the root of that connection. Also, leaves can request to join a point-to-multipoint call independently of whether the call has been active or not. The LIJ capability is not supported in the ATM Forum PNNI 1.0. It is left as a working item for PNNI 1.1. Until this capability is defined in PNNI 1.1, there is no standard to support LIJ in a network that includes different vendors. Point-to-multipoint connections are unidirectional, as illustrated in the Figure 3-15, and are identified as Type 2 by ITU-T. This connection type helps to support multicast services across ATM, as you see the later chapters.

A multipoint-to-point connection, identified as Type 3 connection by the ITU-T, is the exact opposite of the point-to-multipoint connection. It allows the information to arrive from various locations and be reassembled at the central root site. Yet another connection (Type 4) is a multipoint-to-multipoint VC that can support multipoint conferencing. Chapter 4 addresses point-to-multipoint signaling and ATM multicast options.

Anycast

The ATM anycast capability is available only with UNI 4.0, which allows a user to request a point-to-point connection to a single ATM end system that is part of an ATM group. The group concept is not new. You all know that "911" means emergency number in North America. Well, people using that number create point-to-point connections that are part of the "911" group.

The ATM Forum UNI 4.0 Signaling specification (AF-SIG-0061.000) specifies the ATM groups and their corresponding addresses. An ATM group represents a collection of ATM end systems. One of the ways an ATM end system can join a group is through the use of ILMI, which is responsible for client registration and de-registration. Anycast, using PNNI routing, allows connection requests and address registration for group addresses to be limited to specific areas on the network.

WAN Interworking

One of the major deployments of ATM is in the WAN environment. I am sure you are using services of some forms of WAN. Introduction of ATM technology means that it must interoperate with legacy services, such as Frame Relay and Switched Multimegabit Data Services (SMDSs), simply because many users are deploying several types of services due to costs and other criterias.

First, let's examine the ATM's interoperability with the Frame Relay service, then with the SMDS.

ATM and Frame Relay Interworking

The two methods for supporting the integration of Frame Relay networks into ATM are

- **Frame Relay to ATM Interworking (I.555)**—Offers the benefits of using the existing equipment base already installed.
- **Frame Relay UNI (FUNI)**—Offers the benefit of a new encapsulation method with the capability to support ATM singaling, QoS, and ATM management.

I.555 Method of ATM and Frame Relay Interworking

The I.555 method of ATM WAN and Frame Relay interworking, illustrated in Figure 3-16, involves the following criteria:

- RFC 1490, Multiprotocol Interconnect over Frame Relay defines the method of encapsulation of upper layer protocols within a Frame Relay frame.

  Defined in RFC 1490, Network Layer Protocol Identifier (NLPID) is used in conjunction with Subnetwork Access Protocol (SNAP) to allow ATM and Frame Relay interworking. NLPID is really a point of interconnection between Layer 3 protocols and Frame Relay.

- Frame Relay protocol interworking over ATM AAL5.
- ITU-T I.555 recommendation—interworking Frame Relay and ATM.

Figure 3-16 *Frame Relay/ATM Interworking Criteria*

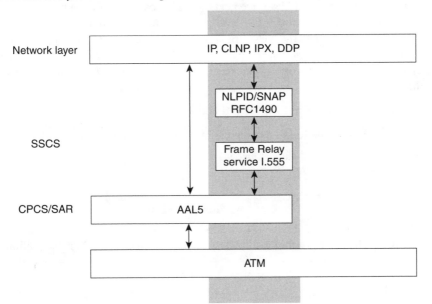

ATM can either interwork with Frame Relay or service as a transport to Frame Relay service. The interworking methods can be categorized further into *service interworking* and *network interworking*, as defined in the sections that follow.

ATM to Frame Relay Service Interworking

In the case of service interworking, one part of the network is ATM and the other part is Frame Relay, as illustrated in Figure 3-17.

Figure 3-17 *ATM/Frame Relay Service Interworking*

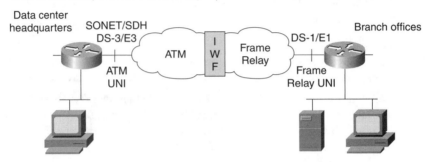

In this example, branch offices are interconnected through the Frame Relay service via DS-1/E1 lines, which are connected to the data center headquarters, which is interconnected to the ATM service via DS-3/E3 lines. This solution is quite feasible because branches do not have enough traffic to justify ATM connectivity. Somewhere within the service provider cloud, the ATM/Frame Relay interworking must take place. This function, called *interworking function (IWF)* is accomplished according to the FRF.8 specification. Service interworking works to convert the components of the two different transmission methods.

In this scenario, IWF performs two functions:

- Remaps Frame Relay parameters into ATM and vice versa
- Changes the data encapsulation

Translating Layer 2

The whole process of service interworking is quite similar to the translational bridging performed by routers—they completely change around Layer 2 encapsulation.

According to Figure 3-18, user data, first encapsulated into RFC 1490, gets introduced to the first Frame Relay switch, and then to the next, and so on, until it reaches the IWF device, which could be a router or an ATM switch.

Figure 3-18 *ATM Frame Relay Service Interworking: Protocol Stacks*

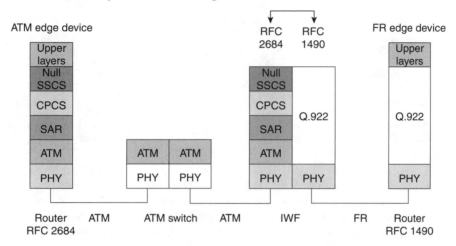

By remapping the RFC 1490 NLPID (known as FRF.3) to the RFC 2684 LLC/SNAP encapsulation, IWF converts between RFC 1490 and RFC 2684 encapsulations (ATM uses RFC 2684, which replaced the original RFC 1483), which are not compatible with each other. Also, IWF is responsible for remapping between Frame Relay data-link connection identifiers (DLCIs) and ATM VPIs/VCIs or NSAP, or E.164 addresses (specified in FRF.8). IWF also is responsible for setting the congestion notification bits in the ATM cell headers, cell loss priority (CLP), according to the Frame Relay settings, DE, or according to the ATM cell header CLP value.

IWF introduces new cells to the ATM cloud, which then forwards them to the ATM edge device.

ATM to Frame Relay Network Interworking

Network interworking (FRF.5) performs the transparent tunneling of Frame Relay user traffic and PVC over ATM. This function often is used to link Frame Relay networks over the ATM backbone. The most distant nodes can be configured to interoperate with one another—in contrast to service interworking—because intact Frame Relay frames are sent over the ATM network. The ATM backbone is used as an alternative to a leased line, and provides cost savings over leased lines. You can have one-to-one relationships between Frame Relay and ATM PVCs or multiple Frame Relay PVCs multiplexed into a single ATM PVC.

IWFs used for network interworking do not remap data encapsulations, but instead rely completely on the ATM end system to support FR-SSCS, which includes RFC 2684 and

NLPID. IWF also maps multiple Frame Relay logical connections into a single ATM VC, taking advantage of the FR-SSCS, which preserves the end-to-end DLCI identity. Figure 3-19 depicts a typical application of network interworking.

Figure 3-19   *Frame Relay/ATM Network Interworking*

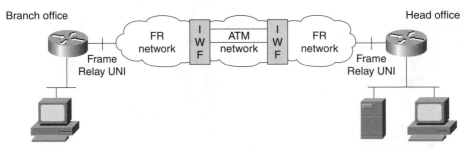

A branch office interconnected via Frame Relay is communicating with the head office that also is interconnected via the Frame Relay network. The two offices are subscribing to a carrier that is using ATM as a transport for Frame Relay service. IWF must be performed twice in this case, but there is no translation of addresses, congestion parameters, or encapsulations. IWF simply embraces the Frame Relay frames as a regular payload, encapsulates that payload into RFC 2684, utilizes AAL5, and manufactures the cell structure to be carried across the ATM network.

Figure 3-20 illustrates the stack of the protocols involved, starting at one edge device and terminating at another. Notice that the ATM network performs the Frame Relay–Service Specific Convergence Sublayer (FR-SSCS) function.

Figure 3-20   *ATM/Frame Relay Network Interworking: Protocol Stacks*

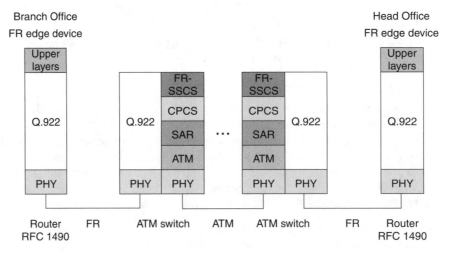

Frame UNI (FUNI) Method of ATM and Frame Relay Interworking

FUNI is the second method of ATM and Frame Relay interworking. FUNI is capable of transparently supporting ATM signaling; ATM network management; ATM traffic shaping; and Operations, Administration, and Maintenance (OAM) of ATM, which Chapter 4 discusses.

From the network perspective, your topology will look as illustrated in Figure 3-21.

Figure 3-21 *FUNI Example*

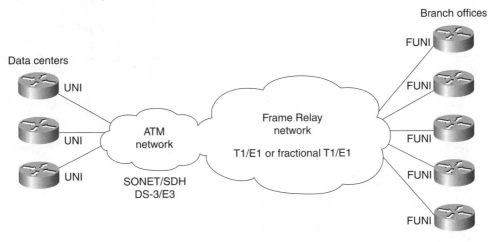

You have a series of branch offices interconnected to the data centers through the Frame Relay and ATM networks. The branch offices are attached to the Frame Relay cloud via FUNI interfaces; whereas, the data centers are attached via ATM UNI interfaces. In this topology, the data centers can request their ATM QoS all the way to the branch offices while setting up the VCs. Both branch offices and data centers are capable of performing ATM traffic shaping at the edge devices. This functionality is most important in the direction of Frame to ATM. Why? So that there are fewer surprises to the ATM cloud, resulting in lowering network congestion.

ATM's Preventative Medicine

I view traffic shaping as a form of "preventative medicine" to the networks. As in medicine, it is much easier to prevent the disease than to cure it after the fact. As you can see later, network congestion could be very debilitating for ATM networks. The subjects of ATM network congestion and the techniques for how to handle it have been around since the inception of ATM. Wouldn't it be simpler to prevent the congestion from happening, maybe not completely, but as much as possible? This is exactly the reasoning behind ATM traffic shaping. Chapter 4 continues your journey into traffic shaping and traffic management.

Figure 3-22 illustrates the FUNI-to-ATM interworking protocol stack.

Figure 3-22 *FUNI/ATM Interworking Protocol Stack*

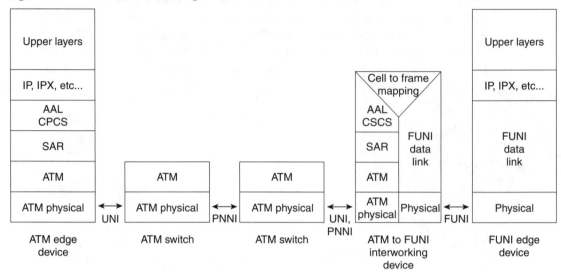

Two types of FUNI frame formats exist:

- FUNI frame with a 2-byte frame header
- FUNI frame with a 4-byte frame header

A FUNI with a 2-byte frame header can support up to 512 user VCCs using combinations of the 16 VPI values and 32 VCI values available for each VPI. A FUNI with a 4-byte frame header can support more than 16,000,000 user VCCs ($256 \times [2^{16}-32]$). Figure 3-23 illustrates the formats of the FUNI frames.

Figure 3-23 *FUNI Frame Formats*

FUNI header = 2 or 4 bytes

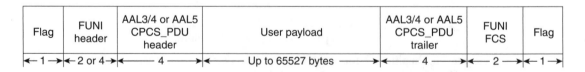

The FUNI header contains information on VPI, VCI, payload type identifier (PTI), CLP, and the type of the frame (signaling, data, or ILMI) that are necessary for the ATM header. The information in the FUNI header is mapped to the 5-byte ATM header. The ATM Forum specification, AF-SAA-0088.000, explains the mapping process in detail.

ATM Forum specification, AF-SAA-0088.000, of July 1997, specifies that FUNI supports only AAL5 and AAL3/4, hence providing interworking with non-real-time variable bit rate (nrt-VBR) and unspecified bit rate (UBR) type services. In February 1999, the

"Multiservice Extensions to FUNI v2.0" specification (AF-SAA-0109.000) was approved, thus extending FUNI support to voice and other real-time data. The ATM Forum specification, "ATM Trunking Using AAL2 for Narrowband Service," (AF-VTOA-0113.000) extended FUNI support to real-time variable bit rate (rt-VBR) traffic as well. This is absolutely revolutionary because it allows you to converge your compressed voice and data over Frame Relay and ATM, utilizing your bandwidth very efficiently. Figure 3-24 illustrates the architecture where voice and data are interconnected to the Frame Relay network at the branch location, and ATM concentrates the traffic at the central site.

Figure 3-24 *Voice and Data over FUNI*

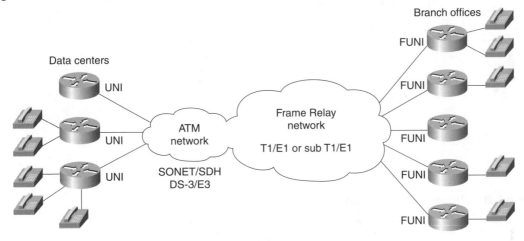

ATM and SMDS Interworking

You can find SMDS in public networks in Europe and the United States. SMDS has been defined by a three-level stack with a Level 3 protocol data unit (PDU) that contains the variable-length packet and E.164 source and destination addressing. The Level 2 PDUs, based on a 53-byte cell, are defined according to the IEEE 802.6 DQDB (Dual Queue Dual Bus) specification on metropolitan-area networks (MANs). These cells have a different format from the ATM cell, including the use of only VCI for locally significant addressing, as illustrated in Figure 3-25. I consider SMDS to be a first cut at a cell relay technology.

With the advent of ATM, there has been considerable interest in replacing Level 2 with a pure ATM Level 1.25 (53-byte ATM cell) using AAL3/4, as depicted in Figure 3-26. This has been standardized by the ITU-T as the I.364 specification. Support of SMDS over ATM is compliant with I.364 and eliminates a need for a separate CDU/DSU, which SMDS otherwise requires.

Figure 3-25 *DQDB and ATM Cell Comparison*

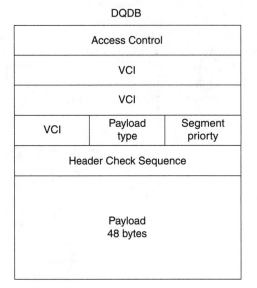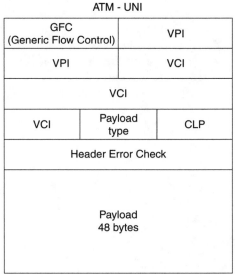

Figure 3-26 *SMDS and ATM Interworking*

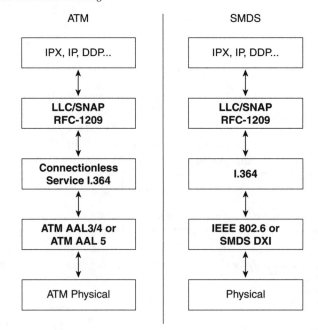

To emulate the SMDS service over ATM networks requires the functionality of a connectionless server function (CLSF). A CLSF, acting as a route server, forwards groups of cells based on the E.164 address in the AAL3/4 packet. As you might recall, AAL3/4 has the sequence number associated with every individual cell. This is the sequence number that CLSF uses to resequence cells. The resequencing is a very important function because cells from multiple packets can be interleaved on the same VC. Next, CLSF can either operate in cell-based mode or frame-based mode:

- If the CLSF is in the frame-based mode, it reassembles the ATM cells into the SMDS data packets. Then, using AAL5 and ATM, CLSF forwards the ATM cells to the appropriate destination.

- If CLSF is in the cell-based mode, it forwards the SMDS cells, sequenced using AAL3/4, to the appropriate destination.

Voice Interworking

One of the major advantages of ATM over any other method of transport is its capability to handle multiple types of services (one of which is voice) simultaneously. The ATM Forum has done tremendous work in that area over the last three years. Starting with the simple voice handling techniques over AAL1 for CBR traffic, there are specifications now to handle compressed voice over AAL2. Table 3-6 summarizes the ATM specifications for voice interworking.

Table 3-6   *Voice and Telephony Over ATM Specifications*

ATM Forum Specification	Description	Date of Approval
AF-VTOA-0078.000	Circuit Emulation Service 2.0	January 1997
AF-VTOA-0083.000	Voice and Telephone over ATM to the Desktop	May 1997
AF-VTOA-0083.001	Voice and Telephony over ATM to the Desktop	February 1999
AF-VTOA-0085.000	Dynamic Bandwidth Utilization in 64 Kbps time slot trunking over ATM Using CES	July 1997
AF-VTOA-0089.000	ATM Trunking Using AAL1 for Narrow Band Services	July 1997
AF-VTOA-0113.000	ATM Trunking Using AAL2 for Narrowband Services	February 1999
AF-VTOA-0119.000	Low Speed Circuit Emulation Service	May 1999
AF-VTOA-0120.000	ICS for ATM Trunking Using AAL2 for Narrowband Services	May 1999
AF-VMOA-0145.000	Loop Emulation Service Using AAL2	July 2000

You can subdivide voice interworking into three different approaches:

- CES, which carries full or fractional rate T1/E1 circuits between endpoints
- Dynamic bandwidth circuit emulation service (DBCES)
- Voice solutions using variable bit rate (VBR) and AAL2

Chapter 8, "Circuit Emulation Service ATM Connectivity and Summary of Cisco ATM Edge Devices," presents Cisco's CES implementation.

CES

CES enables legacy systems not supporting ATM, such as PBX and existing time-division multiplexing (TDM) systems, to be transported over ATM infrastructures. With CES, CBR type of traffic can be carried over an ATM network. With CES, voice simply is encoded into an ATM network as into a regular TDM network using pulse code modulation (PCM), adaptive differential pulse code modulation (ADPCM), or other encoding mechanisms. The CES approach is very simple. You do not need to alter any edge devices; they stay as is, including voice networks.

CES uses the ATM AAL1 mechanism to encapsulate, segment, and reassemble the incoming T1 or E1 traffic into the ATM cell, thus using ATM as the replacement of the network in place.

You can categorize CES into structured and unstructured CES, as depicted in Figure 3-27. The unstructured CES takes the entire T1 or E1 circuit into a single ATM VC; whereas, the structured CES allows independent 64-kbps channels to be mapped to a single ATM VC.

Figure 3-27 *Structured and Unstructured CES*

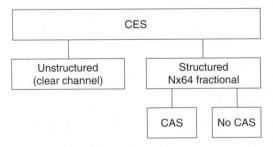

Being simple, CES has its own limitations: it cannot provide statistical multiplexing, and it is implemented as a point-to-point service, which creates problems from the scalability perspective. Furthermore, the nature of the CBR traffic forces the bandwidth reservation, regardless of the voice traffic being present or not, which is rectified with the help of Channel Associated Signaling (CAS). The next section, "DBCES," elaborates more on CAS.

DBCES

DBCES allows for dynamic bandwidth allocation for voice traffic. The ingress switch detects the idle state within a timeslot and drops it from the ATM structure, allowing for the freed up bandwidth to be utilized by other services (UBR, ABR, and VBR type information). This inactivity detection mechanism could vary from vendor to vendor. The most common one is the CAS, which in voice is referred to as *on/off hook detection.*

Terminology Inconsistencies

Although in voice *on-hook* means no traffic and no connection, in data *on* means there is traffic.

From Figure 3-28, you can see that this capability allows for the efficient use of bandwidth allocated for CBR traffic by reclaiming the bandwidth when there is no voice traffic and by freeing up the network bandwidth for bursty data traffic.

Figure 3-28 *On/Off Hook CAS*

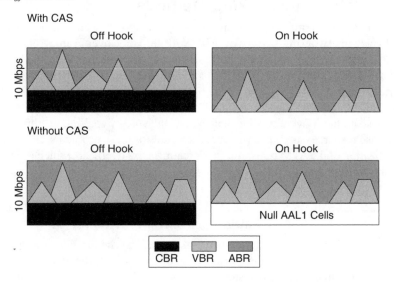

In May 1999, the ATM Forum extended the CES specification to include low-speed circuits, including the rates of 1200, 2400, 4800, and 9600 bps (AF-VTOA-0119.000). This specification documents point-to-point unstructured CES using AAL1 via PVCs and SVCs.

Voice Solutions Using VBR and AAL2

The interesting side of voice is that it is not a constant stream of information. When you talk, you pause between words and sentences. Surely enough, there is no need to occupy the bandwidth when you pause or when one party talks and another listens. Voice compression mechanisms result in efficient bandwidth utilization.

The AF-VTOA-0113.000 specification addresses this issue: it provisions for handling compressed voice over AAL2 and for multiplexing multiple voice channels into a single VC. The specification addresses how the various data streams of voice traffic are combined into a single sequence of cells so that they can be transmitted over a single ATM VC. Chapter 2 illustrates the AAL2 encapsulation. You can see that each ATM cell can contain data from several voice calls. This reduces the packetization delay.

The specification also addresses CAS and common channel signaling (CCS) types of signaling to detect the presence of voice traffic.

The major benefit of ATM trunking using AAL2 is bandwidth savings, which is achieved by voice compression, the use of CAS, and the dynamic routing of call setup.

Summary of Voice Interworking Methods

Before summarizing the voice interworking methods, I want to mention the fourth method of voice interworking—Voice over IP (VoIP) or Voice over Frame Relay (VoFR). The VoIP method can select ATM as the transport mechanism, in which case ATM no longer "knows" that it carries voice traffic. Although the implementation of VoIP networks could be simple, the constraints of ATM being totally unaware of real-time voice should not be ignored. This might result in inefficiency in the ATM networks. Furthermore, being encapsulated into an IP packet, the ATM network is unaware of the voice signaling, resulting in its inability to release resources as calls terminate. As a cure for these problems, IP must manage the utilization of the ATM transport, thus creating extra overhead, which is not necessary if you carry voice directly over ATM.

Efficiency of Voice over IP over ATM

Carrying VoIP over ATM reminds me of tunneling. The inefficiency of tunneling is quite clear: packets are longer, the transport cloud is unaware of the type of traffic it carries, hence you cannot make policy decisions unless you make them before you enter the tunnel. Although I can justify the need for tunnels (one of the justifications might be the dominance of one protocol over another), I cannot justify the need to carry VoIP over ATM. If ATM is used as a transport, why introduce extra overhead from the bandwidth and the complexity perspective? Don't forget, you would need to use additional protocols for IP to realize QoS, especially because ATM was designed to handle QoS natively.

Table 3-7 illustrates the comparison of the methods of voice interworking.

Table 3-7   *Comparison of VTOA Methods*

	Voice Compression	Idle Channel Suppression	Silence Removal
CES	No	No	No
DBCES	No	Yes	No
AAL2 with rt-VBR	Yes	Yes	Yes

ATM Interworking with Existing Protocols

One of the major goals of ATM is to provide dynamic interoperability between existing technologies and ATM. Subjects on WAN and voice interworking speak for that. But there is more. What about the capability of supporting the existing applications that reside on IP, IPX, AppleTalk, and other Layer 3 protocols that require seamless internetworking? Native Mode Network Layer operation is one method for running network layer protocols over ATM networks (this concept is addressed later in the chapter, in the section, "Native Mode Protocols Operation over ATM."

Another method of seamless internetworking of existing applications across the ATM network is LAN Emulation (LANE). The ATM Forum completed the LANE version 2 specification (AF-LANE-0093.000) in February 1999.

ATM Interworking with Existing Protocols via RFC 2684 Encapsulation (Formerly RFC 1483)

Both methods, LANE and Native Mode Network Layer Operation, use the RFC 2684 (formerly RFC 1483—RFC 2684 was released in September 1999) encapsulation method.

The original encapsulation method, RFC 1483, was issued by the IETF Internetworking over NBMA (ION) working group in 1993. In September 1999, RFC 2684 replaced it. RFC 2684 does not obsolete implementations of RFC 1483; rather, it enhances them and provides some clarifications. One of the major enhancements is the addition of the new encapsulation for Virtual Private Networks (VPNs) and the addition of security. RFC 2684 is an encapsulation method of multiple Layer 3 or Layer 2 protocols over ATM, which implies that it can encapsulate routed or bridged traffic, including VPNs.

RFC 2684 uses two techniques of encapsulation: logical link control/Subnetwork Access Protocol (LLC/SNAP) and VC multiplexing.

The LLC/SNAP header, consisting of 3 bytes, is attached to each packet to identify which protocol is contained in the payload. The LLC/SNAP header information includes the LLC, the Organizational Unique Identifier (OUI) field, and the Protocol Identification (PID) field, which allows for various protocols to be differentiated from each other. RFC 1700 lists all the PID codes for various protocols. Being able to distinguish among different protocols "upstairs" LLC/SNAP results in a very efficient use of VC space. It allows for multiple protocols to be carried over a single VC.

The VC multiplexing method creates a binding between an ATM VC and the type of network protocol carried on that VC. Thus, there is no need for PID information to be carried in the payload of each AAL5 CPCS-PDU. This implies that a VC can carry only a single protocol. So, if you have multiple protocols, you need a separate VC for each protocol involved, although the originating and terminating points could be the same. It is interesting to note that the VC multiplexing method can improve the efficiency of your ATM network and your ATM edge devices. How? Simply by reducing the number of cells needed to carry PDUs. Because there is no need for PID information to be carried, the PID size is reduced, which results in the reduction of per-packet processing and number of cells needed to carry PDUs.

Figure 3-29 illustrates the protocol stack for running Layer 3 or Layer 2 protocols, for example LANE, directly over RFC 2684.

Figure 3-29 *RFC 2684 Protocol Stack*

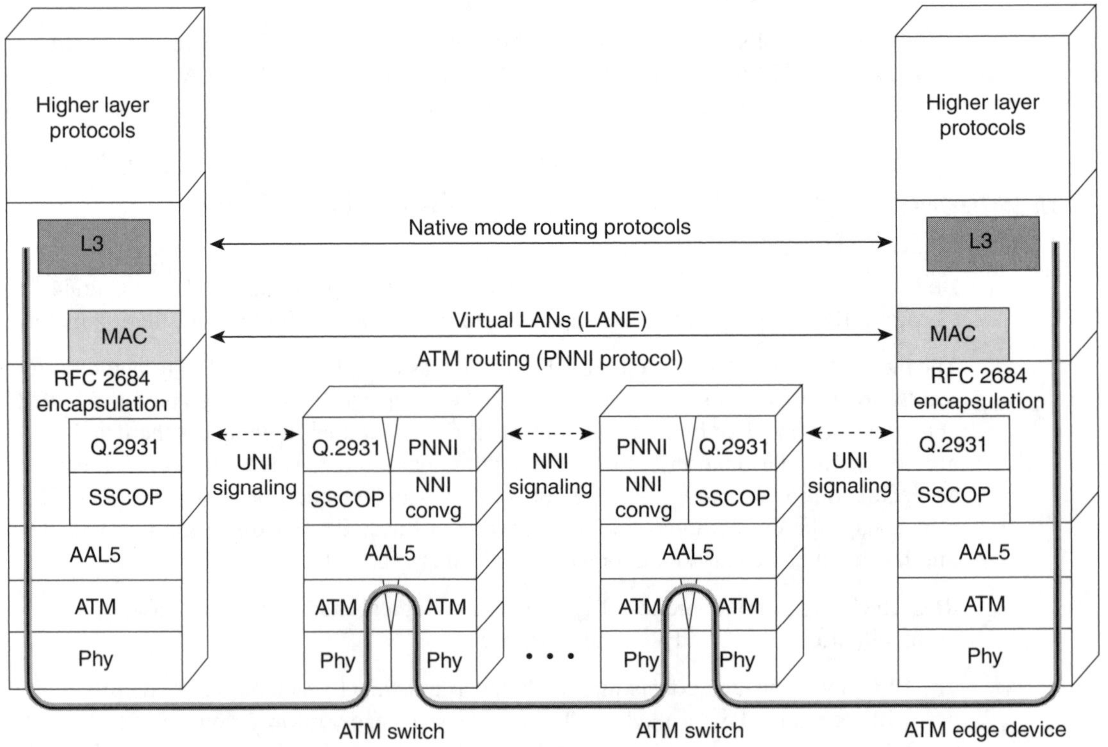

RFC 2684 Explained

RFC 2684 is the multiprotocol encapsulation method. The encapsulation method of multiple protocols (Layer 3 or bridged) over a single VC is accomplished using LLC/SNAP; the encapsulation method of a single protocol over a single VC is done using MUX. Both PVCs and SVCs are supported, provided that the ATM cloud can support PVCs and/or SVCs.

ATM Interworking with Existing Protocols via LANE

LANE's purpose in life is to extend Layer 2 functionality over the ATM cloud, meaning longer distances, without any concern for Layer 3.

Consider legacy LAN, be it Ethernet on Token Ring. Its characteristics include

- A single broadcast domain
- Physical proximity
- Speed of communication

To overcome LAN's limitation of physical proximity, virtual LANs (VLANs) were introduced, with one of the selling factors being "ease of MACs (Moves And Changes)." Now you have LANs that stretch over several floors, if not buildings. What if you need to stretch these LANs even more, over several cities? Here ATM comes to the rescue. LANE extends VLANs throughout the network dynamically, providing total seamless connection to the Ethernet or to Token Ring hosts, which are fully unaware of ATM's existence. The ATM Forum has done tremendous work on LANE since 1995. Table 3-8 summarizes the ATM Forum's efforts in this regard.

Table 3-8   *ATM Forum LANE Specifications*

ATM Forum Specification	Date of Approval	Description
AF-LANE-0021.000	January 1995	LANE over ATM 1.0
AF-LANE-0038.000	September 1995	LANE Client Management Specification
AF-LANE-0050.000	December 1995	LANE 1.0 Addendum
AF-LANE-0057.000	March 1996	LANE Servers Management Specification v1.0
AF-LANE-0084.000	July 1997	LANE v2.0 LUNI Interface
AF-LANE-0093.000	October 1998	LANE Client Management Specification Version 2.0
AF-LANE-0112.000	February 1999	LANE over ATM Version 2 – LNNI Specification

Figure 3-30 illustrates the fundamental concept of LANE. Three different broadcast domains stretch across the ATM network: Engineering, Marketing, and Sales. Each domain has a series of hosts attached to the various Ethernet switches using a native Ethernet connection. Although the Ethernet switches are dispersed geographically, they are required to share a single broadcast domain with other devices that are within the same department.

For example, all four switches of Marketing must be on a single broadcast domain. LANE architecture achieves this kind of connectivity dynamically. All three of the illustrated broadcast domains containing natively attached Ethernet hosts are interconnected via the ATM cloud fully seamlessly, without changing any of the host applications.

Figure 3-30 *LANE*

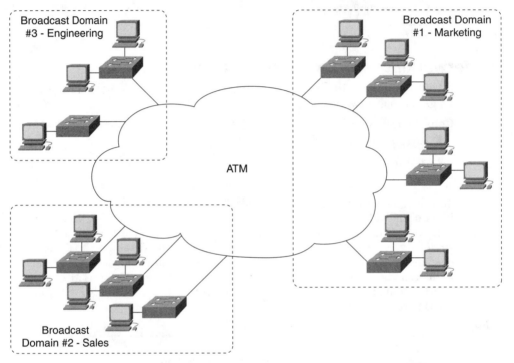

Defining LANE

To avoid the confusion that is so common when there are multiple interworking methods, here is my comparison "formula" of LANE v1 and LANE v2:

LANE v1 is defined by the OSI Layer 2 only, extending the Layer 2 broadcast domain through the ATM cloud. LANE v1 can handle *any* Layer 3 protocol. When the definition of LANE architecture is defined, VCs are set up dynamically, without any static mappings. LANE v1 has no redundancy specified. Cisco has a proprietary solution—Simple Server Redundancy Protocol (SSRP) to handle servers' redundancy in LANE v1.

LANE v2 is defined by LANE v1 + Dynamic Server Redundancy + SNAP encapsulation (implying multiple protocols over a single VC) + QoS + ABR support + Selective Multicast.

Chapter 5, "LAN Emulation (LANE)," addresses LANE v1 and LANE v2 in depth.

Native Mode Protocols Operation over ATM

In contrast to LANE, native mode protocols operation extends Layer 3. Figure 3-31 illustrates the main question here: How do you resolve Layer 3 network addressing to ATM addressing so that data traffic can cross ATM networks seamlessly?

Figure 3-31 *Native Mode Protocols Address Resolution*

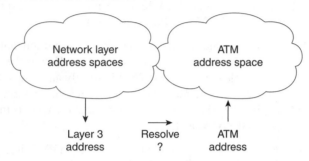

The following sections address the methods for resolving Layer 3 network addressing to ATM addressing.

Resolving Layer 3 Network Addressing to ATM Addressing Manually

To have a Layer 3 protocol transported over ATM, a mechanism of address resolution between the Layer 3 addresses to their corresponding ATM addresses must take place. Let's take IP as an example, as illustrated in Figure 3-32.

Figure 3-32 *IP over ATM: Manually Created Address Resolution Table*

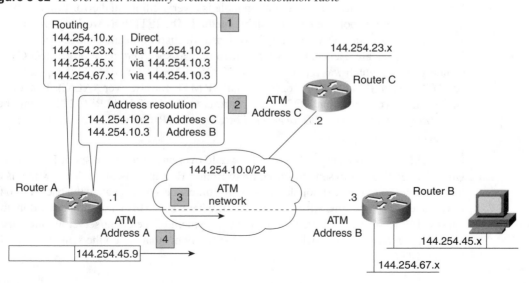

The whole process of packet transfer from Router A to Router B involves four steps:

Step 1   Router A receives a packet across its LAN interface for the destination 144.254.45.9. Depending on the router model, Router A checks its cache (fast, autonomous, silicon, optimum, or NetFlow). If this is the first packet, the router checks its routing tables to identify the next hop for the destination 144.254.45.0/24. Router A finds that the next hop that can be reached via the ATM interface is Router B.

Step 2   Now Router A needs to consult the address resolution table to determine the ATM address of the next hop destination. How is the address resolution table created? RFC 2684 is strictly an encapsulation method here; hence, there are no dynamics in the resolution table creation. The only method here is manual. Assuming that the table is there, the router determines the ATM address.

Step 3   Now Router A is ready to set up a VC. If it is a PVC, it is predetermined already. If it is an SVC, the signaling frame leaves the router, enters into the ATM cloud, and, based on the ATM global address, "paves its way through the ATM network."

Step 4   Finally, the packet can be sent. It is encapsulated into RFC 2684 and then into AAL5. In AAL5, the packet gets segmented, ATM cell headers get attached to the 48-byte payloads, and the traffic is on its way to the destination.

Resolving Layer 3 Network Addressing to ATM Addressing via RFC 2225

Manual creation of the address resolution table is a very tedious and error-prone exercise, and consequently is not a practical scalable method. The IETF ION working group was very eager to introduce ATM technology with as little disruption and change to the existing IP model as possible. Hence, the dynamic method was specified in the original RFC 1577 (January 1994), which was replaced by RFC 2225 in April 1998. RFC 2225 replaced RFC 1577 ("Classical IP") and RFC 1626 ("Default IP MTU for Use over AAL5"). To avoid the confusion between different RFCs, I simply refer to RFC 1577 and RFC 2225 using the *classical* name, as *Classical IP over ATM* or *Classical IP*. Figure 3-33 illustrates the Classical IP protocol stack.

Classical IP tries to behave as IP typically would over any kind of transport. For example, when Router A needs to send information to Router B, it must issue an ARP (which is a local broadcast) to the next hop device so that Router A can encapsulate the packet into the lower layer. As you know, ARP is a broadcast, whereas ATM is a non-broadcast domain. Classical IP resolves this issue through the deployment of the client/server architecture, where the server provides ARP services to the IP clients that are on the same Logical IP Subnet (LIS).

Figure 3-33 *Classical IP Protocol Stack*

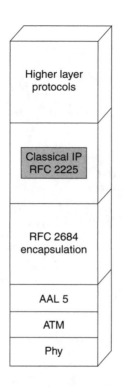

NOTE   In fact, a pretense of any kind of behavior in internetworking is achieved quite successfully by the deployment of a client/server architecture. Other examples of this include LANE and MPOA (discussed in Chapters 4 and 5).

Note that client/server architecture is necessary in the SVC environment. In the PVC environment, as you see later in the chapter, there is no need for ARP servers.

The Classical IP process can be subdivided into two major phases:

- Initialization
- Data transfer

Figure 3-34 depicts the initialization phase of the Classical IP process.

Figure 3-34 *Classical IP Initialization Phase*

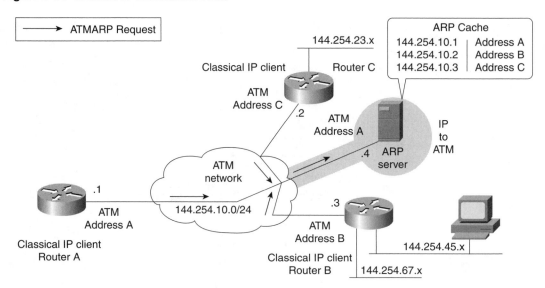

As Figure 3-34 illustrates, the following events take place during the initialization phase of the Classical IP process:

Step 1 Each Classical IP client knows the ARP server NSAP address. When the client becomes part of the IP network, it announces itself to the server via a dynamically setup VC to the server.

Step 2 The client sends normal ATMARP request packets to the server.

Step 3 The ATMARP server examines each ATMARP request packet.

Step 4 If the server detects a duplicate IP address, it does not update the table entry and it raises the duplicate IP address detection condition to the server's management.

Step 5 The server registers the client's NSAP and the corresponding IP address for future reference and stores the information in the ARP cache, entries of which are valid for 20 minutes. If an entry ages beyond 20 minutes without being updated by the client, that entry is deleted from the table regardless of the state of any VCs that might be associated with that entry.

The ARP server maintains IP and ATM addresses, whereas the ARP clients maintain the local ATM address and the ATM address of the ATMARP server. A client must refresh its ATMARP information with the server at least once every 15 minutes.

Figure 3-35 depicts the data transfer phase of the Classical IP process.

Figure 3-35 *Classical IP Using SVC over ATM*

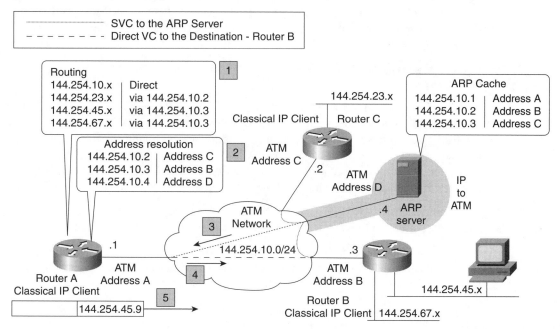

As Figure 3-35 illustrates, the following events take place during the data transfer phase of the Classical IP process:

Step 1   Router A receives a packet across its LAN interface for the destination 144.254.45.9. Depending on the router model, Router A checks its cache (fast, autonomous, silicon, optimum, or NetFlow). If this is the first packet, the router checks its routing tables to identify the next hop for the destination 144.254.45.0/24. Router A finds that the next hop is Router B, which it can reach via the ATM interface.

Step 2   Now Router A needs to consult the address resolution table to determine the ATM address of the next hop destination. To determine the ATM address of the next hop destination, Router A—being a Classical IP ARP client—sends out an ARP request to the ARP server.

Step 3   The ARP server receives the request, looks into its ARP cache, and sends a reply.

Step 4   Now Router A is ready to set up a VC. The signaling frame leaves the router, enters into the ATM cloud, and, based on the ATM global address, paves its way through the ATM network.

Step 5 Finally, the packet can be sent. It is encapsulated into RFC 2684, and then into AAL5 where it is segmented, the ATM Layer attaches the 5-byte cell header to the 48-byte payload, and the traffic is on its way to the destination.

If the ARP server does not have an entry for a destination X, it sends ATMARP_NAK to the requestor.

Classical IP supports PVC and SVC connections. The ARP server is required only in the case of an SVC connection. In the case of the PVC connection, InATMARP is used to resolve VC identifiers to the corresponding IP addresses, without the involvement of an ARP server. It is interesting to note that InATMARP is based on the RFC 1293, which defines the behavior of an InARP in the Frame Relay networks (Frame Relay InARP provides Frame Relay addressing resolution to more than one routed protocol, such as IPX and AppleTalk).

Classical IP uses the LLC/SNAP encapsulation mechanism to allow the sharing of VCs.

A major drawback of the Classical IP implementation using RFC 1577 is the lack of ARP server redundancy. The standard specifies only a single ARP server per LIS, which implies that the ARP server is a single point of failure.

The advantage of multiple ARP servers is obviously clear: more robust operation and high network resiliency. Cisco has a proprietary solution regarding ARP servers, sometimes referred to as "Extensions to Classical IP over ATM." Using Cisco gear, you can achieve full redundancy. RFC 2225 states that it

...recognizes the future development of standards and implementations of multiple-ATMARP-server models that will extend the operations as defined in this memo to provide a highly reliable address resolution service

RFC 2225 specifies that the clients must have a reference to the ATMARP server list, which can contain more than one server. The clients should attempt to communicate with any of the servers until they accomplish a successful registration.

Summary of IP Resolving Layer 3 Network Addressing to ATM Addressing via RFC 2225

Classical IP internetworks IP only. It allows native behavior of IP through the ATM cloud. This implies that the IP ARP function of mapping IP addresses to the ATM PVCs or SVCs happens dynamically. The dynamics occur with the help of the ARP server for the SVC scenario; in the case of the PVCs, InATMARP must be configured for every PVC defined. The SVC scenario does not provide a complete specification on provisioning for redundancy. Cisco has a proprietary solution to provision for redundancy. RFC 1577 and RFC 2225 specify the IP interoperability within a single LIS.

Internetworking Across Multiple LISs Using Next Hop Resolution Protocol (NHRP)

Imagine the following scenario. You diligently create a hierarchical network over ATM to interconnect various sites using all principles of scalable network designs. Figure 3-36 illustrates such a network.

Figure 3-36 *A Hierarchical Network Design over ATM*

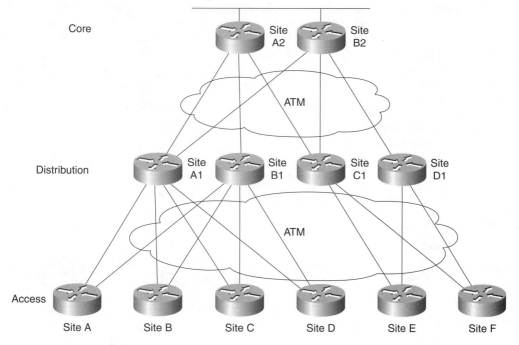

Using a classless IP routing protocol and contiguous IP network numbers, you assign the individual network numbers to maximize the network scalability, such as route summarization, updates frequency, and so on. You provision your network for redundancy in such a way that the access layer sites get connectivity to the distribution should their prime links disappear. The same goes for the interconnectivity between the distribution and the core layers. Each individual link represents a separate IP network number (or subnet, or how about calling it a broadcast domain?). Now, for Site A to communicate with Site F, packets must be segmented into cells and reassembled back into packets eight times (A,A1,A2,C1,F)! This is a bit too much. To cure this problem, which is actually not only ATM's problem but all nonbroadcast multiaccess (NBMA) networks when you are faced with interconnecting multiple LIS' through them, you use a protocol called *Next Hop Resolution Protocol (NHRP)*.

Surprisingly enough, NHRP has been supported in Cisco IOS Software since Release 10.3. Nobody talked about it, simply because the speed of WAN connectivity was slow enough to be taken for granted. Now that you have ATM, which can provide several Gbps, speed becomes an issue.

RFC 2332 of April 1998, defines NHRP and extends Classical IP to allow shortcuts over ATM networks that support several LISs. These shortcuts also are referred to as *cut-through* routing. NHRP breaks the rules of Classical IP by extending the address resolution to multiple hops. NHRP fools Layer 3 protocols by extending the capability of NBMA nodes to talk to each other directly. Using NHRP, your Site A can communicate with Site F directly, bypassing Layer 3 decisions.

NHRP uses Local Address Groups (LAGs). The main difference between LISs and LAGs is that, in the LIS model, the two nodes can talk to each other directly only if they belong to the same LIS, whereas in the LAG model, the two nodes can talk to each other if they belong to the same NBMA network.

NHRP has a client/server architecture. An NHRP Client (NHC) issues the NHRP request, and an NHRP Server (NHS) replies to the NHRP request or forwards it to another server.

Because a single device can act as both client and server, NHRP can function in two modes:

- **Fabric mode**—Occurs when a router functions as both NHC and NHS. Operating in Fabric mode is a good idea in large-scale networks.

- **Server mode**—Occurs when one or more NHSs maintains the address resolution database. Operating in Server mode is more appropriate for smaller networks.

Figure 3-37 illustrates the flow of operation in the NHRP environment.

Figure 3-37 *NHRP: Flow of Operation*

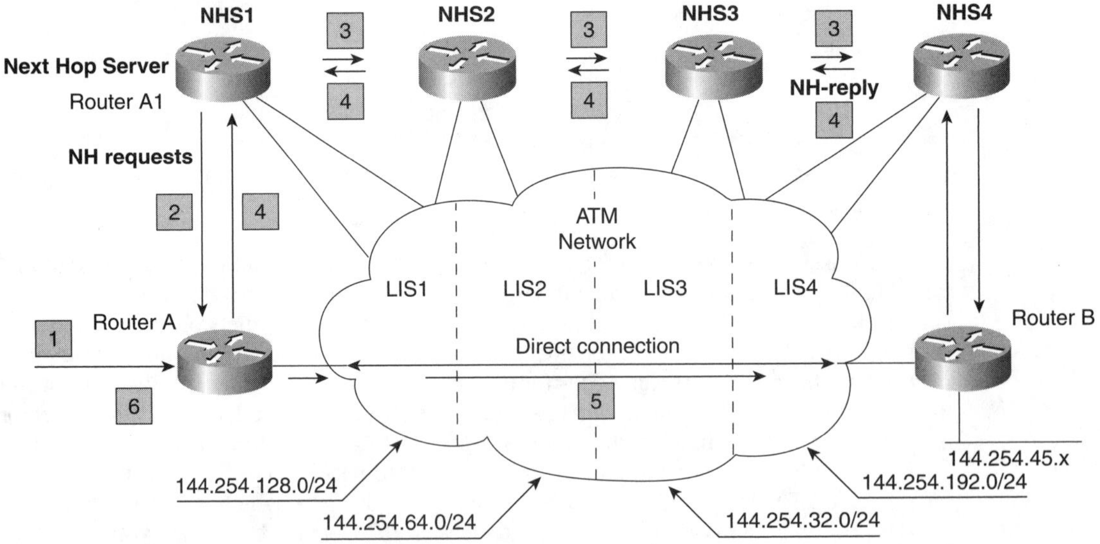

As depicted in Figure 3-37, the flow of operation in the NHRP environment is as follows:

Step 1   Router A receives a packet across its LAN interface for the destination 144.254.45.9. Depending on the router model, Router A checks its cache (fast, autonomous, silicon, optimum, or NetFlow). If this is the first packet, the router checks its routing tables to identify the next hop for the destination 144.254.45.0/24. Router A finds that the next hop is Router A1 via the ATM interface.

Step 2   Now Router A needs to consult the address resolution table to determine the ATM address of the next hop destination. To determine the ATM address of the next hop destination, Router A, being a Classical IP ARP client, sends out an ARP request to the ARP server, which in this case is Router A1, also functioning as NHS1.

Step 3   NHS1 receives the request and looks it up in its ARP cache. If it does not have an entry, it forwards the request to the next NHS, NHS2. NHS2 repeats the same steps as NHS1, and so on. The same algorithm is applied until an NHS is reached that knows the requested mapping.

Step 4   The NHRP response is cached on its way back so that for the next mapping request, the NHS responds directly. The node has the flexibility to request an *authoritative* mapping, which implies that the authoritative mapping cached data is never used.

Step 5   Now Router A is ready to set up a direct VC to Router B. The signaling frame leaves the router, enters the ATM cloud, and, based on the ATM global address, paves its way through the ATM network by cutting through various LISs.

Step 6   Finally, the packet can be sent. It is encapsulated into RFC 2684, and then into AAL5, where it is segmented, ATM cell headers are attached to the 48-byte payloads, and the traffic is on its way to the destination.

NHRP is an integral part of the MPOA specification and can be used in SVC implementations of Classical IP (RFC 2225) or manual SVC setup.

Resolving Layer 3 Network Addressing to ATM Addressing via MPOA

Classical IP is really interconnecting IP only. What about other protocols? What about IPX, AppleTalk, and other desktop protocols that customers do deploy today? How can they be dynamically interworked through the ATM networks without the tedious exercises of manual mapping? The ATM Forum examined this problem and came up with a solution—MPOA.

MPOA is based on LANE, which supports multiple protocols over a single broadcast domain. MPOA extends the idea of LANE into Layer 3 and brings the dynamics of LANE and NHRP to all Layer 3 protocols. MPOA creates a standardized entity of a virtual router, which is really a routing functionality integrated within a dynamically switched ATM network. Chapter 6, "Multiprotocol over ATM (MPOA)," covers MPOA in detail.

Table 3-9 lists the ATM Forum's MPOA specifications that are approved and the ones that are pending completion.

Table 3-9   *MPOA ATM Forum Specification*

ATM Forum Specification	Date of Approval or Expected Approval	Description
AF-MPOA-0087.000	July 1997	Multiprotocol over ATM v1.0
AF-MPOA-0092.000	July 1998	Multiprotocol over ATM v1.0 MIB
AF-MPOA-0114.000	May 1999	Multiprotocol over ATM, v1.1
AF-MPOA-0129.000	October 1999	MPOA v1.1 Addendum for VPN Support

Formula for MPOA

MPOA = LANE + QoS + Redundancy + SNAP encapsulation (implying multiple protocols over a single VC) + ABR support + NHRP + multiple Layer 3 protocols + MARS (Multicast Address Resolution Server).

MPLS and Tag Switching

One of the newest standards that the IETF is working on is Muptiprotocol Label Switching (MPLS). MPLS is a very interesting and innovative method in Layer 3 routing/switching. Within the last year, there have been a number of RFC drafts on MPLS framework and architecture. You can find the summary of all the MPOA drafts and their corresponding URLs at www.ietf.org/ietf/1id-abstracts.txt. A majority of the specifications are based on Cisco's tag switching. At the time of this writing, the specifications have not been standardized yet. Consequently, I am describing how Cisco has implemented MPLS. When the specifications are released, Cisco will comply with the standards.

What are labels? What devices are involved in label switching? How does it integrate with ATM? What benefits do you obtain from MPLS? Before addressing these questions, let's define MPLS terminology.

Table 3-10 lists the MPLS terminology that I use to describe MPLS functionality.

Table 3-10   *MPLS Terminology*

MPLS Term	Definition
Label Switch Router (LSR)	A switch or a router that switches labeled packets based on pre-computed switching tables.
Label	This is a header that is used by LSR to switch/forward packets. The header could vary in format. In the router network, it is a 32-bit header. In the ATM networks, the label is placed into a position of VPI/VCI of the cell header.
Edge Label Switch Router (Edge LSR)	A multilayer switch or a router can do this functionality. Edge LSR is responsible for performing the initial packet processing at Layer 3 and for applying the classification with a corresponding first label.
Label Switch Path (LSP)	This is a path defined by all labels assigned between any end points.

Table 3-10   *MPLS Terminology (Continued)*

MPLS Term	Definition
Label Virtual Circuit (LVC)	This is a hop-by-hop connection that is established at the ATM layer to implement LSP.
Label Distribution Protocol (LDP)	This is a protocol that is responsible for creating labels in the core and edge devices. It works in conjunction with the interior routing protocols, such as OSPF, RIP, EIGRP, and IS-IS.

Figure 3-38 illustrates the MPLS operation.

Figure 3-38   *MPLS Operation*

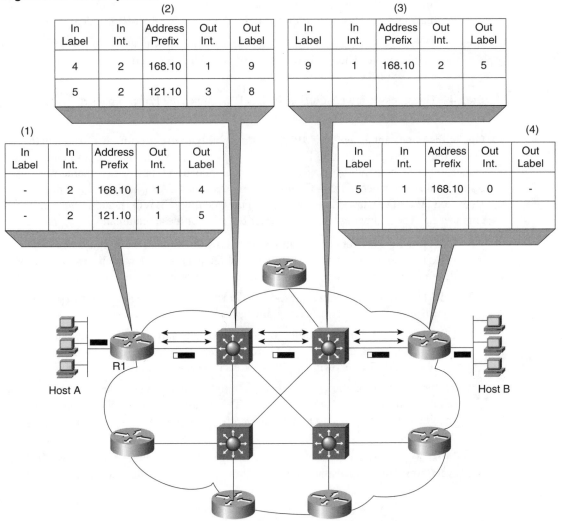

As illustrated in Figure 3-38, the process involved with the MPLS operation is as follows:

Step 1 The network runs a dynamic routing protocol, such as EIGRP. Based on the resulting routing topology, the MPLS edge device (a router, for example) creates a table of label values between adjacent devices using LDP. This is similar to the idea of PVC, except that it is created dynamically, there is no human intervention whatsoever.

Step 2 A packet from Host A enters the ingress MPLS edge device. Here, the packet gets processed for any bandwidth requirements and types of services (QoS—not to be confused with ATM QoS). Based on the results, the Edge LSR selects and applies a label to the packet header and forwards it to the next hop. The labels have local significance only, making them similar to a Frame Relay DLCI or ATM VPI/VCI idea.

Step 3 The next LSR reads the packet label and replaces it with a new one from its label table. Then it forwards the packet. The same action is repeated until the packet gets to the final destination.

Step 4 The egress Edge LSR strips the label, examines the Layer 3 packet header, and forwards the packet to its final destination.

One of the important aspects of MPLS is its capability to use meaningful fixed length labels, thereby avoiding routing based on longest address match found. These labels are associated with the depth of service classes and application types, which includes the use of the 3-bit IP precedence field, Committed Access Rate (CAR), Weighted Random Early Detection (WRED), Class-Based Weighted Fair Queuing (CBWFQ), and Layer 3 traffic engineering. The following list briefly describes each of these features:

- CAR provides packet classification and bandwidth management. It analyzes the packet and assigns a service class based on the packet header, such as source and destination addresses, application type, and the protocol in use.

- WRED prevents network congestion by detecting and slowing the flows to prevent the congestion from expanding. Only selected packets could get dropped.

- CBWFQ provides the capability to re-order packets and control latency within the network. Utilizing different weights for different service classes, a switch manages the bandwidth and its own resources for each service class.

- Traffic engineering allows the network administrators to intervene into the decisions of an interior dynamic routing protocol. This results in the capability to control specific network routes, to load balance across unequal metric routes, and to reduce congestion.

In addition, MPLS results in the packet processing only at the edges of the network instead of at every hop. This reduces the forwarding table look up time significantly.

Positioning MPLS over ATM results in a very interesting synergy. Using MPLS, IP no longer needs NHRP and Classical IP for its dynamics over ATM. Also, ATM does not require manually preset PVC or dynamically allocated SVCs. All that is required is a straightforward mapping between an MPLS label and an ATM VPI/VCI. In fact, the labels are VPI/VCI numbers, which results in a dynamic VC setup.

MPLS Defined

MPLS can be defined as the dynamic generation of locally significant addresses, called labels, through the use of an interior routing protocol and the Label Distribution Protocol to spread the news about labels to everybody plus intelligence on service levels to applications plus direct dynamic mapping between IP and ATM.

Summary

This chapter introduces ATM higher layers. These include ATM signaling, various WAN interworking methods, voice interworking, as well as handling the existing Layer 3 protocols and Layer 2 technologies. The chapter elaborates on various types of ATM virtual circuits, such as PVCs, SVCs, Soft PVCs, and PVP tunneling, and on the processes involved in establishing the connections across the ATM clouds. ATM can handle point-to-point, point-to-multipoint, and anycast types of connections.

ATM, being a technology that is widely deployed in WANs, has the capability to interwork with legacy WAN technologies, such as Frame Relay and SMDSs. Frame Relay services are deployed around the world. SMDS services, although not as widely spread as Frame Relay, can be found within public networks in Europe and the United States.

One of the major advantages of ATM over any other method of transport is its capability to handle multiple types of services (one of which is voice) simultaneously. AAL1 handles your uncompressed voice traffic, whereas AAL2 handles the compressed voice traffic. Although voice connectivity does require a reserved bandwidth, voice interworking methods provide the capability to share the voice-reserved bandwidth dynamically with data applications.

ATM provides the capability of seamless internetworking for the existing applications that reside on IP, IPX, AppleTalk, and other Layer 3 protocols. Several methods run Layer 3 protocols over ATM, including Classical IP and MPOA. Also, ATM can extend your Ethernet and Token Ring LANs across distances without needing to change the currently used technologies or applications. This method is called LAN Emulation.

The chapter also introduces MPLS and Tag Switching. MPLS is a method of Layer 3 routing/switching that deploys meaningful fixed length labels. If you use the ATM network as the transport for the MPLS networks, the labels could provide the ATM VPI/VCI values.

Review Questions

1 What steps are involved in ATM call setup?

2 What types of virtual connections does ATM have? What are the differences between them?

3 How do you set up an SVC connection?

4 What form of addressing is used by a PVC? By an SVC?

5 What forms of ATM global addresses exist? What are the differences?

6 How long is an NSAP prefix?

7 What is ANS?

8 What is ILMI?

9 What is SAAL? What does it consist of?

10 What is Q.2931?

11 What types of connections does ATM support?

12 What is ATM anycast?

13 What is FUNI?

14 What is the difference between FRF.5 and FRF.8?

15 What is SMDS? How do you interwork ATM with SMDS?

16 What is CES?

17 What is CAS?

18 What is RFC 2684?

19 What is the difference between mux and LLC encapsulation?

20 What is LANE?

21 What are the advantages of RFC 2225?

22 What is the disadvantage of using RFC 2225 in multi-LIS networks?

23 What is MPOA, and how does it compare with MPLS?

"To industry, nothing is impossible."—Latin proverb

"Tell me, I'll forget. Show me, I may remember. But involve me, and I'll understand."—Chinese proverb

"Imagination, not invention, is the supreme master of art as of life."—Joseph Conrad (1857–1924)

After reading this chapter, you should be able to understand the following:

- **ATM Traffic Management During Connection Setup**—Covers traffic contract negotiations, traffic parameters and QoS requirements for various service types, and connection admission control.

- **ATM Traffic Management During Data Flow**—Covers contract conformance monitoring, traffic shaping, and congestion control.

- **ATM Routing Protocols**—Covers Interim Interswitch Signaling Protocol (IISP) and PNNI 1.0.

- **ATM Network Management**—Provides an overview of the protocols and the interfaces, including SNMP, ILMI, and OAM, involved in ATM network management.

CHAPTER 4

ATM Traffic and Network Management

ATM connection establishment and traffic management processes are some of the most intriguing aspects of ATM technology. From the overall perspective of traffic management, the principles are quite simple; however, the variety of traffic types, their behaviors, and their unique requirements, make traffic management a complicated subject.

Some of the questions this chapter addresses include

- How does the ATM connection get established?
- What are the principles behind ATM connections? How can ATM provide QoS?
- What happens if the ATM network gets congested?
- How can you prevent congestion from happening?
- What tools and techniques do you employ in ATM network management?

Your knowledge of the ATM lower and higher layers can help you understand and fully appreciate the very logical and intelligent processes involved in ATM traffic management.

ATM technology is a transport method for a variety of services and applications. The service types include real-time voice and video, a variety of data applications, and so on. To provide seamless interconnectivity of these technologies across distances requires a function of traffic management. It is very important to define processes and algorithms for traffic management during ATM connection setup as well as after ATM connection setup (during the data flow).

Preventative Medicine for Traffic Management

The procedures of traffic management during the connection setup remind me of preventative medicine. If you take care of your body and mind, you can avoid many diseases. The same applies to networking—good network design results in easier network maintenance; proper policies applied in traffic management during a connection setup or during the data flow result in less congested ATM networks.

The prime role of traffic management is to protect the network and the end systems from congestion. This ensures the promised network performance and level of QoS. Furthermore, traffic management results in the efficient use of network resources.

The traffic management process occurs in two phases: while the connection is established and during the flow of data.

While the connection is established, traffic management is responsible for the following:

- Traffic contract negotiations
- Traffic parameters
- QoS
- Connection Admission Control (CAC)

During the flow of data, the traffic management responsibilities include the following:

- Contract conformance monitoring
- Traffic shaping
- Congestion control

ATM Traffic Management During Connection Setup

A primary role of ATM traffic management during a connection setup is to ensure a connection from the source end device to the destination that provides the required QoS. To ensure QoS, an application must negotiate a traffic contract with the ATM network for each virtual connection. The contract is a network-level agreement of the service to be provided during the flow of data while the connection is in use.

Guaranteed QoS

Some couples get into the contract signing prior to their marriages. One partner agrees on this, that, and the other stuff. The other partner agrees on whatever. This is before the expected quality of life (QoL) can become a reality, or so they think. Well, a traffic contract in ATM is slightly different. The edge device is *guaranteed* the required QoS, if the network can provide that.

After the traffic contract is defined, the network applies the CAC algorithm to ensure that the QoS can be provided without impacting all other existing connections.

Figure 4-1 illustrates the overall negotiation process during the SVC connection setup. Notice that signaling is responsible for the dynamic negotiations for SVC only. In the PVC world, the network management system provides the similar "handshaking" in a static, manual way.

Figure 4-1   *SVC Connection Establishment Process*

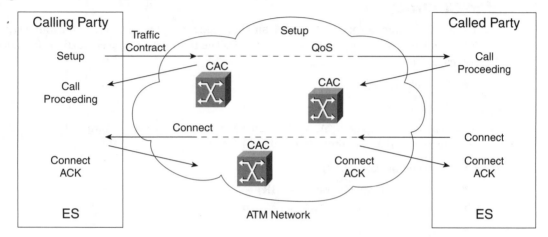

The signaling protocol stack depicted in Figure 4-2 illustrates the ATM signal carrying information to each ATM switch along the predetermined path. How the path is predetermined is another question, which is answered later in the chapter, in the section "ATM Routing Protocols."

Figure 4-2   *SVC Signaling Protocol Stack*

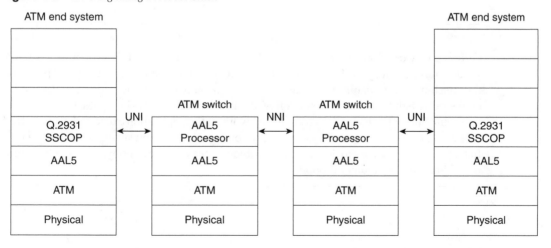

During this flow, the traffic contract is defined with the ingress ATM switch at the UNI level, CAC is checked along the way, and the QoS specification is established.

Now let's examine the UNI traffic contract.

UNI Traffic Contract

The traffic contract is specified at call setup time, depending on the nature of the traffic type (CBR, rt-VBR, nrt-VBR, UBR, ABR, or GFR). The traffic contract specifications fall into two categories:

- Traffic parameters
- Required QoS

As discussed in Chapter 2, "ATM Reference Model: Lower Layers," various traffic types are categorized into different service classes:

- Constant bit rate (CBR)
- Real-time variable bit rate (rt-VBR)
- Non-real-time variable bit rate (nrt-VBR)
- Unspecified bit rate (UBR)
- Available bit rate (ABR)
- Guaranteed frame rate (GFR)

Various service classes have different demands on the ATM network. For example, CBR connections must provide the peak cell rate (PCR), whereas rt-VBR demands PCR and sustainable cell rate (SCR). UBR, on the other hand, does not put any demands on the network, it simply relies on the "best effort" service.

Guaranteed Frame Rate

GFR is a new development from the ATM Forum and the ITU-T. It is similar to ABR and yet different. The major difference lies in the fact that ABR requires a flow-control protocol, thus pushing the probability of congestion from the network onto the edge devices. GFR, on the other hand, does not require a flow control mechanism. It simply guarantees a minimum amount of bandwidth from the network. If the application exceeds the guaranteed minimum, the network does not provide any commitments on how much data might be lost. In fact, the network tries to deal with the problem at the edge devices by dropping the entire frame instead of randomly dropping cells.

Depending on the UNI signaling version, certain parameters are supported. For this chapter's purposes, assume UNI version 4.0.

Traffic Parameters

Traffic parameters include PCR, SCR, maximum burst size (MBS), cell delay variation tolerance (CDVT), minimum cell rate (MCR), and maximum frame size (MFS). As discussed in Chapter 2, various service classes require various traffic parameters. Table 4-1 defines the traffic parameters and their corresponding service classes.

Table 4-1   *Traffic Parameter Descriptions and Associated Service Classes*

Traffic Parameter	Description	Associated Service Classes
PCR	Defines the upper limit on the traffic submitted to the ATM network. As per the ATM Forum definition, "PCR of the ATM connection is the inverse of the minimum inter-arrival time between two basic events." The limitation of the PCR is the physical speed limitation of the edge device's access to the ATM network.	CBR, rt-VBR, nrt-VBR, UBR, ABR, GFR[1]
SCR	An upper bound on the conforming average transmission rate of the ATM connection. The SCR value is typically less than the PCR value.	rt-VBR, nrt-VBR
MBS	Measures the burstiness of a specific connection. It is expressed in the number of cells that can be transmitted at PCR while still complying with the negotiated SCR.	rt-VBR, nrt-VBR
MCR	Represents a guaranteed minimum throughput of the payload cells through the ATM network.	ABR, GFR[1]
CDVT	Defines the maximum amount of cell delay variation (CDV) that a specific connection can tolerate. The next section, "Quality of Service," elaborates on CDV.	CBR, rt-VBR, nrt-VBR, UBR, ABR, GFR[1]
MFS	Defines the maximum size of all packets that are sent through the GFR connection.	GFR[1]

[1]GFR specifications could vary pending approval by the ATM Forum.

Quality of Service

The ultimate goal of quality of service in ATM is for the ATM network to provide the requested network performance from the source to the destination. This network performance is quantified at the ATM layer, meaning at the cell structure. Here, I am talking about cell delay and cell loss, not packet delay/loss, with respect to the impact they might have on a specific type of application (for example, real-time voice, video, file data transfer, and so on).

QoS Defined

The phrase *quality of service* is over used and abused. Vendors, service providers, and customers use the same phrase to refer to so many different aspects of communication. Take, for example, your telephone service. In this scenario, *quality of service* refers to the clarity of your voice, the capability of the service to handle many voice calls simultaneously within a busy hour, and the maintenance of echo-free communication. In contrast, quality of service for videoconferencing includes picture clarity and speed of refreshing.

The ATM Forum divides the negotiable QoS variables into two major categories:

- Cell transfer delay (CTD)

    — **Maximum cell transfer delay (MCTD)**—Refers to the maximum length of time it takes the network to transmit a cell from one endpoint to another.

    — **Peak-to-peak cell delay variation (peak-to-peak CDV)**—Refers to the best and the worst case of cell transfer delay. It is the line distortion caused by a change in the inter-arrival times between cells, also known as *jitter*.

- **Cell loss ratio (CLR)**—Refers to the acceptable percentage of cells that the network can discard due to congestion.

    — CLR = Lost Cells ÷ Total Transmitted Cells.

Negotiable QoS variables imply the capability of the edge device to negotiate dynamically the levels of cell loss and cell delay through signaling, as part of the traffic contract.

The non-negotiable QoS variables include cell error ratio (CER), cell misinsertion rate (CMR), and severely errored cell block ratio (SECBR). Refer to Chapter 2 for more information on the non-negotiable QoS variables.

Table 4-2 documents the categorization of QoS variables.

Table 4-2   *QoS Parameters*

Negotiable QoS Parameters	Non-Negotiable QoS Parameters
CTD	CER
MCTD	CMR
Peak-to-peak CDV	SECBR
CLR	

The requirements for QoS parameters varies depending on the traffic types. Table 4-3 signifies that real-time traffic requires more rigid QoS definitions than non-real time.

Table 4-3   *QoS and Service Classes*

QoS	CBR	rt-VBR	nrt-VBR	UBR	ABR	GFR
MCTD	Must	Must	N/A	N/A	N/A	N/A
Peak-to-peak CDV	Must	Must	N/A	N/A	N/A	N/A
CLR	Must	Must	Must	N/A	Could be	Could be

Cell Transfer Delay

The measured CTD is an elapsed time between a cell exit event at the source UNI and the corresponding cell entry event at the destination UNI for a particular connection. According to the ATM Forum specification AF-TM-0056.000:

The CDV between the two measurement points is a sum of the total inter-ATM node transmission delay and the total ATM node processing delay between measurement point 1 and measurement point 2.

The CTD QoS variable is categorized further into the following:

- Maximum cell transfer delay (MCTD)
- Peak-to-peak cell delay variation (peak-to-peak CDV)

MCTD consists of various inter- and intra-ATM nodal variables, including the transfer time between the nodes of the network and the queuing time within a node. When you impose a specific MCTD on a particular connection, you can reverse-engineer the queue size, Qs, within a node using the following approximation:

$$Qs = MCTD \div \text{Queue Service Rate}$$

As you see later in the chapter, part of the dynamic connection establishment is the CAC algorithm running within an ATM node. Note that CAC uses the Qs value to compute the queue size availability for a specific connection, which is to be allocated for that connection upon the completion of its setup.

The peak-to-peak CDV is

$$\text{Peak-to-peak CDV} = MCTD - \text{fixed CTD}$$

where fixed CTD is the minimum CTD. This actually implies that peak-to-peak CDV is the difference between the best and the worst case of CTD.

Cell Loss Ratio

CLR, as mentioned in Chapter 2, is a ratio of lost cells to the total number of transmitted cells for a specific connection:

CLR = Lost Cells ÷ Total Transmitted Cells

The lost cells include not only cells that are "lost in action," as I call them, but also cells that are received with an invalid header or errors within their payload. The total number of transmitted cells includes only cells that do not break the law, that is, cells that conform to the predetermined contract.

CAC Algorithm

During the establishment of an ATM connection, the signaling frame traverses through various ATM switches on the network, as the ingress switch predetermines (see the section, "Signal Routing: IISP and PNNI," later in the chapter). One of the very important pieces of information that is carried in the frame is the service category of the traffic that will be sent upon establishing the connection. Each of these service categories has a specific requirement for the resources to be allocated, including memory allocation, prioritization, buffer sizes, and bandwidth allocation.

The whole objective of the most efficient CAC algorithm lies in achieving the most accurate resource requirements for a specific connection in such a way that the resources are utilized optimally. It is very easy to simply sum up the maximum values of the required bandwidth, basing your algorithm on the worst case scenario. However, this results in the under-utilization of the network and system resources and its overprovisioning, which is very costly. The efficient CAC algorithm provides the required resources, without overprovisioning, yet meeting what is requested. The art side of this comes in when several types of connections need to be run simultaneously, the types and the frequency of which are calculated statistically.

The ATM Forum does not specify CAC algorithms for the simple reason that they stay within the box. Every vendor could deploy its own algorithm, as long as the system understands the required QoS and traffic parameters. For example, you could deploy a very simple philosophy of providing the required switch resources for CBR traffic under the condition that the total bandwidth of the link must be less than the sum of PCR values for all CBR connections. As far as UBR traffic goes (because there are no guarantees), theoretically, the switch can nod its head to agree to handle this connection. For ABR and GFR traffic types, the switch must be sensitive to the MCR value and, specifically for GFR, to the MFS.

UNI Signaling

User-Network Interface (UNI) signaling, used only for SVCs, is a very responsible component in ATM networks. The signaling frame sets up a connection based on the ATM addressing and the required QoS and traffic parameters. Based on the geography of the signaling, generally speaking, it is subdivided into UNI and Network-to-Network Interface (NNI), where UNI is responsible for the delivery of the requirements from the source to the ingress switch or from the egress switch to the destination. As illustrated in Figure 4-3, the NNI signaling is responsible for carrying the requirement passed along from the source UNI signaling through the ATM network and delivering it at the destination side of the ATM network to another UNI.

Figure 4-3   *Location on UNI/NNI Signaling*

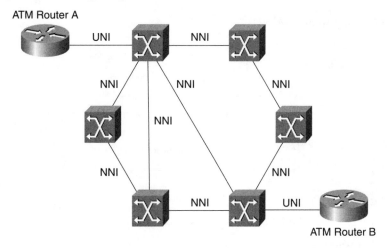

The generic format of the signaling message, depicted in Figure 4-4, includes the protocol discriminator, the call reference, the message type, the message length, and the variable length information elements.

Table 4-4 lists the responsibilities of all the fields in the message format.

Table 4-4   *Signaling Message Format Field Responsibilities*

Field	Description
Protocol discriminator	Distinguishes protocols by the unique identifiers.
Length of call reference value	Specifies the length of the call reference value.
Flag	The call reference flag identifies the source of origination of the call reference value.

Table 4-4 *Signaling Message Format Field Responsibilities*

Field	Description
Call reference value	Identifies the call at UNI. It is assigned at the UNI and is kept for a duration of a call.
Message type	Identifies the function of the message being sent. It could be the following: call proceeding, connect, setup, release, restart, and so on.
Message length	Identifies the length of the message content.
Variable length information elements as required	Used to carry the global ATM addressing information, the AAL parameters, and the QoS parameters.

Figure 4-4 *Signaling Message Format*

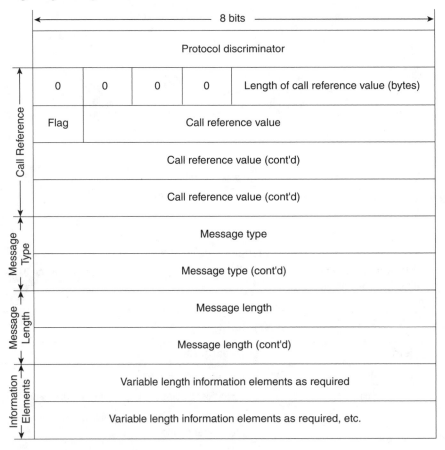

UNI signaling is divided into UNI point-to-point signaling and UNI point-to-multipoint signaling.

UNI Point-to-point Signaling

The result of point-to-point signaling is a bidirectional connection that can remain active for an arbitrary period of time. The originator of the connection is called the *call originator* or the *calling party*, whereas the destination is called the *call destination* or the *called party*, as illustrated in Figure 4-5.

Figure 4-5   *Point-to-point Connection*

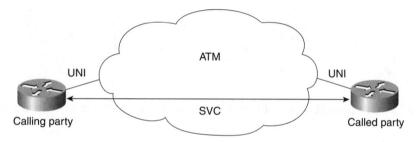

To establish a connection, the network and the end systems must satisfy the following criteria:

- VCs must be available
- End systems must be compatible
- Both network and end system resources must be available to provide the required QoS

Figure 4-6 illustrates the call states that take place at the source and the destination during the connection establishment.

Figure 4-6 *Call States During the Connection Establishment*

Connection Establishment Control Procedures at the Source for Point-to-Point

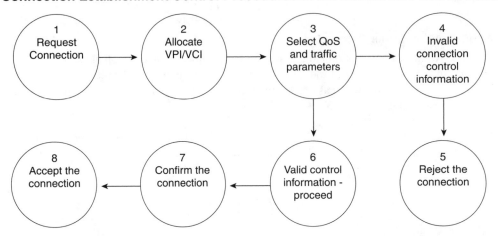

Connection Establishment Control Procedures at the Destination for Point-to-Point

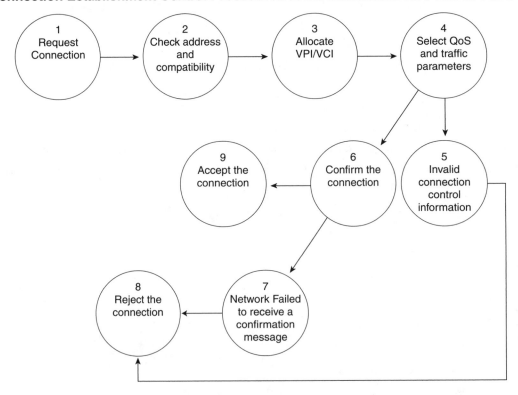

Figure 4-7 illustrates the call states that take place during a call release.

Figure 4-7   *Call States During the Connection Release*

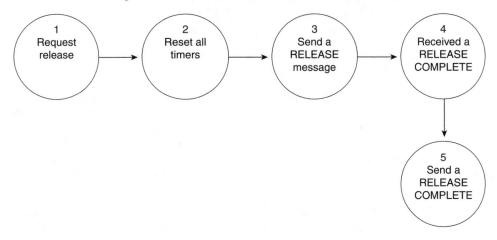

UNI Point-to-Multipoint Signaling

A point-to-multipoint connection, as discussed in Chapter 3, "ATM Reference Model: Higher Layers," allows one edge device to connect to many devices. The device that originates a connection is called the *root*; the other stations are called *leaves*. A point-to-multipoint connection is always unidirectional, from the root to the leaves. Leaves cannot send traffic directly to each either nor can leaves send traffic to the root. Figure 4-8 illustrates a point-to-multipoint connection.

Figure 4-8   *Point-to-multipoint Connection*

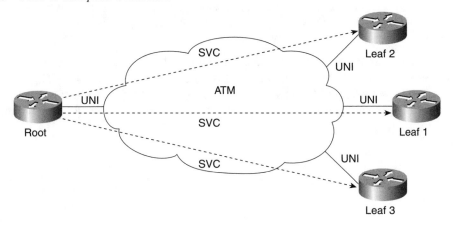

Prior to establishing a point-to-multipoint connection, the root sets up the first point-to-point unidirectional connection to a leaf. The signaling message must convey the fact that the intent of the setup is a point-to-multipoint connection; otherwise, the root cannot add leaves to that one connection. After establishing the first root-to-leaf connection, other leaves can join in. Leaves can be added or deleted from the call at any time.

The ATM Forum UNI 4.0 Signaling specification (AF-SIG-0061.000) identifies two types of Leaf Initiated Join (LIJ) calls:

- **Network LIJ**—The network automatically adds new leaves that request to be added to ongoing calls. With this method, if the leaf's request is for an existing connection, the network handles the request. The root is not notified when each leaf is added or dropped from a connection. When a leaf requests to be added to a totally new connection (that is, when it is the first leaf), the root performs the initial setup of the connection.

- **Root LIJ**—The root adds all leaves manually. A leaf can send a request over a UNI to join a point-to-multipoint connection. The request goes all the way to the root. The root adds leaves or removes leaves from a new or an established connection.

NOTE   It is important to note that the LIJ capability initially is limited to UNIs because neither the ATM Forum PNNI specification, Version 1.0 (AF-PNNI-0055.000), nor the ATM Forum B-ICI specification, Version 2.0 (AF-BICI-0013.003), support the LIJ capability.

Figure 4-9 depicts the call states that take place during the point-to-multipoint connection establishment. These states apply to both types of LIJ calls.

During the initial connection setup, the structure looks very similar to a point-to-point connection. When a new leaf joins a pre-established connection, however, the setup procedure is much less complex than the connection of the first party.

You use point-to-multipoint connections for broadcast and multicast emulations of Layer 3 protocols over ATM (see Chapter 5, "LAN Emulation (LANE)," and Chapter 6, "Multiprotocol over ATM (MPOA)"). Because point-to-multipoint connections are unidirectional, they are not very useful when you require bidirectional communication.

Figure 4-9   *Point-to-multipoint Connection Establishment States*

Connection for the First Party

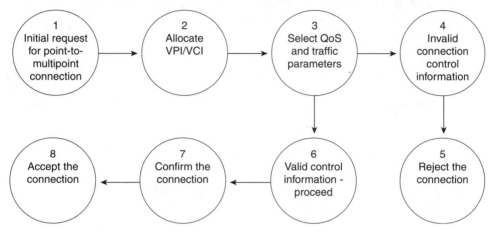

Adding Additional Members

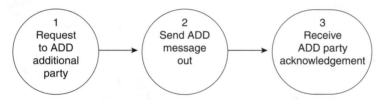

ATM Multicasting

Multicasting is the capability of a select group of devices to communicate with each other without involving broadcasting. Multicasting is positioned exactly between unicast and broadcast. Main efforts into multicast specifications have been happening within the IP community. Typical applications requiring multicast include videoconferencing, stock quotes, interactive games, database replication, and so on.

Positioning multicast over ATM is not a trivial exercise. You are dealing with a non-broadcast domain. IP multicasting uses bidirectional, multipoint-to-multipoint connections, whereas ATM supports unidirectional point-to-multipoint connections. Furthermore, IP membership to a multicast group is open to every system; in ATM (UNI 4.0 only), however, you still require some out-of-band signaling for the root to determine whether a leaf is allowed to join the group. Being a transport method for any kind of traffic, ATM's approach to the "foreign" behavior is, once more, a client/server architecture.

At this point, the two most-common ATM multicast mechanisms are the use of multicast servers and the use of meshed point-to-multipoint connections, as illustrated in Figure 4-10.

Figure 4-10 *Approaches to ATM Multicast*

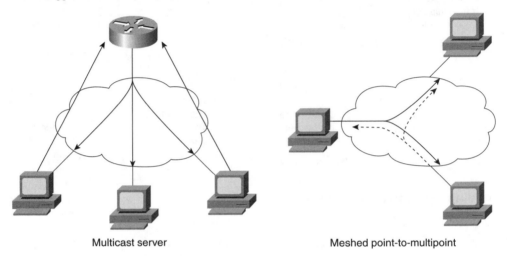

Multicast server   Meshed point-to-multipoint

The multicast server can support dynamic groups because the members can be added and deleted as leaves on the tree, as specified in the UNI 4.0. The LIJ capability allows the edge devices to join point-to-multipoint connections independently. Chapters 5 and 6 address the functionality of multicast servers in detail.

Signal Routing: IISP and PNNI

Signal routing is required if and only if you have SVC. In the PVC world, the VCs are predetermined manually.

Now you have the signaling frame entering the ingress switch, as shown in Figure 4-11. The information element field of the signal contains the destination global ATM address (NSAP or E.164), the QoS it is looking for, and the traffic parameters for an AAL that the specific application is using.

Figure 4-11 *Signaling at the Ingress Switch for SVC Setup*

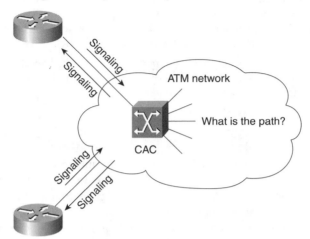

The ingress switch runs the CAC algorithm, and determines that it has enough resources to meet the requirements. Now it is ready to pass along the signaling frame to the next switch down the road. The question is what should be the next hop? Well, it is not good enough to know the next hop, simply because there are no guarantees that the required QoS can be met. The ingress switch needs to provide the entire path, which can handle the required QoS, to the signaling frame. This way, the signaling frame knows exactly what should be the next step.

When you think about the complexities involved in determining the "best path" based on the required QoS (such as keeping that information as accurate as possible, building databases, and so on), you can appreciate fully why the ATM Forum went ahead with the static route as Phase0 of the signal routing. Cisco first suggested that the static routing philosophy had nothing in common with the complexities of the dynamic routing algorithm that is called PNNI Phase1. Hence, instead of calling the static routing PNNI Phase0, the ATM Forum agreed to name it the Interim Interswitch Signaling Protocol (IISP). The purpose of IISP is to provide some routing table–based rerouting without topology discovery or QoS handling. Both IISP and PNNI1 are covered later in this chapter in detail.

ATM Traffic Management During Data Flow

Now that your ATM connections are set up, the payload cells can flow. The connection is set up based on the requested QoS, the contracts are signed, and the network is ready to handle what it's being asked to provide. The traffic contract becomes a temporary "law" for the duration of the connection. Suddenly, an application breaks that law and sends out much more traffic than was contracted. Now, imagine others do the same. What happens to the good old engineering of your circuits, busy hour calculations, and switches provisioning? I leave it to your imagination. The network rumbles, like a volcano, erupts, and then totally collapses. This results in a total devastation of the applications and the entities using those applications—humans. Nobody can talk to each other...

Obviously, you do not want that to happen to the network. Therefore, you need to police the cloud. Imagine a policing function at the ingress switch of the cloud. If the entering traffic exceeds the traffic contract, it gets marked.

ATM Traffic Management

ATM traffic management during the data flow is similar to highway laws, with slightly different rules. Imagine a highway that allows cars to drive with different speed limits, based on pre-agreed contracts that car drivers sign. A contract that allows a car to move faster than other cars costs more. When you enter the highway, your receive a ticket if your entry speed exceeds your contractual speed. If you receive a ticket and the highway becomes congested, your car simply is extracted from the highway. If you do not receive a ticket, your journey is successful. Interesting highway, isn't it?

Traffic management consists of two primary functions:

- **Traffic control**—Preventative operation
- **Congestion control**—Reactive operation

Traffic Control Functions

Consider again the analogy of the highway. If your car is ticketed, it could simply disappear if the highway becomes congested. Consequently, doesn't it make sense to prevent that from happening?

This is exactly the functionality of traffic control—preventative medicine, as I call it.

Traffic control is responsible for the following procedures:

- Smoothing out the bursty traffic into something more predictible; hence, *traffic shaping* (optional)

- *Monitoring* or *policing* the connection and marking the cells that do not conform with the contract (you can say "ticketing the cells")

Traffic Shaping Mechanisms

Although traffic shaping is optional according to the ATM Forum Traffic Management 4.1 specification (AF-TM-0121.000, March 1999), it is an absolutely great idea to implement it at the edge nodes of the ATM networks.

The goal of the traffic shaping mechanism is to prevent congestion from occurring. Going back to the highway analogy, highways do not get congested if the cars are put through a mechanism that orchestrates which car can enter the highway at what speed and when. Sounds like a dream, doesn't it? Well, ATM edge devices are trying to achieve exactly that—prevent the congestion within the ATM networks, as illustrated in Figure 4-12.

Figure 4-12 *Traffic Shaping: Preventative Congestion Control*

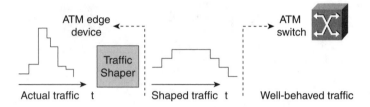

NOTE   Because traffic shaping takes place only at the UNI level (private and/or public), it is possible for multiple well-shaped flows to contend for a link in the ATM network, if the ATM network is not engineered properly. You should use traffic shaping parameters used by the edge devices as guidelines to do traffic engineering of the ATM networks. Knowing the approximate number of users (including growth factors) and the traffic shaping parameters deployed by these users, you can engineer your ATM networks properly.

Traffic shaping controls the bursty nature of typical data traffic before transmitting it into an ATM network by smoothing out the peaks and the valleys of the data traffic into something more predictable. This allows ATM network engineers and architects to design a network that is optimal—enough bandwidth and resources to handle what is required at the minimum cost. Traffic shaping results in fewer cells getting marked (or ticketed); hence, fewer resends of payload data, faster response times to the applications, and happier users. The only reason why a shaped flow of cells can be lost in an ATM cloud is an accident; for example, network topology changes or accidentally marked cells due to a cell stream suffering from jitter in its path.

Traffic shaping occurs at the end device of the ATM cloud, implying the UNI side, public or private. When you interconnect your private ATM network to the public ATM, your traffic shaping occurs on the edge device interconnected to the private network and on the ATM switch of your private cloud that is interconnected to the public ATM (public UNI), as illustrated in Figure 4-13. This includes the ingress or the egress side of your private network.

Figure 4-13 *Traffic Shaping Occurs at the UNI Side*

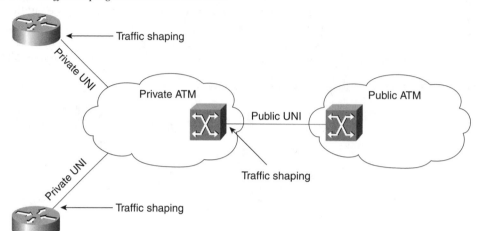

You can use various approaches to traffic shaping algorithms: Leaky Bucket algorithm, Spacing, Scheduling, Priority Queuing, and so on. The traffic shaping algorithm, in conformance with the ATM Forum, specifies that the Generic Cell Rate Algorithm (GCRA)—the Leaky Bucket algorithm—is the most popular, and it is addressed in this book.

In the Leaky Bucket algorithm, you use two parameters: the bucket size, B (which could be the Burst Tolerance [BT]), and the token generation rate (which could be the sustainable cell rate [SCR]). Figure 4-14 demonstrates how this algorithm works.

Token Ring and the Leaky Bucket Algorithm

Which technology behaves predictably, at almost the same rate, without congestion? Token Ring. When I think about Token Ring, I think of a main person (token) without whom nobody can communicate on the ring. A frame cannot leave the source device without an available token. A similar philosophy applies to the Leaky Bucket algorithm. Without a token, cells cannot leave.

Picture this. Tokens rotate on a conveyer belt at a fixed speed, say, SCR. At the end of the conveyer belt, they fall into the bucket. If the number of tokens exceeds the limit, which is of a value of BT, they just overflow into the land of nowhere. When cells come in, each cell takes a token, which leaks down from the bucket. Only then can the cell be transmitted. You could implement the algorithm so that each token takes more than one cell.

The shaper can enforce the use of another traffic parameter—peak cell rate (PCR)—and incorporate a dual Leaky Bucket algorithm, which the next section illustrates.

Figure 4-14 *Leaky Bucket Algorithm*

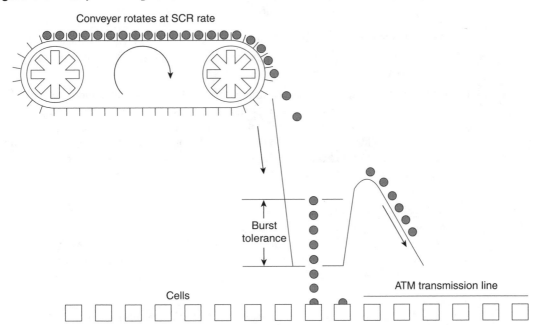

Connection Monitoring

Connection monitoring, which is much like a highway police patrol, is the policing function that I referred to previously. Connection monitoring is responsible for monitoring the traffic flows and for enforcing the previously "signed" traffic contract. Its main purpose is to protect the network's resources from misuse (or even abuse) that intentionally or unintentionally would affect the performance of all other network users.

Connection monitoring can take place at the UNI or the NNI. When it is at the UNI, it is called the *Usage Parameter Control (UPC)*. When it is at the NNI, it is called the *Network Parameter Control (NPC)*. As per the Traffic Management 4.1 specification, UPC is optional at the UNI side. However, it is required that "UPC functions be capable of enforcing the traffic contract" [AF-TM-0121.000]. I use the term *UPC* to refer to both UPC and NPC. You can deploy a very simple methodology in policing the traffic. The ingress switch can simply mark the cells that are not conforming with the contract by setting the cell loss priority (CLP) bit to 1, signifying that the cell has low priority. If a cell conforms to the contract, its CLP bit remains as 0, signifying that the cell has high priority. Later, when the network gets congested, the marked (or low priority) cells are dropped, whereas the unmarked (or high priority) cells, continue their journeys. The methods of checking for conformance are addressed later in this section.

In reality, the rule is not that simple. ATM Forum Traffic Management 4.1 defines two models for the cell conformance definition:

- **CLP-transparent**—The network generally disregards the CLP bit.
- **CLP-significant**—The network pays attention to the CLP bit and deploys the selective discard.

The type of service category used determines which cell conformance model is used. For the cell conformance definition, it is important for the ATM Forum's service categories (CBR, rt-VBR, nrt-VBR, UBR, ABR, and GFR) to correspond to the ITU-T QoS classes (1, 2, and 3). The ITU-T discontinued Recommendation I.362, which defined the traffic classes A, B, C, and D. Instead, the ITU-T defines QoS classes 1, 2, and 3 in its Recommendation I.356.

NOTE   It is important to emphasize that the QoS classes defined in I.356 apply only to public ATM networks; whereas, the ATM Forum's service categories apply to both private and public networks. I.356 does not address the private network's impact on the end-to-end QoS.

Table 4-5 illustrates the association between the ATM Forum service categories and the ITU-T QoS classes.

Table 4-5   *Association Between ATM Forum Service Categories and ITU-T QoS Classes*

ATM Forum Service Category	ITU-T QoS Class
CBR (CBR.1)	1
rt-VBR (VBR.1)	1
nrt-VBR (VBR.1)	2
nrt-VBR (VBR.2)	3
nrt-VBR (VBR.3)	3
ABR	3 and Unspecified QoS Class
UBR (UBR.1, UBR.2)	Unspecified QoS Class
GFR (GFR.1, GFR.2)	3 and Unspecified QoS Class

Cell Conformance Definition: CLP-Transparent Model

Imagine you have two private ATM networks, as illustrated in Figure 4-15.

Figure 4-15 *CLP Transparency*

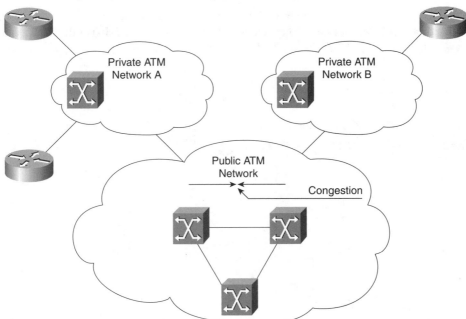

Network A's customers really are pushing their luck with the traffic. This results in approximately 60 percent of the cells being marked with CLP equal to 1. On the other hand, Network B's applications are conforming with the contract, which results in all the cells having high priority, that is, all the cells have CLP equal to 0. Now, these two private networks are connected to the VP of the public carrier with absolutely identical bandwidth requirements. Assume that the public network experiences congestion. Who do you think the congestion affects? Of course, the private ATM, Network A. In fact, Network A discards up to 60 percent of its payload. This is very unfair behavior towards Network A. After all, both customers A and B pay for the same bandwidth and comply with the signed contract when entering the public domain. What is the solution? Simply ignore the CLP bit. This behavior is called *CLP transparency.* Although CLP transparency is designed for VPs, VCs can deploy it. If VCs deploy CLP transparency, all traffic is considered high priority.

CBR.1 and VBR.1 service types of traffic use the CLP-transparent model.

Cell Conformance Definition: CLP-Significant Model

Using the CLP-significant model, the cell marking applies as an option. If it is deployed, the network makes a best-effort attempt to transmit the marked (CLP equals 1) cells and, if the network experiences congestion, it employs selective cell discard.

For a better illustration of UPC rules and actions, see Figure 4-16.

How does UPC police the traffic? What methodology does it use? UPC could use a variety of algorithms: the Leaky Bucket algorithm (refer to Figure 4-14) or the Dual Leaky Bucket algorithm, which utilizes the PCR parameter as well. Figure 4-17 depicts the Dual Leaky Bucket algorithm.

Figure 4-16 *UPC Rules*

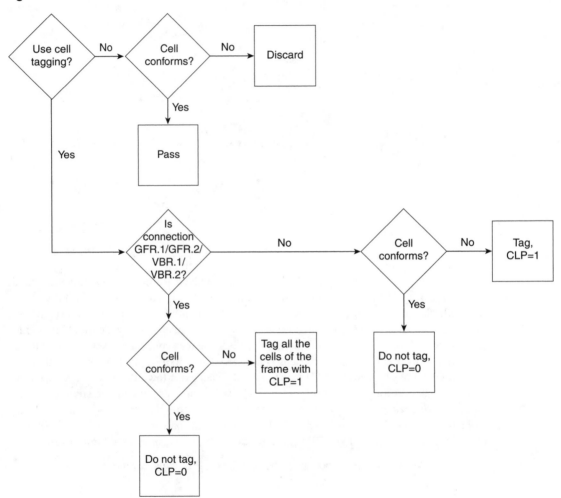

Figure 4-17 *Dual Leaky Bucket Algorithm*

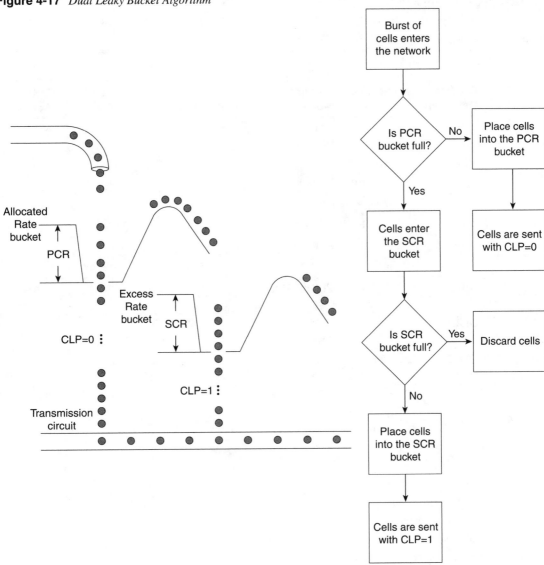

Various service types use either one bucket, the Allocated Rate bucket, or both. For example, VBR traffic uses both buckets because the VBR service type specifies the PCR and SCR parameters; however, CBR traffic uses only the Allocated Rate bucket because CBR specifies only the PCR parameter.

VBR.2, VBR.3, GFR.1, and GFR.2 use the CLP-significant model of the cell conformance definition.

Summary of Cell Conformance Definitions

Table 4-6 summarizes the conformance definitions for all service traffic categories.

Table 4-6   *Conformance Definitions for Various Service Classes*

Conformance Definition	Service Type	Conformance Definition Model	PCR	SCR	MCR	Cell Loss QoS	CLP Marking Option Active
CBR.1	CBR	CLP-transparent	$0+1^8$	NS^1	NS	0+1	N/A^2
VBR.1	rt-VBR nrt-VBR	CLP-transparent	0+1	0+1	NS	0+1	N/A
VBR.2	rt-VBR nrt-VBR	CLP-significant	0+1	0	NS	0	No
VBR.3	rt-VBR nrt-VBR	CLP-significant	0+1	0	NS	0	Yes
ABR	ABR	CLP marking does not apply	0	NS	0	0^6	N/A
GFR.1	GFR	CLP marking does not apply	0+1	NS	0	0^7	No
GFR.2	GFR	CLP-significant	0+1	NS	0	0^7	Yes^5
UBR.1	UBR	CLP marking does not apply	0+1	NS	NS	U^3	No
UBR.2	UBR	CLP marking applies, but does not mean non-conformance	0+1	NS	NS	U	Yes^4

[1]NS means not specified.

[2]N/A means cell marking is not applicable.

[3]U means that cell loss ratio (CLR) is unspecified for both CLP = 0 and CLP = 1.

[4]When a UBR connection uses the CLP marking option, the network can overwrite the CLP bit to 1 for any cell of that connection. Such action does not imply a condition of non-conformance, as it does for other service categories.

[5]CLP marking is applicable to all cells of a frame for which the service guarantee cannot be provided.

[6]CLR is low for sources that adjust cell flow in response to control information.

[7]CLR is low for frames that are eligible for service guarantee.

[8]0+1 implies that the parameter or QoS is applied to all cells, whether their CLP = 0 or CLP = 1.

Congestion Control Functions

Regardless of the preventative efforts involved, the ATM network still can experience congestion. For example, your private network could use OC-3, yet you decide to use DS-3 to interconnect it to the public domain (due to the costs, of course), as illustrated in Figure 4-18.

Figure 4-18 *Congestion in an ATM Network*

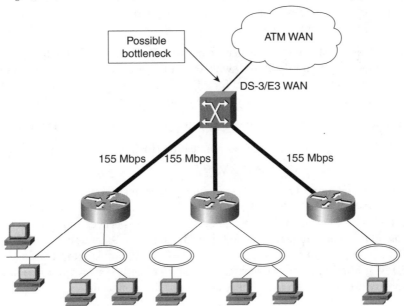

Congestion is a devastating experience for the ATM network. Think about it. A maximum IP packet size over ATM is 9180 bytes, which is 192 cells. An Ethernet frame of 1518 bytes is 32 cells. Now, imagine one of these cells is lost due to congestion. The remainder of the cells arrives to the destination side and gets reassembled. Next, the CRC error checking takes place. The error is detected in the frame, the application does not receive a packet, TCP (if used) or an application becomes an "unhappy camper" and asks for the packet to be resent. Consequently, the source must resend all those packets/frames/cells again. What you just witnessed is a self-inducing behavior: dropping one or more cells causes them to be resent, which causes more traffic on the network, which causes more congestion. The outcome of this behavior is the exponential growth of traffic, which results in the network collapse. To combat this scenario, you can employ various techniques to generate "smart" behavior.

First, a node that experiences congestion must have some means of notifying others about it. Second, the cell dropping should be done much more intelligently than described in the preceding scenario.

Congestion Notification Methods

In a case of non-transparent CLP, the CLP bit is marked. This means that the switch reacts to the network congestion by dropping all the marked cells. You can compare the CLP bit to a Discard Eligible (DE) bit in the Frame Relay networks.

How does a switch know whether the network is congested? There must be some sort of an informer that can notify all the switches in the network about the congestion. This notification process is not trivial for ATM. One of the reasons is speed. By the time the notification about the network congestion comes along, it's already been cleared.

Traffic Management 4.1 defines two methods for congestion notification:

- Explicit Forward Congestion Indication (EFCI)
- Relative Rate Marking (RRM)

As indicated in the Traffic Management 4.1 specification, the use of EFCI is optional for CBR, rt-VBR, nrt-VBR, GFR, and UBR. It is mandatory for ABR traffic to use RRM for ABR's flow control and congestion notification. This is because the ABR source adapts its rate to the changing network conditions dynamically. Although the use of RRM is not defined for control of CBR, rt-VBR, nrt-VBR, GFR, and UBR in Traffic Management 4.1, RRM is allowed on such connections. The RRM cells convey information about the state of network bandwidth availability and impending congestion.

Congestion Notification Method: Explicit Forward Congestion Indication (EFCI)

The traffic types CBR, rt-VBR, nrt-VBR, GFR, and UBR can use the EFCI marking mode. In EFCI marking mode, the switches set a flag in the headers of forwarded data cells to indicate congestion. This congestion indication then is received at the destination end system. Then the destination end system can use this indication to implement a protocol that adaptively lowers the cell rate of the connection during congestion. If such connections use Resource Management cells (RM-cells), they are considered part of the user data cell flow. Consequently, the destination end system can use RM-cells to notify the source about the congestion by setting the Congestion Indication bit in the RM-cell and sending it back to the source end system using backward RM-cells, as illustrated in Figure 4-19.

Figure 4-19 *Congestion Control: EFCI Mode*

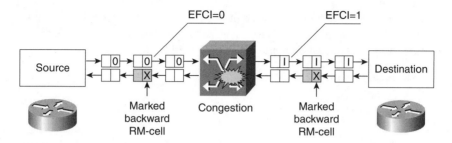

In general terms, although EFCI marking is widely available, especially on WAN switches, it can provide only minor improvements in network performance for two reasons:

- EFCI mode notifies only the destination about the congestion, not the source.

- Even if the destination can deploy RRM backward cells to notify the source, its effectiveness is not that great due to the latency of turning around the forward congestion indication.

As with any feedback mechanism, congestion control schemes operate best when the latency of the feedback path is minimized. Indeed, excessive latencies can be counterproductive because they might cause sources to slow down unnecessarily when the network congestion is eased already.

Congestion Notification Method: Relative Rate Marking

RRM is mandatory for ABR traffic. ABR is a very complex specification with multiple possible modes of operation specifying the behavior of both source and destination end systems and of intermediate switches. Source end systems periodically generate inline RM-cells that are sent intermixed with data cells along all the connections. The destination end systems receive these cells and return them along the backward connection to the source, indicating whether intermediate switches experienced congestion. RM-cells use the VCI equal to 6 value, as illustrated in Table 4-7.

Table 4-7 *Reserved VPI/VCIs*

VPI	VCI	Used for
0	0	Empty cell
x	5	Signaling, UNI
x	6	RM-cells
x	16	ILMI
x	0–31	Reserved by the ATM Forum and the ITU-T

Using RRM mode, switches can set a flag in the backward RM-cells immediately upon experiencing congestion to indicate congestion without going all the way to the destination. RRM delivers much greater performance than the EFCI mode, because it is capable of using the backward RM-cells to send the congestion indication to the source. Figure 4-20 illustrates the congestion control mechanism of RRM.

Figure 4-20 *Congestion Control: Relative Rate Mode*

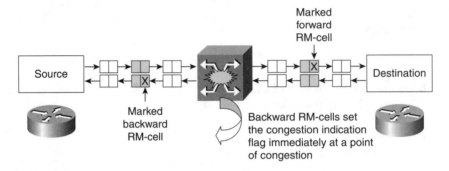

Selective Cell Discard

When an ATM switch experiences congestion, it notifies the source about it (using the EFCI or RRM method). Numerous studies on different algorithms for intelligent cell discard have been performed, focusing mainly on traffic using AAL5. Why? Simply because of the magnitude of the problem when cell drops occur.

The Relativity of Cell Loss

Everything in the world is relative. Using Einstein's theory of relativity, a person sitting in a moving car, when looking outside, might think the car stays still and the houses and trees move. The same applies to applications/packets/cells. A packet loss for an application could mean just another resend. A cell loss, that is one little tiny unit of a huge packet, does not mean much for an application, although it means a lot for an ATM network. Why? Because now dozens of cells that constitute that packet might have to be resent, introducing even more traffic into a potentially congested network.

It is important to realize that not all applications use "resending" to correct errors. An occasional lost cell might not be a significant problem in most asynchronous applications because the destination often conceals the resulting transmission error.

The most efficient techniques of selective cell discard that are available today include

- Tail Packet Discard (TPD)
- Early Packet Discard (EPD)
- Random Early Discard (RED)

Cell Discard Technique: TPD

The TPD mode is very simple and effective. If an ATM switch experiences congestion, it starts dropping marked cells (CLP equals 1). After it drops a cell (which is part of a much larger packet), the rest of the cells become useless anyway. With this in mind, even though the congestion could clear up, the switch continues dropping all the cells that are part of the packet, until it hits the last cell (remember, the intelligent cell header where the End Of Message [EOM] bit is turned on?). The switch cannot drop the last cell. It is very important! Why? Because some cells of that packet might leave the switch before it experiences congestion, meaning that they might reach the destination. Well, guess what the destination does? It waits until it receives the last cell of the packet before it reassembles the cells into a packet. Now, imagine what happens if the last cell never reaches the destination. There is another train of cells that belongs to a totally different packet. Upon receiving these wholesome cells, the edge device tries to concatenate the few cells it received from the first packet with these new ones. The result is not pleasant. Instead of one packet, your source device needs to resend two. Hence, even more traffic for your network. Therefore, the switch deploying TPD resets the CLP bit of the last cell to 0, ensuring that it can reach the final destination, and sends it out.

Figure 4-21 illustrates the TPD mechanism and the flow of the process.

Figure 4-21 illustrates cells 1, 2, 3, 4, 5, 6, and 7 belonging to the same packet. Cells 1, 2, and 3 left the switch successfully. Then, upon receiving the congestion notification, the switch starts dropping the non-conforming cells (CLP equals 1)—4, 5, and 6. The switch does not drop the last cell, 7, however. The switch changes its CLP bit to 0 and sends it out.

Cell Discard Technique: EPD

EPD proactively decides to drop the entire packet before any cell discard occurs that is part of that packet. You can say that TPD is a reactive technique; whereas, EPD is a proactive technique. The switches use threshold measurements to come up with an occupancy factor. Reaching this factor triggers the EPD. Imagine this scenario. The first cell of a long packet arrives at the switch. At this moment, the occupancy factor exceeds the threshold, thus triggering the EPD. This triggers the discard of every arriving cell, including the last cell. After all, if the switch drops all cells, the last cell is useless anyway. After the switch discards the last cell, it resets the EPD mode. Figure 4-22 illustrates the EPD mechanism and the flow of the process.

Figure 4-21 *Tail Packet Discard*

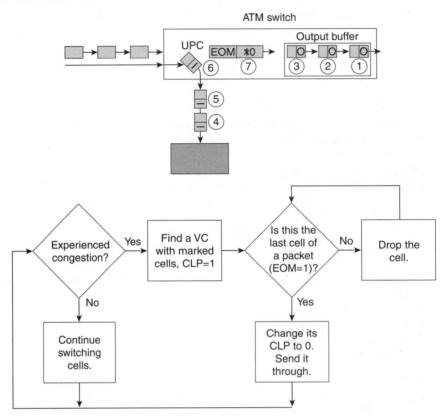

RED

Sally Floyd and Van Jacobson proposed RED (FLJA93) for packet switched networks to avoid congestion in IP networks. ATM networks can adopt the same algorithm. Assume that the switch detects the congestion by using the threshold measurements, as in EPD. When the occupancy factor exceeds the preset threshold, the switch marks each arriving cell with a certain probability of being dropped. The probability factor is a function of the occupancy factor. Consequently, the switch defines several occupancy factors. When the first cell arrives and the current occupancy factor reaches the threshold value of that moment, the switch discards the entire packet, meaning all the cells of that packet. The higher the probability, the more packets are discarded.

Figure 4-22 *Early Packet Discard*

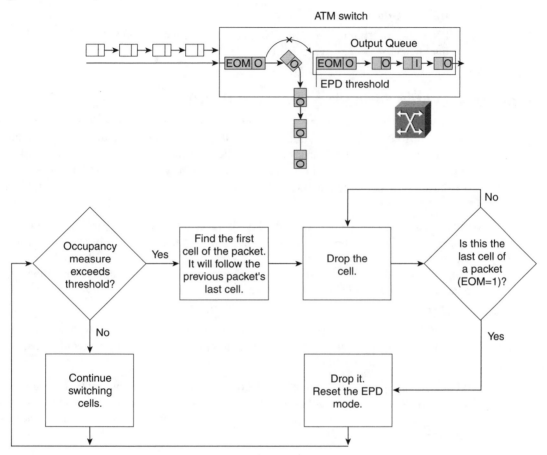

ATM Routing Protocols

Now is the time to unravel the mysteries of how the signal "knows" where to go when establishing the SVC.

SRouter Definition

A lot of confusion exists about the definition of an *srouter*. The ATM cloud routes signaling but forwards payloads. Because the ATM cloud routes signaling, you could call ATM switches *srouters*. Layer 3 routers, however, are switches too—the only difference is that they switch Layer 3 packets. So you might want to call them, using a popular term of the late 1990s, Layer 3 switches.

As mentioned earlier, the ATM Forum developed two standard routing protocols:

- IISP for *static routing*
- PNNI 1.0 for *dynamic routing*. PNNI can route around failed links or links with insufficient resources dynamically.

Interim Interswitch Signaling Protocol (IISP)

The ATM Forum specified IISP in December 1994. The primary responsibility of IISP is to handle static routing. Because it is static, the IISP cannot achieve such ideas as QoS. Where can IISP be used? One of the places could be interconnectivity of private ATM networks to the public ATM cloud. Again, keep in mind that a majority of public ATM networks are PVC-based at this time. So, an SVC with IISP, selected as a routing protocol, would be a major step forward.

IISP does not have the scalability of the PNNI1 protocol. Why? Compare static routing of Layer 3 with OSPF or EIGRP. How many hours does it take to carefully plan static routes in a meshed, average-sized IP environment? What happens if the network topology changes? As you can imagine, the manual configuration of routing tables limits the applicability of any static environment to a very small scale or to security-conscious networks.

How does IISP work? Simple. Can it provide alternate routes? Absolutely. Is it loop free? Absolutely not. IISP requires very careful configuration and planning to avoid loops, especially when planning alternate routes.

IISP is a signaling protocol for interswitch communication. Given the fact that the UNI 3.0/3.1/4.0 signaling procedures are symmetrical, IISP uses UNI signaling for switch-to-switch communication, with nodes arbitrarily taking the role of the network and user side across particular switch-to-switch links, as illustrated in Figure 4-23.

Let's examine the example in the Figure 4-23. The ATM network has four switches: S1, S2, S3, and S4. Each switch has a prime route to one of four destinations: R1, R2, R3, and R4. Also, two alternate routes exist for every destination. Assume R1 has to send data to R3. The signaling VC (x,5) starts setting up a connection at S1. The S1 routing table suggests that the next hop is S3. At this moment, the S1/S3 link disappears. As an alternate route, S1 chooses the path S1,S4. When S4 receives the signal, it checks its routing table. The routing table points to the S4,S3 path. At this point, S4 realizes that the link S4,S3 does not exist, so the next choice is S4,S1. Now, the signaling frame goes to its originator, S1. The signal is in the loop and nothing can fix the problem—there is no Time To Live (TTL).

IISP supports a crankback mechanism that reroutes connections around nodes whose local CAC rejected the connection. Because IISP does not support hierarchies, the signal cranks back to the node originating the call. For example, when S1 chooses the path S1,S4 as an alternate route to set up an SVC link between R1 and R3, S4's CAC could reject the connection. This forces S1 to try the S1,S2 path as an alternative.

Figure 4-23 *IISP Routing Example*

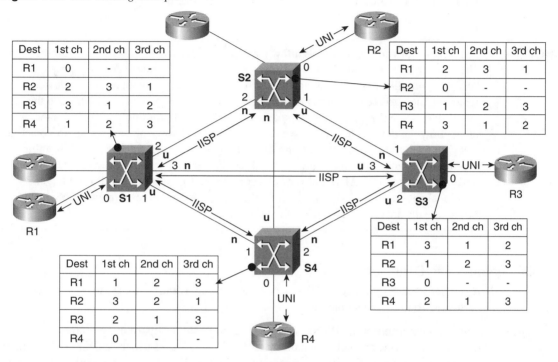

Dest	1st ch	2nd ch	3rd ch
R1	0	-	-
R2	2	3	1
R3	3	1	2
R4	1	2	3

Dest	1st ch	2nd ch	3rd ch
R1	2	3	1
R2	0	-	-
R3	1	2	3
R4	3	1	2

Dest	1st ch	2nd ch	3rd ch
R1	3	1	2
R2	1	2	3
R3	0	-	-
R4	2	1	3

Dest	1st ch	2nd ch	3rd ch
R1	1	2	3
R2	3	2	1
R3	2	1	3
R4	0	-	-

Formula for Understanding IISP

IISP = static routing + no QoS routing + no summarization + no hierarchy.

Private Network-to-Network Interface (PNNI) 1.0

The ATM Forum finalized the PNNI definition in March 1996. The whole purpose of PNNI is to provide the necessary scalability and dynamics for medium- and large-scale networks that can stretch over distances. And PNNI specifications meet that expectation.

PNNI simplifies the configurations in large ATM networks by allowing ATM switches to learn the network topology automatically. PNNI distributes any changes to other switches dynamically as well. PNNI is a dynamic, link-state routing protocol that encompasses a lot of intelligence. The main advantage of a link-state routing protocol is its fast convergence compared to distance vector protocols (with the exception of the third-generation distance vector protocol, EIGRP). The link-state protocol has a couple disadvantages: memory requirements and the CPU resources that are required for the algorithm involved.

NOTE Distance vector routing protocols allow the topology discovery to occur "by rumor," whereas link-state routing protocols allow the topology to be discovered "by propaganda." This really implies that the distance vector routing protocols do not allow the devices deploying them to see the entire network topology and, hence, the computation on the best path is done from the neighbors' perspective. The link-state routing protocols, on the other hand, allow the devices to "see" the entire network topology and, as a result, compute the best path from their perspective. In traditional Layer 3 routing, EIGRP, which is a third-generation distance vector routing protocol, uses a very clever algorithm (the Diffusing Update Algorithm [DUAL]) and very clever metrics. This is sufficient for the Layer 3 traditional routing. In ATM's case, where the routing job involves dynamic QoS as the metric, the distance vector view is not sufficient.

PNNI Features and Definitions

A standards-based protocol, PNNI is extremely scalable and includes two categories of protocols: routing and signaling.

The routing portion of the PNNI protocol is responsible for distributing topology information between switches and clusters of switches. It uses a hierarchical mechanism to ensure scalability and the link-state routing technique. This way, the network convergence time is very minimal.

The signaling portion of PNNI establishes point-to-point or point-to-multipoint connections across the ATM network. It is based on the UNI signaling and includes additional features of source routing, crankback, and alternate routing for call setup requests.

Formula for Understanding PNNI

PNNI = link-state routing + allows partitioned areas + source routing + 104 layers of hierarchy + QoS routing + autosummarization and flexible summarization + multiple routing metrics and attributes.

PNNI is compatible with both the UNI 3.1 and UNI 4.0 specifications.

PNNI Routing

The routing functions of PNNI include the following:

- Discovery of neighbors
- Synchronization of topological databases
- Flooding
- Election of Peer Group Leaders (PGLs)
- Summarization of routes
- Construction of routing hierarchy

Your journey into PNNI begins at the lowest hierarchical level.

Lowest Hierarchical Level

Although there is a lot of magic to PNNI, any "virtual" reality is based on physical reality. Let's look at the sample network topology depicted in Figure 4-24.

Figure 4-24 *Physical Network*

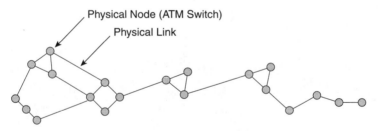

Each line in Figure 4-24 represents a physical link that attaches two ATM switches. A unique ATM address identifies each ATM switch.

Imagine a link-state routing protocol that supports only flat architectures. The scalability of such a protocol is literally non-existent. Every little network change is advertised to all the network nodes, increasing the load on links and disturbing all the nodes. Link-state routing protocols must allow for a hierarchical infrastructure.

Link-state Hierarchies

One of the main characteristics of link-state routing protocols, such as OSPF, IS-IS, or NLSP, is their hierarchical architecture. Hierarchy is the best friend of any network infrastructure. OSPF, for example, uses a "daisy flower," as I call it, architecture—area 0 (the middle of the flower) is surrounded by other areas (the petals). IS-IS is not that rigid in its definition of areas—any area can connect to any area.

Hierarchy allows for hiding network changes from one area to the next, resulting in quieter networks, although propaganda is the link-state philosophy. Using a hierarchical infrastructure, the networks can be summarized. The only drawback of a hierarchical infrastructure is the potential routing of a signal (or a payload in Layer 3 routing) to the land of nowhere. That is, because area A nodes are not aware of the details of networks in area B, the signal might get routed to the edge switch of area B to find out that the path or the node it thought existed does not exist. The advantages of route summarization and hierarchical infrastructures overweigh this disadvantage, however.

The PNNI's hierarchy begins at the lowest level, the physical level, which is organized into logical groups. Each logical group is called a node. So, the word *node* could refer either to a physical node or to a logical node. Nodes form a peer group (PG). Within a PG, nodes exchange information with each other, maintaining the identical view of the topology within a group. Each node has a unique identifier, called a *logical node ID*. Let's look at the example in Figure 4-25.

Figure 4-25   *Lowest Level of PNNI Hierarchical Structure*

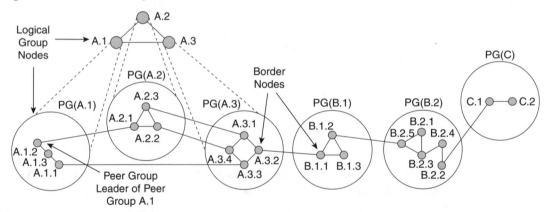

The network is organized into six PGs. PG(A.1) denotes peer group A.1, PG(B.1) denotes peer group B.1, and so on. PG(A.1) forms logical node A.1, PG(B.1) forms logical node B.1, and so on.

A unique peer group identifier (PGI), which is exchanged during the *handshaking* between neighboring nodes, identifies a PG. The handshaking is a Hello protocol that runs between the neighboring nodes, for example, A.1.2 and A.2.1. The Hellos are sent to verify the identity of a node and the status of the link between the nodes. Again, when I say a *node*, it means a physical and a logical node. Consequently, Hellos are sent between physical and logical nodes. Remember Einstein's theory of relativity? When a Hello is shipped between the physical nodes, it traverses between physically attached neighbors, for example, A.1.2 and A.1.3, A.2.3 and A.2.1, and so on. A Hello between logical nodes could traverse between multiple physical nodes via logical links, and recursively, their own Hellos. For example, logical node A.1 is a neighbor of logical node A.2. Hence, a Hello between A.1 and A.2 traverses the path A.1.2, A.2.1, A.2.3, as illustrated in Figure 4-26. Hellos are transmitted periodically every 15 seconds, unless a node dies.

Figure 4-26 *PNNI Hello Protocol*

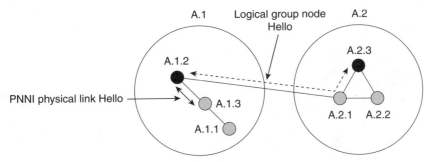

One of the important pieces of information that Hello packets carry is the PGI. Using the PGI, the nodes know if they belong to the same peer group. Through the Hello, nodes also exchange their ATM addresses and their higher level node IDs.

In OSPF, there is a concept of the Area Border Router. Here, the node that has at least one link that belongs to a different peer group is called the *border node*. Referring to Figure 4-25, nodes A.3.2 and B.1.1 are examples of border nodes.

When a logical link is established, the attached nodes set up a PNNI Routing Control Channel (RCC), which a VC uses for a Hello exchange between logical node neighbors.

After establishing the neighbor relationship, the nodes are ready to send to each other PNNI Topology State Elements (PTSEs), which are flooded reliably through the entire peer group. For example, nodes in PG(A.3) flood each other with PTSEs that represent all the links attached to the nodes within PG(A.3). PTSEs are similar to Link-State Advertising (LSA) packets in OSPF. These PTSEs form a topological database within a particular node. This topological database provides enough information for a switch to compute a route from itself to any node that it heard from the PTSE. Now, let's look at the higher levels of hierarchy. Remember that PNNI supports up to 104 levels of hierarchy.

Higher Hierarchical Levels

At the higher hierarchical level, the logical group node is the primary unit. Looking at Figure 4-27, A.2 represents PG(A.2) and A represents PG(A). This is just one method of representing the levels of hierarchy.

Figure 4-27 *Higher Hierarchical Levels of PNNI*

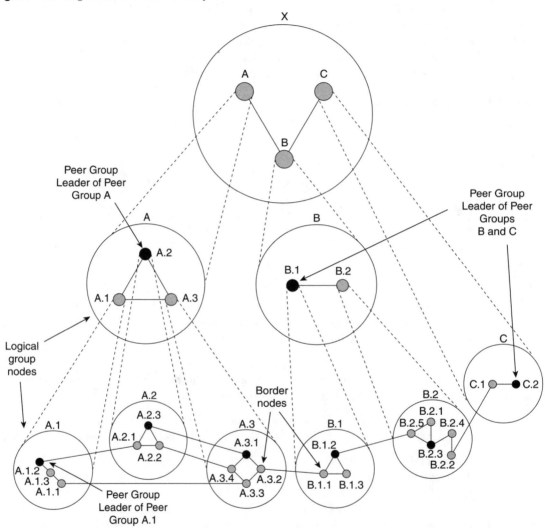

Let's analyze how the peer groups are formed. Nodes {A.1.2,A.1.3,A.1.1} form PG(A.1). Nodes {A.2.3,A.2.1,A.2.2} form PG(A.2). Nodes {A.3.1,A.3.2,A.3.3,A.3.4} form PG(A.3). Each peer group selects a peer group leader (PGL). (Call it the CEO of the peer group.) The PGL represents the peer group to the parent peer group above it. So, within PG(A.1), A.1.2 is elected as the PGL; within PG(A.2), A.2.3 is elected as the PGL; and within PG(A.3), A.3.1 is elected as the PGL. Next, logical nodes A.1, A.2, and A.3 form the parent peer group PG(A), where A.2 is chosen as the PGL. The same logic applies to PG(B) and PG(C). Finally, another parent peer group is formed above the current parent group—

call it the grandparent group—consisting of three logical nodes {A,B,C}. In this structure, the children peer group is at the physical level, the parent peer group is at the next level. Then the parent peer group becomes a child peer group when compared to the next parent peer group above it, and so on. You can call it a grandparent peer group, and then the great-grandparent peer group, and so on.

The PTSEs are exchanged within a peer group only. The border nodes have a special responsibility, though. Border nodes do not ship databases to each other—they send only Hellos. Through that Hello, the information about their respective higher-level peer groups and the logical node representing that peer group is indicated. For example, the border nodes A.3.2 and B.1.1 identify that they have peer group X in common. This mechanism allows each node to know the complete topology within its peer group and the complete summarized topology of the higher-level parent peer groups A and B and the grandparent peer group, X.

Analyzing the third hierarchical level, where only the three nodes {A,B,C} exist, the Hello protocol is executed between the neighbors {A,B} and {B,C}. Considering that A, B, and C are logical nodes, the PNNI Routing Control Channel (RCC) is created between A,B and B,C. The RCC between A and B could take the path {A.2.3,A.3.1,A.3.2,B.1.1,B.1.2}.

A unique ATM addresses all nodes. Be it a logical node or a physical node, the unique ATM address is used. The logical node can correspond to the address of the lowest-level node in the same switch, but with a different Selector value. For example, physical node A.2.3 represents the logical node A. Although the A.2.3 ATM address is 47.0091.8100.0000.0040.0b0a.0481.2222.1111.2222.01, the logical A node's ATM address could be 47.0091.8100.0000.0040.0b0a.0481.2222.1111.2222.04.

A peer group ID identifies each peer group. The peer group ID is expressed, like an ATM address, in hexadecimal notation. In fact, ID numbers are related closely to ATM addresses. An ATM address identifies a child peer group. Its parent peer group ID must be shorter than its ID, but the prefix must be the same, as illustrated in Figure 4-28. The length of the peer group ID indicates the level of that peer group within the PNNI hierarchy. Considering that ATM address prefixes are 104 bits in length, PNNI is capable of 104 layers of hierarchy. PNNI levels are not dense, which implies that not all levels are used in any specific topology. For example, a peer group with an ID length of 104 bits might have a parent peer group whose ID ranges anywhere from 0 to 103 bits in length. Peer group IDs are encoded using 14 bytes—1 byte signifying the level indicator followed by up to 13 bytes of peer group ID, as illustrated in Figure 4-28. The following formula describes how to determine the value of the level indicator:

Level indicator = 104–n

where n is the level number

Figure 4-28   *The ATM Hierarchical Peer Group ID*

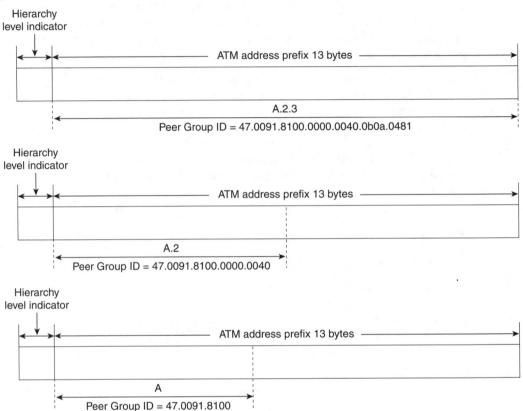

Hierarchy and Summarization

When you examine the hierarchical nature of PNNI, you see a recursive behavior: a group of nodes form a node, a group of which forms another node, a group of which forms another node, and so on. Figure 4-29 illustrates this behavior.

Figure 4-29 *The Recursive Nature of PNNI Hierarchy*

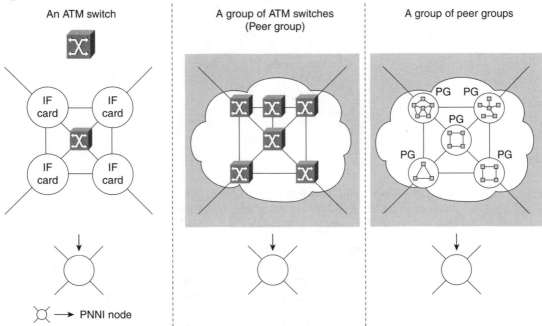

Have you ever seen Russian nesting dolls? Inside a large doll sits a smaller doll; a smaller doll sits inside that doll; another, smaller doll sits inside that doll; and so on. The dolls are nested recursively.

Like the Russian nesting doll example, where a single doll holds all the other dolls, the hierarchy is complete when a single highest-level peer group encompasses the entire network.

The PNNI's hierarchical structure is very flexible. The behavior of a peer group is fully independent of the level that it is at. Everything that applies to one peer group applies to them all, regardless of their level of hierarchy. The only exception to the rule is the highest-level peer group. It does not need a peer group leader because there is no parent peer group in which to represent itself.

The PNNI hierarchy results in the reduction of topological databases as well. For example, referring to Figure 4-27, all the nodes of PG(A) must know about only seven nodes (the nodes are A.1.2, A.1.3, A.1.1, A.2, A.3, B, and C) and seven links (the links are A.1.2–A.1.3, A.1.3–A.1.1, A.1.1–A.3, A.1.2–A.2, A.2–A.3, A.3–B, and B–C). This is quite a substantial reduction from 20 nodes and 25 links that all the nodes of PG(A) would have to know otherwise. Figure 4-30 depicts how this hierarchical model reduces the size of the topological database. All the nodes in Figure 4-30 have an identical view of the topology. This is because flooding within the PG(A) ensures that the topology databases of all its members are identical.

Figure 4-30 *Hierarchy Results in Database Reduction*

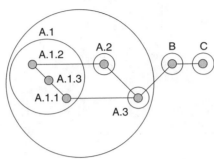

Flexibility in address summarization is very healthy for the network and its nodes because it reduces the amount of addressing information that must be distributed among the nodes and the memory requirements within the nodes.

The summary address associated with a node is either configured or assumed by the system with a default value. A *foreign* address associated with a node does not match any of the node's summary addresses, whereas a *native* address does. When you examine Figure 4-31, A.2.2 is a summary of nodes whose prefixes do not match the summary, whereas A.2.3 nodes match the summary. Nodes Y.1.1.1, Y.1.1.2, Y.1.1.3, Z.2.1.1, and Z.2.2.2 are called *foreign nodes*, and nodes A.2.3.1, A.2.3.2, and A.2.3.3 are called *native nodes*.

Figure 4-31 *Native and Foreign Addresses*

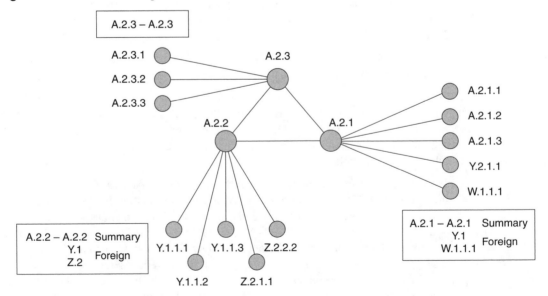

Topology State Parameters

PNNI topology state parameters fall into two categories: topology metric and topology attribute. The *topology metric* is a topology state parameter that requires the values of all links' state parameters along a given path to be combined to determine whether the path is acceptable and/or desirable for a required connection. The topology metrics are cell delay variation (CDV), maximum cell transfer delay (maxCTD), and administrative weight (AW), as listed in Table 4-8.

The *topology attribute* is a topology state parameter that is considered individually to determine whether a given node or link is acceptable and/or desirable for a required connection. The topology attributes are divided further into *performance/resource-related* and *policy-related* attributes. A performance/resource-related attribute provides a measure of the cell transfer performance or a resource constraint associated with the topology, whereas a policy-related attribute provides the characteristic of the level of conformance of the topology to a specific policy constraint. For example, maximum cell rate (MCR) is a performance/resource-related attribute; whereas, restricted transit is a policy-related attribute, which means that a switch does not allow itself to be a transit switch.

Various traffic types require different topology state parameters. Table 4-8 lists the topology state parameters and the corresponding indication of them being a topology metric or a topology attribute for different traffic types.

Table 4-8   *Traffic Types and Topology State Parameters*

Topology State Parameter	Topology State Parameter Category	CBR	rt-VBR	nrt-VBR	UBR	ABR	GFR[4]
Max CTD	Metric	R[1]	R	R	N/A[2]	N/A	N/A
CDV	Metric	R	R	N/A	N/A	N/A	N/A
Administrative weight (AW)	Metric	R	R	R	R	R	R
CLR for CLP = 0	Resource-related attribute	R	R	R	N/A	R	R
CLR for CLP = 0 + 1	Resource-related attribute	R	R	R	N/A	N/A	N/A
Maximum cell rate	Resource-related attribute	OPT[3]	OPT	OPT	R	R	R
Available cell rate	Resource-related attribute	R	R	R	N/A	R	R
Cell rate margin	Resource-related attribute	N/A	OPT	OPT	N/A	N/A	N/A
Variance factor	Resource-related attribute	N/A	OPT	OPT	N/A	N/A	N/A

[1]R means that the indicated topology state parameter is required for the identified service category.

[2]N/A means that the indicated topology state parameter is not applicable for the identified service category.

[3]OPT means that the indicated topology state parameter is optional for the identified service category.

[4]The ATM Forum currently is working on the GFR signaling specification. The values in the GFR column could vary from the actual specification when approved.

AW is the value set by the network administrator. It indicates the desirability of one link versus another. All service categories require this value. The lower the AW, the more desirable is the link. The AW of a path is defined as the sum of the AWs of the links and the nodes contained in the path.

The cell rate margin is the difference between the effective bandwidth allocation and the allocation for SCR for the new VC.

The variance factor is a measure of the cell rate margin normalized by the variance of the total cell rates of all existing connections.

Path Selection

ATM is a connection-oriented technology that provides QoS. This means that prior to any payload, a signaling frame is sent through to establish a connection that meets the required QoS for the duration of that VC. Because PNNI is the protocol that helps this signaling frame find the best-suited path for a requested QoS, PNNI must be very careful. Let's look at it closer.

Basically, two different routing techniques for path selection exist: source routing and hop-by-hop. PNNI uses the source routing mechanism, where the originating (or source) system selects the path to the destination and ignores the hints from the system itself. The information element of the signaling frame contains the entire path, which is supplied by the ingress ATM switch, as illustrated in Figure 4-32.

Figure 4-32 *Source Routing Mechanism*

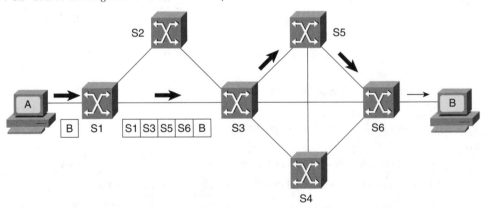

The hop-by-hop path selection mechanism has many disadvantages when compared to the source routing mechanism. Table 4-9 compares the two methods.

Table 4-9   *Comparison of Source Routing and Hop-by Hop Methodology*

Compared Item	Source Routing	Hop-by-Hop
Routing decisions	Is consistent.	Is inconsistent due to the convergence time involved.
Switches' knowledge of the path selection metrics	Not replicated in every device.	Must be replicated from switch to switch. For constantly changing QoS, this is not trivial.
Switches' CPU utilization	Only the ingress switch of every peer group must run SPF algorithm.	The path computation, which in link state involves the SPF algorithm and tree creation, is very CPU-intensive. Every system must perform it.
Switches' memory requirements	Involves only the ingress switches of every peer group.	More memory is required in every switch.
Compatibility between the path selection algorithms deployed by the switches	Because only one switch of a peer group is involved in path selection, the switches can run different path selection algorithms.	Because all the switches are involved in the path selection algorithm, all the algorithms must be compatible with each other.

Path Cost and QoS

It is interesting to note that the definition of the "best path" for PNNI is quite different from the other protocols, such as OSPF. OSPF looks for the best-cost path. PNNI, on the other hand, looks for the path that meets the required QoS for that particular call. Another interesting phenomena is that with such protocols as OSPF, all the packets (regardless of the applications) traverse the network via the same path (provided that the topology does not change), as long as the cost is minimal. In PNNI's case, every call is treated individually. The path, which is provided to the setup message, is based on the QoS specifications that are specific for that call. Overall topology could stay untouched. However, if the QoS changes somewhere, that triggers PTSE flooding, which changes the QoS topological view of the network.

PNNI Signaling

Now that the route is determined, the switches are ready to forward the signaling that originated at source node A. The main objective of PNNI signaling is to complete the delivery of the requested connection from the UNI side, using the source route that the routing portion of PNNI established, with the required QoS parameters.

PNNI signaling is based on a subset of UNI 4.0 signaling. It does not support proxy signaling or leaf initiated join capability, which UNI 4.0 supports. However, PNNI supports the following additional features that are not supported by UNI 4.0:

- PNNI uses PNNI routing information on reachability, connectivity, and available QoS parameters of the network.

- PNNI uses Designated Transit Lists (DTLs) that carry the intelligence of hierarchical infrastructure and the source route path selection mechanism of PNNI.

- PNNI allows for crankback and alternate routing. This helps to manage the topological inconsistencies, should there be any, within the ATM network.

- PNNI uses associated signaling over virtual path connections.

NOTE *Crankback* is a mechanism that allows a partial release of in-progress connection setup due to link failure or topological discrepancies with respect to QoS.

Whereas PNNI's RCCs use the well-known VCI equals 18, with VPI typically equal to 0 for the exchange of PNNI routing protocol packets (Hellos, PTSEs, and so on), the signaling PVC (VCI equals 5) is used for SVC setup/release. Table 4-10 summarizes all the reserved VPI/VCIs that I've talked about so far.

Table 4-10 *Reserved VPI/VCIs*

VPI	VCI	Used for
0	0	Empty cell
x	5	Signaling, UNI
x	6	RM-cells
x	16	ILMI
x	18	PNNI's RCC
x	0–31	Reserved by the ATM Forum and the ITU-T

Figure 4-33 examines a sample, flat topology. PNNI routing computes the topological databases in all the switches. Using the topological database, the ingress switch, S1, creates a tree-like data structure to represent the possible QoS values for various destinations (remember that the tree data structure has QoS values, versus cost values, which OPSF uses).

Figure 4-33 *PNNI Signaling: Flat Topology Network*

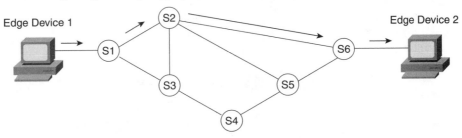

The signaling request comes in on a UNI from Edge Device 1. When S1 receives the request, it executes its locally significant CAC, responds to Edge Device 1 with "call proceeding," and builds the DTL of {S1,S2,S6}. S1 determines the DTL using the pre-built tree data structure. The UNI signaling information element has the QoS parameters for which Edge Device 1 is looking. Using this information and its tree structure with QoS, S1 can approximate the DTL. The DTL is added in the source route form to the information element of the signaling request. The signal goes to the next guy on the list, S2. S2 runs its CAC. Let's assume that it can meet the requirements of Edge Device 1, so it replies with "call proceeding" to S1. Furthermore, S2 uses the generic CAC (GCAC) algorithm to calculate the expected CAC behavior of other nodes using their advertised information. The signal now is forwarded to the next switch on the DTL, S6. S6 performs the same functions as S2. Assume that it replies with "call proceeding" as well. Finally, S6 forwards the request to the destination, Edge Device 2, which also replies with OK. The hole from Edge Device 1 to Edge Device 2 has been drilled (that is, the connection is now set).

Now, assume another scenario where, instead of the six nodes depicted in Figure 4-33, your network consists of 100 nodes. Also, assume that the topology is flat. When the signal starts traversing through the cloud, one of the switches (say number 50) rejects the connection because it cannot meet the requirements that the signaling message is conveying. This becomes a true nightmare. Why? Simply because only the ingress switch of the peer group can provide the source route. How many peer groups do you have in the flat topology? Only one. Hence, the crankback must go all the way to the beginning of your ATM cloud, that is, S1. This increases the call establishment process time and results in extra traffic. What is the solution in the large-scale networks? Implement a hierarchical approach. Let's look at the hierarchical approach in Figure 4-34.

Figure 4-34 *PNNI Signaling: Hierarchical Topology Network*

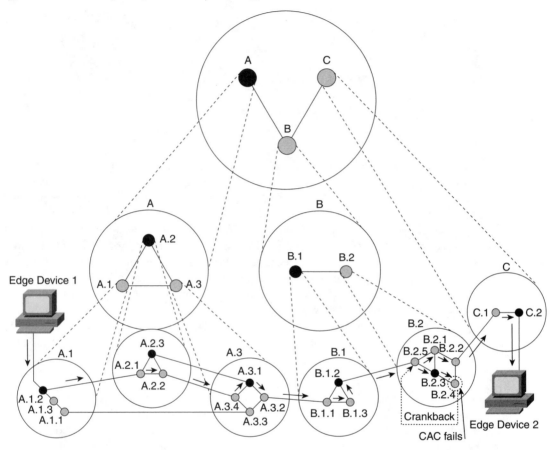

Edge Device 1 needs to communicate with Edge Device 2. Edge Device 1 issues the signaling message to the first ingress switch, A.1.2. The switch runs CAC and replies to Edge Device 1 with "call proceeding." It looks at the required QoS parameters and, based on the QoS tree data structure, comes up with the path {A.1.2,A.2,A.3,B,C}. The path is presented as a sequence of DTLs ordered from the lowest to the highest peer group level and organized as a stack (that is, first in, last out data structure). When the end of the DTL is reached, it is removed from the stack.

The stack of DTLs that it provides to the information element of the signaling message looks like this:

```
-> DTL: {A.1.2}
   DTL: {A.1,A.2,A.3}
   DTL: {A,B,C}
```

where the transit pointer (->) points at the currently examined member of the stack. The DTL being pointed at is always examined first.

Before forwarding the call setup request, A.1.2 stores the content of the SETUP message. This is to remember this signaling request, just in case alternate routing is required. Next, A.1.2 examines the top DTL ({A.1.2}) pointed at by the transit pointer (->), and notices the DTL points to its own node ID. A.1.2 looks for the next entry in the top DTL, but there are no more entries. Consequently, A.1.2 looks at the next DTL, and finds the next destination to be A.2. Because A.1.2 is not part of the peer group A.2, it starts looking for a way to get to A.2. A.1.2 finds that its immediate neighbor, A.2.1, is in the peer group A.2. Hence, it removes the top DTL, {A.1.2}, from the stack and advances the current transit pointer to the next DTL, {A.1,A.2,A.3}:

> -> DTL: {A.1,A.2,A.3}
> DTL: {A,B,C}

A.2.1 looks at the top DTL, and recognizes that the current destination is A.2. Because A.2.1 is in A.2, it looks at the next entry in the DTL and starts routing to A.3. A.2.1 analyzes the topology it is aware of (which is its own peer group), and finds that the path to A.3 that will meet the required QoS is through A.2.2. As a result, A.2.1 pushes that DTL, {A.2.1,A.2.2}, onto the stack:

> -> DTL: {A.2.1,A.2.2}
> DTL: {A.1,A.2,A.3}
> DTL: {A,B,C}

Because A.2.1 added a DTL to the stack and it is the border node, it stores the content of the received SETUP message and the content of DTL that it added to the stack, just in case rerouting might be required. Next, it sends the packet to A.2.2. A.2.2 determines that the top DTL target has been reached and that the DTL list is exhausted. So A.2.2 removes the top DTL, {A.2.1,A.2.2}, from the stack and advances the current pointer to the next DTL:

> -> DTL: {A.1,A.2,A.3}
> DTL: {A,B,C}

Next, the request arrives at A.3.4. Because A.3.4 is in the peer group A.3, the request reaches target of the top list, {A.1,A.2,A.3}. A.3.4 builds a route to B, using its tree data structure to meet the required QoS. It uses nodes A.3.1 and A.3.2. It pushes the new DTL list, {A.3.4,A.3.1,A.3.2}, onto the stack:

> -> DTL: {A.3.4,A.3.1,A.3.2}
> DTL: {A.1,A.2,A.3}
> DTL: {A,B,C}

A.3.4 stores the SETUP request and the DTL that it generated just in case it might be involved in alternate routing. The next node, A.3.1, receives the call setup, runs CAC and GCAC (as all the nodes do), advances the pointer within the top DTL, and forwards the request to A.3.2. A.3.2 receives the setup request and decides to forward the message to its neighbor, B. First, A.3.2 removes the top DTL, {A.3.4,A.3.1,A.3.2}, from the stack, and then removes the next DTL, {A.1,A.2,A.3}, because it has been exhausted:

> -> DTL: {A,B,C}

Node B.1.1 receives the request. Because it is the border node, it builds the path to C by pushing two DTL lists onto the stack:

> -> DTL: {B.1.1,B.1.3,B.1.2}
> DTL: {B1,B2}
> DTL: {A,B,C}

B.1.1 stores the SETUP request and the DTLs that it generated, just in case it needs to do any rerouting.

Here, without going into the recursive nature of the process, the nodes B.1.3 and B.1.2 take the same steps as nodes within the A.3 peer group, for example. When the signaling message reaches the border node of B2, the DTL stack looks like this:

> -> DTL: {B.2.5,B.2.3,B.2.4,B.2.2}
> DTL: {B.1,B.2}
> DTL: {A,B,C}

B.2.5 stores the SETUP request and the DTL that it created because it might need it for rerouting. When the top DTL gets traversed to node B.2.4, node B.2.4 CAC fails—it cannot meet the QoS requirements that the SETUP message requires. The crankback procedure now begins, with B.2.4 sending the RELEASE message to B.2.3, which, in turn, sends it to B.2.5. The RELEASE message now is received by B.2.5, which specified the DTL for this call. Consequently, B.2.5 tries an alternate route, still with a promise to meet the required QoS. It finds the option of using B.2.2. Hence, it removes the top DTL list from the stack and pushes another one:

> -> DTL: {B.2.5,B.2.1,B.2.2}
> DTL: {B.1,B.2}
> DTL: {A,B,C}

The signaling message happily traverses using the top list. When the node B.2.2 is reached, B.2.2 realizes that the two DTLs have been exhausted. It removes them both from the stack. The stack now looks like this:

> -> DTL: {A,B,C}

Finally, when the border node of C is reached, C.1 pushes another DTL, stores the request and the DTL, and forwards it to the next switch:

> -> DTL: {C.1,C.2}
> DTL: {A,B,C}

When C.2 is reached, C.2 removes both lists from the stack because both lists are exhausted. C.2 forwards the request to Edge Device 2 via UNI. The connection between Edge Device 1 and Edge Device 2 is now established with the required QoS.

Recent Enhancements to PNNI1

Since the release of PNNI1 in March 1996, the ATM Forum has been working on its enhancements. Since that time, the ATM Forum has released various addendums with respect to PNNI1. Table 4-11 summarizes these addendums.

Table 4-11   *Recent Enhancements to PNNI1*

Addendum	Date of Release	Summary
AF-PNNI-0075.000	January 1997	PNNI ABR Addendum
AF-CS-0102.000	October 1998	Specifies PNNI/B-QSIG Interworking and Generic Functional Protocol for the Support of Supplementary Services
AF-RA-0104.000	January 1999	PNNI Augmented Routing (PAR), Version 1.0
AF-RA-0123.000	May 1999	PNNI Addendum for Mobility Extensions Version 1.0
AF-CS-0115.000	May 1999	PNNI Transported Address Stack, Version 1.0
AF-CS-0116.000	May 1999	PNNI Version 1.0 Security Signaling
AF-CS-0126.000	July 1999	PNNI Addendum for Generic Application Transport Version 1.0
AF-CS-0127.000	July 1999	PNNI SPVC Addendum Version 1.0
AF-CS-0141.00	March 2000	PNNI Addendum for Path and Connection Trace, Version 1.0
Final Ballot	October 2000	PNNI1.0 Addendum – Secure PNNI Routing
Work in progress	TBD	PNNI1.1 - PNNI Routing
Work in progress	TBD	PNNI1.1 - Control Signaling
Final Ballot	October 2000	Conformance Abstract Test Suite for PNNI Routing, Testing

ATM Network Management

Most network management architectures use the same basic structure and set of relationships. This section provides an overview of the ATM network management protocols and interfaces.

Such managed devices as ATM switches, run software (including management agents or just agents) that allows them to send alerts when they recognize problems. Problems are recognized when user-determined thresholds are exceeded. Upon receiving these alerts, the management entity (the network management application) is programmed to react by executing one, several, or all of a group of actions, including operator notification, event logging, system shutdown, and automatic attempts at system repair. Management entities also can poll managed devices to check the values of certain variables. Agents in the managed devices respond to these polls.

The ATM Forum Management Module Framework is based on a layer model, defined as M1 through M5, as depicted in Figure 4-35.

Figure 4-35 *ATM Forum Management Module Interfaces*

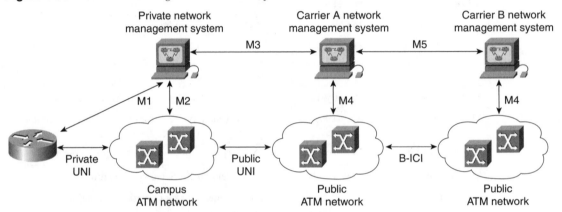

The first management interface that the ATM Forum focused on was M3 and M4. Specifications still are under development for M5- and M3-type interfaces. M1 and M2 are private interfaces that are used in private ATM networks and private network management systems.

The definitions of the management architecture interfaces, M1 through M5, are as follows:

- M1 and M2 define the interface between the NMS at the customer site and the ATM end station (for example, router or Layer 2 switch). M1 and M2 define private interfaces. ILMI, UNI 3.0/3.1/4.0, and RFC 1695 AtoM MIB define how a customer site implements private interfaces (M1 and M2).

- M3, which is a customer network management (CNM) interface, provides a customer view into the carriers network. M3 defines the public interface.

- M4, which is the network management level (NML) and element management level (EML), provides a way to merge public and private network management technologies. When M4 is enabled, it facilitates the outsourcing of end-to-end network management. M4 defines the public interface.

- M5 provides the interfaces between carriers' network management systems. M5 defines the public interface.

The ATM UNI MIB contains the ATM management information. The type of management information available in the ATM UNI MIB is physical data, ATM-layer statistics, VPC, VCC, and address registration information.

ATM uses the following tools for network management:

- Simple Network Management Protocol (SNMP)
- Common Management Information Protocol (CMIP)
- Integrated Local Management Interface (ILMI)
- Operations, Administration, and Maintenance (OAM) cells

The CMIP discussion is outside the scope of this book.

Simple Network Management Protocol (SNMP)

SNMP is the network management protocol used to manage ATM-based networks. Using SNMP, an ATM device, such as an ATM switch, communicates with the NMS manager via an ATM line. SNMP NMS is typically a color graphics, multiple windows, UNIX-based workstation. An ATM switch communicates with the NMS manager over an ATM line via SNMP/UDP/IP/AAL5/ATM. Figure 4-36 depicts a typical SNMP management model.

Table 4-12 lists four SNMP operations.

Table 4-12   *SNMP Operations*

SNMP Operation	Description
Get	Retrieves management information from the agent on a remote device. The NMS initiates the Get operation.
GetNext	Retrieves management information from the agent on a remote device by traversing the MIB within an agent.
Set	The Sets are parameters within an agent, used to set MIB variables.
Trap	Used by the agent to asynchronously inform the NMS of some event (for example, reporting a problem). The remote device initiates the Trap operation.

Figure 4-36 *SNMP Management Model*

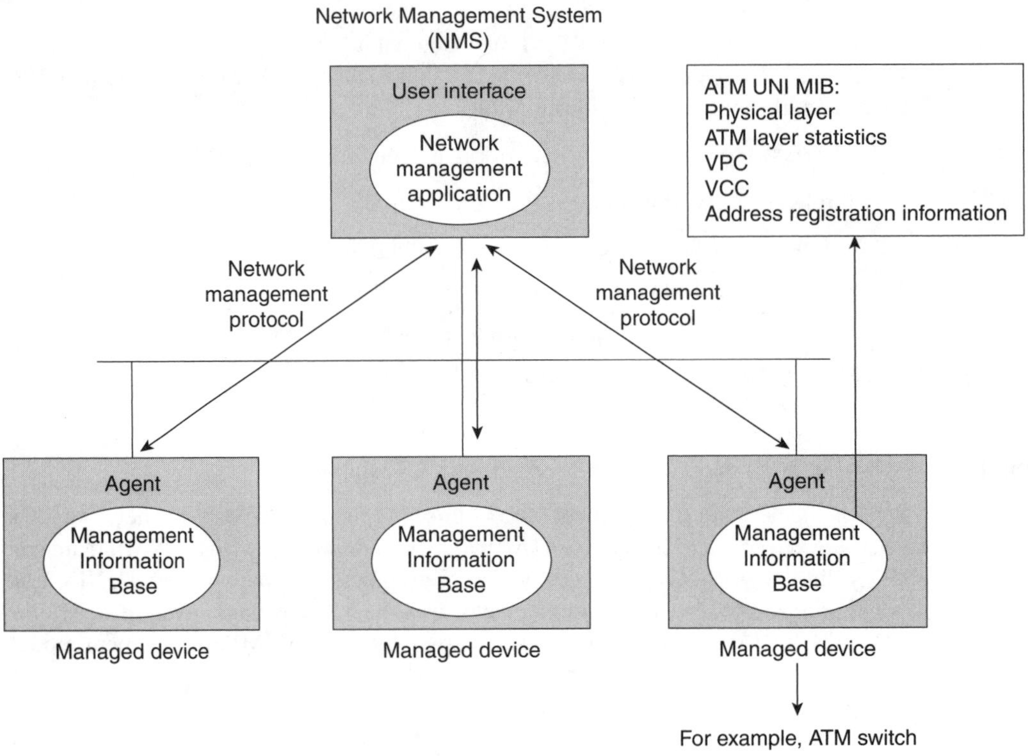

Network Management System
(NMS)

User interface

Network
management
application

ATM UNI MIB:
Physical layer
ATM layer statistics
VPC
VCC
Address registration information

Network
management
protocol

Network
management
protocol

Agent

Management
Information
Base

Agent

Management
Information
Base

Agent

Management
Information
Base

Managed device

Managed device

Managed device

For example, ATM switch

Integrated Local Management Interface (ILMI)

Where SNMP provides communication from the manageable devices (such as switches and routers) to the NMS and back, ILMI is a peer-to-peer protocol that exists between public and private switches or between switches and hosts.

NOTE   In UNI 3.1, ILMI stands for *Interim Local Management Interface*, with the assumption that it would be used temporarily until another standard was agreed on. In UNI 4.0, ILMI stands for *Integrated Local Management Interface*, indicating that the protocol is no longer a temporary solution (there is nothing more permanent than a temporary solution).

ILMI functions for an ATM interface provide configuration, status, and control information about physical and ATM-layer parameters for each ATM interface. Each device that implements ILMI has an ATM Interface Management Entity (IME) that supports the ILMI functions for that UNI. The ILMI bidirectional communication takes place between adjacent IMEs related to the physical and ATM-layer management, as illustrated in Figure 4-37. Also, ILMI has the capability to act as a proxy agent for NMS. It provides NMS access to the ATM interface MIB data for remotely located switches.

Figure 4-37   *ILMI*

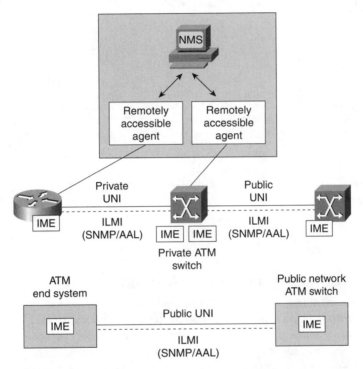

ILMI uses VPI=x,VCI=16 for its cell flows, as depicted in Table 4-10.

ILMI is based on SNMP, and like SNMP, consists of many MIB elements, as defined by the ATM Forum and depicted in Figure 4-38. ILMI is an open protocol. SNMP uses ILMI for management and control operations of information across the ATM interface. The data in ILMI MIBs is useful for general network management functions, such as configuration discovery, fault isolation, and troubleshooting.

Figure 4-38 *ATM Forum ILMI MIB Structure*

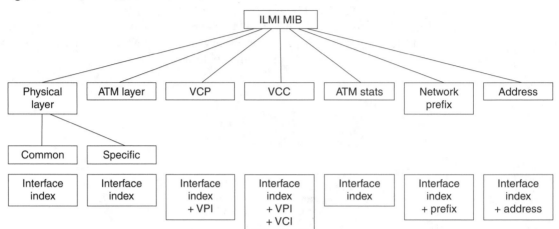

One of the very useful features of ILMI is its great help in the capability to learn and register long ATM addresses fully and dynamically, as illustrated previously in Chapter 3. Another useful feature of ILMI is to locate ATM network services, such as LAN Emulation Configuration Server (LECS) and ATM Name Server (ANS), dynamically.

Operations, Administration, and Maintenance (OAM) Cells

Operations, Administration, and Maintenance (OAM) cells are very critical in the ATM network maintenance. OAM cells are associated with the physical and ATM layers. OAM cells provide fault management, performance management, fault localization, monitoring, and troubleshooting. OAM cells help the network administrators to perform standard loopback (end-to-end or segment) testing to detect network faults on the connections. When there is an OAM state change, such as a loopback failure, OAM software notifies the connection management software. OAM can be enabled or disabled on each interface individually.

Table 4-13 lists the seven different types of OAM flows.

Table 4-13 *OAM Flow Types*

OAM Flow Type	Function
F1	Performance monitoring of the SONET/SDH section. It is used as part of the SONET/SDH overhead structure.
F2	Line error monitoring. It is used as part of the SONET/SDH overhead structure.
F3	Path error monitoring and fault management. It is used as part of the SONET/SDH overhead structure.

Table 4-13   *OAM Flow Types (Continued)*

OAM Flow Type	Function
F4	Performance monitoring of the VPCs.
F5	Performance monitoring of the VCCs.
F6	AAL2-specific performance monitoring.
F7	AAL2-specific performance monitoring.

F4 and F5 flows can be either segment or end-to-end flows, depending on the encoding within the cell header. Figure 4-39 illustrates F4 and F5 cell formats.

Figure 4-39 *F4 and F5 OAM Cell Format*

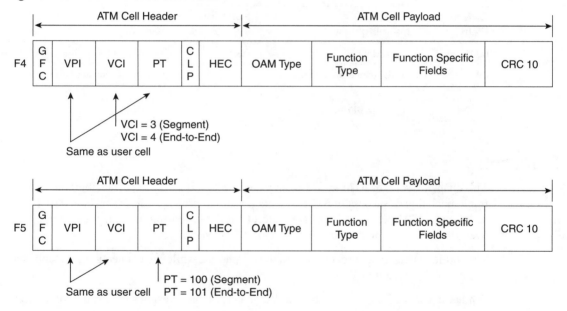

You now can add additional well-known VPI/VCI numbers to the table of reserved VPI/VCIs, as listed in Table 4-14.

Table 4-14   *Reserved VPI/VCIs*

VPI	VCI	Used for
0	0	Empty cell
x	3	F4 OAM, segment monitoring
x	4	F4 OAM, end-to-end monitoring

continues

Table 4-14   *Reserved VPI/VCIs (Continued)*

VPI	VCI	Used for
x	5	Signaling, UNI
x	6	RM-cells
x	16	ILMI
x	18	PNNI's RCC
x	0–31	Reserved by the ATM Forum and the ITU-T

Table 4-15 lists the OAM and function types of F4 and F5 type cells.

Table 4-15   *OAM and Function Type F4 and F5 Cells*

OAM Type Field	Meaning	Function Type Field	Meaning
0001	Fault Management	0000	Alarm Indication Signal (AIS)
0010	Performance Management	0001	Far End Reporting Failure (FERF)
1000	Activation/Deactivation	0010	Loopback

Summary

This chapter discusses ATM traffic management, which is a very important ingredient in the implementation of successful ATM networks. Without proper traffic management tools and techniques, ATM networks either are underutilized, thus costing more money, or are overutilized, thus providing insufficient QoS to its users.

The traffic management process occurs in two phases: while the connection is established and during the data flow.

While the connection is established, traffic management is responsible for the following:

- Traffic contract negotiations
- Traffic parameters
- QoS
- CAC

During the data flow, the traffic management responsibilities include:

- Contract conformance monitoring
- Traffic shaping
- Congestion control

ATM routing protocols, which are used strictly by UNI signaling for an SVC setup, are an essential ingredient of the traffic management. Two types of ATM routing protocols exist: IISP, which is static routing, and PNNI, which is dynamic routing. PNNI enables the edge devices to set up SVCs dynamically across the ATM networks. PNNI provides two basic functions: routing and signaling. The routing function is responsible for topology maintenance and path selection, whereas the signaling function is responsible for forwarding the signaling from the source to the destination.

ATM uses various network management tools, including SNMP, CMIP, ILMI, and OAM cells.

Review Questions

1 What is the role of traffic management? How can you subdivide the ATM traffic management responsibilities?

2 When is the traffic contract specified? What does it consist of?

3 What is ATM QoS?

4 What is CAC? Do switches have to have compatible CAC algorithms?

5 What kind of information is sent within a UNI signal's information element field?

6 What type of connections can be established in ATM, and what are their directions?

7 What are the ATM routing protocols used for? Name them.

8 What type of protocol is IISP? What are its advantages and disadvantages?

9 What are the responsibilities of traffic control function during data flow traffic management?

10 What is the main problem with congested ATM networks?

11 What techniques are used to reduce ATM traffic when congestion occurs?

12 How does an ATM node "know" that there is congestion?

13 What is PNNI?

14 What is a PNNI node?

15 What is a peer group?

16 What is PTSE?

17 How many layers of hierarchy does PNNI have?

18 How does a switch establish the SVC connection using PNNI?

19 What is the difference between F4 and F5 OAM cells?

"Worse than being blind would be to be able to see but not have any vision."—Helen Keller (1880–1968)

"When everything seems to be going against you, remember that the airplane takes off against the wind, not with it."—Henry Ford (1863–1947)

"A hunch is creativity trying to tell you something"—Anonymous

After reading this chapter, you should be able to understand the following:

- **The Role of LANE**—LANE is the extension of the Ethernet or Token Ring broadcast domains through the ATM network. LANE defines a standard method of forwarding Layer 2 data link traffic over ATM, taking advantage of high-speed bandwidth. LANE makes an ATM interface look like one or more separate Ethernet or Token Ring interfaces. This enables the existing LAN applications to run over ATM, without any changes to the host's NICs or their current platforms.

- **LANE Protocol Architecture**—LANE is an ATM application that uses client/server architecture to emulate Layer 2 services, which include MAC addressing, low delay of data transfer, and broadcast behavior. The ATM Forum defined the first version of LANE in 1995. The ATM Forum completed the definition of LANE v2 in 1999. This chapter focuses on LANE v2.

- **LANE Connection Procedures**—LANE's connection procedures include initialization, server redundancy, and data transfer procedures. This chapter discusses each procedure in detail, followed by the example of LANE v2 in operation.

CHAPTER 5

LAN Emulation (LANE)

Although ATM is a transport mechanism for various types of information, the development of ATM has taken a very different approach than any other transport mechanism (Frame Relay, for example). The question is, why take a different approach? One possible reason is due to the speed of ATM and its unique native understanding of Quality of Service (QoS) with respect to various types of applications, such as voice, video, and data. ATM can extend network connectivity with speeds of up to 2.5 Gbps. This makes ATM applicable to LANs, where the speed of connectivity typically is now measured in Mbps and Gbps.

Chapter 3, "ATM Reference Model: Higher Layers," talks about various services over ATM. One of the key ATM services is LAN Emulation (LANE). LANE allows all higher-layer protocols to interconnect using high-speed ATM with guaranteed QoS. LANE is a method of extending the bridged/switched domains (broadcast domains) across the ATM clouds, regardless of the protocol in use. LANE extends virtual LANs (VLANs) throughout the ATM network. When a VLAN is extended through the ATM cloud, it is called an emulated LAN (ELAN). Using LANE, corporations can introduce new applications that require lower latency (for example, multimedia-type applications), better predictability and various levels of QoS. Furthermore, LANE allows corporations to maintain the installed base of LAN-connected devices and still use higher-bandwidth ATM backbone for their interconnectivity.

ELANs and VLANs

It is important to differentiate between a VLAN and an ELAN. A VLAN is a single broadcast domain extending over distances (which could be several floors or nearby buildings) using a LAN technology as its transport (Ethernet, Token Ring, or FDDI). An ELAN is a VLAN that is a single broadcast domain extended over distances using the ATM networks as its transport. You can say that every ELAN is a VLAN, but not every VLAN is an ELAN.

The Role of LANE

Most LAN technologies are optimized for situations in which people in a given physical location (for example, a floor of a building) are all in one workgroup, and people in another physical area belong to another workgroup. VLANs provide the same service to members of a workgroup regardless of whether they are physically separated from each other. With VLANs, workgroups can be redefined as often as new projects require, because physically relocating workgroups for just one project is impractical.

For several years now, various corporations have been deploying VLANs. A VLAN is a logical group of end stations, independent of their physical location, with a common set of requirements. A VLAN can be thought of as an extension of a single broadcast domain over distances, as illustrated in Figure 5-1.

Figure 5-1   *VLAN Example*

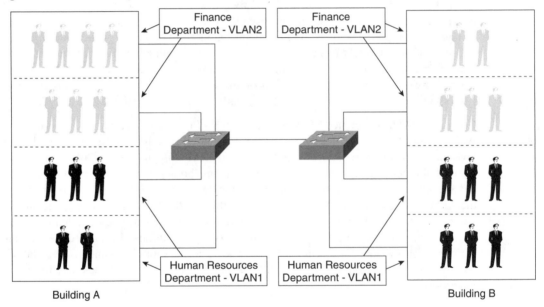

Of course, a single broadcast domain would go as far as the common interest extends it with sensitivity to the scalability of that protocol. For example, a single IP broadcast domain can extend to accommodate up to 1000 hosts without many drawbacks, whereas a single AppleTalk broadcast domain can extend to accommodate up to only 200 hosts before some service degradation occurs due to the chattiness of AppleTalk traffic.

LANE extends VLANs throughout the ATM network. ATM allows VLANs or logical domains to be defined and extended over distances. Computers connected to the same virtual LAN behave as if they are on the same broadcast domain, which means that they receive each other's broadcast messages.

LANE architecture, produced by the ATM Forum, defines a standard method of forwarding Layer 2 data link traffic over ATM, taking advantage of high-speed bandwidth. LANE makes an ATM interface look like one or more separate Ethernet or Token Ring interfaces. This enables the existing LAN applications to run over ATM, without any changes to the host NICs or their current platforms, as depicted in Figure 5-2.

Figure 5-2 *Seamless VLAN-to LANE Migration*

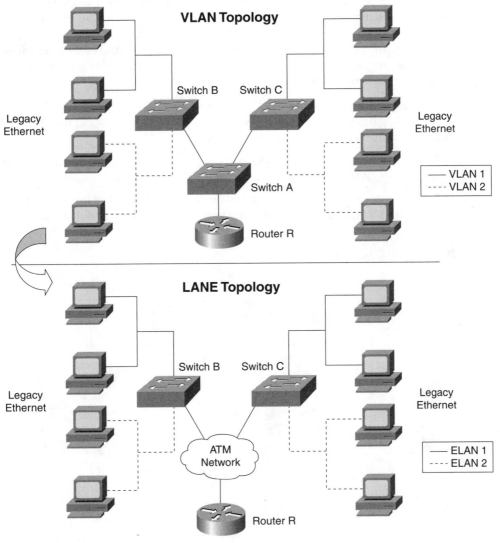

Figure 5-2 shows a typical trunked VLAN with cascading Layer 2 switches. An ATM network can replace the core using ELANs. The edge switches, B and C, and the router must be aware of the change of interface modules and interconnection methods. However, the devices behind switches B and C, as well as behind the router, are fully unaware of the change, making the LANE interconnectivity fully seamless.

LANE uses ATM as a backbone to interconnect existing legacy LANs. LANE emulates a single LAN segment by providing the connectionless broadcast service required by the network layer protocols. For example, VLAN 1 and VLAN 2, illustrated in Figure 5-2, have been extended through the ATM network. Multiple ELANs, which are separated logically, can share the same physical ATM network and the same physical ATM interfaces. Membership of an end system in any of the ELANs is independent of the physical location of the end system. End systems can move easily from one ELAN to another, independent of whether the hardware moves.

LANE service provides connectivity between ATM-attached devices and LAN-attached devices, as illustrated in Figure 5-3. Two primary applications that can use the LANE protocol for integrating networks are as follows:

- Connectivity between LAN-attached stations across an ATM network. Extending existing LANs over a high-speed ATM transport backbone.

- Connectivity between ATM-attached hosts and LAN-attached hosts. Centralized hosts with high-speed ATM adapters to provide services to traditional LAN-attached devices.

Figure 5-3   *Use of LANE in Network Integration*

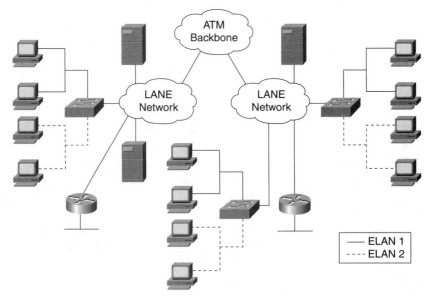

LANE Versus Gigabit Ethernet

Often, I am asked for my opinion about LANE and how it compares to Gigabit Ethernet. As a technology, LANE was finalized prior to Gigabit Ethernet, so a lot of companies have gone the LANE route. Now, some of these companies are questioning their decision—should they convert to Gigabit Ethernet, or should they stay with LANE? The first thing to do is consider the following questions: What are you trying to solve? Does LANE meet the current requirements on the data side? Are you going to bring in voice and video applications (that is, multimedia)? Remember, ATM can support real-time voice and video natively, without anybody's interpretation. There are many "if, then, else" decisions, in my opinion. If you do not have LANE currently, but simple 100BaseT or 10BaseT, the decision is straightforward. If the applications are and will be only data—Gigabit Ethernet is the way to go. If you have already invested in LANE and you will deploy it with only data for the next three years (a dubious prediction in this industry) and it makes economic sense, convert to Gigabit Ethernet. However, if there is a slight chance that you will deploy multimedia in your networks, stay with ATM. ATM with its QoS support for voice and video real-time traffic is a strong candidate as the network technology of choice. Chapter 1, "ATM Introduction," elaborates on this subject.

LANE Protocol Architecture

LANE has a lot of challenges. LANE enables existing applications to access an ATM network via protocol stacks, such as Advanced Peer-to-Peer Networking (APPN), NetBIOS, Internet Packet Exchange (IPX), AppleTalk, Internet Protocol (IP), and so on, as if they are running over traditional, legacy LANs. LANE allows legacy LAN adapters, such as Network Driver Interface Specification (NDIS) and Open Data-Link Interface (ODI), to function without any modifications. In fact, these adapters with the corresponding Layer 2 and Layer 3 protocols are LANE's applications, as depicted in Figure 5-4. Notice that LANE uses the RFC 2684 encapsulation method.

Emulating LANs with LANE

LANE defines a mechanism for emulating an IEEE 802.3 Ethernet and IEEE 802.5 Token Ring LAN. It is important to note that LANE is different for Ethernet and Token Ring. When you say "emulate," the goals of emulation should be all the positive characteristics of a specific behavior. Emulating an unnecessary behavior, as it relates to the physical/data link characteristics, is not a good idea. Hence, LANE does not emulate carrier sense multiple access/collision detect (CSMA/CD) for Ethernet or token passing for Token Ring.

Figure 5-4 *The LANE Protocol Stack*

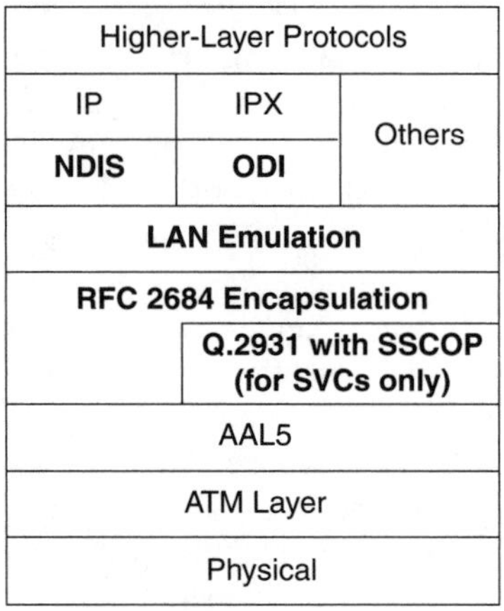

Higher-Layer Protocols		
IP	IPX	Others
NDIS	**ODI**	
LAN Emulation		
RFC 2684 Encapsulation		
	Q.2931 with SSCOP (for SVCs only)	
AAL5		
ATM Layer		
Physical		

The characteristics of traditional LANs are as follows:

- Speed of connectivity and data transfer (for example, 10/100 Mbps for Ethernet)
- Layer 2 addressing use (that is, MAC addresses)
- Broadcasting

Consequently, to enable the seamless interconnectivity, LANE must achieve the following goals:

- Achieve fast data transfer (for it to be similar to an uncongested LAN speed of transfer)
- Translate, somehow, between ATM addressing (40 hexadecimal numbers) and MAC addressing (12 hexadecimal numbers)
- Permit or emulate broadcasting through ATM, which is a nonbroadcast domain

LANE performs the necessary data conversion between LAN packets and ATM cells, resolves MAC addresses to ATM addresses, and emulates the broadcast behavior of a LAN. LANE can interconnect between native ATM hosts and legacy LAN hosts using the translation mechanisms between LAN and ATM, as illustrated in Figure 5-5.

Furthermore, LANE can interconnect your legacy LAN devices through high-speed ATM-aware devices, as illustrated in Figure 5-6.

Figure 5-5 *Existing Applications' Interconnections Between Legacy and ATM Hosts*

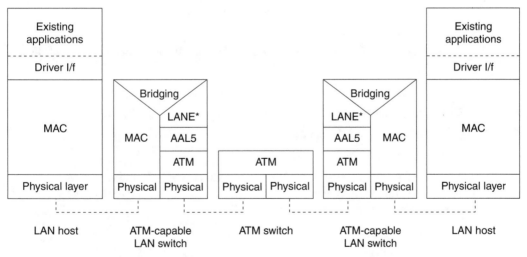

Figures 5-5 and 5-6 demonstrate that an application residing on a legacy LAN host can communicate completely seamlessly with an application that is implemented directly on an ATM host. Similarly, an existing application on a legacy LAN host can communicate with another legacy LAN host's application over an ATM infrastructure.

LANE Client/Server Architecture

LANE is an ATM application deployed with a client/server architecture. One or more ELANs can run over the same ATM network, although they must stay completely independent of each other. Why? Simply because each one represents a separate broadcast domain.

Any client/server architecture requires clients and servers, which implies that each ELAN is composed of a set of LAN Emulation Clients (LECs) and a single LAN Emulation Service (LE Service). The types of services that the LE Service must support include ATM and MAC address resolution, emulation of broadcast, and finding the destination to unknown addresses by deploying broadcasting. To comply with these services, LE Service consists of one or more LAN Emulation Servers (LESs) and one or more Broadcast and Unknown Servers (BUSs). What if you have more than one ELAN? How will a client know which ELAN it belongs to? For this reason, another LE Service has been defined. It is implemented by one or more LE Configuration Servers (LECSs).

NOTE	Some of the most confusing terminology within LANE is with respect to LECs and LECS. Watch out for that "s"! Is it a capital "S" or lowercase "s"? If the "S" is capital, the reference is to the LAN Emulation Configuration Server (LECS). If the "s" is lowercase, the reference is to multiple LAN Emulation Clients (LECs).

Your journey into the LANE architectural model consists of understanding the following items:

- LANE components and how they relate to the client/server principles
- LANE connections and functions
- LANE initialization process
- Data transfer through LANE

Furthermore, a complete list of LANE Version 1.0 (LANE v1) and LANE Version 2.0 (LANE v2) features is provided so that you can contrast and compare the two versions and understand their compatibility.

LANE v1 Versus LANE v2

It is very important to categorize and understand the differences between LANE v1 and LANE v2 due to differences in implementation and scalability issues.

The ATM Forum finalized the first LANE specification in January 1995 (af-lane-0021.000). This specification focuses on basic LANE functionality, without providing for any redundancy, allowing a single VC to support only one protocol. All this means that

LANE v1 does not scale very well. As a result, in July 1997 and February 1999, the ATM Forum released the LANE v2 specifications—LANE v2 LUNI and LANE v2 LNNI. This chapter focuses on LANE v2 features and architecture.

NOTE	You can find PDF versions of the ATM Forum specifications at ftp.atmforum.com/pub/approved-specs/. They are also listed in Appendix A, "Approved ATM Forum Specifications."

Table 5-1 lists and contrasts the features of LANE v1 and LANE v2.

Table 5-1   *LANE v1 Versus LANE v2*

Feature	LANE v1	LANE v2
Support of LE-ARP, MAC-to-ATM address resolution	Yes	Yes
Broadcast support	Yes	Yes
Multicast support through broadcasting	Yes	Yes
Dynamic methods for finding the LES and the BUS	Yes	Yes
LECS, LES, and BUS redundancy	No	Yes
QoS support	No	Yes
Multicast support through a special server—Selective Multicast Server (SMS)	No	Yes
Capability to multiplex multiple flows into a single VC, which results in better LANE scalability	No	Yes
Handles ABR traffic	No	Yes

LANE v2 is fully backward compatible with LANE v1. In fact, when a LANE v2 client interacts with the LANE v1 client, the LANE v2 client must perform only operations of which the LANE v1 client is aware. For example, virtual circuit (VC) multiplexing is not used if the LANE v1 and LANE v2 clients are intermixed.

LANE Components

Now let's define LANE components and their relationships with each other, as well as the types of LANE interfaces. Figure 5-7 illustrates the LANE interfaces and their dependency.

Figure 5-7 *LANE Interfaces*

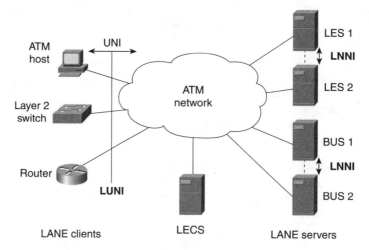

Notice that clients are connected to the servers using LANE User-Network Interface (LUNI), whereas the servers are maintaining LANE Network-Network Interface (LNNI) dependency between each other. LNNI does not exist in LANE v1. In fact, LANE v1 specifies only the interaction between the LANE clients and the various LANE servers. LANE v1 does not specify the interfaces (the LNNI protocols) between the server entities—this is part of the completed LANE v2 protocol specification. Hence, LANE v1 does not offer server redundancy, with the exception of the Cisco proprietary protocol, called Simple Server Redundancy Protocol (SSRP). LANE v2 LNNI specifies redundancy in LANE by provisioning for multiple servers.

Each LEC and/or LES can be implemented in workstations, routers, ATM switches, and ATM-capable LAN switches.

The following list examines all LANE components and their corresponding responsibilities:

- **LAN Emulation Client (LEC)**—The LEC is implemented in an end station. It performs data forwarding, providing a MAC-level emulated Ethernet or Token Ring service interface to the station's higher-level software. The LEC uses the LUNI when communicating with other components within an ELAN.

- **LAN Emulation Server (LES)**—The LES provides a service of resolving unicast and multicast MAC addresses to ATM addresses. The LES is LANE's control center, providing joining, address resolution, and address registration services to clients in a given ELAN. The LES maintains a list of LAN destination MAC addresses and associated ATM addresses. The LES also handles LANE-Address Resolution Protocol (LE-ARP) requests and responses. An LE-ARP is a query to resolve an ATM address for a given MAC address and, if used, a route descriptor (route descriptors are applicable only to IEEE 802.5 Token Ring LANs). One active LES exists per ELAN in LANE v1, and multiple LESs exist in LANE v2. The beauty of multiple LESs is the capability to have distributed and reliable LES functionality within a single ELAN. Each involved LES must maintain a database of all registered LAN destinations and their associated ATM addresses. The LES database includes the ATM address of all BUSs. Also, all active LESs must synchronize their databases so that all servers on the ELAN have complete and up-to-date databases.

- **Broadcast and Unknown Server (BUS)**—The BUS handles data sent by clients to the broadcast MAC address (FFFFFFFFFFFF), in addition to multicast data and initial unicast data, which the LEC sends to unknown destinations prior to the MAC and ATM addresses being resolved. The BUS also is responsible for serializing the frames it receives and retransmitting them directly or indirectly to other clients. The serialization process is required to prevent the cells from different sources that comprise the AAL5 frames from being interleaved. One active BUS exists per ELAN in LANE v1. LANE v2 allows for multiple BUSs to exist per ELAN, which results in distributed and reliable LANE architecture. Each BUS is paired logically with an LES. No protocol is defined for LES/BUS interaction. This is why Cisco implemented LES/BUS functionality in the same physical device. In LANE v2, broadcast frames (received from an LEC) are forwarded not only to all clients but to all BUSs within a single ELAN. A BUS never forwards a frame received from a BUS or an SMS to another BUS or SMS. Should the SMS be unavailable, the BUS handles all the multicast traffic as well.

- **Selective Multicast Server (SMS)**—The SMS is designed for a single purpose only—efficiency in forwarding multicast frames. The SMS service is a LANE v2–specific service and is not available with LANE v1. The BUS performs the functions of the SMS in the event that a specific ELAN fails to have SMS. LANE v2 allows for multiple SMSs in a single ELAN, which results in distributed and redundant functionality of SMS service within that ELAN. The SMS is designed to handle multicast frames efficiently, thus offloading the traffic on the BUS and leaving it to handle broadcast or unknown frames only. The SMS combines a subset of LES and BUS functionality into a single entity. Each SMS maintains a copy of the registration database, which permits the SMS to know which clients registered for which multicast MAC addresses. In this sense, SMS behaves like an LES. Clients, however, do not register with SMS. Clients register only with their LESs. The SMS is separate logically from the LES, unlike the BUS. The SMS uses the same VCs as the BUS to talk to the clients, although these VCs are associated with fully independent senders and receivers, which is not the case for the BUS.

- **LAN Emulation Configuration Server (LECS)**—The LECS serves as a form of directory assistance to clients. One or more LECS assign individual clients to different ELANs. After an LEC is assigned to a particular ELAN, it gets the address of its corresponding LES and/or SMS. LANE v1 allows only one LECS within an entire

ATM domain, whereas LANE v2 allows for more. The capability of LANE v2 to have more than one LECS allows the distribution of LECS responsibility among several servers, thereby avoiding single points of failure. Multiple LECSs are required to know which LESs are serving which ELANs at any given moment.

Table 5-2 summarizes the functions and characteristics of each LANE component.

Table 5-2   *LANE Components*

LANE Component	Characteristics	Within a Single ELAN, Communicates With:
LAN Emulation Client (LEC)	Performs data forwarding. Provides MAC-level emulated Ethernet and Token Ring services.	LECSs LESs SMSs BUSs Other clients
LAN Emulation Server (LES)	Provides joining, address registration, and address resolution for all the clients. Handles LE-ARP requests. Synchronizes the database with other LESs within the same ELAN. Keeps track of SMSs within an ELAN.	Other LESs Clients
Broadcast and Unknown Server (BUS)	Handles broadcast, multicast, and initial unicast data. Serializes the frames it receives and retransmits them directly or indirectly to other clients.	Clients Other BUSs
Selective Multicast Server (SMS)	Handles multicast frames. Maintains a copy of the registration database, allowing SMS to communicate with clients that are part of various multicast groups.	Clients BUSs Other SMSs
LAN Emulation Configuration Server (LECS)	Serves as directory assistance to clients by providing them with the LESs addresses, based on the ELAN identity.	Clients Other LECSs

LANE Connections

Now that you are familiar with the definitions of the LANE service components, let's look at the LANE connection types.

LANE v2 connections can be divided into three categories:

- **Control VCs**—Responsible for client control and registration, address resolution, and LESs discovery
- **Synchronization VCs**—Responsible for peer-to-peer connection between servers and synchronization of server databases.
- **Data VCs**—Responsible for carrying payload frames, including unicast, multicast, and broadcast traffic.

Each of these categories has several types of VCs, which are summarized in Table 5-3. Due to the VCs functionality, they operate between different types of interfaces. The control and data VCs operate using both LUNI and LNNI. The synchronization VCs use only LNNI.

The connection types can be either point-to-point or point-to-multipoint, as illustrated in Table 5-3. All point-to-point connections are bidirectional, whereas all point-to-multipoint connections are unidirectional.

In LANE v1, each VC uses a vc-mux encapsulation, meaning that every LANE flow and protocol has to have its own VC. LANE v2 allows multiplexing several flows into a single VC, which is accomplished by using LLC encapsulation. VC multiplexing results in fewer VCs required to be set up for LANE operation. This results in better LANE scalability.

Table 5-3 summarizes all the VCs and their purposes in LANE.

Table 5-3   *LANE Connections Summary*

VC Type	VC Name	Direction	Encapsulation	Type of Interface	Between Nodes
Control	Configuration Direct	Point-to-point	Mux	LUNI	LECS ↔ LEC
				LNNI	LECS ↔ LES, LECS ↔ SMS
	Control Coordinate	Point-to-point or point-to-multipoint	LLC	LNNI	LESi ↔ LESj or LESi → LESj
	Control Direct	Point-to-point	Mux	LUNI	LES → LEC
	Control Distribute	Point-to-multipoint	Mux	LUNI	LES → multiple LECs
Synchroni-zation	LECS Synchroni-zation	Point-to-point or point-to-multipoint	LLC	LNNI	LECSi ↔ LECSj or LECSi → LECSj

Table 5-3 *LANE Connections Summary (Continued)*

VC Type	VC Name	Direction	Encapsulation	Type of Interface	Between Nodes
	Cache Synchronization	Point-to-point or point-to-multipoint	LLC	LNNI	LESi ↔ LESj
					LES ↔ SMS
					or
					LESi → LESj
					LES → SMS
Data	Multicast Forward	Point-to-multipoint	Mux	LNNI	BUSi → BUSj
					SMS → BUS
				LUNI	BUS → multiple LECs
					SMS → multiple LECs
	Default Multicast Send	Point-to-point	Mux	LUNI	BUS ↔ LEC
	Selective Multicast Send	Point-to-point	Mux	LUNI	SMS ↔ LEC
	Data Direct	Point-to-point	Mux or LLC	LUNI	LECi ↔ LECj

Now, let's define these VCs in greater detail.

Control VCs

Let's go back to the LANE architecture and its purpose. LANE emulates the behavior of a broadcast domain using client/server architecture. Defining BUS, LES, SMS, and LECS LANE services assists the emulation process in accomplishing the required behavior. Prior to transmitting any data frame, LANE must resolve the address translation between ATM and MAC layers of the destination host. In cases of multicast requests, the multicast server (SMS) must know which hosts are part of its multicast group. Furthermore, a single ATM domain can support multiple ELANs (that is, broadcast domains). Consequently, there is a need for the directory assistance type of function, which identifies which client belongs to which ELAN. The purpose of control connections is to help the emulation process by providing these housekeeping services to the clients.

The control connections illustrated in Figure 5-8 are divided as follows:

- Configuration Direct
- Control Coordinate
- Control Direct
- Control Distribute

Figure 5-8   *Control Connections*

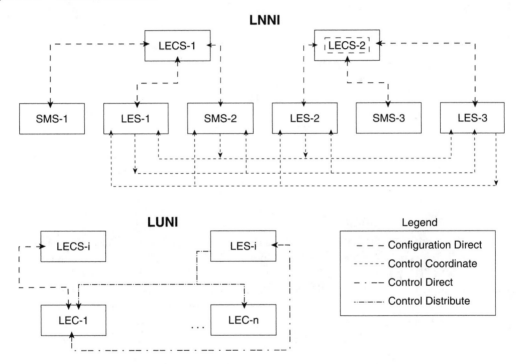

The following sections cover the responsibilities of all the control VCs.

Configuration Direct VC

The Configuration Direct VC is a bidirectional point-to-point VC. This VC is set up on the LUNI side by a client to the LECS. This VC queries the LECS (or *directory assistance*) about the address of the LESs for the ELAN domain to which the client belongs. The VC is set up on the LNNI side by LESs and SMSs to the LECS. The purpose of the Configuration Direct VC on the LNNI side is to download LES and SMS configurations into the LECS. The information downloaded includes the list of all neighboring LESs and

SMSs that must synchronize their databases. Figure 5-9 illustrates a Configuration Direct VC.

Figure 5-9 *Configuration Direct VC Connection*

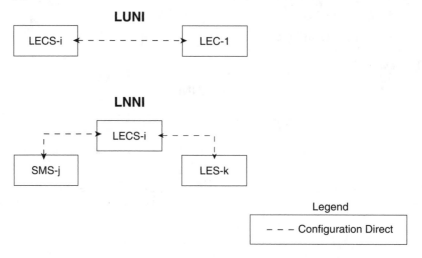

Control Coordinate VC

A Control Coordinate VC connection can be either point-to-point or point-to-multipoint. When it is point-to-point, it is bidirectional. This VC is set by the LES to other LESs using LNNI. The purpose of the VC is to distribute a request from an LEC to other LESs for the unknown ATM address of the destination client, whose MAC address is known (that is, an LE-ARP request). Figure 5-10 illustrates a point-to-point and a point-to-multipoint Control Coordinate VC connection.

Control Direct VC

A Control Direct VC connection is a point-to-point bidirectional VC. This VC is set up on the LUNI side by the client to the LES. The Control Direct VC is a conduit for exchanging control traffic and handling LE-ARP requests between the client and the LES. Through LE-ARP requests, the client resolves MAC and ATM addresses of a destination device when the client needs to send the payload there. Figure 5-11 illustrates a Control Direct VC connection.

Figure 5-10 *Control Coordinate VC Connection*

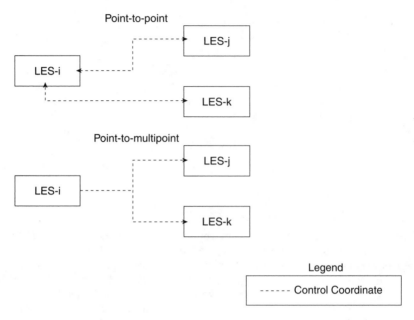

Figure 5-11 *Control Direct VC Connection*

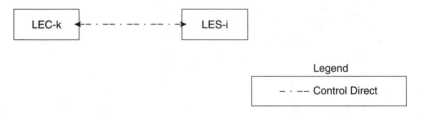

Control Distribute Control VC

A Control Distribute control VC connection is an optional point-to-multipoint VC from an LES to many clients. If an LES cannot resolve an LE-ARP request, the LES uses this VC to other clients to search for help in resolving MAC and ATM addresses for a destination. Figure 5-12 illustrates a Control Distribute control VC connection.

Figure 5-12 *Control Distribute Control VC Connection*

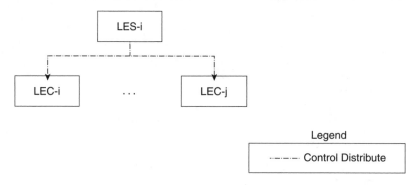

Synchronization VCs

LANE v2 provisions for servers' redundancy. The good health of LANE servers is absolutely essential for seamless LANE connectivity. In the event of an LES failure, any new kind of client-to-client connection becomes impossible. Furthermore, in the event of LES failure, the BUS also fails, because the LES and BUS must reside within a single physical device. Without a BUS, you cannot send broadcasts. Prior to the release of the LNNI specification in February 1999, Cisco invented SSRP to provision for redundancy. The LNNI specification accomplishes servers' redundancy with the help of synchronization VCs. The two types of synchronization VCs, as illustrated in Figure 5-13, are

- LECS Synchronization
- Cache Synchronization

The following sections cover the responsibilities of the synchronization VCs.

LECS Synchronization VC

The LECS Synchronization VC can be point-to-point or point-to-multipoint. It is set between all the LECSs in the ATM domain. The purpose of the LECS Synchronization VC is to synchronize the status information on LESs and SMSs that are part of all ELANs in the ATM domain. The objective of this synchronization is to achieve identical understanding of all LESs and SMSs for all ELANs involved. Figure 5-14 illustrates an LECS Synchronization VC connection.

Figure 5-13 *Synchronization Connections*

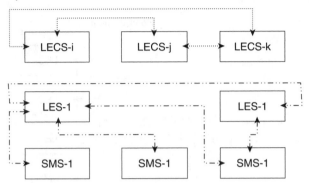

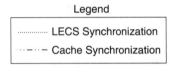

Legend

.... LECS Synchronization

..–..– Cache Synchronization

Figure 5-14 *LECS Synchronization VC Connection*

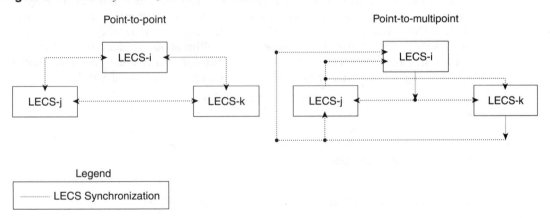

Legend

.... LECS Synchronization

Cache Synchronization VC

The Cache Synchronization VC can be either point-to-point or point-to-multipoint. This VC is set between LESs and SMSs to dynamically synchronize their databases. The database includes information on all LESs, BUSs, SMSs, and clients in the ELAN, and the registrations associated with all clients and servers. Figure 5-15 illustrates a Cache Synchronization VC connection.

Figure 5-15 *Cache Synchronization VC Connection*

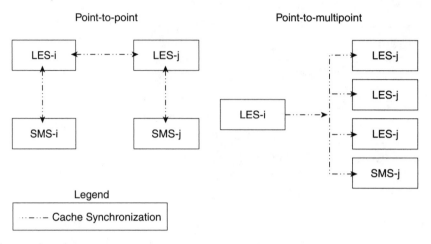

Data VCs

The goal of LANE is to send a payload from one end device to another. The VCs responsible for this important task are data VCs. Various types of data VCs are used in LANE. Why? Shouldn't it be enough to have just one data VC, from a source station to a destination station, after the ATM and MAC addresses have been successfully resolved? Of course not. You cannot use only one VC from source to destination. What about broadcast frames? They should be sent to all the devices across an ELAN. What if your LES does not have a cache entry resolving between MAC and ATM addresses for the destination device?

The data VCs, illustrated in Figure 5-16, are as follows:

- Multicast Forward
- Default Multicast Send
- Selective Multicast Send
- Data Direct

The following sections cover data VCs and their responsibilities.

Multicast Forward VC

The Multicast Forward VC is a point-to-multipoint VC. On the LNNI side, it is located between BUSs and from SMSs to BUSs. Its purpose is to forward broadcast, multicast, and initial unicast data frames to other BUSs and SMSs, when receiving the frames from a local LEC. On the LUNI side, the VC is between BUSs and the clients, or SMSs and the clients. Its purpose is to deliver broadcast, multicast, and initial unicast data frames to the clients. Figure 5-17 illustrates a Multicast Forward VC connection.

Figure 5-16 *Data Connections*

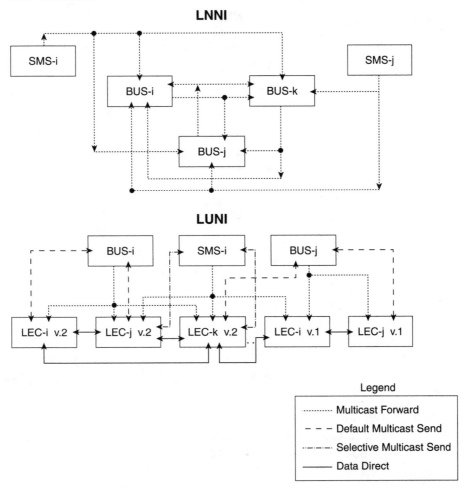

Default Multicast Send VC

The Default Multicast Send VC is a bidirectional point-to-point VC. Upon finding the BUS's address from an LES, the client establishes the VC to a BUS. Using this VC, the client sends the frames to the broadcast address and the initial data to unicast or multicast destinations. Figure 5-18 illustrates a Default Multicast Send VC connection.

Figure 5-17 *Multicast Forward VC Connection*

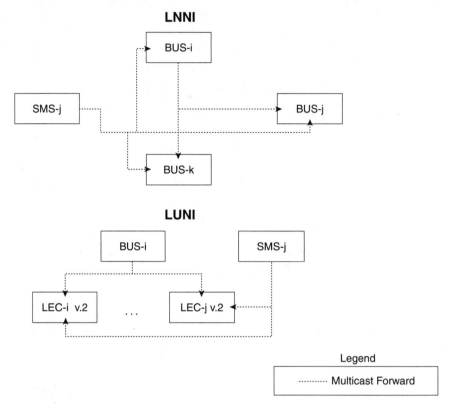

Figure 5-18 *Default Multicast Send VC Connection*

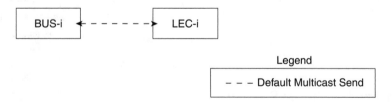

Selective Multicast Send VC

The Selective Multicast Send VC is a bidirectional point-to-point VC. Upon finding the address of an SMS, a client can set up a VC to an SMS. This allows a client to propagate all its multicast frames to its members. Figure 5-19 illustrates a Selective Multicast Send VC connection.

Figure 5-19 *Selective Multicast Send VC Connection*

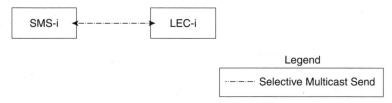

Data Direct VC

The Data Direct VC is a bidirectional point-to-point VC that is set up between clients to exchange unicast data traffic. Figure 5-20 illustrates a Data Direct VC connection.

Figure 5-20 *Data Direct VC Connection*

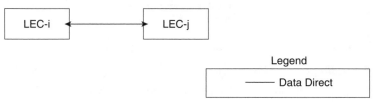

Server Cache Synchronization Protocol (SCSP)

The Server Cache Synchronization Protocol (SCSP) is used to accomplish dynamic redundancy of services in LANE v2. The responsibility of SCSP is to synchronize the databases between LANE servers. RFC 2334 defines SCSP, and af-lane-0112.000 specifies its relation to the LNNI.

NOTE   You can find RFC 2334 at www.ietf.org/rfc/rfc2334.txt. You can find the af-lane-0112.000 specification at ftp.atmforum.com/pub/approved-specs/.

You can view SCSP as being an ATM application, because it is a part of LANE architecture, which is the ATM application. SCSP consists of two sublayers, as illustrated in Figure 5-21. The protocol-independent sublayer relates to all the housekeeping functions between the servers that are independent of the type of server being maintained.

Figure 5-21 *Functions and Protocols of SCSP*

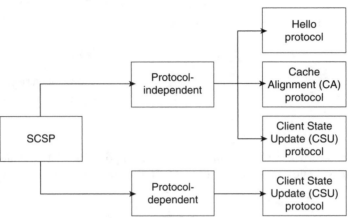

The protocols that belong to the protocol-independent sublayer include the following:

- **Hello protocol**—Maintains SCSP connectivity between neighboring servers.

- **Cache Alignment (CA) protocol**—Synchronizes the server's caches.

- **Client State Update (CSU) protocol**—The protocol-independent sublayer uses a portion of the CSU protocol, which is independent of the synchronized server type.

The protocol-dependent layer contains another part of the CSU protocol that is related to the type of server being synchronized.

Before the protocol-dependent layer can be executed, protocol-independent functions must be performed. Let's examine the entire SCSP process. When the LES or the SMS establishes the Cache Synchronization VC to the neighbor servers, it initiates the Hello protocol to those servers. When the neighbor servers recognize each other, the CA protocol ensures database synchronization. When the CA protocol completes its mission, the registration databases in all the involved servers are identical. The CSU protocol is responsible for keeping the servers up-to-date on any changes with the help of the CSU messages, which contain zero or more Client State Advertisement records (CSA records). For example, when a new server is added, a CSA record is sent, notifying all the servers; when an LEC leaves the ELAN, its local LES deletes the information from the database and sends the CSA record, notifying all the servers about the change. All the CSA records are acknowledged to confirm that the sending servers are sending the updates to all the appropriate destinations and not to electronic limbo.

QoS in LANE

LANE v2 permits higher-layer protocols to access the QoS feature of an ATM network. This implies that in addition to unspecified bit rate (UBR) support, LANE v2 supports variable bit rate (VBR) and available bit rate (ABR) traffic. QoS capability, residing in LEC, allows higher layers to specify unique ATM QoS parameters. LANE v2 allows each LEC to define QoS sets. Each QoS set defines call setup parameters and indicates whether this VC can be shared with other flows. During the establishment of a Data Direct VC, the QoS sets ensure that the required call setup parameters are met. If no QoS sets are defined, an LEC uses the default parameters of a UBR QoS set, as in LANE v1. When LEC binds a QoS set to a VC, QoS binding is created automatically.

LANE Connection Procedures

You can divide the connection procedures involved in LANE into the following:

- Initialization
- Server redundancy
- Data transfer

The initialization procedures prepare LANE components for the actual data transfer by pre-establishing all the necessary VCs that are and will be necessary for the seamless connection that LANE offers. This includes clients finding their own servers and establishing VCs to all the BUSs, SMSs, and so on.

The server redundancy procedures include preparing the servers to back up each other by establishing the VCs between them and exchanging the databases dynamically.

The data transfer procedures include sending the actual legacy frames across the pre-established VCs. The only VC that does get set up here is the Data Direct VC, extending one LEC to another.

The following sections examine these procedures in more depth.

Initialization Procedures

Locating a Friend

The following analogy represents the LANE initialization procedures. Imagine that you are trying to locate a long lost-friend in a big city. You know that your friend lives in that city, but you have no address or telephone number. What do you do? The first thing you do is call directory assistance, which provides you with the phone number for your lost friend, if you are lucky. It could very well be that there are several individuals with the same last name and initials. In that case, you get several telephone numbers from directory assistance. If you receive more than one telephone number, you simply call one at a time, narrowing down your search. Finally, when you talk to your friend and arrange a meeting, the friend can tell you how to get to his or her place so that you can meet. You travel using the bus, the train, and the bus again until you reach the destination. Finally, you meet. You talk and talk and talk. Nothing can stop you....

LANE's goal, like yours in the preceding story, is for one client to talk to another—that is, for one host to talk to another. How does the requestor find out the address of the destination client? The requestor knows only the MAC address of the destination. Also, to which broadcast domains do the requestor and the destination belong? Who can help the requestor? Well, LANE has the LECS (directory assistance). LECS provides the address of the LES, which is like the telephone number of your lost friend. Then, before one client actually can talk to another, you need to understand the ATM address of the destination and establish the connection to the destination. Similar to the preceding analogy, the LEC finds out from the LES the ATM address of the destination client. All these activities, called the *initialization procedures*, take place when the LANE starts up.

The initialization procedure of an LEC on the LUNI side is divided into an initial state and six phases as follows:

1 Initial state

2 LECS Connect Phase

3 Configuration Phase

4 Join Phase

5 Initial Registration Phase

6 BUS/SMS Connect Phase

The initialization process, which takes place at the beginning of any LANE operation and before any payload transmission, is completed after the completion of registration and BUS connectivity. Upon the completion of the initialization process, the LEC becomes operational. The following sections cover the initial state and the six phases of the initialization procedure.

Phase 1: Initial State

The initial state exists for a client as well as for a server. A client or a server enters the initial state when it is abnormally terminated from any of the LANE phases, initialization or operational. When a client or a server enters the initial state, which I call the "state at the beginning of time," various parameters are defined. These parameters are defined for both the impacted client and/or the impacted server. Some of the client's parameters are LAN type, ATM addresses, maximum data frame size, ELAN name, local route descriptor (used only in the source-route bridging), various timers, and multicast addresses for clients. The parameters that are applied to the LES include LES ATM address, LAN type, BUS address, ELAN-ID, and various timers.

The parameters cannot be smaller than the minimum value, nor can they be larger than the maximum value. For example, one of the timer parameters is *Aging Time*. Aging Time is the maximum time that an LEC can maintain an ATM address of the unicast LAN destination. The Aging Time minimum value is 10 seconds, which implies that it cannot be less than 10 seconds; its maximum value is 300 seconds, which implies that it cannot exceed 300 seconds. The af-lane-0084.000 document details the complete list of LEC and LES parameters in the initial state. You can find the document at ftp.atmforum.com/pub/approved-specs/.

Phase 2: LECS Connect Phase

The goal of the LECS Connect Phase is for the LEC to establish a bidirectional Configuration Direct VC to the LECS so that an LEC can determine where the LES is.

For the LEC to establish a VC to the LECS, it must know the address of the LECS. How does the LEC "know" the address of the LECS? Well, there are several methods to locate the address of the LECS, including the following:

1 Preconfigure the LECS address in the clients.

2 Obtain the LECS address using the Integrated Local Management Interface (ILMI).

3 Use the well-known LECS address.

The LEC attempts to locate the LECS in the order in which the methods appear in the preceding list. That is, if there is a preconfigured LECS address, the LEC uses it. Otherwise, the LEC tries to locate LECS with the help of ILMI (Chapter 3 elaborates on ILMI). If the ILMI does not help, it searches for a well-known LECS address.

Method 1 is error-prone and does not scale well. Imagine the nightmare of typing LECS addresses into hundreds of ATM edge devices. Methods 2 and 3 are more dynamic.

If using ILMI (method 2), you must establish an ILMI PVC between the edge device and the immediately attached ATM switch (ingress ATM switch). The ingress ATM switch must have the LECS(s) address(es) configured. The LEC issues an ILMI Get or GetNext request to obtain the ATM address of the LECS from the ingress switch.

If you use the well-known LECS address (method 3), the LEC uses the well-known LECS address **C50079000000000000000000-00A03E000001-00**. The ATM Forum assigns **00A03E000001**. If the LEC cannot establish the VC to this well-known address, another well-known LECS address must be used, as specified in the LANE v1: **47007900000000000000000-00A03E000001-00**. The ATM Forum specification af-lane-0084.000 specifies the full, well-known LECS address.

At the end of the LECS Connect Phase, LEC establishes the Configuration Direct VC to the LECS, as illustrated in Figure 5-22.

Figure 5-22 *Initialization Procedures: LECS Connect Phase*

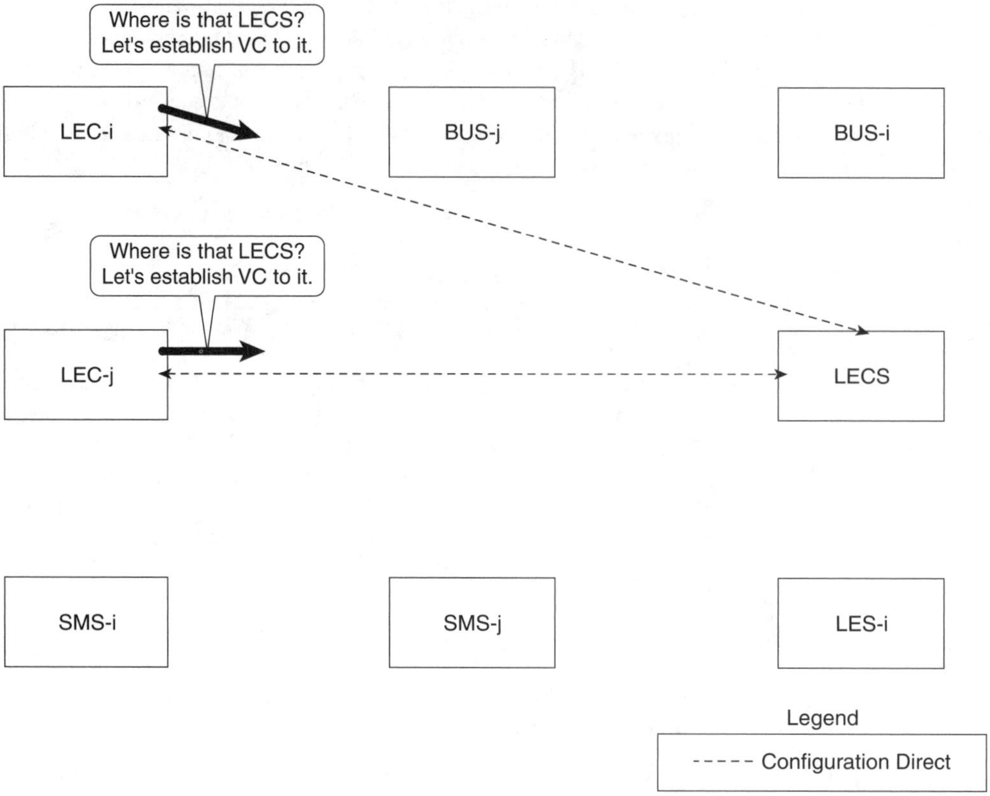

You can configure an LEC to bypass the LECS Connect Phase entirely if you program it to bypass the Configuration Phase and manually assign the addresses for LESs, which otherwise are obtained dynamically. Assuming that the LEC cannot bypass this phase, let's look at the Configuration Phase more closely.

Phase 3: Configuration Phase

The goal of the Configuration Phase is to obtain the ATM address of the LES from the LECS database. The Configuration Phase prepares the LEC for the Join Phase, which is the next phase of the initialization process. If the LEC is preconfigured with the LES address and the ELAN name, the Configuration Phase is bypassed.

During the Configuration Phase, the LEC obtains the information about which ELAN it belongs to and the operational parameters of that ELAN, such as the maximum frame size. Based on the information provided by the client, the LECS assigns the LES to the client by providing the client with the ATM address for the LES, as illustrated in Figure 5-23.

Figure 5-23 *Initialization Procedures: Configuration Phase*

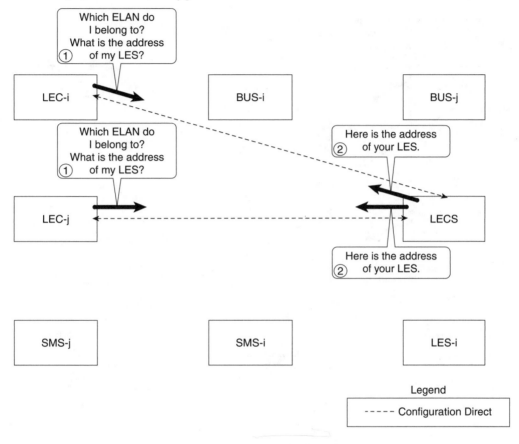

Upon completing the Configuration Phase, the LEC releases the Configuration Direct VC. It is important to note that the Configuration Direct VCs across LNNI interfaces, which are between the LECS and the LES and between the LECS and the SMS, are not torn down. This is discussed further in the "Server Redundancy Procedures" section of this chapter.

Phase 4: Join Phase

Now that the client knows the address of the LES and the ELAN it belongs to, it can establish a VC to its LES, which is exactly the goal of the Join Phase. The LEC initiates the call to the LES and establishes a point-to-point bidirectional Control Direct VC. When the VC is established, the client sends a request to join the ELAN over the Control Direct VC.

When the client sends a request to join the ELAN, the LES must decide whether to confirm the success of the join request based on the ELAN name matching and the maximum frame size. If the request is successful, the LES establishes a Control Distribute VC to that client. Figure 5-24 illustrates the Join Phase.

Figure 5-24 *Initialization Procedures: Join Phase*

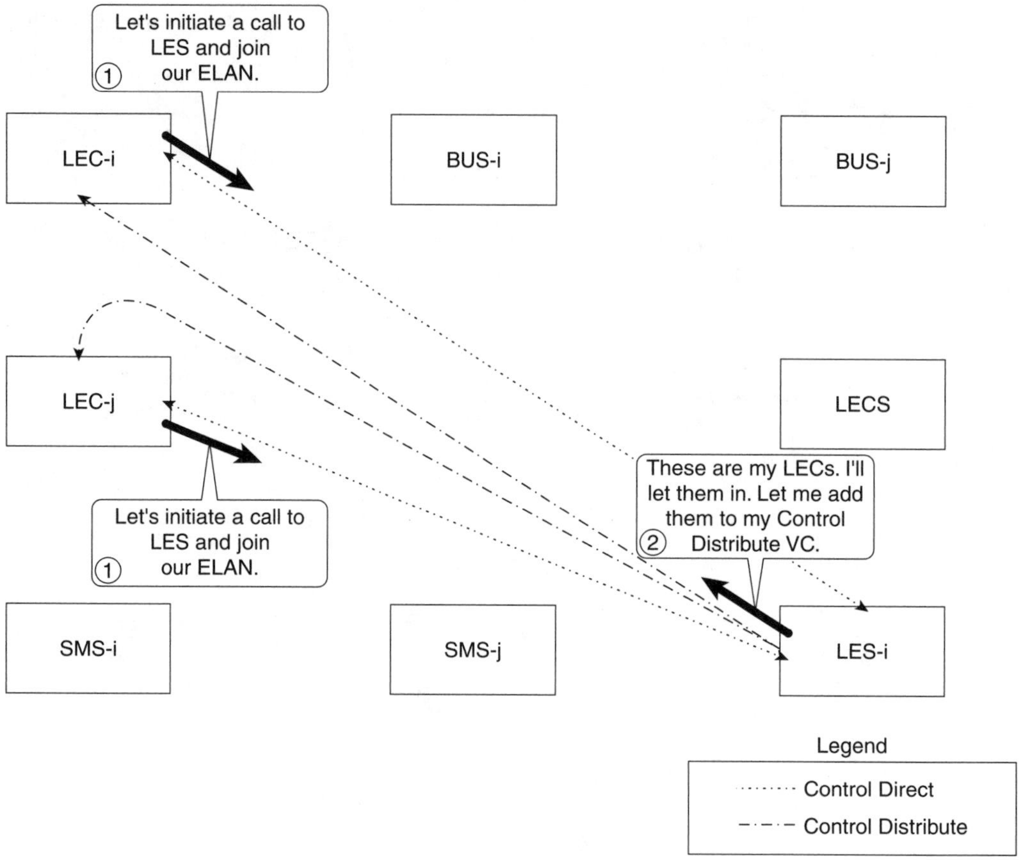

The Control Direct and Control Distribute VCs remain during the lifetime of the client.

Phase 5: Initial Registration Phase

After successfully completing the Join Phase, the LEC might attempt to register any number of unicast or multicast LAN destinations, as illustrated in Figure 5-25. The Initial Registration Phase allows the LEC to verify the uniqueness of its local address.

Figure 5-25 *Initialization Procedure: Initial Registration Phase*

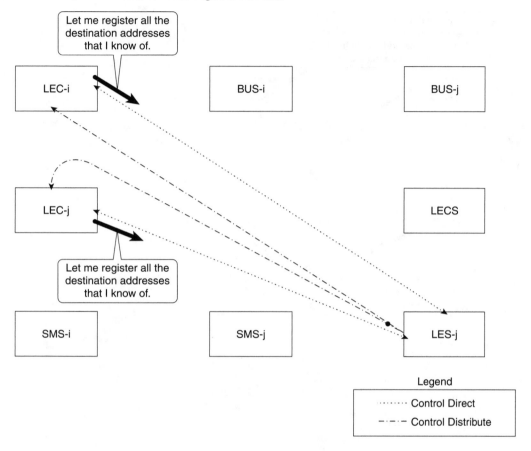

Phase 6: BUS/SMS Connect Phase

In this phase, the client must connect to the BUS and to the SMS. The client determines the address for the BUS from the LES using the address resolution procedure, LE-ARP. The LEC sends a request to the broadcast MAC address (FFFFFFFFFFFF). The LES, hearing the request, replies with the BUS ATM address, as depicted in Figure 5-26. Using LE-ARP, the client also finds the address of the SMS.

Figure 5-26 *Initialization Procedures: Bus Connect Phase, Part 1*

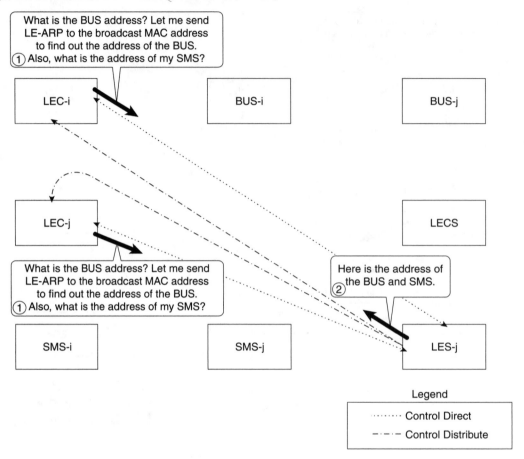

Upon learning the ATM address of the BUS, the client establishes the Default Multicast Send VC to the BUS, which is a point-to-point bidirectional VC. At the same time, knowing the SMS address (should it be used), the client sets a Selective Multicast Send point-to-point VC to the SMS. Next, the BUS connects back to the client using the Multicast Forward VCs. These are point-to-multipoint connections, as illustrated in Figure 5-27.

Figure 5-27 *Initialization Procedures: Bus Connect Phase, Part 2*

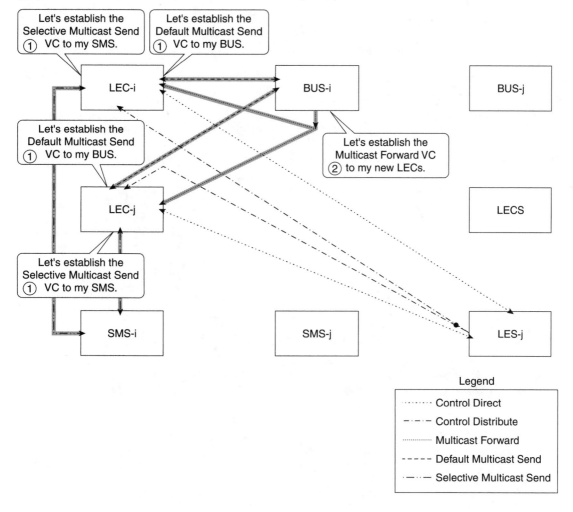

Server Redundancy Procedures

Part of LANE v2 is the provision of dynamic server redundancy capability. Server redundancy procedures run parallel to the initialization procedures and include the following steps:

Step 1 Configuration and status communication

Step 2 LECS synchronization

Step 3 LES-SMS database synchronization

Step 4 LANE control communications

Step 5 BUS data communications

Step 6 SMS data communications

Step 1: Configuration and Status Communication

As specified in the LNNI portion of LANE v2, af-lane-0112.000, Configuration Direct VCs are established from LESs and SMSs to the LECS, as illustrated in Figure 5-28.

Figure 5-28 *Server Redundancy Procedures: Configuration and Status Communication*

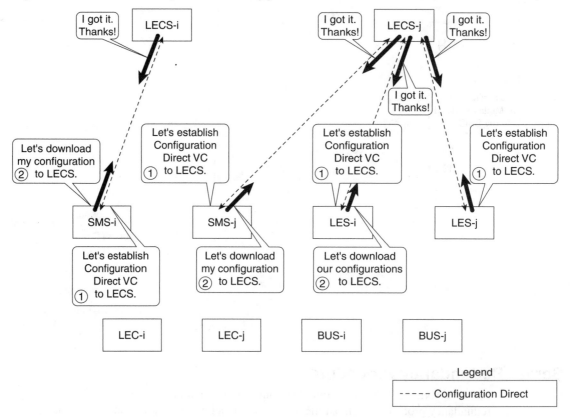

Upon establishing these VCs, each LES and SMS must download its configuration dynamically into the LECS. This configuration includes the list of neighboring LESs and SMSs, and an ID that identifies this server (LES or SMS) within the ELAN. LNNI Configuration Direct VCs stay up while the LESs and SMSs are operational. Through these VCs, LESs and SMSs notify the LECS that they are operational using the keepalive messages. The LECS sends the keepalive responses as an answer to each keepalive message. Through the help of these keepalive messages, the LECS knows which LES and SMS can be assigned to a client.

Step 2: LECS Synchronization

Because each LES or SMS connects to a single LECS, any given LECS does know about all the service components. Therefore, LECSs must exchange the information about their own LESs and SMSs. To achieve this sharing of information, LECSs set up LECS Synchronization VCs to all the other LECSs, as illustrated in Figure 5-29. LECSs learn about other LECSs either through static configurations or with the help of the ILMI.

Figure 5-29 *Server Redundancy Procedures: LECS Synchronization*

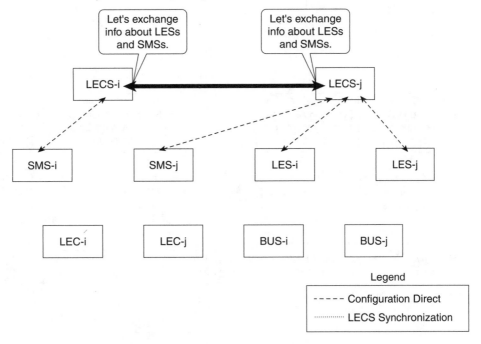

Step 3: LES-SMS Database Synchronization

Through the Configuration Direct VC, the servers (LESs and SMSs) receive a list of neighboring servers from the LECS. The neighboring server is the peer server, performing a similar function. To synchronize the neighboring databases, the LES and SMS servers establish Cache Synchronization VCs to their neighbors. The ATM Forum suggests using point-to-point VCs.

You can configure a set of servers at each LECS. Each server can have a set of neighboring servers with which it needs to synchronize. Each LECS uses a combination of the configured neighbors and the active servers for those neighbors when returning a neighbor list to its servers. The situation is so dynamic that you do not need to configure the list of servers—LECSs learn about them dynamically and send the information about them dynamically to all the servers.

When the LES or the SMS becomes operational, or when the LES or the SMS becomes aware of the new server, it establishes a Cache Synchronization VC to all of its neighbors, as illustrated in Figure 5-30.

Figure 5-30   *Servers Redundancy Procedures: LES-SMS Database Synchronization*

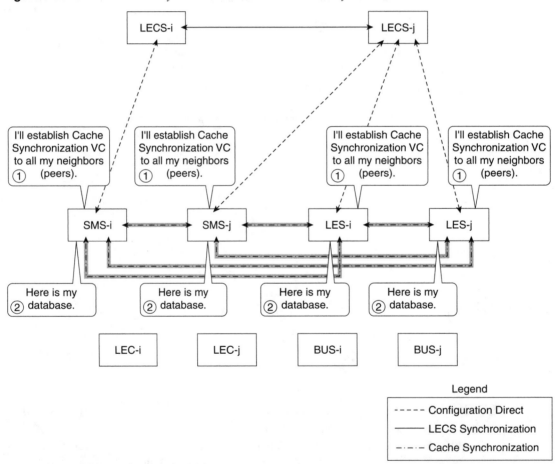

As a result of this connectivity, each server maintains a complete and up-to-date list of LNNI databases, which includes information about LESs, BUSs, SMSs, and LE clients in the ELAN.

Step 4: LANE Control Communications

During this step, each LES forwards its local LE-ARP requests for clients with unknown destinations to other LESs and to other local clients. The LES also is responsible for returning the reply to the originator. To accomplish this task, the LES either sets up a Control Coordinate VC or multiplexes the Control Coordinate VC's function with the Cache Synchronization VC, as illustrated in Figure 5-31.

Figure 5-31 *Server Redundancy Procedures: LANE Control Communications*

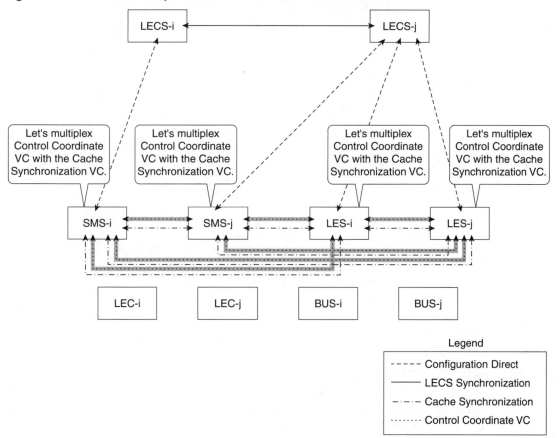

Step 5: BUS Data Communications

Each BUS is paired logically with an LES. Consequently, each LES knows the address of its associated BUS. The LES database includes the ATM address of all BUSs. BUSs establish Multicast Forward VCs to each other and to all the clients. Multicast Forward VC connectivity between a BUS and the clients is established already during the BUS Connect Phase of the initialization procedures. When redundant BUSs exist, BUS-to-BUS connections also are established using Multicast Forward VCs. A BUS forwards a data frame to other BUSs when sending a broadcast, a multicast, or a first unicast payload. A BUS cannot propagate a frame from one BUS to another, leaving this responsibility to the originating BUS. Figure 5-32 depicts BUS-to-BUS connectivity.

Figure 5-32 *Server Redundancy Procedures: BUS Data Communications*

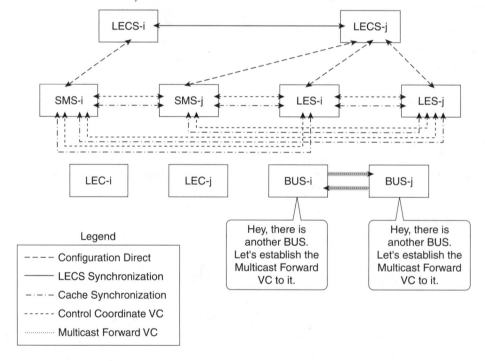

Step 6: SMS Data Communications

The purpose of an SMS is to send data to the selected multicast group (that is, a few clients) as opposed to all clients. Every SMS obtains a complete copy of the other SMSs and BUSs from the LES via Cache Synchronization VCs.

When a LUNI v2 client sends an LE-ARP request for a multicast address, the LES assigns a client to an SMS, if that SMS can help. The LES maintains a complete set of SMSs and the MAC addresses that each SMS can serve.

SMSs can operate in one of two modes—standalone or distributed, as defined by a network administrator. In the standalone mode, each SMS maintains a point-to-multipoint Multicast Forward VC to all clients associated with a particular multicast address. SMS is responsible for transmitting multicast frames to all LANE v2 clients and to all BUSs, which, in turn, pass this information to the LANE v1 clients. This step is what makes LANE v1 and LANE v2 backward compatible.

In distributed mode, more than one SMS participates. Each SMS maintains two sets of point-to-multipoint Multicast Forward VCs. One set connects the SMS with other SMSs, BUSs, and clients. The other VC set connects strictly to clients.

The distributed mode is more efficient due to the lower number of VCs required. Figure 5-33 illustrates the distributed mode of SMS data communications.

Figure 5-33 *Servers Redundancy Procedures: SMS Data Communications*

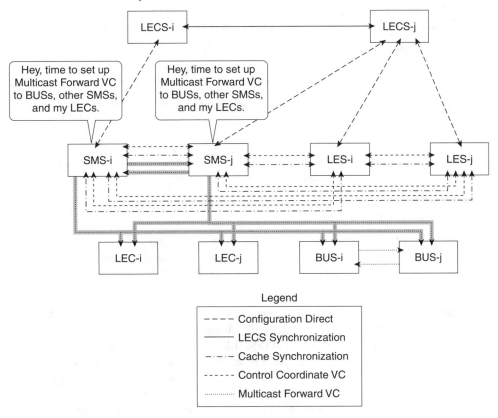

Data Transfer Procedures

Now that the initialization and server redundancy procedures are complete, the payload data transfer can take place.

Data flows connect the clients to the BUS, the SMS, and other clients. These flows actually refer to the LAN frames, be they Ethernet or Token Ring LAN frames. The Ethernet or Token Ring frames carry traffic that could be an upper-layer application such as Telnet for example.

The following sections examine the data transfer phase and the Flush Message protocol, which ensures that data frames are delivered in the same order in which they are transmitted.

Data Transfer Phase

Figure 5-34 examines the flow of Telnet packets/frames across the LANE network.

Figure 5-34 presents HostA connected to LECi and HostB connected to LECj. LECi and LECj could be any Layer 2 switch, but for our purposes, let's say they are Catalyst 5000 switches. The steps for the Data Transfer Phase of LANE are as follows:

Step 1   HostA wants to Telnet to HostB. Telnet is an IP application that requires IP ARP first.

Step 2   HostA sends an IP ARP broadcast searching for HostB's MAC address. The ARP frame has an unknown MAC address destination and a source MAC address of HostA.

Step 3   LECi hears the IP ARP broadcast and forwards it to the BUSi, using the Default Multicast Send VC.

Step 4   BUSi, hearing a broadcast and being a broadcast server, propagates the IP ARP broadcast to all the clients and the other BUSs using Multicast Forward VCs. The IP ARP broadcast carries HostA's IP address and its MAC. The question is what is the HostB's MAC address?

Step 5   LECj, being one of the clients of BUSi, hears the message. HostB is attached directly to LECj. LECj, being a transparent bridge, learns the MAC address of HostB. If LECj has not learned the HostB MAC address, it propagates the broadcast to HostB's segment. Host B hears and replies. In any case, LECj knows HostB's MAC address. LECj also knows the source MAC address of HostA from the IP ARP request. What LECj does not know is the source's ATM address. Hence, it asks LESj via the Control Direct VC with the help of an LE-ARP request about the ATM address of the HostA.

Figure 5-34 *Data Transfer over LANE*

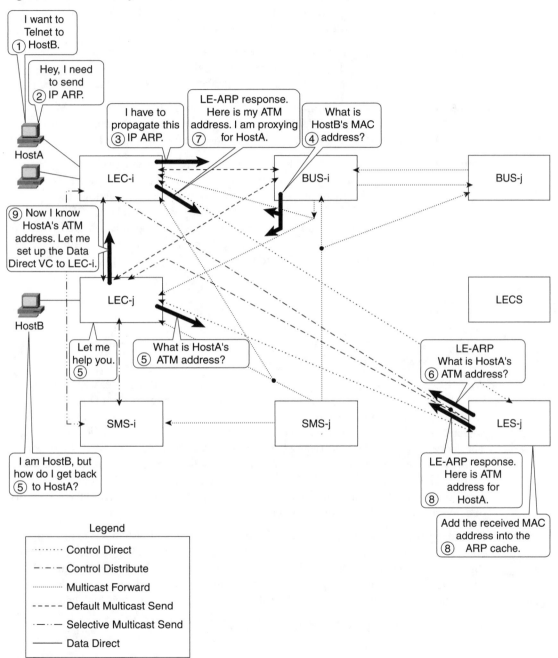

Step 6   Assume that LESj does not have an answer for LECj. This forces LESj to send out an LE-ARP request using the Control Distribute VC to all clients, asking for the ATM address for HostA.

Step 7   LECi hears the LE-ARP request. It knows that HostA is its Ethernet client. Therefore, LECi replies to LESj on behalf of HostA (proxy) via the Control Direct VC. This reply is called an LE-ARP response.

Step 8   LESj receives the information and adds the HostA MAC address to ATM address mapping into its ARP cache. Also, using Control Distribute VCs, LESj sends HostA's ATM address to all the clients—that is, to LECj.

Step 9   LECj receives the ATM address for HostA. Remember the goal of all these steps? HostA wants to Telnet to HostB, so it sends out an IP ARP, which LECj and, therefore, HostB received. Now, when LECj knows the ATM address of HostA, which is really an ATM address on LECi, LECj can reply by setting up a Data Direct VC to LECi. The goal is achieved! HostA gets a response to its IP ARP. The Telnet protocol can now begin using the direct VC from LECi to LECj.

Flush Message Protocol

Figure 5-34 illustrates the sequence of events that take place when a Telnet session starts up from HostA to HostB. Prior to issuing a Telnet, IP ARP must be resolved. Upon IP ARP resolution, HostA sends out a Telnet frame.

When LECi receives the Telnet frame, it can send frames to the LAN destination using the Default Multicast Send VC (going to the BUS) prior to its using the Data Direct VC (going to LECj). This creates a problem. Remember that ATM is connection-oriented, so cells do not have sequence numbers. Therefore, all cells must arrive at the destination in sequence. The concept of multiple paths (using Default Multicast Send VC—via BUS—and Data Direct VC—via LECj) compromises the sequential delivery characteristic of ATM. The solution to this problem is the ATM Forum Flush Message protocol. The Flush Message protocol prevents total chaos in cell arrival at the destination. It helps avoid the possibility of delivering unicast frames out of order.

Prior to any use of a Data Direct VC, the sender must transmit a Flush message down the old path. Then it sets table entries to stop any further frames from traveling to that destination. The Flush message is a very special frame, different from a data frame and recognizable as such. The sender will not be happy until it receives the sent Flush frame from the destination. When the sender receives the returned Flush message, the use of the new path can begin.

There are two types of Flush Protocol messages:

- Flush Request
- Flush Response

Using the example in Figure 5-35, the following are the steps involved in Flush Message protocol:

Step 1   The source client, LECi, sends a Flush Request message to the BUSi via the Default Multicast Send VC.

Step 2   BUSi distributes the Flush Request message using the Multicast Forward VC to all the clients and the other BUSs, should they be involved. A BUS never forwards the Flush Request message to other BUSs if it received the message from another BUS.

Step 3   When a targeted client receives the request, it responds with the Flush Response message using the Control Direct VC. Other clients simply ignore the request message.

Step 4   When LESj receives the Flush Response message, it forwards the frame to the client that is specified in the Flush Request message (LECi in this example). If LESj does not know about that particular client, it simply forwards the message to all the clients it knows about.

Step 5   Finally, the LECi receives the Flush Response message. Now, it can start using the Data Direct VC to the LECj.

Summary

This chapter closely examined LANE v2 architecture and functionality. LANE is a dynamic Layer 2 extension of single broadcast domains (VLANs) across ATM networks. These broadcast domains are called *ELANs* when extended across ATM using LANE architecture. Because LANE is emulating Layer 2, it can handle multiple Layer 3 protocols.

When compared to LANE v1, LANE v2 handles ATM QoS, Layer 2 multicasting, and VC multiplexing, and it is fully redundant. LANE is based on client/server architecture. In trying to emulate Layer 2 functionality, LANE architecture includes services to handle broadcast traffic and traffic to unknown destinations (BUS), multicast traffic (SMS), and MAC- to-ATM address resolution (LES), and it includes directory assistance of various ELANs (LECS). LANE v2 architecture uses three types of VCs: control, synchronization, and data. The control VCs are used for housekeeping reasons, the synchronization VCs are used to synchronize the servers' databases, and the data VCs are used to carry the actual data.

LANE architecture allows you to preserve the investment into current topologies and technologies—the natively attached Ethernet and Token Ring hosts do not need any changes in the hardware or software. The legacy devices simply are attached to the LANE-aware devices that extend legacy topologies, bringing their broadcast domains across distances using ATM networks. LANE architecture is used in campus solutions carrying only data or multimedia applications.

Figure 5-35 *Flush Message Protocol Functionality*

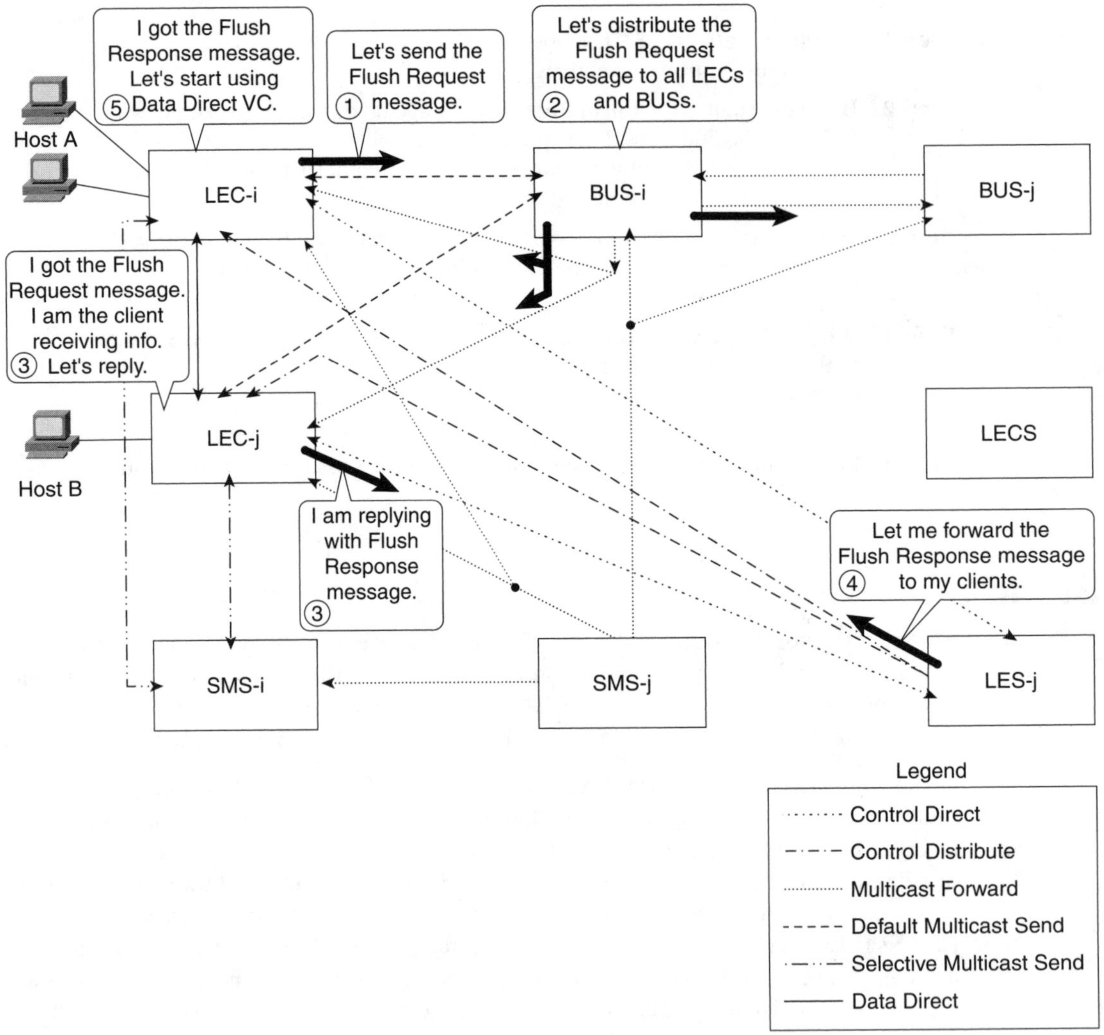

Review Questions

1 What is an ELAN? How does it compare to a VLAN?

2 What processing architecture does a LANE implementation use?

3 What is the purpose of the LECS, LES, BUS, SMS, and LEC?

4 How can you divide various LANE VCs?

5   What VCs are generated in LANE?

6   What are the differences between LANE v1 and LANE v2?

7   What is the Cache Synchronization VC used for?

8   How does LANE ensure that the cells are received in order at the destination?

9   How many BUSs and LESs can your LANE have?

10   How many LECSs can your LANE have?

"Without a purpose, nothing should be done"—Marcus Aurelius (121–180)

"There is one thing which gives radiance to everything. It is the idea of something around the corner"—G.K. Chesterton (1874–1936)

"The most absurd and reckless aspirations have sometimes led to extraordinary success"—Vauvenargues (1715–1747)

After completing this chapter, you should be able to understand the following:

- **Role of MPOA**—Where MPOA permits multiple Layer 3 networks, positioned over ATM, to carry internetworking traffic using shortcuts or cut-through routing. MPOA plays the role of a virtual router stretched across an ATM domain.

- **MPOA Architecture**—Consists of three major components—Next Hop Resolution Protocol (NHRP), LANE v2, and Multicast Address Resolution Server (MARS). The MPOA client/server architecture and the types of connections are discussed.

- **MPOA Layer 3 Protocol Support**—Includes IP and IPX protocols. Issues of Layer 3 routing protocols convergence, IP Strict Source Routing, and a variety of IPX Layer 2 encapsulations are discussed.

- **MPOA Data Transfer Process**—Demonstrates a trace of a packet through the MPOA architecture.

CHAPTER 6

Multiprotocol over ATM (MPOA)

As discussed in Chapter 5, "LAN Emulation (LANE)," LANE allows Layer 2 connectivity (between broadcast domains) to be extended across ATM clouds in a seamless manner, with no changes to the edge devices' platforms or the applications. When applications use Layer 3 protocols, such as IP, IPX, Datagram Delivery Protocol (DDP used by AppleTalk architecture), and so on, to send data from one broadcast domain to another, LANE, being a single broadcast domain, is no longer a viable option due to its Layer 2 nature. Layer 3 protocols require that hosts on different broadcast networks communicate via intermediate routers, which slows down the packet throughput significantly when packets are sent between various ELANs. Why? Simply because each router has to reassemble cells of the Layer 3 packet for routing, and then segment the packet back into cells again for ATM forwarding.

This is where Multiprotocol over ATM (MPOA) comes into the picture to handle the Layer 3 functionality that LANE cannot handle. Although LANE extends VLANs throughout the ATM network, providing seamless intra-VLAN connectivity, MPOA is a dynamic internetworking method between logical Layer 3 domains, which are based on Layer 3 addressing, across an ATM cloud. MPOA allows inter-ELAN (VLAN) connectivity by direct forwarding of Layer 3 packets from one ELAN to another, without involving any intermediate reassembly and segmentation procedures. Within a subnet, MPOA uses LANE. Using LANE and MPOA, corporations can introduce new applications that require lower latency, better predictability, and various levels of QoS.

MPOA is a rare instance of joint development by the ATM Forum and the IETF, with its prime emphasis on IP as a Layer 3 protocol. The ATM Forum released the first MPOA specification, MPOA 1.0 (AF-MPOA-0087.000), in July 1997. Almost two years later, in May 1999, the ATM Forum released the MPOA 1.1 specification (AF-MPOA-0114.000). Although the MPOA 1.0 concentrates on IP, it extends the specification to IPX. This chapter is based on the MPOA 1.1 specification.

NOTE You can find the approved ATM Forum specifications at www.atmforum.com/atmforum/specs/approved.html.

The MPOA definition includes IETF's developments on NHRP (RFC 2332, RFC 2677, RFC 2333, RFC 2603, RFC 2336, RFC 2491) and MARS (RFC 2443, RFC 2022, RFC 2149).

MPOA 1.1 introduced the following functional enhancements to MPOA architecture:

- NHRP Authentication (refer to Chapter 3, "ATM Reference Model: Higher Layers," for a description of NHRP)
- MPOA Authentication

MPOA 1.0 is based on the draft of the NHRP RFC, which provides an optional authentication. MPOA 1.1 is based on the finalized NHRP RFC 2332.

MPOA optional authentication provides the compatibility with NHRP authentication, should it be used.

When you grasp the principles of the main building blocks of MPOA, MPOA becomes a very simple and sound concept. Just look at MPOA as a synthesis of bridging and routing over ATM. MPOA uses LANE for the bridging function within a single broadcast domain. When it comes to Layer 3 forwarding, MPOA adopts NHRP, which gives MPOA the capability to forward traffic between various broadcast domains with a net delay of a single router hop over ATM. The actual complexity of the architecture lies in the integration details.

Role of MPOA

Traditionally, computers break down data into packets and send it over LANs and WANs, using Layer 3 technology (routers). Each packet is processed by a router, which forwards it to another router if the destination is not an immediately attached network. Because every single packet must be processed every hop of the way, the process can add significant delays to the delivery of the packet. Just picture the scenario illustrated in the Figure 6-1.

Host A, located on network 111, sends a file to Host X, located on network 333. Host A breaks down the data into packets, encapsulates them into Ethernet frames, and, upon discovery of the gateway, sends them to Router A. Router A receives the Ethernet frame, decapsulates it, and examines Layer 3 information that contains the logical Layer 3 addressing. For Router A to forward the packet to the next hop, which leads the packet to the desired destination, Router A examines its routing tables, determines that the packet must be sent through the atm 1/0 interface, does all the necessary conversions into ATM cells, and presents them to the ATM network. Should the application involve 100 packets to be sent from Host A to Host X, Router A (as do the other routers) examines the routing tables to understand the *next-hop* interface and its corresponding Layer 2 encapsulation. This is the very original Layer 3 routing methodology.

Years ago, Cisco modified the routing process significantly with various enhancements to the routers' architectures, by introducing various caches within a router and distributed processing, creating a distributed router positioned within the same chassis. Figure 6-2 elaborates on the distributed router idea.

Figure 6-1   *Traditional Layer 3 Routing*

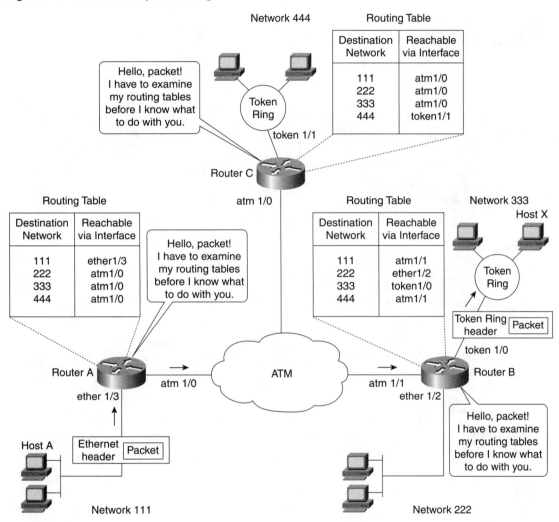

Figure 6-2 *Distributed Router*

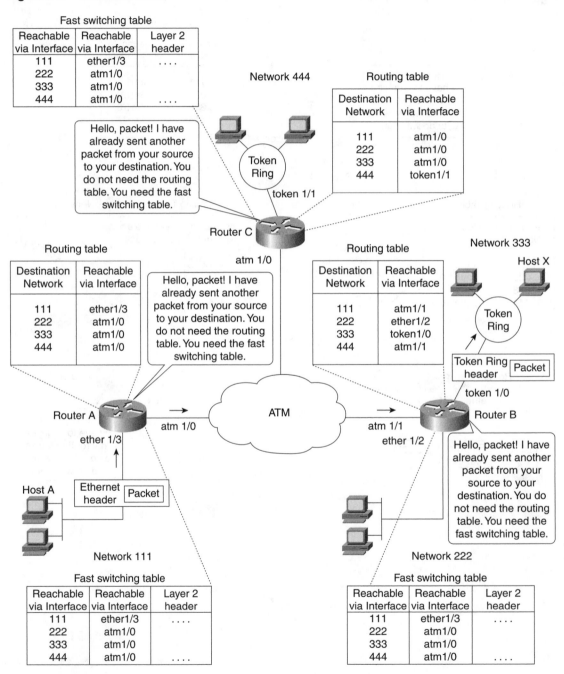

Let's assume that Host A needs to send 100 packets to Host X. Only the first packet can be routed the traditional way by Routers A and B. The remaining 99 packets can be fast-switched, silicon-switched, or Netflow-switched, depending on the router's model (the versatility of the switching modes with cached information depends on the Cisco router type).

Now, let's focus on the router's processes. The very first packet from a source to a destination has to undergo a routing table lookup (route processing), which is a CPU-intensive process. Every other consecutive packet bypasses that. It uses the cached information (forwarding table) that is created when the first packet is sent. Some Cisco routers, such as the 7500 and 12000 series routers, cache the forwarding information on the interfaces, thereby bringing the information as close as possible to the source/destination ports. These types of routers are called *distributed routers* and this type of routing is called *distributed routing*.

MPOA takes the idea of the distributed router, extends it over the ATM network, and turns it into a virtual router, as illustrated in Figure 6-3.

If each router has the routing intelligence in traditional Layer 3 routing (that is, it can perform route processing), MPOA architecture dictates that a Route Server represents the intelligence of the overall topology and dynamically tracks the topology of the entire network with the assistance from a dynamic routing protocol. This can be viewed as separating the route processing and fast/silicon/Netflow switching functionalities and positioning them into separate physical entities, where the Route Server performs the Route Processing functionality. In the centralized management environments, this could be very plausible.

NOTE   Here are the formulas of traditional and virtual routers:

Traditional router = (route server + packet forwarding) in a single physical box.

Virtual router = route server + packet forwarding in different boxes.

Because MPOA architecture is based on LANE v2, MPOA provides QoS with guaranteed bandwidth. In an MPOA environment, LAN traffic is aggregated into various shortcut ATM paths.

MPOA separates routing and forwarding processes, thus providing a very scalable architecture that is very useful in mission-critical applications and multimedia applications (such as videoconferencing, distance learning, image transfers for hospital use, and so on). Separating routing and forwarding processes allows MPOA to reduce the cumulative latency in a multiprotocol routed network by reducing the number of intermediate hops, thus allowing the traffic to be forwarded to its destination over an ATM VC with a delay of a single router hop.

Figure 6-3 *MPOA Virtual Router*

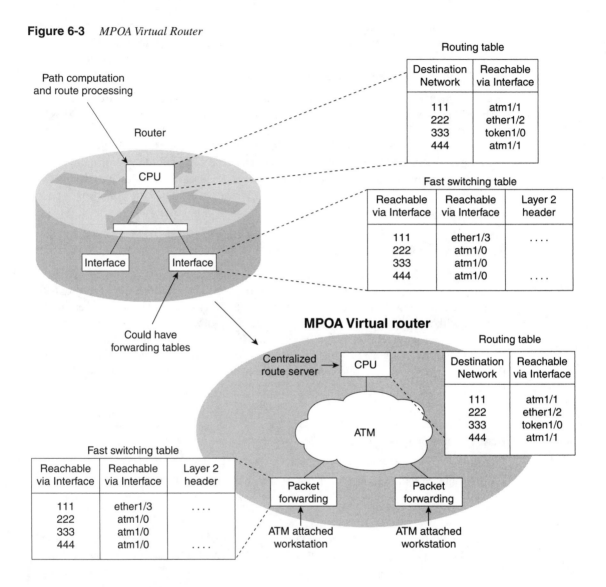

MPOA Architecture

MPOA integrates LANE and NHRP, consequently enabling dynamic internetworking over ATM VCs. This integration provides a method of seamless communication among various broadcast domains using a virtual router.

Path computation is a router's job; whereas, any network device can do packet forwarding along a pre-established path. MPOA banks on this idea and establishes a direct path or connection from one port to another over an ATM network.

Similar to LANE, MPOA is an application to ATM that uses LANE v2 as its Layer 2, as depicted in Figure 6-4. The responsibility of MPOA is to simulate various processes of Layer 3 networks, for example, finding gateway routers.

Figure 6-4   *MPOA Protocol Stack*

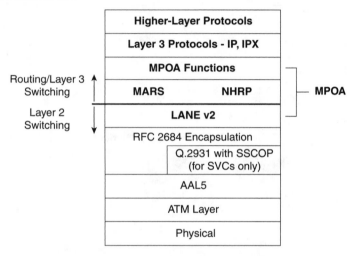

MPOA Building Blocks

The three building blocks of MPOA are as follows:

- **LANE v2**—Supports Layer 2 forwarding
- **NHRP**—(RFC 2332) Supports Layer 3 cut-through routing
- **MARS**—(RFC 2022, RFC 2149) Supports Layer 3 multipoint/multicast communication

LANE v2

Chapter 5 expands on LANE v2, which is the foundation for MPOA. LANE v2 provides QoS, Layer 2 redundancy, and Layer 2 forwarding mechanism.

NHRP

The NHRP (RFC 2332), which is another one of the building blocks of MPOA, provides for cut-through routing, thus avoiding multihop routing. Cut-through routing results in reduced delays when transferring packets between several broadcast domains, as described in Chapter 3. Figure 6-5 illustrates NHRP functionality.

Figure 6-5 *MPOA Building Blocks: NHRP*

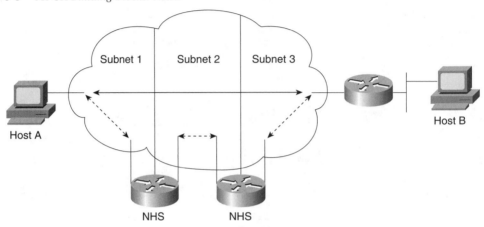

MARS

The third building block of MPOA is MARS, as defined in RFCs 2022 and 2149. There are two methods that are specified to handle the internetwork layer multicast—either have a meshed point-to-multipoint VC through the ATM domain or have a proxy Multicast Server (MCS) that is responsible for distributing the data to the appropriate end systems. This section focuses on the second option—the use of the MCS.

MARS, illustrated in Figure 6-6, allows dynamic IP multicast group registration for support of Layer 3 multicast over ATM.

MARS maintains a mapping of Layer 3 multicast group addresses to ATM addresses. You can say that MARS is an extension of the ATM ARP Server introduced in RFC 1577 (obsoleted by RFC 2225). Chapter 3 elaborates on the ATM ARP server further. Hosts in the ATM network use MARS to resolve Layer 3 multicast addresses into ATM addresses. The domain for MARS is specified as the MARS-cluster, which is defined in RFC 2022 as the set of ATM interfaces that participate in direct ATM connections to achieve multicasting. MARS serves end systems in a MARS-cluster within a single broadcast domain or subnet, where the word *cluster* refers to the set of endpoints that choose to use the same MARS to register their membership to a multicast group.

Figure 6-6   *MPOA Building Blocks: MARS*

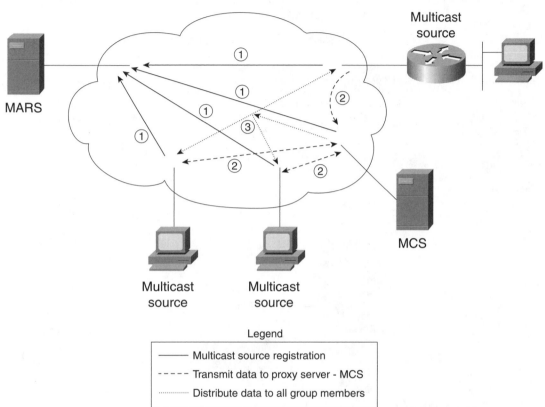

As illustrated in Figure 6-6, all multicast sources and MCSs register themselves with the MARS (designated as Step 1). The MCS acts as a proxy server multicasting data received from a source to the group members in the cluster. All multicast sources send the data to the MCS (designated as Step 2 in Figure 6-6), which then, acting on behalf of the sender (this is why it is called *proxy*), forwards it further to all the group members in the cluster (Step 3).

MPOA Client/Server Environment

As LANE deploys client/server architecture to simulate a single broadcast domain, MPOA deploys client/server architecture to simulate Layer 3 forwarding processes between multiple broadcast domains. In any client/server architecture, there are clients and servers. MPOA provides MPOA Clients (MPCs) and MPOA Servers (MPSs), as illustrated in Figure 6-7. MPOA defines the series of protocols that are used for MPCs and MPSs to communicate.

Figure 6-7 *MPOA Client/Server Environment*

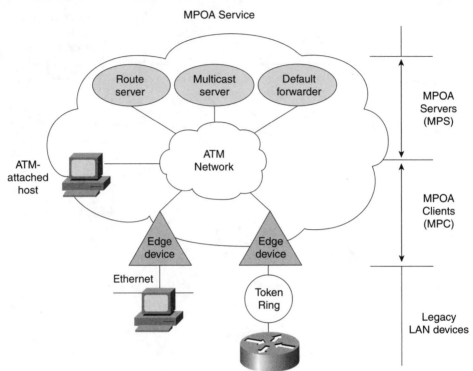

The MPOA Servers consists of three main components:

- **Route servers**—Perform routing function for the MPCs.
- **Default forwarders**—Perform default forwarding.
- **Multicast servers**—Perform multicast function for the MPCs.

There are two types of MPOA Clients:

- **Edge devices**—ATM-attached devices that connect traditional LANs to the MPOA-capable networks.
- **ATM hosts**—MPOA-enhanced LANE hosts directly attached to the MPOA network.

MPOA architecture allows for full interoperability with existing Layer 3 devices and the Layer 3 routing protocols, such as OSPF, EIGRP, and so on.

MPOA Components

Now let's discuss the MPOA components in more detail. Based on a client/server architecture, MPOA architecture dictates the need for two logical components—clients and servers.

MPOA Client

An MPC is a user of MPOA services. MPC functionality can reside in any ATM-attached edge device—a host, a LAN switch, or a router. The primary function of the MPC is "to source and sink" (allocate the circuit and nail it) internetwork shortcuts (AF-MPOA-0114.000), which implies that the MPC must be able to perform Layer 3 forwarding, but does not have to run the internetwork routing protocol. Recall that MPOA separates Route Processing, which requires every packet to examine the routing tables, and packet forwarding, and puts these functions into separate boxes.

Figure 6-8 illustrates the packet flow from Network A to Network B. When MPC 1 detects this flow of packets, it requests the information required to establish a shortcut so that these packets can reach the destination directly, using a shortcut VC. The very first packet from Network A to Network B transpires through Router 1, which serves an MPS function. Remember, the first packet going through the router is always process switched, which is the function of the MPS in the MPOA architecture. MPC 1 utilizes the NHRP protocol to request the shortcut information.

Figure 6-8 *MPC Functionality*

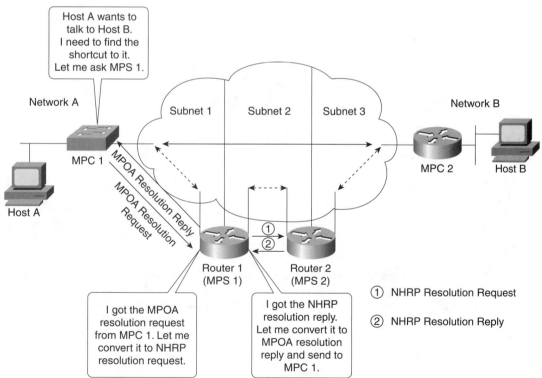

MPOA Server

The MPS is the second logical component of MPOA. The MPS is collocated with a Layer 3 device (router) and acts as a route server for MPOA target resolution requested by MPCs. A Layer 3 router acts as a default forwarder. The default router forwards the packets outside subnet boundaries.

MPS provides Layer 3 forwarding information to MPCs, as illustrated in Figure 6-8. MPS functionality includes the use of the Next Hop Server (NHS), as defined in the NHRP specification. When MPC 1 sends an MPOA Resolution Request to MPS 1, this MPS translates the request to the NHRP resolution request and forwards it on the routed path. On the way back, when the NHRP resolution reply returns to the MPS 1, it translates the reply to the MPOA resolution reply and returns it to the MPC 1.

MPOA Client/Server Relationship with LANE Components

Because MPOA uses LANE architecture within a single broadcast domain, the MPC can service one or more LANE clients (LECs), as illustrated in Figure 6-9.

Figure 6-9   *Relationship Between LECs and MPC*

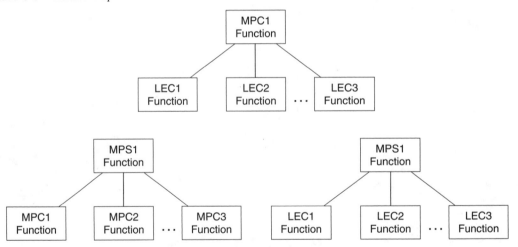

Notice that a single LEC can be associated with only one MPC. However, each MPC can communicate with more than one LEC. Likewise, a single MPS can be associated with more than one LEC; however, an LEC can be associated with only a single MPS. Why? Simply because multiple LECs belong to a single broadcast domain, which is represented by MPCs and MPSs.

MPOA Redundancy

MPOA provides resiliency because multiple routers can service as MPSs and/or MPCs. Hence, there is no single point of failure. With MPOA, traditional routers, each acting as the MPS for its respective network or subnetwork, work together through the exchange of common protocols,

just as they did before the introduction of MPOA. Also, each MPC subnet can have a backup
MPS by employing the same method used to provide inter-VLAN router redundancy—the Hot
Standby Router Protocol (HSRP). This feature is available for Cisco ATM LANE networks.

MPOA Connections

MPOA uses two types of connection flows: Control and Data flows. Control flows are used
for housekeeping of the MPOA architecture; whereas, Data flows are used for packet
transfer between various hosts. Both flow types use Logical Link Control (LLC)/
Subnetwork Access Protocol (SNAP) encapsulation, as defined in RFC 2684. Because
LLC/SNAP encapsulation permits a single VC to handle multiple protocols, it results in
efficient VC utilization in an MPOA environment.

Because the MPOA protocols require LANE transport between its components, all
LANE v2 control flows are applicable to MPOA. As discussed in Chapter 5, each LEC has
a Configuration Direct VC to the LECS. Because the MPC and/or MPS includes an LEC,
each MPC and/or MPS has a Configuration VC (called *flow*, as defined in the ATM Forum)
to the LECS, as illustrated in Figure 6-10. With the help of the Configuration flow VC, the
MPC and the MPS retrieve configuration information.

Figure 6-10 *MPOA Control and Data Flows*

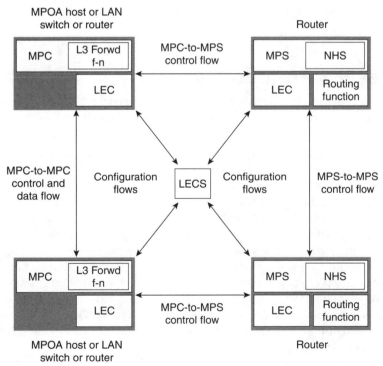

Source: ATM Forum MPOA 1.1 Specification

The flow types between MPOA clients and servers vary depending on the tasks to be performed. For example, MPC-to-MPS communication is done via Control flow only; whereas, MPC-to-MPC communication is accomplished using Control and Data flows. Table 6-1 lists all the MPOA connection flows and their purposes.

Table 6-1   *MPOA Connection Flow Types*

Connection Flow	Purpose

Configuration:
  MPC-to-LECS
  MPS-to-LECS
	Used to retrieve configuration information from the LECS.

MPC-to-MPS Control	Manages the MPC cache, which contains shortcut information that enables cut-through routing.
MPS-to-MPS Control	Standard Layer 3 routing protocols and NHRP use this control flow.
MPC-to-MPC Control	When the egress MPC receives misdirected packets from the ingress MPC, the egress MPC sends the invalidate cache signal to the ingress MPC using MPC-to-MPC Control flow.
MPC-to-MPC Data	Used for data transfer between MPCs over MPOA, using shortcut VCs.
MPC-to-NHS Data	Used to send unicast data to the NHS, which is then passed to another MPC.

MPOA Layer 3 Protocol Support

MPOA has a lot of challenges, one of which is to extend the architecture to all Layer 3 protocols (other challenges include providing multicast routing, cut-through routing, and so on).

CAUTION   Be careful not to underestimate the functionality of MPOA. Although requiring routers to perform the initial internetwork routing between various broadcast domains, MPOA performs cut-through routing for the consecutive packets of a conversation. It is a very powerful mechanism with very high throughput. Positioning 1.25 Layer switching gear—ATM—into the core and Layer 2 and 3 switching gear—LAN switches and routers—at the edges of your networks, you create a very high throughput machine that understands and implements QoS natively. By contrast, Classical IP (RFC 2225) concentrates only on IP; whereas, MPOA expands the idea to all Layer 3 protocols. Furthermore, MPOA provides QoS (because it uses LANE v2, which understands QoS), which Classical IP does not. Although Classical IP can work in conjunction with an NHRP algorithm, it does not provide cut-through routing mechanism dynamically as MPOA does. Also, MPOA architecture is fully redundant.

Each Layer 3 protocol provides its own logical addressing and forwarding function. Also, every protocol uses different encapsulations on top of LANs. For example, IPX uses four different encapsulations over Ethernet. Due to all these differences, MPOA components are required to have protocol-specific knowledge. This enables MPOA to perform flow detection, address resolution, and shortcut data transformation. MPC-to-MPC shortcut transformations are defined individually for every protocol that is supported.

Routing Protocol Interaction

Routing protocols, such as OSPF, EIGRP, IP RIP, IPX RIP, and so on, are executed between routers across MPOA domains in a standard way. The difference here lies in NHRP requests and replies. NHS supplies the routing information to MPOA through the help of the MPS. MPSs interact with NHSs to initiate and answer resolution requests. The whole objective of the NHSs and MPSs is to maintain the most up-to-date forwarding information so that optimal cut-through routing is possible. If there is a change in the network topology, the NHSs' and, consequently, the co-located MPSs' databases are updated accordingly. Next, MPSs purge or update relevant MPC caches, as illustrated in 6-11.

Figure 6-11 *MPOA and Routing Protocol Interaction*

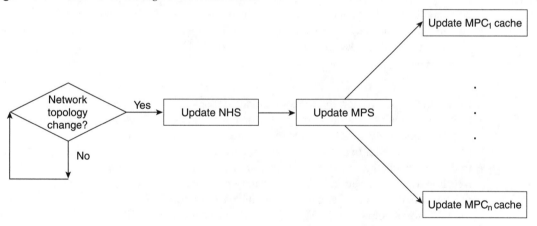

NOTE   It is important to associate ATM QoS within MPOA properly. Because LANE v2 provides QoS within the ATM infrastructure and MPOA uses LANE v2 for intranetwork connectivity, MPOA provides QoS to its edge devices. When Layer 3 routing protocols converge or reconverge, the MPS's and MPC's routers (Layer 3) are fully unaware of QoS. Why? Simply because traditional routing does not offer QoS. MPOA's QoS goes as far as intra-ATM connectivity, which means setting up VCs from Location A to Location B (cut-through routing or not) using the paths within the ATM network that guarantees the required ATM throughput.

IP Handling

The MPOA specification supports IPv4 and IPv6. MPOA carries IP packets that use three standard formats of frames—Ethernet, IEEE 802.3, or IEEE 802.5 carrying IP packets.

NOTE   IPv6 over ATM has not been specified in the ATM Forum specification. However, RFC 2491 and RFC 2492 provide specific details on how to apply the IPv6 over ATM architectures. The standard extends the use of MARS and NHRP, which are the main ingredients of MPOA Layer 3 architecture, to IPv6. This extends MPOA to IPv6.

Co-located with a router, the MPS processes IP packets just as a regular router does. The MPC's role is slightly more complicated than the MPS's role. Beyond performing basic IP forwarding, the MPC must be able to forward a packet that "wants" to be forwarded using Strict Source Route. In this case, what if the MPC does not have access to the routing table to determine whether the next hop given in the Strict Source Routing option is the current next hop to the destination? This uncertainty prevents the MPC from forming an independent decision on what to do with the packet—forward it or drop it. In this instance, the MPC seeks help from the MPS and sends the packet to the MPS via LANE. If the MPC is aware of the next hop, then it exercises the shortcut. This extra step of packet forwarding from the MPC to the MPS does not modify the TTL field in the packet header.

NOTE   By definition, should a packet have a Strict Source Route, which means the entire path from source to destination is in its header, a router must forward the packet, as identified in the Source Route. If the router does not have a route, as identified in the Source Route, the packet is dropped.

Should the ingress MPC encounter some errors, it must send the applicable ICMP message (for example, *message unreachable*, *time exceeded*, and so on). In addition, the ingress MPC might fragment the packets if the incoming packets exceed the accepted maximum transmission unit (MTU). If the MPC must exercise fragmentation, it should be careful enough to avoid packet misordering. This fragmentation problem can be avoided very easily by using a single path for a given flow of packets.

IPX Handling

The MPOA specification supports the IPX environment. IPX Ethernet encapsulation is quite unique. IPX uses four encapsulation types: raw Ethernet (Novell proprietary), Ethernet II, LLC, and LLC/SNAP. MPOA handles IPX encapsulations over a shortcut using three methods: RFC 2684, Tagged, and RFC 2684 NULL. The ingress MPC (where an inbound data flow enters the MPOA system) removes the LAN encapsulations and adds one of the shortcut encapsulations. The egress MPC (where the outbound data flow exits the MPOA system) removes the shortcut encapsulations and adds the LAN encapsulation.

NOTE   The MPOA 1.1 specification refers to RFC 1483, not RFC 2684. This is because RFC 2684 was released after the MPOA 1.1 specification.

One of the characteristics of IPX RIP is hop count limitation. Because MPOA performs IPX routing, the MPS must include a hop counter. IPX does not have Time to Live (TTL), like IP does. Instead, IPX uses Transport Control (TC), which counts up to 16 or 128 hops (IPX hosts start up with the TC equal to 0). To behave natively, the ingress MPC must increment the TC before sending the IPX packet. When TC reaches the limit of 16, in RIP's case, or 128, in the case of NetWare Link Service Protocol (NLSP), the MPC must drop the packet.

MPOA Data Transfer Process

To better understand the MPOA data transfer process, take a look at the sample scenario illustrated in Figure 6-12.

The MPOA network consists of two ELANs, ELAN1 and ELAN2, which implies two VLANs. The communication of the hosts within an ELAN is performed using LANE architecture. Intra-VLAN flows use LANE address resolution and data transfer, as illustrated in Figure 6-12.

For interVLAN communication, there are two data transfer modes: default flow and shortcut flow. With default flow, the MPC sends the data to the router, avoiding direct client-to-client VC connectivity, as illustrated in Figure 6-13.

Figure 6-12 *2MPOA Data Transfer: Intra-VLAN*

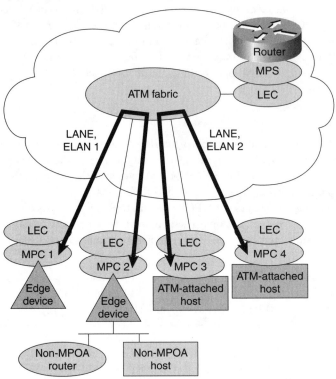

This data transfer mode is similar to the route process switching mode in a Cisco router, where every router must examine the routing table before sending a packet out of the interface.

The interVLAN communication using the shortcut flow is much more efficient. As shown in Figure 6-14, ingress MPC 1 establishes VC connectivity with MPS 1 and sends an MPOA resolution request to ingress MPS 1. MPS 1 translates the MPOA resolution request to the NHRP resolution request and forwards the request on the routed path to the MPS 2, which is the egress MPS. Because MPS 2 is egress, it translates the NHRP resolution request to an MPOA cache imposition request and sends it to egress MPC 2. Egress MPC 2 responds to the cache imposition request by returning an MPOA cache imposition reply to egress MPS 2. Then MPS 2 translates the MPOA cache imposition reply to an NHRP resolution reply, and forwards the reply on the routed path to the ingress MPS address. When the ingress MPS 1 receives the NHRP resolution reply, it translates the reply to an MPOA resolution reply and returns it to MPC 1. MPC 1 caches the information.

Figure 6-13 *MPOA Data Transfer: InterVLAN, Default Flow*

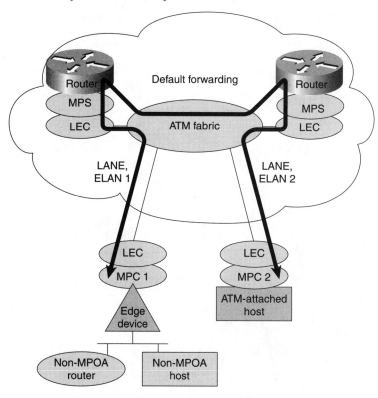

MPS 1 provides the Layer 3 forwarding information to MPC 1. When the next packet enters MPC 1, MPC 1 examines its Layer 3 header and realizes that it can handle it using the shortcut. Then, it simply sends it to the MPC 2 directly, as illustrated in Figure 6-15.

The mission of cut-through routing is accomplished. Every consecutive packet is now going directly from source to destination with the required QoS along an ATM shortcut.

Summary

This chapter focused on the role of MPOA and its architecture, and presented examples of MPOA traffic flows. MPOA is a Layer 3 internetworking method that allows connectivity of multiple broadcast domains (networks) across ATM clouds in one hop. The concept is quite simple: connectivity from any network to any other network, not necessary directly connected, is done in one hop (when all networks are over ATM). The MPOA architecture results in many benefits, including faster network throughput (segmentation and reassembly occurs only twice, although the traffic could be carried through multiple

Layer 3 networks), native ATM QoS provided to the ATM edge devices, and the preservation of existing network topologies and applications.

Figure 6-14 *MPOA Data Transfer: Establishing a Shortcut*

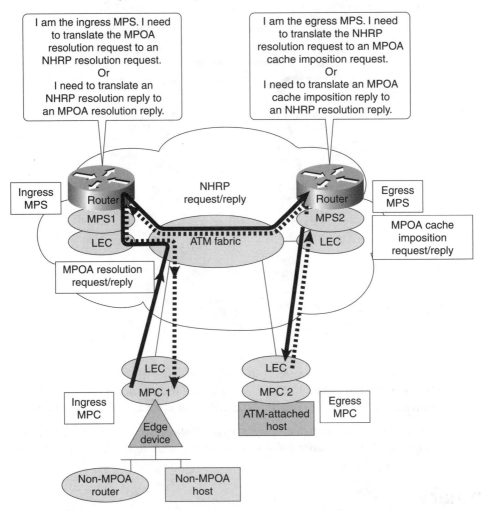

Figure 6-15 *MPOA Data Transfer: Using a Shortcut*

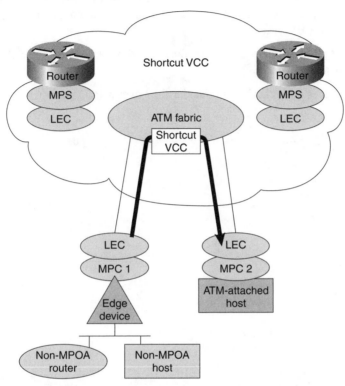

MPOA consists of three building blocks: LANE v2, NHRP, and MARS. MPOA intranetwork communication is achieved using LANE. MPOA internetwork communication is achieved using shortcuts or cut-through routing. MPOA deploys client (MPC)/server (MPS) philosophy, where MPCs create shortcuts to other MPCs with the assistance of MPSs. MPOA architecture is fully redundant.

Review Questions

1 What is MPOA?

2 How do LANE and MPOA compare?

3 What is MPOA based on?

4 What is MARS?

5 What does MPOA architecture consist of, and what are the functions of its components?

6 Name and describe the MPOA connection types.

7 What happens when an MPC receives a packet with no TTL (for IP) or maximum TC value (for IPX)?

8 What types of interVLAN data transfer flows does MPOA have? Which one is the most scalable one?

9 How does intraVLAN data transfer flow over MPOA occur?

"We must dare, and dare again, and go on daring."—Georges Jacques Danton (1759–1794)

"Minds are like parachutes; they function only when they are open."—Unknown

"If you can dream it, you can do it."—Walt Disney (1901–1966)

"Action is eloquence."—William Shakespeare (1564–1616)

Cisco ATM Edge Device Interfaces and Implementations

Now, let's put theory to practice! This part concentrates on various types of edge devices that Cisco Systems offers to interface with ATM networks. This part approaches Cisco's implementation of ATM networks from the edge device perspective, including the high-end routers (such as the 7500 and 7200 series), the 8500 multilayer switches, and the mid-range products.

The chapters in this part of the book include

- Chapter 7, "ATM Interface Processor (AIP), Port Adapter (PA), and Network Port Module (NPM) Features and Functions," concentrates on the 7500 and 4500/4700 series routers.

- Chapter 8, "Circuit Emulation Service ATM Connectivity and Summary of Cisco ATM Edge Devices," provides an overview of the multilayer switches and the lower end routers.

- Chapter 9, "Multiprotocol Encapsulation (RFC 2684), Classical IP and ARP over ATM (RFC 2225), and NHRP Implementation," provides some sound implementation examples of RFC 2684, RFC 2225, and NHRP using both PVCs and SVCs. Lab exercises follow the implementation examples so that you can experiment in your own environments.

- Chapter 10, "LANE Implementation," discusses Cisco's implementation of LANE using routers and Layer 2 switches. A few lab exercises also are provided.

- Chapter 11, "MPOA Implementation," addresses Cisco's implementation of MPOA with lab exercise.

"When one door closes, another opens. But we often look so long and so regretfully upon the closed door that we do not see the one which has opened for us."—Helen Keller (1880–1968)

"The only menace is inertia."—Saint-John Perse (1887–1975)

"If you aren't going all the way, why go at all?"—Joe Namath (1943–)

After reading this chapter, you should be able to understand the details of supported features and functions of Cisco routers when connected to ATM networks. In particular, this chapter helps you understand the following:

- ATM Interface Processor (AIP)/Port Adapter (PA)/ATM Network Processor Module (NPM) physical interface support. This includes supported bandwidth and cabling infrastructure.

- ATM virtual circuit support, which includes PVCs and SVCs.

- Router support of internetworking features, which include RFC 2684, RFC 2225, LANE, and MPOA.

- ATM interface types and encapsulations types, which include the necessary encapsulations for SMDS, signaling, ILMI, and data ATM cells.

- ATM interface support for traffic shaping and algorithm deployment. These include rate queues, continuous-state Leaky Bucket algorithm, and calendar scheduling algorithm.

- ATM interfaces SNMP management support and MIBs.

CHAPTER 7

ATM Interface Processor (AIP), Port Adapter (PA), and Network Module (NPM) Features and Functions

Connectivity to ATM can be done either natively or through an additional device that converts frames into ATM cells. Native ATM connectivity implies that a specific platform performs the encapsulation, segmentation, and reassembly tasks. The ATM User-Network Interface (UNI) begins directly from the interface level of that device. For example, the Cisco 7500 and 4500/4700 series routers have native ATM connectivity.

Devices that can connect to an ATM WAN only through serial interfaces are interconnected to the ATM network using an external device called an ATM data service unit (ADSU), as illustrated in Figure 7-1.

Figure 7-1   *ATM Edge Devices with Non-native ATM Interfaces*

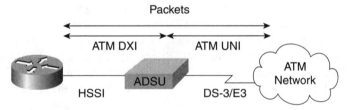

The router is attached to the ADSU via a High-Speed Serial Interface (HSSI), which is then attached to the ATM network via DS-3/E3. The ADSU receives the data from the router in the ATM Data Exchange Interface (DXI) format over HSSI. The ATM DXI addressing consists of a DXI Frame Address (DFA), which is the equivalent of a Frame Relay data-link connection identifier (DLCI). The ADSU performs the functions of segmentation and reassembly and maps the DFA to the appropriate VPI and VCI values in the ATM cell. The ADSU provides the UNI interfaces to the ATM networks.

NOTE   You can find more information on the ATM DXI connection to an ADSU at www.cisco.com/univercd/cc/td/doc/cisintwk/idg4/nd2008.htm.

This chapter concentrates on the native ATM interfaces, use of which eliminates the need for the ADSU.

Cisco has a rich variety of products that offer native ATM connectivity. For example, the 7000 series high-end routers use either ATM Interface Processors (AIPs) or ATM Port Adapters (PAs), and the 4000 series routers use ATM Network Port Modules (NPMs).

Cisco Router Physical Interface Support for ATM

The 7000 series routers have the following ATM interface modules:

> AIP
> PA-A1
> PA-A3

The 4500/4700 series routers use only ATM NPMs. The following sections examine the features of each module.

AIP Module

The AIP module was the industry's first commercially available, standards-based ATM router interface. The AIP module supports native ATM connectivity in the Cisco 7000, Cisco 7010, and Cisco 7500 routers starting with Cisco IOS 10.0. The AIP has one ATM port that supports different ATM physical layers using various daughter cards called physical layer interface modules (PLIMs), as indicated in Figure 7-2. These PLIMs are not interchangeable in the field. Depending on the PLIM type, different physical connections are supported. For example, the PMC-Sierra SUNI is used for the SONET/SDH PLIM; the AMD Transparent Asynchronous Transmitter/Receiver Interface (TAXI) is used for the 4B/5B PLIM; the Brooktree BT8222 framer is used for both the E3 and the DS3 PLIMs.

NOTE   You can find a thorough guide to AIP installation and configuration at www.cisco.com/univercd/cc/td/doc/product/core/cis7000/7000cfig/1214aip.htm.

AIP supports online insertion and removal (OIR). The OIR function allows you to install and replace the AIP while the system is operating—there is no need to preconfigure the software or to shut down the system power.

NOTE   Very frequently people confuse the terms *hot-swappable* and *online insertion and removal*. *Hot-swappable* implies that you can remove the module and nobody would notice. This is not the case with the AIP module, which has network connectivity. Hence, this capability is called *online insertion and removal (OIR)*.

Figure 7-2   *AIP*

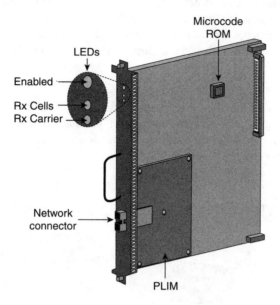

The three AIP LEDs can be read as follows:

- **Enabled**—"On" indicates that the AIP is enabled for operation. The interface ports might not be functional or enabled. "Off" indicates that the AIP is not enabled for operation. You should suspect that the AIP board connector is not fully seated in the backplane.

- **RX cells**—"On" indicates that the AIP received an ATM cell. "Off" indicates that the AIP did not receive any ATM cells. This LED flickers in normal operation, indicating traffic passing through.

- **RX carrier**—"On" indicates that the AIP detected a carrier on the RX cable. For a fiber-optic interface, this simply means that light is detected. "Off" indicates that the AIP did not detect a carrier on the RX cable.

AIP has only one ATM interface per module and runs at transmission rates up to 155 Mbps.

CAUTION   When you engineer your system, you should be very careful about bandwidth allocation. Don't overprovision your router! Be sensitive to the following facts:

- The aggregate bandwidth for the CxBus in the 70xx series routers is 0.533 Gbps.

- The aggregate bandwidth for the CyBus in the 7505 series routers is 1.067 Gbps.

- The aggregate bandwidth for the dual CyBus in the 7507 and 7513 series routers is 2.134 Gbps.

Traffic from multiple ATM network interfaces theoretically could exceed the bandwidth of the system bus, causing the packets to be dropped. As a practical limit, install no more than two AIP modules per CxBus in the Cisco 7000 series routers or per CyBus in the Cisco 7500 series router. With the dual 2-Gbps CyBus, you can install multiple AIPs.

An ATM interface cable connects your router to an ATM network or to two routers back-to-back. Figure 7-3 illustrates the connector types that AIP supports, and Table 7-1 provides information about the wiring type, the connection speed, and the distance limitation for each connector type.

Figure 7-3 *AIP Connection Types*

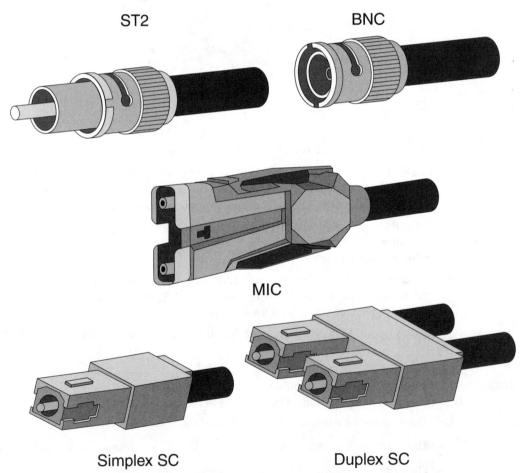

Table 7-1   *AIP Connector Types*

Connector Type	Type of Wiring	Connection Speed	Distance Limitation
Duplex SC[1]	SONET/SDH, MMF	155 Mbps	Up to 3 km
Simplex SC	SONET/SDH, MMF	155 Mbps	Up to 3 km
ST2[2]	SONET/SDH, SMF	155 Mbps	Up to 15 km
MIC (media interface connector)	TAXI 4B/5B, MMF	100 Mbps	Up to 3 km
BNC[3]	DS-3, E3, RG-59 coax	45 Mbps, 34 Mbps	Up to 500 meters

[1]SC connector stands for Snap Click connector.

[2]ST2 connector is a single-mode bayonet-style twist-lock connector.

[3]The letter B in *BNC connector* stands for a bayonet-type connection (similar to the attachment of a bayonet to a rifle) and NC stands for the inventors of the connector—Neil and Concelman.

WARNING   Unless you want to have "free" laser eye surgery, please do not stare into open ports of the single mode ATM products when no fiber optic cable is connected.

The AIP can send and receive frames up to 9188 bytes in length, which allows it to support the IP maximum transmission unit (MTU) of 9180 bytes, as specified in RFC 2225 (RFC 2225 obsoletes RFCs 1626 and 1577). The AIP default MTU is set to 4470 bytes to match FDDI buffers, which results in avoiding unnecessary fragmentation. The AIP hardware MTU size must be set to be equal to or larger than the largest desired MTU size on any of its subinterfaces.

ATM Port Adapters (PAs)

The ATM Port Adapter is the first of a new generation of ATM interface modules for the 7200 and 7500 series routers. It is fully compliant with the ATM Forum specifications.

There are two types of ATM Port Adapters: PA-A1 and PA-A3. The PA-A3 port adapter is referred to as the *Enhanced ATM Port Adapter.*

PA-A1 supports Synchronous Optical Network/Synchronous Digital Hierarchy (SONET/SDH) 155-Mbps physical interfaces using multimode fiber (MMF) and single-mode fiber (SMF). PA-A3 supports not only the Optical Carrier-3 (OC-3) connectivity, but DS-3/E3, which is very useful for WAN interconnectivity.

ATM Network Port Modules (NPMs)

The ATM Network Processor Module (NPM) provides native ATM cell processing support on Cisco 4500-M/4700 midrange routers, eliminating the need for an external ATM data service unit (DSU) or similar converter. ATM NPMs support OC-3, DS-3, and E3 physical layer interfaces using MMF and SMF.

ATM NPMs support up to 1023 active VCs and can segment and reassemble up to 192 packets simultaneously. NPMs support ATM AAL5 and AAL3/4 encapsulation types. AAL3/4 enables service interworking between SMDS and ATM, whereas AAL5 enables the support of typical packet-based data traffic.

NPM Versus AIP Versus ATM PAs

It is very important to compare NPM, AIP, and ATM PAs, because too often confusion abounds between them with respect to supported interfaces and capacity.

The AIP was the industry's first commercially available standards-based ATM router interface. You can install the AIP in the Cisco 7000 and 7500 series routers. The ATM PA was released later and is the only solution when you must support the 7200 router platform. AIP, on the other hand, is the preferred solution when you must support SMDS networking. PA-A3 is the preferred solution when you require high throughput. Before you make any decision on which interface to deploy, you need to carefully examine all the applications and the potential traffic patterns, and compare the advantages and the limitations of each interface type. The NPM is used strictly on the 4xxx platforms.

Table 7-2 compares the features of NPM, AIP, and two types of ATM Port Adapters.

Table 7-2   *NPM, AIP, ATM PA-A1, and ATM PA-A3 Comparison*

Physical Interfaces→ Features/Functions↓	NPM	AIP	ATM PA-A1	ATM PA-A3
Platform	4500, 4700	7000, 7500	7200, VIP2-based 7500	7200, VIP2-based 7500
OC-3 MMF	Yes	Yes	Yes	Yes
OC-3 SMF	Yes	Yes	Yes	Yes
DS-3/E3	Yes	Yes	No	Yes
TAXI	No	Yes	No	No
UNI	3.0 / 3.1 / 4.0	3.0 / 3.1	3.0 / 3.1	3.0 /3.1 /4.0
LANE	Yes	Yes	Yes	Yes
RFC 2684, 2225	Yes	Yes	Yes	Yes

Table 7-2   *NPM, AIP, ATM PA-A1, and ATM PA-A3 Comparison (Continued)*

Physical Interfaces→ Features↓	NPM	AIP	ATM PA-A1	ATM PA-A3
Types of VCs Supported	PVCs, SVCs	PVCs, SVCs	PVCs, SVCs	PVCs (as per 11.1(22)C) SVCs (IOS 12.0)
Maximum pps (64 byte, bidirectional)	N/A	110,000 pps	150,000 pps	170,000 pps
Simultaneous SARs (number of packets)	192	256 (can be up to 512)	512	1024
Maximum number of VCs	1023	2048	2048	4096
AAL	AAL5	AAL3/4, AAL5	AAL5	AAL5
ATM Service Category	UBR, ABR	UBR	UBR	nrt-VBR, UBR, ABR
Traffic Shaping Support	Yes	Yes	None	Yes
OAM Support	F4, F5	F4, F5 (as of 11.3(2)T Cisco IOS)	F4, F5 (as of 11.3(2)T Cisco IOS and 11.1(22)CC)	F4, F5 (special release 11.1(22)CC and 12.0)

ATM Virtual Circuit Support

AIPs, NPMs, and PA-A1s support point-to-point and point-to-multipoint PVCs and switched virtual circuits (SVCs). Unless you have Cisco IOS 12.0, PA-A3s do not support these connections. LANE, multicast traffic, and other ATM internetworking services require point-to-multipoint VCs.

ATM PVC Support

Figure 7-4 depicts how an ATM environment supports PVCs. ATM encapsulations are specified in RFC 2684. The network layer datagram first is encapsulated in a standard SNAP encapsulation frame. The SNAP frame format is equivalent to SNAP encapsulation, which also is used in Ethernet, Token Ring, and FDDI LANs.

Figure 7-4 *ATM PVC Support*

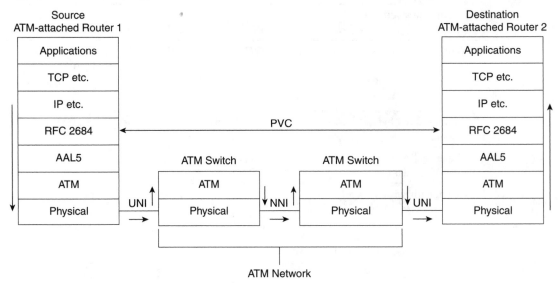

The ATM port on the Router 1 side chops the SNAP frame into 48-byte payload (performed at the AAL5 layer) and attaches the 5-byte header, making up a 53-byte cell. Then the ATM port wraps the cells into Layer 1 frames and sends them out into the ATM network. On the receiving site, Router 2 extracts or recovers the cells from the Layer 1 frames, performs a cell header check (at Layer 1), detaches the cell header from the 48-byte payload, and re-assembles the 48-byte payloads into a SNAP frame. Notice that the PVC ATM cloud functions exclusively at the ATM layer and below.

ATM SVC Support

Figure 7-5 depicts how an ATM environment supports SVCs. Each SVC requires at least one PVC, the signaling PVC, which uses VPI/VCI = x/5 (where x is any number). The signaling protocol Q.2931, as defined by the ATM Forum, establishes an SVC between routers. With IOS 12.05 (T), the negotiation that establishes the SVC includes QoS parameters requested by the router, which must be agreed to by all the switches in the path as well as the destination router. SVCs are disconnected automatically after a period of inactivity. The default value of the inactivity period is 5 minutes.

Figure 7-5   *ATM SVC Setup Support*

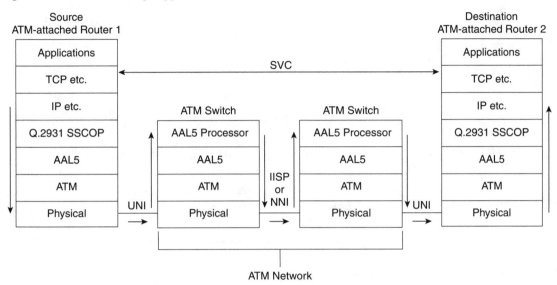

ATM Network

After the packet arrives at the edge router and the router determines that the packet must be sent through the ATM cloud, the router initiates a "call" into the ATM network (using the signaling PVC), requesting an ATM connection to be set up. Signaling is an ATM application, which implies that it must be processed by ATM switches along the path dictated by the ATM routing protocol in use (Interim-Interswitch Signaling Protocol [IISP] or Private Network-to-Network Interface 1 [PNNI1]). Notice that every switch along the way performs the segmentation and reassembly (SAR) function of the signaling frame to assess if it can provide the required QoS (only if Cisco IOS supports QoS).

While the SVC is getting established, the switches create VPIs/VCIs dynamically. When the SVC is established between routers, the SVC can be used for data transmission. When you compare the dynamically established VC protocol stack, illustrated in Figure 7-6, with the PVC protocol stack (see Figure 7-4), you cannot see any noticeable differences. There is a difference, however. With dynamically established VCs (that is, SVCs) your path has guaranteed QoS (under UNI 4.0). By default, Cisco routers use LLC/SNAP (instead of mux) encapsulation for payload cells with SVCs, thus conforming to RFC 2684. Recall that mux encapsulation also conforms to RFC 2684, but it allows a single VC to carry only a single protocol, whereas LLC/SNAP encapsulation allows a single VC to carry multiple protocols.

Figure 7-6 *Data Flow Over the Established SVC*

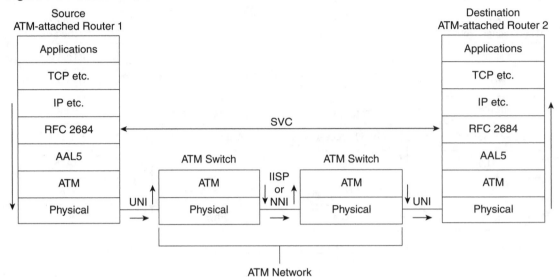

Cisco Router Support for ATM Internetworking Features

Cisco ATM-attached routers support various ATM internetworking services, including the following:

- Native protocol support using multiprotocol encapsulation, as defined in RFC 2684
- ATM ARP services for Classical IP over ATM, as defined in RFC 2225
- LANE and VLAN internetworking services
- SMDS and ATM interworking

RFC 2684 enables multiprotocol support over ATM with static address mappings in environments where LANE and/or RFC 2225 is not deployed. Static mapping resolves network layer address to ATM address using RFC 2684. RFC 2684 specifies the use of an LLC/SNAP 3-byte header to identify the encapsulated protocol. RFC 2684 also specifies a null encapsulation for VC Mux, which creates a separate VC per protocol. Chapter 3, "ATM Reference Model: Higher Layers," discusses RFC 2684 in greater detail. Chapter 9, "Multiprotocol Encapsulation (RFC 2684), Classical IP and ARP over ATM (RFC 2225), and NHRP Implementation," covers the Cisco IOS commands associated with the RFC 2684 internetworking feature

An ATM network, running an RFC 2225–compliant IP protocol stack, supports IP over ATM more efficiently because of the reduced overhead that is required to resolve

IP-to-ATM addresses. RFC 2684 requires static mapping, whereas RFC 2225, discussed in Chapter 3, relies on IP ARP functionality. Cisco routers support both PVC- and SVC-based classical IP (RFC 2225). Chapter 9 addresses Cisco IOS commands and examples associated with RFC 2225. It is interesting to note that RFC 2225 addresses the redundancy issue by allowing the existence of multiple ARP servers within an LIS. The previous Classical IP specification, RFC 1577, did not provision for server redundancy. As a result, Cisco created a proprietary solution that allows your network to have redundant ARP servers within each LIS.

Cisco routers also support LANE and VLAN internetworking services. The router's functionality includes the capability to act as an LEC, LES/BUS, and LECS. Also, of course, routers enable inter-VLAN/inter-ELAN communications. Chapter 5, "LAN Emulation (LANE)," covers LANE in greater detail. Chapter 10, "LANE Implementation," presents LANE-related Cisco IOS commands and LANE configuration examples.

MPOA also is supported by the Cisco IOS. Chapter 11, "MPOA Implementation," illustrates some configuration examples for MPOA.

Cisco Router Support for ATM Encapsulation Types

Table 7-3 lists the ATM encapsulation types supported by Cisco routers. The encapsulation types listed reflect the acronyms used by Cisco IOS.

Table 7-3 *Supported Encapsulation Types*

Encapsulation Type	Description
aal5snap	RFC 2684 LLC/SNAP, multiprotocol VC.
aal5mux	RFC 2684 VC-Mux, one protocol per VC.
aal5nlpid	NLPID, used with HSSI/Frame Relay interface.
aal34smds	Switched Multimegabit Data Service (SMDS) framing preceeds the protocol datagram. This is not supported by the Cisco 4500/4700.
qsaal	Signaling ATM adaptation layer used by signaling PVC.
ilmi	Encapsulation type used by ILMI PVC.

If you define a VC as aal5snap, the standard SNAP frame is used. If you define a VC as aal5mux, a protocol must be specified, and only that protocol traffic will use that VC, as illustrated in Figure 7-7.

Figure 7-7   *Encapsulation: aal5snap and aal5mux*

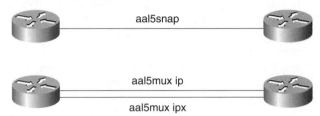

You can configure AAL3/4 on an ATM interface to handle Switched Multimegabit Data Service (SMDS) services over ATM networks. With this configuration, the SMDS encapsulation can provide SMDS capabilities over ATM, as depicted in Figure 7-8.

Figure 7-8   *Encapsulation: aal34smds*

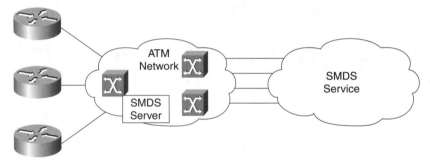

SMDS-over-ATM specification requires an SMDS server (rather than an SMDS switch). The SMDS-over-ATM specification preserves the SMDS packet formats and features the integrated access of connectionless and connection-oriented services over a single ATM UNI.

NOTE   The SMDS service offers an interface from Bellcore. SMDS provides a packet-switched service, where a packet has about a 40-byte header plus up to 9188 bytes of data. The packets themselves might or might not be transported on top of a connection-oriented ATM service. SMDS, like ATM, uses E.164 addresses. Therefore, SMDS is not a cell-relay service; it is a connectionless packet-switched service. It is important to realize that SMDS is a service, not a technology. As such, multiple protocols can access it, as long as those protocols support the features of SMDS. You can use either IEEE 802.6 Distributed Queue Dual Bus (DQDB) access, or DXI, or Frame Relay, or ATM. DQDB is a form of cell relay.

It fragments the SMDS packets into cells with a 5-byte header and 48-byte payload. The payload itself has a 2-byte header, 44 bytes of data, plus a 2-byte trailer. This makes the SMDS cell nearly identical to an AAL3/4 ATM cell. When ATM is used to access SMDS, SMDS is treated as an ATM application, where an SMDS server is deployed. You can find the complete specification on the ATM access to SMDS in ITU-TI.364 and in the ATM Forum B-ICI specification af-bici-0013.001

When configuring a native ATM interface (such as AIP) to communicate with a Cisco router that uses ATM DXI to connect to the ATM network, the native ATM interface requires network layer protocol identifier (NLPID) encapsulation or you need to configure ATM DXI with the LLC/SNAP encapsulation. aal5nlpid encapsulation enables ATM interfaces to interoperate with HSSI devices that use an ADSU and run ATM DXI, as illustrated in Figure 7-9.

Figure 7-9   *Encapsulation—AAL5NLPID*

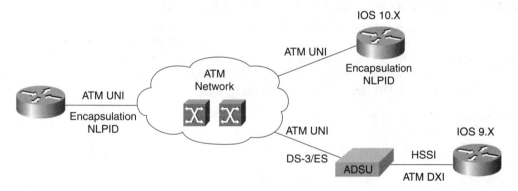

NLPID also provides compatibility with HSSI/Frame Relay, NLPID encapsulation—multiprotocol over FR/SSCS, and implementations based on RFC 1490.

Traffic Management and Traffic Shaping

It is the responsibility of an edge device to perform *preventive medicine* in the form of traffic shaping prior to sending packets through the ATM network.

Pre-sales Versus Post-sales

My favorite analogy between pre-sales and post-sales is *preventive medicine* and *surgical procedures*. If everybody, including myself, were very diligent about eating correctly, exercising often, sleeping well, and so on, doctors would be out of their jobs (most of them, anyway). If networks are designed and engineered properly, allowing for maximum scalability from all aspects—hardware platforms, bandwidth, addressing schemes, protocols in use, and so on—post-sales engineers (most of them) would be out of their jobs.

Traffic shaping smoothes out the peaks and valleys of traffic before transmitting it to an ATM network, thereby controlling the burstiness of typical data traffic.

First, let's examine the segmentation/reassembly processes that take place in the router.

Packet Forwarding to and from an ATM Interface

A packet arrives at Router A through an Ethernet interface, as illustrated in Figure 7-10. The destination network is Network X across the ATM cloud. The Ethernet encapsulation is stripped off so that the router can examine the packet header using the Route/Switch processor. I am not going to get into the details of different cache mechanisms available on Cisco routers. The idea is that the packet is forwarded to the ATM interface of the router.

Figure 7-10 *Packet Forwarding Process: Source*

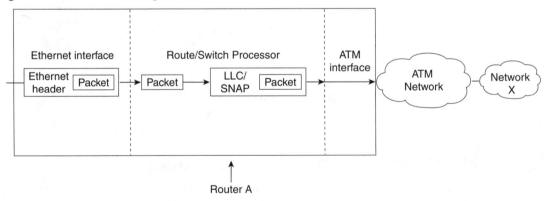

When the ATM interface (AIP, ATM NPM, or ATM PA) receives the packet, after completing all the necessary encapsulations, it must segment the packet. Cisco routers can segment and reassemble up to 1024 packets simultaneously (refer to Table 7-2). AAL5 segments the encapsulated frame (either LLC/SNAP or VC mux) into payloads of 48 bytes, which then are converted into cells when the ATM layer attaches the 5-byte headers to all these payloads. Figure 7-11 illustrates the segmentation process.

Figure 7-11 *Segmentation Process at the Transmitting End*

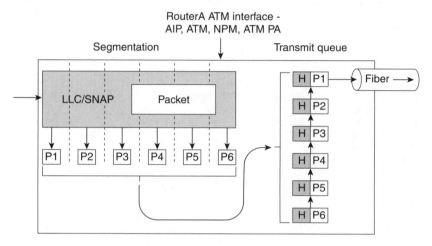

After the frames are converted into cells, the cells are introduced to the transmitting queue, and traffic shaping takes place.

The cell headers are checked first upon cell arrival at the destination site. If there are any errors, the cell is discarded. Otherwise, the ATM layer reads the VPI/VCI and the PTI fields. The reassembly of cells into Layer 2 frames, illustrated in the Figure 7-12, then takes place.

Figure 7-12 *Reassembly Process at the Receiving End*

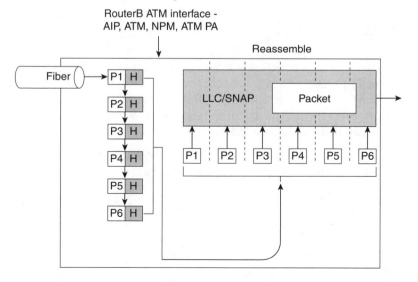

After completing the reassembly process, the router checks the frame for any errors. If the frame is good, the packet is extracted from the frame, and the packet routing proceeds on the packet as usual. The frame is forwarded to the interface that leads it to its destination, Network X, as depicted in Figure 7-13.

Figure 7-13 *Packet Forwarding Process: Destination*

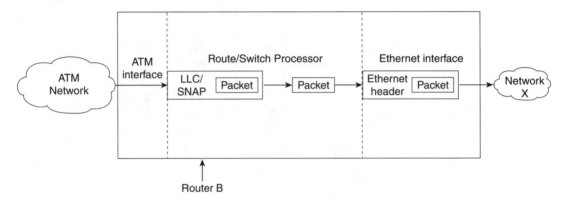

Traffic Shaping Algorithms

When the packet is introduced to the ATM interface on its way into the ATM network, the ATM interface chipset performs segmentation and traffic shaping. Depending on the SAR firmware deployed by a router, the traffic shaping algorithms vary. Some ATM interfaces use rate queues and the continuous-state Leaky Bucket algorithm, whereas others use the calendar scheduling algorithm.

Rate Queues

The AIP card uses the FRED/SARA chip for SAR functionality. National Semiconductor sells the FRED chipset and Transwitch sells the SARA chipset. These chipsets can support AAL5 and AAL3/4 simultaneously. One SAR chip supports the segmentation of packets into cells in the transmit direction, and the other SAR chip supports the reassembly of cells into packets in the receive direction.

AIP uses the continuous-state Leaky Bucket algorithm combined with eight rate queues. There are two sets of rate queues, high-priority and low-priority, as illustrated in Figure 7-14.

Figure 7-14 *AIP Traffic Shaping Rate Queues*

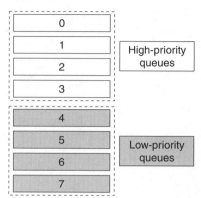

Rate queues 0 through 3 belong to the high-priority set, and rate queues 4 through 7 belong to the low-priority set. The packets linking to the low-priority set are blocked from transmission as long as the rate queues in the high-priority set are not empty.

Each rate queue is programmable with a peak data rate in Mbps. Virtual circuits can be assigned to one of the eight rate queues, each of which is programmable for a different peak rate. The VC's PCR determines the best match with the queues' peak data rate. When you define a VC, you can configure three parameters that are used to manage the traffic flow over AIP:

- **Peak cell rate (PCR)**—Decides the rate queue to which the VC is attached.

- **Sustainable cell rate (SCR)**—Determines the time period of one token to be put into the bucket—that is, the speed of the wheel rotation, as illustrated in Figure 4-16 in Chapter 4, "ATM Traffic and Network Management."

- **Burst size (BT)**—Determines the maximum number of tokens to be put into the Leaky Bucket. Each token can carry 32 cells (if they are there)!

Packets to be transmitted first are linked to the corresponding VC structure, and then that VC structure is linked to the appropriate rate queue. On a per-rate queue basis, the SAR chip round robins through the linked VCs. When a rate queue requests service, one packet, segmented into cells, from the currently selected VC is sent, and the round robin pointer increments to the next VC linked to that rate queue, as illustrated in Figure 7-15.

If VC1, VC2, and VC3 belong to the same rate queue, say, queue #1, Packet A1 gets segmented and shipped out using the Leaky Bucket algorithm. Next, using the round-robin technique, Packet B1 gets shipped, and so on.

Figure 7-15 *Logical Rate Queue Structure*

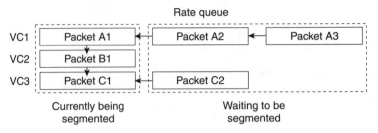

CAUTION   You should be sensitive to the Cisco IOS in use when deploying the AIP card. Prior to 11.2, there were no default rate queues. This means that if you create a PVC with some PCR value and forget to define the rate queue with that value, the packets associated with that VC are dropped. As of IOS Release 11.2, there is a default queue that is generated for you dynamically based on the PCR value of the VC.

The number of times that a specific rate queue is serviced depends on the individual rate queue values and the total number of rate queues in use. I use the following formula to determine the number of times that the queue is serviced before the service pointer progresses to the next queue:

$$N = \frac{(PCR)q_k}{\displaystyle\sum_{i=1}^{m}(PCR)q_i}$$

where

N is the number of instances (times) that cells are dispatched from queue$_k$ (q$_k$)
m is the total number of queues (statically and dynamically defined)

How do you know which PCR to assign to a specific VC? Well, no solid formula exists that is associated with the PCR assignment. Create rate queues around the total bandwidth that you have, starting with small numbers so that you minimize the impact of one VC overpowering another.

Let's look at the following example. Say you create three VCs, as identified in Table 7-4. Also, say you define the rate queues, corresponding to the VCs' PCR values.

Table 7-4   *Rate Queue Example*

VC number	PCR (Mbps)	Rate Queue Defined	Upper-Layer Protocol Association
1	100	0	IP
2	35	1	IPX
3	20	2	AppleTalk

The rate queue assignment and the PCR values imply that IP is dispatched 100/155 times; IPX—35/155 and AppleTalk—20/155 (where 155 = 100+35+20, as per the formula). This means that IP packets have precedence over other protocols.

Now imagine that you define another VC that carries DECnet. Assume that you do not define the rate queue associated with it, nor do you bother to define its VC PCR. What happens now? Well, if you have Cisco IOS 11.1 or below, nothing exciting—DECnet is ignored and the packet is dropped before reaching the ATM cloud. If you run Cisco IOS 11.2 or higher, however, interesting things begin to happen. Suddenly, your IP service starts experiencing more delays. When it comes to IPX and AppleTalk, those users are just sitting and wondering if they are attached to any network at all! What happened? When you create another VC for DECnet with the default PVC at 155 Mbps, Cisco IOS 11.2 and above creates a rate queue matching the new PVC value, which is 155 Mbps in this case. Furthermore, because the last occupied rate queue is #2, the new rate queue is #3, which still belongs to the category of "high priority" queues. All this implies that IP now is dispatched 100/310 times, IPX—35/310, AppleTalk—20/310, and DECnet—155/310 (where 310 = 100+35+20+155, as per the previously defined formula).

TIP

To eliminate the chance of this kind of surprise occurring, you should always create a default rate queue of 155 Mbps, for example, and associate it with one of the queues in the "low priority" category, such as queue #4.

ATM NPM on the Cisco 4500/4700 series routers uses a similar traffic-shaping philosophy, with a few exceptions. One of the exceptions is that NPM uses only four rate queues, 0 through 3, all of which are of the same priority. Another difference is that burst size tokens represent one cell, not 32 cells, as in AIP's case.

Determining the Type of VC Encapsulation to Use

I often am asked a question regarding the type of encapsulation to use for traffic over ATM. My answer is—it depends (the favorite consultant's answer, right?). Well, it does depend on what you are trying to achieve. Remember, when you use LLC/SNAP encapsulation, you save on the number of VCs that need to be set up through your ATM network. However, if you need to perform traffic shaping on a per-VC basis, taking into account various upper-layer protocols, you need to use VC-mux encapsulation. This allows each upper-layer protocol to be uniquely recognized and shaped.

Calendar Scheduling

ATM PA-A3 modules, used by the 7200 and 7500 series routers, use LSI Logic ATMizer II SAR firmware. The module supports traffic shaping in hardware on a per-VC basis.

The ATM PA-A3 supports non-real-time variable bit rate (nrt-VBR), available bit rate (ABR), and unspecified bit rate (UBR) traffic. For each ATM service class, the ATM PA-A3 supports peak cell rate (PCR), sustainable cell rate (SCR), maximum burst size (MBS), and minimum cell rate (MCR) parameters, which are VC-definable. Table 7-5 lists the parameters and the corresponding service classes.

Table 7-5   *ATM PA-A3 Service Classes Parameters*

nrt-VBR Parameters	ABR Parameters	UBR Parameters
PCR	PCR	PCR
SCR	MCR	N/A
MBS	N/A	N/A

The ATM PA-A3 firmware "shapes" the VC to the specific parameters using a wheel-based calendar scheduling algorithm. This ensures fairness across the ATM interface. In the event that two cells compete for the same time slot, the VCs are prioritized in the following order (starting with the highest priority):

1 OAM cells and signaling

2 nrt-VBR

3 ABR

4 UBR

Prioritizing the VCs in this manner ensures that the high-priority traffic and the guaranteed traffic have precedence over the best-effort traffic.

The wheel-based scheduling algorithm involves managing a Calendar Table. Each entry in the Calendar Table corresponds to one cell slot. An entry contains the identifiers of VCs to be serviced in that slot. The scheduler supports four Calendars (0 through 3). All four Calendars operate either in Priority or Flat mode. The Priority mode has six priority classes—0 through 5. Class 0 has the highest priority and class 5 the lowest. In Flat mode, all connections have the same priority.

SNMP Management and OAM

The ATM interfaces of the Cisco 4XXX/7XXX series routers support not only Simple Network Management Protocol (SNMP), but also Operations, Administration, and Maintenance (OAM) protocol. The ATM interfaces can initiate loopback F5 OAM cells for proactive verification of good VC connectivity. Chapter 12, "LightStream 1010 Features and Functions," elaborates more on OAM.

When it comes to SNMP, the Cisco 4XXX/7XXX series routers have a very rich selection of manageable objects. First, a little reminder about SNMP.

SNMP is not a single protocol, but three protocols that make up a family of protocols designed to help network management and administration. The three protocols are

- **Simple Network Management Protocol (SNMP)**—A method of communicating between managed devices

- **Management Information Base (MIB)**—A database containing status information

- **Structure and Identification of Management Information (SMI)**—Specification defining the entries in a MIB

Every SNMP-managed device maintains databases that are called MIBs. The SNMP MIB attributes are readable and writable across the ILMI using SNMP. The SNMP MIBs relating to ILMI are as follows:

- **Physical interface MIB**—Interface index, interface address, transmission type, media type, and operational status

- **Per-VCC statistics**—Packets received/transmitted, packets broadcast, packets fast-switched, packets autonomous-switched, and OAM 5 cells received/transmitted

- **ATM layer interface MIB**—Interface index, maximum number of VPCs, maximum number of VCCs, number of configured VPCs, number of configured VCCs, maximum number of active VPI bits, maximum number of active VCI bits, and ATM UNI port type (public/private)

- **ATM-layer statistics**—Interface index, ATM cells received, ATM cells dropped on receipt, and ATM cells transmitted

- **Virtual channel MIB**—Interface index, VPI, VCI, transmit traffic descriptor, receive traffic descriptor, operational status, transmit QoS, and receive QoS

The following ATM MIBs are supported:

- SONET MIB (RFC 1595)
- AToM MIB (RFC 1695)
- DS3/E3 MIB (RFC 1407)
- ATM ILMI MIB
- LANE MIB

Summary

This chapter focused on Cisco router connectivity to the ATM networks. Cisco routers use a variety of ATM network modules, which include ATM Interface Processor (AIP)/Port Adapter (PA)/ATM Network Processor Module (NPM).

These modules support SONET and DS-3/E3 connectivity. The capability of routers to support PVCs and SVCs makes PVCs and SVCs viable for deployment in various ATM networks. Cisco routers support various ATM internetworking features utilizing AAL3/4 and AAL5. The features include support of RFC 2684, RFC 2225, LANE, and MPOA.

Being an edge device, Cisco routers provide ATM traffic shaping before the traffic is introduced to the ATM cloud. This smoothes out the peaks and valleys of the bursty LAN traffic and allows for some predictability in the ATM networks. The routers use various traffic-shaping algorithms, which include rate queues, continuous-state Leaky Bucket algorithm, and calendar scheduling algorithm.

You can manage Cisco ATM connection using SNMP management and OAM.

Review Questions

1 What is an ATM "native" interface?

2 What types of interfaces do 7000 series routers support? What are the differences between them?

3 What types of connections do the Cisco 4000 and 7000 series routers support?

4 What are all the encapsulations that ATM edge routers (4000 and 7000 series) support?

5 What is traffic shaping?

6 Why is traffic shaping recommended?

7 What technique does the 7000 series router use to shape the traffic?

8 What PCR values should be assigned to VCs?

"Leaders don't force people to follow—they invite them on a journey."—Charles S. Lauer (1930–)

"If one is forever cautious, can one remain a human being?"—Alexander Solzhenitsyn (1918–)

"Unless you enter the tiger's den, you cannot take the cubs."—Japanese proverb

After reading this chapter, you should be able to understand the following:

- **The features and the functionality of the ATM CES Port Adapter**—Includes the circuit emulation service interworking function (CES-IWF), which enables ATM User-Network Interfaces (UNIs) to carry CBR traffic, unstructured CES, structured CES, channel-associated signaling with and without on-hook detection, and networking clocking.

- **Cisco ATM edge devices**—Includes the summary of all Cisco ATM edge devices. The summary details the payload types supported on all the platforms, the ATM access speeds, and the ATM Adaptation Layers support.

CHAPTER 8

Circuit Emulation Service ATM Connectivity and Summary of Cisco ATM Edge Devices

This chapter describes how Cisco ATM edge devices support voice communications over ATM. Whereas Chapter 7, "ATM Interface Processor (AIP), Port Adapter (PA), and Network Port Module (NPM) Features and Functions," focused on devices to support data transfer through an ATM network, this chapter emphasizes interconnection through ATM networks for voice traffic. Furthermore, this chapter summarizes all the Cisco ATM edge products that support both voice and data. The summary categorizes the products by switching levels, ATM access speeds supported, ATM Adaptation Layers (AAL) supported, and types of traffic supported.

This chapter covers unique features and characteristics of the circuit emulation service Port Adapters (CES PAs), which are available in the 3600, 3800, and 7200 series routers, Catalyst 5XXX switches, and 8500 multilayer switches.

How do Cisco routers handle voice over an ATM network? What happens when voice and data are sent over ATM together? How can edge devices handle the dynamic bandwidth allocation as dictated by traffic and still provide QoS to voice, which is what ATM is all about? This chapter answers these questions and more.

First, let's examine the methodology behind voice handling by Cisco routers and switches, using ATM CES Port Adapters.

ATM CES Port Adapters

Traditional enterprise networks have evolved into two separate networks: one for data and one for voice/video traffic. These separate infrastructures resulted in increased service costs, separate network management, and increased costs for support staff.

NOTE

For years, various standards committees and corporations have talked about voice/data integration. The first *integrator*-type device was DS-1/E1 multiplexer (mux), which was born more than two decades ago. The mux gave corporations the capability to throw voice and data on the same wire, thus saving a substantial amount of money for voice/data lines. Companies talked about integrating voice and data departments. Voice/data integration was on the verge. Years have passed, and voice and data worlds still are separate. Why? Because the terminating equipment is separate. Corporate voice departments plan for and monitor PBXs that are connected to muxs, and data departments take care of routers, controllers, and servers. This will change, however. In fact, it's changing already. ATM technology and its convergence with IP are bringing voice and data closer than ever.

Today, a majority of enterprises are looking for a scalable solution that allows them to easily and effectively move to a single physical network by integrating voice, data, and video traffic. Because ATM is a transport method that enables this integration, enterprises need to adopt the ATM edge devices that enable the integration to occur. Cisco's ATM CES Port Adapter is one of the methods that you could adopt at the edges of an ATM network.

The ATM CES Port Adapter is an "ATM access concentrator on a card." It concentrates multiple circuit streams, such as voice, video, and data, into a single broadband link for transport across an ATM network, as illustrated in Figure 8-1.

Figure 8-1 *ATM CES Port Adapter Application*

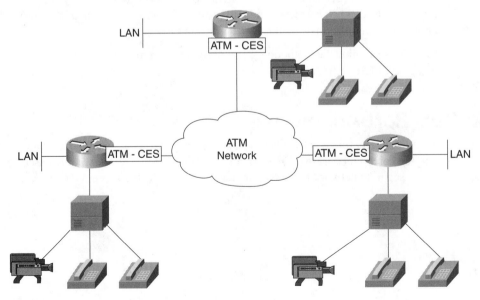

CES allows DS-1/E1 to connect natively to the ATM networks directly from private branch exchanges (PBXs) and DS-1/E1 multiplexors (MUXs). This reduces the need for unnecessary equipment, such as data service units (DSUs), MUXs, and so on, that are required for separate infrastructures.

CAUTION   You should be quite careful when configuring clocking for CES. Improper configuration could cause problems. This chapter addresses CES clocking in the upcoming sections.

ATM CES PA Feature Summary

The ATM CES is a dual-wide module. It has four DS-1/E1 ports and one T3 port, or four DS-1/E1 ports and one OC-3 port. The target application for the ATM CES Port Adapter is access to the public or private ATM cloud, where consolidation of multimedia traffic over a single ATM link is a requirement. Table 8-1 lists ATM CES Port Adapter features and benefits.

Table 8-1   *ATM CES Features and Benefits*

Software Feature	Benefits
Supports AAL5	Allows for the support of high-speed LAN data traffic, such as IP over ATM.
Supports AAL1	Allows for the support of voice and video traffic over ATM.
Supports constant bit rate (CBR)	Allows for guaranteed delivery of voice and video traffic over ATM.
Supports variable bit rate (VBR)	Allows for the efficient support of best effort data traffic with data delivery guarantee.
Supports unspecified bit rate (UBR)	Allows for the support of commonly used LAN traffic without data delivery guarantee.
Cisco IOS Software	Allows for common network services.
Structured CES[1]	Allows for the efficient use of CBR bandwidth by supporting nx64-kbps circuits on one link.
Unstructured CES[1]	Allows for the support of non-channelized DS-1/E1 circuits, thus emulating point-to-point DS-1/E1.
On-hook/off-hook channel-associated signaling (CAS)[1]	Allows for the efficient use of bandwidth allocated for CBR traffic by recognizing the absence of voice traffic and making it available for ABR or UBR data traffic.
Clocking from WAN	Provides flexibility for the user to use clocking from PBXs that are connected to the CES ports.
F4 and F5 Operations, Administration, and Maintenance (OAM) support	Enables performance monitoring, failure detection, performance information, and fault isolation.

[1]Structured/unstructured CES and on-hook/off-hook CAS are discussed later in the chapter.

NOTE	Confusion often exists distinguishing between T1 and DS-1. Are they the same? If not, what is the difference? The answer is that a T1 (the same applies to a T3) is a physical facility implementation of a line that operates at 1.544 Mbps, whereas DS-1 represents a signal format. Parts of the DS-1 specification include framing and channelization. Typically, a T1 carries a DS-1 signal, which is why they are linked together in many references. For example, although Cisco documentation refers to T1, the reference is to a DS-1 signal, as identified in the ATM Forum CES specification af-vtoa-0078.000.

ATM CES Functions

CES extends traditional DS-1/E1 services by carrying real-time voice and video traffic directly from a traditional TDM to an ATM network. CES modules provide four configurable key functions:

- Circuit emulation services interworking function (CES-IWF) enables ATM User-Network Interfaces (UNIs) to carry CBR traffic.

- DS-1/E1 unstructured CES, also called *clear channel or non-channelized DS-1/E1*, allows DS-1/E1 to be emulated across ATM networks.

- DS-1/E1 structured CES, also called *channelized DS-1/E1*, allows mapping of one or multiple digital signal level 0 (DS-0), 64-kbps channels across ATM networks.

- Channel-associated signaling (CAS) and on-hook detection enable the efficient use of bandwidth. With CAS, CES is capable of detecting on-hook situations and thus allocating CBR bandwidth to the ABR/UBR traffic.

The following sections examine each key function that CES provides.

CES-IWF

CES-IWF enables interworking between non-ATM telephones and other devices (such as PBX systems or TDM systems) and ATM devices (such as ATM switches) or ATM edge devices (such as routers or Layer 2 switches). Recall that real-time, uncompressed voice uses AAL1. Well, CES-IWF is responsible for packaging incoming native DS-1/E1 frames into ATM adaptation layer 1 (AAL1) frames, breaking them into payloads, forming the cells at the ingress location, and then performing the opposite function at the egress location. Figure 8-2 illustrates the use of CES-IWF between traditional PBXs, routers, and Ethernet switches (for example, Catalyst 5500).

Figure 8-2 *CES-IWF Functionality in the ATM Network*

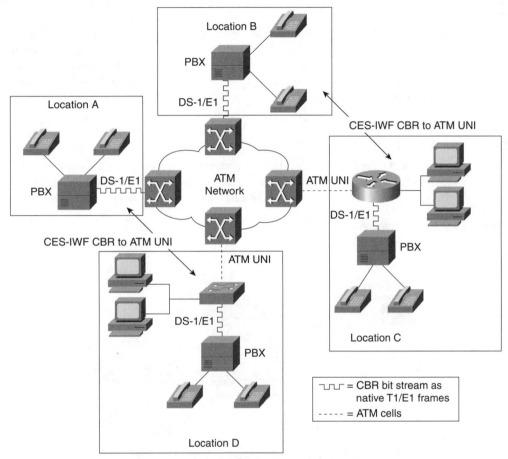

Locations A and B have traditional PBXs; whereas, Location C has the ATM-attached router and Location D has the ATM-attached Layer 2 switch. For Locations A and B to communicate, the following transactions occur:

Step 1 CBR data in the native DS-1 format is received from the edge PBX at the Location A ingress switch. The data is encapsulated into AAL1, segmented into 53-byte ATM cells, and propagated into the ATM network.

Step 2 After traversing the network, the ATM cells are reassembled at the egress ATM switch into a CBR bit stream that matches the original data.

Step 3   This native DS-1 CBR data then is passed out of the network to the edge
PBX at Location B.

For Locations B and C to communicate, where the traditional PBX and the ATM-attached
router are involved, the ATM-attached router performs the reassembly (or segmentation)
into the CBR bit stream for the attached PBX. Similarly, the ATM-attached Layer 2 switch
in Location D performs the reassembly (or segmentation) into the CBR bit stream for the
attached PBX.

Unstructured CES

Unstructured CES through the ATM network emulates a point-to-point connection over a
DS-1/E1 leased line. The entire DS-1/E1 bandwidth is used across the ATM network
without any decoding or altering to the CBR data, as illustrated in Figure 8-3.

Figure 8-3   *DS-1/E1 Unstructured CES*

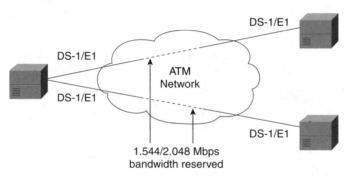

The CES DS-1 Port Adapters support DS-1 unstructured (clear channel) services at 1.544
Mbps, and the CES E1 Port Adapters support E1 unstructured (clear channel) services at
2.048 Mbps. As Figure 8-3 illustrates, each unstructured connection reserves 1.544/2.048
Mbps of bandwidth across the ATM network.

Structured CES

Structured CES is designed to emulate point-to-point fractional DS-1/E1 connections.
Fractional DS-1/E1 connection refers to a circuit bandwidth M, where $M = N \times 64$ kbps.
That is, M is the aggregation of $N \times 64$-kbps channels (N is the number of 64-kbps
channels). The 64-kbps data rate, also called DS0, is the basic building block of the T
carrier systems (DS-1, DS-2, and DS-3). The structured CES results in simplified networks,
because TDM devices can be eliminated.

Two types of CES modules exist. One of them, the CES DS-1 Port Adapter, provides DS-1 channelized data transmission services at a rate of 1.544 Mbps. With the DS-1 Port Adapter, you can map one or more DS0 channels to an ATM virtual circuit to be connected across an ATM network. Each DS-1 port has up to 24 DS0 time slots per DS-1 port for allocating structured CES circuits. Each time slot can transmit CBR data at a rate of 64 kbps. Another CES module uses an E1 Port Adapter and supports data transmission services at a rate of 2.048 Mbps. Each E1 port has up to 31 DS0 available time slots, each of which can transmit CBR data at a rate of 64 kbps.

NOTE   If you enabled the channel-associated signaling (CAS) feature, the effective data transfer rate of your circuit is limited to 56 kbps. The CAS feature is covered later in this chapter.

When I think about the functionality of the structured CES module, it reminds me of a classic DACS (Digital Access and Cross-Connect System) switch. Figure 8-4 illustrates a network using the structured CES module. You can see that either single or multiple DS0 time slots can be mapped across the ATM network.

Figure 8-4   *DS-1/E1 Structured CES*

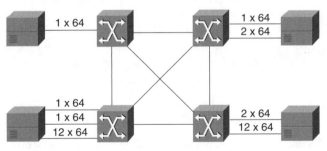

It is interesting to note that the DS0 channels at the source can be mapped to different DS0 channels at the destination, as long as the total number of time slots at both ends is the same.

Channel-associated Signaling and On-hook Detection

Because the CES DS-1/E1 Port Adapters emulate CBR services over ATM networks, they must be able to support channel-associated signaling (CAS) information. PBXs and TDMs introduced CAS, also called *robbed bit signaling*, into structured CES circuits for connection control.

NOTE	North America's and Japan's DS-1 framing uses 8 kbps out of each 64-kbps channel to carry signaling information, leaving 56 kbps for voice channel. So, you see, DS-1 CAS literally *robs* every 64 kbps of 8 kbps—hence the name *robbed bit signaling*. Outside North America and Japan, E1 framing and signaling use 32 channels. Rather than robbing each 64-kbps channel for signaling, E1 CAS uses two whole time slots—slot 1 for framing information and slot 16 for signaling for all the other time slots.
	The alternative to CAS is common channel signaling (CCS). CCS also is called *out-of-band signaling*. CCS uses an entire separate 64-kbps channel for signaling. CES DS-1/E1 Port Adapters do not support CCS.

Using CAS, on-hook detection allows other virtual connections to use the 56 kbps of bandwidth associated with a quiet DS0 channel (a channel is considered *quiet* if no traffic is on it). This feature frees unused CBR bandwidth for other preexisting ABR or UBR circuits, allowing for bursty traffic to occur. Sounds great, doesn't it? Instead of shipping empty AAL1 cells, deallocate the VCs that CBR traffic had allocated.

NOTE	Typically, data people are greatly confused by the expression *on-hook*. When it comes to data, "on" anything means "the data is there!" In voice, however, the terminology is the opposite. *On-hook* means that the handset is sitting on the telephone set; therefore, no voice traffic exists, because the circuit is not connected. When you pick up the telephone handset to answer a call or to make a call, it becomes "off-hook."

Structured CES can be configured using a variety of methods:

- **CAS not enabled**—In this state, the CES module does not sense the CAS information and does not provide the CAS support. The CAS information is carried as ABCD bits in the CBR bit stream.

- **CAS enabled without on-hook detection**—The CES module in the ingress ATM switch or the ATM-attached router senses the ABCD bit patterns in the incoming data, incorporates these patterns into the ATM cell streams, and propagates the cells to the destination. At the egress switch or the ATM-attached router, the CES module strips off the ABCD bit patterns carried by the ATM cells, reassembles the CAS ABCD bits and the user CBR data into their original form, and passes them to the appropriate destination.

- **CAS and on-hook detection enabled**—The CAS and on-hook detection features work together to allow the ingress node in the ATM network to monitor on-hook and off-hook conditions. On-hook is the condition when the circuit is idle or unconnected.

Off-hook is the condition when the circuit is in use and connected. When you configure CAS, the ingress CES module monitors the ABCD bits in the incoming CBR bit stream to detect on-hook and off-hook conditions in the circuit.

The off-hook condition uses all the bandwidth to transport ATM AAL1 cells across the network. In the on-hook condition, the network periodically sends dummy ATM cells from the ingress node to the egress node to maintain the connection. These dummy cells occupy only a fraction of the bandwidth, leaving a huge chunk of it available for other network traffic. This bandwidth release feature allows bursting of oversubscribed traffic to use the unused bandwidth, thereby making more efficient use of the network's resources. Figure 8-5 illustrates the differences in loading. Note that the released bandwidth cannot be reserved by a new virtual connection.

Figure 8-5   *On-hook/Off-hook CAS*

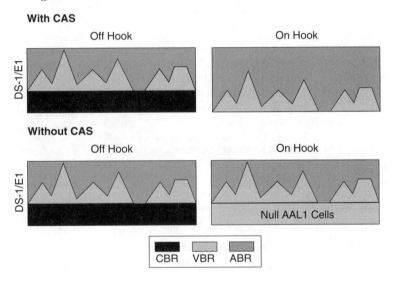

NOTE   DS-1 can use two types of framing: super framing (SF) and extended super framing (ESF). SF CAS uses the least-significant bits in frames 6 and 12 as *robbed bit signaling*. These are identified as A and B bits, or AB bit signaling. ESF CAS uses four bits—in frames 6, 12, 18, and 24—that are identified as ABCD bit signaling.

Network Clocking for CES and CBR Traffic

For your CES environment to function properly, you must carefully set up clocking. The CES Port Adapters can use three clocking modes:

- Synchronous
- Synchronous residual time stamp (SRTS)
- Adaptive

Table 8-2 summarizes the advantages and the disadvantages of the CES clocking modes.

Table 8-2   *Summary of CES Clocking Modes*

Clocking Mode	Advantages	Disadvantages
Synchronous	Supports structured and unstructured CBR traffic. Shows superior wander[1] and jitter[2] characteristics.	Requires network clock synchronization services.
Synchronous residual time stamp (SRTS)	Provides an independent clocking signal for each CES circuit. Allows equipment at the edges of a network to use a different and completely independent clocking signal from the one being used by the ATM network.	Requires network clock synchronization services. Supports only unstructured CBR traffic. Shows moderate wander characteristics.
Adaptive	Is used when other methods are not available. It does not require network clock synchronization services.	Supports only unstructured CBR traffic. Shows poorest wander characteristics.

[1]Wander is a long-term variation of an interpacket arrival time

[2]Jitter is a short-term variation of an interpacket arrival time.

With *synchronous* clocking, every device must get its clocking from a single device, which in many cases is a PBX connecting to a public telephone network. This is the only mode that supports the full CES functionality. Synchronous clocking typically is used in public telephone systems, making a precision reference signal widely and readily available. This is why it is the default mode on the ATM CES Port Adapters.

The *SRTS* clocking mode typically is used when multiple clocking sources exist. A good example of how this happens is when your ATM network uses one clock source and your edge devices (PBXs, for example) use another clock source (of a carrier, for example).

The word *adaptive* in *adaptive clocking mode* means that the rate at which CBR traffic is propagated through the ATM network is driven by the rate at which CBR data is introduced into the network by the user's edge equipment. As you can see, the reason why it is called adaptive is because the clock is trying to adapt to whatever clocking mechanism is available. Adaptive clocking infers timing for data transport by calculating an average arrival rate for the data. Relative to the other clocking sources, adaptive clocking is the simplest, because you do not need any external network clock synchronization services. The major drawback of adaptive clocking, as indicated in Table 8-2, is that is does not support structured CESs.

Summary of Cisco ATM Edge Device Connectivity

Cisco has a variety of products that can interconnect various networks via ATM. These products include Layer 2 switches, routers (or you can use the most recent buzzword and say *Layer 3 switches*), and multilayer switches.

Table 8-3 summarizes the current Cisco ATM edge devices and lists the types of supported connections, AAL types, bandwidth, and so forth.

Table 8-3   *Cisco ATM Edge Devices Summary Table[1]*

Edge Device Model	Switch Type	Supported Traffic Type	Supported ATM Interface Speeds	Supported AAL	Supported UNI	Supported ATM Service Categories
26XX	Layer 3	Voice and Data	1x25 Mbps 4xDS-1/E1 with (IMA) 8xDS-1/E1 with IMA DS-3/E3	AAL1, AAL2, AAL5	UNI3.0, UNI3.1, UNI4.0	UBR, rt-VBR, nrt-VBR, ABR, CBR
36XX	Layer 3	Voice and Data	1x25 Mbps 1x (OC-3)/ (STM-1) 4xDS-1/E1 with IMA 8xDS-1/E1 with IMA DS-3/E3	AAL1, AAL2, AAL5	UNI3.0, UNI3.1, UNI4.0	UBR, rt-VBR, nrt-VBR, ABR, CBR, GFR
3810	Layer 3	Voice and Data	1xDS-1/E1	AAL1, AAL2, AAL5	UNI3.0, UNI3.1, UNI4.0	UBR, ABR, CBR, nrt-VBR, rt-VBR
4500	Layer 3	Data	1xOC-3/STM-1	AAL5, AAL3/4	UNI3.0, UNI3.1, UNI4.0	UBR, ABR, nrt-VBR

continues

Table 8-3 *Cisco ATM Edge Devices Summary Table[1] (Continued)*

Edge Device Model	Switch Type	Supported Traffic Type	Supported ATM Interface Speeds	Supported AAL	Supported UNI	Supported ATM Service Categories
4700	Layer 3	Data	1xOC-3/STM-1	AAL5, AAL3/4	UNI3.0, UNI3.1, UNI4.0	UBR, ABR, nrt-VBR
6400	Layer 3	Voice and Data	1xOC-3/STM-1 1xOC-12/STM-4	AAL5, AAL1	UNI3.0, UNI3.1, UNI4.0	CBR, UBR, nrt-VBR, ABR
7100	Layer 3	Data	T3/E3 2xOC-3/STM-1	AAL5	UNI3.0 UNI3.1 UNI4.0	UBR, nrt-VBR, ABR
72XX	Layer 3	Voice and Data	8xDS-1/E1 with IMA 1xOC-3/STM-1 1xOC-12/STM-4 1xDS-3/E3	AAL5, AAL1	UNI3.0, UNI3.1, UNI4.0	CBR, UBR, ABR, nrt-VBR
75XX	Layer 3	Data	1xOC-3/STM-1 1xOC-12/STM-4 1xDS-3/E3 8xDS-1/E1 with IMA	AAL5, AAL3/4	UNI3.0, UNI3.1, UNI4.0	UBR, ABR, GFR, nrt-VBR
12000	Layer 3	Data	1xOC-12/STM-4 4xOC-3/STM-1	AAL5	UNI3.0, UNI3.1, UNI4.0	UBR, nrt-VBR, ABR
Catalyst 2820	Layer 2	Data	1xOC-3/STM-1	AAL5	UNI3.0, UNI3.1, UNI4.0	UBR, nrt-VBR, ABR
Catalyst 2900	Layer 2	Data	1xOC-3/STM-1	AAL5	UNI3.0, UNI3.1, UNI4.0	UBR, nrt-VBR, ABR,
Catalyst 3900	Layer 2	Data	1xOC-3/STM-1	AAL5	UNI3.0, UNI3.1, UNI4.0	UBR, nrt-VBR, ABR

Table 8-3 *Cisco ATM Edge Devices Summary Table[1] (Continued)*

Edge Device Model	Switch Type	Supported Traffic Type	Supported ATM Interface Speeds	Supported AAL	Supported UNI	Supported ATM Service Categories
Catalyst 5XXX	Layer 2	Voice and Data	25 Mbps DS-1/E1 DS-3/E3 1xOC-3/STM-1 1xOC-12/STM-4	AAL5	UNI3.0, UNI3.1, UNI4.0	CBR, UBR, nrt-VBR, ABR
Catalyst 6000	Layer 2	Data	1xOC-12/STM-4	AAL5	UNI3.0, UNI3.1, UNI4.0	UBR, nrt-VBR, ABR
Catalyst 85XX	Layer 2, Layer 3, Layer 1.25[2]	Voice and Data	Up to 64xDS-1/E1 Up to 64xDS3/E3 96x25 Mbps 128xOC-3/STM-1 32xOC-12/STM-4 8xOC-48/STM-16	AAL1, AAL2, AAL5	UNI3.0, UNI3.1, UNI4.0	UBR, ABR, rt-VBR, nrt-VBR, CBR, GFR

[1]Table 8-3 information is based on Cisco's product catalog as of April 2000.

[2]A member of the Catalyst 8500 family, the Catalyst 8540MSR, also can be an ATM switch. It can accept not only new modules, but also existing LightStream 1010 modules.

Inverse Multiplexing over ATM (IMA)

Table 8-3 references the Inverse Multiplexing over ATM (IMA) feature. Recall from Chapter 2, "ATM Reference Model: Lower Layers," that IMA is essentially a single stream of high-speed ATM cells distributed over multiple lower-speed links and recombined at the destination. This aggregation of bandwidth occurs between several DS-1/E1 links, enabling it to be altered to best suit customer requirements. ATM cells are transported over IMA links by placing them in a variable-length IMA frame. The IMA frames are controlled in turn by the IMA Control Protocol (ICP). The ICP's job is to ensure their safe delivery and the correct sequencing of ATM cells. Remember that ATM is connection-oriented, which implies that the recombined cells at the far end must be in the same sequence as they were before they entered IMA. ICP also sets up and maintains the link. Figure 2-11 illustrates the IMA operation.

The other significant part of IMA is its link management function, which enables DS-1/E1 links to be added to or removed from the IMA bundle dynamically. In fact, you can purchase your DS-1/E1 links from different ATM service providers and ensure greater resiliency for your network this way. Should one DS-1/E1 from the bundle die, IPC simply removes it painlessly and uses the healthy links.

Summary

This chapter introduced circuit emulation service (CES) ATM connectivity and described its features and functionality. These include circuit emulation services interworking function (CES-IWF), which enables ATM User-Network Interfaces (UNIs) to carry CBR traffic; unstructured CES; structured CES; channel-associated signaling with and without on-hook detection; and networking clocking.

This chapter also summarized Cisco ATM edge devices by detailing the payload types supported on all platforms, the ATM access speeds, and the ATM Adaptation Layers supported.

Review Questions

1 What is the main disadvantage of having separate networks for voice and data?

2 What is the advantage of CES?

3 What four key functions does a CES module provide?

4 How does structured DS-1/E1 differ from the unstructured DS-1/E1?

5 What is CAS?

6 Why is CAS called *robbed bit signaling*?

7 What clocking modes does CES use?

8 What is the limitation of the SRTS clocking mode?

"It is no longer our resources that limit our decisions; it's our decisions that limit our resources."—U Thant (1909–1974)

"Perseverance is falling nineteen times and succeeding the twentieth."—Julie Andrews (1935–)

"The fishermen know that the sea is dangerous and the storm terrible, but they have never found these dangers sufficient reason for remaining ashore."—Vincent van Gogh (1853–1890)

After reading this chapter, you should be able to understand Cisco's implementation of the following:

- Multiprotocol encapsulation (RFC 2684)
- Classical IP (RFC 2225)
- NHRP

Multiprotocol Encapsulation (RFC 2684), Classical IP and ARP over ATM (RFC 2225), and NHRP Implementation

This chapter provides the syntax of the relevant IOS commands, the implementation examples using the 7XXX and 4XXX series routers, and the references to the laboratory exercises with configurations.

Remember that the job here is to implement connectivity to through ATM cloud. The ATM cloud is being designed for you to interconnect various offices using various methods.

Multiprotocol encapsulation (RFC 2684) allows you to transport various upper-layer protocols; however, it involves a lot of manual labor. Classical IP (RFC 2225) takes care of IP only and allows some form of dynamics. NHRP fools the upper-layer protocols and interconnects various broadcast domains by cutting through the ATM cloud instead of deploying next-hop mentality.

Implementing Multiprotocol Encapsulation (RFC 2684)

RFC 2684 is a multiprotocol encapsulation method. There is no magic with RFC 2684, meaning there are no associated dynamics. Why? Simply because a Layer 3 protocol, such as IP, IPX, and so on, needs to be encapsulated into something that a lower-layer cloud can understand. Think about it! A Layer 3 packet must be passed to the ATM, or to the Frame Relay, or to whatever type of network is being used as the underlying physical infrastructure. This network must be able to ship the packet to the intended destination using its own rules and regulations, not those of the upper-layer protocol. This is why the Layer 3 packet needs to be encapsulated into the ATM-related frame, which is exactly what RFC 2684 specifies.

NOTE   RFC 2684 is the method for encapsulating multiple protocols (Layer 3 or bridged) over a single VC using LLC/SNAP. Both PVCs and SVCs can be supported. VC multiplexing is used to encapsulate a single protocol over a single VC. Chapter 3, "ATM Reference Model: Higher Layers," elaborates on these aspects of RFC 2684.

Because RFC 2684 does not have any magic, or should I say dynamics, the correlation between upper-layer protocol addresses (such as IP, IPX, or AppleTalk) and the ATM addressing must be done manually.

Implementing PVC Connections Using Multiprotocol Encapsulation (RFC 2684)

First, let's examine how you implement a PVC connection using RFC 2684. Remember that the ATM cloud is already preconfigured for you. If it is the public ATM, you have to obtain VPI/VCI numbers from the carrier; if it is a private ATM network, you must obtain the VPI/VCI numbers within your own organization. Recall that the VPI/VCI numbers are locally significant only. It is absolutely critical for them to match the VPI/VCI numbers for which the ingress ATM switch is waiting. Remember, when the ingress switch receives cells, it does cell forwarding based on the incoming VPI/VCI values. Hence, with the correct correlation of VPI/VCI numbers, your cells are forwarded to the right destinations.

Figure 9-1 illustrates that VPI=1, VCI=87 is the VPI/VCI pair that the ingress switch A expects to see. At the receiving side, VPI=4, VCI=93 is the expected VPI/VCI pair.

Figure 9-1 *VPI/VCI Assignment for PVC*

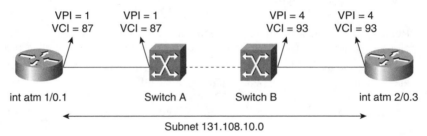

What to Do: Syntax for PVC Creation Using Multiprocol Encapsulation (RFC 2684)

The steps involved in PVC creation using RFC 2684 are as follows:

Step 1 Create a PVC. Assign an identifier and a VPI/VCI to the PVC.

Step 2 Define the encapsulation type. Will this VC carry a single protocol or multiple protocols? Is this an ILMI VC; a signaling VC; an Operation, Administration, and Maintenance (OAM) VC; or a regular payload VC?

Step 3 Optionally, identify the rate queue(s).

Step 4 Map the protocol address to the VC identifier that represents this VC.

Steps 1 and 2: Creating a PVC; Assigning a VCD, VPI/VCI to the VC; and Defining an Encapsulation Type

The **atm pvc** command incorporates Steps 1 and 2 involved in the PVC creation. The PVC command is either the major interface or a subinterface-level command. The full syntax for the **atm pvc** command is as follows:

```
atm pvc vcd vpi vci aal-encap [[midlow midhigh] [peak average [burst]]] [inarp
[minutes]] [oam [seconds]]
```

Figure 9-2 provides a more robust dissection of the **atm pvc** command.

Figure 9-2   **atm pvc** *Command*

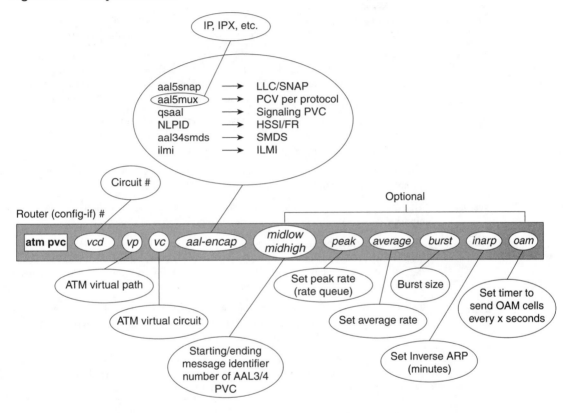

Table 9-1 provides a description of the **atm pvc** command arguments.

Table 9-1   *Descriptions of the* **atm pvc** *Command Arguments*

Field	Description
vcd	The virtual circuit descriptor (VCD) uniquely identifies the PVC in the router. It must be unique in the entire router because there will be a reference to that number from the global configuration level. The VCD numbers stay in the routers.
vpi	The virtual path identifier (VPI) is part of the ATM VC address. It must match the carrier-provided VPI for a specific destination and must be unique within a physical interface of the router[1].

continues

Table 9-1   *Descriptions of the* **atm pvc** *Command Arguments (Continued)*

vci	The virtual channel identifier (VCI) is part of the ATM VC address. It must match the carrier-provided VCI for a specific destination and must be unique within a physical interface of the router[1].
aal-encap	This is a mandatory parameter that identifies the ATM adaptation layer (AAL) and the encapsulation type. Figure 9-2 identifies the various encapsulation types.
midlow	This optional parameter is set for the aal34smds encapsulation only. It is the starting message identifier (MID) number for this PVC. The default is 0. If you set the *peak* and *average* (*burst* is optional) values for aal34smds encapsulation, you also must set the *midlow* and *midhigh* values. This option is not available for the ATM port adapter.
midhigh	This optional parameter is set for the aal34smds encapsulation only. It is the ending MID number for this PVC. The default is 0. If you set the *peak* and *average* (*burst* is optional) values for aal34smds encapsulation, you also must set the *midlow* and *midhigh* values.
peak	This is an optional parameter that signifies the maximum rate at which this virtual circuit can transmit in kbps. By default, peak = 155000 kbps.[2]
average	This is an optional parameter that signifies the average rate at which this virtual circuit can transmit in kbps. By default, average = 155,000 kbps.[2]
burst	This is an optional parameter, the value of which relates to the maximum number of ATM cells that the VC can transmit to the network at the peak rate of the PVC. The default value varies, based on the model of the router. For example, the 7XXX series default burst value = 94.[2,3]
inarp x	This is an optional parameter to enable Inverse ARP on the PVC (it works only for IP, which is RFC 2225—Classical IP). The Inverse ARP datagrams are sent every *x* minutes on this PVC. The default value is 15 minutes.
oam x	This is an optional parameter that configures the transmission of OAM F5 loopback cells every *x* seconds. The OAM F5 cells verify connectivity on the virtual circuit. The remote end must respond by echoing back such cells.

[1]The reference to the physical interface should not be confused with the subinterface notation. Cisco routers treat the subinterfaces as real physical interfaces, each of which is a separate broadcast domain that can have unique traffic control and policy definitions, using access lists, for example. The VPI/VCI must be unique within an actual physical interface range. Why? Simply because an ingress ATM switch has no idea how to spell the word subinterface.

[2]The *peak*, *average*, and *burst* numbers are the PCR, SCR, and BT values that are used by the router to perform traffic shaping using the leaky bucket algorithm. This is discussed in Chapter 4, "ATM Traffic and Network Management."

[3]The default *burst* value of 94 for the 7XXX series signifies that the default burst tolerance is 94 tokens. Each token in the 7XXX series handles 32 cells. In the 4XXX series, each token handles only one cell. Hence, in the Cisco literature, you sometimes see a reference to "cells" in the 4XXX commands, and to "tokens" in the 7XXX commands.

Example 9-1 lists some sample PVC configurations.

Example 9-1   *Sample PVC Configurations*

```
atm pvc 22 0 67 aal5snap
atm pvc 78 0 78 aal5mux IP
atm pvc 85 0 85 aal5mux IPX
atm pvc 1 0 5 qsaal
```

In the first sample configuration in Example 9-1, all protocols use the same circuit because the encapsulation is based on aal5snap. If a VC is defined as aal5mux, as in the second and third sample configurations, the VC is dedicated for a single network layer protocol. In the second and third examples, the protocol has to be specified (the examples show IP and IPX). Different protocols use different VCs. To support the IP network layer protocol, for example, the dedicated VCD# 78 is defined, which uses VPI = 0, VCI = 78. To support the Novell IPX network layer protocol, a dedicated VCD# 85 is defined, which uses VPI=0, VCI=85. The last example illustrates the signaling PVC, using VCD# 1, VPI = 0, VCI= 5. Notice the encapsulation type, qsaal, which is used for signaling PVC. The VCI must be equal to 5 in accordance with ATM Forum specifications.

Step 3: Identify the Rate Queue

The **atm rate-queue** command establishes the maximum transmit speed for a VC linked to this rate queue. The **atm rate-queue** command is a major interface configuration command, the syntax for which is as follows:

```
atm rate-queue queue-number speed
```

Table 9-2 provides descriptions of the **atm rate-queue** command arguments.

Table 9-2   **atm rate-queue** *Command Arguments*

Argument	Description
queue-number	This is the rate queue number that the PVC uses for traffic shaping. For the 7XXX series, the value for this argument is a number from 0 to 7. For the 4XXX series, the value for this argument is a number between 0 and 3. For a complete description of the algorithm used for traffic shaping, please refer to Chapter 7, "ATM Interface Processor (AIP), Port Adapter (PA), and Network Port Module (NPM) Features and Functions."
speed	Speed in megabits per second (Mbps) in the range from 1 to 155. The type of interface card determines the maximum speed. For example, the speed limit is 45 Mbps for DS3, whereas TAXI type can support 100 Mbps. Traffic, whose PCR (from the **atm pvc** command) matches the *speed* specified, is placed in the corresponding queue.

CAUTION   Please be aware of which Cisco IOS Release is in use. If, for example, you are using an AIP card and IOS Release 11.1, you need to create all the rate queues to match the peak cell rates (PCRs) of the specified PVCs. Otherwise, if the matching PCR is not found, the traffic is dropped. As of IOS Release 11.2, the rate queues are generated dynamically, matching the specified PCRs of the PVCs. Remember that the PCRs specified in the **atm pvc** command are in kilobits per second (kbps), whereas the **atm rate-queue** command specifies PCRs in megabits per second (Mbps).

For example, the following **atm rate-queue** configuration:

```
atm rate-queue 1 155
```

specifies **1** as the queue number and **155** as the speed (data rate) in Mbps.

TIP   Please be sensitive to the type of encapsulation used by a PVC. If you need to distinguish IP traffic and shape IP traffic differently from IPX traffic, you need to use separate PVCs with aal5mux encapsulation and an individual rate queue.

Step 4: Mapping the Protocol Address to the VC Identifier

The final step in implementing multiprotocol encapsulation (RFC 2684) is the manual creation of a map list that provides a correlation between the upper-layer protocol address and the router's reference to the ATM address, which is a virtual circuit descriptor (VCD).

Example 9-2 lists the syntax of the **map-list** command and its reference from the major interface or a subinterface level. The map list is created from the global configuration level, whereas the reference to a map list is done at the interface/subinterface level. The **map-group** command is used to link a particular map list to an interface.

Example 9-2   *PVC Address Configuration with the **map-list** Command*

```
Router (config)#map-list name
Router (config-map-list)#protocol protocol-address atm-vc vcd
Router (config-if)#map-group name
```

Table 9-3 identifies the **map-list** arguments involved with PVC address configuration and their meanings.

Table 9-3   **map-list** *Command Arguments*

Argument	Description
name	The name of the map list. It can be any arbitrary name; however, the *name* value used in the **map-group** and the **map-list** commands must match.
protocol	An actual protocol name, such as **ip**, **ipx**, **vines**, **appletalk**, **decnet**, **bridge**, **clns**, or **xns**.
protocol-address	The next-hop address that is being mapped to this PVC. This is the next-hop address that is identified in the routing table to reach a specific destination.
vcd	The virtual circuit descriptor for the PVC that is being defined during PVC creation.

TIP

Here is a piece of advice. Too many times I've seen people deploying RFC 2684 and using a single map list for all the upper-layer protocols. I prefer a modular method of programming, which, in this instance, means the creation of independent modules that can be inserted into or removed from the configuration file. Create a separate map list for each upper-layer protocol. Then refer to each of them with a separate **map-group** statement from the interface/subinterface layer. This allows you to lift off a **map-group** statement for IP without impacting IPX traffic, should you decide to deploy Classical IP (RFC 2225) instead of multiprotocol encapsulation (RFC 2684) for the IP protocol.

Example 9-3 provides a sample **map-list** configuration applicable to an ATM interface.

Example 9-3   *Sample Map List Configurations for IP and IPX on a 4XXX Series Router*

```
Router (config)#map-list test-ip
Router (config-map-list)#ip 10.0.0.1 atm-vc 78
Router (config-map-list)#ip 10.0.0.2 atm-vc 79
Router (config)#map-list test-ipx
Router (config-map-list)#ipx 40.0000.0123.48e5 atm-vc 85
Router (config-map-list)#ipx 40.0000.0321.5e84 atm-vc 58
Router (config)# interface atm 0.1 multipoint
Router (config-if)#map-group test-ip
Router (config-if)#map-group test-ipx
```

Separate map lists are defined for IP and IPX, thus allowing modularity in the router configuration.

How to Do: Configuration Examples for PVC Creation Using Multiprotocol Encapsulation (RFC 2684)

Figure 9-3 presents three routers connected to an ATM network that is implementing multiprotocol encapsulation (RFC 2684).

Figure 9-3 *Multiprotocol Encapsulation PVC Configuration Example—Network Diagram*

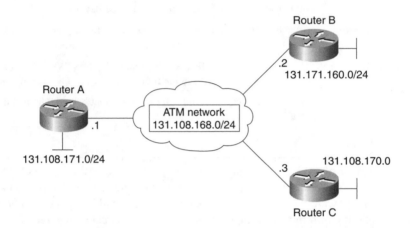

The ATM cloud is treated as a single Layer 3 network, 131.108.168.0/24, with all directly connected routers. On Router A, you configure a multipoint subinterface atm 0.1 and assign an IP address of 131.108.168.1/24 (as demonstrated in Example 9-4). Routers B and C also configured to route IP, as demonstrated in Examples 9-5 and 9-6.

Example 9-4 *4XXX Series Router A PVC Configuration for Multiprotocol Encapsulation*

```
interface atm 0.1 multipoint
ip address 131.108.168.1 255.255.255.0
atm pvc 1 0 100 aal5snap
atm pvc 2 0 200 aal5snap
map-group pvc-routerA

map-list pvc-routerA
ip 131.108.168.2 atm-vc 1 broadcast
ip 131.108.168.3 atm-vc 2 broadcast
```

Example 9-5   *4XXX Series Router B PVC Configuration for Multiprotocol Encapsulation*

```
interface atm 0.1 multipoint
ip address 131.108.168.2 255.255.255.0
atm pvc 1 0 200 aal5snap
atm pvc 2 0 210 aal5snap
map-group pvc-routerB
map-list pvc-routerB
ip 131.108.168.1 atm-vc 1 broadcast
ip 131.108.168.3 atm-vc 2 broadcast
```

Example 9-6   *4XXX Series Router C PVC Configuration for Multiprotocol Encapsulation*

```
interface atm 0.1 multipoint
ip address 131.108.168.3 255.255.255.0
atm pvc 2 0 210 aal5snap
atm pvc 4 0 220 aal5snap
map-group pvc-routerC

map-list pvc-routerC
ip 131.108.168.1 atm-vc 2 broadcast
ip 131.108.168.2 atm-vc 4 broadcast
```

In Router A, you create two PVCs using the following VCD and VPI/VCI information:

- VCD# = 1, with VPI = 0, VCI = 100
- VCD# = 2, with VPI = 0, VCI = 200

In Router B, you create two PVCs using the following VCD and VPI/VCI information:

- VCD# = 1, with VPI = 0, VCI = 200
- VCD# = 2, with VPI = 0, VCI = 210

In Router C, you create two PVCs using the following VCD and VPI/VCI information:

- VCD# = 2, with VPI = 0, VCI = 210
- VCD# = 4, with VPI = 0, VCI = 220

The type of encapsulation that the VCs use is aal5snap, meaning that multiple protocols could use those VCs, should the need arise. Then the **map-group pvc-routerA** command line links to the **map-list pvc-routerA** module, which then links the next-hop address 131.108.168.2 to VCD# 1 and 131.108.168.3 to VCD# 2.

Similarly, the **map-group pvc-routerB** and **map-group pvc-routerC** command lines link to their corresponding map-lists, which then link next-hop IP addresses to the corresponding VCD#s.

CAUTION One keyword that you might have not seen before is **broadcast**. Remember that ATM is a *nonbroadcast multiaccess (NBMA)* network. The **broadcast** keyword specifies that this map entry sends the corresponding protocol broadcast requests through the interface atm 0.1. If you do not specify **broadcast**, the ATM software prevents from sending routing protocol updates to the remote hosts.

IOS Online Help

I always tell my students that it does not hurt to type a space, followed by a **?**. You might be amazed at what you discover. Cisco IOS's wonderful online help (**?**) feature helps you complete the commands entered. Sometimes, you might not have access to the Cisco command manuals in hard or electronic copy. Do not be squeamish about using the online help feature to help you on the job—IOS has the online help feature for a reason.

If you deploy the 7XXX series routers, your reference to the subinterface is

```
interface atm 1/0.1 {multipoint | point-to-point}
```

If you need to interconnect two routers back to back at the SONET/SDH speed, you can accomplish that as demonstrated in Examples 9-7 and 9-8.

Example 9-7 *Interconnecting Two Routers Back-to-Back at SONET/SDH Speed—Router 1*

```
Router 1

interface atm3/0
ip address 1.0.0.1 255.0.0.0
no keepalive
map-group hello
atm clock internal
atm rate-queue 2 34
atm pvc 50 1 150 aal5snap

map-list hello
ip 1.0.0.2 atm-vc 50 broadcast
```

Example 9-8 *Interconnecting Two Routers Back-to-Back at SONET/SDH Speed—Router 2*

```
Router 2

interface atm3/0
ip address 1.0.0.2 255.0.0.0
no keepalive
map-group hello
atm rate-queue 2 34
```

Example 9-8   *Interconnecting Two Routers Back-to-Back at SONET/SDH Speed—Router 2 (Continued)*

```
atm pvc 5 1 150 aal5snap

map-list hello
ip 1.0.0.1 atm-vc 5 broadcast
```

NOTE   Later in this chapter, Lab 9-1, "Configuring PVCs on Cisco 4500 Routers, RFC 2684,"
provides you with an opportunity to dabble with IP internetworking using PVCs over ATM.
Likewise, Lab 9-2, "Configuring IPX over PVCs Using AAL5SNAP, RFC 2684," provides
you with the same opportunity, this time focusing on IPX internetworking using PVCs over
ATM.

Implementing SVC Connections Using Multiprotocol Encapsulation (RFC 2684)

You might find that configuring an SVC is much easier than configuring a PVC. SVC-based
ATM clouds are more reliable—should the link go down somewhere within the SVC
network, a new VC is set up dynamically for you if there is a requirement.

As is the case with PVCs, the ATM cloud is preconfigured for you. The big difference
between PVC and SVC clouds is that PVCs use a predefined set of locally significant VPI/
VCI numbers, whereas SVCs use global ATM addressing (remember those long 40 hex
numbers). PVCs are set up manually within the ATM cloud; SVCs are generated
dynamically when traffic needs to be sent. The addresses used by an SVC must be obtained
from the carrier, or whoever is maintaining your ATM network, even though they are
globally significant.

Correlating ATM Addresses

One point I want to stress is that regardless of how your ATM addresses are obtained, you
need to correlate them with your carrier/ATM network provider to ensure that the ATM
network knows those addresses. This measure is necessary so that when a signaling request
to connect to a location X is received, the ATM switches can find a route for the ATM
address of that location.

Chapter 3 covered the format of globally significant ATM addresses. If your ATM network is private, ATM addressing is NSAP-based; if your ATM network is public, your ATM addressing uses E.164. Figure 9-4 illustrates the format of a typical NSAP address.

Figure 9-4 *Typical ATM Address*

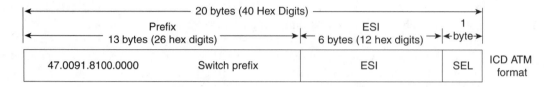

NSAP addresses can be assigned manually at every edge device or automatically constructed using ILMI. Lab 9-3, "Configuring SVCs on Cisco 4500 Routers, RFC 2684," provides you with exercises for IP internetworking using SVCs with manually assigned NSAP addresses.

Figure 9-5 illustrates how to use ILMI to assign ATM addresses.

Figure 9-5 *ATM Address Assignment Using ILMI*

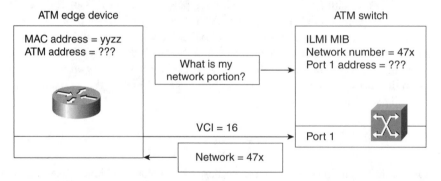

ILMI requires the availability of a PVC with VPI/VCI values of X,16, correspondingly, where VPI value(X) can be anything.

Manually assigned NSAP addresses do not require the use of ILMI. Figure 9-6 illustrates a typical SVC connection, where Routers A and B use manually assigned addresses (NSAP A and NSAP B).

Figure 9-6   *ATM SVC*

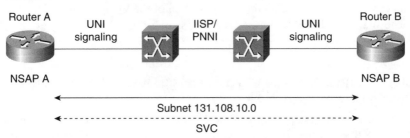

What to Do: Syntax for SVC Creation Using Multiprotocol Encapsulation (RFC 2684)

Before beginning with the syntax for creating SVCs using multiprotocol encapsulation, keep in mind that any SVC requires a single special PVC. Just one special PVC is sufficient for one or thousands of SVCs. What PVC is that? QSAAL signaling, of course, which uses VPI=x, VCI=5. Remember the one that drills the hole through the ATM cloud and sets up a VC with QoS? Please always remember this.

To configure ATM SVCs using multiprotocol encapsulation (RFC 2684), you must perform the following steps:

Step 1   Set up a PVC for establishing a signaling channel.

Optionally, set up a PVC for ILMI. You should always check with the ATM network administration to see if the ingress switch is using ILMI. If it is, you need to set up a PVC for ILMI. If you don't set up the PVC, the ILMI keepalive messages cannot be acknowledged, and the signaling function fails. Some ATM switches (such as the LightStream 1010, which is discussed in Part III, "ATM Cloud: LightStream 1010 ATM Switch") have ILMI enabled by default. If you assign ATM addresses manually, you do not need to set up an ILMI PVC. Just make sure that the ingress switch does not have it enabled.

Step 2   If you are not using ILMI for automatic ATM address assignment, define a 40-byte ATM address for the SVC located on the interface/subinterface of the router using the NSAP format, for example. If you do use ILMI for the address assignment function, you should define the end-system identifier (ESI) portion of the address. Remember that the prefix is obtained dynamically from the ingress ATM switch by ILMI.

Step 3   Establish map statements to map the protocol addresses to the ATM addresses. Notice that for PVCs, the mapping of the protocol addresses is done to the VCD numbers, which are locally significant. For SVCs, the mapping of the protocol addresses is done to the globally significant ATM addresses.

NOTE	You can use Step 4 to set up the encapsulation of the VC to be mux. The default encapsulation of the SVC-type VCs is aal5snap for data VCs.

Steps 1 and 2: Establishing a Signaling Channel (PVC) and Optionally Setting Up a PVC for ILMI

Example 9-9 depicts the syntax of the commands for establishing the signaling and ILMI PVCs. Notice that the signaling and ILMI PVCs need to be established only at the major interface level, not the subinterface!

Example 9-9 *Establishing Signaling and ILMI PVCs*

```
Router(config)#interface atm 1/0
! or
Router(config)#interface atm 0
Router(config-if)#atm pvc 1 0 5 qsaal
Router(config-if)#atm pvc 2 0 16 ilmi
```

Example 9-9 illustrates that the VPI is set as 0. It can be any number, remember? However, the VCI values of 5 for the signaling PVC and 16 for the ILMI PVC must be used to comply with the ATM Forum specifications. Within the ATM network, as addressed in Part III of this book, you do not need to configure signaling and ILMI PVCs—they are generated for you dynamically. For vendor compatibility, if you happen to have various vendor ATM switches, they all have the same VCIs for signaling and ILMI, as specified by the ATM Forum.

Steps 3 and 4: Defining the ATM NSAP Address/End Station System Identifier (ESI) to the Interface/Subinterface, and Mapping the Protocol Address to the Global ATM address

Example 9-10 illustrates the syntax for the commands required to configure the source ATM NSAP address and the map list that associates the ATM addresses with a Layer 3 protocol address.

Example 9-10 *Configuring Source ATM NSAP Addresses and Map Lists*

```
Router (config-if)#atm nsap-address nsap-address
!  or
Router (config-if)#atm esi-address esi
Router (config-if)#map-group name
Router (config)#map-list name
Router (config-map-list)# protocol protocol-address atm-nsap atm-nsap-address
[class class-name][broadcast]
```

The SVC commands are at either the major interface or subinterface level.

Table 9-4 identifies the arguments in the commands illustrated in Example 9-10.

Table 9-4   *Argument Description for the SVC-Associated Commands*

Argument	Description
nsap-address	Source address, specified as 40 hexadecimal digits.
esi	End-system identifier (esi), specified as 12 hexadecimal digits. To form a full NSAP address, the 26 hexadecimal digit prefix is learned dynamically from the ingress ATM switch with the help of ILMI.
name	This is the name of the map list that is created at the global configuration mode. The map list name has to be referenced from the interface/subinterface mode using **map-group** to activate the map list.
protocol	One of the following keywords: **ip**, **ipx**, **appletalk**, **decnet**, **vines**, **apollo**, and so on, depending on the Layer 3 protocol in use.
protocol-address	The destination address that is being mapped to this SVC.
atm-nsap-address	The destination ATM NSAP address.
class-name	A reference to the traffic parameters **map-class** lists. This is available optionally to change the traffic parameter values from their default values. With the help of **map-class** statements, you can customize the traffic-shaping parameters for various types of traffic.
broadcast	This keyword is necessary if protocol broadcast traffic, such as routing updates, needs to use the ATM interface.

If you need to customize traffic shaping of the data that is shipped through the established SVCs, use the following **map-class** subcommands:

```
broadcast
atm forward-peak-cell-rate-clp0 rate
atm backward-peak-cell-rate-clp0 rate
atm forward-peak-cell-rate-clp1 rate
atm backward-peak-cell-rate-clp1 rate
atm forward-sustainable-cell-rate-clp0 rate
atm backward-sustainable-cell-rate-clp0 rate
atm forward-sustainable-cell-rate-clp1 rate
atm backward-sustainable-cell-rate-clp1 rate
atm forward-max-burst-size-clp0 cell-count
atm backward-max-burst-size-clp0 cell-count
atm forward-max-burst-size-clp1 cell-count
atm backward-max-burst-size-clp1 cell-count
```

The commands in the preceding list change the traffic parameters from their default values. The syntax of the commands should be self-explanatory. To be more specific:

- You can change the following traffic parameters: peak cell rate (PCR), sustainable cell rate (SCR), and burst size.

- You can shape traffic from source to destination (using the keyword **forward**) and from destination to source (using the keyword **backward**), making traffic shaping bi-directional.

- You can shape traffic of high- and/or low-priority cells (using the keyword **clp0** for high priority and **clp1** for low-priority).

After you create the map class, you have to refer to it from the **map-list** level using the **map-list** command, as demonstrated in Example 9-11.

Example 9-11 *Use the* **map-list** *Command to Refer to Map Classes After Creating Them*

```
Router (config)# map-class atm lets-contract
Router(config-map-class)# atm forward-peak-cell-rate-clp0 123000

Router(config)# map-list hello
ip 144.254.100.1 atm-nsap 11.1111.00.000000.0000.0000.0000.0000.0000.0000.00
class lets-contract
```

Example 9-11 depicts the definition of the PCR for high-priority cells (**clp0**) to 123 Mbps for the source to destination (forward) direction.

Example 9-12 demonstrates an SVC configuration using static ATM addresses. Notice that the example illustrates the use of a 7XXX series model. The configuration of the signaling PVC is done at the major interface level.

Example 9-12 *SVC Configuration: Static ATM Addresses*

```
Router(config)# int atm 4/0
Router(config-if)# atm pvc 5 0 5 qsaal
Router(config-if)# int atm 4/0.1 multipoint
Router(config-subif)# atm nsap-address
47.0081.01.234567.890A.0000.F012.3456.7890.1234.12
Router(config-subif)# ip address 144.254.10.2 255.255.255.0
Router(config-subif)# map-group svclines
Router(config)# map-list svclines
Router(config-map-list)# ip 144.254.10.1 atm-nsap 47.0081.01.AA4567.890A.0000.
F012.3456.7890.1111.12 broadcast
```

At the subinterface level, atm 4/0.1, IP and NSAP addresses are assigned. Then, because the example illustrates the use of the multiprotocol encapsulation, manual mapping of the next-hop IP address to its ATM address must be done.

Example 9-13 demonstrates an SVC configuration where ILMI is used to obtain the prefix of the ATM address. The only part of the address that needs to be statically assigned is the ESI.

Example 9-13 *SVC Configuration: ILMI Obtains ATM Address Prefixes*

```
Router(config)# int atm 4/0
Router(config-if)# atm pvc 5 0 5 qsaal
Router(config-if)# atm pvc 16 0 16 ilmi
Router(config-if)# int atm 4/0.1 multipoint
```

Example 9-13 *SVC Configuration: ILMI Obtains ATM Address Prefixes (Continued)*

```
Router(config-subif)# atm esi 3456.7890.1234.12
Router(config-subif)# ip address 144.254.10.2 255.255.255.0
Router(config-subif)# map-group svclines
Router(config)# map-list svclines
Router(config-map-list)# ip 144.254.10.1
  atm-nsap 47.0081.01.AA4567.890A.0000.F012.3456.7890.1111.12 broadcast
```

At the major interface, you create two PVCs: one for signaling and another for ILMI. Then, on the subinterface level, you assign the *atm esi* value. The router uses ILMI to obtain the ATM prefix value dynamically from the ingress switch. The **map-group svclines** points to the map-list svclines, where the destination IP and ATM NSAP addresses are mapped. The broadcast keyword at the end of the statement enables the dynamic routing protocols to send their routing updates.

How to Do: Configuration Examples for SVC Creation Using Multiprotocol Encapsulation (RFC 2684)

Figure 9-7 illustrates an SVC configuration example using multiprotocol encapsulation (RFC 2684). You have three routers, Router A, Router B, and Router C, interconnected via ATM network. The routed protocol in use is IP. All three routers use a single broadcast domain through the ATM network, the IP address of which is 131.108.175.0/24.

Figure 9-7   *Multiprotocol Encapsulation SVC Configuration Example: Network Diagram*

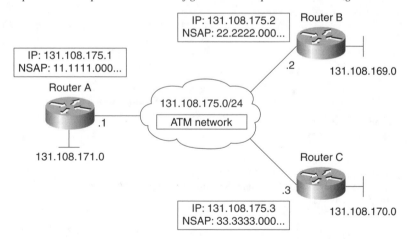

On all three routers, you must assign the signaling and ILMI PVC at the major interface level. On the Router A subinterface, you assign the IP address 131.108.175.1/24; on the

Router B subinterface, you assign the IP address 131.108.175.2/24; and on the Router C subinterface, you assign the IP address 131.108.175.3/24.

Next, you need to assign ATM addresses to the routers' subinterfaces. In this example, I use private NSAP addresses instead of automatically building an ATM address with the help of ILMI. Because this example illustrates the implementation of multiprotocol encapsulation (RFC 2684), you are required to statically map the destination ATM addresses to the next-hop IP addresses. The keyword **broadcast** enables the dynamic routing protocol, such as IGRP, to send its routing updates through the ATM network, which is an NBMA-type network. Examples 9-14, 9-15, and 9-16 show the configurations for all three routers depicted in Figure 9-7.

Example 9-14 *SVC Multiprotocol Encapsulation: Router A Configuration (4XXX Series)*

```
interface atm 0
atm pvc 5 0 5 qsaal

interface atm 0.1 multipoint
ip address 131.108.175.1 255.255.255.0
atm nsap-address 11.1111.0000000000000000000000.000000000000.00
map-group svc-ip-routerA
map-group svc-ipx-routerA


map-list svc-ip-routerA
ip 131.108.175.2 atm-nsap 22.2222.0000000000000000000000.000000000000.00 broadcast
ip 131.108.175.3 atm-nsap 33.3333.0000000000000000000000.000000000000.00 broadcast

map-list svc-ipx-routerA
ipx 100.0000.0123.012e atm-nsap 22.2222.0000000000000000000000.000000000000.00
  broadcast
ipx 100.0000.0543.0231 atm-nsap 33.3333.0000000000000000000000.000000000000.00
  broadcast
```

Example 9-15 *SVC Multiprotocol Encapsulation: Router B Configuration (4XXX Series)*

```
interface atm 0
atm pvc 5 0 5 qsaal

interface atm 0.1 multipoint
ip address 131.108.175.2 255.255.255.0
atm nsap-address 22.2222.0000000000000000000000.000000000000.00
map-group svc-ip-routerB
map-group svc-ipx-routerB


map-list svc-ip-routerB
ip 131.108.175.1 atm-nsap 11.1111.0000000000000000000000.000000000000.00
  broadcast
ip 131.108.175.3 atm-nsap 33.3333.0000000000000000000000.000000000000.00
  broadcast
```

Example 9-15 *SVC Multiprotocol Encapsulation: Router B Configuration (4XXX Series) (Continued)*

```
map-list svc-ipx-routerB
ipx 100.0000.0987.1e43 atm-nsap 11.1111.00000000000000000000.000000000000.00
  broadcast
ipx 100.0000.0543.0231 atm-nsap 33.3333.00000000000000000000.000000000000.00
  broadcast
```

Example 9-16 *SVC Multiprotocol Encapsulation: Router C Configuration (4XXX Series)*

```
atm pvc 5 0 5 qsaal

interface atm 0.1 multipoint
ip address 131.108.175.3 255.255.255.0
atm nsap-address 33.3333.00000000000000000000.000000000000.00
map-group svc-ip-routerC
map-group svc-ipx-routerC


map-list svc-ip-routerC
ip 131.108.175.1 atm-nsap 11.1111.00000000000000000000.000000000000.00 broadcast
ip 131.108.175.2 atm-nsap 22.2222.00000000000000000000.000000000000.00 broadcast

map-list svc-ipx-routerC
ipx 100.0000.0987.1e43 atm-nsap 11.1111.00000000000000000000.000000000000.00
  broadcast
ipx 100.0000.0123.012e atm-nsap 22.2222.00000000000000000000.000000000000.00
  broadcast
interface atm 0
```

TIP   As was the case with PVCs, I recommend using a separate map list for each routed protocol. This creates modularity in your configurations. If you choose to implement some magic with your IP (for example, if you implement Classical IP instead of just multiprotocol encapsulation), you can lift off the IP-related map group from the interface/subinterface level without impacting other routed protocols, such as IPX or DECnet.

Lab 9-3, "Configuring SVCs on Cisco 4500 Routers, RFC 2684," can help you with IP internetworking using SVCs and multiprotocol encapsulation (RFC 2684).

Implementing Classical IP and ARP over ATM (RFC 2225)

Whereas RFC 2684 is a method for encapsulating multiple protocols, including bridging, RFC 2225 allows you to have some magic, but only with a single protocol—IP. This is why it is also referred to as *Classical IP*. Classical IP uses RFC 2684 for encapsulating IP.

<table>
<tr><td>NOTE</td><td>Why do I say magic? Well, because RFC 2225 specifies a dynamic mechanism for mapping Layer 3 addressing (the IP address) to the ATM address. RFC 2225 allows for the implementation of both PVC and SVC types of VCs. The Inverse ATM Address Resolution Protocol (InATMARP) is the magic wand used to resolve IP and ATM addressing.</td></tr>
</table>

SVC implementations use a client/server architecture to resolve IP and ATM addressing. Recall from Chapter 3 that each Logical IP Subnet (LIS) requires its own ARP server (this is defined in RFC 2225). Also, unlike the original Classical IP specification (RFC 1577), RFC 2225 allows for ARP server redundancy. Cisco had a proprietary solution even before RFC 2225 was released that allowed for the redundancy of ARP servers within a single LIS. Chapter 3 elaborates on the Classical IP theory.

Implementing PVC Connections Using Classical IP and ARP over ATM (RFC 2225)

Classical IP implementation via the use of PVCs is very simple. ATM ARP (as used in ATM networks) is similar to the Inverse ARP (InARP) used in Frame Relay networks. ATM ARP dynamically announces to the edge routers the IP addresses that are associated with the predefined PVCs. This allows all involved routers to build a dynamic map table between the IP addresses and the corresponding PVCs' VCD numbers.

Figure 9-8 depicts four routers, Router A, Router B, Router C, and Router D, that are interconnected via the ATM network. All routers are fully meshed using PVCs, which means there are direct connections between each of them.

Figure 9-8 *Classical IP Implementation, PVC-based ATM Network*

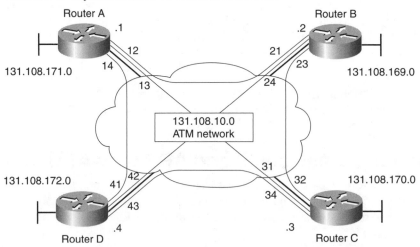

Using InATMARP, each router dynamically builds a table, associating the IP addresses with the locally significant VCD numbers, as listed in Table 9-5.

Table 9-5   *Dynamic IP and VCD Number Assignment*

Router	IP Address	VCD Number
A	138.108.10.2	12
	138.108.10.3	13
	138.108.10.4	14
B	138.108.10.1	21
	138.108.10.3	23
	138.108.10.4	24
C	138.108.10.1	31
	138.108.10.2	32
	138.108.10.4	34
D	138.108.10.1	41
	138.108.10.2	42
	138.108.10.3	43

Now, let's look at the commands involved in implementing Classical IP using PVCs across your ATM network.

What to Do: Syntax for PVC Creation Using Classical IP and ARP over ATM (RFC 2225)

The syntax of commands for PVC Classical IP is very simple. All you have to do is create PVCs, as you would for a multiprotocol encapsulation (RFC 2684) implementation, using exactly the same PVC commands. There are only two differences:

- Specify **inarp** at the end of the **atm pvc** command as follows:

  ```
  atm pvc vcd vpi vci aal-encap [[midlow midhigh] [peak average [burst]]]
  [inarp [minutes]] [oam [seconds]]
  ```

- Omit the **map-group** statement reference to a map list globally configured at the interface level, or the subinterface level.

Table 9-1 provides an explanation of the **atm pvc** command arguments. The optional *oam* argument generates OAM F5 loopback cells every *x* seconds. The default value is 10 seconds. The *inarp* option enables InATMARP. The *minutes* field following *inarp* specifies how long (in minutes) a particular router can maintain IP address-to-VCD number resolution. Upon the expiration of the defined time, InATMARP kicks in again. The default expiration time is 15 minutes.

How to Do: Configuration Examples for PVC Creation Using Classical IP and ARP over ATM (RFC 2225)

Let's go back to the network illustrated in Figure 9-8. For the dynamic mappings to take effect, you must implement the configurations listed in Examples 9-17, 9-18, 9-19, and 9-20.

Example 9-17 *PVC Classical IP Implementation: Router A Configuration*

```
interface atm 1/0
no shutdown

interface atm 1/0.1 multipoint
ip address 138.108.10.1 255.255.255.0
atm pvc 12 0 77 aal5snap inarp 5
atm pvc 13 0 78 aal5snap inarp 5
atm pvc 14 0 79 aal5snap inarp 5
```

Example 9-18 *PVC Classical IP Implementation: Router B Configuration*

```
interface atm 1/0
no shutdown

interface atm 1/0.1 multipoint
ip address 138.108.10.2 255.255.255.0
atm pvc 21 0 87 aal5snap inarp 5
atm pvc 23 0 88 aal5snap inarp 5
atm pvc 24 0 89 aal5snap inarp 5
```

Example 9-19 *PVC Classical IP Implementation: Router C Configuration*

```
interface atm 1/0
no shutdown

interface atm 1/0.1 multipoint
ip address 138.108.10.3 255.255.255.0
atm pvc 31 0 97 aal5snap inarp 5
atm pvc 32 0 98 aal5snap inarp 5
atm pvc 34 0 99 aal5snap inarp 5
```

Example 9-20 *PVC Classical IP Implementation: Router D Configuration*

```
interface atm 1/0
no shutdown

interface atm 1/0.1 multipoint
ip address 138.108.10.4 255.255.255.0
atm pvc 41 0 107 aal5snap inarp 5
atm pvc 42 0 108 aal5snap inarp 5
atm pvc 43 0 109 aal5snap inarp 5
```

Each router has three PVCs configured, creating a fully meshed environment. Each PVC has *inarp* enabled, which ensures dynamic ATM VCD number to IP address mapping. The number 5 specifies that all routers can send Inverse ARP datagrams every 5 minutes.

Implementing SVC Connections Using Classical IP and ARP over ATM (RFC 2225)

Implementing Classical IP and ARP over ATM (RFC 2225) over an SVC is based on a client/server architecture, which implies that there must be a server to provide the services to many clients. In the case of Classical IP, the service provided by the server, which is called an ATMARP server, is IP ARP. You do not have to perform static mappings between the globally significant ATM addresses and IP addresses—the ATMARP server takes care of it dynamically.

When you define an ARP client, it automatically announces itself to the ATMARP server. In fact, the ATMARP server is leading quite a passive life—it waits for a client to initiate VCs to it and to tell it the client's IP address and the ATM global address. After a client announces itself to the ATMARP server, the server builds the dynamic ARP table, containing the cross-reference between the client's IP and ATM addresses.

Let's look at the example illustrated in Figure 9-9.

Figure 9-9   *Classical IP Implementation, SVC-Based ATM Network*

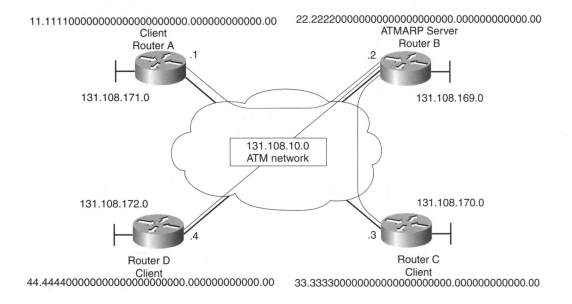

Router B contains the ATMARP server. Routers A, C, and D are its clients. After you define the clients, they automatically set up VCs to the ATMARP server, Router B. Then each client sends normal ATMARP request packets to the ATMARP server. Router B examines each ATMARP request packet and uses the information to build its ATMARP cache, as identified in Table 9-6. This information is used to generate replies to any ATMARP requests that it receives.

Table 9-6 *Dynamically Generated ATMARP Server Cache Entries*

IP Address	ATM (NSAP) Address
138.108.10.1	11.1111000000000000000000.000000000000.00
138.108.10.2	22.2222000000000000000000.000000000000.00
138.108.10.3	33.3333000000000000000000.000000000000.00
138.108.10.4	44.4444000000000000000000.000000000000.00

Using the ARP table entries, clients can communicate with each other without the need for static map list entries.

What to Do: Syntax for Client Identification and ARP Server Creation in an SVC-Based ATM Network Using Classical IP and ARP over ATM (RFC 2225)

To define a Classical IP ATMARP server for Classical IP, you need to perform configurations at the client and server sites. At the client site, you are required to point to the ATMARP server. At the server site, you need to tell the server that it is the ATMARP server.

Example 9-21 identifies the syntax of commands for the ARP client.

Example 9-21 *Command Syntax for the Client in an SVC-Based ATM Network*

```
Router (config)# int atm 0/0.1 multipoint
Router (config-if)# atm nsap nsap-address
Router (config-if)# atm arp-server nsap nsap-address
```

The **atm nsap** command assigns the NSAP address to the client. The **atm arp-server nsap** command points to the NSAP address of the ATMARP server.

Example 9-22 identifies the syntax of commands for the ATMARP server.

Example 9-22 *Command Syntax for the ARP Server in an SVC-Based ATM Network*

```
Router (config)# int atm 0/0.1 multipoint
Router (config-if)# atm nsap nsap-address
Router (config-if)# atm arp-server self [time-out minutes]
```

The **atm nsap** command assigns the ATM address to the ATMARP server. The **atm arp-server self** command declares to the router that it is the ATMARP server and, optionally, specifies the number of minutes a destination entry listed in the ARP table (cache) can be kept before the server takes any action to verify or time out the entry. The default value of the ATMARP cache timeout is 20 minutes, as per RFC 2225.

Cisco's implementation permits the redundancy of ATMARP servers within a single LIS. Example 9-23 illustrates the command syntax that enables ATMARP server redundancy. Redundancy of ATMARP servers is essential in environments where network downtimes cannot be tolerated. You can very well imagine the nightmares of non-redundant networks. In the Classical IP implementation, if the ATMARP server is dysfunctional, the remote sites cannot communicate with each other through the ATM network.

Example 9-23 *Command Syntax for ATMARP Server Redundancy in an SVC-Based ATM Network*

```
Router (config)# int atm 0/0.1 multipoint
Router (config-if)# atm classic-ip-extensions bfi
```

After you input the commands of Example 9-23, the Cisco IOS allows you to enter more than one ATMARP server address into the configuration. In fact, you can create a list of ATMARP servers in every client. As per RFC 2225, the client tries to find a server, one at a time. When the chosen server becomes unavailable, the client tries the next server on the list.

How to Do: SVC Configuration Using Classical IP and ARP over ATM (RFC 2225)

Using the network diagram from Figure 9-9, you can define a configuration for the clients and the ATMARP server. Notice that the **map-group** reference to the map list is no longer required.

Examples 9-24, 9-26, and 9-27 illustrate the configurations of the ARP clients. Example 9-25 illustrates the configuration of the ATMARP server.

Example 9-24 *Classical IP Implementation Using SVCs, Router A (Client)*

```
interface atm 1/0
atm pvc 1 0 5 qsaal
no shutdown

interface atm 1/0.1 multipoint
ip address 138.108.10.1 255.255.255.0
atm nsap-address 11.11110000000000000000000000.000000000000.00
atm arp-server nsap 22.22220000000000000000000000.000000000000.00
```

Example 9-25 *Classical IP Implementation Using SVCs, Router B (ATMARP Server)*

```
interface atm 1/0
atm pvc 1 0 5 qsaal
no shutdown

interface atm 1/0.1 multipoint
ip address 138.108.10.2 255.255.255.0
atm nsap-address 22.222200000000000000000000.000000000000.00
atm arp-server self
```

Example 9-26 *Classical IP Implementation Using SVCs, Router C (Client)*

```
interface atm 1/0
atm pvc 1 0 5 qsaal
no shutdown

interface atm 1/0.1 multipoint
ip address 138.108.10.3 255.255.255.0
atm nsap-address 33.333300000000000000000000.000000000000.00
atm arp-server nsap 22.222200000000000000000000.000000000000.00
```

Example 9-27 *Classical IP Implementation Using SVCs, Router D (Client)*

```
interface atm 1/0
atm pvc 1 0 5 qsaal
no shutdown

interface atm 1/0.1 multipoint
ip address 138.108.10.4 255.255.255.0
atm nsap-address 44.444400000000000000000000.000000000000.00
atm arp-server nsap 22.222200000000000000000000.000000000000.00
```

The **atm pvc 1 0 5 qsaal** command creates the signaling PVC, which is absolutely essential for any SVC-based ATM network. The command **atm arp-server self** signifies that the Router B is the ATMARP server.

Examples 9-28, 9-29, 9-30, and 9-31 illustrate an example of ATMARP server redundancy within Routers A, B, C, and D, where the redundant ATMARP server is Router D.

Example 9-28 *Redundant Classical IP Implementation Using SVCs, Router A (Client)*

```
interface atm 1/0
atm pvc 1 0 5 qsaal
no shutdown

interface atm 1/0.1 multipoint
ip address 138.108.10.1 255.255.255.0
atm classic-ip-extensions bfi
atm nsap-address 11.111100000000000000000000.000000000000.00
atm arp-server nsap 22.222200000000000000000000.000000000000.00
atm arp-server nsap 44.444400000000000000000000.000000000000.00
```

Example 9-29 *Redundant Classical IP Implementation Using SVCs, Router B (Primary ATMARP Server)*

```
interface atm 1/0
atm pvc 1 0 5 qsaal
no shutdown

interface atm 1/0.1 multipoint
ip address 138.108.10.2 255.255.255.0
atm classic-ip-extensions bfi
atm nsap-address 22.2222000000000000000000000.000000000000.00
atm arp-server self
atm arp-server nsap 44.444400000000000000000000.000000000000.00
```

Example 9-30 *Redundant Classical IP Implementation Using SVCs, Router C (Client)*

```
interface atm 1/0
atm pvc 1 0 5 qsaal
no shutdown

interface atm 1/0.1 multipoint
ip address 138.108.10.3 255.255.255.0
atm classic-ip-extensions bfi
atm nsap-address 33.3333000000000000000000000.000000000000.00
atm arp-server nsap 22.222200000000000000000000.000000000000.00
atm arp-server nsap 44.444400000000000000000000.000000000000.00
```

Example 9-31 *Redundant Classical IP Implementation Using SVCs, Router D (Secondary ATMARP Server)*

```
interface atm 1/0
atm pvc 1 0 5 qsaal
no shutdown

interface atm 1/0.1 multipoint
ip address 138.108.10.4 255.255.255.0
atm classic-ip-extensions bfi
atm nsap-address 44.4444000000000000000000000.000000000000.00
atm arp-server nsap 22.222200000000000000000000.000000000000.00
atm arp-server self
```

The **atm classic-ip-extensions bfi** command is added to all the clients and ATMARP servers. This allows for ATMARP server redundancy. Initially, clients Router A and Router C use Router B as their ATMARP servers. Should Router B become unavailable, the clients can use Router D as their ATMARP server.

Lab 9-4, "Configuring Classical IP Using PVCs and SVCs on Cisco 4500 Routers, RFC 2225," provides you with an opportunity to practice implementing Classical IP and ARP over ATM (RFC 2225) using SVCs.

Implementing NHRP

Regardless of whether a PVC or an SVC method is used for Layer 3 protocol interconnection, a single LIS implementation results in two hops—one into and another out of the ATM cloud. On the way into the ATM cloud, packets are segmented into cells, transferred through the ATM network, and finally reassembled into packets on the way out of the ATM cloud.

Multi-LIS implementations involve multiple hops through the ATM network, which is the IP paradigm—hop by hop. This results in increased latency and extra overhead for the router's CPU because Layer 3 routing requires that a packet be forwarded on a hop-by-hop basis. The existence of multiple LIS implementations through the ATM cloud results in packet forwarding one hop at a time through the ATM cloud, which also means that the packets are segmented and reassembled many times. In fact, the formula for the number of segmentations/reassemblies is quite simple:

Number of segmentations and reassemblies = number of LISs × 2

NHRP, discussed in Chapter 3, allows ATM (in fact, any NBMA-type network) to fool a Layer 3 protocol. Recall that basically NHRP operates in a client/server mode, where Next-Hop Servers (NHSs) are responsible for maintaining the *next-hop resolution cache* by mapping ATM and IP addresses, regardless of which LIS the ATM address belongs to. The next-hop resolution cache is built when the client sends its initial request, which does go through all the necessary hops, as dictated by the IP routing tables. The NHRP response is cached on its way back, so that for the next mapping request, the NHS responds with the ATM address of the destination, as opposed to the ATM address of the next-hop. NHRP results in cut-through routing, where the laws of Layer 3 forwarding (hop-by-hop) are totally abandoned.

NHRP provides an ARP-like solution that alleviates a hop-by-hop paradigm of IP and multiple-LIS over NBMA network problems (such as latency). With NHRP, systems attached to the ATM network dynamically learn the ATM addresses of the other systems that are part of that network but are part of other LISs, allowing these systems to communicate directly without requiring traffic to use intermediate hops.

NHRP supports two modes of operation, fabric and server, both of which Cisco routers support. In the fabric mode implementation, which is best suited to large networks, each router operates as a next-hop Server (NHS). In the server mode implementation, suitable for smaller networks, each LIS has an NHS with other routers pointing to it. Cisco routers, running IOS Release 10.3 or later, are capable of implementing NHRP in either mode and thus can act as NHSs.

Figure 9-10 illustrates a typical NHRP server mode implementation.

Figure 9-10 *Multiple-LIS Implementation*

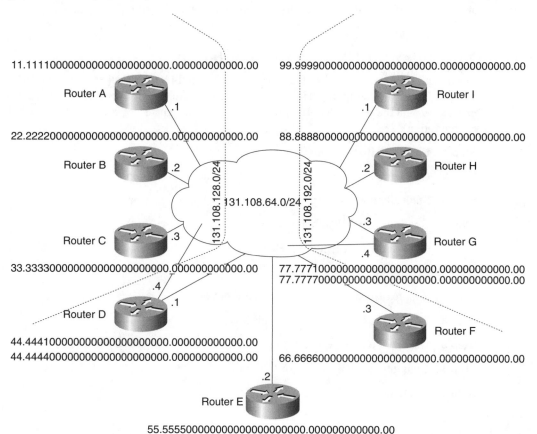

11.111100000000000000000000.000000000000.00   99.999900000000000000000000.000000000000.00

Router A   .1   .1   Router I

22.222200000000000000000000.000000000000.00   88.888800000000000000000000.000000000000.00

Router B   .2   .2   Router H

131.108.128.0/24   131.108.192.0/24

131.108.64.0/24

.3

Router C   .3   Router G
.4

33.333300000000000000000000.000000000000.00   77.777100000000000000000000.000000000000.00
.4   77.777700000000000000000000.000000000000.00
.1
Router D   .3

44.444100000000000000000000.000000000000.00   Router F
44.444400000000000000000000.000000000000.00   66.666600000000000000000000.000000000000.00

.2

Router E

55.555500000000000000000000.000000000000.00

Routers A, B, C, and D belong to LIS 131.108.128.0/24. Routers D, E, F, and G belong to
LIS 131.108.64.0/24. Routers I, H, and G belong to LIS 131.108.192.0/24. Routers within
the same LIS are one hop away from each other (they are directly connected). Routers in
LISs 131.108.128.0 and 131.108.64.0 are two hops away from each other (for example,
Routers B and E). LISs 131.108.128.0 and 131.108.192.0 are three hops away from each
other. For example, packets from Router A to Router I take the following path:

> Router A to Router D
> Router D to Router G
> Router G to Router I

When you enable NHRP, the routers build the cache of ATM and IP addresses. The very
first packet traverses through the multihop path and learns the direct route. Then the path

from Router A to Router I becomes direct—Router A to Router I! NHRP breaks all the rules of next-hop forwarding that normally take place in Layer 3 routing!

What to Do: Syntax for NHRP Implementation

Cisco's implementation of NHRP supports the IPv4 and Internet Packet Exchange (IPX) network layers. To configure NHRP, you need to perform the following tasks. Step 1 is mandatory, and the remainder are optional (Steps 5 through 11 are considered advanced configuration).

Step 1 Enable NHRP on a router interface.

Step 2 Configure a station's static IP-to-NBMA address mapping.

Step 3 Statically configure an NHS.

Step 4 Configure NHRP authentication.

Step 5 Control the triggering of NHRP.

Step 6 Control the NHRP packet rate.

Step 7 Suppress forward and reverse record options.

Step 8 Specify the NHRP responder address.

Step 9 Change the time period NBMA addresses are advertised as valid.

Step 10 Configure a GRE tunnel for multipoint operation.

Step 11 Configure NHRP server-only mode.

Step 1: Enable NHRP on a Router Interface

To enable NHRP on an interface of a router, use the following command:

```
Router (config-if)# ip nhrp network-id number
```

In general, you can configure all NHRP stations within a logical NBMA network (such as ATM, Frame Relay, and X.25) with the same network identifier. When you implement NHRP in a fabric mode, you must use this command in all the routers because every router is an NHRP server. In server mode, only NHSs must have this command.

Step 2: Configure a Station's Static IP-to-NBMA Address Mapping

When you implement NHRP in server mode, you must configure all stations connected to the ATM cloud with the IP and ATM addresses of their NHSs.

These NHSs also might be the station's default or peer routers, so their addresses can be obtained from the station's network layer forwarding table.

To configure static IP-to-NBMA address mapping on a station (host or router), use the following command:

```
Router (config-if)# ip nhrp map ip-address nbma-address
```

Step 3: Statically Configure an NHS

An NHS normally uses the network layer forwarding table to determine where to forward NHRP packets and to find the egress point from an NBMA network.

Alternately, an NHS can be configured statically with a set of IP address prefixes that correspond to the IP addresses of the stations it serves and their logical NBMA network identifiers.

To statically configure an NHS, use the following command:

```
Router (config-if)# ip nhrp nhs nhs-address [net-address [netmask]]
```

To configure multiple networks for that NHS, repeat the same **ip nhrp nhs** command with the same NHS address but different IP network addresses. To configure additional NHSs, repeat this command with a different NHS address.

Step 4: Configure NHRP Authentication

You also can configure authentication for NHRP, which ensures that only those routers configured with the same authentication string can intercommunicate using NHRP. Therefore, if you decide to use the authentication scheme, you must configure the same string in all devices configured for NHRP in fabric mode. To specify the authentication string for NHRP on an interface, use the following command:

```
Router (config-if)# ip nhrp authentication string
```

Steps 5–11: Advanced Configuration

Other advanced NHRP commands exist. You can find details of them in the Cisco Command Reference Documentation (www.cisco.com/univercd/cc/td/doc/product/software/ios120/12cgcr/np1_c/1cprt2/1cipadr.htm).

These commands include advances that allow your routers to trigger NHRP under specific rules only. For example, NHRP can be triggered not by just any IP packet, but by a packet type that you specify using access lists. Another method is the capability to trigger NHRP only after a specified number of data packets have been sent to a particular destination. These advanced features are very useful, especially because NHRP takes up memory and CPU resources.

Furthermore, IOS Release 12.0 has the capability to trigger NHRP and to tear down the shortcut SVCs based on the traffic rate. This enhancement results in further network scalability. This feature works in conjunction with Cisco Express Forwarding (CEF) platforms, ATM networks, and BGP. You can find further information in the Cisco Online Documentation.

CAUTION   Please be aware! Cisco IOS releases prior to Release 12.0 implemented NHRP draft version 4. Cisco IOS Release 12.0 implements NHRP draft version 11. These versions are incompatible. Therefore, all routers running NHRP in a network must run the same version of NHRP to communicate with each other. All routers must run Cisco IOS Release 12.0, or all routers must run a release prior to Release 12.0, but not a combination of the two.

How to Do: Configuration Examples for NHRP Implementation

Refer to the network depicted in Figure 9-10 for the following configuration examples. Examples 9-32, 9-33, and 9-34 illustrate the configurations for Routers C, D, and E as depicted in Figure 9-10.

Example 9-32 *NHRP Configuration for Router C*

```
interface atm 0/0
 atm pvc 1 0 5 qsaal
 atm rate-queue 1 10

interface atm 0/0.1 multipoint
 ip address 131.108.128.3 255.255.255.0
 ip nhrp network-id 1
 ip ospf network multipoint
 map-group c
 atm nsap-address 33.33330000000000000000000.000000000000.00

router ospf 1
 network 131.108.128.0 0.0.0.255 area 1

map-list c
   ip 131.108.128.4 atm-nsap 44.44410000000000000000000.000000000000.00
   ip 131.108.128.1 atm-nsap 11.11110000000000000000000.000000000000.00
   ip 131.108.128.2 atm-nsap 22.22220000000000000000000.000000000000.00
```

Example 9-33 *NHRP Configuration for Router D*

```
interface atm 0/0
 no ip address
 atm rate-queue 1 10
 atm pvc 2 0 5 qsaal

interface atm 0/0.1 multipoint
 ip address 131.108.128.4 255.255.255.0
 ip nhrp network-id 1
 ip ospf network multipoint
 map-group d1
 atm nsap-address 44.44410000000000000000000.000000000000.00

interface atm 0/0.2 multipoint
 ip address 131.108.64.1 255.255.255.0
```

Example 9-33 *NHRP Configuration for Router D (Continued)*

```
ip nhrp network-id 1
ip ospf network multipoint
map-group d2
atm nsap-address 44.44440000000000000000000.000000000000.00

router ospf 1
network 131.108.128.0 0.0.0.255 area 1
network 131.108.64.0 0.0.0.255 area 0

map-list d1
  ip 131.108.128.3 atm-nsap 33.33330000000000000000000.000000000000.00
  ip 131.108.128.1 atm-nsap 11.11110000000000000000000.000000000000.00
  ip 131.108.128.2 atm-nsap 22.22220000000000000000000.000000000000.00
map-list d2
ip 131.108.64.2 atm-nsap 55.55550000000000000000000.000000000000.00
ip 131.108.64.3 atm-nsap 66.66660000000000000000000.000000000000.00
ip 131.108.64.4 atm-nsap 77.77710000000000000000000.000000000000.00
```

Example 9-34 *NHRP Configuration for Router E*

```
interface atm 0/0
 atm pvc 1 0 5 qsaal
 atm rate-queue 1 10

interface atm 0/0.1 multipoint
 ip address 131.108.64.2 255.255.255.0
 ip nhrp network-id 1
 ip ospf network multipoint
 map-group e
 atm nsap-address 55.55550000000000000000000.000000000000.00

router ospf 1
 network 131.108.0.0 0.0.255.255 area 0

map-list e
  ip 131.108.64.1 atm-nsap 44.44440000000000000000000.000000000000.00
  ip 131.108.64.3 atm-nsap 66.66660000000000000000000.000000000000.00
  ip 131.108.64.4 atm-nsap 77.77710000000000000000000.000000000000.00
```

The preceding configuration examples use the OSPF routing protocol. Router C obtains an OSPF route that it can use to reach the LIS where Router E resides. Router C can then initially reach Router E through Router D. Router C and Router E can communicate directly without Router D when NHRP has resolved Router C's and Router E's respective NSAP addresses. The interface command **ip nhrp network-id 1** enables NHRP on every router.

Summary

This chapter provided details on Cisco's implementation of multiprotocol encapsulation (RFC 2684), Classical IP (RFC) 2225, and NHRP over PVC and SVC ATM network. The chapter provided syntax of the relevant IOS commands, implementation examples using the 7XXX and 4XXX series routers, and references to the laboratory exercises with configurations.

Multiprotocol encapsulation (RFC 2684) allows you to transport various upper-layer protocols; however, it involves a lot of manual labor. Classical IP (RFC 2225) takes care of IP only and allows some form of dynamics, where you are not required to map ATM to IP addresses manually. NHRP fools the upper-layer protocols and interconnects various broadcast domains by cutting through the ATM cloud instead of deploying next-hop mentality.

Labs 9-1 through 9-6 in the following sections provide you with an opportunity to apply what you learned in this chapter.

Lab 9-1: Configuring PVCs on Cisco 4500 Routers, RFC 2684

Appendix C, "Lab Solutions," provides the solutions to the exercises for this lab.

Objectives: At the end of the lab, you will have completed the following:

- Configure the Cisco router for operation
- Configure a full-mesh PVC environment
- Configure RFC 2684

Purpose: Because this is the first lab, you need to configure the router to route IP, including an IP routing protocol and IP addresses. In addition, passwords, hostname, and so forth are required. After the router is configured, you need to set up eight permanent virtual circuits (PVCs) to the other routers in a full-mesh topology, as well as give the Layer 3 protocol, IP, the capability to use these PVCs.

Table 9-7 lists and describes the commands you need to be familiar with to complete this lab.

Table 9-7   *Lab 9-1 Command Summary*

Command	Description
router igrp	Turns on the IGRP routing protocol on the router.
atm pvc	Sets up bidirectional permanent virtual circuits.
map-list	Maps a Layer 3 network address to a PVC.
show atm vc	Displays the configured virtual circuits on the router.

Table 9-7   *Lab 9-1 Command Summary (Continued)*

Command	Description
show atm interface atm	Displays more detail about the specified interface.
show atm map	Displays the map-lists that the user created.
debug atm events	Displays the creation of PVCs between the router and the ATM switch.
show ip route	Displays the IP routing table.
ping	Tests connectivity at Layer 3.

Figure 9-11 shows the network topology and the addressing scheme that must be implemented.

Figure 9-11   *PVCs for IP*

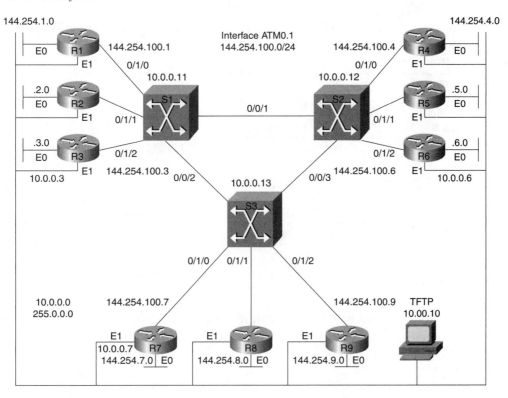

Exercises

Refer to Figure 9-11 to complete the following exercises for Lab 9-1.

1 Configure your router either via the SETUP utility or the command-line interface (CLI) with the following parameters:

— Hostname: **Rn** (where **n** is the router number)

— Enable secret password: **geotrain**

— Enable password: **sanfran**

— Virtual Terminal/Console password: **cisco**

— SNMP: no

— IP Routing: IGRP

— IGRP Autonomous System Number: 100

— IP is your *only* routed protocol thus far

2 Configure your Ethernet 0 and ATM 0.1 interfaces, as identified in Table 9-8.

Table 9-8   *IP Address Assignment*

Router	E0	ATM0.1
R1	144.254.1.1/24	144.254.100.1/24
R2	144.254.2.2/24	144.254.100.2/24
R3	144.254.3.3/24	144.254.100.3/24
R4	144.254.4.4/24	144.254.100.4/24
R5	144.254.5.5/24	144.254.100.5/24
R6	144.254.6.6/24	144.254.100.6/24
R7	144.254.7.7/24	144.254.100.7/24
R8	144.254.8.8/24	144.254.100.8/24
R9	144.254.9.9/24	144.254.100.9/24

3 Configure a PVC to every other router to create a fully meshed ATM PVC network. Use AAL5SNAP. Use Table 9-9 for the VPI/VCI number assignment.

Table 9-9   *VPI/VCI Assignment*

From	To	VCD	VPI	VCI
R1	R2		0	112
	R3		0	113
	R4		0	114

Table 9-9   *VPI/VCI Assignment (Continued)*

From	To	VCD	VPI	VCI
	R5		0	115
	R6		0	116
	R7		0	117
	R8		0	118
	R9		0	119
R2	R1		0	121
	R3		0	123
	R4		0	124
	R5		0	125
	R6		0	126
	R7		0	127
	R8		0	128
R3	R1		0	131
	R2		0	132
	R4		0	134
	R5		0	135
	R6		0	136
	R7		0	137
	R8		0	138
	R9		0	139
R4	R1		0	141
	R2		0	142
	R3		0	143
	R5		0	145
	R6		0	146
	R7		0	147
	R8		0	148
	R9		0	149
R5	R1		0	151
	R2		0	152

continues

Table 9-9 *VPI/VCI Assignment (Continued)*

From	To	VCD	VPI	VCI
	R3		0	153
	R4		0	154
	R6		0	156
	R7		0	157
	R8		0	158
	R9		0	159
R6	R1		0	161
	R2		0	162
	R3		0	163
	R4		0	164
	R5		0	165
	R7		0	167
	R8		0	168
	R9		0	169
R7	R1		0	171
	R2		0	172
	R3		0	173
	R4		0	174
	R5		0	175
	R6		0	176
	R8		0	178
	R9		0	179
R8	R1		0	181
	R2		0	182
	R3		0	183
	R4		0	184
	R5		0	185
	R6		0	186
	R7		0	187
	R9		0	189

Table 9-9   *VPI/VCI Assignment (Continued)*

From	To	VCD	VPI	VCI
R9	R1		0	191
	R2		0	192
	R3		0	193
	R4		0	194
	R5		0	195
	R6		0	196
	R7		0	197
	R8		0	198

4 Map your neighbor's IP network number to the appropriate PVC.

5 Test your configuration.

Remember to save your configuration!

Lab 9-2: Configuring IPX over PVCs Using AAL5SNAP, RFC 2684

Appendix C, "Lab Solutions," provides the solutions to the exercises for this lab.

Objectives: At the end of the lab, you will have completed the following:

- Configure IPX routing
- Enable IPX to flow over the PVCs that were created in Lab 9-1

Purpose: Most environments have multiple Layer 3 protocols. This lab demonstrates how you can implement several protocols over ATM using the same virtual circuit.

Table 9-10 lists and describes the commands you need to be familiar with to complete this lab.

Table 9-10   *Lab 9-2 Command Summary*

Command	Description
ipx routing	Turns on IPX routing.
atm pvc	Sets up bidirectional permanent virtual circuits.
map-list	Maps a Layer 3 network address to a PVC.

continues

Table 9-10 *Lab 9-2 Command Summary (Continued)*

Command	Description
show atm vc	Displays the configured virtual circuits on the router.
show atm interface atm	Displays more detail about the specified interface.
show atm map	Displays the map lists that were created by the user.
debug atm events	Displays the creation of PVCs between the router and the ATM switch.
show ipx route	Displays the IPX routing table.
ping ipx	Tests connectivity at Layer 3.

Figure 9-12 shows the network diagram with all the necessary addressing for the lab.

Figure 9-12 *PVCs for IPX*

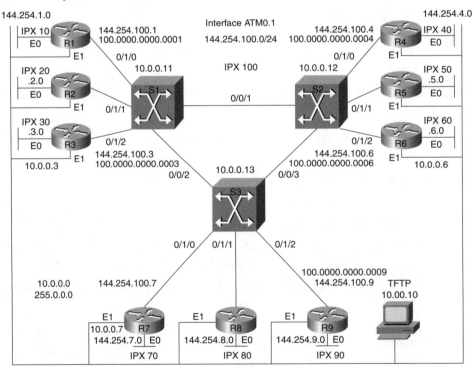

Exercises

Refer to Figure 9-12 to complete the following exercises for Lab 9-2.

1   Turn on IPX routing using the **ipx routing 0000.0000.000x** command, where *x* is your router number.

2   On interface ATM 0.1, assign IPX Network 100.

3   Assign the proper mapping of IPX network addresses to their respective PVCs.

4   Assign an IPX network number to your Ethernet 0 interface (Router 1 uses Network 10, Router 2 uses Network 20, and so on).

5   Test your connectivity.

Remember to save your configuration!

Lab 9-3: Configuring SVCs on Cisco 4500 Routers, RFC 2684

Appendix C, "Lab Solutions," provides the solutions to the exercises for this lab.

Objectives: At the end of the lab, you will have completed the following:

* Configure a signaling PVC

* Assign AESA (NSAP format)

* Configure RFC 2684

Purpose: Although PVCs are good and stable, they are rather cumbersome to set up. SVCs are a bit easier to set up because the ATM switch does all the work—all the end station has to do is signal an SVC request.

Table 9-11 lists and describes the commands you need to be familiar with to complete this lab.

Table 9-11   *Lab 9-3 Command Summary*

Command	Description
atm pvc	Sets up a bidirectional PVC, as well as a signaling PVC.
atm nsap-address	Configures your ATM address (AESA).
map-list	Maps a Layer 3 network address to a PVC (Layer 2).
map-group	Enables or activates a particular map list for an interface.
show atm vc	Displays the configured virtual connections on the router.
show atm interface atm	Displays more detail about the specified interface.

continues

Table 9-11 *Lab 9-3 Command Summary (Continued)*

Command	Description
show atm map	Displays the map lists that the user created.
debug atm events	Displays the creation of PVCs between the router and the ATM switch.
show ip route	Displays the IP routing table.
ping	Tests connectivity at Layer 3.

Figure 9-13 shows the network diagram with all the necessary addressing for the lab.

Figure 9-13 *SVCs for IP*

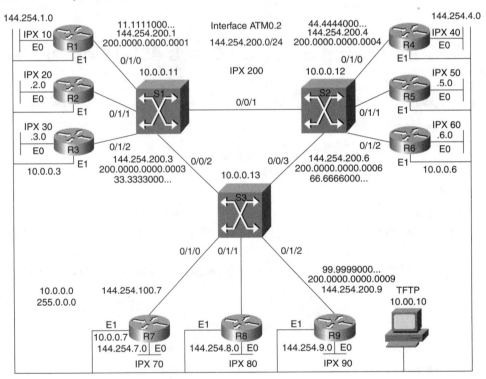

Exercises

Refer to Figure 9-13 to complete the following exercises for Lab 9-3.

   1 Set up signaling PVC between your router and the ingress switch (VPI=0, VCI=5).

2 On subinterface ATM 0.2, configure an AESA address, an IP address, and an IPX address, given the parameters in Table 9-12.

Table 9-12   *AESA Address Assignment*

Router	AESA	IP Address
R1	11.11110000000000000000000.000000000000.00	144.254.200.1
R2	22.22220000000000000000000.000000000000.00	144.254.200.2
R3	33.33330000000000000000000.000000000000.00	144.254.200.3
R4	44.44440000000000000000000.000000000000.00	144.254.200.4
R5	55.55550000000000000000000.000000000000.00	144.254.200.5
R6	66.66660000000000000000000.000000000000.00	144.254.200.6
R7	77.77770000000000000000000.000000000000.00	144.254.200.7
R8	88.88880000000000000000000.000000000000.00	144.254.200.8
R9	99.99990000000000000000000.000000000000.00	144.254.200.9

3 Much like PVCs, your Layer 3 connectivity cannot work unless you map the Layer 3 addresses to the proper ATM addresses using SVCs (remember, RFC 2684 is only an encapsulation method—hence, no magic).

4 Test your connectivity. Make sure you are using the newly created SVCs, not the previously created PVCs.

Remember to save your work!

Lab 9-4: Configuring Classical IP Using PVCs and SVCs on Cisco 4500 Routers, RFC 2225

Appendix C, "Lab Solutions," provides the solutions to the exercises for this lab.

Objectives: At the end of the lab, you will have completed the following:

- Enable Classical IP on the existing PVC network (RFC 2225)
- Enable Classical IP of the SVC network (RFC 2225)
- Configure the ARP Server and Client (RFC 2225)
- Implement a single logical IP subnet (LIS)
- Enable Cisco's extensions to Classical IP and ARP over ATM

Purpose: So far, you have implemented RFC 2684 to carry multiprotocol traffic over ATM. Yet, if you only want to carry IP traffic through your ATM network, you might want to consider RFC 2225, which allows your implementation to be more dynamic and is not as configuration-intensive.

Table 9-13 lists and describes the commands you need to be familiar with to complete this lab.

Table 9-13 *Lab 9-4 Command Summary*

Command	Description
atm pvc	Sets up bidirectional permanent virtual connections; add the **inarp** keyword to activate RFC 2225.
atm arp-server self	Configures the ARP server for one LIS.
atm arp-server nsap	Configures the ARP server client.
atm nsap-address	Configures the ATM NSAP (AESA) address.
atm classic-ip-extensions bfi	Enables Cisco's extensions for server redundancy.
debug atm events	Displays the creation of PVCs between the router and the switch.
debug atm arp	Displays the ATM ARP events.
show ip route	Displays the IP routing table.
ping	Tests connectivity at Layer 3.

Figure 9-14 shows the network diagram and addressing scheme to be deployed in this lab.

Figure 9-14 *Classical IP*

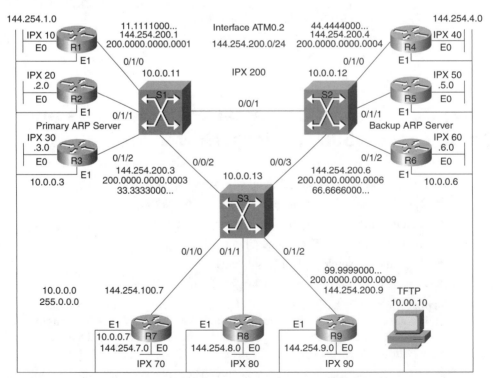

Exercises

Refer to Figure 9-14 to complete the following exercises for Lab 9-4.

1 Remove the **ip map-group** statement from ATM 0.2 to allow dynamic mapping to occur.

2 Initially, R3 will be the only ARP server for the network, with all other routers set up as clients pointing themselves to R3.

3 Test your configuration and IP connectivity. Also, ensure that IPX connectivity is working as expected.

4 Implement a second redundant ARP server, R6, using Cisco's proprietary solution.

5 Verify your configuration and test the failover capability.

Remember to save your work!

Lab 9-5: Configuring next-hop Resolution Protocol on Routers

Appendix C, "Lab Solutions," provides the solutions to the exercises for this lab.

Objectives: At the end of the lab, you will have completed the following:

- Configure NHRP on the Cisco 4500 routers
- Implement three logical IP subnets (LISs) over the ATM backbone
- Demonstrate the advantages of NHRP

Purpose: Lab 9-4, using RFC 2225, allowed you to map Layer 3 IP addresses to ATM addresses dynamically to set up SVCs. This solution was deployed on a single LIS. This lab demonstrates how that simple model can be extended, allowing you to deploy multiple LISs over ATM. You can use NHRP to demonstrate how cut-through routing enables you to bypass intermediate router hops.

NHRP is designed to eliminate the suboptimal routing that results from the LIS model. Routers running Release 10.3 or later are capable of implementing NHRP and thus can act as next-hop servers. A host or router that is not an NHRP server must be configured with the identity of the next-hop server that serves it. NHRP supports two modes of operation: fabric and server. In this lab, you deploy NHRP in fabric mode—allowing each router to operate as a NHS.

In fabric mode, it is expected that all routers within the NBMA network are NHRP-capable. A next-hop server serving a destination must lie along the routed path to that destination. In practice, this means that all egress routers must double as next-hop servers serving the destinations beyond them, and that hosts on the NBMA network are served by routers that double as next-hop servers.

Please note that the implementation of this lab requires the same version of NHRP. Cisco IOS releases prior to Release 12.0 implemented NHRP draft version 4. Cisco IOS Release 12.0 implements NHRP draft version 11. These versions are incompatible.

Table 9-14 lists and describes the commands you need to be familiar with to complete this lab.

Table 9-14 *Lab 9-5 Command Summary*

Command	Description
atm pvc	Sets up bidirectional PVC, as well as a signaling PVC.
atm nsap-address	Configures your ATM address (AESA).
ip nhrp network-id	Specifies an NHRP logical network identifier (enables NHRP).
show atm vc	Displays the configured virtual connections on the router.
show atm int atm	Displays more detail about the specified interface.
show atm map	Displays the map lists that the user created.
debug atm events	Displays the creation of PVCs between the router and the ATM switch.
debug ip nhrp	Displays NHRP messages (such as service requests).
show ip nhrp	Displays NHRP information.
show ip route	Displays the IP routing table.
ping	Tests connectivity at Layer 3.
show ip arp	Displays the contents of the IP ARP table.

Figure 9-15 shows the network topology, illustrating three IP broadcast domains and the addressing schemes involved.

Exercises

Refer to Figure 9-15 to complete the following exercises for Lab 9-5.

1 You are to use new subinterfaces—ATM 0.3 and, on some routers, ATM 0.4—to implement this lab solution. Migrate your router NSAP (AESA) address from ATM 0.2 to subinterface ATM 0.3 and shut down your ATM 0.2 subinterface.

2 RFC 2225 is deployed in the lab within an LIS. This implies that you require a separate ARP server (because you are using SVCs) within a single LIS. Have R3 be the ARP server in the LIS1, R8 be the ARP server in the LIS2, and R5 be the ARP server in the LIS3.

Figure 9-15 *NHRP Implementation*

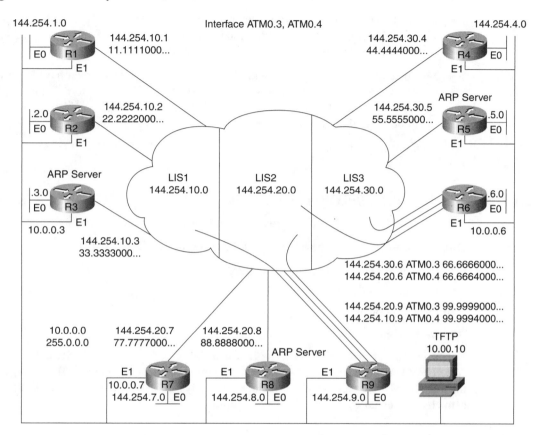

3   As per the lab schematic in Figure 9-15, R9 and R6 both are associated logically with two logical IP subnets. They require a second NSAP address and a second IP address to support the second subnet, associated with subinterface ATM 0.4. Note that you are still using the same Layer 3 IP routing protocol, IGRP.

4   Configure your ATM 0.3 (and ATM 0.4) subinterfaces and ensure that you are associating the correct ARP servers to the correct subinterfaces.

5   Verify that you have full IP connectivity between all routers. Using pings and the **show ip route** command, ensure that the IGRP routing strategy is working as expected. You have not yet turned on or activated NHRP.

6   Use the **trace** command to demonstrate the path taken when you forward packets to remote IP destinations from your router—for example, from R2, **trace 144.254.7.7**, **trace 144.254.4.4**.

7 Configure NHRP at the subinterface level with the **ip nhrp network-id 1** command.

8 Use the **trace** command on your router to demonstrate that IP, as per the IP routing table information, can take an extra hop to go to the 144.254.4.X and 144.254.5.X destinations. For example, from R2 or R3, trace IP address 144.254.4.4.

9 Now that all routers participate in the NHRP, verify that you no longer have to go via extra hop to reach destinations 144.254.4.X and 144.254.5.X, as before. For example, on R3 or R2, repeat the **trace** test to IP destinations used previously. You can see the cut-through routing event.

Do *not* save your work!

Lab 9-6: ATM NPM-to-ATM NPM Configuration

Appendix C, "Lab Solutions," provides the solutions to the exercises for this lab.

Objectives: At the end of the lab, you will have completed the following:

• Configure a router-to-router ATM NPM configuration

• Configure PVCs across an OC-3 link

• Configure the internal clocks

• Verify connectivity

Purpose: This lab sets up connectivity between two ATM NPMs directly. By default, the ATM NPM expects a connected ATM switch to provide transmit clocking. To specify that the ATM NPM generates the transmit clock internally for SONET, the user needs to add the **atm clock internal** command to the configuration.

NOTE   For SONET, E3, or DS3 interfaces, at least one of the ATM AIPs must be configured to supply its internal clock to the line.

After the link is up, PVCs can be configured with traffic mapped across the link. The user then can see that other than clocking issues, the setup is the same as the first PVC lab. Because you do not have a link to an ATM switch, you no longer have a UNI interface for signaling. For this format, PVCs are the only type of connection available.

Table 9-15 lists and describes the commands you need to be familiar with to complete this lab.

Table 9-15 *Command Summary*

Command	Description
map-group	Associates a list of addresses to a subinterface.
atm clock internal	Generates the transmit clock internally.
atm pvc	Configures a PVC.
map-list	Creates a list of mapped addresses.

Figure 9-16 shows the network topology and the addressing scheme to be deployed in this lab.

Figure 9-16 *NPM-to-NPM Diagram*

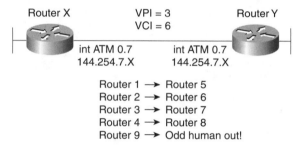

Exercises

Refer to Figure 9-16 to complete the following exercises for Lab 9-6.

1   Using Figure 9-16 for configuration, assign the IP address to the subinterface.

2   Associate your list of mapped addresses to this subinterface.

3   Change the clocking to rely on the internal clock of the router (routers 1, 2, 3, and 4 *only*).

4   Create your PVC segment using the addresses shown in Figure 9-16.

5   Create your list of mapped addresses.

6   Check for connectivity of the 144.254.7.x cloud.

Do *not* save your work!

Review Questions

1 What steps are necessary to implement RFC 2684 using PVCs?

2 What is VCD? Is it locally significant?

3 What does "aal5mux" stand for?

4 How do you configure RFC 2225 using PVCs?

5 How does the RFC 2684 implementation vary for SVCs when compared to its use with a PVC?

6 What does RFC 2225 SVC implementation use as a model?

7 What is the major difference between RFC 2225 and RFC 1577?

8 What types of NHRP implementations do Cisco routers support?

9 What should you be careful of when implementing NHRP?

"I have made mistakes, but I have never made the mistake of claiming that I never made one."—James Gordon Bennett (1795–1872)

"To conquer without risk is to triumph without glory."—Pierre Corneille (1606–1684)

"Only those who attempt the absurd will achieve the impossible."—Albert Einstein (1879–1955)

After reading this chapter, you should be able to understand the following:

- LANE design considerations and what to watch out for in your designs
- LANE scalability issues
- The limitations of LANE v1
- Cisco's redundant LANE architecture
- The syntax of commands and configuration examples

CHAPTER 10

LANE Implementation

Chapter 9, "Multiprotocol Encapsulation (RFC 2684), Classical IP and ARP over ATM (RFC 2225), and NHRP Implementation," elaborated on implementations of multiprotocol encapsulation over ATM (RFC 2684) and Classical IP (RFC 2225) in a single LIS or multiple LISs (with the help of NHRP). This chapter discusses Cisco's LANE v1 implementation. Remember that, as with Classical IP, LANE uses RFC 2684 encapsulation.

This chapter presents four LANE laboratories, including Simple Server Redundancy Protocol (SSRP) and multi-ELAN examples. Appendix C, "Lab Solutions," presents the solutions for the labs.

LANE Design Considerations

Let's recall the definition of LANE. LANE is a method for supporting legacy LAN technologies over an ATM infrastructure. It is an extension of Layer 2 over ATM. The edge devices are totally unaware of ATM's involvement. They think that the communication is over a LAN technology—Ethernet or Token Ring. LANE positions ATM to support any Layer 3 protocol because it provides bridging capabilities that are very similar to those of any other LAN technology. The net result is that all the devices attached to the emulated LAN (ELAN) appear to be one bridged segment. In this way, the performance characteristics of IP, IPX, AppleTalk, DecNet, and any other protocol are very similar to a traditional bridged environment. LANE, as with any other ATM internetwork method, uses the multiprotocol encapsulation over ATM method that is defined in RFC 2684.

It is important to distinguish between ELANs and LANE. ELAN is the VLAN over ATM, whereas LANE is the supporting architecture. You can equate a VLAN to an ELAN—each ELAN is a separate broadcast domain. Although more than one ELAN can run on the same ATM network, each ELAN is completely independent of the others. Users of separate ELANs cannot communicate directly, as is true of users on separate VLANs. Communication between ELANs is possible only through routers. Refer to Chapter 5, "LAN Emulation (LANE)," for full details on LANE architecture and operation.

LANE functionality is supported in a variety of Cisco products. This includes the families of Catalyst switches and routers that support ATM, which are listed in Table 8-3 in Chapter 8, "Circuit Emulation Service ATM Connectivity and Summary of Cisco ATM Edge Devices."

You have to define the LANE functions on the ATM physical interfaces and subinterfaces. A subinterface is a logical interface and is part of a physical interface, such as an OC-3 fiber. ATM interfaces on the Cisco routers and the ATM module of the Catalyst 5000 switch can be subdivided into up to 255 logical subinterfaces.

When designing LANE networks, you should be aware of the following design considerations:

- Capacity of the ATM interface switching fabric for transmitting and receiving data
- Overhead needed to be handled by LANE servers
- Virtual circuit (VC) types in your ATM network for use by LANE
- ELAN Spanning-Tree Protocol functionality
- Server redundancy in the LANE architecture

The following sections analyze each of these design considerations.

Capacity of the ATM Switching Fabrics

When you examine the switching capacity of the ATM interface, you should be sensitive to the limitations on the number of VCs. For example, Cisco 7500 routers can handle up to 4096 VCs, whereas Cisco 4500/4700 routers can handle up to 1023 VCs. As discussed in Chapter 5, the LANE architecture results in VC consumption in both the edge devices and the ATM switch cloud.

The total number of VCs consumed by LANE is calculated as follows:

$$\frac{N \times (N-1)}{2} + 3 \times N + 2$$

where N is the number of LANE clients.

The logic behind the formula is quite simple. The total number of VCs depends on the number of control and data VCs. For a fully meshed LANE architecture, which the majority of them are, the total number of Data Direct VCs is N×(N-1)÷2. Then you have three point-to-point VCs for each LEC (Configuration Direct, Control Direct, and Multicast Send VCs) plus two point-to-multipoint VCs (Control Distribute and Multicast Forward VCs).

Figure 10-1 presents a LANE example of two ELANs, involving two departments— Marketing and Engineering. The Marketing ELAN has four clients (LEC1–LEC4), and the Engineering ELAN has six clients (LEC1–LEC6). Using the formula for VC consumption, the total number of VCs for the entire LANE implementation is 55 (20 VCs for the Marketing ELAN {[(4×(4–1)÷2)+3×4+2]= 20} and 35 VCs for the Engineering ELAN {[(6×(6–1)÷2)+3×6+2]= 35}).

Figure 10-1 *Illustration of Total VC Count*

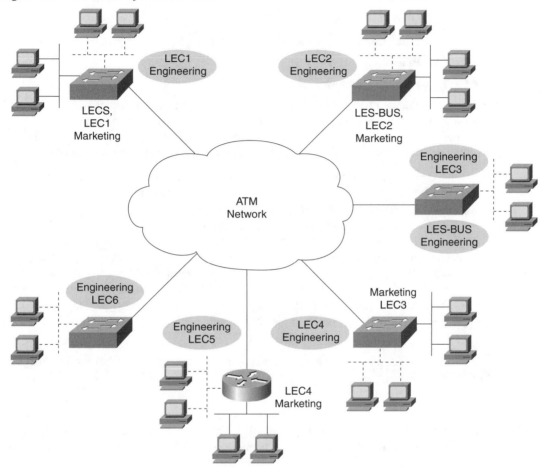

Another aspect of capacity planning is the call setup capability of ATM switches inside the ATM network. This is especially important if there is a failure in the cloud in an SVC-based network scenario where VCs are created dynamically. In this case, the ATM switches can experience many call setup requests simultaneously and could be overloaded. For example, the call handling capability of a LightStream 1010 switch is approximately 110 calls per second.

Overhead Handled by LANE Servers

Three types of servers exist in LANE architecture:

- LAN Emulation Configuration Server (LECS)
- LAN Emulation Server (LES)
- Broadcast and Unknown Server (BUS)

Cisco implemented LES and BUS functions on a single platform, which makes absolute sense. Why? Because the LANE v1 specification does not specify any method of interconnection between the LES and the BUS, yet the LES must somehow know the address of the BUS and is responsible for providing the BUS's address to an LEC.

If you examine which of the servers has the highest volume of traffic, you discover that it is the BUS. The LECS has only one VC to every client—namely, a Configure Direct VC. Although the LES and the BUS have the same number of VCs for every client, BUS services are used much more frequently than those of the LES. Why? Simply because a single ELAN is a broadcast domain and, depending on the protocol in use, there could be numerous broadcasts. In LANE v1 architecture, it is the BUS's responsibility to handle the broadcast, multicast, and unknown traffic. Be extra careful when selecting the right platform for BUS services (which actually are LES-BUS services in a Cisco environment). For example, the LANE card for the Catalyst 5000 has a BUS processing capability of approximately 120 kbps, whereas the 7500 AIP card's capability is approximately 60 kbps.

When you consider the dynamics of LANE, the burden on the devices running LANE services becomes apparent. Therefore, it is a good idea to spread LANE services across multiple devices if possible.

TIP   Some implementations use ATM switches as LANE edge devices, typically performing the functions of a server(s). Generally, this is not a good idea. Leave the ATM switches to do what they are designed to do—switch ATM cells. Remember that LANE server/client functions are ATM applications, so your ATM switch must segment and reassemble the payload cells. Why invest money in a cell relay technology when all you need is an Ethernet or a Token Ring emulation server?

Types of VCs in ATM Networks for Use with LANE

LANE VCs can be either SVC-based or PVC-based. Although a PVC-based LANE can exist, the complexity of its setup and the manual labor involved are absolutely monstrous. Think about it! You must configure PVCs for all control and data VCs. Typing is very error-prone and time-consuming. A PVC-based LANE is almost impossible to administer. Consider the sample LANE architecture illustrated in Figure 10-2. Just two LANE clients result in nine VCs!

Figure 10-2 *PVC-based LANE*

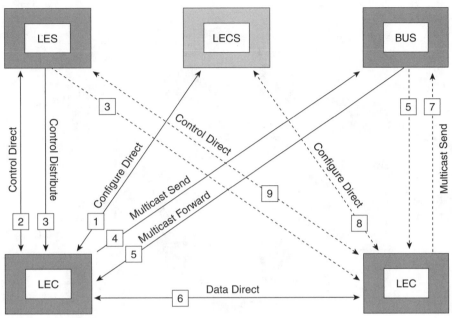

An SVC-based LANE is much more flexible and is easier to administer and set up. You can deploy Private Network-to-Network Interface (PNNI) as a routing protocol for ATM signaling, which enables dynamic bandwidth allocation, traffic distribution, and path redundancy. Within the ATM cloud, PNNI allows you to

- Load balance call setup requests across multiple paths
- Support path redundancy with fast convergence
- Provide excellent call setup performance across multiple hops using the background routing feature

Figure 10-3 illustrates how ATM networks support load balancing.

NOTE   Please do not confuse connection-oriented ATM load balancing with connectionless IP load balancing. In ATM, you load balance call setup only, not the actual data; whereas in IP, you load balance the data itself.

Figure 10-3 *Load Balancing ATM Call Setup*

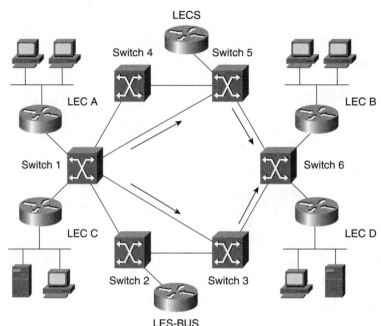

Load balancing of calls is enabled by default on the LightStream 1010 switch. As illustrated in Figure 10-3, connection from LEC A to LEC B can be established via the {Switch 1, Switch 5, Switch 6} path, whereas a connection from LEC C to LEC D could be established using the {Switch 1, Switch 3, Switch 6} path.

The background routing process consists of routing call setups with the help of a pre-computed route database. With the background routing process, the LightStream 1010 switches compute a list of possible paths to all destinations for all service categories. When a call is placed from LEC A to LEC B, PNNI picks a cached route from the background route table in ingress Switch 1, instead of computing a route on demand. This eases the CPU load on the switches and provides a faster rate of call setup processing.

ELAN Spanning-Tree Protocol Functionality

The Spanning-Tree Protocol is implemented in Layer 2 switches/bridges to prevent loops in networks that have redundant paths. Because LANE bridges Ethernet/Token Ring traffic across an ATM network, the Spanning Tree bridge protocol data units (BPDUs) are transmitted over the entire ELAN. The ATM network appears to the Spanning Tree process from the Layer 2 edge devices—it simply thinks of the ATM network as a shared Ethernet/Token Ring network.

Because all clients cache their ARP information for a relatively long period of time, there is a danger that these clients might end up using "old" information until the ARP table is refreshed. While the "old" cache information is used, the clients can send the data into the "land of nowhere" using the previously established Data Direct VCs.

To speed up Spanning Tree convergence over LANE, the LANE protocol specifies two types of messages: the LE-Topology-Request and the LE-NARP. LANE clients that support the Spanning Tree process generate the LE-Topology-Request message and send it to the LES (whenever they detect the network topology change). In turn, the LES distributes this request to all the other clients on the LANE. Upon receipt of such a message, each of the clients reduces the aging period of its cached ARP information. The LANE clients use another message type, the LE-NARP, to inform the LES that a MAC address, which was remote for a given LEC, is now local. In turn, the LES distributes this information to all other clients. As a result, the clients update their cache information with the new MAC address.

The moral of the story about Spanning Tree over LANE is to be sensitive to network stability. If your LANE clients appear and reappear frequently, you need to lower the ARP cache timing to reduce the traffic into the "land of nowhere."

Server Redundancy in the LANE Architecture

Although LANE allows you to connect your legacy LANs to an ATM network, LANE v1 does not define any mechanisms for building redundancy and fault tolerance into LANE services. This makes LANE services a single point of failure for the network. Furthermore, because ELAN-to-ELAN connectivity is achieved at Layer 3, router redundancy is another issue.

You can use the following techniques to build fault-tolerant LANE networks:

- Deploy Simple Server Redundancy Protocol (SSRP) to provide for server redundancy.
- Deploy Hot Standby Router Protocol (HSRP) to provide for router redundancy.
- Implement dual-attached LANE cards in the Catalyst 5000 switches for multiple ATM uplinks. Lab 10-4, "Configuring LANE for Dual-Homed Catalyst Switches with Redundancy," illustrates the example of a dual-attached Catalyst 5000 providing quadruple redundancy.

The most important redundancy issue in the LANE v1 architecture is that LANE clients can access only one set of LANE services at any given time—that is, a single LECS supports all the ELANs, and a single LES-BUS supports a single ELAN. If any one of these services fails, the whole LANE collapses. An LECS failure impacts all ELANs. Any existing connections would operate normally under these conditions, but new clients would not be able to communicate. An LES/BUS failure impacts all clients because the LES-BUS pair provides vital functions to the clients with respect to MAC-to-ATM address resolution and broadcasting.

It is clear that LANE v1 has limited robustness, and in many instances this is a deciding factor as to whether to proceed with a LANE v1 architecture.

Now, let's examine how SSRP and HSRP can provide for server and router redundancy when using LANE v1.

SSRP

SSRP uses a primary-secondary combination of LANE services to provide server resiliency.

For LECS redundancy, multiple secondary LECSs back up the primary one.

LES-BUS redundancy is handled in a similar fashion, with multiple secondary LESs-BUSs backing up the primary one.

TIP   I often am asked about the number of LECSs and redundant LESs-BUSs. You are not limited theoretically to how many servers you can configure using SSRP. However, you should use a commonsense philosophy here. How much redundancy do you want, and how much do you really need? You should evaluate the complexity of the implementation versus the quantity of redundant servers. Typically, two or three servers should be enough. Any more could result in very complex topologies, and the benefits would not justify the extra cost.

LECS Redundancy

How is LECS redundancy implemented? Before answering this question, you should review the three methods that clients use to discover the ATM address of the LECS. According to Cisco's LANE v1 implementation, which complies with the ATM Forum LANE v1 specification (af-LANE-0021.000), LEC uses the following mechanisms to locate the LECS:

- Use ILMI to find the LECS ATM address.
- Use the well-known LECS address. Look for a fixed ATM address that is specified by the ATM Forum as the LECS ATM address.
- Use the LECS PVC. The well-known PVC uses VPI/VCI = 0/17. This option rarely is used and is not included as an option on Cisco LECs; thus, it is omitted from further discussion in this book.

In addition to these options, Cisco implemented the capability to use the preconfigured LECS address in the clients (as specified in the LANE v2 ATM Forum specification, af lane-0084.000). This method is simple to accomplish—all you have to do is statically enter LECS addresses into every LEC. However, this method does not scale well due to the manual labor involved. Just imagine, every single client (and there could be many) must have LECS addresses preconfigured!

Using ILMI to Find the LECS ATM Address   Using this method, a client sends queries to the ingress ATM switch using ILMI. The switch has a MIB variable set up with the ATM address of the LECS. Although this method involves static LECS address entries into ATM ingress switches, it scales better than the previous method. Why? Simply because typically fewer ATM ingress switches exist than LECs.

Because a client uses ILMI to discover the LECS address, the ILMI PVC (using VPI/VCI =0/16) must be defined in your clients. Figure 10-4 depicts the process for LECS address discovery with the help of ILMI.

Figure 10-4 *Auto-Discovery of LECS Address Using ILMI*

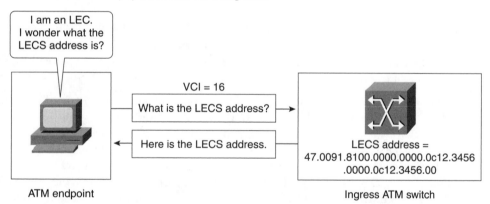

Every ingress ATM switch that has LANE clients connected to it must have the LECS address preprogrammed. The command for defining an LECS address in an ATM switch is as follows:

```
atm lecs-address-default lecsaddress index
```

Example 10-1 illustrates the configuration command within a LightStream 1010 of an LECS address.

Example 10-1 *Definition of LECS Address in an ATM Switch*

```
Switch(config)#atm lecs-address-default
  47.0091.8100.0000.00e0.142b.4a01.00e0.f966.4a43.00 1
Switch(config)#atm lecs-address-default
  47.0091.8100.0000.0000.0c12.3456.0000.0c12.3456.00 2
```

When you implement SSRP, you need to configure multiple LECS addresses into your ingress ATM switches. When an LEC requests the LECS address from the ATM switch, it gets the entire table of LECS addresses in response. The client's job is to connect to the highest-ranked LECS address. If this fails, the client tries the next one on the list, and so on, until it finally connects to an active LECS.

It is the SSRP's responsibility to ensure that only one LECS responds to the Configure Request queries that come from the LEC. How does SSRP determine which LECS is the primary one? This question goes to the heart of SSRP. When LANE is initialized, the LECS obtains the LECS address table from the switch. Then the LECS tries to connect to all the other LECSs that are below itself in the rank. The index entry in the LECS address table located in the ATM switches (see Example 10-1) determines the rank. The index entry is assigned dynamically by the switch, based on the order of entry of the LECS addresses. That is, if you first enter the address **47.0091.8100.0000.00e0.142b.4a01.00e0.f966.4a43.00** into an ingress ATM switch, and then you enter the address **47.0091.8100.0000.0000.0c12.3456.0000.0c12.3456.00**, the switch automatically assigns the index of 1 to the first entry and the index of 2 to the second entry.

If the LECS has a connection from an LECS that is ranked higher than its own (the lower the number, the higher the rank), it assumes it is supposed to be in the backup mode. The highest-ranking LECS (the one with the lowest number) does not have any other LECS that connect to it from above; thus, it assumes the role of the primary LECS.

Figure 10-5 illustrates the procedure for a backup in case a primary LECS fails. Assume that the LANE defined five LECSs: A, B, C, D, and E. After startup, when you configure all the ATM switches with the same LECS address table, LECS A obtains the LECS address table from the ATM switch to which it is attached and finds out that it has four LECSs below itself. Consequently, it tries to connect to LECS B, LECS C, LECS D, and LECS E. Similarly, LECS B connects to LECS C, LECS D, and LECS E. LECS C connects to LECS D and LECS E. LECS D connects to LECS E. There is a downward cascading effect of established VCs. Because LECS A does not have any VCs from above it, it becomes the primary LECS.

During normal network operation, LECS A responds to all of the Configure Request queries, and the backup LECS do not respond to any queries. If the primary LECS A becomes unavailable for any reason, LECS B, LECS C, LECS D, and LECS E lose their VCs from LECS A. When that happens, LECS B no longer has any VCs from above; thus, it assumes the role of the primary LECS. LECS C, LECS D, and LECS E still have connections from higher-ranking LECSs and, therefore, continue to operate in the backup mode.

Figure 10-5 *LECS Redundancy*

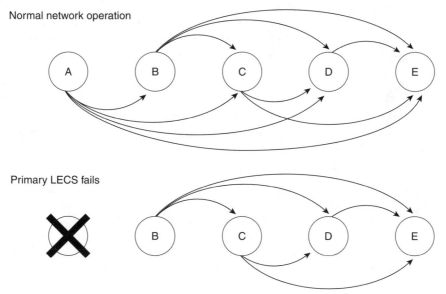

Normal network operation

Primary LECS fails

Using a Well-Known ATM Address Specified by ATM Forum to Find the LECS

ATM Address   SSRP also works with the LECS well-known address
(0x47.0079.0000000000000000000.00A03E000001.00), which the LANE v1
specification defines.

The Cisco LECS can listen on multiple ATM addresses simultaneously—the well-known
and the autoconfigured addresses. You need to configure LECS to listen to the well-known
address using the following command:

```
Router (config-if)#lane config fixed-config-atm-address
```

When the LECS is enabled to listen to the well-known address, it registers the address with
the ATM switch so that the ATM switches can advertise routes to the well-known address
and route any call setup requests. Implementing SSRP allows for multiple LECSs in the
network. If each LECS registers the well-known address with the ATM switch to which it
is directly attached, call setups are routed to different places in the network. Therefore, first
you want the master LECS to be chosen, using the autoconfigured addresses that are preset
in all Cisco LANE-capable devices. To accomplish this, you need to enable
autoconfiguration of the LECS address. When the master LECS fails, the well-known
address moves with the master LECS. PNNI routing handles advertising the new route to
the well-known address when the LECS mastership changes.

WARNING	SSRP with well-known addresses does not work properly if two LECS are attached to the same ATM switch due to possible duplicate address registration on the same switch. Consequently, please ensure that each LECS is attached to a separate ATM switch.

LES-BUS Redundancy

LES-BUS redundancy supports the configuration of multiple LES-BUS pairs that work as a primary or a secondary. The mechanism used here is different from the one used in LECS redundancy.

You need to configure the addresses of multiple LESs for a given ELAN into the LECS database. Within this database, each LES is assigned a priority. Upon completion of the LANE initialization, each LES opens a VC with the primary LECS using the LECS address discovery mechanism. The LES with the highest priority that has an open VC to the LECS is assigned as the primary LES-BUS by the primary LECS. Remember that BUS redundancy follows LES redundancy because Cisco's implementation positions both the LES and the BUS functions within the same physical platform.

SSRP Interoperability

Cisco's deployment of SSRP does not violate the LANE v1 specification; thus, it is interoperable with other vendors. Because SSRP is transparent to all LANE clients that use ILMI or the well-known LECS NSAP address, independent third-party LANE clients can use SSRP if they use ILMI for LECS address discovery and can handle multiple LECS addresses returned by the ATM switch. It is important to understand that SSRP is proprietary and no other vendor implements it. Therefore, it is not compatible with the redundancy schemes used by other vendors.

SSRP Configuration Guidelines

To correctly support server redundancy, you must adhere to the configuration rules listed in Table 10-1. Failure to do so results in improper SSRP operation.

Table 10-1   *SSRP Configuration Guidelines*

Rule	Description
1	Each LECS must maintain the same database of ELANs.
2	Each ATM switch must define the LECS address table in the same order.
3	When using SSRP with the well-known address, do not place more than one LECS on the same ATM switch.

Fast Simple Server Replication Protocol

To improve upon SSRP, Cisco introduced the Fast Simple Server Replication Protocol (FSSRP). The difference between SSRP and FSSRP is that all LANE servers are always active with FSSRP. With FSSRP, LANE clients have VCs established to all servers, up to a maximum of four at any given time. If a single LANE server becomes unavailable, the LANE client instantly switches to the next LES-BUS, resulting in no loss of the LANE service.

With the SSRP, when the primary server fails, the client must clear its Data Direct VCs to other clients, clear out its LE-ARP entries, and start sending signals to establish new VCs to the backup LES-BUS. FSSRP alleviates these problems by allowing a client to join up to four LES-BUSs simultaneously. FSSRP still maintains the concept of the primary LES-BUS, where the clients do use the primary LES-BUS. With FSSRP, however, when the primary LES-BUS goes down, the client is already connected to up to three backup LES-BUSs. The client simply uses the next backup LES-BUS, which becomes the primary one. The FSSRP ranking order of primary and backup servers is identical to the SSRP's.

The only disadvantage of the FSSRP is the number of simultaneous VCs that must be set up. On a per-client basis, up to 12 additional VCs could be created. These include the additional Control Direct, Control Distribute, Multicast Send, and Multicast Forward VCs. If you decide to use FSSRP, you should calculate whether the number of the existing VCs in your network can be maintained with the additional VC connections to all the backup servers.

The good news is that FSSRP is designed to interoperate seamlessly with SSRP. From a configuration perspective, FSSRP requires only one additional line to the SSRP configuration, as follows:

```
Router (config-if)#lane fssrp
```

HSRP over LANE

HSRP is the protocol that provides redundancy for the Layer 3 devices (routers) that are required for the ELAN's interconnection. When the HSRP protocol is used between two routers, one of the routers is elected as the primary router interface (or subinterface) for a given broadcast domain (subnet). The other router acts as the *hot standby* router.

HSRP requires that routers implementing HSRP share a default IP and MAC address, which is called the *virtual address*. The *virtual* IP address is used as the default gateway for all IP devices on that network. Therefore, when the primary router fails, the hot standby router takes over without needing to reprogram the default addresses in the edge devices.

Because HSRP requires a MAC address, it is possible to implement HSRP-based recovery over LANE. The mechanisms used are the same as for any Ethernet interface.

LANE Configuration

Prior to examining the steps that are necessary to configure LANE functions in the edge devices, let's review the ATM addressing scheme that is used by the Cisco platforms.

Notice that this section focuses on the SVC method of LANE implementation. If you implement a PVC-based LANE, you do not require NSAP addresses.

The good news is that you do not have to worry about typing long 40-hex numbers to assign NSAP addresses to the edge devices.

Cisco products that support the LANE architecture have preprovisioned the end system identifier (ESI) portions of the NSAP address for the LECS, the LES, the BUS, and the LEC functions in case the device is required to be one of them. The prefix of the NSAP address is obtained from the ingress ATM switch using ILMI. Recall that the ESI portion of the address is 6 bytes long and the prefix is 13 bytes long, as illustrated in Figure 10-6.

Figure 10-6 *Edge Device Address Autoconfiguration*

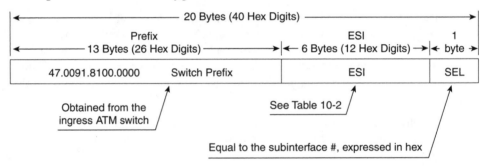

Cisco's prefix is 0x47.0091.8100.0000. This prefix is concatenated with the 6-byte switch identifier, which is the switch's MAC address that is obtained from the Ethernet port located in the switch. This makes up for the prefix portion of the ATM edge device. The ESI is obtained from the MAC address of the first LAN port located in the edge device. This is followed by the Selector byte, which must be equal to the subinterface number that is expressed in hexadecimal notation.

Well, so far the edge devices have obtained only one NSAP address dynamically (with the help of ILMI). The question is, what if that edge device performs all the LECS, LES-BUS, and LEC functions? Every server and client in the LANE architecture must have its own unique NSAP address. To conform to the ATM addressing uniqueness requirements, different ESIs apply to the different functions of the LANE architecture. Cisco uses the ESI and the Selector byte number conventions listed in Table 10-2.

Table 10-2   *NSAP Address Assignment*

ESI for a Component of	Selector Byte	Edge Device is Catalyst 5000	Edge Device is a Router
LEC	= 0xSubint #	MAC + 0	MAC - 1
LES	= 0xSubint #	MAC + 1	MAC + 0
BUS	= 0xSubint #	MAC + 2	MAC + 1
LECS	= 0x00	MAC + 3	MAC + 2

The term *MAC* in Table 10-2 represents the MAC address of the first LAN port in the device.

The use of the Selector byte and the modification of the last digit of the ESI ensures a unique ATM address assignment for each LANE component for each ELAN, even if the components share the same physical interface.

Table 10-3 illustrates an example of ESI assignment for the Catalyst 5000, if it is required to participate in implementing LANE. The assumption here is that the MAC address of the first LAN port is 0800.200c.1000.

Table 10-3   *ESI Assignment Example for Catalyst 5000*

ESI for	Catalyst 5000
LEC	0800.200c.1000
LES	0800.200c.1001
BUS	0800.200c.1002
LECS	0800.200c.1003

As stated earlier, Cisco edge devices in a LANE implementation assume the NSAP addresses dynamically. You are required to set up an ILMI PVC in the edge device for the prefix to be announced dynamically. The command syntax for creating the ILMI PVC creation is as follows:

```
Router (config-if)#atm pvc 4 0 16 ilmi
```

Please note that for the preceding command line, **4** is the VCD number, **0** is the VPI number, **16** is the VCI number (which is reserved by the ATM Forum for ILMI), and **ilmi** is the encapsulation method.

To view the dynamic NSAP addresses that would be used by the edge device when it participates in a LANE implementation, use the following command:

```
Router#show lane default-atm-addresses
```

NOTE	Some people become confused when viewing the NSAP addresses for all the LANE functions. Just remember this: a device does not have to be an LES in a particular LANE to have an NSAP address for the LES function. The addresses that you see when you type the **show lane default-atm-addresses** command are default values that are given to that edge device if it is required to perform an LEC, LES, BUS, or LECS function. If you did not configure that device to be an LECS, for example, the LECS address exists but cannot be used.

Prior to discussing the configuration commands for the various LANE components, let's lay out the interface and subinterface rules that you should conform to when configuring LANE in routers (or Layer 3 switches):

- The LECS should always be assigned to the major interface because one LECS serves all ELANS.

- The assignment of any other component to the major interface is identical to assigning that component to the 0 subinterface.

- The LES-BUS should be assigned to a subinterface because each subinterface is a single broadcast domain, and each ELAN requires its own LES-BUS pair.

- The LEC should be assigned to a subinterface because each subinterface is a single broadcast domain.

- Clients of two different ELANs cannot be configured on the same subinterface.

- Servers of two different ELANs cannot be configured on the same subinterface.

- The LES-BUS and the LEC for a given ELAN should be on the same subinterface within a single platform, belonging to the same ELAN.

LANE Example

Let's examine a sample LANE, illustrated in Figure 10-7. There are two ELANs—Marketing and Engineering. Because there are two ELANs, you need to configure two LES-BUSs—one per ELAN—and one LECS for the whole network. Each ELAN can have as many clients as necessary (of course there is a limit, which is associated with the physical limitations for the platforms that you are using).

Figure 10-7 *LANE Example*

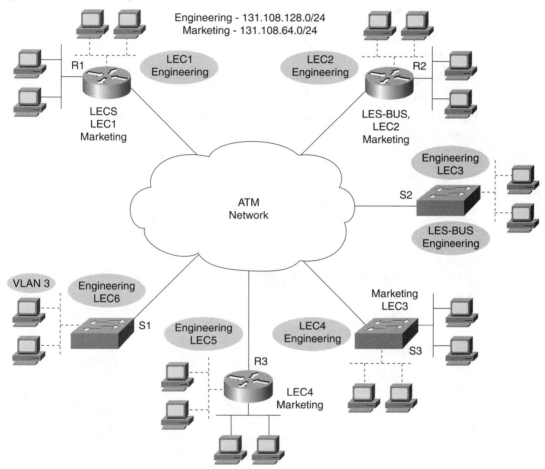

Before you dive into the configurations for all the LANE components, you should create a LANE plan and worksheet. The plan and worksheet should contain the following information (leave spaces for the ATM address of each LANE component on each subinterface of each participating router or switch):

- The component and the interface where the LECS is located.

- The component, the interface, and the subinterface where the LES and the BUS for each ELAN are located. Each ELAN can have multiple servers for fault-tolerant operation.

- The component, the interfaces, and the subinterfaces where the clients for each ELAN are located.
- The LECS database name and its components.
- The name of the default ELAN (optional).
- The names of the ELANs that have unrestricted membership.
- The names of the ELANs that have restricted membership.

The last three items in this list are very important; they determine how you set up each ELAN in the LECS database.

Table 10-4 provides a sample LANE plan and worksheet based on the LANE network topology illustrated in Figure 10-7.

Table 10-4   *LANE Plan and Worksheet*

Name of ELAN	LAN Type to Be Emulated	LANE Component	Location	Interface to Be Used on the Device	ATM Address
N/A	N/A	LECS	R1	atm 1/0	47.00918100000000E0 4FACB401.0801.200c.1 003.00
Marketing	Ethernet	LES	R2	atm 1/0.16	47.00918100000000E0 4FBCA401.0801.300c. 1001.10
		BUS	R2	atm 1/0.16	47.00918100000000E0 4FBCA401.0801.300c. 1002.10
		LEC 1	R1	atm 1/0.16	47.00918100000000E0 4FACB401.0801.200c.1 000.10
		LEC 2	R2	atm 1/0.16	47.00918100000000E0 4FBCA401.0801.300c. 1000.10
		LEC 3	S3	atm 0.16	47.00918100000000E0 4FCBA401.0801.100c. 1000.10
		LEC 4	R3	atm 1/0.16	47.00918100000000E0 4FABD401.0801.400c. 1000.10

Table 10-4   *LANE Plan and Worksheet (Continued)*

Name of ELAN	LAN Type to Be Emulated	LANE Component	Location	Interface to Be Used on the Device	ATM Address
Engineering	Ethernet	LES	S2	atm 0.17	47.00918100000000E0 4FDBA401.0801.000c. 1001.11
		BUS	S2	atm 0.17	47.00918100000000E0 4FDBA401.0801.000c. 1002.11
		LEC 1	R1	atm 1/0.17	47.00918100000000E0 4FACB401.0801.200c.1 000.11
		LEC 2	R2	atm 1/0.17	47.00918100000000E0 4FBCA401.0801.300c. 1000.11
		LEC 3	S2	atm 0.17	47.00918100000000E0 4FDBA401.0801.000c. 1000.11
		LEC 4	S3	atm 0.17	47.00918100000000E0 4FCBA401.0801.100c. 1000.11
		LEC 5	R3	atm 1/0.17	47.00918100000000E0 4FABD401.0801.400c. 1000.11
		LEC 6	S1	atm 0.17	47.00918100000000E0 4FBAD401.0800.000c. 1000.11

Please note that VLANs need to be configured on the LAN edge switches. These VLANs must be mapped to the appropriate ELANs. This is illustrated in a moment in Example 10-5.

Because the discussion here is about SVC-based LANE, you are required to configure the signaling PVC on the major interface. In addition, because you are using the dynamic

NSAP addresses, you are required to configure an ILMI PVC. Example 10-2 illustrates how to configure the signaling and the ILMI PVCs.

Example 10-2 *Configuring the Signaling and the ILMI PVCs*

```
Router (config-if)#atm pvc 1 0 5 qsaal
Router (config-if)#atm pvc 2 0 16 ilmi
```

Now, let's examine the necessary steps involved in configuring a LANE client (LEC).

LEC Configuration

Configuring the LEC is very simple. All you have to do is enable the automatic LANE address assignment on the major interface and declare the device to be a LANE client for a specific ELAN, emulating an Ethernet or Token Ring LAN. Example 10-3 demonstrates the command syntax required for LEC configuration.

Example 10-3 *Command Syntax for LEC Configuration*

```
Router (config-if)#lane auto-config-atm-address
Router (config-subif)#lane client {ethernet ¦ tokenring} [elan-name]
```

Example 10-4 demonstrates the complete configuration for LEC 1 for both of the ELANs from the example in Figure 10-7 (Engineering and Marketing).

Example 10-4 *LEC1 Configuration for LANE in Figure 10-7*

```
R1(config)#interface atm 1/0
R1(config-if)#atm pvc 1 0 5 qsaal
R1(config-if)#atm pvc 2 0 16 ilmi
R1(config-if)#lane auto-config-atm-address
R1(config-if)#interface atm 1/0.17 multipoint
R1(config-subif)#ip address 131.108.128.1 255.255.255.0
R1(config-subif)#lane client ethernet engineering
R1(config-if)#interface atm 1/0.16 multipoint
R1(config-subif)#ip address 131.108.64.1 255.255.255.0
R1(config-subif)#lane client ethernet marketing
```

Example 10-5 demonstrates the configuration for LEC 6 of the Engineering ELAN depicted in Figure 10-7. The subinterface command **lane client ethernet 3 engineering** binds VLAN 3 to the ELAN Engineering.

Example 10-5 *LEC6 Configuration for LANE in Figure 10-7*

```
ATM(config)#interface atm 0
ATM(config-if)#atm pvc 1 0 5 qsaal
ATM(config-if)#atm pvc 2 0 16 ilmi
ATM(config-if)#lane auto-config-atm-address
ATM(config-if)#interface atm 0.17 multipoint
ATM(config-subif)#lane client ethernet 3 engineering
```

LES-BUS Configuration

LES-BUS configuration is very similar to LEC configuration. The only difference is in the definition of the LANE component. As illustrated in Example 10-6, all you have to say is that a specific device is performing a function of the LES-BUS component.

Example 10-6 *Command Syntax for LES-BUS Configuration*

```
Router (config-if)#atm pvc 1 0 5 qsaal
Router (config-if)#atm pvc 2 0 16 ilmi
Router (config-if)#lane auto-config-atm-address
Router (config-subif)#lane server-bus {ethernet ¦ tokenring} [elan-name]
```

Examples 10-7 and 10-8 demonstrate the configurations for the LES-BUSs for the Engineering and Marketing ELANs shown in Figure 10-7.

Example 10-7 *LES-BUS Configuration for Marketing ELAN in Figure 10-7*

```
R2(config)#interface atm 1/0
R2(config-if)#atm pvc 1 0 5 qsaal
R2(config-if)#atm pvc 2 0 16 ilmi
R2(config-if)#lane auto-config-atm-address
R2(config-if)#interface atm 1/0.16 multipoint
R2(config-subif)#lane server-bus ethernet marketing
```

Example 10-8 *LES-BUS Configuration for Engineering ELAN in Figure 10-7*

```
ATM(config)#interface atm 0ATM(config-if)#atm pvc 1 0 5 qsaal
ATM(config-if)#atm pvc 2 0 16 ilmi
ATM(config-if)#lane auto-config-atm-address
ATM(config-if)#inteface atm 0.17 multipoint
ATM(config-subif)#lane server-bus ethernet engineering
```

NOTE   I call the LES and BUS (LES-BUS) components the Siamese twins. In Cisco's implementation, one cannot live without the other.

LECS Configuration

LECS configuration is a little bit more involved than LEC or LES-BUS configuration. Think about it! In what way does LECS differ from the LES-BUS or the LEC? First, only one LECS exists for the entire ATM network (unless you implement SSRP or FSSRP), implying that the LECS must be configured on the major interface. Next, because an LEC will be asking the LECS about its corresponding LES address, the LECS must have a form of database containing the addresses of all LESs for all ELANs involved.

Example 10-9 illustrates the syntax of commands involved in LECS configuration on an ATM-connected router or an ATM-attached Catalyst switch (reference to the switch is ATM).

Example 10-9 *Command Syntax for LECS Configuration*

```
Router/ATM(config)#lane database database-name
Router/ATM(lane-config-database)#name elan-name1 server-atm-address atm-address1
Router/ATM(lane-config-database)#name elan-name2 server-atm-address atm-address2
Router/ATM(lane-config-database)#default name elan-name
Router/ATM(config-if)#atm pvc 1 0 5 qsaal
Router/ATM(config-if)#atm pvc 2 0 16 ilmi
Router/ATM(config-if)#lane config database-name
Router/ATM(config-if)#lane config auto-config-atm-address
```

Notice that the LANE database is created at the *global configuration* level in a router or a switch. Then, at the major interface, the reference to the previously created database is made. The optional, default *elan-name* argument provides a default ELAN for LANE clients that are not explicitly bound to a specific ELAN. Also, notice that all the commands involved are executed on the major interface only.

WARNING   Prior to Cisco IOS Release 11.2, the LECS command **lane config auto-config-atm-address** did not have the word **config**. If you ever see LANE in an environment that uses a release of software earlier than Cisco IOS 11.2, make sure to add the word **config** when you upgrade the IOS. Otherwise, your LECS will not work!

Example 10-10 demonstrates the configuration for the LECS shown in Figure 10-7. Note that I obtained the LES addresses from Table 10-4.

Example 10-10 *LECS Configuration Example for LANE in Figure 10-7*

```
R1(config)#lane database it-is-simple
R1(lane-config-database)#name engineering server-atm-address
  47.00918100000000E04FDBA401.0801.000c.1001.11
R1(lane-config-database)#name marketing server-atm-address
  47.00918100000000E04FBCA401.0801.300c.1001.10
R1(lane-config-database)#default name engineering
R1(config)#interface atm 1/0
R1(config-if)#atm pvc 1 0 5 qsaal
R1(config-if)#atm pvc 2 0 16 ilmi
R1(config-if)#lane config it-is-simple
R1(config-if)#lane config auto-config-atm-address
```

If you want to set up the LECS with restricted membership, you must use the additional **client-atm-address** command, as highlighted in Example 10-11. For LECS to authenticate which LEC can join in, it must know which clients are allowed in. You must enter this command for *each client* that is allowed in.

Example 10-11 *LECS Configuration with Restricted Membership*

```
Router/Switch (config)#lane database database-name
Router/Switch (lane-config-database)#name elan-name1 server-atm-address atm-address1
Router/Switch (lane-config-database)#name elan-name2 server-atm-address atm-address2
Router/Switch (lane-config-database)#default name elan-name
Router/Switch (lane-config-database)#client-atm-address lec-atm-address1
  name elan-name
Router/Switch (config-if)#atm pvc 1 0 5 qsaal
Router/Switch (config-if)#atm pvc 2 0 16 ilmi
Router/Switch (config-if)#lane config database-name
Router/Switch (config-if)#lane config auto-config-atm-address
```

LANE Monitoring

Troubleshooting LANE is a very complex process. Usually, the problem is either LANE connectivity or the performance of the LES-BUS. You can avoid the LES-BUS performance issue by properly engineering the necessary platforms involved in the LANE architecture. Incorrect LECS database, improper LECS addressing specified in the ATM switches, and so on can cause connectivity problems. Cisco IOS is very rich in its capability to perform LANE monitoring. Table 10-5 lists all the **show** commands and their corresponding meanings. These commands help you identify whether the client joined the LANE successfully, what control and data VCs are set up, the state of the LES for each ELAN, and so on. These commands help you narrow your search for the cause of the LANE connectivity problem.

Table 10-5 *LANE **show** Commands for the 4xxx Router Series*

Command	What It Does
show lane [**interface atm** *slot/ port*[*.subinterface-number*] | **name** *elan-name*] [**brief**]	Displays the global and the per-VC connection LANE information for all the LANE components and the ELANs configured on an interface or subinterfaces.
show lane bus [**interface atm** *number* [*.subinterface-number*] | **name** *elan-name*] [**brief**]	Displays the global and the per-VC LANE information for the BUS.
show lane client [**interface atm** *number* [*.subinterface-number*] | **name** *elan-name*] [**brief**]	Displays the global and the per-VCC LANE information for all LANE clients.
show lane config [**interface atm** *number*]	Displays the global and the per-VCC LANE information for the LECS.
show lane database [*database-name*]	Displays the LECS database.

continues

Table 10-5 *LANE **show** Commands for the 4xxx Router Series (Continued)*

Command	What It Does
show lane le-arp [**interface atm** *number*[*.subinterface-number*] | **name** *elan-name*]	Displays the LANE ARP table of the LANE client configured on the specified subinterface.
show lane server [**interface atm** *number* [*.subinterface-number*] | **name** *elan-name*] [**brief**]	Displays the global and the per-VC LANE information for the LES.

Summary

This chapter discussed LANE design considerations and Cisco's implementation of LANE architecture. Before implementing LANE, you should perform a careful examination of the current network architectures and traffic flows. The knowledge of traffic flows can help you avoid LANE scalability issues and position the right groups and departments into ELANs.

The chapter focused on LANE v1 implementation, including proprietary redundancy solutions using SSRP and FSSRP. These protocols allow you to have a completely redundant LANE architecture. The configuration examples elaborate on the syntax and the steps necessary to build LANE.

The chapter presents four LANE laboratories, including Simple Server Redundancy Protocol (SSRP) and multi-ELAN examples. Appendix C, "Lab Solutions," presents the solutions for the labs.

Lab 10-1: Configuring LANE for a Single ELAN

Objectives: At the end of the lab, you will complete the following:

- Configure the LECS address onto the switches
- Configure the LECS database for the ELAN
- Configure the LES and the BUS
- Configure the ILMI PVC for learning AESA
- Configure the routers as clients
- Verify the connectivity of the ELAN

Purpose: This lab sets up connectivity using LANE. PNNI is the routing protocol. The ILMI PVC is necessary to learn where the LECS is located after it is configured on the switches as well as for dynamic ATM address prefix assignment. When this process is complete, the LECS must be configured with the database of the ELAN called "easy." Next, you must configure the LES and the BUS for ELAN "easy." All other routers must be configured as clients. After you do this, you can see your routers come up as clients and you can accomplish full connectivity.

NOTE   In this first of the four LANE labs, Router 6 is the LECS, the LES, and the BUS for ELAN "easy." All other routers are clients.

Table 10-6 lists and describes the commands you need to be familiar with to complete this lab.

Table 10-6   *Lab 10-1 Command Summary*

Command	Description
show lane default	Shows the NSAP address for the LANE components
show atm address	Shows the prefix for the switch
atm lecs-address	Assigns the LECS address on the switch
lane database	Configures a database
name server-atm-address	Associates an LES with an NSAP
default-name	Sets the default ELAN if a request is not in the database
mtu	Sets the requested MTU size for the ELAN
atm pvc	Creates a PVC on an ATM interface needed for ILMI
lane config database	Associates a database with the configuration server on the selected ATM interface
lane auto-config-atm-address	Turns on address autoconfiguration
lane config auto-config-...	Turns on address autoconfiguration for LECS
lane client	Declares the subinterface as a client
lane server-bus	Declares the subinterface a LES and a BUS
show lane config	Displays details of LECS operation
show lane le-arp	Displays the client's cache of mapped addresses
show lane database	Displays the ELAN-to-LES NSAP mapping
show lane client	Displays the operations of a client
show lane server	Displays the operations of the LES
show lane bus	Displays the operations of the BUS

Figure 10-8 shows the network topology with a single ELAN stretched across the ATM cloud.

Figure 10-8 *Single ELAN Topology*

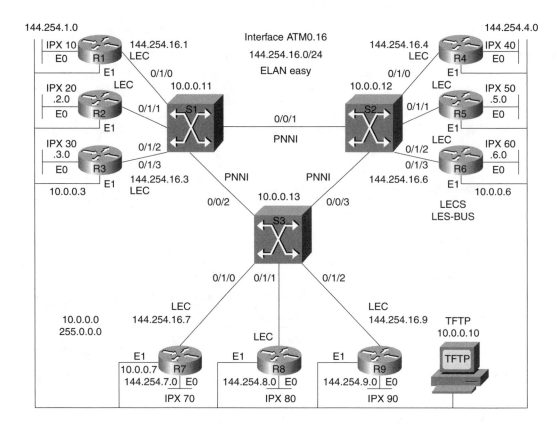

Exercises

Refer to Figure 10-8 to complete the following exercises for Lab 10-1.

1 Telnet to R6 using the 10.0.0.6 address. Record the ESI portion of the address of R6.

LECS ESI for R6:_____

2 Telnet to Switch 2. R6 is connected directly to Switch 2. Therefore, the prefix portion of the LECS's AESA is Switch 2's prefix. What is the prefix?

Switch 2 Prefix:_____

3 What is the LECS AESA?

LECS Address:_____

4   What is the R6 LES address for this ELAN? Note that the port selector field of the LES must be changed from ** to the interface number where you put the LES. You put this functionality on subinterface 16. Remember that the subinterface must be expressed in hexadecimal notation when associated as part of the ATM address.

R6 LES ESI Address:_____

R6 LES NSAP Address:_____

5   R6 also must create the database. Call the database **cisco**.

6   Add the ELAN called **easy** to the database. Use the AESA found in Task 4.

7   R6 also must enter the default ELAN for this domain. The default is the ELAN named **easy**.

8   On the major ATM interface, each client must enter some basic information. This includes the **MTU size**, the **ilmi** PVC, and the capability to learn where the LECS is located.

NOTE   We already created the signaling PVC; otherwise, you also would need to create this PVC.

---

9   R6 on the major ATM interface also must enter the command to start up the LECS software and to associate with the database **cisco**.

10   All LECs (clients) must declare themselves as such. Therefore, on **subinterface 16**, enter the IP address as shown in Figure 10-8 (144.254.16.x, where x is your router number) and declare your subinterface as a client joining the **easy** ELAN.

11   R6, on subinterface 16, also must declare itself to be the LES and the BUS.

12   Verify that your clients are seeing the correct LECS.

13   Verify that your clients are operational.

14   Check your LANE cache to see which destinations you have addresses for.

15   Check for connectivity of the 144.254.16.x cloud.

16   Telnet to R6 and check to see if your router is in R6's server cache.

Lab 10-2: Configuring LANE for a Single ELAN with SSRP

Objectives: At the end of the lab, you will complete the following:

- Configure a backup LECS, LES, and BUS
- Replicate the LECS database

- Configure the LS1010 switches and the appropriate routers to support SSRP

Purpose: LANE version 1 does not have any built-in redundancy, so Cisco built the Simple Server Redundancy Protocol. You will configure this protocol in this lab. Note that LANE Version 2 supports redundancy.

Table 10-7 lists and describes the commands you need to be familiar with to complete this lab.

Table 10-7 *Lab 10-2 Command Summary*

Command	Description
atm lecs-address	Assigns the LECS address on the ATM switch
show lane config	Displays details of LECS operation
show lane default	Displays the NSAP address for LANE components
show atm address	Displays the prefix for the switch
lane database	Configures a LANE database
name server-atm-address	Associates an LES with an NSAP
default-name	Sets the default ELAN if a request is not in the database
lane config database	Associates a database with the configuration server on the selected ATM interface
lane server-bus	Declares the subinterface offering LES-BUS
show lane config	Displays details of LECS operation
show lane le-arp	Displays the client's cache of mapped addresses
show lane database	Displays the ELAN-to-LES NSAP mapping
show lane client	Displays the operations of a client
show lane server	Displays the operations of the LES
show lane bus	Displays the operations of the BUS

Figure 10-9 shows the network topology depicting R1 as the secondary LECS and R8 as the secondary LES-BUS.

Figure 10-9 *LANE Redundancy with SSRP, Single ELAN*

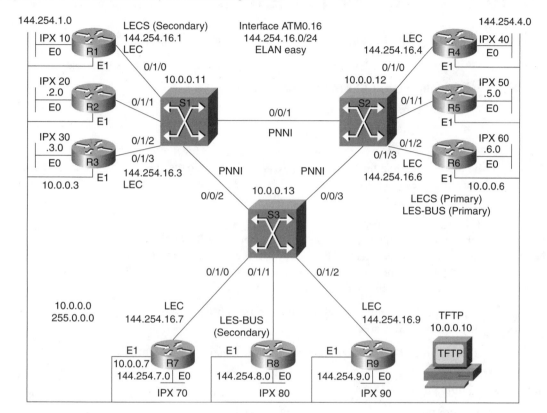

Exercises

Refer to Figure 10-9 to complete the following exercises for Lab 10-2.

1 Copy the LECS database from R6 exactly.

2 Add R1's AESA to the LECS list.

3 Set up R8 as an LES-BUS.

4 Change the LECS database of R1 to reflect R8 as the secondary LES-BUS.

5 Change the LECS database of R6 to reflect R8 as the secondary LES-BUS.

Lab 10-3: Configuring LANE for Multiple ELANs

Objectives: At the end of the lab, you will complete the following:

- Configure the LES address and the ELAN name into the LECS database
- Configure the LES and the BUS for each ELAN
- Configure the routers as clients
- Verify connectivity of the ELAN

Purpose: This lab sets up connectivity using LANE for multiple ELANs. The concept being shown is that nine separate ELANs can coexist in the cloud (administrative domain). Each router establishes itself as the LES, the BUS, and the client of one ELAN, while also being a client of multiple other ELANs.

Each router needs to add its ELAN to the database **cisco** that was established in the previous lab. To do so, you need to locate your LES address. When the LES address is in the database, you need to set up the location of the LES by mapping it to the associated AESA. Configurations for declaring the subinterfaces as the LES, the BUS, and the client, or only as a client, also must be completed.

When you have configured all devices, you can **ping** or Telnet to any other router across any of the ELANs created.

Table 10-8 lists and describes the commands you need to be familiar with to complete this lab.

Table 10-8 *Lab 10-3 Command Summary*

Command	Description
show lane default	Displays the NSAP address for the LANE components
lane database	Configures a database
name server-atm-address	Associates an LES with an NSAP
lane client	Declares the subinterface as a client
lane server-bus	Declares the subinterface as an LES and a BUS
show lane config	Displays details of LECS operation
show lane le-arp	Displays the client's cache of mapped addresses
show lane database	Displays the ELAN-to-LES NSAP mapping
show lane client	Displays the operations of a client
show lane server	Displays the operations of the LES
show lane bus	Displays the operations of the BUS

Figure 10-10 shows the network topology illustrating all nine broadcast domains.

Figure 10-10 *Multiple ELANs*

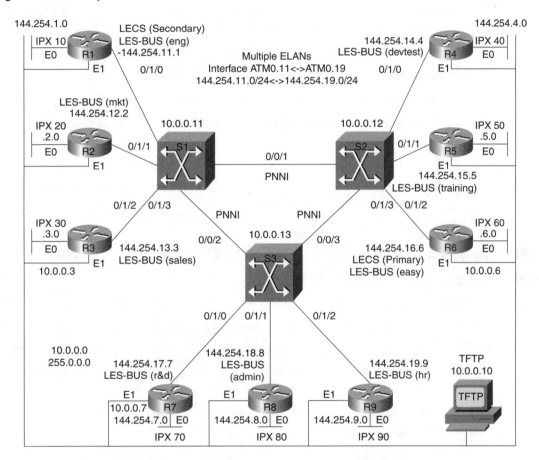

Exercises

Refer to Figure 10-10 to complete the following exercises for Lab 10-3.

    1 What is the LES AESA for every router (remember that the selector field is in hex)?

        LES AESA:_____

    2 Telnet to R6. Enter all ELANs into the **cisco** database.

3 Using Figure 10-10, on the correct subinterfaces, configure the LES, the BUS, and the LEC of the ELANs assigned to every router. Also, configure all routers to be part of each other's broadcast domains by assigning the addresses 144.254.*y.x* to the *y* subinterfaces. *x* is the destination router number, as depicted in Figure 10-10. Note that you configured R6 for this already in Lab 10-2.

4 On the other subinterfaces listed, declare yourself as a client only.

5 Verify that every LEC is operational.

6 Check your LANE cache to see which destinations you have AESAs for.

7 Check for connectivity of the 144.254.*y.x* cloud, where *y* is the subinterface and *x* is the destination router.

8 Telnet to R6 and check to see if your server is in the database.

9 Check to see if you have all the clients registered in your server's database. How many connections do you currently have?

Lab 10-4: Configuring LANE for Dual-Homed Catalyst Switches with Redundancy

Objectives: At the end of the lab, you will complete the following:

- Configure Catalyst 5000 switches as primary and secondary LECS, LES-BUS
- Configure two Catalyst 5000 switches to interconnect their VLAN 2 to ELAN "easy"
- Configure the LES addresses and the ELAN names into the LECS databases
- Configure the LES and the BUS for the appropriate ELAN
- Configure the routers as LANE clients
- Verify the connectivity for the appropriate ELAN
- Verify a particular design's physical redundancy with SSRP redundancy

Purpose: This lab provides the opportunity to implement a more robust, higher-performance ATM LANE backbone design by connecting the dual-port LANE module of the Catalyst 5000 switches to two different LS1010 ATM switches. By offering LES-BUS services on the Catalyst 5000 switches, you can achieve higher BUS performance and implement additional physical redundancy.

This lab is an extension of Lab 10-1, where you implemented a single ELAN, "easy," on the ATM backbone running PNNI. All LANE services are to be implemented on the Catalyst switches with all routers still configured as LANE clients only for ELAN "easy." SSRP functionality is demonstrated here again, with redundant LANE servers implemented on the Catalyst switches.

Table 10-9 lists and describes the commands you need to be familiar with to complete this lab.

Table 10-9   *Lab 10-4 Command Summary*

Command	Description
show lane default	Displays the NSAP address for the LANE components
lane database	Configures a database
name server-atm-address	Associates an LES with an NSAP
lane client	Declares the subinterface as a client
lane server-bus	Declares the subinterface as an LES and a BUS
show lane config	Details the LECS operation
show lane le-arp	Displays the client's cache of mapped addresses
show lane database	Displays the ELAN-to-LES NSAP mapping
show lane client	Displays the operations of a client
show lane server	Displays the operations of the LES
show lane bus	Displays the operations of the BUS

Figure 10-11 shows the two Catalyst switches, CAT1 and CAT2, added to the network infrastructure.

Figure 10-11 *LANE with Dual-Homed Catalyst*

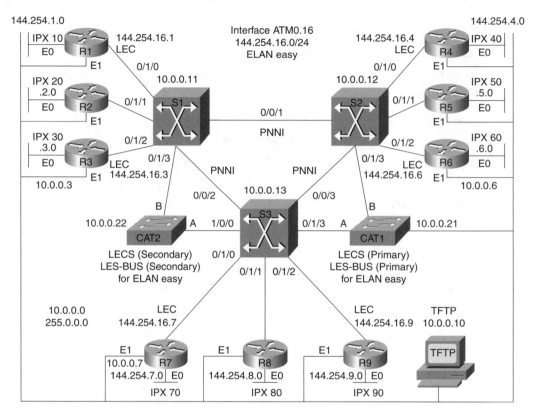

Exercises

Refer to Figure 10-11 to complete the following exercises for Lab 10-4.

1 Configure the Catalyst 5000 switches. Ensure that you establish physical and IP connectivity to the 5000 switches.

2 Configure two Catalyst 5000 switches to interconnect their VLAN 2 to ELAN "easy."

3 On the Catalyst 5000 switches, configure the ATM interface with the appropriate terminating PVCs (signaling PVC and ILMI PVC) and the MTU size.

4 Identify the appropriate LECS addresses for CAT1 and CAT2 based on the associated ATM switch prefix to be used, depending on the appropriate LANE port A or port B to be active at one time.

CAT1 LECS address:_____

CAT1 LECS address:_____

CAT2 LECS address:_____

CAT2 LECS address:_____

5 Configure the LS1010 switches with the appropriate LECS addresses to be used. Identify CAT1 as the primary LECS and CAT2 as the secondary LECS. Ensure that all appropriate LECS addresses are being used and are taking physical redundancy into consideration.

6 As per Lab 10-1, where you implemented ELAN "easy," you can use subinterface ATM0.16 on the Catalyst 5000 to enable the LANE client and the LES-BUS services. Map VLAN2 with ELAN "easy."

7 As in the previous labs for this chapter, identify the AESA LES addresses pertaining to CAT1 and CAT2. Configure the appropriate LANE databases on CAT1 and CAT2, identifying all required LES AESA address entries to provide full physical redundancy, as per the design. Activate the LECS service with the appropriate database on both CAT 5000 switches.

8 Ensure that ELAN "easy" is up and working with full membership, with CAT1 as the primary LECS, LES-BUS. Verify the design's reliability by disabling the appropriate ATM interface on the ATM switch that currently provides connectivity to CAT1. Verify that CAT1 still remains active in support of the ELAN services using the second physical port on the LANE module.

9 Shut down the appropriate LS1010 ATM interface port to isolate CAT1 and the provided LANE services, and verify that CAT2 indeed provides the required LANE services redundancy. Ensure that full ELAN "easy" membership is reestablished.

10 Similar to Exercise 7, ensure that CAT2 can provide LANE services when connectivity to its default LANE module port A is terminated. Again, verify full ELAN "easy" membership.

Review Questions

1 What are the differences between LANE, ELAN, and VLAN?

2 What are the main design considerations that you should be aware of when planning for LANE?

3 What are the advantages and disadvantages of PVC-based LANE?

4 Which LANE server is most heavily utilized? Why?

5 How is Spanning Tree convergence improved over LANE?

6 How does a LANE client learn the address of the LECS in LANE v1?

7 What is SSRP?

8 How does SSRP determine which LECS is the primary one?

9 What is the difference between SSRP and FSSRP?

10 What are the important rules for proper SSRP operation?

11 How can you obtain the LANE component NSAP addresses?

12 What is the value of the Selector byte in the LANE NSAP address?

13 What is the main difference between configuring LECS and other LANE components?

"Action will remove the doubts that theory cannot solve."—Tehyi Hsieh

"The only limit to our realization of tomorrow will be our doubts of today. Let us move forward with strong and active faith."—Franklin Delano Roosevelt (1882–1945)

"Do not be too timid and squeamish…. All life is an experiment. The more experiments you make, the better."—Ralph Waldo Emerson (1803–1882)

After reading this chapter, you should understand the following:

- **MPOA Operation**—MPOA is based on both LANE v2 and the Next Hop Resolution Protocol (NHRP). MPOA combines the benefits of LANE and NHRP to allow very efficient transfer of packets among various broadcast domains. NHRP minimizes the hop count for interdomain traffic over an ATM network by dividing the ATM network into logical subnets. NHRP enables various broadcast domains to interconnect using cut-through routing. LANEv2 provides redundancy within a broadcast domain and QoS.

- **MPOA Configuration**—MPOA implementation and configuration are based on client/server architecture, hence requiring the configuration of the MPOA Server (MPS) and the MPOA Client (MPC). Because MPOA resides on LANE, LANE configuration must be intact. Furthermore, LANE's LECs must be bound to the MPC/MPS.

This chapter presents a lab exercise that elaborates more on the MPOA implementation. Appendix C, "Lab Solutions," presents the solutions to the lab.

CHAPTER 11

MPOA Implementation

Chapter 6, "Multiprotocol over ATM (MPOA)," discussed the theory of MPOA; this chapter focuses on Cisco's implementation of MPOA. What products and IOS releases provide support for MPOA? How do you implement MPOA? What should you be aware of when implementing MPOA? Beyond the MPOA examples in this chapter, you can find the MPOA lab examples in Appendix C.

MPOA Operation

MPOA enables Layer 3 protocols to communicate across ATM networks natively, providing for fast routing using the cut-through routing technique. MPOA replaces multihop routing with point-to-point routing using direct VCs between ingress and egress edge devices, bypassing the need for multiple logical IP subnet (LIS) domains.

NOTE   As a reminder, an *ingress device* is the point at which an inbound flow of traffic enters, whereas an *egress device* is the point at which the outbound traffic flow exits.

MPOA is based on both LANE v2 and the Next Hop Resolution Protocol (NHRP). MPOA combines the benefits of LANE and NHRP to allow very efficient transfer of packets among various broadcast domains. LANE provides for effective bridging within a broadcast domain across an ATM network. However, communication between different broadcast domains (that is, traffic between ELANs) is routed using NHRP. NHRP minimizes the hop count for interdomain traffic over an ATM network by dividing the ATM network into logical subnets. Although Layer 3 devices are required still to connect these subnets, NHRP allows traffic to bypass the intermediate routers by providing address resolution of the next-hop IP address (which is exactly how IP forwarding is performed) to the destination ATM address.

With the help of the NHRP shortcut VCs, MPOA increases performance and reduces latency for communication between the edge devices. Similar to LANE, MPOA uses a client/server architecture, except the server must have Layer 3 functionality. Remember, LANE is an emulation of Layer 2 over ATM, whereas MPOA is an emulation of Layer 3 over ATM. MPOA Clients (MPCs) establish shortcuts with the help of MPOA Servers

(MPSs) that reside on routers. Figure 11-1 illustrates the MPOA message flow sequence between MPCs and MPSs. Chapter 6 elaborates more on MPOA theory.

Figure 11-1 *MPOA Communication Between MPCs and MPSs*

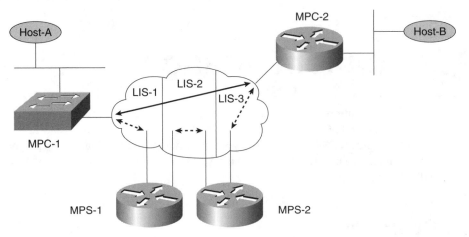

Assume that Host A wants to Telnet to Host B. For Host A to communicate with Host B, the following events must take place:

Step 1   Host A sends an IP ARP.

Step 2   Because the IP ARP is intraLAN traffic, LANE functions kick in. MPC-1 hears the ARP message and, using the LANE facilities, sends it to the BUS of LIS-1.

Step 3   MPS-1 (which is a router) hears the IP ARP request, checks its routing tables, realizes that it is aware of the destination network, and sends a proxy IP ARP reply to MPC-1. In turn, MPC-1 forwards the ARP reply to Host A.

Step 4   Host A sends traffic to Host B. MPC-1, detecting the packet flow to a destination IP address, sends an MPOA resolution request to MPS-1, trying to resolve a destination IP address to an ATM address in order to establish a shortcut VC to the egress device MPC-2.

Step 5   MPS-1 converts the MPOA resolution request to an NHRP resolution request and sends it to its neighboring MPS/NHS, MPS-2.

Step 6   When the NHRP resolution request reaches the egress MPS, MPS-2, it sends the MPOA cache-imposition request to MPC-2, providing the MAC rewrite information for a destination IP address.

Step 7   MPC-2 sends a cache-imposition reply to MPS-2, acknowledging an MPOA cache-imposition request. Within the reply, MPC-2 adds a tag that allows the originator of the MPOA resolution request, MPC-1, to receive the ATM address of MPC-2.

Step 8   MPS-2 sends the NHRP resolution reply to MPS-1, which MPS-1 converts into an MPOA resolution reply.

Step 9   MPS-1 sends the MPOA resolution reply to MPC-1, thereby resolving the IP address to the ATM address.

Step 10 MPC-1 establishes a shortcut VC to MPC-2, over which MPC-1 and MPC-2 will now be able to send packets.

Step 11 MPC-1 uses the shortcut VC to send the Telnet traffic.

When traffic flows from Host A to Host B, MPC-1 is the ingress MPC and MPC-2 is the egress MPC. The ingress MPC, MPC-1, contains a cache entry for Host B with the ATM address of the egress MPC, MPC-2. The ingress MPC, MPC-1 switches packets destined to Host B on the shortcut VC with the appropriate tag as received in the MPOA resolution reply. On the other hand, the egress MPC, MPC-2, contains a cache entry that associates the IP address of Host A and the ATM address of the ingress MPC-1. This is how ATM "fools" a Layer 3 protocol.

Because MPOA configuration works in conjunction with LANE, let's look at how MPOA interacts with LANE.

MPOA Interaction with LANE

The MPSs and MPCs use LANE control frames to discover each other's presence in the LANE network. An MPC or an MPS can function as an LEC. In turn, the LEC can be associated with any MPS/MPC function in the router. A single LEC can be attached to both an MPC and an MPS simultaneously under the condition that the association is with only a single MPC/MPS. Figure 11-2 illustrates the LEC-MPC and the LEC-MPS relationships.

To summarize, here are the MPOA-LANE interaction rules.

- The MPS and the MPC can serve one or more LECs.
- A single LEC can be associated with any MPC and MPS.
- A single LEC can be attached to both an MPC and an MPS simultaneously, but only to one pair at any given moment.

The next section reviews the MPC's operation.

Figure 11-2 *LEC-MPC and LEC-MPS Relationships*

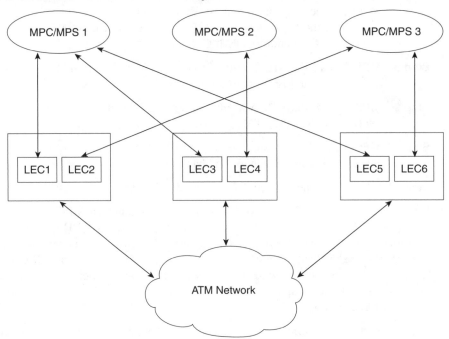

MPC Operation

The MPC connects the LANE client, which is a Layer 2 function, to the next higher internetworking layer (Layer 3). As mentioned earlier, each MPC can serve more than one LEC, but each LEC must be associated with only one MPC. Each MPC has its own MPC control ATM address, which might coincide with the ATM address of one of its subordinate LECs. The MPC supplies each subordinate LEC with its control ATM address. Each time an LEC sends an LE_ARP response, it includes the control ATM address of the MPC with which it is associated.

The MPC identifies packets sent to an MPOA router over ATM and establishes shortcut VCs to the egress MPC. To summarize, the MPC's functions are as follows:

- Ingress/egress cache management
- MPOA frame processing
- MPOA flow detection
- Shortcut VC establishment and management
- LEC connectivity to Layer 3

MPS Operation

How do MPCs know the VC shortcut? It is the MPS that supplies forwarding information to the MPCs. An MPS uses NHRP to support the query and response messages issued by MPC. The MPS uses MPOA frames that are identical to NHRP frames with a few modifications.

When MPS interacts with NHRP, the following actions take place:

Step 1 MPS converts the MPOA resolution requests to the NHRP requests.

Step 2 MPS searches for the next hop routing information to determine the outbound interface and sends the requests to the next hop MPS or NHS, depending on the configuration.

Step 3 NHS sends resolution requests to MPSs when the next hop is within a LANE cloud or when NHS is unsure where to send the packet.

Step 4 NHS sends resolution replies to the MPS when the next hop interface is LANE or when the replies terminate in the router.

Step 5 The MPS converts the NHRP replies into MPOA replies. Then it sends the MPOA resolution replies to the MPC.

Figure 11-3 illustrates the MPS-NHRP interaction.

Figure 11-3 *MPS-NHRP Interaction*

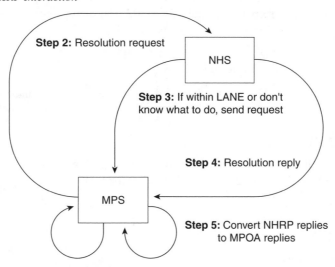

MPOA Configuration

Configuring MPOA includes the following general steps of the MPC and MPS components configurations:

Step 1 Define the ELAN ID.

Step 2 Define a name for the MPC/MPS.

Step 3 Attach the MPC/MPS to an interface.

Step 4 Assign an ATM address to the MPC/MPS.

Step 5 Bind the MPC/MPS to multiple LECs.

Step 6 Define MPC/MPS variables.

The definition of the ELAN is absolutely essential because MPOA resides on LANE. It is important to keep in mind that you can attach each MPC/MPS to only one hardware interface; however, you can attach more than one MPC/MPS to the same interface provided that they have different control ATM addresses. When you attach an MPC/MPS to a single interface for its control traffic, you cannot attach it to another interface unless you break the first attachment.

You can bind any LEC running on any subinterface of a hardware interface to any MPC/MPS; however, when you bind a client to a particular MPC/MPS, you cannot bind it to another MPC/MPS at the same time. If you need to change the binding, you must first unbind the client from the original MPC/MPS, and then you can bind it to another MPC/MPS.

You must ensure that all LECs bound to an MPC/MPS can reach the hardware interface attached to that MPC/MPS directly through the ATM network.

The following sections discuss the details of configuring MPC and MPS.

Configuring MPC

Table 11-1 lists the tasks that are involved in configuring an MPOA client. Please note that some of the tasks are optional, as indicated in the table.

Table 11-1   *MPC Configuration Tasks*

Task Number	Task	Mandatory (M)/ Optional (O)
1	ELAN ID Configuration:	M
1.1	Define an ELAN ID for the LEC.	
1.2	Configure the LEC with the ELAN ID.	

Table 11-1   *MPC Configuration Tasks (Continued)*

Task Number	Task	Mandatory (M)/ Optional (O)
2	MPC Configuration:	M
2.1	Define an MPC with a specified name.	
2.2	Attach the MPC to the ATM physical interface.	
2.3	Bind LECs to the specified MPC.	
3	MPC Variable Configuration:	O
3.1	Specify the control ATM address that the MPC should use.	
3.2	Specify the maximum number of times a packet can be routed to the default router within the shortcut-frame-time before the MPOA resolution request is sent.	
3.3	Set the shortcut-setup-frame for the MPC.	

Now, let's look at the syntax of the commands for each of these tasks.

For MPOA to work properly, LECs and MPCs must have the same ELAN ID. When an LEC wants to communicate across the ATM network using MPOA, it must belong to an ELAN that has a defined ELAN ID. The MPC, bound to this LEC, also must have the same ELAN ID. Usually, the LEC obtains the ELAN ID from the LECS database during registration. Sometimes, however, it is possible to provide an LEC with the LES ATM address manually. If that is the case, the LEC might not receive the ELAN ID, so you also must provide the LEC with the ELAN ID manually.

Task 1: ELAN ID Configuration

The following commands are necessary for Task 1, which involves defining and configuring an ELAN ID for the LEC.

```
Router(config-lane-database)#name elan-name elan-id id
Router(config-subif)#lane client ethernet elan-name [elan-id id]
```

Please note that you should supply the same value for the **elan id** argument in both commands.

Task 2: MPC Configuration

To configure an MPC on your network, use the following commands in the appropriate configuration modes.

```
Router(config)#mpoa client config name mpc-name
Router(config-if)#mpoa client name mpc-name
Router(config-subif)#lane client mpoa client name mpc-name
```

The value supplied for the *mpc-name* variable in the **lane client** command must match the value supplied for the *mpc-name* variable in the **mpoa client** command of the global configuration mode.

Task 3: MPC Variable Configuration

If you decide to change the MPC's variables, the commands are as follows:

```
Router(mpoa-client-config)#atm-address atm-address
Router(mpoa-client-config)#shortcut-frame-count count
Router(mpoa-client-config)#shortcut-frame-time time
```

First, you should define an MPC with the specified name, as mentioned before. Next, you optionally can specify the control ATM address that the MPC uses and the maximum number of times a packet can be routed to the default router within the **shortcut-frame-time** before the MPOA resolution request is sent. The default **shortcut-frame-count** is 10 frames. The **shortcut-frame-time** is measured in seconds; the default value is 1 second. Using the default parameters, the MPC routes a packet up to 10 times to the default router within 1 second before it sends the MPOA resolution request. You can tweak the parameters of the two commands to impact the paths of different traffic flows in your network. If you want to use cut-through shortcuts for longer type session flow, you should increase these parameters. This ensures that the MPOA cut-through path is used only after the **shortcut-frame-time** elapses and the **shortcut-frame-count** frames pass through a normal switching path.

MPC Configuration Example

Figure 11-4 provides a sample ATM network with MPC configuration.

Your network has two ELANs: eng and mkt. The eng ELAN has three LECs, and the mkt ELAN has two LECs. Each ELAN has its own LES-BUS. The entire LANE structure has one LECS. Notice that the binding between MPOA and LANE is totally arbitrary. For example, LEC2 of eng and LEC1 of mkt are both bound to the MPS, whereas LEC1 of eng is bound to the MPC1. As long as you follow the rules of MPOA-LANE interaction, which were identified earlier in this chapter, you can bind an LEC to an MPC and/or an MPS.

This configuration example includes both routers and switches. Remember that, when you are operating with the Catalyst 5000 or 6000 family ATM module, you must establish a connection with the ATM module first, next enter privilege mode, and then enter configuration mode.

Figure 11-4 *MPC Configuration Example*

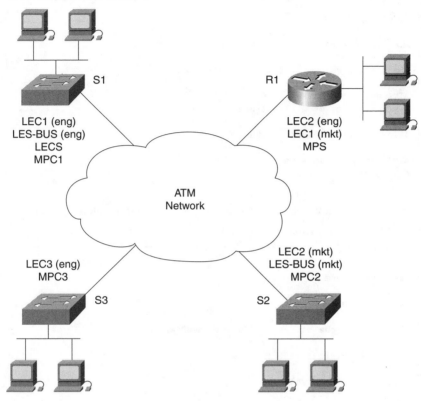

Example 11-1 shows the configuration for MPC1 that is illustrated in Figure 11-4.

Example 11-1 *MPC1 Configuration Example*

```
! Define the MPC1

ATM#config term

!Define the ELAN ID and ATM address of LES

ATM(config)#lane database mpoa-one
ATM(lane-config-database)#name eng server-atm-address 47.00918100000000624E5AAAAA.
007070175522.01
ATM(lane-config-database)#name eng elan-id 101

ATM(lane-config-database)#name mkt  server-atm-address 47.00918100000000624E5BBBBB.
007070175522.01
ATM(lane-config-database)#name mkt elan-id 102
```

continues

Example 11-1 *MPC1 Configuration Example (Continued)*

```
!MPC1_eng definition

ATM(config)#mpoa client config name MPC1_eng

!Bind the physical interface to the MPC1

ATM(config)#interface atm0
ATM(config-if)#mpoa client name MPC1_eng

!Bind the LANE client to the MPC1

ATM(config-if)#interface atm0.1 mul
ATM(config-subif)#lane client mpoa client name MPC1_eng
```

Example 11-2 shows the configuration for MPC2, as illustrated in Figure 11-4.

Example 11-2 *MPC2 Configuration Example*

```
!Define the MPC2

ATM#config term

!MPC2_mkt definition

ATM(config)#mpoa client config name MPC2_mkt

!Bind the physical interface to the MPC2

ATM(config)#interface atm0
ATM(config-if)#mpoa client name MPC2_mkt

!Bind the LANE client to the MPC2

ATM(config-if)#interface atm0.1 mul
ATM(config-subif)#lane client mpoa client name MPC2_eng
```

Example 11-3 shows the configuration for MPC3, as illustrated in Figure 11-4.

Example 11-3 *MPC3 Configuration Example*

```
!Define the MPC3

ATM#config term

!MPC3_eng definition

ATM(config)#mpoa client config name MPC3_eng

!Bind the physical interface to the MPC3

ATM(config)#interface atm0
```

Example 11-3 *MPC3 Configuration Example (Continued)*

```
ATM(config-if)#mpoa client name MPC3_eng

!Bind the LANE client to the MPC3

ATM(config-if)#interface atm0.1 mul
ATM(config-subif)#lane client mpoa client name MPC3_eng
```

NOTE   When referencing the subinterface **interface atm0.1 mul**, you must specify the **mul** keyword (mul stands for multipoint); otherwise, the CLI does not accept the command.

Please remember that the configurations in Examples 11-1 through 11-3 are not complete. You are required to set up the LEC appropriately as well. The complete MPOA lab appears at the end of this chapter, with solutions presented in Appendix C.

You can use the **show** commands to monitor and maintain the MPC. Again, as with any other configuration, think about what you need to see: the **mpoa client** statistics and details. Use the power of the help command (**?**). The MPC **show** commands include the following:

```
Router# show mpoa client [name mpc-name][brief]
Router# show mpoa client [name mpc-name]cache[ingress¦egress][ip-address ip-
address]
Router# show mpoa client [name mpc-name] statistics
```

Example 11-4 illustrates the output of the **show mpoa client** command. This is a very important command that verifies whether your MPC is operational. The whole objective of this command is to illustrate the resolution between the destination IP address and the destination ATM address, as signified by the highlighted portion of the output.

Example 11-4 show mpoa client *Example*

```
MPC Name: r2, Interface: ATM0, State: Up
MPC actual operating address: 47.009181000000001007399E01.00E0145505C5.00
Shortcut-Setup Count: 10, Shortcut-Setup Time: 60
Number of Ingress cache entries: 1
MPC Ingress Cache Information:
Dst IP addr      State    Egress MPC Atm address
144.254.60.8     RSVLD    47.009181000000000100739C301.00E0145502C5.00
    Expires in 107:56, vcd 43, mpsid 2
Number of Egress cache entries: 1
MPC Egress Cache Information:
Dst IP addr      Dst MAC        Src MAC      MPSid  Elan Expires  CacheId  Tag
144.254.50.2     00e0.1455.05c0 00e0.1455.0470    2    50  119:48        2    1
```

Configuring MPS

You need to perform the tasks listed in Table 11-2 to configure an MPS on your network. Some tasks are required, and some are optional.

Table 11-2 *MPS Configuration Tasks*

Task Number	Task	Mandatory (M)/ Optional (O)
1	ELAN ID Configuration:	M
1.1	Define an ELAN ID in the LECS database.	
1.2	Configure the LES with the ELAN ID.	
2	MPS Configuration:	M
2.1	Define an MPC with a specified name.	
2.2	Attach the MPC to the ATM physical interface.	
2.3	Bind LANE clients to the specified MPS.	
3	MPS Variable Configuration:	O
3.1	Specify the control ATM address that MPS should use.	
3.2	Specify the network ID of the MPS.	
3.3	Specify the keepalive time value for the MPS.	
3.4	Specify the duration that a keepalive message from the MPS is considered valid by the MPC; the specified duration is the keepalive-lifetime.	
3.5	Set the holding time value for the MPS.	

WARNING Be careful with the ELAN ID. For LECs to reach each other through an MPC and an MPS, all components must have the same ELAN ID. If you configure the ELAN IDs manually, make sure they are identical.

Task 1: ELAN ID Configuration

For MPOA to work properly, a LANE client must have an ELAN ID for all ELANs represented by the LECs. You should perform ELAN ID configuration in the interface configuration mode when starting up the LES for the ELAN and/or in the LANE database configuration mode.

The following command syntax demonstrates how to define and configure the ELAN ID for an MPS.

```
Router(config-lane-database)#name elan-name elan-id id
Router(config-subif)#lane server-bus {ethernet ¦ tokenring} elan-name [elan-id id]
```

Make sure that you provide the same value for the **elan-id** argument in both commands.

Task 2: MPS Configuration

The MPS configuration is very similar to the configuration for an MPC. First, you must define the MPS name, then attach the MPS to the physical interface, and finally, bind an LEC to the MPS, as illustrated by the following sequence of commands.

```
Router(config)#mpoa server config name mps-name
Router(config-if)#mpoa server name mps-name
Router(config-subif)#lane client mpoa server name mps-name
```

Task 3: MPS Variable Configuration

As was the case with MPCs, you can change the MPS variables, which include the **atm-address**, the **network-id**, and the **keepalive-time**, **holding-time**, and the **keepalive-lifetime** timers. The command syntax for changing the MPS variables is as follows:

```
Router(mpoa-server-config)#atm-address atm-address
Router(mpoa-server-config)#network-id id
Router(mpoa-server-config)#keepalive-time time
Router(mpoa-server-config)#holding-time time
Router(mpoa-server-config)#keepalive-lifetime time
```

The default value for **keepalive-time** is 10 seconds, the default value for **keepalive-lifetime** is 35 seconds, and the default value for **holding-time** is 20 minutes. The **keepalive-time** is the frequency that a keepalive message is sent from the MPS to the MPC. The **keepalive-lifetime** value must be greater than or equal to three times the value of **keepalive-time**. Any increase in these timers will cause extra traffic over your ATM network.

MPS Configuration Example

Let's look at the example of MPS configuration demonstrated by Example 11-5 (refer to Figure 11-4).

Example 11-5 *MPS Configuration Example*

```
!Define the MPS "MPS_all"

R1(config)#mpoa server config name MPS_all

!Bind the physical interface to the MPS

R1(config)#interface atm 1/0
R1(config-if)#mpoa server name MPS_all
```

continues

Example 11-5 *MPS Configuration Example (Continued)*

```
!Bind both LECs to MPS

R1(config-if)#interface atm 1/0.1 mul
R1(config-subif)#lane client ethernet eng
R1(config-subif)#lane client mpoa server name MPS_all

R1(config-subif)#interface atm 1/0.2 mul
R1(config-subif)#lane client ethernet mkt
R1(config-subif)#lane client mpoa server name MPS_all
```

You can use the **show** commands to monitor and maintain the MPS, as you can for the MPC. Again, as with any other configuration, think about what you need to see: the **mpoa server** statistics and details. Use the power of the help command (**?**). You might be surprised at what you discover. The MPS **show** commands include the following:

```
Router# show mpoa server [name mps-name]
Router# show mpoa server [name mps-name]cache[ingress¦egress][ip-address ip-
address]
Router# show mpoa server [name mps-name] statistics
```

The **show mpoa server** command displays information about any specified MPS or all MPSs in the system. The command displays information about server configuration parameters and LECs that are bound to the MPC and the MPS. The command **show mpoa server cache** displays ingress and egress cache entries associated with that MPS. The command **show mpoa server statistics** displays the statistics pertaining to the ingress/egress cache entry creation, deletion, and failures collected by that MPS.

Summary

This chapter focused on Cisco's implementation of MPOA. Recall that if LANE is a Layer 2 emulation, MPOA is a Layer 3 emulation. MPOA is based on LANE v2 and the NHRP, combining the benefits of both. LANE v2 allows MPOA to rely on LANE for communication within a single LIS. NHRP allows MPOA to deploy a cut-through routing mechanism between various broadcast domains, bypassing the traditional "next-hop" Layer 3 routing paradigm.

This chapter illustrated Cisco's MPOA implementation, presenting command syntax and implementation examples. MPOA implementation and configuration are based on client/server architecture, hence requiring the configuration of the MPOA Server (MPS) and the MPOA Client (MPC). Because MPOA resides on LANE, LANE configuration must be intact. Furthermore, LANE's LECs must be bound to the MPC/MPS. This chapter presents a lab that elaborates more on the MPOA implementation. Appendix C presents solutions to the lab.

Lab 11-1: Configuring MPOA

Objectives: At the end of the lab, you can complete the following:

- Configure MPOA on the Cisco 4500 routers
- Implement three logical IP subnets (LISs) over the ATM backbone
- Implement three logical IPX networks over the ATM backbone
- Demonstrate the advantages of MPOA

Purpose: Labs 9-4 and 9-5 allowed you to map Layer 3 IP addresses to ATM addresses dynamically to set up SVCs and illustrated the implementation over a single LIS and multiple LISs. To deploy multiple LISs with cut-through routing capability, NHRP was used.

This lab illustrates the same LISs, but in the MPOA view. MPOA uses NHRP and LANE. LANE helps the intra-LIS connectivity; whereas, NHRP with MPOA is responsible for inter-LIS connectivity.

Notice that MPOA is based on LANE Version 2, which requires UNI4.0. This is available in the Cisco IOS Release 12.05(T).

Table 11-3 lists and describes the commands you need to be familiar with to complete this lab.

Table 11-3   *Lab 11-1 Command Summary*

Command	Description
lane client mpoa server name *mps-name*	Binds a LANE client to the specified MPS.
mpoa server config name *mps-name*	Defines the MPS with the specified name.
mpoa server name *mps-name*	Attaches the MPS to the ATM interface.
lane database *database-name*	Configures a database.
name elan-name server-atm-address atm-address	Associates an LES with an NSAP.
mpoa client config name *mpc-name*	Defines an MPC with a specified name.
mpoa client name *mpc-name*	Attaches an MPC to the ATM interface.
lane client mpoa client name *mpc-name*	Binds a LANE client to the specified MPC.
lane client ethernet *elan-name*	Declares the subinterface as a client.
lane server-bus ethernet *elan-name*	Declares the subinterface an LES and a BUS.

Figure 11-5 shows three broadcast domains: mkt, sales, and engineering. R1, R2, and R3 belong to the mkt broadcast domain; R7, R8, and R9 are part of the sales broadcast domain; and R4, R5, and R6 are part of the engineering broadcast domain. Within each broadcast domain, MPOA devices use LANE. When communicating between several broadcast domains, NHRP comes to the rescue. This results in cut-through routing. For example, MPOA provides a direct connection between R1 and R5, cutting through three LISs.

Figure 11-5 *MPOA Implementation*

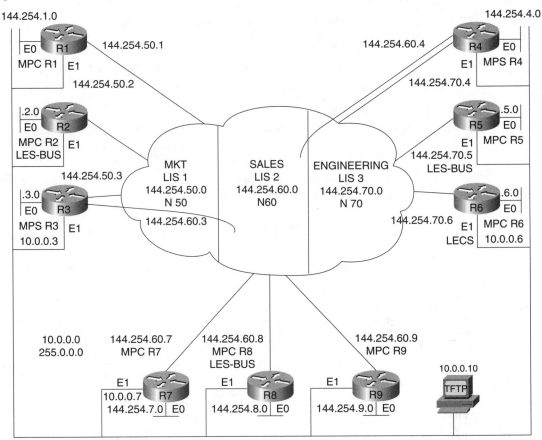

Exercises

Refer to Figure 11-5 to complete the following exercises for Lab 11-1.

1 Use the new subinterfaces ATM 0.50, ATM 0.60, and ATM 0.70 to implement this lab solution. Notice that because MPOA is based on LANE, you can rely on the dynamic AESA address registration. Configure the subinterfaces according to Table 11-4.

Table 11-4 *IP Addressing Scheme*

Router Number	Subinterface Number	IP Address	IPX Address
R1	ATM 0.50	144.254.50.1/24	50
R2	ATM 0.50	144.254.50.2/24	50

Table 11-4   *IP Addressing Scheme (Continued)*

Router Number	Subinterface Number	IP Address	IPX Address
R3	ATM 0.50	144.254.50.3/24	50
	ATM 0.60	144.254.60.3/24	60
R4	ATM 0.60	144.254.60.4/24	60
	ATM 0.70	144.254.70.4/24	70
R5	ATM 0.70	144.254.70.5/24	70
R6	ATM 0.70	144.254.70.6/24	70
R7	ATM 0.60	144.254.60.7/24	60
R8	ATM 0.60	144.254.60.8/24	60
R9	ATM 0.60	144.254.60.9/24	60

2 LANE is deployed in the lab within an LIS. This implies that you require a separate LES-BUS server within a single broadcast domain. Configure R2 as the LES-BUS server in LIS1, R8 as the LES-BUS Server in LIS2, and R5 as the LES-BUS Server in LIS3.

3 As per the lab schematic, R3 and R4 both are associated logically with two logical IP subnets. They require a second AESA address, which they obtain dynamically, and a second IP address to support the second subnet, which is associated with another subinterface, as depicted in Table 11-4. Note that you are still using the same Layer 3 IP routing protocol, IGRP.

4 Configure the LECs on all the routers, identifying ELANs according to Figure 11-5.

5 Configure R6 as the LECS, as you did for the LANE labs in Chapter 10, "LANE Implementation."

6 Configure the MPC and MPS binding to the LANE clients, as indicated in Figure 11-5.

7 Verify that you have full IP connectivity between all routers. Use the **ping** command and the **show ip route** command to ensure that the IGRP routing strategy works as expected.

8 Use another **trace** command on your router to demonstrate that ATM "fools" IP by providing cut-through routing. For example, on R3 or R2, repeat the **trace** test to the IP destinations used previously. You will see the cut-through routing event.

9 Verify that you have full IPX connectivity between all routers.

Review Questions

1 What is MPOA?

2 What are the advantages of MPOA?

3 What is the implementation of MPOA based on?

4 What are the components of the MPOA architecture, and what are their functions?

5 What is the relationship between MPOA and the LANE components?

6 What are the MPC's functions?

7 What are the MPS's functions?

8 What are the general steps involved in configuring an MPC and an MPS?

9 What could be one of the possible reasons for MPOA failure?

"Our greatest glory consists not in never falling, but in rising every time we fall."
—Confucius (551–479 B.C.)

"I attempt a difficult work, but there is no excellence without difficulty."—Ovid (43 B.C.–18 A.D.)

"What great things would you attempt if you knew you could not fail?"
—Robert Fuller (1845–1919)

PART **III**

ATM Cloud: LightStream 1010 ATM Switch

This part dives into the ATM cloud, concentrating on Cisco's implementation of the ATM switches for campus solutions. The prime product for accomplishing this is the LightStream 1010 switch.

Cisco discontinued the use of the *LightStream* brand name in June 1999, but continues to offer the award-winning LightStream 1010 platform and technology. The LightStream 1010 is available as is, and is now one of the platforms in the Catalyst 8500 MSR family, where it offers the same functionality as the original LightStream 1010 plus much more.

The chapters in this part of the book include

- Chapter 12, "LS1010 Features and Functions," focuses on the LightStream 1010 features and functions. Complementing Chapter 4, "ATM Traffic and Network Management," which covers the theory of traffic management and congestion control mechanisms, Chapter 12 discusses the deployment of these functions by the switch.

- Chapter 13, "LightStream 1010 Configuration," discusses the implementation of PVCs, SVCs using static and dynamic routing, soft PVCs, and tunnels using LightStream 1010 switches.

"It is difficult to say what is impossible, for the dreams of yesterday are the hopes of today, and the realities of tomorrow."—Robert H. Goddard (1882–1945)

"True vision is always twofold. It involves emotional comprehensions as well as physical perception." —Ross Parmenter

"Nothing is permanent but change."—Heraclitus (c. 540–c. 480 B.C.)

After reading this chapter, you should be able to understand the following:

- LightStream 1010 features, architecture, and components. This includes the physical and logical interfaces, ATM connection types, supported traffic parameters, and QoS parameters for various traffic classes.

- LightStream's traffic management and congestion control during the connection setup phase and during data transfer.

- LightStream 1010 management, which includes auto-configuration, ILMI, and OAM support.

CHAPTER 12

LightStream 1010 Features and Functions

The LightStream 1010 (LS1010) ATM switch is designed for workgroup LAN and campus backbone applications and supports ATM to the desktop with interfaces for unshielded twisted-pair and fiber-optic cabling. Figure 12-1 illustrates an example of the LS1010 application to the desktop.

Figure 12-1 *LightStream 1010: Workgroup ATM Application*

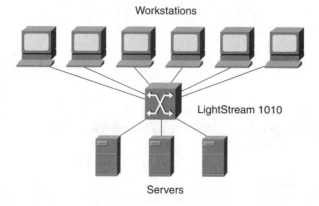

The primary application of the LS1010 is its use in the campus or building backbone, where the LS1010 provides interconnection to ATM-capable switches and routers (for example, Cisco 3600, 4*XXX* series, and Catalyst 5500 and 8500, to name a few). Furthermore, your LS1010 can provide an interface to switched LANs across an ATM network and can extend your voice connectivity by reaching to your in-place PBXs. Figure 12-2 illustrates a typical campus ATM application for the LS1010.

Figure 12-2 *LightStream 1010: Campus ATM Application*

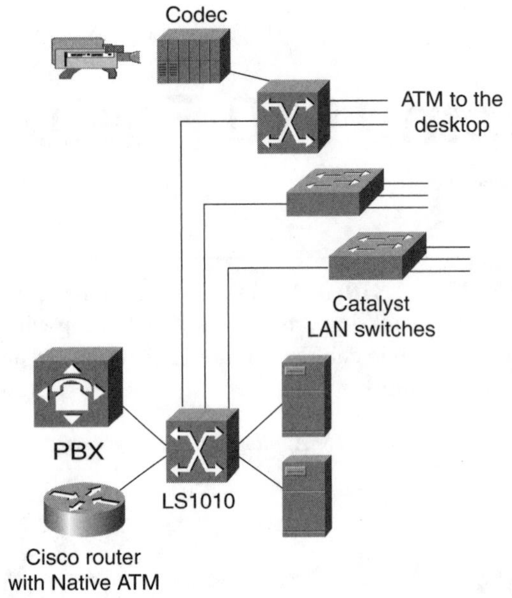

The LS1010 has multiple personalities. Not only can it function as your high-speed backbone switch, allowing multiple ATM interconnection methods, but it can perform the edge device functions, such as LANE functions and the Classical IP roles of server or client.

NOTE	Although the multiple personalities functionality exists, you should treat an LS1010 switch like what it actually is—an ATM switch designed to switch your Layer 1.25 cells. Any other job, such as LANE, is considered an ATM *application*. So, to gain maximum performance out of LS1010s, leave them to switch ATM cells, which is exactly what they are designed to do. Catalyst switches and routers should perform the LANE and/or Classical IP functions.

Figure 12-3 illustrates the LANE application for the LS1010 in both situations—LS1010 is used as an ATM switch and as an edge device, providing LANE services.

Figure 12-3 *LightStream 1010: LANE Support*

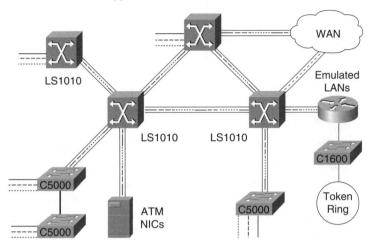

The LS1010 is very rich in features, one of which is complete support of ATM Forum specifications on traffic management and congestion control. The switch has a totally non-blocking, 5-Gbps architecture, which is addressed later in this chapter. A non-blocking architecture achieves optimum delay-throughput performance for various traffic types. It ensures that the switch can support parallel, fully meshed communications between all its ports with no head-of-line blocking.

The LS1010 can work with your Catalyst 5500 and Catalyst 8500 MSRs, complementing your campus network architecture.

This chapter first addresses LS1010 architecture, then traffic management and congestion control, and then closes with a discussion of LS1010 management. Remember that traffic management and congestion control are the two inevitable functions that the ATM cloud must provide to ensure the best network utilization and performance. Using these features, the LS1010 integrates support for different types of ATM services, such as voice, video, and data; avoids conditions where congestion can occur and minimizes the effects of congestion when it does happen; and prevents the spread of congestion to other parts of the network.

LightStream 1010 Switch Architecture

The LS1010 is a modular, non-blocking, 5-Gbps ATM switch that can support up to 32 full-duplex ATM ports at OC-3 or STS-3c (155 Mbps) or eight ports at OC-12 (622 Mbps). The fabric includes 65,536 cells of shared buffers, with control over buffer allocation policies and thresholds permitting flexible support of multiple service classes.

LS1010 supports Quality of Service (QoS) on demand, Private Network-to-Network Interface (PNNI) 1 routing, and User-Network Interface (UNI) signaling (ranging from 3.0 to 4.0). The LS1010 provides the capability to monitor cells as they flow through the switch, allowing ATM analyzers to snoop into the port and observe the traffic. In addition, the LS1010 supports Simple Network Management Protocol (SNMP) management and Operation, Administration, and Maintenance (OAM) flows.

Cell Switching Fabric

Traditionally, you can divide switching fabric types into four broad categories:

- **Shared medium**—Similar to a ring or a bus type topology, the shared medium switches are limited in bandwidth and therefore in scale. Their buffers must operate at the shared medium speed, which is much faster than the port speed and places a physical limitation on the throughput of the switch. Also, because the output buffers are not shared, the total number of buffers is greater than that of the shared memory switch.

- **Fully interconnected**—Requires independent paths between all possible pairs of inputs and outputs, consequently broadcasting arriving cells on several busses to all the ports, which results in the appropriate necessity of filtering. Although this approach is scalable in speed, due to the quadratic growth of buffers, practical reasons limit the number of output ports.

- **Space division**—A matrix-like space division fabric physically interconnects any number of input ports to any number of output ports. One of the popular types of switching architectures, deploying space division approach, is Banyan networks. The main issue with the Banyan networks design is the possibility of internal blocking, which occurs when the routes of two cells addressed to two different outputs might conflict. Various workarounds are available and are being worked on regarding this issue, which is outside the scope of this book.

- **Shared memory**—Shared memory is an output queueing approach where the output buffers all belong to a common memory block. This approach minimizes the amount of buffer memory required to achieve a specified cell loss rate. The shared memory switch architecture achieves 100 percent throughput under a heavy load. Why? Simply because if one output port receives a large burst of traffic, the shared memory can absorb as much of that traffic as possible. Compared to the shared medium switch, the shared memory switch has the advantages of more efficient hardware utilization and higher buffering efficiency, which reduce the total buffer and memory requirements.

The LS1010 is a *shared memory switch.* By definition, a shared memory switch is totally non-blocking and achieves the optimal delay-throughput performance for unicast or point-to-point traffic. The architecture of the shared memory fabric also facilitates easy field upgradability to support future standards or advanced capabilities, because all value-added switch machanisms are centralized on the field-upgradable feature card on the ASP module.

Components

The LS1010 uses a five-slot modular chassis that features the option of dual fault-tolerant, load-sharing power supplies, as illustrated in Figure 12-4. It is interesting to note that the chassis for the LS1010 is the same as the Cisco Catalyst 5000 switch, which allows sharing of spares and ease of administration. Furthermore, you can integrate the LS1010 into the Catalyst 5500 chassis to have a single chassis for both Ethernet and ATM connectivity.

Figure 12-4 *LightStream 1010 Components*

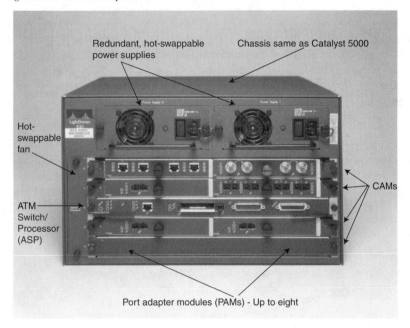

The LS1010 components include the following:

- ATM switch processor (ASP) module
- Chassis
- Carrier Adapter Module (CAM)
- Port Adapter Module (PAM)
- Dual power supplies

The central (third) slot in the LS1010 is dedicated to a single field-replaceable ASP module, which supports a switch fabric, a RISC processor, and a feature card. The CPU uses the R4600 processor, which runs at 100 MHz. The remaining slots support a variety of interface modules. The chassis fits a standard 19-inch rack and includes mounting hardware and cable guides.

The slots not occupied by ASP support up to four CAMs in total for the entire LS1010. Each CAM supports up to two PAMs for a maximum of eight PAMs per switch. Each PAM supports up to four ports. You can pull out all PAMs and CAMs of the chassis while the LS1010 is powered up, which implies that you can insert and remove the cards while the switch is turned on.

NOTE   There is a difference between *hot-swappability* and *online insertion and removal (OIR)*. Hot-swappable means that the removal of a card is totally transparent to the end user. But if you remove a card, guess what—the traffic cannot flow through that card anymore. OIR, on the other hand, means that you can remove cards without powering down the equipment, which is exactly what applies here.

Figure 12-5 illustrates the rear view of an LS1010, showing CAMs, PAMs, and ports. Your reference to a port of an LS1010 includes three numbers: the CAM number, followed by the PAM number, followed by the port number within the PAM. For example, a reference to second CAM, first PAM, and third port within that PAM is 1/0/2, as illustrated in Figure 12-5.

Figure 12-5 *Rear View of LightStream 1010*

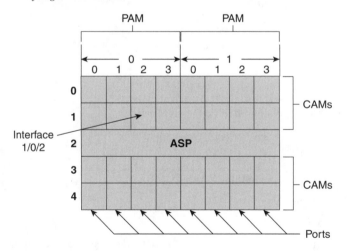

The ASP module, illustrated in Figure 12-6, interfaces to the switch fabric through an integral 155-Mbps ATM UNI port and an AAL5-capable SAR process.

Figure 12-6 *LightStream 1010 ASP Module*

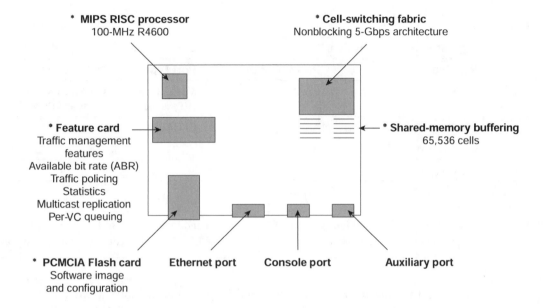

The ASP module can handle 2.5 million cells per second and runs elements of the Cisco IOS software for ATM, including ATM signaling and routing protocols, traffic management mechanisms, and ATM internetworking capabilities for access across the ATM ports. The ASP module supports up to 64 MB of DRAM (16 MB is the standard) on a single SIMM bank, 8 MB of Flash EPROM (expandable internally up to 16 MB), and 128 KB of NVRAM. The Flash EPROM allows downloads of software images for field-upgradability and for the storage of permanent connection information. NVRAM supports static configuration parameters to permit continuous operation upon reboot. As illustrated in Figure 12-6, ASP houses the feature card, which is a daughter card of the ASP module. The feature card supports the whole series of features, which are discussed later in the chapter.

Physical and Logical Ports

The LS1010 has several types of external physical and logical ports, as defined in Table 12-1.

Table 12-1   *LS1010 Physical and Logical Ports*

LightStream 1010 Physical Ports		LightStream 1010 Logical Ports	
Port Type	**Port Location**	**Port Type**	**Port Location**
ATM interfaces	CAMs and PAMs	Virtual Path (VP) tunnel	Associated with CAMs and PAMs
10-Mbps Ethernet	ASP	CPU port	ASP
Console port	ASP		
Auxiliary (AUX) port	ASP		

NOTE   Cisco IOS uses the word *interface* to refer to physical and logical ports of LS1010. For the purposes of this chapter, where the discussion is on the LS1010 architecture, I use the word *port*.

The logical VP tunnel port connects two switches via a transit public network. One application of the VP tunnel might be to interconnect two private SVC-based ATM networks via a public ATM cloud, as illustrated in Figure 12-7.

Figure 12-7   *LightStream 1010 ATM VP Tunneling*

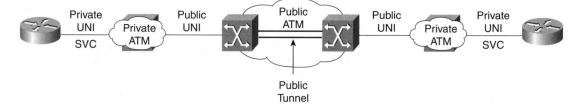

With VP tunneling, as discussed in Chapter 3, "ATM Reference Model: Higher Layers," a VP interconnects two LS1010s, one on each side, through the public network, across two public UNIs. Signaling traffic is mapped into the VP tunnel, and the switches allocate a virtual channel connection (VCC) on that VP, allowing signaling to pass transparently through the public network. Connections can be either permanent virtual circuits (PVCs), configured manually, or switched virtual circuits (SVCs) across the ATM ports using UNI signaling. The LS1010 also supports soft PVC/permanent virtual path (PVP). (The section "Connection Types" later in this chapter covers the benefits of this support.) The NVRAM memory of the ASP can store all PVCs, which are reestablished automatically following a reboot.

The LS1010 treats the CPU as a port, with a reference to the port number 2/0/0 (remember, the CPU resides in the middle of the switch, utilizing slot 2). Traffic destined for the LS1010 terminates on the CPU port 2/0/0 as it does with signaling, OAM, and ILMI.

NOTE   You can delete any logical port on the switch except the CPU port. I always say that only the hammer can delete the CPU port.

The LS1010's port assignment flexibility includes the capability to place any PAM into a CAM, which adds to the versatility of the switch and its flexible use in various network topologies.

The LS1010 can support a variety of connection types. Table 12-2 provides a complete list of all the ATM physical interfaces on an LS1010.

Table 12-2   *LightStream 1010 ATM Physical Interfaces*

Interface Type	Rate	Media	Maximum Distance	Quantity of Ports per PAM	Quantity of Ports per Switch
SONET STS-3c/ SDH STM1	155 Mbps	MMF	2 km	4	32
		SMF	40 km	4	32
		UTP5	100 m	4	32
Mixed Mode SONET STS-3c/ SDH STM1	155 Mbps	MMF	2 km and 30 km	3	24
		SMF	40 km	1	8
SONET STS-12c/SDH STM 4c	622 Mbps	MMF	500 m	1	8
		SMF	40 km	1	8
DS-3	45 Mbps	Coax	396 m	2/4	16/32
E3	34 Mbps	Coax	396 m	2/4	16/32
25.6 Mbps UNI	25.6 Mbps	UTP/ STP	50–100 m	12	96
T1/E1 ATM Trunk	1.544 Mpbs 2.048 Mbps	UTP (T1/ E1) Coax (E1)	304.8 m	4	32
T1/E1 CES	1.544 Mpbs 2.048 Mbps	UTP (T1/E1) Coax (E1)	304.8 m	4	32

The LS1010 supports traffic pacing that shapes the outgoing traffic on an individual port at the UNI side, as discussed in Chapter 4, "ATM Traffic and Network Management."

Table 12-3 lists and describes the clocking options supported by LS1010 ports.

Table 12-3   *LS1010 Port Clocking Options*

Clocking Option	Definition
Loop timing	Any interface can operate in loop timing mode, deriving its transmit clock from the incoming (received) line clock. Loop timing is required when connecting to public networks.
Derived master clock	Any appropriate synchronous (for example, STS-3c/STM-1) interface of an LS1010 can be a clock master interface, from which all other appropriate ports on the switch receive clock. This allows you, if desired, to synchronize all other interconnected switches and end systems throughout the network. Synchronization is important if you want to operate such synchronous services as circuit emulation, using AAL1, across a network. This is because AAL1 requires all attached end systems to use a common master clock (typically derived from a public network interface).
Free-running local clock	Each LS1010 switch also has an internal, free-running clock with the accuracy of a Stratum 4 clock (20 parts per million). You can use this interface clock in the absence of any external clock source. A switch deriving from and distributing a master clock also switches to its local clock if the master clock is lost, so that network-wide synchronization can be maintained and services are not disrupted.

High-speed Physical Interfaces

SONET/SDH at 155 Mbps comes in different flavors: over multimode fiber for connecting routers and LAN switches; over single-mode fiber for long distance runs; or over unshielded, twisted-pair category 5 (UTP5) for desktop connections.

The mixed-mode 155 Mbps SONET STS-3c/SDH STM-1 PAM supports three-port multimode and one-port single-mode (for a total of four ports per PAM) fiber intermediate reach plus, which can span to 30 km. It is a very effective interface for connecting devices, such as routers and LAN switches, locally and for connecting to another ATM switch in the backbone, which could be a service provider.

The single-mode fiber 155 Mbps SONET STS-3c/SDH STM-1 PAM supports four ports. With an intermediate reach, it can span up to 15 km; the long reach allows it to span to 40 km. It uses an SC-type connector.

The UTP-5 155 Mbps PAM supports standard RJ-45 connectors for ease of use and supports cable runs up to 100 meters in length. The UTP-5 PAM also works with 150-ohm shielded twisted-pair (STP) and 120-ohm Category 5 foiled twisted pair.

The single-mode fiber 622 Mbps SONET STS-12c/SDH STM-4 PAM supports a single port, and with higher-power laser output, supports connectivity up to 40 km. You can use the single-mode fiber for trunk connections among switches. The multimode fiber 622 Mbps spans up to 500 m and supports an SC-type connector.

The 25.6-Mbps rate allows high-density workgroup connections. The 25.6 Mbps ATM PAM has 12 ATM UNI ports, each with a standard throughput rate of 25.6 Mbps full duplex. Each port is compatible with the ATM Forum 25.6 Mbps physical sublayer specification for UTP Category 3 (UTP-3) or STP cable plants.

Low-Speed Physical Interfaces

The LS1010 supports the following low-speed physical interfaces:

* DS-3/E3
* T1/E1

Connections across a WAN to link multiple campuses or to connect to public networks use DS3 at 45 Mbps or E3 at 34 Mbps. You can configure each of the DS3/E3 ports to support various clock options, including self-timing based on the LS1010 processor clock, loop timing from the received data stream, and synchronized timing from a selected master clock port.

The LS1010 has a two-faced identity for the T1/E1 speed cards (1.544/2.048 Mbps). The first one, T1/E1 ATM trunk, supports AAL5, whereas the second one, T1/E1 CES, supports AAL1. The ATM trunk PAM adds broadband and narrowband trunking capability for the LS1010 switch. The T1/E1 ATM port adapter modules are ideal for intercampus, MAN, or WAN links. Deployed in combination with the T1/E1 CES PAM, the ATM trunk PAM enables the LS1010 platform for voice and data trunking applications.

CES T1 PAM supports physical interfaces for T1 unstructured and structured CBR data transmission services through LS1010 switches. The unstructured CES emulates point-to-point PVCs over T1/E1 trunks. This service maps the entire bandwidth on a T1/E1 trunk across an ATM network to interconnect PBXs, TDMs, and videoconferencing equipment. With the CES port adapter, customers can add voice transport by interconnecting PBXs over the same dark fiber to avoid local telephone charges. The T1/E1 structured (Nx64) CES enables the CES module to function very similarly to a classic Digital Access and Cross-Connect System (DACS). Using a CES T1/E1, you can map a single DS-0 channel of 64 kbps or multiple DS-0 channels across the ATM network. T1/E1 structured CES allows you to use LS1010, instead of a TDM, to allocate T1/E1 bandwidth to PBXs and teleconferencing equipment.

The LS1010 T1/E1 CES PAM supports three modes of clocking (see Chapter 8, "Circuit Emulation Service ATM Connectivity and Summary of Cisco ATM Edge Devices," for more detailed definitions):

- Adaptive clocking, as defined in AF-SAA-0032.000
- Synchronous residual time stamp (SRTS) clocking, as defined in ITU-T 363
- Synchronous timing for CBR traffic

The CES PAM supports CAS (channel-associated signaling) for on-hook/off-hook detection on CBR ports. Chapter 8 elaborates on CES functionality and uses of CAS.

Feature Card

The LS1010 feature card is a daughter card of the ASP, and implements a number of value-added capabilities over and above the basic switch mechanisms. These capabilities include support for statistics gathering, high-speed multicast replication, per-VC queuing, and traffic management mechanisms. Traffic management mechanisms, discussed in the section "Traffic Management and Congestion Control" later in this chapter, include usage parameter control (traffic policing), intelligent packet discard, and ABR congestion control.

By supporting these capabilities on the feature card, the LS1010 can be enhanced easily with new and advanced mechanisms that meet your needs.

Multicast and Broadcast Traffic

First, let's examine how the feature card handles multicast and broadcast traffic, which is point-to-multipoint.

Whereas a shared medium switch physically stores multiple copies of the multicast cell at different output ports, the LS1010, using its shared memory fabric, stores only a single copy of a multicast cell in the common cell memory, thus reducing buffer requirements for multicast traffic.

Furthermore, the LS1010 differs from other shared memory fabrics in that it uses a specialized Fast Multicast Engine (FME), which replicates only pointers to the buffer location for each leaf of the point-to-multipoint connection. The LS1010 can include its own switch processor as a leaf on point-to-multipoint connections, which becomes handy in LANE architecture (which treats a client as a leaf on the point-to-multipoint connections from the LES and BUS).

Delay-Service Classes

The LS1010 breaks traffic service classes into delay-service classes. LS1010 supports four delay-service classes, each with two loss priority classes. The four delay-service classes are as follows:

Class 1, CBR, supports CBR traffic
Class 2, VBR, supports rt-VBR and nrt-VBR
Class 3, ABR, supports ABR and GFR traffic
Class 4, UBR, supports UBR traffic

The LS1010 reserves a minimum amount of buffer for each delay-service class on each output port. The same is done in the CPU queue to avoid the situation of *buffer starvation*, which occurs when the appropriate buffer space is not available.

The LS1010 provides a very flexible buffer control mechanism, which you can adjust for each delay-service class. This chapter addresses the buffer controls in the section, "Output Priority." For now, you need to understand only that each delay-service class has a system-wide, programmable maximum queue limit and that each delay-service class has the programmable maximum queue limits per port. Also, cell loss priority (CLP) and early packet discard (EPD) have programmable thresholds for each delay-service class, per port.

The LS1010 records a bundle of information on its performance, including the following:

- Input and output cell count per connection
- Input and output cell count per port
- Header Error Control (HEC) errors
- Internal parity errors
- Delay-service queue sizes—call it S_{ij}, where S is the queue size, i is the delay class (i equals 1, 2, 3, 4), and j is the queue limit (measured in cells, j equals 1, 2, 3,...32)
- Invalid cell count
- Total number of cells discarded due to a reason, which includes buffer space problems or UPC violations, and the maximum queue limit being exceeded

Connection Types

The LS1010 supports the following point-to-point and point-to-multipoint connections:

- PVC
- SVC
- Soft PVC

The LS1010 supports up to 32,000 point-to-point and up to 32,000 point-to-multipoint connections, shared across all ports. Each port can support up to 8 bits of the virtual path identifier (VPI) space and up to 14 bits of the virtual channel identifier (VCI) space. The switch supports VCC switching, in which the connections are switched on the basis of the VPI and VCI values, and virtual path connection (VPC) switching, in which only VPI space is used and the VCI value passes through unchanged.

Extending the idea of VCC and VPC switching, LS1010s support soft permanent virtual circuit connection (PVCC) and soft permanent virtual path connection (PVPC). Soft PVCs are the solution to environments that do not support signaling at the edges of the cloud, or when an ATM service provider needs to reroute the connection, should any failures exist within the network. Within the soft PVC environment, the connection setup uses signaling protocols to set up connections between two switches terminating UNI PVC, as illustrated in Figure 12-8.

Figure 12-8 *LightStream 1010 ATM Connections—ATM Soft PVC*

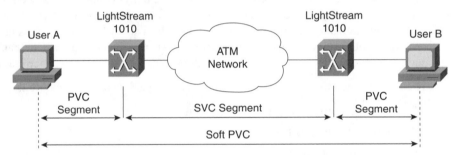

Soft PVCs can greatly ease the setup of PVCs by precluding the need to configure each hop of the PVC manually. Instead, you can use network management at the ingress switch to simply designate the desired endpoint switch and the target UNI PVC value. Then the ingress ATM switch invokes ATM signaling and the PNNI routing protocol to route, and sets up the connection across the network. Being signaled within the network, such soft PVCs also benefit from the automatic call rerouting capabilities of SVCs, ensuring that such connections can be reestablished and rerouted across failed links of nodes.

ATM Traffic Descriptor, QoS, and Service Classes

Recall that the goal of ATM networks is to carry multiple types of traffic (voice, video, and data) characterized by various delay sensitivity and delay tolerance factors. Consequently, an ATM switch must provide some methods for users or applications to describe the characteristics of the transmitted traffic and their QoS. Furthermore, the ATM network must ensure that each traffic type experience the acceptable delay and/or loss using traffic management mechanisms. In other words, if someone requests you to provide a certain service and you agree, you must comply with your agreement.

Beyond "keeping the promise," an ATM switch must provide mechanisms to avoid network congestion (preventive medicine) and to react to network congestion should it occur. Reacting to congestion is an imperative task—you want to minimize the intensity and the spread of the problem.

In a nutshell, an ATM switch must

- Define the traffic parameters and QoS, which constitutes the service contract
- Find the path guaranteeing QoS
- Deliver the promise—the guaranteed agreement

Chapter 4 identifies these traffic parameters:

- Peak cell rate (PCR)
- Sustainable cell rate (SCR)
- Burst tolerance (BT)
- Maximum burst size (MBS)
- Cell delay variation tolerance (CDVT)

UNI 4.0 contains the QoS values that identify end-to-end network performance. These include cell delay variation (CDV), maximum cell transfer delay (maxCTD), and cell loss ratio (CLR). The end systems and the network agree on these QoS parameters by using UNI and NNI signaling protocols.

Various traffic types, broken into service categories, have various traffic characteristics and QoS requirements. Based on the required service category, traffic parameters, and QoS, the source system generates the request with the traffic contract to establish the connection to the destination system, as illustrated in Figure 12-9.

Figure 12-9 *Typical Traffic Flow in an ATM Network*

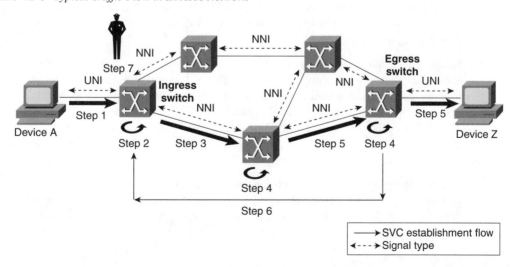

The following steps establish the connection to the destination system:

Step 1 The request is passed from the edge device A to the ingress LS1010 via UNI.

Step 2 Upon receiving this call setup message, the ingress switch performs the local connection admission control (CAC) function to determine the sufficiency of the local resources. If the resources are there, the ingress switch uses a PNNI VC routing protocol to find a source route through the network.

Step 3 The ingress switch forwards the request, using the PNNI signaling protocol.

Step 4 All switches along the suggested source route execute their own CAC algorithms.

Step 5 Upon the successful result of the CAC algorithm, all switches forward the request according to the source route in the request.

Step 6 When the connection is routed to the final destination and is accepted there, the egress LS1010 completes the connection setup and informs the requesting source about it.

Step 7 Upon the establishment of the connection, the edge LS1010s police the conformance of the entering traffic to the agreed traffic contract. The switches take proper actions should the contract be broken.

Traffic Management and Congestion Control

Let's recall that congestion within the ATM networks is something real and probably occurs at the connectivity to the WANs because the WAN connectivity is usually at a lower speed than the campus environment.

Network congestion can be a very debilitating phenomenon for ATM. Why? Well, think about the cell size when compared to the packet or frame size. Should your ATM network lose one cell, the whole packet, segmented into cells, must be resent, which adds to the congestion problem. For example, IP over ATM packet size is 9180 bytes, which constitutes 192 cells. Imagine losing just one cell—all 192 cells must be retransmitted. The more you lose, the more you retransmit. The more you retransmit, the heavier the traffic becomes, ultimately resulting in worse congestion.

Under a heavy load, an ATM switch can discard a cell from several different packets, which results in more traffic on your network. An exponential collapse of an ATM network is possible under the heavy load, which becomes heavier should congestion occur in the first place.

Hence, congestion control is a very important aspect of ATM network performance. The ATM switch must provide mechanisms to avoid network congestion and to react to network congestion in a manner that does not increase congestion so that the intensity of the congestion remains minimized.

LS1010 uses different traffic control approaches for different types of traffic categories. The following two major service types summarize all traffic categories:

- Guaranteed service, which includes constant bit rate (CBR), real-time variable bit rate (rt-VBR), and non–real-time variable bit rate (nrt-VBR)

- Best-effort service, which includes unspecified bit rate (UBR), available bit rate (ABR), and guaranteed frame rate (GFR)

You can subdivide the traffic management and congestion control into two different procedures:

- During the connection setup phase (at the call level)
- During the data transfer phase (at the cell level)

Let's examine now how the LS1010 handles the preventive and reacting measurements regarding traffic management and congestion control.

The Connection Setup Phase

During the connection setup phase, the LS1010 tries to prevent network congestion from happening. What must it do to prevent congestion? Well, somehow the switch must reserve enough of its own resources to meet the requested QoS, if it can. If the connection cannot be established at that particular time, the ingress LS1010 must reject the connection request.

The LS1010 includes the following steps in the connection setup:

Step 1   "Sign" the traffic contract, involving traffic parameters and QoS.

Step 2   Use CAC/GCAC.

Step 3   Use QoS routing (PNNI).

"Signing" the Traffic Contract

The traffic contract is specified at the call setup time, depending on the values of the service parameters (CBR, rt-VBR, and so on). These parameters fall into two categories: those specifying traffic parameters and those specifying QoS. The contract supports certain parameters depending on the UNI signaling version (refer to Tables 4-1 and 4-2 in Chapter 4 for various types of traffic parameters and QoS values). For purposes of demonstration here, assume that UNI 4.0 is used.

An ATM switch receiving a call request checks its local CAC first. If it's acceptable, it passes the request to the PNNI process for route calculation across the ATM network.

LS1010 uses the Connection Traffic Table (CTT) to help facilitate the resource management function. As illustrated in Table 12-4, the CTT specifies the service category and the traffic parameters. Please note that "Tolerance" refers to CDVT.

Table 12-4   *Sample Connection Traffic Table*

Row in the CTT	Service Category	Peak Cell Rate	Sustainable Cell Rate	Tolerance
1	UBR	7113539	N/A	None
2	CBR	424	N/A	None
3	rt-VBR	424	424	50
4	nrt-VBR	424	424	50
5	ABR	424	N/A	None
6	UBR	424	N/A	None

CAC/GCAC

Connection admission control (CAC) is the set of actions and procedures that the ATM switch takes in the connection setup phase to determine whether it can accept the VC request. This decision is based on two criteria:

- **Resource criteria**—Can the LS1010 provide the requested bandwidth and QoS values with respect to delay and loss?

- **Policy criteria**—Does this request conform with the LS1010 rules imposed by the administrator? The rules might include the maximum number of connections allowed within a service category or access lists based on various parameters, such as ATM network addresses.

WARNING   Although policy criteria is available in the LS1010, you should avoid implementing the policy if you use your LS1010 in the backbone of your infrastructure. Follow the design principles of leaving the backbone to send data as quickly as possible. The policy decisions should be performed at the distribution/access layers.

When the ingress LS1010 receives a signaling packet, it performs a CAC function to determine whether local resources exist to support the requested connection, as illustrated in Figure 12-10. Because the CAC function stays within a switch, the algorithm itself can be proprietary.

If the CAC result is positive, the LS1010 now needs to determine whether the network can support the request. The LS1010 uses PNNI to determine a potential source route through the network. Then the LS1010 uses the ATM Forum–specified Generic CAC (GCAC) to determine whether a potential route has sufficient resources to support a connection. This route must offer a high probability of meeting the QoS of the new connection request. The GCAC tries to provide a good prediction of a typical node CAC algorithm. After completing the GCAC, the ingress LS1010 routes the request to the next switch identified in the source route. If and when the connection is routed through to the final destination, and is accepted, the LS1010 completes the connection and informs the requesting endsystem about the success, thus accepting the traffic guarantee.

Figure 12-10 *Resource Management—CAC/GCAC*

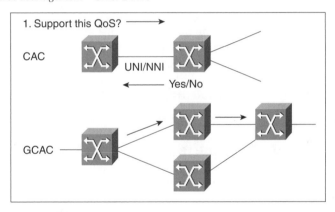

If the CAC result is negative, the crankback mechanism, described in Chapter 4, pushes the request back to the source.

The LS1010 CAC Algorithm

Now, let's look closer at the LS1010 CAC algorithm. The CAC algorithm uses the following parameters:

- Traffic parameters, including PCR, SCR, MBS, and CDVT
- QoS values, if they are provided, including CLR, CTD, and CDV

The proprietary CAC algorithm considers the measured network load to predict the system performance and to maximize switch utilization, while still meeting the performance objectives.

For a multilink trunk group (MLTG), PNNI provides a port list that allows CAC to select a specific physical or logical port to be used by a connection. Depending on the traffic type, the LS1010 supports two modes of operation for MLTG, as documented in Table 12-5.

Table 12-5 *LightStream 1010 Modes of Operation for MLTG*

Traffic Type	Modes of Operation
Guaranteed	**Load balancing**—Evenly distributes traffic load over MTLG in both directions, in and out.
	Best fit (first fit)—Searches for the first link with enough bandwidth.
Best effort	**Load balancing**—Uses even load approximation.
	Least queuing—Uses average queue occupancy of each link within MLTG.

You have enough flexibility within the switch to customize the resource management parameters used by CAC. For example, you can specify the minimum and maximum bandwidth as a percentage of the link bandwidth that is allowed for CBR, VBR, and so on. You also can provide the maximum bandwidth for combined CBR and VBR connections. If you specify these values, the LS1010 applies the following constraints:

min_CBR_BW + min_VBR_BW <= 1
and
min_CBR_BW <= max CBR_BW
and
min_VBR_BW <= max_VBR_BW
and
CBR_BW <= min {1-min_VBR_BW, max_CBR_BW} × LinkBW
and
VBR_BW <= min {1-min_CBR_BW, max_VBR_BW} × LinkBW

The use of VPCs greatly simplifies the CAC algorithm, because you can establish individual VCCs by making admission control decisions at nodes where the VPC terminates. This allows for VPC group settings of QoS for all the VCCs. One flexibility that needs to be worked on is for the LS1010 to allow individual QoS parameters for various VCCs that can be grouped into VPCs.

QoS Dynamic Routing

PNNI is the protocol responsible for providing QoS routing. This section examines PNNI with respect to the LS1010. Refer to Chapter 4 for a more in-depth discussion of PNNI.

The goal of PNNI routing is to provide a path that at the absolute least meets the QoS requirements of a connection request. Remember that the path might not necessarily be optimal from the perspective of number of hops or bandwidth. The main concern of PNNI is to minimize cell delay and loss, as identified by a particular traffic category.

The LS1010 implements the following metrics for PNNI:

- Administrative weight (AW)
- Maximum cell transfer delay (maxCTD) for CBR and VBR traffic
- Peak-to-peak cell delay variation (peak-to-peak CDV) for CBR and VBR
- Available cell rate (AvCR) per service category
- Maximum cell rate (maxCR) per line
- MaxCLR for high priority cells (CLP=0) of CBR and VBR traffic
- Cell rate margin (CRM)
- Variance factor (VF)

The GCAC uses the PNNI protocol to provide an accurate prediction of a typical path to meet the requirements.

This completes the setup call process. Does it mean that congestion won't occur? Absolutely not! The careful planning process of a call setup only *tries* to prevent the congestion; it cannot prevent it from happening.

The Data Transfer Phase

During the data transfer phase, the LS1010 reacts to congestion. First, let's examine the cell flow through the LS1010 traffic management and congestion control functions, as illustrated in Figure 12-11.

Figure 12-11 *LightStream 1010 Traffic Management/Congestion Control Cell Flow*

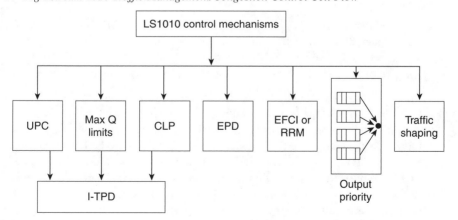

Figure 12-11 illustrates the relationships between various control mechanisms that the LS1010 has to offer, which include the following:

- Usage Parameter Control (UPC)
- Maximum queue limits
- Cell loss priority (CLP) control
- Intelligent Tail/Early Packet Discard (I-TPD/EPD) options
- Congestion control using Explicit Forward Congestion Indication (EFCI)/Relative Rate Marking (RRM) cells
- Output priority
- Traffic shaping

Notice that Figure 12-11 does not resemble a flow chart horizontally. Vertically, however, there is dependency between the functions. The congestion control mechanisms together make the LS1010 emulate a packet switch. For example, a LAN switch or router drops entire packets when experiencing congestion. These packet discard mechanisms work in close conjunction with higher-layer protocols, such as TCP, which are designed to adjust packet flow rate rapidly in response to network congestion, as signaled by packet discards. Conversely, they can increase packet throughputs rapidly by taking advantage of network bandwidth availability.

The following sections examine each control mechanism.

Traffic Policing—UPC

Traffic policing is when an ATM switch monitors a VC to make sure that the traffic patterns are what was agreed to when the call was set up. The cell stream is monitored and checked for conformity, and a VC of cells in conformity is said to be compliant.

The ATM Forum calls traffic policing *Usage Parameter Control (UPC)*. UPC is a set of actions taken by the LS1010 to monitor and control traffic at the UNI. Notice that UPC is applied at the edges of your ATM network, strictly at the UNI side, be it private or public. The objective of the UPC is to protect the network from the misbehavior of another network user.

The LS1010 uses the Leaky Bucket algorithm (referred to as the Generic Cell Rate Algorithm [GCRA] in the ATM Forum and discussed in Chapter 4) to check the conformity of every cell arriving from a connection with the stated traffic contracts. It sometimes is referred to as Dual-Mode Leaky Bucket algorithm, because LS1010s can use either peak cell rate (PCR) and cell delay variation tolerance (CDVT) parameters, or sustained cell rate (SCR) and burst tolerance (BT)/maximum burst size (MBS) parameters, depending on the service category of the flowing traffic. Upon detecting a violation, the LS1010 takes one of the following actions on a per-connection basis:

- Forwards the cell.

- Tags the cell by setting the CLP equal to 1 in the cell header. This allows other switches in the network to drop the cell, should there be network congestion.

- Drops non-conforming cells.

Figure 12-12 illustrates traffic policing with UPC during the data transfer.

Figure 12-12 *Traffic Policing with UPC During the Data Transfer Phase for the LightStream 1010*

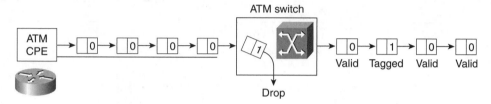

In the case of discarding, the LS1010 supports a unique and patented Intelligent Packet Discard (IPD) mechanism, which is discussed in Chapter 4.

The UPC uses two parameters: I, the *incremental* parameter, which determines the maximum PCR and SCR allowed; and L, the *limit* parameter, which defines the averaging interval used (which determines the CDVT or BT).

Table 12-6 shows the range of bit rates that can be policed as a function of I, where I represents PCR. It allows relatively fine adjustment of policed or allocated data rates in which the lowest bit rate that the LS1010 can police is 40 kbps.

Table 12-6 *Range of Bit Rates That Can Be Policed on LS1010*

The I Parameter	Bit Rates (Mbps)
1	2650.00
2	1325.00
3	833.33
4	662.50
5	530.00
6	441.67
…	…
17	155.88
18	147.22
19	139.47
…	…
26	101.92

continues

Table 12-6 *Range of Bit Rates That Can Be Policed on LS1010 (Continued)*

The I Parameter	Bit Rates (Mbps)
27	98.15
…	…
58	45.69
59	44.91
…	…
165	16.06
166	15.96
…	…
265	10.00
…	…
663	4.00
…	…
65535	0.04

Table 12-7 shows different effects of L settings, such as the number of cells or packets that can be accepted as a single burst of back-to-back cells.

Table 12-7 *Effects of Various Averaging Intervals on LS1010*

L Value (ms)	Bit Rates (Mbps)	Cells/Burst	Ethernet 1500-byte Packets/Burst	IP 9200-byte Packets/Burst
671.09	0.064	103	3.2	0.5
	0.348	611	19.1	3.2
	0.512	814	25.4	4.2
	1.5	2396	74.8	12.4
	4	6488	202.7	33.7
	10	16839	526.2	87.7
	16	28015	875.4	145.9
	34	67606	2112.6	352.1
	45	97568	3049.0	508.1
	100	395690	12365.3	2060.8
2.72	0.064	1	0.0	0.0

Table 12-7   *Effects of Various Averaging Intervals on LS1010 (Continued)*

L Value (ms)	Bit Rates (Mbps)	Cells/Burst	Ethernet 1500-byte Packets/Burst	IP 9200-byte Packets/Burst
	0.348	4	0.0	0.0
	1.5	11	0.3	0.0
	4	28	0.8	0.1
	10	70	2.1	0.3
	16	115	3.5	0.5
	34	275	8.5	1.4
	45	396	12.3	2.0
	100	1605	50.1	8.3

Maximum Queue Limits

As discussed in the section "Delay-Service Classes" earlier in this chapter, LS1010 supports four delay-service classes, which are associated with various traffic types (CBR, ABR, rt-VBR, nrt-VBR, UBR, and GFR). Each delay-service class has a predefined buffer that handles traffic types of the corresponding class.

The buffering of the LS1010 switch, which is discussed in the section "Output Priority" later in this chapter, can be allocated flexibly between each delay-service class and the output port to ensure that the switch can be tuned for any particular traffic profile or deployment scenario. When the tuning of the buffers for each delay-service class does not meet the requirements for the actual traffic types, the maximum queue limits are reached. This causes cell drops.

Cell Loss Priority (CLP) Control

The LS1010 implements two levels of cell loss priority. You can set a configurable threshold on each per–service-class port buffer beyond which the switch can accept cells only with the CLP bit not set—that is, CLP equals 0—hence favoring conforming traffic.

Cells with the CLP bit set to 1 are dropped preferentially, as illustrated in Figure 12-13. Such cells (particularly for the best-effort services) are not dropped arbitrarily, because the LS1010 uses the intelligent packet discard mechanism. This mechanism dictates the dropping of useless cells, once a cell of a packet is dropped, with the exception of the last cell of a packet/frame. Why is the last cell so important? Remember, the last cell has an end of message (EOM) bit turned on, which helps the destination edge device reassemble all the cells into the original frame. As discussed in Chapter 4, if the last cell is dropped as well, the cells from the other frames/packets are concatenated with the cells of the frame whose last cell was dropped, now causing two frames to be resent. This creates more traffic on the ATM network, causing more congestion.

Figure 12-13 *CLP Control During the Data Transfer Phase for the LightStream 1010*

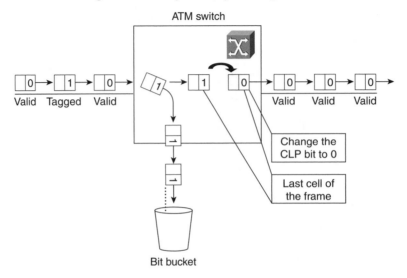

CLP control is a very powerful feature. When voice is transmitted over ATM, the degradation in quality that results from consecutive cell loss at a switch queue can be avoided through CLP marking and selective discard within the network. You can use CLP tagging in conjunction with compressed video, where VBR service class is used.

Intelligent Tail/Early Packet Discard

As discussed in Chapter 4, when one or more cells are dropped for a particular application, the remaining cells become useless. Furthermore, when a cell is dropped, a bunch of useless cells are delivered to the egress switch, occupying bandwidth "for fun" and resulting in wasted resources. To rectify this problem, the LS1010 switch implements a unique, patented I-TPD/EPD scheme that intelligently and selectively discards cells belonging to the "incomplete" packet that lost some of its cells. The goal of this scheme is to emulate a packet switch, which drops the entire packet/frame when experiencing congestion.

The LS1010 allows you to set individual thresholds for Explicit Forward Congestion Indication (EFCI) or Relative Rate Marking (RRM) mode, and a higher threshold for early packet and CLP discard. When a cell is dropped for any reason, such as UPC enforcement, buffer overflow, CLP selective discard, or queue limits, the ITPD discards all the other cells, except the last one (the EOM cell), which is identified in the cell header.

EPD is a technique in which the switch starts discarding all cells except the EOM cell from the newly arriving packets. EPD discards cells when the switch buffer queues reach a threshold level. Figure 12-14 illustrates the dependency between the threshold parameters and the corresponding action that the LS1010 takes.

Figure 12-14 *LightStream 1010 Threshold/Action*

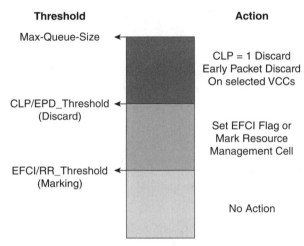

As long as buffer space exists, the EOM cell is not dropped because the EOM cell is required to delimit packet boundaries. In addition, the LS1010 switch always resets the CLP bit to 0 for all EOM cells to maximize their chances of being transmitted successfully to the destination point.

Congestion Control

LS1010 switches can use two methods to indicate and control congestion at their queuing points. The methods, listed in the order of their complexity, are as follows:

1 **EFCI marking mode**—The switch sets the EFCI state in the headers of forward data cells to indicate congestion. When the destination receives an EFCI flag set, it marks the congestion indication bit in the backward RRM cells to indicate congestion and sends the cells back to the source.

2 **RR marking mode**—The switch sets the congestion indication bit in forward and/or backward RRM cells to indicate congestion (the setting for this bit must be specified and is mandatory for ABR traffic type for flow and congestion control).

In all cases, sources send RRM cells regularly, and destinations return them to the sources. Depending on the feedback received, the source system either increases or decreases its rate. Chapter 4 discusses the functionality and the structure of the RRM cells in detail.

Both methods involve two important functions:

- Detect the congestion
- Provide feedback to the source

The RR marking mode, because of its capability to use backward RRM cells to notify the source, greatly reduces the feedback delays and delivers much better performance than the EFCI marking mode, which relies on the destination end system to reflect the notification back.

Both modes, EFCI and RR, can be used for congestion control as well as flow control. As discussed in Chapter 4, any flow control is optional for CBR, VBR, UBR, and GFR traffic, but is mandatory for ABR. The LS1010 switch allows you to set up individual thresholds for either EFCI or RRM modes.

Output Priority

The role of buffer sharing and management in the LS1010 is to select the cells that must be dropped in an overload situation and to control the trade-off between complete buffer sharing and fairness approaches.

The LS1010 has four system-wide configurable maximum buffer limits for each delay-service class, as described in the section "Delay-Service Classes" earlier in this chapter. By supporting so many priority levels, the LS1010 switch ensures full separation of the various traffic classes. This consequently ensures absolute priority for the guaranteed services over the best-effort services. Also, fixed minimum buffer limits preclude the possibility of buffer starvation when high-priority traffic consumes all available switch buffers.

The following configurable buffer controls, which apply to all four buffers, are available:

- Per-switch controls on maximum buffer limits for each delay-service class
- Per delay-service class maximum buffer sizes per port
- Per delay-service class thresholds for CLP/EPD and EFCI/RRM

The default values of all buffer limits (Li, where i = 1,2,…,32) are the same and are equal to 65,536 cells. You can modify the maximum buffer controls for the service classes simply by adjusting the oversubscription factor (OSF) of the switch fabric. The default value of OSF is 8 in a value range from 1 to 32. OSF controls the degree of buffer sharing and hence the amount of effective buffering within the switch. Within the LS1010, the single OSF value is mapped into multiple optimal buffer thresholds, which allows you to simplify the tuning of the buffer allocation.

Figure 12-15 illustrates the effect of the OSF setting on the switch buffer.

Figure 12-15 *The Effect of OSF on the LightStream 1010 Switch Buffer*

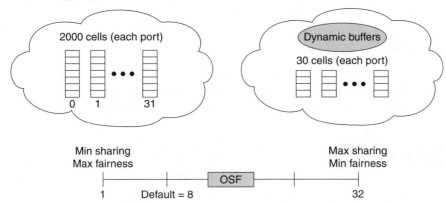

Traffic Shaping

The LS1010 supports a traffic shaping mechanism that allows you to limit the rate at which traffic is sent across a port to a variety of peak traffic rates. This capability is important when connecting to a public UNI, because many public ATM network carriers base their tariffs on the access bandwidth.

LS1010's traffic shaping mechanism, deploying the Leaky Bucket algorithm, can shape up to 128 VP tunnels and each VP tunnel can have up to 128 VCs. Chapter 4 elaborates on the Leaky Bucket algorithm.

LightStream 1010 Management

The LS1010 builds on the infrastructure of the Cisco IOS software, which allows the LS1010 to utilize all aspects of Cisco IOS software functionality and the specific capabilities of the Cisco IOS for ATM.

The LS1010 incorporates both a complete TCP/IP stack plus all the associated protocols—BOOTP, Telnet, TFTP, and so forth—required to access the switch. Upon initial power up, the switch attempts to use BOOTP across its serial and Ethernet ports to determine its IP addresses and any other configuration information. Using a local terminal also can provide such information.

After you configure the switch with the required IP addressing, you can use any of its ports—the ATM interfaces, the Ethernet port, and the two serial ports—to access the switch for further configuration. The LS1010 offers the familiar Cisco router command-line interface (CLI) for switch configuration and monitoring. You can download software releases into the switch online using the TFTP protocol and remote reset capabilities.

The LS1010 offers the versatility in access protection using multiple password levels and TACACS for remote access validation.

The LS1010 also is manageable through SNMP management systems, and it supports standard device and ATM MIBs, together with private extensions to standard MIBs.

LS1010 MIBs are accessible through dual SNMPv1 and SNMPv2 stacks and support all SNMP operations, including both SET and GET. The operation of the LS1010's functionality can be monitored and configured through SNMP applications.

Autoconfiguration

LS1010s operating with the PNNI image (IOS 11.2) are preconfigured with Cisco ATM address prefixes, which consist of the following:

- An ICD ATM format
- A Cisco-specific ICD in the first three bytes
- A Cisco-assigned next four bytes
- A preconfigured, unique MAC address for the switch

This 13-byte prefix results in a unique node identifier, as illustrated in Figure 12-16.

Figure 12-16 *Cisco's LightStream 1010 Autoconfigured Address*

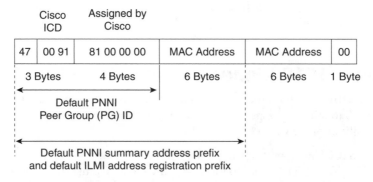

To complete the entire ATM address for the switch, the prefix is concatenated with the switch's MAC address. Should the end station require an automatic ATM address, the switch announces the unique prefix (via ILMI) and attaches the end device's MAC address to complete the ATM address. When you deploy IOS Release 11.2 and later, the switches automatically bring up the PNNI routing hierarchy, hence offering true plug-and-play operation.

These autoconfigured addresses are sufficient for a small peer group of a few dozen switches, permitting you to deploy small-scale ATM internetworks. Autoconfiguring gives you time to obtain and allocate your own ATM address prefixes. If and when autoconfiguration is required, mechanisms implemented on the LS1010 facilitate automatic address reassignment.

Such mechanisms, when combined with IP address autoconfiguration mechanisms (such as BOOTP), allow the LS1010 to be fully self-configuring with no manual configuration whatsoever, as illustrated in Figure 12-17. Upon obtaining the IP addresses (using DHCP), LS1010s obtain their configuration files. This is very handy, especially if you are new to ATM.

Figure 12-17 *LightStream 1010 Autoconfiguration*

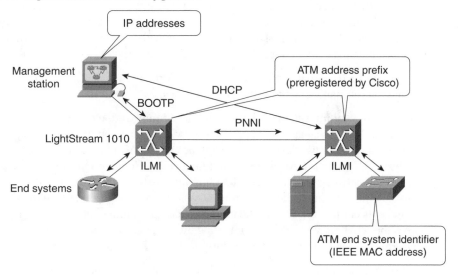

Preconfigured ATM addresses allow a network of LS1010 switches to come up totally automatically, PNNI routing protocol allows the automatic switch discovery, and the ILMI protocol automatically configures the addresses of the ATM end systems. Furthermore, BOOTP capability allows the LS1010 to obtain IP address configuration automatically.

ILMI and OAM

The ILMI protocol uses the SNMP format across the UNI (and across NNI links) to access an ILMI MIB associated with the link within each node. Recall that the ILMI protocol runs across a well-known virtual channel: VPI = 0, VCI = 16. The ILMI protocol allows adjacent nodes to determine various characteristics of the other node. One example of this is the type of signaling used. One of the most-used features of ILMI, which greatly facilitates the administration of ATM addressing, is address registration.

The LS1010 also uses the ILMI protocol to recognize the nature of any new ATM interface automatically—that is, whether it is a UNI or NNI, public interface or private interface, again contributing to the autoconfiguration discussed previously.

The LS1010 supports OAM, receiving and generating F4 and F5 cells and making OAM ping available. You actually can ping ATM switches by their ATM addresses, by the VPI/VCI identifiers, and this ping has nothing to do with the ICMP (IP) ping.

LightStream 1010 Monitoring

The LS1010 allows online passive monitoring. You can connect an external ATM analyzer to LS1010 and transparently monitor all the connections. You can use this capability to troubleshoot ATM systems. ATM analyzers provide the statistics in cells, which is a much more accurate measurement for ATM than packets/frames.

To simplify LS1010 management, you can use AtmDirector, which is a GUI-based application for management of the ATM switches.

AtmDirector simplifies the installation and the administration of ATM. It is a graphical, system-level ATM management application for configuring, monitoring, and troubleshooting a network of LS1010 switches and ATM-attached Cisco routers and Catalyst LAN switches. AtmDirector automatically discovers and illustrates the topology of the ATM network, displays real-time link information, and facilitates ATM network interrogation and troubleshooting. You can select any virtual connection on an ATM link and trace its entire path. The application provides an intuitive interface for creating PVCs across the ATM network. You can integrate the package with other network management platforms, or you can run it independently just for ATM network management.

CiscoView also can be part of your ATM network management package. When you point and double-click on any Cisco ATM device icon, it launches CiscoView, which provides a configuration GUI configuration tool and monitoring.

Summary

This chapter focused on Cisco's LS1010 ATM switching platform. The LS1010 can reside as a stand-alone unit or in your Catalyst 5500 or 8500 platforms. It is based on a non-blocking, shared memory fabric with a 5-Gbps capacity.

The LS1010 uses Cisco IOS software, which results in the same command set used to run Cisco routers. The LS1010 supports connectivity starting at the T1/E1 level up to OC-12.

The LS1010 comes with a dual, hot-swappable power supply with cards that you can insert and remove online with OIR.

The LS1010's feature card supports advanced traffic management, traffic shaping, and congestion control. The system fully supports ATM Forum specifications, including UNI

4.0 and PNNI. The system provides full network management capabilities and autoconfiguration with the help of ILMI, PNNI, BOOTP, and Telnet capabilities.

Review Questions

1 What is the application of the LS1010?

2 What kind of switching architecture does the LS1010 use?

3 What two types of switching architectures exist, and what are the differences?

4 What is the difference between "hot-swappable" and "OIR"? Which one applies to LS1010 components?

5 What kinds of ports are available on an LS1010 switch?

6 How would you refer to the interface associated with the CAM located in the second slot, the first PAM, and the third port in the PAM?

7 When you see traffic terminating in port 2/0/0, what does it mean?

8 How does the LS1010 handle multicast and broadcast traffic?

9 What clocking sources does the LS1010 use when connecting via T1/E1 CES interface?

10 What connection types does the LS1010 support?

11 What are the LS1010 responsibilities during the connection setup phase?

12 What is the difference between CAC and GCAC?

13 How does PNNI contribute to QoS?

14 What is the purpose of UPC?

15 How does the LS1010 react to full buffer condition?

16 How does the LS1010 react when it sees low-priority cells?

17 What kind of management capabilities does the LS1010 provide?

"Far away there in the sunshine are my highest aspirations. I may not reach them, but I can look up and see their beauty, believe in them, and try to follow where they lead."—Louisa May Alcott (1832–1888)

"Once the 'what' is decided, the 'how' always follows. We must not make the 'how' an excuse for not facing and accepting the 'what.'"—Pearl Buck (1892–1973)

"Simplicity, carried to an extreme, becomes elegance."—Jon Franklin

After reading this chapter, you should be able to understand the methods and the mechanics of ATM network implementation using LightStream 1010 switches, including the following:

- **LightStream 1010 ATM Interfaces**—LightStream 1010 has physical and logical ports, which are deployed for physical and logical connectivity. The logical ports are deployed in tunneling.

- **LightStream 1010 Virtual Circuit Connectivity**—This includes support of PVCs, PVPs, Soft VCs, and SVCs. SVCs allow the maximum network flexibility. SVC networks require signaling and signaling routing protocols. Your understanding includes the implementation of static routing and dynamic routing protocols.

- **LightStream 1010 Internetworking Support and Troubleshooting**—This includes various methods of troubleshooting and support deployed in ATM networks, such as gathering information on cell flow through the switches with the help of port snooping and the **debug** and **show** Cisco IOS commands.

CHAPTER 13

LightStream 1010 Configuration

In this chapter, you put theory to practice in relation to the implementation of the ATM cloud itself. After examining the theory of events within the ATM network and knowing what must be done at its edges, the question becomes: "What do I have to do to implement a permanent virtual circuit (PVC) ATM network in the cloud?" or "How do I configure the SVC network?" Another question might be "What choices do I have when configuring dynamic routing for signaling?"

Well, this chapter covers that and more. You learn how to configure PVC-based, switched virtual circuit (SVC)-based, permanent virtual path (PVP)-based, and Soft VC-based networks. Because ATM SVC networks require a signaling routing protocol, you learn how to configure Interim Interswitch Signaling Protocol (IISP) and Private Network-to-Network Interface (PNNI), and you become familiar with the flexibilities involved. The ATM switch that is used for examples in this chapter is the LightStream 1010 (LS1010). Similar philosophies do apply to other ATM switches with different syntax, of course. But, hey, when you learn how to ride a bicycle, it becomes irrelevant what model you ride. You know how to speed up, how to slow down, to turn, and so on.

This chapter concludes with some laboratory exercises to enhance your learning of how to configure ATM switches. The exercises include configurations of PVC, Soft VC, and SVC ATM networks and VP tunneling.

LightStream 1010 ATM Interfaces

The naming of ATM interfaces in the LS1010 is as follows:

- Reference to the physical card number—Carrier Adapter Module (CAM)
- Reference to the physical subcard number—Port Adapter Module (PAM)
- Reference to the physical port number

For example, a reference to the ATM interface on card 3, subcard 0, port 1 is 3/0/1. A reference to the CPU port is 2/0/0. Why 2? Because the ATM switch processor (ASP) is located in the slot 2, as discussed in Chapter 12, "LightStream 1010 Features and Functions." Furthermore, when you refer to a tunnel, it has a subinterface flavor to it. An example of the tunnel reference is 1/1/3.100, which means that you are referring to a logical port on card 1, subcard 1, port 3 with virtual path tunnel (VPT) number 100.

In contrast to Cisco routers, ATM interfaces are created when a switch boots up and the port card is plugged in. The LS1010 uses autoconfiguration, by default, which includes running Integrated Local Management Interface (ILMI). The autoconfiguration derives the following parameters using ILMI:

- Interface type—User-Network Interface (UNI)/Network-to-Network Interface (NNI)
- UNI version (3.0, 3.1, 4.0)
- Interface side (network/user)
- max-vpi-bits
- max-vci-bits

The autoconfiguration is off when the interface type is IISP, or ILMI is turned off.

If you do not want to use autoconfiguration mode, please follow these steps:

Step 1   Shut down the interface.

Step 2   Turn off autoconfiguration if it is enabled.

Step 3   Change the configuration parameters, as indicated in Table 13-1.

Step 4   Execute **no shutdown**.

Do not forget to save the new changes to the NVRAM, just as you would for a Cisco router.

Interface Parameters

Table 13-1 lists the interface configuration parameters of the LS1010.

Table 13-1   *LightStream 1010 Interface Configuration Parameters*

Parameter Type	Parameter Value
Interface location	Card/subcard/port
Port type	External/logical/CPU
Interface type	UNI/IISP/NNI
Interface side	User/network
UNI type	Private/public
UNI version	3.0/3.1/4.0

Table 13-1   *LightStream 1010 Interface Configuration Parameters (Continued)*

Parameter Type	Parameter Value
Maximum number of bits used in addressing	max-vpi-bits, max-vci-bits
Maximum number VPs or VCs	max-vp, max-vc

The maximum number of virtual path identifier (VPI) and virtual channel identifier (VCI) bits used for addressing as well as the maximum number of VPs or VCs are optional parameters. Table 13-2 shows their default values and the configurable ranges. Notice that the defaults are set to the specifications, which is important for interoperability.

Table 13-2   *VPI/VCI Space Configuration*

Parameter	Default Value	Value Range
max-vpi-bit	8	0–8
max-vci-bit	14	0–14
max-vp for physical port	255	0–255
max-vc for any port	32768	0–32768
max-vp for CPU and logical port	0	N/A

In addition to the flexibility of the VPI/VCI assignment, you should follow VPI/VCI space management rules, which are as follows:

1   VCI values ranging from 0 to 31 (0 and 31 inclusive) are reserved by the International Telecommunication Union-Telecommunication (ITU-T) and the ATM Forum. So you cannot assign those values.

2   For logical ports, the VPI for all VCs should be equal to the VPI of the tunneling VP.

3   For the CPU port, the VPI must be 0.

4   For PVCs, it is highly recommended that you use high VCI numbers.

5   For SVCs, the LS1010 switch chooses the first available VCI under the following conditions:

— The LS1010 is not the network side of UNI.

— The LS1010 is on the network side of IISP.

— The LS1010 is NNI and has the higher node ID.

The LS1010 treats the CPU port as a regular port of the LS1010 switch; hence, you can have terminating VCs on the CPU port. The CPU port is always operational for obvious reasons. Certain rules apply strictly to the CPU port. I call them "NOT" rules, which are

1   The UNI/NNI/IISP cannot be configured on the CPU port.

    2 The virtual path cannot be configured on the CPU port.

    3 The VP-tunnel cannot be configured on the CPU port.

    4 The CPU port cannot be shutdown.

    5 The CPU port cannot be deleted.

Basic Interface Configuration

The LS1010 runs Cisco IOS, which means that LS1010s have the same command syntax as Cisco routers. To change any interface parameters, you need to refer to an interface,

```
LS1010(config)#interface atm card/subcard/port [.vpt#]
```

where *vpt#* is the virtual path tunnel number that is used when you are deploying tunneling.

Then you can change some of the interface parameters, such as interface signaling type, version type, and so on. Entered in the interface configuration mode—LS1010 (config-ig)# —Table 13-3 presents some of these commands.

Table 13-3   *Interface Parameter Commands*

Command	What It Does
atm uni [**side** *side*] [**version** *ver*] [**type** *type*]	Configures ATM UNI on the specified physical or logical port. The default for the *side* value is **network**; for *ver*, it depends on the Cisco IOS release; for *type*, it is **private**.
atm nni	Configures ATM NNI on the specified physical or logical port.
atm iisp [**side** *side* [**version** *ver*]]|[**version** *ver* [**side** *side*]]	Configures ATM IISP, the interface type, and the version on a specific physical or logical port. Values of *side* could be **user** or **network**. Values of *ver* could be 3.0, 3.1, or 4.0 (the default is 3.0).
[**no**] **atm maxvp-number** *max_vp*	Configures the maximum number of virtual paths supported (0–255; the default is 255).
[**no**] **atm maxvc-number** *max_vc*	Configures the maximum number of virtual channels (0–32768; the default is 32768).
[**no**] **atm maxvpi-bits** *max_vpi_bits*	Configures the maximum number of VPI bits supported on the ATM interface (0–8; the default is 8).
[**no**] **atm maxvci-bits** *max_vci_bits*	Configures the maximum number of VCI bits (0–14; the default is 14).

TIP

When you want to change the type of signaling for an interface (for example, from NNI to IISP), you cannot remove the type of signaling and enter another one. You simply need to enter the desired signaling type over the existing one. Just remember that the interface must be of one specific type at any given moment. If the IOS allowed the negation of the interface type, what would it be? It cannot be "nothing!" It must be "something." This is why you simply override the existing signaling type with the desired new one.

The ATM interface can be in either a *down* or an *up* state. When the interface is down, either the physical link is down or the interface is administratively down (using the **shut** command). When the logical interface is down, you need to check the status of the underlying ATM interface. When the interface status shows up, the physical link is up or the interface is administratively up. You can delete the logical interfaces.

NOTE

Why would you want to delete the logical interface? Suppose that you have configured tunneling between the two SVC-based ATM clouds across the PVC-based one. You have joined the SVC networks, and they are in full operation. The business is growing and the amount of locations connecting to your ATM backbone has multiplied. Now, the time has come to change your existing tunneling infrastructure across the ATM network. Because the tunneling is configured with the help of the logical interfaces, you are now required to delete and/or alter the existing logical interfaces and create the other ones.

To display the status of the interface, enter the commands illustrated in Table 13-4 in global configuration mode (LS1010#).

Table 13-4   *Interface Parameters Commands*

Command	What It Does
show atm interface [**atm** *card/subcard/ port*[.*vpt#*]]	Displays the ATM interface configuration, including the logical tunnel interface.
show atm interface [**atm** *card/subcard/ port*[.*vpt#*]] **traffic**	Displays the number of input/output packets on the specified physical or logical interface. The output includes Operations, Administration, and Maintenance (OAM) cells sent and received.
show atm interface [**atm** *card/subcard/ port*[.*vpt#*]] **status**	Displays the ATM interface status.

Example 13-1 illustrates one of the **show** commands.

Example 13-1 show atm interface *Example*

```
LS1010#show atm interface atm 1/0/0.99
    Interface:          ATM1/0/0.99
    Port-type:          vp tunnel
    IF Status:          UP
    Admin Status:       up
    Auto-config:        disabled
    AutoCfgState:       not applicable
    IF-Side:            Network
    IF-type:            UNI
    Uni-type:           Private
    Uni-version:        V3.0
    Max-VPI-bits:       8
    Max-VCI-bits:       14
    Max-VP:             0
    Max-VC:             32768
ATM Address for Soft VC: 47.0091.8100.0000.0060.3e5a.db01.4000.0c80.0000.63
    Configured virtual links: PVCLs SoftVCLs   SVCLs  Total-Cfgd  Installed-Conns
                                 5      0        0        5            5
    Input cells: 0, Output cells: 0
    5 minute input rate: 0 bits/sec, 0 cells/sec
    5 minute output rate: 134028000 bits/sec, 2528830 cells/sec
```

Example 13-1 shows that it is a logical interface (**vp tunnel**), that its status is functional (**UP**), the interface type, and the UNI version numbers. It also shows the output rate of the interface.

Table 13-5 shows the ILMI configuration commands that you would enter in interface configuration mode—LS1010(config-if)#.

Table 13-5 *ILMI Interface Configuration Commands*

Command	What It Does
[no] atm ilmi-enable	Enables ILMI on a port.
[no] atm address-registration	Enables the switch to engage its address registration on an interface using the ILMI protocol.
[no] auto-link-determination	Enables the ILMI link determination feature.
[no] atm ilmi-keepalive [*t* **retry** [*number*]]	Changes the ILMI keepalive poll interval. The default values are polled every 5 seconds (t) and retried 5 times (number).

The default status for **atm ilmi**, **atm address-registration**, and **auto-link-determination** is **enable**, and the default value of **atm ilmi-keepalive** is 5 seconds.

To view the ILMI, execute the following **show** commands in global configuration mode:

```
show atm ilmi-status card/subcard/port
show atm ilmi-config
```

LightStream 1010 Virtual Circuit Connectivity

When the physical interfaces are up and running, LS1010s automatically generate VCs for well-known connections, such as ILMI, PNNI, and signaling. These connections are terminating connections that are treated as non-real-time variable bit rate (nrt-VBR) service category at the physical port level. For the logical port or the VP tunnel, the service category equals to the service category of the VP.

The LS1010 can handle the following VC types (which are discussed in Chapter 3, "ATM Reference Model: Higher Layers"):

- PVC
- PVP
- PVP tunneling
- Soft VC
- SVC

Let's begin with the permanent circuits first.

Permanent Circuits

Permanent circuits include

- PVCs
- PVPs
- PVP tunneling
- Soft VCs

Let's recall what the differences are between a virtual channel connection (VCC) and a virtual path connection (VPC). As illustrated in Figure 13-1, a VCC is established with the help of both VPI and VCI numbers, whereas a VPC connection is accomplished strictly with VPI. The central switch is shown as a VP switch for the VC. The switch is configured to inspect only the VPI portion of the cell address for VPI = 12 and to output the cell with a modified VPI = 26 on the next link.

Figure 13-1 *VPC versus VCC*

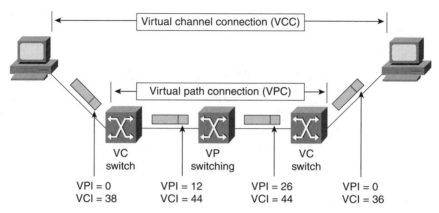

<table>
<tr><td>TIP</td><td>

Be careful when creating PVCs. They don't always work. Why? The reasons for possible VPI/VCI failures are:

For a VCC—The VPI/VCI is used already by an existing connection; the VPI is used by an existing transit VP; the VCI is less than 32. (Values less than 32 are reserved by the ITU-T and the ATM Forum.)

For a VPC—The VPI has been used by an existing connection; the VPI is equal to 0 (it must be of a nonzero value).

For a logical port—The VPI is different from the VPI of the VP tunnel.

For the CPU port—The VPI is nonzero. It must be equal to 0. The VPI nonzero values apply strictly to tunnels and/or VPCs.

For all ports and connection types—The maximum VPC number and/or the maximum VCC number and/or *max-vpi-bits* and/or *max-vci-bits* values have been violated.

</td></tr>
</table>

Table 13-6 lists the common parameters involved in the creation of permanent circuits, including PVCs, PVPs, and Soft VCs. The commands for these circuits are listed in the sections that follow.

Table 13-6 *Permanent Circuit Parameters*

Parameter	Meaning and Value(s)	Default Values	Required or Optional
Source interface	Reference to the source interface of the PVC in the switch.	N/A	Required
VPI	VPI value to use for this VC at the source interface (0-255).	None	Required

Table 13-6 *Permanent Circuit Parameters (Continued)*

Parameter	Meaning and Value(s)	Default Values	Required or Optional
VCI	VCI value to use for this VC at the source interface (0-32768).	None	Required
Destination interface	Reference to the destination interface of the PVC in the switch.	None	Required
VPI	VPI value to use for this VC at the destination interface (0-255).	None	Required
VCI	VCI value to use for this VC at the source interface (0-32768).	None	Required
Cast-type	Reference to the circuit type. It can be point-to-point, point-to-multipoint leaf, and point-to-multipoint root.	Point-to-point	Optional
Upc	Reference to the UPC in a permanent way. It can be either "drop," "pass," or "tag."	Pass	Optional
Pd	Activate packet discard. Values can be "on" or "off."	Off	Optional
rx-cttr	Connection traffic table row index in the received direction. The connection traffic table row should be configured before using this option.	1	Optional[1]
tx-cttr	Connection traffic table row index in the transmit direction. The connection traffic table row should be configured before using this option.	1	Optional[1]

[1] The LS1010 Connection Traffic Table (CTT) has fixed by default six rows that cannot be erased. When you create VCs, you have the flexibility to attach the configured PVC or PVP to a pre-specified row of the CTT. The CTT enables you to specify the traffic parameters values for the corresponding VCs statically.

Entered in global configuration mode—LS1010(config)#—the syntax of the commands that create a table entry in the CTT for various traffic types are as follows:

```
atm connection-traffic-table-row [index row-index] cbr pcr rate [cdvt cdvt]
atm connection-traffic-table-row [index row-index] {vbr-rt | vbr-nrt} pcr rate {scr0
  |
   scr10}scrval [mbs mbsval] [cdvt cdvtval]
atm connection-traffic-table-row [index row-index] abr pcr rate [cdvt cdvtval] [mcr
mcrval]
atm connection-traffic-table-row [index row-index] ubr pcr rate [cdvt cdvtval] [mcr
mcrval]
```

Table 13-7 lists the description of the parameters used in the CTT modification.

Table 13-7   *Parameters Description of CTT Command*

Parameter	Description
cdvt	The value of the cell delay variation tolerance, in the range of 0 to 2,147,483,647, expressed in cell-times (2.72 microseconds at 155.2 Mbps).
mbs	The value of the maximum burst size, in the range of 0 to 2,147,483,647, expressed in the number of cells.
mcr	The minimum cell rate is a positive integer, measured in kbps, in the range of 0 to 910,533,065.
pcr	The peak cell rate is a positive integer, measured in kbps, in the range of 0 to 910,533,065.
scr0	Sustained cell rate for the CLP 0 flow measured in kbps per second, in the range of 0 to 910,533,065.
scr10	Sustained cell rate for the CLP 0+1 flow measured in kbps per second, in the range of 0 to 910,533,065.

The sections that follow on the various permanent circuit types use the network topology illustrated in Figure 13-2.

Figure 13-2   *ATM Network Topology for Permanent Circuit Examples*

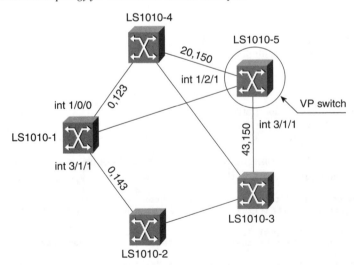

PVC Configuration

The full syntax of the command to create a PVC is as follows:

```
LS1010(config)# interface atm [card/subcard/port]
LS1010(config-if)# atm pvc vpi# vci# cast-type cast-type upc upc pd pd
  rx-cttr rx-cttr tx-cttr tx-cttr interface atm [card/cubcard/port] vpi# vci#
cast-type cast-type upc upc pd pd rx-cttr rx-cttr tx-cttr tx-cttr
```

Using Figure 13-2, the configuration in Example 13-2 shows the use of all the parameters.

Example 13-2 *PVC Configuration Example Using All Parameters*

```
! Configure PVC on LS1010-1 from interface atm 1/0/0 to interface atm 3/1/1

LS1010-1(config)# interface atm 1/0/0
LS1010-1(config-if)# atm pvc 0 123 cast-type p2mp-root upc tag pd on rx-cttr 12
tx-cttr 45 interface atm 3/1/1 0 143 cast-type p2mp-leaf upc tag pd on
  rx-cttr 45 tx-cttr 12
!
LS1010-1(config)# atm connection-traffic-table-row index 45 ubr pcr 100000
LS1010-1(config)# atm connection-traffic-table-row index 12 ubr pcr 155000
```

The **atm pvc** command on the **interface atm 1/0/0** states that this PVC is for traffic coming to and leaving from the LS1010 through the interface 1/0/0 on the VPI/VCI = 0/123, and leaving from and coming to the LS1010 through the interface 3/1/1 on the VPI/VCI = 0/143. This PVC is point-to-multipoint. It is tagged, and packet discard is activated. The PVC uses the CTT parameters specified in row 12 when receiving traffic. It uses CTT parameters specified in row 45 when transmitting the traffic. The CTT indexes of **45** and **12** have to be created before the PVC can use them. Example 13-3 illustrates the same PVC creation using only mandatory parameters.

Example 13-3 *Basic PVC Configuration*

```
! Configure PVC on LS1010-1 from interface atm 1/0/0 to interface atm 3/1/1

LS1010-1(config)# interface atm 1/0/0
LS1010-1(config-if)# atm pvc 0 123 interface atm 3/1/1 0 143
```

PVP Configuration

The full syntax for the commands used to configure PVP switching is as follows:

```
LS1010(config)# interface atm [card/subcard/port]
LS1010(config-if)# atm pvp vpi# cast-type cast-type upc upc rx-cttr rx-cttr
  tx-cttr tx-cttr interface atm [card/cubcard/port] vpi# cast-type cast-type
  upc upc rx-cttr rx-cttr tx-cttr tx-cttr
```

Referring to the network topology in Figure 13-2, Example 13-4 shows the configuration of the LS1010-5 switch as a VP switch.

Example 13-4 *LS1010 PVP Configuration Example Using All Parameters*

```
! Configure PVP on LS1010-5 from interface atm 1/2/1 to  interface atm 3/1/1
!
LS1010(config)# interface atm 1/2/1
LS1010(config-if)# atm pvp 20 cast-type p2p upc drop rx-cttr 12
  tx-cttr 45 interface atm 3/1/1 43 cast-type p2p upc drop
  rx-cttr 45 tx-cttr 12
!
LS1010(config)# atm connection-traffic-table-row index 45 ubr pcr 100000
LS1010-1(config)# atm connection-traffic-table-row index 12 ubr pcr 155000
```

The LS1010-5 performs switching based on VPIs only, from/to VPI= 20 to/from VPI= 43. Because you used the new indexes in the CTT, you must create them as in Example 13-2 for PVC configuration. Example 13-4 shows this creation process.

PVP Tunneling Configuration

PVP tunneling is used to connect two private ATM switches via a transit public network. Tunneling results in connectivity transparency as illustrated in Figure 13-3.

Figure 13-3 *VP Tunnel*

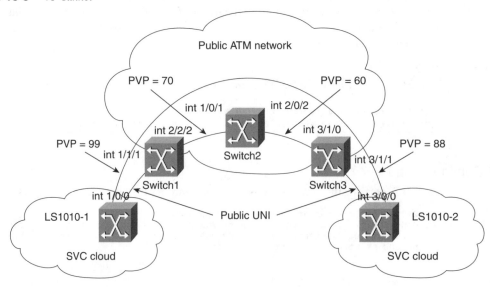

Two private SVC ATM clouds are interconnected via a public PVC ATM network. The beauty of this design is complete independence of the private networks from the public one. Suppose that the ATM service provider does not supply an SVC-based network. Your traffic requires the Quality of Service (QoS) parameters to be sent all the way to another SVC network. How do you accomplish this? By tunneling the SVC signal from one network to another. Even if the public ATM network is SVC-based, you could use tunneling to distinguish your QoS requirements from those of the public network.

The main characteristics of the VP tunnels are

- UNI/NNI/IISP can be configured on a VP tunnel.
- Virtual channels can be configured within a VP tunnel.
- Virtual paths cannot be configured within a VP tunnel.
- Well-known channels are created within a VP tunnel, which includes signaling, PNNI, and ILMI.
- The logical port represents a VP tunnel.
- You can delete the logical port.
- You can administratively **shut / no shut** the logical port.

The configuration steps involved in setting up a VP tunnel are as follows:

Step 1 Create the logical port at the edges of two private ATM networks.

Step 2 Assign the VP tunnel numbers to match the logical port numbers in the same switches.

Step 3 Have the public provider give you PVP switching inside the public ATM network.

Example 13-5 shows the configurations for LS1010-1, LS1010-2, and the intermediate public switches, as illustrated in Figure 13-3.

Example 13-5 *PVP Tunnel Configuration Example*

```
!Configuration of the edge private LS1010-1 - Step 1 and Step 2
LS1010-1(config)# interface atm 1/0/0
LS1010-1(config-if)# atm pvp 99
LS1010-1(config-if)# interface atm 1/0/0.99

!Configuration of the edge private LS1010-2 - Step 1 and Step 2
LS1010-2(config)# interface atm 3/0/0
LS1010-2(config-if)# atm pvp 88
LS1010-2(config-if)# interface atm 3/0/0.88

!Configuration of the public Switch1 - Step 3
```

continues

Example 13-5 *PVP Tunnel Configuration Example (Continued)*

```
Switch1(config)# interface atm 1/1/1
Switch1(config-if)# atm pvp 99 interface atm 2/2/2 70

!Configuration of the public Switch2 - Step 3
Switch2(config)# interface 1/0/1
Switch2(config-if)# atm pvp 70 interface atm 2/0/2 60

!Configuration of the public Switch3 - Step 3
Switch3(config)# interface 3/1/0
Switch3(config-if)# atm pvp 60 interface atm 3/1/1 88
```

Notice that the PVP number at the two sides of the tunnel does not have to be the same. This is because PVP numbers are significant locally. It is customary, however, to have the same PVP number for ease of administration.

Soft VC Configuration

Recall that the Soft VCs can greatly ease the setup of PVCs by precluding the need to configure each hop of the PVC manually, which is, no doubt, a very tedious and error prone exercise. The Soft VCs are needed when

- The host or edge switch does not support signaling
- There is a need to set up PVCs without too much manual configuration overhead
- There is a need for PVCs with reroute or retry capability if there is any failure within the network

Figure 13-4 illustrates a typical Soft VC scenario.

Figure 13-4 *ATM Soft VC*

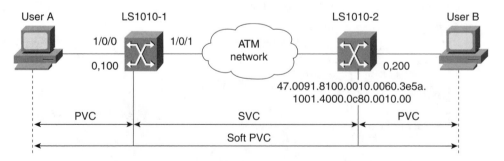

A Soft VC is built from the incoming interface of LS1010-1 to the outgoing interface of LS1010-2, or vice versa. It is, by default, a bidirectional VC. The configuration statements are required only in LS1010-1. If the circuit is torn down due to network outages, LS1010-

1 attempts to reestablish the Soft VC. The circuit is checked periodically to see whether a more efficient path exists.

The LS1010 supports two types of Soft VCs: Soft PVCs and Soft PVPs. The configuration parameters of the Soft VC are

- Source interface
- Source VPI/VCI
- Destination Soft VC ATM address
- Destination VPI/VCI
- Optional parameters, as identified in Table 13-3

NOTE   Be careful in identifying what is meant by "destination Soft VC ATM address." This is where the majority of misconfigurations occur. The "destination" address is the address of the terminating SVC switch, not the address of a switch, or end user station that does not know how to spell the word "ATM global address," because they do not understand ATM signaling.

The main idea here is to somehow "bind" the PVC's method of addressing, which is locally significant VPI/VCI numbers, and the SVC's method of addressing, which is the NSAP or E.164 form of globally significant value. Recall that LS1010s have a whole bunch of predefined ATM global addresses. Each ATM interface on an LS1010 is assigned automatically an ATM address for Soft VC purposes.

The ATM address is 20 bytes in length and has the following format:

- Obtains 13 bytes from the prefix of the switch
- Obtains 3 bytes from the Cisco OUI with local-admin-bit set to 1
- Obtains 4 bytes from the internal interface ID

You can view the Soft VC addresses by entering

```
LS1010-2> show atm addresses
```

The LS1010 responds with the list of all ATM addresses that are associated with the physical LS1010 interfaces, as illustrated in Example 13-6.

Example 13-6   **show atm addresses** *Output*

```
LS1010-2> 47.0091.8100.0010.0060.3e5a.1001.4000.0c80.0000.00 atm 0/0/0
47.0091.8100.0010.0060.3e5a.1001.4000.0c80.0010.00 atm 0/0/1
```

Similar to a regular PVC configuration syntax, you have the option of specifying either all of the parameters or only the mandatory parameters when configuring a Soft VC. The syntax of the Soft VC configuration, including Soft PVC and Soft PVP, is

```
LS1010(config)# interface atm [card/subcard/port]

! Soft PVC syntax

LS1010(config-if)# atm soft-vc vpi vci dest-address address dest-vpi dest-vci
  upc upc pd pd rx-cttr rx-cttr tx-cttr tx-cttr retry-interval first interval
  maximum interval

! Soft PVP syntax

LS1010(config-if)# atm soft-vp vpi dest-address address dest-vpi upc upc
  rx-cttr rx-cttr tx-cttr tx-cttr retry-interval first interval maximum interval
```

NOTE   **retry-interval** signifies that the retry interval timers for a Soft-VC will be configured.

first *interval* signifies the retry interval for the first retry after the first failed attempt specified in milliseconds. If the first retry after the first failed attempt also fails, the subsequent attempts are made at intervals computed using the first retry interval as follows:

$2^{(k-1)} \times \text{first} = \text{retry-interval}$

Where the value of k is 1 for the first retry after the first failed attempt. Then it increments by 1 for every subsequent attempt. The range of values is 100 to 3,600,000 milliseconds. The default is 5,000 milliseconds.

maximum *interval* represents the maximum retry interval between any two attempts specified in seconds. When the retry interval is computed in the first retry interval and becomes equal to or greater than the maximum retry interval configured, the subsequent retries are done at regular intervals of maximum retry-interval seconds until the call is established. The range of values is 1 to 65,535 seconds. The default is 60 seconds.

Using Figure 13-4, the configuration of the LS1010-1 is illustrated in Example 13-7. Notice that you are required to configure only one of the switches because the Soft VCs are bidirectional. Because I am configuring LS1010-1, I refer to the LS1010-2's destination ATM address.

Example 13-7 *ATM Soft VC Configuration*

```
LS1010-1(config)# interface atm 1/0/0
LS1010-1(config-if)# atm soft-vc 0 100 dest-address
  47.0091.8100.0010.0060.3e5a.1001.4000.0c80.0010.00 0 200
```

Switched Circuits

SVC-based ATM networks provide maximum flexibility and scalability in ATM connectivity. Why? Simply because the link failures within the ATM cloud are detected dynamically, which results in the new SVCs being established by the switches.

Signaling plays the critical role in the dynamics of the VC setup. To set up an SVC, signaling—carrying the global ATM address of the destination along with the other parameters (like QoS)—gets routed through the ATM network with the help of the ATM routing protocol. When the signaling goes through the cloud successfully, the VC is set up and its functionality becomes no different from the permanent circuit. While the signaling is routed, every switch generates a VPI/VCI pair that could be used for that potential VC if the setup is successful.

This section of the chapter concentrates on the configuration of two different methods of routing protocols used for signal routing while setting up SVCs. The methods are

- Static routing using IISP
- Dynamic routing using PNNI

IISP: Static Routing Configuration

The basic configuration of IISP requires you to do the following:

Step 1   Create static routes to the desired destinations.

Step 2   Adjust the interfaces to be the IISP type.

Step 3   Optionally restrict ATM routing software to operate in static mode.

Static routes are necessary when interfacing with parts of an ATM network running IISP. If the ILMI is not registering the addresses of end systems, it also is necessary to use static routes to indicate where end station addresses can be found, that is, out of which ATM interface a call request should be directed.

The syntax of commands involved in IISP routing is as follows:

```
!Create static routes to the desired destinations.
LS1010(config)# atm route addr-prefix atm card/subcard/port[.sub_inter #]

!Select the interface that will run IISP.
LS1010(config)# interface atm card/subcard/port[.vpt#]

!Disable autoconfiguration on the interface.
LS1010(config-if)# no atm autoconfiguration

!Configure the ATM IISP interface
LS1010(config-if)# atm iisp [side {network ¦ user}]
        [version {3.0 ¦ 3.1 ¦ 4.0}]

!Optionally, restrict the ATM routing software to operate in static mode.
LS1010(config)# atm routing-mode static
```

What is really exciting to note is that LS1010s allow you to enter prefixes in the **atm route** command. You do not need to specify all 40 hexadecimal values of the long ATM address, as long as the addressing is not ambiguous.

Remember the following rules while configuring LS1010s:

1   At any given time, the LS1010's interfaces are either UNI, NNI, or IISP. To change the interface type, you always must shut down the interface first, and then change the type.

2   The IISP interface type requires you to disable ATM autoconfiguration. Make sure to do that prior to enabling IISP on the interface.

3   IISP versions between immediately connected switches should be the same.

4   When configured, IISP's sides must be user-to-network, or visa versa, between two immediately connected switches.

5   If you want to have the LS1010 function strictly in static mode, you should reload the switch after enabling the static mode.

Let's examine Figure 13-5.

Figure 13-5   *Sample ATM Network Topology Using IISP*

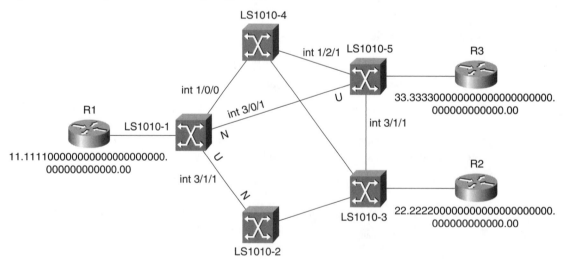

Example 13-8 demonstrates the configuration of LS1010-1 in Figure 13-5.

Example 13-8   *IISP Configuration*

```
!Create static routes to R2 and R3.
LS1010-1(config)# atm route 22... atm 3/1/1
LS1010-1(config)# atm route 33... atm 3/0/1
```

Example 13-8 *IISP Configuration (Continued)*

```
!Select the interface that will run IISP.
LS1010-1(config)# interface atm 3/1/1

!Disable autoconfiguration on the atm 3/1/1.
LS1010-1(config-if)# shut
LS1010-1(config-if)# no atm autoconfiguration

!Configure the ATM IISP interface
LS1010-1(config-if)# atm iisp side user
LS1010-1(config-if)# no shut

!Select the interface that will run IISP.
LS1010-1(config)# interface atm 3/0/1

!Disable autoconfiguration on the atm 3/0/1.
LS1010-1(config-if)# shut
LS1010-1(config-if)# no atm autoconfiguration

!Configure the ATM IISP interface
LS1010-1(config-if)# atm iisp side network
LS1010-1(config-if)# no shut
```

PNNI: Dynamic Routing Configuration

As discussed in Chapter 4, "ATM Traffic and Network Management," PNNI is a dynamic routing protocol for ATM signaling that provides you with enormous scalability, dynamics of configuration, and QoS routing.

As of Cisco IOS Release 11.2, LS1010s are configured to run PNNI by default. PNNI is a dynamic routing protocol because it learns the network topology and reachability information with minimal configuration. It automatically adapts to network changes by advertising topology state information.

Recall that PNNI uses source routing, where the ingress ATM switch dynamically computes the best QoS-based route, which is included in the call setup signaling message.

NOTE   As previously expressed in Chapter 4, the PNNI formulation is as follows:

PNNI = link-state routing + allowed partitioned areas + source routing + 104 layer of hierarchy + QoS routing + autosummarization and flexible summarization + multiple routing metrics and attributes.

Although Chapter 4 provides the theory behind PNNI functionality, this chapter concentrates on the configuration steps required for PNNI implementation.

The PNNI configuration can be subdivided into three types:

- Configuration of PNNI without hierarchy
- Configuration of PNNI with hierarchy at the lowest level of hierarchy
- Configuration of PNNI with hierarchy at the higher levels of hierarchy

Because manual configuration is not required for PNNI without hierarchy, let's proceed into hierarchical PNNI configuration.

When configuring hierarchical PNNI, it is important to "think" in a hierarchical way. Remember that any virtual reality resides on top of physical reality (so far, anyway). Consequently, you need to configure the lower levels before you proceed to the higher levels.

Configuration of PNNI with Hierarchy at the Lowest Level of Hierarchy

The lowest level PNNI configuration includes these steps:

Step 1   Configure the ATM address and the PNNI Node Level.

Step 2   Optionally, configure a static route (if it is required), to a non-PNNI speaking switch.

Step 3   Optionally, configure a summary address.

Step 4   Optionally, configure the scope of addresses.

Step 1: Configuring ATM Address and PNNI Node Level   The PNNI Node Level is a numeric number. The lower numeric number identifies the higher level of the PNNI hierarchy. For example, Node Level of 56 identifies the higher hierarchical PNNI level when compared to the Node Level 64.

By default, the LS1010's PNNI is preconfigured as a single lowest-level PNNI node (identified as node 1) with a Node Level of 56. The system calculates the node ID and the peer group ID based on the current active ATM address.

Typically, when configuring hierarchy, you need to change the active ATM address. The process of changing the ATM address involves the steps and the command syntax listed in Table 13-8.

Table 13-8   *Active ATM Address Change*

Command Syntax	Description
LS1010(config)# **atm address** *new-address*	Configure the new ATM address of the switch.
LS1010# **show atm addresses**	Verify the new address.
LS1010(config)# **no atm address** *old-address*	Remove the old ATM address from the switch.
LS1010(config)# **atm router pnni**	Enter ATM router PNNI mode.

Table 13-8 *Active ATM Address Change (Continued)*

Command Syntax	Description
LS1010(config-atm-router)# **node 1 disable**	Disable the PNNI node.
LS1010(config-atm-router)# **node 1 level** *level* **enable**	Re-enable the node, and, optionally, change the node level.

Step 2: Configuring a Static Route   Step 2 is not optional. Because PNNI is a dynamic routing protocol, static routes are not necessary between nodes that support PNNI. However, you can extend the routing capability of PNNI beyond nodes that support it to connect to nodes that do not support PNNI. Configuration of a static route requires configuring the interface as an IISP and configuring a static route to a reachable address prefix. The section, "IISP: Static Routing Configuration," earlier in this chapter, addresses the steps involved in configuring a static route.

Step 3: Configuring a Summary Address   Address summarization allows scalability across multiple networks. By default, each lowest-level node has a summary address equal to the 13-byte address prefix of the ATM address of the switch. This address prefix is advertised to its peer group.

You can configure multiple addresses, which are used during ATM address migration, for a single switch. ILMI registers end systems with multiple prefixes during this period until an old address is removed. PNNI automatically creates 13-byte summary address prefixes from all of its ATM addresses.

You can configure customized address summarization on each node, especially when your ATM network has systems, addresses of which match the first 13 bytes of the ATM addresses attached to different switches. Table 13-9 presents the configuration steps and the command syntax involved in flexible address summarization.

Table 13-9 *ATM Address Summarization*

Command Syntax	Description
LS1010(config)# **atm router pnni**	Enter ATM router PNNI mode.
LS1010(config-atm-router)# **node** *node_index*	Enter node configuration mode.
LS1010(config-pnni-node)# **no auto-summary**	Remove the default summary addresses.
LS1010(config-pnni-node)# **summary-address** *address-prefix*	Configure the ATM PNNI summary address prefix.

Step 4: Configuring the Scope of Addresses   The PNNI address scope, a numeric value between 1 and 15, allows you to constrain advertised reachability information within configurable bounds. The higher the value of the scope, the larger is the network reachability.

The important thing to understand is that a source node routes to the node that advertises the longest address prefix that matches the destination; however, scope checking takes precedence over longest-prefix match routing. Note that if two destination nodes have the same address prefix, the node closest to the source is selected.

LS1010s have automatic scopes that are based on the PNNI Routing Level Indicator, which coincides with the ATM Forum UNI default scope. You can change the scope value. When autoconfigured, LS1010 forms a peer group at PNNI Node level 56, which dynamically coincides with the Routing Level Indicator 56 of the PNNI hierarchy. Also, when autoconfigured, the suitable UNI scope-to-PNNI level mapping is provided automatically. Table 13-10 lists the PNNI Routing Level Indicators and the corresponding UNI default scope values assumed by the LS1010 and the ATM Forum.

Table 13-10 *Scope Mapping Table*

PNNI Routing Level Indicator	UNI Default Scope Number (Automatic)	UNI Default Scope Number (ATM Forum)	Description of Advertised Reachability
96	N/A	1–3	Local
80	N/A	4–5	Local plus site
72	N/A	6–7	Intrasite
64	N/A	8–10	Intra-organization
56	1–10	N/A	Default node level for LS1010 autoconfiguration
48	11–12	11–12	Intracommunity
32	13–14	13–14	Regional and Interregional
0	15	15	Global

WARNING   By changing the PNNI routing levels to values that are greater than the node level, the reachability information scope becomes smaller than the node scope, and the reachability cannot be advertised.

In automatic mode, the UNI to PNNI level mapping is automatically reconfigured each time you modify the level of the node 1. The automatic reconfiguration prevents misconfigurations caused by node level modifications.

You can configure scopes manually as well. To configure the PNNI scope, execute the commands listed in Table 13-11.

Table 13-11   *Manual PNNI Scope Configuration Steps*

Step	Command	Description
1	LS1010(config)# **atm router pnni**	Enter ATM router PNNI mode.
2	LS1010(config-atm-router)# **node** *node_index*	Enter node configuration mode.
Step	**Command**	**Description**
3	LS1010(config-pnni-node)# **scope mode** {**automatic** I **manual**}	Configure the scope as manual.
4	LS1010(config-pnni-node)# **scope map** *low-org-scope* [*high-org-scope*] **level** *level-number*	Configure node scope mapping.

Configuration of PNNI with Hierarchy at the Highest Level of Hierarchy

After you configure the lowest level of the PNNI hierarchy, you need to configure the Peer Group Leaders (PGLs) and the Logical Group Nodes (LGNs). A PGL is a logical node within the peer group that collects data about the peer group to represent it as a single node to the next PNNI hierarchical level.

Upon becoming a PGL, a PGL creates a parent LGN, which represents the PGL's peer group within the next, higher-level peer group. The LGN aggregates and summarizes information about its child peer group and floods that information into its own peer group. To create the PNNI hierarchy, perform the following tasks:

- Select switches that are eligible to become PGLs at each level of the hierarchy.
- Ensure that the election priority is a non-zero for the potential PGL candidates.

- Ensure that the lowest-level nodes are preferred as PGLs to reduce processing overhead.

The configuration steps consist of the following:

Step 1   Configure the LGN and the peer group identifier (PGI).

Step 2   Configure the node name.

Step 3   Configure a parent node.

Step 4   Configure the node election leadership priority.

Step 5   Configure a summary address.

Let's examine all the steps in sequence and then look at the configuration example.

Step 1: Configuring the LGN and the Peer Group Identifier   The LGN is created only when the child node in the same switch is elected to be a PGL. The PGI does not need to be specified. It defaults to a value created from the first part of the child peer group identifier. You do have the option, however, like in everything else, of changing the defaults.

If you decide to configure your own PGI, you must configure all logical nodes within a peer group with the same PGI number.

The command syntax for LGN and PGI configuration is as follows:

```
LS1010(config)# atm router pnni
LS1010(config-atm-router)# node node-index level level [lowest]
  [peer-group-identifier dd:xxx] [enable ¦ disable]
```

Step 2: Configuring a Node Name   PNNI node names default to names based on the host name. If you want to use another name of the peer group, you can change the default. After you configure a node name, the system distributes it to all other nodes. This allows the node to be identified by its node name from anywhere on the network.

To configure the node name, you must enter the following commands in sequence:

```
LS1010(config)# atm router pnni
LS1010(config-atm-router)# node node-index
LS1010(config-pnni-node)# name name-string
```

Step 3: Configuring a Parent Node   For a node to be eligible to become a PGL within its own peer group, you must configure a parent node and an election leadership priority. If the node is elected as a PGL, the node specified by the **parent** command becomes the parent node and represents the peer group at the next hierarchical level.

The commands involved in the parent node configuration are

```
LS1010(config)# atm router pnni
LS1010(config-atm-router)# node node-index
LS1010(config-pnni-node)# parent node-index
```

Step 4: Configuring the Node Election Leadership Priority   Typically, a node with the highest election leadership priority is elected PGL. If two nodes share the same election priority, the node with the highest node identifier becomes the PGL. To kill the chances of a node becoming a PGL, you must set its priority to zero. It is a good idea to configure multiple nodes in a peer group with non-zero leadership priority so that if one PGL becomes unreachable, the node configured with the next highest election priority becomes the new PGL.

NOTE   The PGL election is somewhat similar to the OSPF Designated Router (DR) / Backup Designated Router (BDR) concept. The higher the priority, the better. A priority of zero guarantees that the node cannot be a DR or a BDR. Similarly, a priority of zero guarantees that the node cannot be a PGL.

It is recommended that the leadership priority be divided into three tiers:

> First tier: 1 to 49
> Second tier: 100 to 149
> Third tier: 200 to 205

The tier classification exists because the node, after it becomes PGL, increases the advertised leadership priority by the value of 50 to avoid instabilities after the election. I guess the node wants to be absolutely sure of being in charge!

If among the PGL candidates you do not want to force anyone to be a PGL, then assign all priority values within the first tier. If you require certain nodes to take precedence over other nodes, however, then assign their priority value from the second tier. You should never have only one candidate to be within a tier level for redundancy reasons. The third tier provides a master leader.

The syntax of commands required to configure leadership priority is

```
LS1010(config)# atm router pnni
LS1010(config-atm-router)# node node-index
LS1010(config-pnni-node)# election leadership-priority number
```

Remember that the **election leadership-priority** command takes effect only after you configure a parent node.

Step 5: Configuring a Summary Address   Summarization increases network scalability by reducing PNNI routing tables, decreasing memory and CPU resources, and resulting in quieter networks.

The syntax of commands for configuring a summary address is identical to the syntax of summary address commands specified in Table 13-9.

PNNI Hierarchical Configuration Example

This section presents the configuration example illustrating the hierarchical PNNI network shown in the Figure 13-6.

Figure 13-6 *Three-Layer Hierarchical PNNI Network*

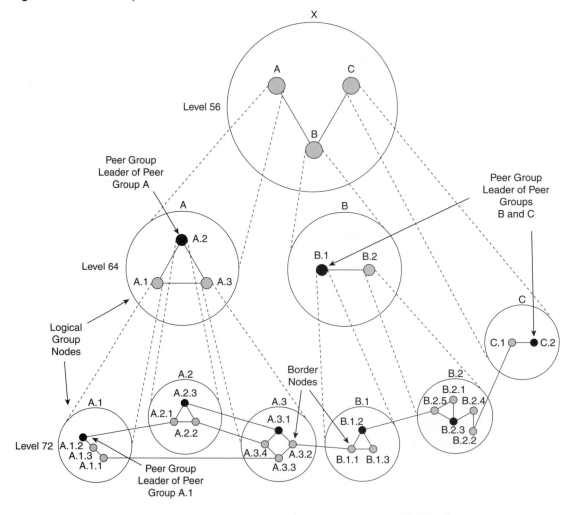

At the lowest level, 72, the hierarchy represents six separate peer groups. In the first peer group, Switches A.1.1 and A.1.3 do not have ancestor nodes configured; thus, they cannot become PGLs. Switch A.1.2 of the first group and switches A.2.1 and A.2.3 of the second group each have two ancestor nodes (a parent node and a grandparent node) and, hence, are eligible to become PGLs at two levels.

The configuration in Example 13-9 illustrates the configuration of nodes A.1.1, A.1.2, A.2.1, and A.2.3. Switch A.2.3 has the highest election priority (45), which means that PNNI will choose it to be PGL.

Example 13-9 *PNNI Hierarchical Configuration*

```
!Configuration of A.1.1 switch; static routes, if any, are redistributed dynamically
!
A.1.1(config)# atm address 47.0091.4455.6677.1144.1011.1233.0060.3e7b.3a01.00
A.1.1(config)# atm router pnni
A.1.1(config-atm-router)# node 1 level 72 lowest
A.1.1(config-pnni-node)# redistribute static
!
!Configuration of A.1.2 switch
!
A.1.2(config)# atm address
    47.0091.4455.6677.1144.1011.1244.0060.3e5b.bc01.00
A.1.2(config)# atm router pnni
A.1.2(config-atm-router)# node 1 level 72 lowest
A.1.2(config-pnni-node)# parent 2
A.1.2(config-pnni-node)# redistribute atm-static
A.1.2(config-pnni-node)# election leadership-priority 40
!
A.1.2(config-atm-router)# node 2 level 64
A.1.2(config-pnni-node)# parent 3
A.1.2(config-pnni-node)# election leadership-priority 40
A.1.2(config-pnni-node)# name A.1
!
A.1.2(config-atm-router)# node 3 level 56
A.1.2(config-pnni-node)# name A
!
!
!Configuration of A.2.1 switch
!
A.2.1(config)# atm address
    47.0091.4455.6677.2233.1011.1266.0060.3e7b.2001.00
A.2.1(config)# atm router pnni
A.2.1(config-atm-router)# node 1 level 72 lowest
A.2.1(config-pnni-node)# parent 2
A.2.1(config-pnni-node)# redistribute atm-static
A.2.1(config-pnni-node)# election leadership-priority 30
!
A.2.1(config-atm-router)# node 2 level 64
A.2.1(config-pnni-node)# parent 3
A.2.1(config-pnni-node)# election leadership-priority 30
A.2.1(config-pnni-node)# name A.2
!
A.2.1(config-atm-router)# node 3 level 56
A.2.1(config-pnni-node)# name A
!
!
!Configuration of A.2.3 switch
!
```

continues

Example 13-9 *PNNI Hierarchical Configuration (Continued)*

```
A.2.3(config)# atm address
  47.0091.4455.6677.2233.1011.1244.0060.3e7b.2401.00
A.2.3(config)# atm router pnni
A.2.3(config-atm-router)# node 1 level 72 lowest
A.2.3(config-pnni-node)# parent 2
A.2.3(config-pnni-node)# redistribute atm-static
A.2.3(config-pnni-node)# election leadership-priority 45
!
A.2.3(config-atm-router)# node 2 level 64
A.2.3(config-pnni-node)# parent 3
A.2.3(config-pnni-node)# election leadership-priority 45
A.2.3(config-pnni-node)# name A.2
!
A.2.3(config-atm-router)# node 3 level 56
A.2.3(config-pnni-node)# name A
!
```

Advanced PNNI Configuration

The advanced features are not required to enable PNNI. Their purpose is to allow you to fine-tune your PNNI functionality.

The advanced features used to tune the PNNI are

- Route selection
- Topology attributes
- Protocol parameters

Table 13-12 summarizes each category of the advanced feature and its description.

Table 13-12 *PNNI Advanced Configuration Options Summary*

Effect of the Parameter on...	Configurable Parameter	Description
Route selection	Background route computation	Determines the use of the background tree.
	Link selection	Allows the selection of a specific link between multiple parallel links.
	Precedence	Allows the selection of preferred routes prior to applying the AW.
	Administrative Weight (AW)	Allows changing of the AW value.
	Maximum Administrative Weight percentage	Allows preventing the use of alternate routes that consume too many network resources.

Table 13-12 *PNNI Advanced Configuration Options Summary (Continued)*

Effect of the Parameter on...	Configurable Parameter	Description
Topology Attributes	Transit restriction	Restricts transit traffic through the switch.
	Redistribution	Instructs PNNI to distribute reachability information from non-PNNI sources.
	Aggregation	Allows representation of aggregate of parallel physical links at the higher PNNI level.
	Significant change thresholds	Allows control of the origination of PNNI Topology State Elements (PTSEs).
Protocol parameters	PNNI Hello, flooding parameters, database synchronization	Allows adjustment of Hello, Database synchronization, and other PNNI parameters.

Now let's walk through all of the configurable parameters.

Configuring Background Route Computation   Most calls are routed using precomputed routing trees. To satisfy QoS requirements, multiple background trees are precomputed.

The LS1010s support two types of route selection modes:

- On-demand
- Background routes

On-demand is a separate route computation that is performed each time a SETUP or ADD PARTY message is received over a UNI or an IISP interface. In this mode, the most recent topology information received by this node is always used for each setup request.

Background routes means that you can route calls using precomputed routing trees. In this mode, multiple background trees are precomputed for several service categories and QoS metrics. If no route can be found in the background trees that satisfies the QoS requirements of a particular setup request, route selection reverts to on-demand route computation.

The background routes mode should be enabled in large networks where it usually exhibits less-stringent processing requirements and better scalability. Route computation is performed at almost every poll interval when a significant change in the topology of the network is reported and when significant threshold changes have occurred since the last route computation.

To configure the background route computation, you need to execute the following commands in sequence:

```
LS1010(config)# atm router pnni
LS1010(config-atm-router)# background-routes-enable
```

```
{insignificant-threshold value ¦ poll-interval seconds}
```

- Background is off by default.

- **poll-interval** is a value from 1 to 60 seconds.

- **insignificant-threshold** is a value from 1 to 100.

Example 13-10 demonstrates enabling the background routes and configuring the poll interval to be 30 seconds.

Example 13-10 *Enabling and Configuring Background Routes*

```
LS1010-1(config)# atm router pnni
LS1010(config-atm-router)# background-routes-enable poll-interval 30
```

Configuring Link Selection   The link selection feature allows you to configure the criteria for selecting a link out of multiple parallel links.

When multiple parallel links are configured inconsistently, the order of precedence of configured values is as follows:

1 admin-weight-minimize

2 blocking-minimize

3 transmit-speed-maximize

4 load-balance

For example, if one out of the two parallel links is configured as **admin-weight-minimize**, then it is used for the entire link group.

The link selection syntax is as follows:

```
LS1010(config)# interface atm card/subcard/port#
LS1010(config-if)# atm pnni link-selection {admin-weight-minimize ¦
   blocking-minimize ¦ load-balance ¦ transmit-speed-maximize}
```

Example 13-11 illustrates how to configure an ATM interface to use the **transmit-speed-maximize** link selection mode.

Example 13-11 *PNNI Link Selection*

```
LS1010(config)# interface atm 1/0/0
LS1010(config-if)# atm pnni link-selection transmit-speed-maximize
```

Configuring Precedence   The PNNI route selection algorithm chooses routes to particular destinations using the longest match reachable address prefixes known to the switch.

When multiple longest match reachable address prefixes known to the switch exist, the route selection algorithm first attempts to find routes to reachable addresses with the greatest precedence values. Next, among multiple longest match reachable address prefixes of the same precedence value, routes with the least total AW are chosen first.

The highest precedence number is numerically lowest in its value. Local internal reachable addresses, learned through ILMI or as static routes, receive the highest precedence, or a precedence value of 1. The precedence of other reachable address types is configurable.

The following are the configuration steps and the syntax required to configure the precedence values:

```
LS1010-1(config)# atm router pnni
LS1010(config-atm-router)# precedence [pnni-remote-exterior value_2-4 ¦
  pnni-remote-exterior-metrics value_2-4 ¦
pnni-remote-internal value_2-4 ¦ pnni-remote-internal-metrics value_2-4 ¦
  static-local-exterior value_2-4 ¦ static-local-exterior-metrics value_2-4 ¦
  static-local-internal-metrics value_2-4]
```

Table 13-13 explains the meaning of the precedence command options.

Table 13-13 *Precedence Command Options*

Option	Meaning
pnni-remote-exterior *value_2-4*	Sets the priority for the remote exterior prefixes without metrics. The default is 4.
pnni-remote-exterior-metrics *value_2-4*	Sets the priority for the remote exterior prefixes with metrics. The default is 2.
pnni-remote-internal *value_2-4*	Sets the priority for the remote internal prefixes without metrics. The default is 2.
pnni-remote-internal-metrics *value_2-4*	Sets the priority for the remote internal prefixes with metrics. The default is 2.
static-local-exterior *value_2-4*	Sets the priority for the static exterior prefixes without metrics. The default is 3.
static-local-exterior-metrics *value_2-4*	Sets the priority for the static prefixes with metrics. The default is 2.
static-local-internal-metrics *value_2-4*	Sets the priority for the static internal prefixes with metrics. The default is 2.

NOTE   *value_2-4* Specifies the precedence of a reachable address type. Smaller values take precedence over larger values. The possible values are 2, 3, and 4.

Configuring Administrative Weight   AW is the main routing metric that PNNI uses for minimizing the use of network resources. You can configure AW to indicate the relative desirability of using a link.

You can configure AW as the global AW for the node or at the interface level. The global AW changes the default AW assignment for all the interfaces on the node.

The syntax of the **administrative-weight** command at the node and interface levels is as follows:

```
!AW command at the node level
LS1010-1(config)# atm router pnni
LS1010(config-atm-router)# administrative-weight {linespeed ¦ uniform}
!
!AW command at the interface level
LS1010(config)# interface atm card/subcard/port#
LS1010(config-if)# atm pnni administrative-weight number traffic-class
```

- The *number* parameter for the **atm pnni administrative-weight** command ranges from 1 to 1,000,000.

- The *traffic-class* parameter for the **atm pnni administrative-weight** command could be CBR, VBR-RT, VBR-NRT, ABR, UBR, or ALL.

The **uniform** mode of **administrative-weight** is the default, and it assigns the AW value of 5040 to the interfaces. In **linespeed** mode, the LS1010 assigns the default AW based on the linespeed of individual lines—the higher the speed of the links, the smaller the AW value is. This assignment is based on the reference AW of 5040 for an OC-3 link.

Figure 13-7 and Example 13-12 provide good examples of PNNI AW.

The links between LS1010-1/LS1010-4 and LS1010-4/LS1010-5 are much faster than the slower OC-3 link between LS1010-1/LS1010-5. As you adjust the AW to be equal to the linespeed, PNNI prefers the faster links.

Example 13-12 *Administrative Weight Adjustment*

```
!Adjust LS1010-1
LS1010-1(config)# atm router pnni
LS1010-1(config-atm-router)# administrative-weight linespeed
!Adjust LS1010-4
LS1010-4(config)# atm router pnni
LS1010-4(config-atm-router)# administrative-weight linespeed
!Adjust LS1010-5
LS1010-5(config)# atm router pnni
LS1010-5(config-atm-router)# administrative-weight linespeed
```

Configuring Maximum Administrative Weight Percentage   The maximum AW percentage allows you to prevent the use of alternate routes that consume too many network resources. This feature provides a generalized form of hop count limit.

The maximum acceptable AW is equal to the specified percentage of the least AW of any route to the specific destination. It is derived from the background routing tables. For example, if the least AW to the destination is 5040 and the configured percentage is 200, then the maximum acceptable AW for the call is 5040 * 200 / 100 = 10,080.

Figure 13-7   *PNNI Administrative Weight*

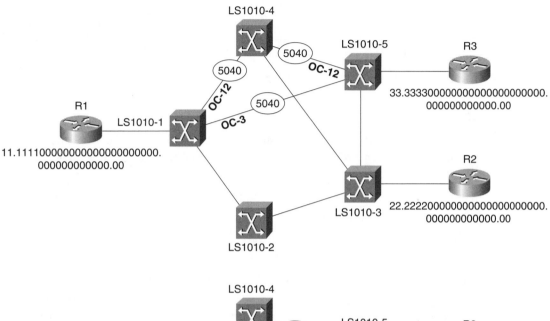

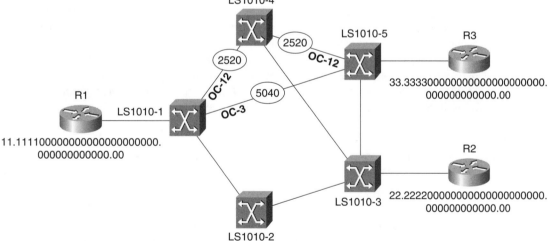

The command syntax to assign the maximum AW percentage is as follows:

```
LS1010(config)# atm router pnni
LS1010(config-atm-router)# max-admin-weight-percentage percentage
```

- The *percentage* value ranges from 100 to 2000.

- The **max-admin-weight-percentage** command takes effect only if background route computation is enabled.

Configuring Transit Restriction   Transit calls are calls originating from another ATM switch and passing through the switch. You might want to eliminate this transit traffic for the edge switches and allow only traffic originating or terminating at this switch to reduce the demand on switch resources, such as memory and processing power. Why loop around through the edge device?

To configure transit restrictions, you need to execute the following commands in sequence:

```
LS1010(config)# atm router pnni
LS1010(config-atm-router)# node node-index
LS1010(config-pnni-node)# transit restricted
```

Configuring Redistribution   Redistribution instructs PNNI to inject reachability information from non-PNNI sources into the PNNI routing domain. Static routes are redistributed into PNNI by default.

If you disabled the default, use the following command syntax to re-enable redistribution.

```
LS1010(config)# atm router pnni
LS1010(config-atm-router)# node node-index
LS1010(config-pnni-node)# redistribute atm-static
```

Configuring PNNI Aggregation   One of the tasks performed by LGN is link aggregation. First, let's define the terms *upnodes*, *uplinks*, and *aggregate links*.

An *uplink* is a link to a higher level node, called an *upnode*. "Higher" refers to a higher level in the hierarchy compared to the level of the peer group. The *aggregation token* controls the grouping of multiple physical links into logical links. Figure 13-8 shows four physical links between four nodes in the two lower-level peer groups, A.1 and A.2. Two physical links between two nodes in different peer groups are assigned the PNNI aggregation token value of 221; the other two are assigned the value of 100. These four links are summarized and represented as two links in the next higher PNNI level, A.

It is wise to deploy the following guidelines when configuring the PNNI aggregation token:

- Configure the interface on one side of the link. If the configured aggregation token value of one side is zero and the other side is nonzero, both sides use the nonzero value as the aggregation token value.

- If you choose to configure an aggregation token value on both interfaces, make sure the aggregation token values match. If the values do not match, the configuration is invalid and the default aggregation token value of zero is used.

- If the metrics for uplinks with the same aggregation token differ widely from each other, no single set of metrics can accurately represent them at the LGN level. Therefore, when you assign separate aggregation tokens to some of the uplinks, they are treated as separate higher-level horizontal links that more accurately represent their metrics.

Figure 13-8 *PNNI Aggregation Token*

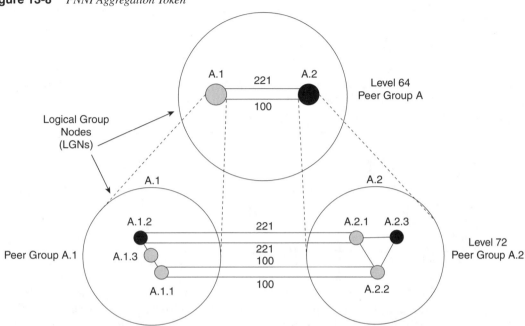

LS1010 has two algorithms to perform link aggregation that control how the metrics for the higher-level links are derived from the individual parallel links that have the same aggregation token:

- The *best link algorithm* selects a single optimal uplink, based on a selected parameter. The LS1010 uses the best link algorithm by default.

- The *aggressive algorithm*, on the other hand, examines each parameter and selects the most optimal value over all aggregate links. The algorithm is repeated for each parameter, resulting in a best case aggregate link, which might not be the case for the existing uplinks. It tends to overestimate the available resources.

In addition, you have the flexibility of controlling the grouping of multiple physical links into logical links through the aid of aggregation tokens. By default, aggregation token values are equal to zero, which means that all parallel links between peer groups are aggregated at higher levels. If the metrics of various parallel links differ by very large amounts, you can improve the routing accuracy by changing the value of the aggregation token for some links. This ensures a separate treatment by PNNI at the higher levels.

The syntax to configure the aggregation for a traffic class is as follows:

```
LS1010(config)# atm router pnni
LS1010(config-atm-router)# node node-index
LS1010(config-pnni-node)# aggregation-mode {link} traffic-class {best-link |
aggressive}
```

The command syntax to change the aggregation token is

```
LS1010(config)# interface atm card/subcard/port#
LS1010(config-if)# atm pnni aggregation-token value
```

NOTE   The aggregation token needs to be configured on only one side of the link. If you choose to configure an aggregation token value on both sides of the link, the values of the aggregation token must be the same. Otherwise, the configuration becomes invalid, and the token is reset to 0.

Configuring Significant Change Threshold   Link-state routing protocols are infamous for potentially flooding the networks when the networks are unstable. In the case of PNNI, the instability of the network topology not only triggers PTSEs, but it also changes in the network parameters because PNNI is based on QoS routing. PTSEs can overwhelm the network if they are transmitted each time a parameter in the network changes.

To avoid this problem, PNNI uses significant change thresholds that control the conditions of the origination of PTSEs. Changes in CDV, MaxCTD, or AvCR are measured in terms of a proportional difference from the last advertised value. A proportional multiplier threshold, expressed as a percentage, provides flexible control over the definition of significant change. The only exception to the rule is AW and CLR—any change in AW or CLR is considered significant and triggers the origination of a new PTSE.

Significant change variables include the following:

- **acr-mt**—Available cell rate maximum threshold percentage
- **acr-pm**—Available cell rate proportional multiplier
- **cdv-pm**—Cell delay variation proportional multiplier
- **ctd-pm**—Max CTD proportional multiplier

To configure the PTSE significant change threshold, execute the following commands in sequence:

```
LS1010(config)# atm router pnni
LS1010(config-atm-router)# node node-index
LS1010(config-pnni-node)# ptse significant-change {acr-mt percentage |
  acr-pm multiplier | cdv-pm multiplier | ctd-pm multiplier}
```

The configuration in Example 13-13 shows how to configure a PTSE being sent only if the available cell rate changes 30 percent from the current metric.

Example 13-13 *Significant Change Configuration*

```
LS1010-1(config)# atm router pnni
LS1010-1(config-atm-router)# node 1
LS1010(config-pnni-node)# ptse significant-change acr-pm 30
```

Configuring PNNI Parameters   You can fine-tune PNNI protocol parameters, such as Hello timers; database synchronization and flooding parameters; poll intervals; and the PTSE significant change percent number.

The resource management poll interval specifies the frequency with which PNNI polls resource management to update the values of link metrics. This parameter helps you to control the trade-off between the processing load and the accuracy of PNNI information. The larger the poll interval, the smaller is the number of PTSE updates. Conversely, the smaller the poll interval value, the greater is the accuracy in tracking resource information.

The command syntax for configuring PNNI parameters is as follows:

```
!Syntax for fine-tuning PNNI parameters
!
LS1010(config)# atm router pnni
LS1010(config-atm-router)# node node-index
LS1010(config-pnni-node)# timer [ack-delay tenth-of-seconds][hello-holddown
  tenth-of-seconds][hello-interval seconds][inactivity-factor number]
  [retransmit-interval seconds]
LS1010(config-pnni-node)# ptse [lifetime-factor percentage-factor]
  [min-ptse-interval tenth-of-seconds] [refresh-interval seconds]
  [request number] [significant-change acr-mt-percent]
  [significant-change acr-pm-percent] [significant-change cdv-pm-percent]
  [significant-change ctd-pm-percent]
!
! Syntax for Resource Management Poll Interval Command
!
LS1010(config)# atm router pnni
LS1010(config-atm-router)# resource-poll-interval seconds
```

LightStream 1010 Internetworking Support and Troubleshooting

LightStream 1010s support basic IP functionality, such as RFC 2225, LAN Emulation (LANE), and Simple Network Management Protocol (SNMP) management via an Ethernet port located in the ASP. You can configure IP functionality on the LS1010 as you would on any other IP client (remember, LS1010 is *not* a router). Also, LS1010s can support internetworking functions, such as LANE and Classical IP.

Internetworking Support

To ensure the proper use of IP ARP or proxy ARP and to direct LS1010 to use the default gateway for non-local network access, you need to execute the following commands:

```
LS1010(config)# ip host-routing
LS1010(config)# ip default-gateway ip-address
LS1010(config)# ip classless
```

The **ip classless** command forwards all non-locally known network and subnetwork addresses to the default gateway.

The LS1010 CPU port (2/0/0) can be configured as an RFC 2225 client, a LANE client, an LES-BUS, or an LECS. Example 13-14 demonstrates how to accomplish these configurations.

Example 13-14 *Configuring the LightStream 1010 CPU Port as an RFC 2225 Client, a LANE Client, an LES-BUS, or an LECS*

```
! RFC 2225 Client Configuration
!
LS1010(config)# interface atm 2/0/0.1
LS1010(config-subinf)# atm nsap-address
   47.0091.8100.0000.1111.1111.1111.1111.1111.1111.00
LS1010(config-subif)# ip address 10.0.0.2 255.0.0.0
LS1010(config-subif)# atm arp-server nsap
   47.0091.8100.0000.0000.1000.0000.0000.0c00.aaaa.00
!
! LANE Client, LES-BUS Configuration
LS1010(config)# interface atm 2/0/0.2
LS1010(config-subif)# ip address 10.100.10.1 255.255.255.0
LS1010(config-subif)# lane client ethernet mis
LS1010(config-subif)# lane server-bus ethernet mis
!
! LANE LECS Configuration
LS1010(config)# lane database mis_dbase
LS1010(lane-config-database)# name mis server-atm-address
47.00918100000000E04FACB401.00E04FACB403.00
LS1010(lane-config-database)# default-name mis
LS1010(config)# interface atm 2/0/0
LS1010(config-if)# lane config database mis_dbase
LS1010(config-if)# lane config auto-config-atm-address
```

WARNING   Although client and server functionalities for Classical IP and LANE are supported, I strongly recommend leaving the LS1010 to do what it is designed to do—switch cells. You do not want to have an ATM switch act as the edge device on your network.

LightStream 1010 Troubleshooting

The LS1010 provides excellent capabilities for checking network connectivity and reachability. The LS1010 supports the ATM **ping** command, which should not be confused with the ICMP **ping**. The ICMP **ping** uses IP packets, whereas the ATM **ping** uses OAM cells.

You can **ping** an ATM network prefix or IP address of another ATM switch ASP, or do a segment loopback to verify ATM connectivity on a specific LS1010 port. By default, the **ping** uses end-to-end OAM loopback cells.

Figures 13-9, 13-10, 13-11, and 13-12 illustrate variations of ATM pings, all of which LS1010s support.

Figure 13-9 *LightStream 1010 ping: Segment Loopback*

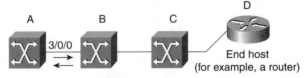

ping atm int atm 3/0/0 100 200 seg-loopback

Figure 13-10 *LightStream 1010 ping: End-to-End Loopback*

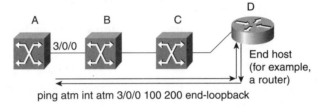

ping atm int atm 3/0/0 100 200 end-loopback

Figure 13-11 *LightStream 1010 ping: IP Address*

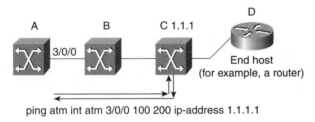

ping atm int atm 3/0/0 100 200 ip-address 1.1.1.1

Figure 13-12 *LightStream 1010 ping: NSAP Prefix*

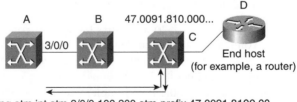

ping atm int atm 3/0/0 100 200 atm-prefix 47.0091.8100.00...

Not only does the LS1010 allow you to check the network topology it also allows you attach an ATM sniffer to the highest system port (located on card 4, subcard 1) and monitor any LS1010 port (except the CPU port). This monitoring also is called *snooping*.

The snoop test port configuration can be changed only while the port is shutdown. The snoop test port shows as interface status = SNOOPING while it is actively in the snoop mode. While the interface status = SNOOPING, any prior connections on the snoop test port remain in place but are in the down state.

The snoop test port requires a port adapter module with a bandwidth large enough to monitor the full bandwidth of the monitored port.

To enable the interface for port snooping, execute the following commands in sequence:

```
LS1010(config)# interface atm card/subcard/port
LS1010(config-if)# shutdown
LS1010(config-if)# atm snoop interface atm card/subcard/port direction dir
LS1010(config-if)# no shutdown
```

- Reference to the *card/subcard/port* in the **atm snoop** command refers to the port that will be monitored.

- The *dir* argument signifies either receive or transmit.

To disable snooping, you need to shut down the interface, execute the **no atm snoop** command, and then re-enable the interface.

The LS1010 is absolutely rich with **show** and **debug** commands to enhance your troubleshooting. You can find the complete set of these commands on CCO at the following URLs:

www.cisco.com/univercd/cc/td/doc/product/atm/c8540/wa5/12_0/3a_11/cmdref/show.htm

www.cisco.com/univercd/cc/td/doc/product/atm/c8540/wa5/12_0/12_3/cm_ref/ch5_d.htm

Summary

This chapter reviews the methods and the mechanics of the ATM network implementation of the cloud itself using LightStream 1010 switches.

The main focus of the chapter is to demystify the creation of PVC, PVP, Soft VC, and SVC networks. You learn that the maximum network flexibility is achieved with SVC-based networks. SVCs networks, requiring signaling, do need the signaling routing protocol. The chapter examines the implementation of the two that are available: IISP and PNNI. The chapter focuses on the PNNI implementation, the most scalable and flexible protocol of the two, elaborating on flat and hierarchical topologies.

Lab 13-1: PVC Segment Setup on the LS1010

Objectives: At the end of this lab, you can complete the following:

- Map PVC addressing through the switches
- Configure PVC segments on the LS1010
- Verify connectivity

Purpose: This lab sets up the PVC environment. Only the segments on the LS1010s need to be added because in Lab 9-1 you created the segments out to the routers. You are required to fill in the chart showing all the segments necessary for a fully meshed ATM PVC environment. You also need to set up the seven stated segments on the switches.

The addressing *must* match what you entered on the routers in Lab 9-1. Therefore, you need to have this chart available for the VPI/VCI addressing. This ensures connectivity.

Table 13-14 lists and describes the commands you need to be familiar with to complete this lab.

Table 13-14   *Lab 13-1 Command Summary*

Command	Description
ip address 255.0.0.0	Defines an IP address for the interface.
media 10baset	Defines the media type.
atm pvc int atm	Defines the port/addressing assignments.
show ip route	Displays which devices can be reached.
show atm vc	Displays all VCs and their statuses.

Parameters for Lab 13-1

Use Table 9-13 in Chapter 9, "Multiprotocol Encapsulation (RFC 2684), Classical IP and ARP over ATM (RFC 2225), and NHRP Implementation," for the VPI/VCI assignment for the PVCs. The numbering convention for the terminating VPI/VCI is quite simple:

VPI = 0, VCI = 1 <from R#> <to R#>.

For the illustration of the PVCs within an LS1010, see Figure 13-13.

Figure 13-13 *PVC Setup on the LightStream 1010*

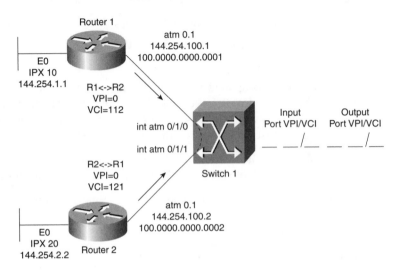

For the illustration of the PVCs between LS1010s, see Figure 13-14.

Figure 13-14 *Setup Between the LightStream 1010*

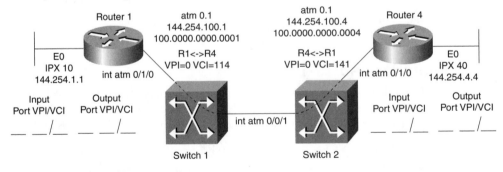

For the PVCs that contain PVC segments that must go through both switches, the following guideline must be used:

The VPI/VCI value used between the switches must be the VPI/VCI values of the UNI segment of the lower number switch.

Figure 13-15 illustrates the overall network topology.

Figure 13-15 *PVC Setup on the LightStream 1010*

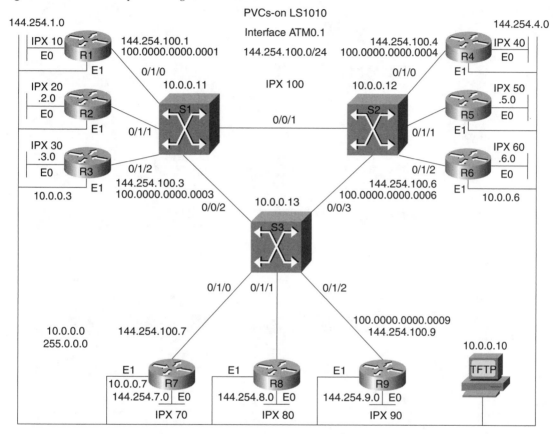

Table 13-15 through Table 13-20 provide the PVC mapping you need to be familiar with to complete this lab. It is highly recommended that you fill out these tables before proceeding to the configurations. These tables serve as your guide to proper PVC configuration. The first row in each table illustrates the examples of what you need to fill out. The tables should read: "PVC from R1 to R2 is configured on Switch 1 as follows: port 0/1/0 using VPI/VCI = 0/112 to port 0/1/1 using VPI/VCI = 0/121."

Table 13-15 *Lab 13-1 PVC Mapping Charts: Switch 1 Local PVC Mapping*

From Router #	In Port	In VPI	In VCI	Out Port	Out VPI	Out VCI	To Router #
R1	0/1/0	0	112	0/1/1	0	121	R2
R2							R3
R3							R1

Table 13-16 *Lab 13-1 PVC Mapping Charts: Switch 2 Local PVC Mapping*

From Router #	In Port	In VPI	In VCI	Out Port	Out VPI	Out VCI	To Router #
R4	0/1/0	0	145	0/1/1	0	154	R5
R5							R6
R6							R4

Table 13-17 *Lab 13-1 PVC Mapping Charts: Switch 3 Local PVC Mapping*

From Router #	In Port	In VPI	In VCI	Out Port	Out VPI	Out VCI	To Router #
R7	0/1/0	0	178	0/1/1	0	187	R8
R8							R9
R9							R7

Table 13-18 *Lab 13-1 PVC Mapping Charts: Interswitch Mapping from Switch 1's Perspective*

Switch 1								Switch 2 or Switch 3						
From Router	In Port	In VPI	In VCI	Out Port	Out VPI	Out VCI	NNI	In Port	In VPI	In VCI	Out Port	Out VPI	Out VCI	To Router
R1	0/1/0	0	114	0/0/1	0	114	0/0/1	0/0/1	0	114	0/1/0	0	141	R4
R1														R5
R1														R6
R1														R7
R1														R8
R1														R9

Table 13-18   *Lab 13-1 PVC Mapping Charts: Interswitch Mapping from Switch 1's Perspective (Continued)*

Switch 1								Switch 2 or Switch 3						
From	In	In	In	Out	Out	Out		In	In	In	Out	Out	Out	To
Router	Port	VPI	VCI	Port	VPI	VCI	NNI	Port	VPI	VCI	Port	VPI	VCI	Router
R2														R4
R2														R5
R2														R6
R2														R7
R2														R8
R2														R9
R3														R4
R3														R5
R3														R6
R3														R7
R3														R8
R3														R9

Table 13-19   *Lab 13-1 PVC Mapping Charts: Interswitch Mapping from Switch 2's Perspective*

Switch 2								Switch 1 or Switch 3						
From	In	In	In	Out	Out	Out		In	In	In	Out	Out	Out	To
Router	Port	VPI	VCI	Port	VPI	VCI	NNI	Port	VPI	VCI	Port	VPI	VCI	Router
R4	0/1/0	0	141	0/0/1	0	114	0/0/1	0/0/1	0	114	0/1/0	0	114	R1
R4														R2
R4														R3
R4														R7
R4														R8
R4														R9
R5														R1
R5														R2
R5														R3
R5														R7
R5														R8
R5														R9

Table 13-19 *Lab 13-1 PVC Mapping Charts: Interswitch Mapping from Switch 2's Perspective*

Switch 2								Switch 1 or Switch 3						
From Router	In Port	In VPI	In VCI	Out Port	Out VPI	Out VCI	NNI	In Port	In VPI	In VCI	Out Port	Out VPI	Out VCI	To Router
R6														R1
R6														R2
R6														R3
R6														R7
R6														R8
R6														R9

Table 13-20 *Lab 13-1 PVC Mapping Charts: Interswitch Mapping from Switch 3's Perspective*

Switch 3								Switch 1 or Switch 2						
From Router	In Port	In VPI	In VCI	Out Port	Out VPI	Out VCI	NNI	In Port	In VPI	In VCI	Out Port	Out VPI	Out VCI	To Router
R7	0/1/0	0	171	0/0/2	0	117	0/0/2	0/0/2	0	117	0/1/0	0	117	R1
R7														R2
R7														R3
R7														R4
R7														R5
R7														R6
R8														R1
R8														R2
R8														R3
R8														R4
R8														R5
R8														R6
R9														R1
R9														R2
R9														R3
R9														R4
R9														R5
R9														R6

Exercises

NOTE	If you want to test any PVC connectivity prior to filling out all the tables and configuring all the PVCs, you can do that by just configuring one PVC (for example, from R1 to R4) using VPI/VCI numbers as illustrated in Table 13-18.

1 Complete the charts in Table 13-15 through Table 13-20.

2 Set up the E1 interface on all routers, as shown in Figure 13-15.

3 Add all the PVC segments in all LS1010s.

4 Check for full connectivity between your router and every other router attached to the IP 144.254.100.X cloud.

Please save your work!

Lab 13-2: Configuring SVCs Using IISP

Objectives: At the end of this lab, you can complete the following:

- Map the AESA destinations to the exit port for that destination
- Verify connectivity of the SVC cloud

Purpose: This lab sets up connectivity for SVCs. You can enable static routes for the SVC when using IISP. These static routes map the destination addresses of the routers to the exit port on the switches. Set up the static routes so that the 144.254.200.x cloud again has full connectivity. Also, you need to check for full connectivity.

Table 13-21 lists and describes the commands you need to be familiar with to complete this lab.

Table 13-21 *Lab 13-2 Command Summary*

Command	Description
atm route atm	Defines the exit port for the IISP.
show atm route	Displays the PNNI prefix (route) information.
atm ping	Pings from various points along the path of the connection.

Figure 13-16 shows the ATM network topology, illustrating the IISP as the signaling routing protocol and the globally significant NSAP addresses assigned to all the routers.

Figure 13-16 *SVC ATM Network, Using IISP*

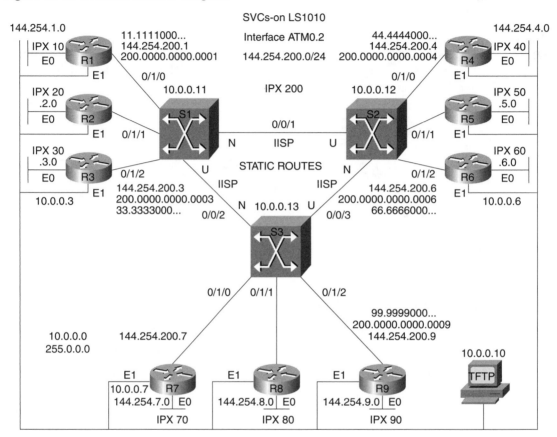

Exercises

Refer to Figure 13-16 to complete the following exercises for Lab 13-2.

1 Configure the two ATM route statements into the switch as designated in the following list:

- On Switch 1:
    — Routes for Routers 1, 4, and 7
    — Routes for Routers 2, 5, and 8
    — Routes for Routers 3, 6, and 9

- On Switch 2:
    — Routes for Routers 1, 4, and 7

— Routes for Routers 2, 5, and 8

— Routes for Routers 3, 6, and 9

- On Switch 3:

   — Routes for Routers 1, 4, and 7

   — Routes for Routers 2, 5, and 8

   — Routes for Routers 3, 6, and 9

For example, the configuration command on Switch 1 of a route to R1 is:

```
atm route 1... atm 0/1/0
```

2   Check for full connectivity between your router and every other router attached to the IP 144.254.200.x cloud.

3   Try the various **atm ping** commands to show connectivity at the switch level.

Remember to save your configuration!

Lab 13-3: Configuring Virtual Path Tunnels (VPTs) Through ATM Networks Using LS1010

Objectives: At the end of the lab, you can complete the following:

- Configure VPTs on an LS1010
- Configure VPTs for IISP support
- Allow VPTs to support router SVCs

Purpose: This lab allows you to simulate a larger ATM backbone environment where VPTs can be used to provide end-to-end SVC connectivity between ATM-equipped router sites. The VPTs implemented in the ATM cloud are used to offer SVC support by supporting IISP across the tunnels. You could use PNNI across the tunnels, if you want to do so. This lab assumes the successful completion on the SVC router lab, where routers made use of subinterface ATM 0.2. If you run into problems completing the SVC Lab 13-2, you can use the configuration samples provided in the solutions in Appendix C, "Lab Solutions."

Table 13-22 lists and describes the commands you need to be familiar with to complete this lab.

Table 13-22 *Lab 13-3 Command Summary*

Command	Description
atm route 1... atm0/1/0	Sets up the IISP static route
atm pvp 17	Creates the ATM PVP
interface atm0/0/2.17 point-to-point	Sets up the PVP subinterface

continues

Table 13-22 *Lab 13-3 Command Summary (Continued)*

Command	Description
show atm interface atm0/0/2.17	Displays useful ATM-related interface information
atm pvp 47 interface atm0/0/1 47	Creates a translation table entry for VP mapping
show atm route	Displays PNNI (routing table) prefix information
show atm vp	Displays existing VP tunnel information
sho atm vp conn-type pvp ...	Displays particular VP connection types
show atm vc conn-type svc ...	Displays particular VC information

Figures 13-17, 13-18, and 13-19 show the details of tunnels that need to be configured using Table 13-23 tunnel assignments.

Figure 13-17 *ATM Tunneling from S1 to S2*

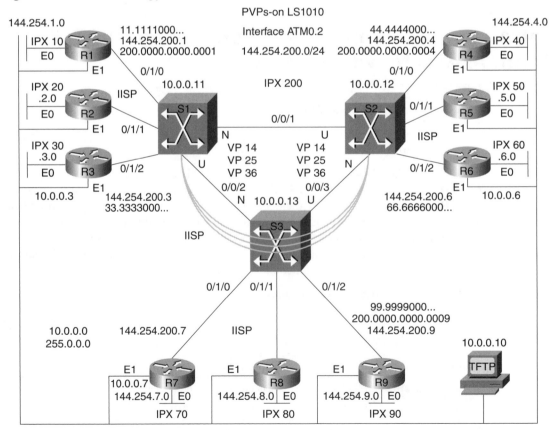

Figure 13-18 *ATM Tunneling from S1 to S3*

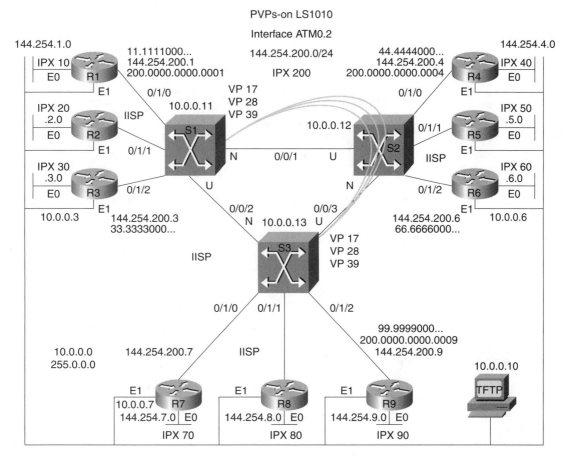

Exercises

Refer to Figures 13-17, 13-18, and 13-19 to complete the following exercises for Lab 13-3.

1 Configure the primary ATM interswitch links as IISP links and ensure that the secondary inter-switch links are shutdown. The routers are making use of their SVC-based solution with their ATM0.2 subinterface and appropriate AESA address—the ATM 0.1 subinterface is shutdown.

2 Ensure that switch S1 has only the appropriate static routes to reach the AESA address prefixes 1..., 2..., 3.... Remove any additional static routes, and verify with the **show atm route** command.

Figure 13-19 *ATM Tunneling from S2 to S3*

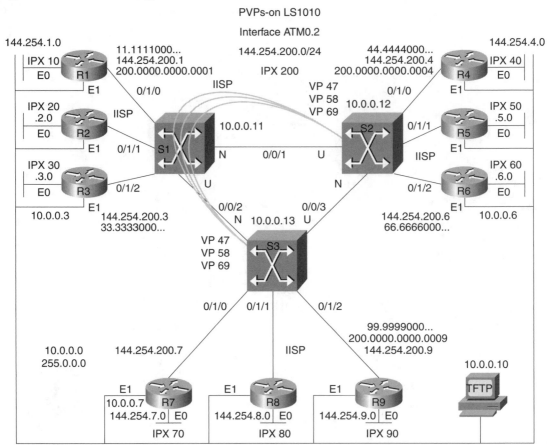

3 Similarly, ensure that switch S2 has only the appropriate static routes to reach AESA address prefixes 4..., 5..., 6.... Remove any additional static routes, and verify with the **show atm route** command.

4 Similarly, ensure that switch S3 has only the appropriate static routes to reach AESA address prefixes 4..., 5..., 6.... Remove any additional static routes, and verify with the **show atm route** command.

5 Verify that routers locally attached to the same switch can successfully set up SVCs between themselves and can provide Layer 3 connectivity. Currently, connectivity cannot be established between remote routers. Verify with the appropriate **show** commands.

6 Set up VPTs 14, 47, and 17 to allow connectivity between R1, R4, and R7.

7 Set up VPTs 25, 58, and 28 to allow connectivity between R2, R5, and R8.

8 Set up VPTs 36, 69, and 39 to allow connectivity between R3, R6, and R9.

9 Set up IISP through the tunnels. Make sure the IISP sides are "user" to "network," or visa versa.

10 Verify that the ATM switches are discovering additional required AESA address via IISP through the tunnels. Also, verify that SVCs between remote routers (routers not connected to the same ATM switch) are being supported via the VPTs. Verify that from the router's perspective, you now have full Layer 3 connectivity.

Please do not save the configurations!

Use Table 13-23 to identify the administrator's configuration tasks.

Table 13-23 *Tunnels Configuration Tasks*

VPT	Router Connectivity	ATM Switch Interfaces Involved	PVP Mapping On
VP=14	R1 to R4	S1 0/0/2–S2 0/0/3	S3
VP=25	R2 to R5	S1 0/0/2–S2 0/0/3	S3
VP=36	R3 to R6	S1 0/0/2–S2 0/0/3	S3
VP=47	R4 to R7	S2 0/0/1–S3 0/0/2	S1
VP=58	R5 to R8	S2 0/0/1–S3 0/0/2	S1
VP=69	R6 to R9	S2 0/0/1–S3 0/0/2	S1
VP=17	R1 to R7	S1 0/0/1–S3 0/0/3	S2
VP=28	R2 to R8	S1 0/0/1–S3 0/0/3	S2
VP=39	R3 to R9	S1 0/0/1–S3 0/0/3	S2

Lab 13-4: Private Network-to-Network Interface (PNNI)

Objectives: At the end of the lab, you can complete the following:

* Configure ILMI
* Configure QSAAL
* Configure the End Station Identifier (ESI)

Purpose: IISP might not be suitable for larger ATM environments, so you can use PNNI as your routing protocol. PNNI code from Cisco encompasses IISP as a "static route."

The switch no longer needs *any* configuration for routing to work in a one peer-group environment. When you want to go to two peer-groups, configuration is required.

Table 13-24 lists and describes the commands you need to be familiar with to complete this lab.

Table 13-24   *Lab 13-4 Command Summary*

Command	Description
atm esi-address	Configures the 7-byte ESI.
show lane default	Displays the NSAP address for LANE components.
atm pvc	Sets up ILMI and QSAAL as well as PVCs.
show atm route	Displays the ATM (PNNI) routing table.

Figure 13-20 shows the network topology required for this lab. Notice that the interface types between the switches is now PNNI.

Figure 13-20   *PNNI Configuration*

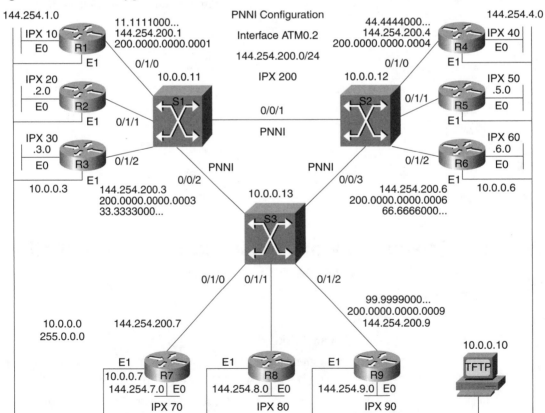

Exercises

Refer to Figure 13-20 to complete the following exercises for Lab 13-4.

1 Configure a signaling PVC on your router.

2 Configure ILMI on your router.

3 Create a subinterface ATM 0.32 on your router. Assign an IP address of 144.254.32.#, where # is your router number. For Router 8, for example, the address is 144.254.32.8.

4 On the ATM0.32 subinterface (on the router), configure your 7-byte ESI. The ESI is <RRRRRRRRRRRR.20>. For Router 8, for example, the ESI is 888888888888.20.

5 Configure every switch with a new ATM address, which consists of the following prefixes:

Switch 1: 11.1111.1111.1111.1111.1111.1111

Switch 2: 22.2222.2222.2222.2222.2222.2222

Switch 3: 33.3333.3333.3333.3333.3333.3333

To complete the ATM addresses, copy the ESIs from the existing ATM addresses in the switches. The routers do not use these because each router has its own pre-configured ESI (as per Exercise 4).

6 Ensure that the prefix of your switch has been downloaded via **show atm ilmi**.

7 To test the connectivity, implement RFC 2684 between the routers. The implementation steps of RFC 2684 are described in Lab 9-3, "Configuring SVCs on Cisco 4500 Routers, RFC 2684." Remember, static mappings must be done between the NSAP addresses and the IP addresses of the edge devices (in this case, routers).

8 Log into your respective switch and show the routing table via **show atm route**. Ensure that your port in the switch has a routing entry.

Please save the configurations!

Lab 13-5: Configuring Soft PVC ATM Networks

Objectives: At the end of the lab, you can complete the following:

- Modify the LS1010 forwarding table entries to eliminate existing PVC mappings
- Verify that router connectivity is no longer supported end-to-end at Layer 3
- Configure Soft PVCs on LS1010 to re-establish end-to-end VC connectivity
- Verify end-to-end router Layer 3 connectivity based on Soft PVC implementation

Purpose: This lab is intended to clearly demonstrate the benefits of implementing Soft PVCs in the ATM backbone. In providing PVC support to the ATM-equipped routers, Soft PVCs can be deployed on the ATM switches to provide key benefits:

- Requiring less configuration work
- Reducing the probability of introducing configuration errors
- Providing automatic rerouting capability without human intervention when hardware failures occur.

This lab also simulates the implementation tasks to be followed when migrating from a complete end-to-end (across ATM cloud) PVC solution to one based on Soft PVCs.

Table 13-25 lists and describes the commands you need to be familiar with to complete this lab.

Table 13-25 *Lab 13-5 Command Summary*

Command	Description
no atm pvc	Eliminates the PVC mapping entry in the forwarding table.
show atm vc conn-type soft-vc	Displays the status of the Soft PVC on the ATM switch.
show atm address	Displays the ATM switch Soft VC addresses.
show atm interface atm	Displays the useful ATM configuration information.
atm soft-vc dest-add ...	Sets up the Soft PVC on the ATM switch.

Figure 13-21 shows the network topology of the Soft PVC setup.

Exercises

Refer to Figure 13-21 to complete the following exercises for Lab 13-5.

1 Restore router configurations to the PVC lab solution using ATM 0.1 subinterface. Ensure that subinterface ATM 0.2 is shutdown. Restore the ATM switch configurations, if required, to ensure that the PVC mapping support is still provided. Verify from the routers' viewpoint that full Layer 3 connectivity is present for IP and IPX.

2 Ensure that the ATM interswitch links are currently configured for PNNI.

Figure 13-21 *Soft PVC Configurations*

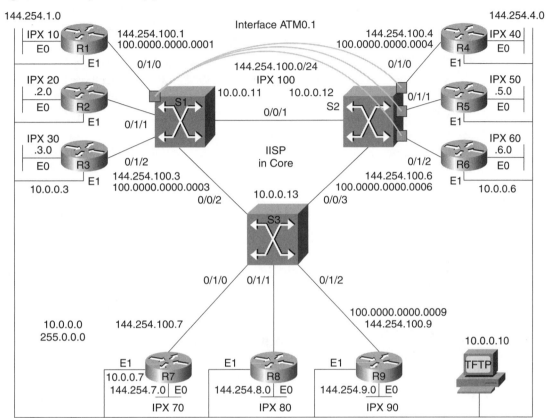

3 On ATM switch S1, eliminate the PVC mappings that support connectivity between R1 and R4, R1 and R5, and R1 and R6 only—three PVC mappings need to be eliminated on S1. Verify from the routers' Layer 3 perspective that connectivity is no longer working between these routers.

4 Introduce a Soft PVC on the S1 switch to re-establish connectivity between R1 and R4. First, on S2, you need to identify the appropriate Soft VC address that pertains to R4's ATM switch port.

S2 Soft VC address:_____

Make use of this Soft VC address to set up a Soft PVC on S1 with the following command:

```
atm soft-vc vpi vci dest-address soft-vc nsap address vpi vci
```

Make use of the **show atm vc conn-type soft-vc** command to verify the status of the VC. Make the necessary changes on S2 to eliminate the local PVC mapping that supports the R1 to R4 connectivity. Make the necessary configuration changes on S1's ATM interface 0/1/0 to ensure that the Soft VC works properly. Use the **show atm vc conn-type soft-vc** switch command.

5 Verify from the perspective of S1 and S2 that the Soft PVC is operational. From R1's and R4's Layer 3 perspective, verify that the IP connectivity is re-established and the IGRP routing strategy is working as expected.

6 Introduce a Soft PVC on the S1 switch to re-establish connectivity between R1 and R5. First, on S2, you need to identify the appropriate Soft VC address that pertains to R5's ATM switch port.

S2 Soft VC address:_____

Make use of this Soft VC address to set up a Soft PVC on S1 with the following command:

```
atm soft-vc vpi vci dest-address soft-vc nsap address vpi vci
```

Make the necessary changes on S1 to eliminate the local PVC mapping that supports the R1 to R5 connectivity. Make use of the **show atm vc conn-type soft-vc** command to verify the status of VC. Make any necessary configuration changes on S1's ATM interface 0/1/0 to ensure the Soft VC works properly.

7 Verify from S1's and S2's perspective that the two Soft PVCs are operational now. From R1's and R5's Layer 3 perspective, verify that IP connectivity is re-established and that the IGRP routing strategy is working as expected.

8 Introduce a Soft PVC on the S1 switch to re-establish connectivity between R1 and R6. First, on S2, you need to identify the appropriate Soft VC address that pertains to R6's ATM switch port.

S2 Soft VC address:_____

Make use of this Soft VC address to set up the Soft PVC on S1 with the following command:

```
atm soft-vc vpi vci dest-address soft-vc nsap address vpi vci
```

Make use of the **show atm vc conn-type soft-vc** command to verify the status of the Soft VC. Make the necessary changes on S2 to eliminate the local PVC mapping that supports the R1 to R6 connectivity. Make the necessary configuration changes on S1's ATM interface 0/1/0 to ensure that the Soft VC works properly. Use the **show atm vc conn-type soft-vc** switch command.

9 Verify from S1's and S2's perspective that the two Soft PVCs are operational now. From R1's and R6's Layer 3 perspective, verify that IP connectivity is re-established and that the IGRP routing strategy is working as expected.

10 Verify from S1's and S2's perspective that the three Soft PVCs are now operational and that full IP connectivity has been re-established between the routers. Verify that all is okay from IGRP's viewpoint.

11 Verify that the three Soft PVCs introduced are using interswitch link(s) between S1 and S2. Disable the physical connectivity between S1 and S2 to verify that the Soft PVC can reroute automatically around the failure and can set up again via the ATM switch S3.

12 Notice the impact to the Soft PVCs when physical connectivity is re-established between S1 and S2.

Review Questions

1 What type of UNIs does the LightStream 1010 support?

2 What are the VPI/VCI space management rules?

3 What are the restrictions of the CPU port?

4 What types of VCs does the LS1010 support?

5 What must you do prior to using the **rx-cttr** or **tx-cttr** options in the **pvc** command?

6 Can you configure virtual paths within a VP tunnel? Within virtual channels?

7 Can you delete all logical ports on the LS1010?

8 When configuring a Soft VC, how many switches have to be involved in the configuration?

9 What configuration steps are required to configure PNNI without hierarchy?

10 What is the meaning of PNNI address scope?

11 What are the rules on PGL election?

12 In what cases does it make sense to deploy the background routes mode?

13 What role does precedence play in the PNNI algorithm?

14 Why is configuring the significant change threshold an important feature to have for PNNI?

"Science and technology multiply around us. To an increasing extent they dictate the languages in which we speak and think. Either we use those languages, or we remain mute."—J.G. Ballard (1930–)

"It takes little talent to see clearly what lies under one's nose, a good deal of it to know in which direction to point that organ."—W. H. Auden (1907–1973)

"You'll come to learn a great deal if you study the Insignificant in depth."—Odysseus Elytis (1911–1996)

Appendixes and Glossary

This part provides up-to-date documentation on the latest approved ATM Forum specifications as well as those specifications that are still works in progress. In addition, Appendix C provides the configuration solutions to the exhaustive labs presented in Chapters 9, 10, 11, and 13. Appendix D provides the answers to the questions that are designed to test your accumulated knowledge at the end of every chapter. Finally, ATM technology brings a sometimes overwhelming wealth of acronyms, terms, and concepts that is easy to lose track of. The Glossary can help you keep tabs on your newly found or enriched ATM vocabulary. This final part of the book consists of the following elements:

Appendix A   Approved ATM Forum Specifications

Appendix B   Pending Approval ATM Forum Specifications

Appendix C   Lab Solutions

Appendix D   Answers to Review Questions

Glossary

Approved ATM Forum Specifications

Table A-1 lists all specifications completed and approved by The ATM Forum since its inception in 1991.

Table A-1 *Approved ATM Forum Specifications*

Technical Working Group	Approved Specifications	Specification	Approved Date
Control Signaling	PNNI Addendum on PNNI/B-QSIG Interworking and Generic Functional Protocol for the Support of Supplementary Services	af-cs-0102.000	Oct, 1998
	Addressing Addendum for UNI Signaling 4.0	af-cs-0107.000	Feb, 1999
	PNNI Transported Address Stack, Version 1.0	af-cs-0115.000	May, 1999
	PNNI Version 1.0 Security Signaling Addendum	af-cs-0116.000	May, 1999
	UNI Signaling 4.0 Security Addendum	af-cs-0117.000	May, 1999
	ATM Inter-Network Interface (AINI) Specification	af-cs-0125.000	July, 1999
	PNNI Addendum for Generic Application Transport Version 1.0	af-cs-0126.000	July, 1999
	PNNI SPVC Addendum Version 1.0	af-cs-0127.000	July, 1999
	PHY/MAC Identifier Addendum to UNI Signaling 4.0	af-cs-0135.000	Nov, 1999

continues

Table A-1 *Approved ATM Forum Specifications (Continued)*

Technical Working Group	Approved Specifications	Specification	Approved Date
	Network Call Correlation Identifier v1.0	af-cs-0140.000	Mar, 2000
	PNNI Addendum for Path and Connection Trace, Version 1.0	af-cs-0141.000	Mar, 2000
Data Exchange Interface	Data Exchange Interface Version 1.0	af-dxi-0014.000	Aug, 1993
Frame-based ATM	Frame-based ATM Transport over Ethernet (FATE)	af-fbatm-0139.000	Mar, 2000
ILMI (Integrated Local Management Interface)	ILMI 4.0	af-ilmi-0065.000	Sep, 1996
LAN Emulation/ MPOA	LAN Emulation over ATM 1.0	af-lane-0021.000	Jan, 1995
	LAN Emulation Client Management Specification	af-lane-0038.000	Sep, 1995
	LANE 1.0 Addendum	af-lane-0050.000	Dec, 1995
	LANE Servers Management Specification v1.0	af-lane-0057.000	Mar, 1996
	LANE v2.0 LUNI Interface	af-lane-0084.000	July, 1997
	LAN Emulation Client Management Specification Version 2.0	af-lane-0093.000	Oct, 1998
	LAN Emulation over ATM Version 2—LNNI Specification	af-lane-0112.000	Feb. 1999
	Multiprotocol Over ATM Specification v1.0	af-mpoa-0087.000	July, 1997
	Multiprotocol Over ATM Version 1.0 MIB	af-mpoa-0092.000	July, 1998
	Multiprotocol Over ATM Specification, Version 1.1	af-mpoa-0114.000	May, 1999
	MPOA v1.1 Addendum on VPN Support	af-mpoa-0129.000	Oct, 1999
Network Management	Customer Network Management (CNM) for ATM Public Network Service	af-nm-0019.000	Oct, 1994
	M4 Interface Requirements and Logical MIB	af-nm-0020.000	Oct, 1994

Table A-1 *Approved ATM Forum Specifications (Continued)*

Technical Working Group	Approved Specifications	Specification	Approved Date
	M4 Interface Requirements and Logical MIB: ATM Network Element View	af-nm-0020.001	Oct, 1998
	CMIP Specification for the M4 Interface	af-nm-0027.00	Sep, 1995
	CMIP Specification for the M4 Interface: ATM Network Element View, Version 2	af-nm-0027.001	July, 1999
	M4 Public Network view	af-nm-0058.000	Mar, 1996
	M4 Interface Requirements and Logical MIB: ATM Network View, Version 2	af-nm-0058.001	May, 1999
	M4 "NE View"	af-nm-0071.000	Jan, 1997
	Circuit Emulation Service Interworking Requirements, Logical and CMIP MIB	af-nm-0072.000	Jan, 1997
	M4 Network View CMIP MIB Specification v1.0	af-nm-0073.000	Jan, 1997
	M4 Network View Requirements and Logical MIB Addendum	af-nm-0074.000	Jan, 1997
	ATM Remote Monitoring SNMP MIB	af-nm-test-0080.000	July, 1997
	SNMP M4 Network Element View MIB	af-nm-0095.001	July, 1998
	Network Management M4 Security Requirements and Logical MIB	af-nm-0103.000	Jan, 1999
	Auto-configuration of PVCs	af-nm-0122.000	May, 1999
Physical Layer	Issued as part of UNI 3.1:	af-uni-0010.002	
	44.736 DS3 Mbps Physical Layer		
	100 Mbps Multimode Fiber Interface Physical Layer		
	155.52 Mbps SONET STS-3c Physical Layer		
	155.52 Mbps Physical Layer		

continues

Table A-1   *Approved ATM Forum Specifications (Continued)*

Technical Working Group	Approved Specifications	Specification	Approved Date
	ATM Physical Medium Dependent Interface Specification for 155 Mbps over Twisted Pair Cable	af-phy-0015.000	Sep, 1994
	DS1 Physical Layer Specification	af-phy-0016.000	Sep, 1994
	Utopia	af-phy-0017.000	Mar, 1994
	Mid-range Physical Layer Specification for Category 3 UTP	af-phy-0018.000	Sep, 1994
	6,312 kbps UNI Specification	af-phy-0029.000	June, 1995
	E3 UNI	af-phy-0034.000	Aug, 1995
	Utopia Level 2	af-phy-0039.000	June, 1995
	Physical Interface Specification for 25.6 Mbps over Twisted Pair	af-phy-0040.000	Nov, 1995
	A Cell-based Transmission Convergence Sublayer for Clear Channel Interfaces	af-phy-0043.000	Jan, 1996
	622.08 Mbps Physical Layer	af-phy-0046.000	Jan, 1996
	155.52 Mbps Physical Layer Specification for Category 3 UTP (See also UNI 3.1, af-uni-0010.002)	af-phy-0047.000	Nov, 1995
	120 Ohm Addendum to ATM PMD Interface Specification for 155 Mbps over TP	af-phy-0053.000	Jan, 1996
	DS3 Physical Layer Interface Spec	af-phy-0054.000	Mar, 1996
	155 Mbps over MMF Short Wave Length Lasers, Addendum to UNI 3.1	af-phy-0062.000	July, 1996
	WIRE (PMD to TC layers)	af-phy-0063.000	July, 1996
	E-1 Physical Layer Interface Specification	af-phy-0064.000	Sep, 1996
	155 Mbps over Plastic Optical Fiber (POF) Version 1.0	af-phy-0079.000	May, 1997
	155 Mbps Plastic Optical Fiber and Hard Polymer Clad Fiber PMD Specification Version 1.1	af-phy-0079.001	Jan, 1999
	Inverse ATM Mux Version 1.0	af-phy-0086.000	July, 1997

Table A-1   *Approved ATM Forum Specifications (Continued)*

Technical Working Group	Approved Specifications	Specification	Approved Date
	Inverse Multiplexing for ATM (IMA) Specification Version 1.1	af-phy-0086.001	Mar, 1999
	Physical Layer High-Density Glass Optical Fiber Annex	af-phy-0110.000	Feb, 1999
	622 and 2488 Mbps Cell-Based Physical Layer	af-phy-0128.000	July, 1999
	ATM on Fractional E1/T1	af-phy-0130.000	Oct, 1999
	2.4 Gbps Physical Layer Specification	af-phy-0133.000	Oct, 1999
	Physical Layer Control	af-phy-0134.000	Oct, 1999
	Utopia 3 Physical Layer Interface	af-phy-0136.000	Nov, 1999
	Specification of the Device Control Protocol (DCP) Version 1.0	af-phy-0138.000	Mar, 2000
	Multiplexed Status Mode (MSM3)	af-phy-0142.000	Mar, 2000
	Frame-Based ATM Interface (Level 3)	af-phy-0143.000	Mar, 2000
	UTOPIA Level 4	af-phy-0144.001	Mar, 2000
P-NNI	Interim Inter-Switch Signaling Protocol	af-pnni-0026.000	Dec, 1994
	P-NNI V1.0	af-pnni-0055.000	Mar, 1996
	PNNI 1.0 Addendum (soft PVC MIB)	af-pnni-0066.000	Sep, 1996
	PNNI ABR Addendum	af-pnni-0075.000	Jan, 1997
	PNNI v1.0 Errata and PICs	af-pnni-0081.000	July, 1997
Routing and Addressing	PNNI Augmented Routing (PAR) Version 1.0	af-ra-0104.000	Jan, 1999
	ATM Forum Addressing: User Guide Version 1.0	af-ra-0105.000	Jan, 1999
	ATM Forum Addressing: Reference Guide	af-ra-0106.000	Feb, 1999
	PNNI Addendum for Mobility Extensions Version 1.0	af-ra-0123.000	May, 1999
Residential Broadband	Residential Broadband Architectural Framework	af-rbb-0099.000	July, 1998
	RBB Physical Interfaces Specification	af-rbb-phy-0101.000	Jan, 1999

continues

Table A-1 *Approved ATM Forum Specifications (Continued)*

Technical Working Group	Approved Specifications	Specification	Approved Date
Service Aspects and Applications	Frame UNI	af-saa-0031.000	Sep, 1995
	Circuit Emulation	af-saa-0032.000	Sep, 1995
	Native ATM Services: Semantic Description	af-saa-0048.000	Feb, 1996
	Audio/Visual Multimedia Services: Video on Demand v1.0	af-saa-0049.000	Jan, 1996
	Audio/Visual Multimedia Services: Video on Demand v1.1	af-saa-0049.001	Mar, 1997
	ATM Names Service	af-saa-0069.000	Nov, 1996
	FUNI 2.0	af-saa-0088.000	July, 1997
	Native ATM Services DLPI Addendum Version 1.0	af-saa-dlpi-0091.000	Feb, 1998
	API Semantics for Native ATM Services	af-saa-0108.000	Feb, 1999
	FUNI Extensions for Multimedia	af-saa-0109.000	Feb, 1999
	H.323 Media Transport over ATM	af-saa-0124.000	July, 1999
Security	ATM Security Framework Version 1.0	af-sec-0096.000	Feb, 1998
	ATM Security Specification Version 1.0	af-sec-0100.001	Feb,1999
Signaling (See UNI 3.1, af-uni-0010.002)	UNI Signaling 4.0	af-sig-0061.000	July, 1996
	Signaling ABR Addendum	af-sig-0076.000	Jan, 1997
Testing	Introduction to ATM Forum Test Specifications	af-test-0022.000	Dec, 1994
	PICS Proforma for the DS3 Physical Layer Interface	af-test-0023.000	Sep, 1994
	PICS Proforma for the SONET STS-3c Physical Layer Interface	af-test-0024.000	Sep, 1994
	PICS Proforma for the 100 Mbps Multimode Fiber Physical Layer Interface	af-test-0025.000	Sep, 1994
	PICS Proforma for the ATM Layer (UNI 3.0)	af-test-0028.000	Apr, 1995

Table A-1 *Approved ATM Forum Specifications (Continued)*

Technical Working Group	Approved Specifications	Specification	Approved Date
	Conformance Abstract Test Suite for the ATM Layer for Intermediate Systems (UNI 3.0)	af-test-0030.000	Sep, 1995
	Interoperability Test Suite for the ATM Layer (UNI 3.0)	af-test-0035.000	Apr, 1995
	Interoperability Test Suites for Physical Layer: DS-3, STS-3c, 100 Mbps MMF (TAXI)	af-test-0036.000	Apr, 1995
	PICS Proforma for the DS1 Physical Layer	af-test-0037.000	Apr, 1995
	Conformance Abstract Test Suite for the ATM Layer (End Systems) UNI 3.0	af-test-0041.000	Jan, 1996
	PICS for AAL5 (ITU spec)	af-test-0042.000	Jan, 1996
	PICS Proforma for the 51.84 Mbps Mid-Range PHY Layer Interface	af-test-0044.000	Jan, 1996
	Conformance Abstract Test Suite for the ATM Layer of Intermediate Systems (UNI 3.1)	af-test-0045.000	Jan, 1996
	PICS for the 25.6 Mbps over Twisted Pair Cable (UTP-3) Physical Layer	af-test-0051.000	Mar, 1996
	Conformance Abstract Test Suite for the ATM Adaptation Layer (AAL) Type 5 Common Part (Part 1)	af-test-0052.000	Mar, 1996
	PICS for ATM Layer (UNI 3.1)	af-test-0059.000	July, 1996
	Conformance Abstract Test Suite for the UNI 3.1 ATM Layer of End Systems	af-test-0060.000	June, 1996
	Conformance Abstract Test Suite for the SSCOP Sublayer (UNI 3.1)	af-test-0067.000	Sep, 1996
	SSCOP Conformance Abstract Test Suite, Version 1.1	af-test-0067.001	May, 1999
	PICS for the 155 Mbps over Twisted Pair Cable (UTP-5/STP-5) Physical Layer	af-test-0070.000	Nov, 1996
	PICS for Direct Mapped DS3	af-test-0082.000	July, 1997

continues

Table A-1   *Approved ATM Forum Specifications (Continued)*

Technical Working Group	Approved Specifications	Specification	Approved Date
	Conformance Abstract Test Suite for Signaling (UNI 3.1) for the Network Side	af-test-0090.000	Sep, 1997
	Abstract Test Suite for UNI 3.1 ATM Signaling for the Network Side v2.0	af-test-0090.001	Mar, 2000
	PICS for Signaling (UNI v3.1) for the User Side	af-test-0097.000	Apr, 1998
	Implementation Conformance Statement (ICS) Proforma Style Guide	af-test-0137.000	Mar, 2000
	ATM Test Access Function (ATAF) Specification Version 1.0	af-test-nm-0094.000	Feb, 1998
	Interoperability Test for PNNI Version 1.0	af-test-csra-0111.000	Feb, 1999
	PICS Proforma for UNI 3.1 Signalling (Network Side)	af-test-csra-0118.000	May, 1999
	ATM Forum Performance Testing Specification	af-test-tm-0131.000	Oct, 1999
Traffic Management (See UNI 3.1, af-uni-0010.002)	Traffic Management 4.0	af-tm-0056.000	Apr, 1996
	Traffic Management ABR Addendum	af-tm-0077.000	Jan, 1997
	Traffic Management 4.1	af-tm-0121.000	Mar, 1999
Voice and Telephony over ATM	Circuit Emulation Service 2.0	af-vtoa-0078.000	Jan, 1997
	Voice and Telephony Over ATM to the Desktop	af-vtoa-0083.000	May, 1997
	Voice and Telephony over ATM to the Desktop	af-vtoa-0083.001	Feb, 1999
	(DBCES) Dynamic Bandwith Utilization in 64 kbps Time Slot Trunking Over ATM—Using CES	af-vtoa-0085.000	July, 1997
	ATM Trunking Using AAL1 for Narrow Band Services v1.0	af-vtoa-0089.000	July, 1997
	ATM Trunking Using AAL2 for Narrowband Services	af-vtoa-0113.000	Feb, 1999

Table A-1   *Approved ATM Forum Specifications (Continued)*

Technical Working Group	Approved Specifications	Specification	Approved Date
	Low-Speed Circuit Emulation Service	af-vtoa-0119.000	May, 1999
	ICS for ATM Trunking Using AAL2 for Narrowband Services	af-vtoa-0120.000	May, 1999
	Low-Speed Circuit Emulation Service (LSCES) Implementation Conformance Statement Proformance	af-vtoa-0132.000	Oct, 1999
User-Network Interface (UNI)	ATM User-Network Interface Specification V2.0	af-uni-0010.000	June, 1992
	ATM User-Network Interface Specification V3.0	af-uni-0010.001	Sep, 1993
	ATM User-Network Interface Specification V3.1	af-uni-0010.002	1994

Pending Approval ATM Forum Specifications

Table B-1 lists all specifications pending approval by The ATM Forum.

NOTE The ATM Forum Specifications pending approval are updated frequently. For the most recent list and status of specifications pending approval, visit www.atmforum.com/atmforum/specs/specwatch.html.

Table B-1 *Pending Approval ATM Forum Specifications*

Technical WG	Major Work Efforts	Status	Approval Status
Control Signaling	Connection Modification	Final Ballot	Jul-00
	UBR with MDCR	Final Ballot	Jul-00
	BICC Support	Final Ballot	Jul-00
	GFR Signaling	Work in Progress	TBD
	DiffServ Signaling	Straw Ballot	Oct-00
	Connection Rerouting	Work in Progress	TBD
	Priority	Work in Progress	TBD
	Loop Detection	Work in Progress	TBD
	PNNI 1.1	Work in Progress	TBD
	Proxy Enhancements	Work in Progress	TBD
ATM-IP Collaboration	MPOA v1.1 Addendum for QoS	Work in Progress	TBD
	MPOA Addendum for Frame Relay Links	Straw Ballot	Oct-00
DANSx	ATM Name System v2.0	Final Ballot	Jul-00
FBATM	Fast-Framed Based ATM over SONET/ SDH	Final Ballot	Jul-00

continues

Table B-1   *Pending Approval ATM Forum Specifications (Continued)*

Technical WG	Major Work Efforts	Status	Approval Status
Network Management	Usage Measurement Requirements and Logical MIB	Straw Ballot	Oct-00
	CORBA for M4 Network View (Req and IDL)	Baseline Text	Jan-01
	Customer Service Provider Interface M3-V2	Work in Progress	Dec-00
	ATM Layer Automatic Protection Switching Req.	Work in Progress	Jul-00
	ILMI Auto Configuration Req. and MIB-V2	Straw Ballot	Jul-00
	Billing Requirements Reference Model	Work in Progress	Dec-00
	PVC Auto Configuration	Straw Ballot	Oct-00
	Path and Connection Trace	Straw Ballot	May-00
Physical Layer	1.0 Gbit Cell Based PHY	Work in Progress	TBD
	Frame-Based ATM Interface (Level 4)	Straw Ballot	Oct-00
	High Speed I/O Study	Work in Progress	TBD
Routing and Addressing	PAR Addendum: Interoperability with ILMI-based Server Discovery	Work in Progress	TBD
	PNNI 1.0 Addendum: Secure PNNI Routing	Work in Progress	TBD
	Bi-Level Addressing (Level 4)	Straw Ballot	Oct-00
	PNNI v1.1	Work in Progress	TBD
	IAP	Work in Progress	TBD
Security	Security Specification Version 1.1	Work in Progress	Jul-00
	Security Specification PICS	Work in Progress	TBD
SAA	Java ATM API	Work in Progress	TBD
	Frame Based ATM over Sonet/SDH	Work in Progress	TBD
	ATM Name Server v.2	Straw Ballot	Feb-00
	Frame Based ATM over Ethernet	Final Ballot	Jan-00
	Frame Based ATM over Blue Tooth	Work in Progress	TBD

Table B-1 *Pending Approval ATM Forum Specifications (Continued)*

Technical WG	Major Work Efforts	Status	Approval Status
Testing	Extensions to Performance Testing Specification	Work in Progress	TBD
	Conformance Abstract Test Suite for ILMI Registration	Inactive	TBD
	UNI Signaling Performance Test Suite	Straw Ballot	Sep-00
	Introduction to ATM Forum Test Specifications V2.0	Baseline Text	Jan-01
	Conformance Abstract Test Suite for PNNI Signaling	Straw Ballot	Sep-00
	Conformance Abstract Test Suite for PNNI Routing	Straw Ballot	Sep-00
	Conformance Abstract Test Suite for Signaling (UNI 3.1) for the Network side v2.0 Errata	Work in Progress	TBD
	Conformance Abstract Test Suite for ABR Source and Destination Behaviors	Straw Ballot	Sep-00
Traffic Management	Addendum to TM4.1 Supporting IP Differentiated Services and IEEE 802.10	Final Ballot	Jul-00
	Addendum to TM4.1 Supporting Specification of a MDCR for UBR	Final Ballot	Jul-00
	Tip Sheet on Support of IP Differentiated Services and IEEE 802.10 User Priorities over ATM Tip Sheet on Delay Estimation in ATM Networks	Baseline Text	Jan-01
	Tip Sheet on Delay Estimation in ATM Networks	Baseline Text	Jan-01
Voice and Telephony over ATM	Local Loop Emulation using AAL2	Final Ballot	Jul-00

Work in Progress: All work up to release of working document for Straw Ballot.

Inactive: Material introduced and possibly progressed but no contributions for several meetings.

Straw Ballot: Specification released for test vote with comments (may require two or more rounds). Discussion phase follows.

Final Ballot: Final specification presented for vote of membership.

Lab Solutions

Initial Configurations of Switches

Example C-1 provides the initial configuration for Switch 1. This initial configuration for Switch 1 is required if and only if you do not have a preconfigured ATM cloud.

Example C-1 *Switch 1 Initial Configuration*

```
!
version 11.3
no service pad
no service udp-small-servers
no service tcp-small-servers
!
hostname Switch_1
!
enable password sanfran
!
no ip domain-lookup
!
atm address 47.0091.8100.0000.0010.0739.9e01.0010.0739.9e01.00
atm router pnni
 node 1 level 56 lowest
   redistribute atm-static
!
!
interface ATM0/0/0
 shutdown
 no ip address
!
interface ATM0/0/1
 no ip address
!
interface ATM0/0/2
 no ip address
!
interface ATM0/0/3
 no ip address
 shutdown
!
interface ATM0/1/0
 no ip address
 no atm auto-configuration
 atm uni version 3.1
 atm maxvpi-bits 3
 atm maxvci-bits 10
```

continues

Example C-1 *Switch 1 Initial Configuration (Continued)*

```
 atm pvc 0 114  interface  ATM0/0/1 0 114
 atm pvc 0 115  interface  ATM0/0/1 0 115
 atm pvc 0 116  interface  ATM0/0/1 0 116
 atm pvc 0 117  interface  ATM0/0/2 0 117
 atm pvc 0 118  interface  ATM0/0/2 0 118
 atm pvc 0 119  interface  ATM0/0/2 0 119
!
interface ATM0/1/1
 no ip address
 no atm auto-configuration
 atm uni version 3.1
 atm maxvpi-bits 3
 atm maxvci-bits 10
 atm pvc 0 121  interface  ATM0/1/0 0 112
 atm pvc 0 124  interface  ATM0/0/1 0 124
 atm pvc 0 125  interface  ATM0/0/1 0 125
 atm pvc 0 126  interface  ATM0/0/1 0 126
 atm pvc 0 127  interface  ATM0/0/2 0 127
 atm pvc 0 128  interface  ATM0/0/2 0 128
 atm pvc 0 129  interface  ATM0/0/2 0 129
!
interface ATM0/1/2
 no ip address
 no atm auto-configuration
 atm uni version 3.1
 atm maxvpi-bits 3
 atm maxvci-bits 10
 atm pvc 0 120  interface  ATM0/1/0 0 120
 atm pvc 0 131  interface  ATM0/1/0 0 113
 atm pvc 0 132  interface  ATM0/1/1 0 123
 atm pvc 0 134  interface  ATM0/0/1 0 134
 atm pvc 0 135  interface  ATM0/0/1 0 135
 atm pvc 0 136  interface  ATM0/0/1 0 136
 atm pvc 0 137  interface  ATM0/0/2 0 137
 atm pvc 0 138  interface  ATM0/0/2 0 138
 atm pvc 0 139  interface  ATM0/0/2 0 139
!
interface ATM0/1/3
 no ip address
!
interface ATM2/0/0
 no ip address
 atm maxvp-number 0
!
interface Ethernet2/0/0
 ip address 10.0.0.11 255.0.0.0
!
ip classless
atm route 1... ATM0/1/0
atm route 2... ATM0/1/1
```

Example C-1 *Switch 1 Initial Configuration (Continued)*

```
atm route 3... ATM0/1/2
!
line con 0
 exec-timeout 0 0
 password cisco
 login
line aux 0
line vty 0 4
 exec-timeout 0 0
 password cisco
 login
!
end
```

Example C-2 provides the initial configuration for Switch 2. Again, this initial configuration for Switch 2 is required if and only if you do not have a preconfigured ATM cloud.

Example C-2 *Switch 2 Initial Configuration*

```
!
version 11.3
no service pad
no service udp-small-servers
no service tcp-small-servers
!
hostname Switch_2
!
enable password sanfran
!
no ip domain-lookup
!
atm address 47.0091.8100.0000.0010.0739.a101.0010.0739.a101.00
atm router pnni
 node 1 level 56 lowest
   redistribute atm-static
!
!
interface ATM0/0/0
 shutdown
 no ip address
!
interface ATM0/0/1
 no ip address
!
interface ATM0/0/2
 shutdown
 no ip address
!
interface ATM0/0/3
```

continues

Example C-2 *Switch 2 Initial Configuration (Continued)*

```
 no ip address
 !
interface ATM0/1/0
 no ip address
 no atm auto-configuration
 atm uni version 3.1
 atm maxvpi-bits 3
 atm maxvci-bits 10
 atm pvc 0 141   interface   ATM0/0/1 0 114
 atm pvc 0 142   interface   ATM0/0/1 0 124
 atm pvc 0 143   interface   ATM0/0/1 0 134
 atm pvc 0 147   interface   ATM0/0/3 0 147
 atm pvc 0 148   interface   ATM0/0/3 0 148
 atm pvc 0 149   interface   ATM0/0/3 0 149
 !
interface ATM0/1/1
 no ip address
 no atm auto-configuration
 atm uni version 3.1
 atm maxvpi-bits 3
 atm maxvci-bits 10
 atm pvc 0 151   interface   ATM0/0/1 0 115
 atm pvc 0 152   interface   ATM0/0/1 0 125
 atm pvc 0 153   interface   ATM0/0/1 0 135
 atm pvc 0 154   interface   ATM0/1/0 0 145
 atm pvc 0 157   interface   ATM0/0/3 0 157
 atm pvc 0 158   interface   ATM0/0/3 0 158
 atm pvc 0 159   interface   ATM0/0/3 0 159
 !
interface ATM0/1/2
 no ip address
 no atm auto-configuration
 atm uni version 3.1
 atm maxvpi-bits 3
 atm maxvci-bits 10
 atm pvc 0 161   interface   ATM0/0/1 0 116
 atm pvc 0 162   interface   ATM0/0/1 0 126
 atm pvc 0 163   interface   ATM0/0/1 0 136
 atm pvc 0 164   interface   ATM0/1/0 0 146
 atm pvc 0 165   interface   ATM0/1/1 0 156
 atm pvc 0 167   interface   ATM0/0/3 0 167
 atm pvc 0 168   interface   ATM0/0/3 0 168
 atm pvc 0 169   interface   ATM0/0/3 0 169
 !
interface ATM0/1/3
 no ip address
 !
interface ATM2/0/0
 no ip address
 atm maxvp-number 0
```

Example C-2 *Switch 2 Initial Configuration (Continued)*

```
!
interface Ethernet2/0/0
 ip address 10.0.0.12 255.0.0.0
!
ip classless
atm route 5... ATM0/1/1
atm route 6... ATM0/1/2
atm route 4... ATM0/1/0
!
line con 0
 exec-timeout 0 0
 password cisco
 login
line aux 0
line vty 0 4
 exec-timeout 0 0
 password cisco
 login
!
end
```

Example C-3 provides the initial configuration for Switch 3. Again, this initial configuration for Switch 3 is required if and only if you do not have a preconfigured ATM cloud.

Example C-3 *Switch 3 Initial Configuration*

```
!
version 11.3
no service pad
no service udp-small-servers
no service tcp-small-servers
!
hostname Switch_3
!
boot system flash bootflash:ls1010-wp-mz.113-0.8.TWA4.2.bin
enable password sanfran
!
no ip domain-lookup
!
atm address 47.0091.8100.0000.0010.0739.c301.0010.0739.c301.00
atm router pnni
 node 1 level 56 lowest
 redistribute atm-static
!
!
interface ATM0/0/0
 shutdown
 no ip address
!
```

continues

Example C-3 *Switch 3 Initial Configuration (Continued)*

```
interface ATM0/0/1
 shutdown
 no ip address
!
interface ATM0/0/2
 no ip address
!
interface ATM0/0/3
 no ip address
!
interface ATM0/1/0
 no ip address
 no atm auto-configuration
 atm uni version 3.1
 atm maxvpi-bits 3
 atm maxvci-bits 10
 atm pvc 0 171  interface  ATM0/0/2 0 117
 atm pvc 0 172  interface  ATM0/0/2 0 127
 atm pvc 0 173  interface  ATM0/0/2 0 137
 atm pvc 0 174  interface  ATM0/0/3 0 147
 atm pvc 0 175  interface  ATM0/0/3 0 157
 atm pvc 0 176  interface  ATM0/0/3 0 167
!
interface ATM0/1/1
 no ip address
 no atm auto-configuration
 atm uni version 3.1
 atm maxvpi-bits 3
 atm maxvci-bits 10
 atm pvc 0 181  interface  ATM0/0/2 0 118
 atm pvc 0 182  interface  ATM0/0/2 0 128
 atm pvc 0 183  interface  ATM0/0/2 0 138
 atm pvc 0 184  interface  ATM0/0/3 0 148
 atm pvc 0 185  interface  ATM0/0/3 0 158
 atm pvc 0 186  interface  ATM0/0/3 0 168
 atm pvc 0 187  interface  ATM0/1/0 0 178
!
interface ATM0/1/2
 no ip address
 no atm auto-configuration
 atm uni version 3.1
 atm maxvpi-bits 3
 atm maxvci-bits 10
 atm pvc 0 191  interface  ATM0/0/2 0 119
 atm pvc 0 192  interface  ATM0/0/2 0 129
 atm pvc 0 193  interface  ATM0/0/2 0 139
 atm pvc 0 194  interface  ATM0/0/3 0 149
 atm pvc 0 195  interface  ATM0/0/3 0 159
 atm pvc 0 196  interface  ATM0/0/3 0 169
 atm pvc 0 197  interface  ATM0/1/0 0 179
```

Example C-3 *Switch 3 Initial Configuration (Continued)*

```
 atm pvc 0 198  interface  ATM0/1/1 0 189
!
interface ATM0/1/3
 no ip address
!
interface ATM1/0/0
 no ip address
!
interface ATM1/0/1
 no ip address
!
interface ATM1/0/2
 no ip address
!
interface ATM1/0/3
 no ip address
!
interface ATM2/0/0
 no ip address
 atm maxvp-number 0
!
interface Ethernet2/0/0
 ip address 10.0.0.13 255.0.0.0
!
ip classless
atm route 7... ATM0/1/0
atm route 8... ATM0/1/1
atm route 9... ATM0/1/2
!
line con 0
 exec-timeout 0 0
 password cisco
 login
line aux 0
line vty 0 4
 exec-timeout 0 0
 password cisco
 login
!
end
```

Solutions for Lab 9-1: Configuring PVCs on Cisco 4500 Routers, RFC 2684

Examples C-4 through C-12 provide the configuration solutions that satisfy all the exercises for Lab
9-1. Specifically, the exercises asked for the following:

1   Configure each router using the parameters stipulated in the Exercises section of Lab 9-1.

2   Configure the Ethernet 0 and ATM 0.1 interfaces for each router using the parameters specified by Table 9-8 on page 348.

3   Configure a PVC to every other router to create a fully meshed ATM PVC network using AAL5SNAP encapsulation. VPI/VCI number assignment is specified in Table 9-9 on page 348.

4   Map your neighbor's IP network number to the appropriate PVC.

5   Test your configuration.

Example C-4   *Router 1 Configuration for Lab 9-1*

```
!
version 11.2
no service password-encryption
no service udp-small-servers
no service tcp-small-servers
!
hostname R1
!
enable password sanfran
!
no ip domain-lookup

!
interface Ethernet0
 ip address 144.254.1.1 255.255.255.0
!
interface Ethernet1
 ip address 10.0.0.1 255.0.0.0
 media-type 10BaseT
!
interface ATM0
 no ip address
!
interface ATM0.1 multipoint
 ip address 144.254.100.1 255.255.255.0
 atm pvc 112 0 112 aal5snap
 atm pvc 113 0 113 aal5snap
 atm pvc 114 0 114 aal5snap
 atm pvc 115 0 115 aal5snap
```

Example C-4 *Router 1 Configuration for Lab 9-1 (Continued)*

```
 atm pvc 116 0 116 aal5snap
 atm pvc 117 0 117 aal5snap
 atm pvc 118 0 118 aal5snap
 atm pvc 119 0 119 aal5snap
 map-group ipPvc
!
interface FastEthernet0
 no ip address
 shutdown
!
router igrp 100
 network 144.254.0.0
!
no ip classless
!
map-list ipPvc
 ip 144.254.100.2 atm-vc 112 broadcast
 ip 144.254.100.3 atm-vc 113 broadcast
 ip 144.254.100.4 atm-vc 114 broadcast
 ip 144.254.100.5 atm-vc 115 broadcast
 ip 144.254.100.6 atm-vc 116 broadcast
 ip 144.254.100.7 atm-vc 117 broadcast
 ip 144.254.100.8 atm-vc 118 broadcast
 ip 144.254.100.9 atm-vc 119 broadcast
!
!
line con 0
 exec-timeout 0 0
line aux 0
line vty 0 4
 exec-timeout 0 0
 password cisco
 login
!
end
```

Example C-5 *Router 2 Configuration for Lab 9-1*

```
!
version 11.2
no service password-encryption
no service udp-small-servers
no service tcp-small-servers
!
hostname R2
!
enable password sanfran
!
no ip domain-lookup
```

continues

Example C-5 *Router 2 Configuration for Lab 9-1 (Continued)*

```
!
interface Ethernet0
 ip address 144.254.2.2 255.255.255.0
!
interface Ethernet1
 ip address 10.0.0.2 255.0.0.0
 media-type 10BaseT
!
interface ATM0
 no ip address
!
interface ATM0.1 multipoint
 ip address 144.254.100.2 255.255.255.0
 atm pvc 121 0 121 aal5snap
 atm pvc 123 0 123 aal5snap
 atm pvc 124 0 124 aal5snap
 atm pvc 125 0 125 aal5snap
 atm pvc 126 0 126 aal5snap
 atm pvc 127 0 127 aal5snap
 atm pvc 128 0 128 aal5snap
 atm pvc 129 0 129 aal5snap
 map-group ipPvc
!
interface FastEthernet0
 no ip address
 shutdown
!
router igrp 100
 network 144.254.0.0
!
no ip classless
!
map-list ipPvc
 ip 144.254.100.1 atm-vc 121 broadcast
 ip 144.254.100.3 atm-vc 123 broadcast
 ip 144.254.100.4 atm-vc 124 broadcast
 ip 144.254.100.5 atm-vc 125 broadcast
 ip 144.254.100.6 atm-vc 126 broadcast
 ip 144.254.100.7 atm-vc 127 broadcast
 ip 144.254.100.8 atm-vc 128 broadcast
 ip 144.254.100.9 atm-vc 129 broadcast
!
!
line con 0
 exec-timeout 0 0
line aux 0
line vty 0 4
 exec-timeout 0 0
 password cisco
 login
```

Example C-5 *Router 2 Configuration for Lab 9-1 (Continued)*

```
!
end
```

Example C-6 *Router 3 Configuration for Lab 9-1*

```
version 11.2
no service password-encryption
no service udp-small-servers
no service tcp-small-servers
!
hostname R3
!
enable password sanfran
!
no ip domain-lookup
!
interface Ethernet0
 ip address 144.254.3.3 255.255.255.0
!
interface Ethernet1
 ip address 10.0.0.3 255.0.0.0
 media-type 10BaseT
!
interface ATM0
 no ip address
!
interface ATM0.1 multipoint
 ip address 144.254.100.3 255.255.255.0
 atm pvc 131 0 131 aal5snap
 atm pvc 132 0 132 aal5snap
 atm pvc 133 0 133 aal5snap
 atm pvc 134 0 134 aal5snap
 atm pvc 135 0 135 aal5snap
 atm pvc 136 0 136 aal5snap
 atm pvc 137 0 137 aal5snap
 atm pvc 138 0 138 aal5snap
 atm pvc 139 0 139 aal5snap
 map-group ipPvc
!
interface FastEthernet0
 no ip address
 shutdown
!
router igrp 100
 network 144.254.0.0
!
no ip classless
!
map-list ipPvc
 ip 144.254.100.1 atm-vc 131 broadcast
```

continues

Example C-6 *Router 3 Configuration for Lab 9-1 (Continued)*

```
 ip 144.254.100.2 atm-vc 132 broadcast
 ip 144.254.100.4 atm-vc 134 broadcast
 ip 144.254.100.5 atm-vc 135 broadcast
 ip 144.254.100.6 atm-vc 136 broadcast
 ip 144.254.100.7 atm-vc 137 broadcast
 ip 144.254.100.8 atm-vc 138 broadcast
 ip 144.254.100.9 atm-vc 139 broadcast
!
!
line con 0
 exec-timeout 0 0
line aux 0
line vty 0 4
 password cisco
 login
!
end
```

Example C-7 *Router 4 Configuration for Lab 9-1*

```
version 11.2
no service password-encryption
no service udp-small-servers
no service tcp-small-servers
!
hostname R4
!
enable password sanfran
!
no ip domain-lookup
!
interface Ethernet0
 ip address 144.254.4.4 255.255.255.0
!
interface Ethernet1
 ip address 10.0.0.4 255.0.0.0
 media-type 10BaseT
!
interface ATM0
 no ip address
!
interface ATM0.1 multipoint
 ip address 144.254.100.4 255.255.255.0
 atm pvc 141 0 141 aal5snap
 atm pvc 142 0 142 aal5snap
 atm pvc 143 0 143 aal5snap
 atm pvc 145 0 145 aal5snap
 atm pvc 146 0 146 aal5snap
 atm pvc 147 0 147 aal5snap
 atm pvc 148 0 148 aal5snap
```

Example C-7 *Router 4 Configuration for Lab 9-1 (Continued)*

```
 atm pvc 149 0 149 aal5snap
 map-group ipPvc
!
interface FastEthernet0
 no ip address
 shutdown
!
router igrp 100
 network 144.254.0.0
!
no ip classless
!
map-list ipPvc
 ip 144.254.100.1 atm-vc 141 broadcast
 ip 144.254.100.2 atm-vc 142 broadcast
 ip 144.254.100.3 atm-vc 143 broadcast
 ip 144.254.100.5 atm-vc 145 broadcast
 ip 144.254.100.6 atm-vc 146 broadcast
 ip 144.254.100.7 atm-vc 147 broadcast
 ip 144.254.100.8 atm-vc 148 broadcast
 ip 144.254.100.9 atm-vc 149 broadcast
!
!
line con 0
 exec-timeout 0 0
line aux 0
line vty 0 4
 exec-timeout 0 0
 password cisco
 login
!
end
```

Example C-8 *Router 5 Configuration for Lab 9-1*

```
!
version 11.2
no service password-encryption
no service udp-small-servers
no service tcp-small-servers
!
hostname R5
!
enable password sanfran
!
no ip domain-lookup
!
interface Ethernet0
 ip address 144.254.5.5 255.255.255.0
!
```

continues

Example C-8 *Router 5 Configuration for Lab 9-1 (Continued)*

```
interface Ethernet1
 ip address 10.0.0.5 255.0.0.0
 media-type 10BaseT
!
interface ATM0
 no ip address
!
interface ATM0.1 multipoint
 ip address 144.254.100.5 255.255.255.0
 atm pvc 151 0 151 aal5snap
 atm pvc 152 0 152 aal5snap
 atm pvc 153 0 153 aal5snap
 atm pvc 154 0 154 aal5snap
 atm pvc 156 0 156 aal5snap
 atm pvc 157 0 157 aal5snap
 atm pvc 158 0 158 aal5snap
 atm pvc 159 0 159 aal5snap
 map-group ipPvc
!
interface FastEthernet0
 no ip address
 shutdown
!
router igrp 100
 network 144.254.0.0
!
no ip classless
!
map-list ipPvc
 ip 144.254.100.1 atm-vc 151 broadcast
 ip 144.254.100.2 atm-vc 152 broadcast
 ip 144.254.100.3 atm-vc 153 broadcast
 ip 144.254.100.4 atm-vc 154 broadcast
 ip 144.254.100.6 atm-vc 156 broadcast
 ip 144.254.100.7 atm-vc 157 broadcast
 ip 144.254.100.8 atm-vc 158 broadcast
 ip 144.254.100.9 atm-vc 159 broadcast
!
!
line con 0
 exec-timeout 0 0
line aux 0
line vty 0 4
 exec-timeout 0 0
 password cisco
 login
!
end
```

Example C-9 *Router 6 Configuration for Lab 9-1*

```
version 11.2
no service password-encryption
no service udp-small-servers
no service tcp-small-servers
!
hostname R6
!
enable password sanfran
!
no ip domain-lookup
!
interface Ethernet0
 ip address 144.254.6.6 255.255.255.0
!
interface Ethernet1
 ip address 10.0.0.6 255.0.0.0
 media-type 10BaseT
!
interface ATM0
 no ip address
!
interface ATM0.1 multipoint
 ip address 144.254.100.6 255.255.255.0
 atm pvc 161 0 161 aal5snap
 atm pvc 162 0 162 aal5snap
 atm pvc 163 0 163 aal5snap
 atm pvc 164 0 164 aal5snap
 atm pvc 165 0 165 aal5snap
 atm pvc 167 0 167 aal5snap
 atm pvc 168 0 168 aal5snap
 atm pvc 169 0 169 aal5snap
 map-group ipPvc
!
interface FastEthernet0
 no ip address
 shutdown
!
router igrp 100
 network 144.254.0.0
!
no ip classless
!
map-list ipPvc
 ip 144.254.100.1 atm-vc 161 broadcast
 ip 144.254.100.2 atm-vc 162 broadcast
 ip 144.254.100.3 atm-vc 163 broadcast
 ip 144.254.100.4 atm-vc 164 broadcast
 ip 144.254.100.5 atm-vc 165 broadcast
 ip 144.254.100.7 atm-vc 167 broadcast
 ip 144.254.100.8 atm-vc 168 broadcast
```

continues

Example C-9   *Router 6 Configuration for Lab 9-1 (Continued)*

```
ip 144.254.100.9 atm-vc 169 broadcast
!
!
line con 0
 exec-timeout 0 0
line aux 0
line vty 0 4
 exec-timeout 0 0
 password cisco
 login
!
end
```

Example C-10   *Router 7 Configuration for Lab 9-1*

```
!
version 11.2
no service password-encryption
no service udp-small-servers
no service tcp-small-servers
!
hostname R7
!
enable password sanfran
!
no ip domain-lookup
!
interface Ethernet0
 ip address 144.254.7.7 255.255.255.0
!
interface Ethernet1
 ip address 10.0.0.7 255.0.0.0
 media-type 10BaseT
!
interface ATM0
 no ip address
!
interface ATM0.1 multipoint
 ip address 144.254.100.7 255.255.255.0
 atm pvc 171 0 171 aal5snap
 atm pvc 172 0 172 aal5snap
 atm pvc 173 0 173 aal5snap
 atm pvc 174 0 174 aal5snap
 atm pvc 175 0 175 aal5snap
 atm pvc 176 0 176 aal5snap
 atm pvc 178 0 178 aal5snap
 atm pvc 179 0 179 aal5snap
 map-group ipPvc
!
interface FastEthernet0
```

Example C-10 *Router 7 Configuration for Lab 9-1 (Continued)*

```
 no ip address
 shutdown
!
router igrp 100
 network 144.254.0.0
!
no ip classless
!
map-list ipPvc
 ip 144.254.100.1 atm-vc 171 broadcast
 ip 144.254.100.2 atm-vc 172 broadcast
 ip 144.254.100.3 atm-vc 173 broadcast
 ip 144.254.100.4 atm-vc 174 broadcast
 ip 144.254.100.5 atm-vc 175 broadcast
 ip 144.254.100.6 atm-vc 176 broadcast
 ip 144.254.100.8 atm-vc 178 broadcast
 ip 144.254.100.9 atm-vc 179 broadcast
!
!
line con 0
 exec-timeout 0 0
line aux 0
line vty 0 4
 exec-timeout 0 0
 password cisco
 login
!
end
```

Example C-11 *Router 8 Configuration for Lab 9-1*

```
!
version 11.2
no service password-encryption
no service udp-small-servers
no service tcp-small-servers
!
hostname R8
!
enable password sanfran
!
no ip domain-lookup
!
interface Ethernet0
 ip address 144.254.8.8 255.255.255.0
!
interface Ethernet1
 ip address 10.0.0.8 255.0.0.0
 media-type 10BaseT
!
```

continues

Example C-11 *Router 8 Configuration for Lab 9-1 (Continued)*

```
interface ATM0
 no ip address
!
interface ATM0.1 multipoint
 ip address 144.254.100.8 255.255.255.0
 atm pvc 181 0 181 aal5snap
 atm pvc 182 0 182 aal5snap
 atm pvc 183 0 183 aal5snap
 atm pvc 184 0 184 aal5snap
 atm pvc 185 0 185 aal5snap
 atm pvc 186 0 186 aal5snap
 atm pvc 187 0 187 aal5snap
 atm pvc 189 0 189 aal5snap
 map-group ipPvc
!
interface FastEthernet0
 no ip address
 shutdown
!
router igrp 100
 network 144.254.0.0
!
no ip classless
!
map-list ipPvc
 ip 144.254.100.1 atm-vc 181 broadcast
 ip 144.254.100.2 atm-vc 182 broadcast
 ip 144.254.100.3 atm-vc 183 broadcast
 ip 144.254.100.4 atm-vc 184 broadcast
 ip 144.254.100.5 atm-vc 185 broadcast
 ip 144.254.100.6 atm-vc 186 broadcast
 ip 144.254.100.7 atm-vc 187 broadcast
 ip 144.254.100.9 atm-vc 189 broadcast
!
!
line con 0
 exec-timeout 0 0
line aux 0
line vty 0 4
 exec-timeout 0 0
 password cisco
 login
!
end
```

Example C-12 *Router 9 Configuration for Lab 9-1*

```
!
version 11.2
no service password-encryption
```

Example C-12 *Router 9 Configuration for Lab 9-1 (Continued)*

```
no service udp-small-servers
no service tcp-small-servers
!
hostname R9
!
enable password sanfran
!
no ip domain-lookup
!
interface Ethernet0
 ip address 144.254.9.9 255.255.255.0
!
interface Ethernet1
 ip address 10.0.0.9 255.0.0.0
 media-type 10BaseT
!
interface ATM0
 no ip address
!
interface ATM0.1 multipoint
 ip address 144.254.100.9 255.255.255.0
 atm pvc 191 0 191 aal5snap
 atm pvc 192 0 192 aal5snap
 atm pvc 193 0 193 aal5snap
 atm pvc 194 0 194 aal5snap
 atm pvc 195 0 195 aal5snap
 atm pvc 196 0 196 aal5snap
 atm pvc 197 0 197 aal5snap
 atm pvc 198 0 198 aal5snap
 map-group ipPvc
!
interface FastEthernet0
 no ip address
 shutdown
!
router igrp 100
 network 144.254.0.0
!
no ip classless
!
map-list ipPvc
 ip 144.254.100.1 atm-vc 191 broadcast
 ip 144.254.100.2 atm-vc 192 broadcast
 ip 144.254.100.3 atm-vc 193 broadcast
 ip 144.254.100.4 atm-vc 194 broadcast
 ip 144.254.100.5 atm-vc 195 broadcast
 ip 144.254.100.6 atm-vc 196 broadcast
 ip 144.254.100.7 atm-vc 197 broadcast
 ip 144.254.100.8 atm-vc 198 broadcast
!
```

continues

Example C-12 *Router 9 Configuration for Lab 9-1 (Continued)*

```
!
line con 0
 exec-timeout 0 0
line aux 0
line vty 0 4
 exec-timeout 0 0
 password cisco
 login
!
end
```

Solutions for Lab 9-2: Configuring IPX over PVCs Using AAL5SNAP, RFC 2684

Examples C-13 through C-21 provide the configuration solutions that satisfy all the exercises for Lab 9-2. Specifically, the exercises asked for the following:

1 Turn on IPX routing using the **ipx routing 0000.0000.000***x* command, where *x* is your router number.

2 On interface ATM 0.1, assign IPX Network 100.

3 Assign the proper mapping of IPX network addresses to their respective PVCs. I advise you to use a different map group for IPX than you used for IP, simply because this makes the IP solution "portable."

4 Assign an IPX network number to your Ethernet 0 interface (Router 1 uses Network 10, Router 2 uses Network 20, and so on).

5 Test your connectivity.

Example C-13 *Router 1 Configuration for Lab 9-2*

```
!
version 11.2
no service password-encryption
no service udp-small-servers
no service tcp-small-servers
!
hostname R1
!
enable password sanfran
!
no ip domain-lookup
ipx routing 0000.0000.0001
!
!
interface Ethernet0
```

Example C-13 *Router 1 Configuration for Lab 9-2 (Continued)*

```
 ip address 144.254.1.1 255.255.255.0
 ipx network 10
!
interface Ethernet1
 ip address 10.0.0.1 255.0.0.0
 media-type 10BaseT
!
interface ATM0
 no ip address
!
interface ATM0.1 multipoint
 ip address 144.254.100.1 255.255.255.0
 atm pvc 112 0 112 aal5snap
 atm pvc 113 0 113 aal5snap
 atm pvc 114 0 114 aal5snap
 atm pvc 115 0 115 aal5snap
 atm pvc 116 0 116 aal5snap
 atm pvc 117 0 117 aal5snap
 atm pvc 118 0 118 aal5snap
 atm pvc 119 0 119 aal5snap
 map-group ipPvc
 map-group ipxPvc
 ipx network 100
!
interface FastEthernet0
 no ip address
 shutdown
!
router igrp 100
 network 144.254.0.0
!
no ip classless
!
map-list ipPvc
 ip 144.254.100.2 atm-vc 112 broadcast
 ip 144.254.100.3 atm-vc 113 broadcast
 ip 144.254.100.4 atm-vc 114 broadcast
 ip 144.254.100.5 atm-vc 115 broadcast
 ip 144.254.100.6 atm-vc 116 broadcast
 ip 144.254.100.7 atm-vc 117 broadcast
 ip 144.254.100.8 atm-vc 118 broadcast
 ip 144.254.100.9 atm-vc 119 broadcast
!
map-list ipxPvc
 ipx 100.0000.0000.0002 atm-vc 112 broadcast
 ipx 100.0000.0000.0003 atm-vc 113 broadcast
 ipx 100.0000.0000.0004 atm-vc 114 broadcast
 ipx 100.0000.0000.0005 atm-vc 115 broadcast
 ipx 100.0000.0000.0006 atm-vc 116 broadcast
 ipx 100.0000.0000.0007 atm-vc 117 broadcast
```

continues

Lab 9-2 Solution

Example C-13 *Router 1 Configuration for Lab 9-2 (Continued)*

```
 ipx 100.0000.0000.0008 atm-vc 118 broadcast
 ipx 100.0000.0000.0009 atm-vc 119 broadcast
!
line con 0
 exec-timeout 0 0
line aux 0
line vty 0 4
 exec-timeout 0 0
 password cisco
 login
!
end
```

Example C-14 *Router 2 Configuration for Lab 9-2*

```
!
version 11.2
no service password-encryption
no service udp-small-servers
no service tcp-small-servers
!
hostname R2
!
enable password sanfran
!
no ip domain-lookup
ipx routing 0000.0000.0002
!
!
interface Ethernet0
 ip address 144.254.2.2 255.255.255.0
 ipx network 20
!
interface Ethernet1
 ip address 10.0.0.2 255.0.0.0
 media-type 10BaseT
!
interface ATM0
 no ip address
!
interface ATM0.1 multipoint
 ip address 144.254.100.2 255.255.255.0
 atm pvc 121 0 121 aal5snap
 atm pvc 123 0 123 aal5snap
 atm pvc 124 0 124 aal5snap
 atm pvc 125 0 125 aal5snap
 atm pvc 126 0 126 aal5snap
 atm pvc 127 0 127 aal5snap
 atm pvc 128 0 128 aal5snap
 atm pvc 129 0 129 aal5snap
```

Example C-14 *Router 2 Configuration for Lab 9-2 (Continued)*

```
 map-group ipPvc
 map-group ipxPvc
 ipx network 100
!
interface FastEthernet0
 no ip address
 shutdown
!
router igrp 100
 network 144.254.0.0
!
no ip classless
!
map-list ipPvc
 ip 144.254.100.1 atm-vc 121 broadcast
 ip 144.254.100.3 atm-vc 123 broadcast
 ip 144.254.100.4 atm-vc 124 broadcast
 ip 144.254.100.5 atm-vc 125 broadcast
 ip 144.254.100.6 atm-vc 126 broadcast
 ip 144.254.100.7 atm-vc 127 broadcast
 ip 144.254.100.8 atm-vc 128 broadcast
 ip 144.254.100.9 atm-vc 129 broadcast
!
map-list ipxPvc
 ipx 100.0000.0000.0001 atm-vc 121 broadcast
 ipx 100.0000.0000.0003 atm-vc 123 broadcast
 ipx 100.0000.0000.0004 atm-vc 124 broadcast
 ipx 100.0000.0000.0005 atm-vc 125 broadcast
 ipx 100.0000.0000.0006 atm-vc 126 broadcast
 ipx 100.0000.0000.0007 atm-vc 127 broadcast
 ipx 100.0000.0000.0008 atm-vc 128 broadcast
 ipx 100.0000.0000.0009 atm-vc 129 broadcast
!
!
line con 0
 exec-timeout 0 0
line aux 0
line vty 0 4
 exec-timeout 0 0
 password cisco
 login
!
end
```

Example C-15 *Router 3 Configuration for Lab 9-2*

```
!
version 11.2
no service password-encryption
no service udp-small-servers
```

Lab 9-2 Solution

Example C-15 *Router 3 Configuration for Lab 9-2 (Continued)*

```
no service tcp-small-servers
!
hostname R3
!
enable password sanfran
!
no ip domain-lookup
ipx routing 0000.0000.0003
!
!
interface Ethernet0
 ip address 144.254.3.3 255.255.255.0
 ipx network 30
!
interface Ethernet1
 ip address 10.0.0.3 255.0.0.0
 media-type 10BaseT
!
interface ATM0
 no ip address
!
interface ATM0.1 multipoint
 ip address 144.254.100.3 255.255.255.0
 atm pvc 131 0 131 aal5snap
 atm pvc 132 0 132 aal5snap
 atm pvc 133 0 133 aal5snap
 atm pvc 134 0 134 aal5snap
 atm pvc 135 0 135 aal5snap
 atm pvc 136 0 136 aal5snap
 atm pvc 137 0 137 aal5snap
 atm pvc 138 0 138 aal5snap
 atm pvc 139 0 139 aal5snap
 map-group ipPvc
 map-group ipxPvc
 ipx network 100
!
interface FastEthernet0
 no ip address
 shutdown
!
router igrp 100
 network 144.254.0.0
!
no ip classless
!
map-list ipPvc
 ip 144.254.100.1 atm-vc 131 broadcast
 ip 144.254.100.2 atm-vc 132 broadcast
 ip 144.254.100.4 atm-vc 134 broadcast
 ip 144.254.100.5 atm-vc 135 broadcast
```

Example C-15 *Router 3 Configuration for Lab 9-2 (Continued)*

```
ip 144.254.100.6 atm-vc 136 broadcast
ip 144.254.100.7 atm-vc 137 broadcast
ip 144.254.100.8 atm-vc 138 broadcast
ip 144.254.100.9 atm-vc 139 broadcast
!
map-list ipxPvc
 ipx 100.0000.0000.0001 atm-vc 131 broadcast
 ipx 100.0000.0000.0002 atm-vc 132 broadcast
 ipx 100.0000.0000.0004 atm-vc 134 broadcast
 ipx 100.0000.0000.0005 atm-vc 135 broadcast
 ipx 100.0000.0000.0006 atm-vc 136 broadcast
 ipx 100.0000.0000.0007 atm-vc 137 broadcast
 ipx 100.0000.0000.0008 atm-vc 138 broadcast
 ipx 100.0000.0000.0009 atm-vc 139 broadcast
!
!
line con 0
 exec-timeout 0 0
line aux 0
line vty 0 4
 password cisco
 login
!
end
```

Example C-16 *Router 4 Configuration for Lab 9-2*

```
!
version 11.2
no service password-encryption
no service udp-small-servers
no service tcp-small-servers
!
hostname R4
!
enable password sanfran
!
no ip domain-lookup
ipx routing 0000.0000.0004
!
!
interface Ethernet0
 ip address 144.254.4.4 255.255.255.0
 ipx network 40
!
interface Ethernet1
 ip address 10.0.0.4 255.0.0.0
 media-type 10BaseT
!
interface ATM0
```

continues

Lab 9-2 Solution

Example C-16 *Router 4 Configuration for Lab 9-2 (Continued)*

```
 no ip address
!
interface ATM0.1 multipoint
 ip address 144.254.100.4 255.255.255.0
 atm pvc 141 0 141 aal5snap
 atm pvc 142 0 142 aal5snap
 atm pvc 143 0 143 aal5snap
 atm pvc 145 0 145 aal5snap
 atm pvc 146 0 146 aal5snap
 atm pvc 147 0 147 aal5snap
 atm pvc 148 0 148 aal5snap
 atm pvc 149 0 149 aal5snap
 map-group ipPvc
 map-group ipxPvc
 ipx network 100
!
interface FastEthernet0
 no ip address
 shutdown
!
router igrp 100
 network 144.254.0.0
!
no ip classless
!
map-list ipPvc
 ip 144.254.100.1 atm-vc 141 broadcast
 ip 144.254.100.2 atm-vc 142 broadcast
 ip 144.254.100.3 atm-vc 143 broadcast
 ip 144.254.100.5 atm-vc 145 broadcast
 ip 144.254.100.6 atm-vc 146 broadcast
 ip 144.254.100.7 atm-vc 147 broadcast
 ip 144.254.100.8 atm-vc 148 broadcast
 ip 144.254.100.9 atm-vc 149 broadcast
!
map-list ipxPvc
 ipx 100.0000.0000.0001 atm-vc 141 broadcast
 ipx 100.0000.0000.0002 atm-vc 142 broadcast
 ipx 100.0000.0000.0003 atm-vc 143 broadcast
 ipx 100.0000.0000.0005 atm-vc 145 broadcast
 ipx 100.0000.0000.0006 atm-vc 146 broadcast
 ipx 100.0000.0000.0007 atm-vc 147 broadcast
 ipx 100.0000.0000.0008 atm-vc 148 broadcast
 ipx 100.0000.0000.0009 atm-vc 149 broadcast
!
line con 0
 exec-timeout 0 0
line aux 0
line vty 0 4
 exec-timeout 0 0
```

Example C-16 *Router 4 Configuration for Lab 9-2 (Continued)*

```
 password cisco
 login
!
end
```

Example C-17 *Router 5 Configuration for Lab 9-2*

```
!
version 11.2
no service password-encryption
no service udp-small-servers
no service tcp-small-servers
!
hostname R5
!
enable password sanfran
!
no ip domain-lookup
ipx routing 0000.0000.0005
!
!
interface Ethernet0
 ip address 144.254.5.5 255.255.255.0
 ipx network 50
!
interface Ethernet1
 ip address 10.0.0.5 255.0.0.0
 media-type 10BaseT
!
interface ATM0
 no ip address
!
interface ATM0.1 multipoint
 ip address 144.254.100.5 255.255.255.0
 atm pvc 151 0 151 aal5snap
 atm pvc 152 0 152 aal5snap
 atm pvc 153 0 153 aal5snap
 atm pvc 154 0 154 aal5snap
 atm pvc 156 0 156 aal5snap
 atm pvc 157 0 157 aal5snap
 atm pvc 158 0 158 aal5snap
 atm pvc 159 0 159 aal5snap
 map-group ipPvc
 map-group ipxPvc
 ipx network 100
!
interface FastEthernet0
 no ip address
 shutdown
!
```

continues

Example C-17 *Router 5 Configuration for Lab 9-2 (Continued)*

```
router igrp 100
 network 144.254.0.0
!
no ip classless
!
map-list ipPvc
 ip 144.254.100.1 atm-vc 151 broadcast
 ip 144.254.100.2 atm-vc 152 broadcast
 ip 144.254.100.3 atm-vc 153 broadcast
 ip 144.254.100.4 atm-vc 154 broadcast
 ip 144.254.100.6 atm-vc 156 broadcast
 ip 144.254.100.7 atm-vc 157 broadcast
 ip 144.254.100.8 atm-vc 158 broadcast
 ip 144.254.100.9 atm-vc 159 broadcast
!
map-list ipxPvc
 ipx 100.0000.0000.0001 atm-vc 151 broadcast
 ipx 100.0000.0000.0002 atm-vc 152 broadcast
 ipx 100.0000.0000.0003 atm-vc 153 broadcast
 ipx 100.0000.0000.0004 atm-vc 154 broadcast
 ipx 100.0000.0000.0006 atm-vc 156 broadcast
 ipx 100.0000.0000.0007 atm-vc 157 broadcast
 ipx 100.0000.0000.0008 atm-vc 158 broadcast
 ipx 100.0000.0000.0009 atm-vc 159 broadcast
!
line con 0
 exec-timeout 0 0
line aux 0
line vty 0 4
 exec-timeout 0 0
 password cisco
 login
!
end
```

Example C-18 *Router 6 Configuration for Lab 9-2*

```
!
version 11.2
no service password-encryption
no service udp-small-servers
no service tcp-small-servers
!
hostname R6
!
enable password sanfran
!
no ip domain-lookup
ipx routing 0000.0000.0006
!
```

Example C-18 *Router 6 Configuration for Lab 9-2 (Continued)*

```
!
interface Ethernet0
 ip address 144.254.6.6 255.255.255.0
 ipx network 60
!
interface Ethernet1
 ip address 10.0.0.6 255.0.0.0
 media-type 10BaseT
!
interface ATM0
 no ip address
!
interface ATM0.1 multipoint
 ip address 144.254.100.6 255.255.255.0
 atm pvc 161 0 161 aal5snap
 atm pvc 162 0 162 aal5snap
 atm pvc 163 0 163 aal5snap
 atm pvc 164 0 164 aal5snap
 atm pvc 165 0 165 aal5snap
 atm pvc 167 0 167 aal5snap
 atm pvc 168 0 168 aal5snap
 atm pvc 169 0 169 aal5snap
 map-group ipPvc
 map-group ipxPvc
 ipx network 100
!
interface FastEthernet0
 no ip address
 shutdown
!
router igrp 100
 network 144.254.0.0
!
no ip classless
!
map-list ipPvc
 ip 144.254.100.1 atm-vc 161 broadcast
 ip 144.254.100.2 atm-vc 162 broadcast
 ip 144.254.100.3 atm-vc 163 broadcast
 ip 144.254.100.4 atm-vc 164 broadcast
 ip 144.254.100.5 atm-vc 165 broadcast
 ip 144.254.100.7 atm-vc 167 broadcast
 ip 144.254.100.8 atm-vc 168 broadcast
 ip 144.254.100.9 atm-vc 169 broadcast
!
map-list ipxPvc
 ipx 100.0000.0000.0001 atm-vc 161 broadcast
 ipx 100.0000.0000.0002 atm-vc 162 broadcast
 ipx 100.0000.0000.0003 atm-vc 163 broadcast
 ipx 100.0000.0000.0004 atm-vc 164 broadcast
```

continues

Lab 9-2 Solution

Example C-18 *Router 6 Configuration for Lab 9-2 (Continued)*

```
ipx 100.0000.0000.0005 atm-vc 165 broadcast
ipx 100.0000.0000.0007 atm-vc 167 broadcast
ipx 100.0000.0000.0008 atm-vc 168 broadcast
ipx 100.0000.0000.0009 atm-vc 169 broadcast
!
!
line con 0
 exec-timeout 0 0
line aux 0
line vty 0 4
 exec-timeout 0 0
 password cisco
 login
!
end
```

Example C-19 *Router 7 Configuration for Lab 9-2*

```
!
version 11.2
no service password-encryption
no service udp-small-servers
no service tcp-small-servers
!
hostname R7
!
enable password sanfran
!
no ip domain-lookup
ipx routing 0000.0000.0007
!
!
interface Ethernet0
 ip address 144.254.7.7 255.255.255.0
 ipx network 70
!
interface Ethernet1
 ip address 10.0.0.7 255.0.0.0
 media-type 10BaseT
!
interface ATM0
 no ip address
!
interface ATM0.1 multipoint
 ip address 144.254.100.7 255.255.255.0
 atm pvc 171 0 171 aal5snap
 atm pvc 172 0 172 aal5snap
 atm pvc 173 0 173 aal5snap
 atm pvc 174 0 174 aal5snap
 atm pvc 175 0 175 aal5snap
```

Example C-19 *Router 7 Configuration for Lab 9-2 (Continued)*

```
 atm pvc 176 0 176 aal5snap
 atm pvc 178 0 178 aal5snap
 atm pvc 179 0 179 aal5snap
 map-group ipPvc
 map-group ipxPvc
 ipx network 100
!
interface FastEthernet0
 no ip address
 shutdown
!
router igrp 100
 network 144.254.0.0
!
no ip classless
!
map-list ipPvc
 ip 144.254.100.1 atm-vc 171 broadcast
 ip 144.254.100.2 atm-vc 172 broadcast
 ip 144.254.100.3 atm-vc 173 broadcast
 ip 144.254.100.4 atm-vc 174 broadcast
 ip 144.254.100.5 atm-vc 175 broadcast
 ip 144.254.100.6 atm-vc 176 broadcast
 ip 144.254.100.8 atm-vc 178 broadcast
 ip 144.254.100.9 atm-vc 179 broadcast
!
map-list ipxPvc
 ipx 100.0000.0000.0001 atm-vc 171 broadcast
 ipx 100.0000.0000.0002 atm-vc 172 broadcast
 ipx 100.0000.0000.0003 atm-vc 173 broadcast
 ipx 100.0000.0000.0004 atm-vc 174 broadcast
 ipx 100.0000.0000.0005 atm-vc 175 broadcast
 ipx 100.0000.0000.0006 atm-vc 176 broadcast
 ipx 100.0000.0000.0008 atm-vc 178 broadcast
 ipx 100.0000.0000.0009 atm-vc 179 broadcast
!
line con 0
 exec-timeout 0 0
line aux 0
line vty 0 4
 exec-timeout 0 0
 password cisco
 login
!
end
```

Example C-20 *Router 8 Configuration for Lab 9-2*

```
!
version 11.2
```

Example C-20 *Router 8 Configuration for Lab 9-2 (Continued)*

```
no service password-encryption
no service udp-small-servers
no service tcp-small-servers
!
hostname R8
!
enable password sanfran
!
no ip domain-lookup
ipx routing 0000.0000.0008
!
!
interface Ethernet0
 ip address 144.254.8.8 255.255.255.0
 ipx network 80
!
interface Ethernet1
 ip address 10.0.0.8 255.0.0.0
 media-type 10BaseT
!
interface ATM0
 no ip address
!
interface ATM0.1 multipoint
 ip address 144.254.100.8 255.255.255.0
 atm pvc 181 0 181 aal5snap
 atm pvc 182 0 182 aal5snap
 atm pvc 183 0 183 aal5snap
 atm pvc 184 0 184 aal5snap
 atm pvc 185 0 185 aal5snap
 atm pvc 186 0 186 aal5snap
 atm pvc 187 0 187 aal5snap
 atm pvc 189 0 189 aal5snap
 map-group ipPvc
 map-group ipxPvc
 ipx network 100
!
interface FastEthernet0
 no ip address
 shutdown
!
router igrp 100
 network 144.254.0.0
!
no ip classless
!
map-list ipPvc
 ip 144.254.100.1 atm-vc 181 broadcast
 ip 144.254.100.2 atm-vc 182 broadcast
 ip 144.254.100.3 atm-vc 183 broadcast
```

Example C-20 *Router 8 Configuration for Lab 9-2 (Continued)*

```
 ip 144.254.100.4 atm-vc 184 broadcast
 ip 144.254.100.5 atm-vc 185 broadcast
 ip 144.254.100.6 atm-vc 186 broadcast
 ip 144.254.100.7 atm-vc 187 broadcast
 ip 144.254.100.9 atm-vc 189 broadcast
!
map-list ipxPvc
 ipx 100.0000.0000.0001 atm-vc 181 broadcast
 ipx 100.0000.0000.0002 atm-vc 182 broadcast
 ipx 100.0000.0000.0003 atm-vc 183 broadcast
 ipx 100.0000.0000.0004 atm-vc 184 broadcast
 ipx 100.0000.0000.0005 atm-vc 185 broadcast
 ipx 100.0000.0000.0006 atm-vc 186 broadcast
 ipx 100.0000.0000.0007 atm-vc 187 broadcast
 ipx 100.0000.0000.0009 atm-vc 189 broadcast
!
line con 0
 exec-timeout 0 0
line aux 0
line vty 0 4
 exec-timeout 0 0
 password cisco
 login
!
end
```

Example C-21 *Router 9 Configuration for Lab 9-2*

```
!
version 11.2
no service password-encryption
no service udp-small-servers
no service tcp-small-servers
!
hostname R8
!
enable password sanfran
!
no ip domain-lookup
ipx routing 0000.0000.0008
!
!
interface Ethernet0
 ip address 144.254.9.9 255.255.255.0
 ipx network 90
!
interface Ethernet1
 ip address 10.0.0.9 255.0.0.0
 media-type 10BaseT
!
```

continues

Example C-21 *Router 9 Configuration for Lab 9-2 (Continued)*

```
interface ATM0
 no ip address
!
interface ATM0.1 multipoint
 ip address 144.254.100.9 255.255.255.0
 atm pvc 191 0 191 aal5snap
 atm pvc 192 0 192 aal5snap
 atm pvc 193 0 193 aal5snap
 atm pvc 194 0 194 aal5snap
 atm pvc 195 0 195 aal5snap
 atm pvc 196 0 196 aal5snap
 atm pvc 197 0 197 aal5snap
 atm pvc 198 0 198 aal5snap
 map-group ipPvc
 map-group ipxPvc
 ipx network 100
!
interface FastEthernet0
 no ip address
 shutdown
!
router igrp 100
 network 144.254.0.0
!
no ip classless
!
map-list ipPvc
 ip 144.254.100.1 atm-vc 191 broadcast
 ip 144.254.100.2 atm-vc 192 broadcast
 ip 144.254.100.3 atm-vc 193 broadcast
 ip 144.254.100.4 atm-vc 194 broadcast
 ip 144.254.100.5 atm-vc 195 broadcast
 ip 144.254.100.6 atm-vc 196 broadcast
 ip 144.254.100.7 atm-vc 197 broadcast
 ip 144.254.100.8 atm-vc 198 broadcast
!
map-list ipxPvc
 ipx 100.0000.0000.0001 atm-vc 191 broadcast
 ipx 100.0000.0000.0002 atm-vc 192 broadcast
 ipx 100.0000.0000.0003 atm-vc 193 broadcast
 ipx 100.0000.0000.0004 atm-vc 194 broadcast
 ipx 100.0000.0000.0005 atm-vc 195 broadcast
 ipx 100.0000.0000.0006 atm-vc 196 broadcast
 ipx 100.0000.0000.0007 atm-vc 197 broadcast
 ipx 100.0000.0000.0008 atm-vc 198 broadcast
!
line con 0
 exec-timeout 0 0
line aux 0
line vty 0 4
```

Example C-21 *Router 9 Configuration for Lab 9-2 (Continued)*

```
 exec-timeout 0 0
 password cisco
 login
!
end
```

Solutions to Lab 9-3: Configuring SVCs on Cisco 4500 Routers

Examples C-22 through C-30 provide the configuration solutions that satisfy all the exercises for Lab 9-3. Specifically, the exercises asked for the following:

1 Set up the signaling PVC between your router and the ingress switch (VPI=0, VCI=5).

2 On subinterface ATM 0.2, configure an AESA address, an IP address, and an IPX address, given the parameters in Table 9-12 on page 355.

3 Much like PVCs, your Layer 3 connectivity cannot work unless you map the Layer 3 addresses to the proper ATM addresses using SVCs (remember, RFC 2684 is only an encapsulation method—hence, no magic).

4 Test your connectivity. Make sure you are using the newly created SVCs, not previously created PVCs.

Example C-22 *Router 1 Configuration for Lab 9-3*

```
!
version 11.2
no service password-encryption
no service udp-small-servers
no service tcp-small-servers
!
hostname R1
!
enable password sanfran
!
no ip domain-lookup
ipx routing 0000.0000.0001
ipx maximum-paths 2
!
!
interface Ethernet0
 ip address 144.254.1.1 255.255.255.0
 ipx network 10
!
interface Ethernet1
 ip address 10.0.0.1 255.0.0.0
 media-type 10BaseT
```

continues

Example C-22 *Router 1 Configuration for Lab 9-3 (Continued)*

```
!
interface ATM0
 no ip address
 atm pvc 5 0 5 qsaal
!
interface ATM0.1 multipoint
 ip address 144.254.100.1 255.255.255.0
 atm pvc 112 0 112 aal5snap
 atm pvc 113 0 113 aal5snap
 atm pvc 114 0 114 aal5snap
 atm pvc 115 0 115 aal5snap
 atm pvc 116 0 116 aal5snap
 atm pvc 117 0 117 aal5snap
 atm pvc 118 0 118 aal5snap
 atm pvc 119 0 119 aal5snap
 map-group ipPvc
 map-group ipxPvc
 ipx network 100
!
interface ATM0.2 multipoint
 ip address 144.254.200.1 255.255.255.0
 atm nsap-address 11.111100000000000000000000.000000000000.00
 map-group ipSvc
 map-group ipxSvc
 ipx network 200
!
interface FastEthernet0
 no ip address
 shutdown
!
router igrp 100
 network 144.254.0.0
!
no ip classless
!
map-list ipPvc
 ip 144.254.100.2 atm-vc 112 broadcast
 ip 144.254.100.3 atm-vc 113 broadcast
 ip 144.254.100.4 atm-vc 114 broadcast
 ip 144.254.100.5 atm-vc 115 broadcast
 ip 144.254.100.6 atm-vc 116 broadcast
 ip 144.254.100.7 atm-vc 117 broadcast
 ip 144.254.100.8 atm-vc 118 broadcast
 ip 144.254.100.9 atm-vc 119 broadcast
!
map-list ipxPvc
 ipx 100.0000.0000.0002 atm-vc 112 broadcast
 ipx 100.0000.0000.0003 atm-vc 113 broadcast
 ipx 100.0000.0000.0004 atm-vc 114 broadcast
 ipx 100.0000.0000.0005 atm-vc 115 broadcast
```

Example C-22 *Router 1 Configuration for Lab 9-3 (Continued)*

```
 ipx 100.0000.0000.0006 atm-vc 116 broadcast
 ipx 100.0000.0000.0007 atm-vc 117 broadcast
 ipx 100.0000.0000.0008 atm-vc 118 broadcast
 ipx 100.0000.0000.0009 atm-vc 119 broadcast
!
map-list ipSvc
 ip 144.254.200.1 atm-nsap 11.11110000000000000000000.000000000000.00 broadcast
 ip 144.254.200.2 atm-nsap 22.22220000000000000000000.000000000000.00 broadcast
 ip 144.254.200.3 atm-nsap 33.33330000000000000000000.000000000000.00 broadcast
 ip 144.254.200.4 atm-nsap 44.44440000000000000000000.000000000000.00 broadcast
 ip 144.254.200.5 atm-nsap 55.55550000000000000000000.000000000000.00 broadcast
 ip 144.254.200.6 atm-nsap 66.66660000000000000000000.000000000000.00 broadcast
 ip 144.254.200.7 atm-nsap 77.77770000000000000000000.000000000000.00 broadcast
 ip 144.254.200.8 atm-nsap 88.88880000000000000000000.000000000000.00 broadcast
 ip 144.254.200.9 atm-nsap 99.99990000000000000000000.000000000000.00 broadcast
!
map-list ipxSvc
 ipx 200.0000.0000.0001 atm-nsap 11.11110000000000000000000.000000000000.00
  broadcast
 ipx 200.0000.0000.0002 atm-nsap 22.22220000000000000000000.000000000000.00
  broadcast
 ipx 200.0000.0000.0003 atm-nsap 33.33330000000000000000000.000000000000.00
  broadcast
 ipx 200.0000.0000.0004 atm-nsap 44.44440000000000000000000.000000000000.00
  broadcast
 ipx 200.0000.0000.0005 atm-nsap 55.55550000000000000000000.000000000000.00
  broadcast
 ipx 200.0000.0000.0006 atm-nsap 66.66660000000000000000000.000000000000.00
  broadcast
 ipx 200.0000.0000.0007 atm-nsap 77.77770000000000000000000.000000000000.00
  broadcast
 ipx 200.0000.0000.0008 atm-nsap 88.88880000000000000000000.000000000000.00
  broadcast
 ipx 200.0000.0000.0009 atm-nsap 99.99990000000000000000000.000000000000.00
  broadcast
!
line con 0
 exec-timeout 0 0
line aux 0
line vty 0 4
 exec-timeout 0 0
 password cisco
 login
!
end
```

Example C-23 *Router 2 Configuration for Lab 9-3*

```
!
version 11.2
```

Example C-23 *Router 2 Configuration for Lab 9-3 (Continued)*

```
no service password-encryption
no service udp-small-servers
no service tcp-small-servers
!
hostname R2
!
enable password sanfran
!
no ip domain-lookup
ipx routing 0000.0000.0002
ipx maximum-paths 2
!
!
interface Ethernet0
 ip address 144.254.2.2 255.255.255.0
 ipx network 20
!
interface Ethernet1
 ip address 10.0.0.2 255.0.0.0
 media-type 10BaseT
!
interface ATM0
 no ip address
 atm pvc 5 0 5 qsaal
!
interface ATM0.1 multipoint
 ip address 144.254.100.2 255.255.255.0
 atm pvc 121 0 121 aal5snap
 atm pvc 123 0 123 aal5snap
 atm pvc 124 0 124 aal5snap
 atm pvc 125 0 125 aal5snap
 atm pvc 126 0 126 aal5snap
 atm pvc 127 0 127 aal5snap
 atm pvc 128 0 128 aal5snap
 atm pvc 129 0 129 aal5snap
 map-group ipPvc
 map-group ipxPvc
 ipx network 100
!
interface ATM0.2 multipoint
 ip address 144.254.200.2 255.255.255.0
 atm nsap-address 22.222200000000000000000000.000000000000.00
 map-group ipSvc
 map-group ipxSvc
 ipx network 200
!
interface FastEthernet0
 no ip address
 shutdown
!
```

Example C-23   *Router 2 Configuration for Lab 9-3 (Continued)*

```
router igrp 100
 network 144.254.0.0
!
no ip classless
!
map-list ipPvc
 ip 144.254.100.1 atm-vc 121 broadcast
 ip 144.254.100.3 atm-vc 123 broadcast
 ip 144.254.100.4 atm-vc 124 broadcast
 ip 144.254.100.5 atm-vc 125 broadcast
 ip 144.254.100.6 atm-vc 126 broadcast
 ip 144.254.100.7 atm-vc 127 broadcast
 ip 144.254.100.8 atm-vc 128 broadcast
 ip 144.254.100.9 atm-vc 129 broadcast
!
map-list ipxPvc
 ipx 100.0000.0000.0001 atm-vc 121 broadcast
 ipx 100.0000.0000.0003 atm-vc 123 broadcast
 ipx 100.0000.0000.0004 atm-vc 124 broadcast
 ipx 100.0000.0000.0005 atm-vc 125 broadcast
 ipx 100.0000.0000.0006 atm-vc 126 broadcast
 ipx 100.0000.0000.0007 atm-vc 127 broadcast
 ipx 100.0000.0000.0008 atm-vc 128 broadcast
 ipx 100.0000.0000.0009 atm-vc 129 broadcast
!
map-list ipSvc
 ip 144.254.200.1 atm-nsap 11.11110000000000000000000.000000000000.00 broadcast
 ip 144.254.200.2 atm-nsap 22.22220000000000000000000.000000000000.00 broadcast
 ip 144.254.200.3 atm-nsap 33.33330000000000000000000.000000000000.00 broadcast
 ip 144.254.200.4 atm-nsap 44.44440000000000000000000.000000000000.00 broadcast
 ip 144.254.200.5 atm-nsap 55.55550000000000000000000.000000000000.00 broadcast
 ip 144.254.200.6 atm-nsap 66.66660000000000000000000.000000000000.00 broadcast
 ip 144.254.200.7 atm-nsap 77.77770000000000000000000.000000000000.00 broadcast
 ip 144.254.200.8 atm-nsap 88.88880000000000000000000.000000000000.00 broadcast
 ip 144.254.200.9 atm-nsap 99.99990000000000000000000.000000000000.00 broadcast
!
map-list ipxSvc
 ipx 200.0000.0000.0001 atm-nsap 11.11110000000000000000000.000000000000.00
  broadcast
 ipx 200.0000.0000.0002 atm-nsap 22.22220000000000000000000.000000000000.00
  broadcast
 ipx 200.0000.0000.0003 atm-nsap 33.33330000000000000000000.000000000000.00
  broadcast
 ipx 200.0000.0000.0004 atm-nsap 44.44440000000000000000000.000000000000.00
  broadcast
 ipx 200.0000.0000.0005 atm-nsap 55.55550000000000000000000.000000000000.00
  broadcast
 ipx 200.0000.0000.0006 atm-nsap 66.66660000000000000000000.000000000000.00
  broadcast
 ipx 200.0000.0000.0007 atm-nsap 77.77770000000000000000000.000000000000.00
```

continues

Lab 9-3 Solution

Example C-23 *Router 2 Configuration for Lab 9-3 (Continued)*

```
  broadcast
 ipx 200.0000.0000.0008 atm-nsap 88.88880000000000000000000000.000000000000.00
  broadcast
 ipx 200.0000.0000.0009 atm-nsap 99.99990000000000000000000000.000000000000.00
  broadcast
!
!
line con 0
 exec-timeout 0 0
line aux 0
line vty 0 4
 exec-timeout 0 0
 password cisco
 login
!
end
```

Example C-24 *Router 3 Configuration for Lab 9-3*

```
!
version 11.2
no service password-encryption
no service udp-small-servers
no service tcp-small-servers
!
hostname R3
!
enable password sanfran
!
no ip domain-lookup
ipx routing 0000.0000.0003
ipx maximum-paths 2
!
!
interface Ethernet0
 ip address 144.254.3.3 255.255.255.0
 ipx network 30
!
interface Ethernet1
 ip address 10.0.0.3 255.0.0.0
 media-type 10BaseT
!
interface ATM0
 no ip address
 atm pvc 5 0 5 qsaal
!
interface ATM0.1 multipoint
 ip address 144.254.100.3 255.255.255.0
 atm pvc 131 0 131 aal5snap
 atm pvc 132 0 132 aal5snap
```

Example C-24 *Router 3 Configuration for Lab 9-3 (Continued)*

```
 atm pvc 133 0 133 aal5snap
 atm pvc 134 0 134 aal5snap
 atm pvc 135 0 135 aal5snap
 atm pvc 136 0 136 aal5snap
 atm pvc 137 0 137 aal5snap
 atm pvc 138 0 138 aal5snap
 atm pvc 139 0 139 aal5snap
 map-group ipPvc
 map-group ipxPvc
 ipx network 100
!
interface ATM0.2 multipoint
 ip address 144.254.200.3 255.255.255.0
 atm nsap-address 33.333300000000000000000000.000000000000.00
 map-group ipSvc
 map-group ipxSvc
 ipx network 200
!
interface FastEthernet0
 no ip address
 shutdown
!
router igrp 100
 network 144.254.0.0
!
no ip classless
!
map-list ipPvc
 ip 144.254.100.1 atm-vc 131 broadcast
 ip 144.254.100.2 atm-vc 132 broadcast
 ip 144.254.100.4 atm-vc 134 broadcast
 ip 144.254.100.5 atm-vc 135 broadcast
 ip 144.254.100.6 atm-vc 136 broadcast
 ip 144.254.100.7 atm-vc 137 broadcast
 ip 144.254.100.8 atm-vc 138 broadcast
 ip 144.254.100.9 atm-vc 139 broadcast
!
map-list ipxPvc
 ipx 100.0000.0000.0001 atm-vc 131 broadcast
 ipx 100.0000.0000.0002 atm-vc 132 broadcast
 ipx 100.0000.0000.0004 atm-vc 134 broadcast
 ipx 100.0000.0000.0005 atm-vc 135 broadcast
 ipx 100.0000.0000.0006 atm-vc 136 broadcast
 ipx 100.0000.0000.0007 atm-vc 137 broadcast
 ipx 100.0000.0000.0008 atm-vc 138 broadcast
 ipx 100.0000.0000.0009 atm-vc 139 broadcast
!
map-list ipSvc
 ip 144.254.200.1 atm-nsap 11.111100000000000000000000.000000000000.00 broadcast
 ip 144.254.200.2 atm-nsap 22.222200000000000000000000.000000000000.00 broadcast
```

continues

Lab 9-3 Solution

Example C-24 *Router 3 Configuration for Lab 9-3 (Continued)*

```
 ip 144.254.200.3 atm-nsap 33.33330000000000000000000.000000000000.00 broadcast
 ip 144.254.200.4 atm-nsap 44.44440000000000000000000.000000000000.00 broadcast
 ip 144.254.200.5 atm-nsap 55.55550000000000000000000.000000000000.00 broadcast
 ip 144.254.200.6 atm-nsap 66.66660000000000000000000.000000000000.00 broadcast
 ip 144.254.200.7 atm-nsap 77.77770000000000000000000.000000000000.00 broadcast
 ip 144.254.200.8 atm-nsap 88.88880000000000000000000.000000000000.00 broadcast
 ip 144.254.200.9 atm-nsap 99.99990000000000000000000.000000000000.00 broadcast
!
map-list ipxSvc
 ipx 200.0000.0000.0001 atm-nsap 11.11110000000000000000000.000000000000.00
  broadcast
 ipx 200.0000.0000.0002 atm-nsap 22.22220000000000000000000.000000000000.00
  broadcast
 ipx 200.0000.0000.0003 atm-nsap 33.33330000000000000000000.000000000000.00
  broadcast
 ipx 200.0000.0000.0004 atm-nsap 44.44440000000000000000000.000000000000.00
  broadcast
 ipx 200.0000.0000.0005 atm-nsap 55.55550000000000000000000.000000000000.00
  broadcast
 ipx 200.0000.0000.0006 atm-nsap 66.66660000000000000000000.000000000000.00
  broadcast
 ipx 200.0000.0000.0007 atm-nsap 77.77770000000000000000000.000000000000.00
  broadcast
 ipx 200.0000.0000.0008 atm-nsap 88.88880000000000000000000.000000000000.00
  broadcast
 ipx 200.0000.0000.0009 atm-nsap 99.99990000000000000000000.000000000000.00
  broadcast
!
line con 0
 exec-timeout 0 0
line aux 0
line vty 0 4
 password cisco
 login
!
end
```

Example C-25 *Router 4 Configuration for Lab 9-3*

```
!
version 11.2
no service password-encryption
no service udp-small-servers
no service tcp-small-servers
!
hostname R4
!
enable password sanfran
!
no ip domain-lookup
```

Example C-25 *Router 4 Configuration for Lab 9-3 (Continued)*

```
ipx routing 0000.0000.0004
ipx maximum-paths 2
!
!
interface Ethernet0
 ip address 144.254.4.4 255.255.255.0
 ipx network 40
!
interface Ethernet1
 ip address 10.0.0.4 255.0.0.0
 media-type 10BaseT
!
interface ATM0
 no ip address
 atm pvc 5 0 5 qsaal
!
interface ATM0.1 multipoint
 ip address 144.254.100.4 255.255.255.0
 atm pvc 141 0 141 aal5snap
 atm pvc 142 0 142 aal5snap
 atm pvc 143 0 143 aal5snap
 atm pvc 145 0 145 aal5snap
 atm pvc 146 0 146 aal5snap
 atm pvc 147 0 147 aal5snap
 atm pvc 148 0 148 aal5snap
 atm pvc 149 0 149 aal5snap
 map-group ipPvc
 map-group ipxPvc
 ipx network 100
!
interface ATM0.2 multipoint
 ip address 144.254.200.4 255.255.255.0
 atm nsap-address 44.444400000000000000000000.000000000000.00
 map-group ipSvc
 map-group ipxSvc
 ipx network 200
!
interface FastEthernet0
 no ip address
 shutdown
!
router igrp 100
 network 144.254.0.0
!
no ip classless
!
map-list ipPvc
 ip 144.254.100.1 atm-vc 141 broadcast
 ip 144.254.100.2 atm-vc 142 broadcast
 ip 144.254.100.3 atm-vc 143 broadcast
```

continues

Example C-25 *Router 4 Configuration for Lab 9-3 (Continued)*

```
 ip 144.254.100.5 atm-vc 145 broadcast
 ip 144.254.100.6 atm-vc 146 broadcast
 ip 144.254.100.7 atm-vc 147 broadcast
 ip 144.254.100.8 atm-vc 148 broadcast
 ip 144.254.100.9 atm-vc 149 broadcast
!
map-list ipxPvc
 ipx 100.0000.0000.0001 atm-vc 141 broadcast
 ipx 100.0000.0000.0002 atm-vc 142 broadcast
 ipx 100.0000.0000.0003 atm-vc 143 broadcast
 ipx 100.0000.0000.0005 atm-vc 145 broadcast
 ipx 100.0000.0000.0006 atm-vc 146 broadcast
 ipx 100.0000.0000.0007 atm-vc 147 broadcast
 ipx 100.0000.0000.0008 atm-vc 148 broadcast
 ipx 100.0000.0000.0009 atm-vc 149 broadcast
!
map-list ipSvc
 ip 144.254.200.1 atm-nsap 11.11110000000000000000000.000000000000.00 broadcast
 ip 144.254.200.2 atm-nsap 22.22220000000000000000000.000000000000.00 broadcast
 ip 144.254.200.3 atm-nsap 33.33330000000000000000000.000000000000.00 broadcast
 ip 144.254.200.4 atm-nsap 44.44440000000000000000000.000000000000.00 broadcast
 ip 144.254.200.5 atm-nsap 55.55550000000000000000000.000000000000.00 broadcast
 ip 144.254.200.6 atm-nsap 66.66660000000000000000000.000000000000.00 broadcast
 ip 144.254.200.7 atm-nsap 77.77770000000000000000000.000000000000.00 broadcast
 ip 144.254.200.8 atm-nsap 88.88880000000000000000000.000000000000.00 broadcast
 ip 144.254.200.9 atm-nsap 99.99990000000000000000000.000000000000.00 broadcast
!
map-list ipxSvc
 ipx 200.0000.0000.0001 atm-nsap 11.11110000000000000000000.000000000000.00
  broadcast
 ipx 200.0000.0000.0002 atm-nsap 22.22220000000000000000000.000000000000.00
  broadcast
 ipx 200.0000.0000.0003 atm-nsap 33.33330000000000000000000.000000000000.00
  broadcast
 ipx 200.0000.0000.0004 atm-nsap 44.44440000000000000000000.000000000000.00
  broadcast
 ipx 200.0000.0000.0005 atm-nsap 55.55550000000000000000000.000000000000.00
  broadcast
 ipx 200.0000.0000.0006 atm-nsap 66.66660000000000000000000.000000000000.00
  broadcast
 ipx 200.0000.0000.0007 atm-nsap 77.77770000000000000000000.000000000000.00
  broadcast
 ipx 200.0000.0000.0008 atm-nsap 88.88880000000000000000000.000000000000.00
  broadcast
 ipx 200.0000.0000.0009 atm-nsap 99.99990000000000000000000.000000000000.00
  broadcast
!
!
line con 0
 exec-timeout 0 0
```

Example C-25 *Router 4 Configuration for Lab 9-3 (Continued)*

```
line aux 0
line vty 0 4
 exec-timeout 0 0
 password cisco
 login
!
end
```

Example C-26 *Router 5 Configuration for Lab 9-3*

```
!
version 11.2
no service password-encryption
no service udp-small-servers
no service tcp-small-servers
!
hostname R5
!
enable password sanfran
!
no ip domain-lookup
ipx routing 0000.0000.0005
ipx maximum-paths 2
!
!
interface Ethernet0
 ip address 144.254.5.5 255.255.255.0
 ipx network 50
!
interface Ethernet1
 ip address 10.0.0.5 255.0.0.0
 media-type 10BaseT
!
interface ATM0
 no ip address
 atm pvc 5 0 5 qsaal
!
interface ATM0.1 multipoint
 ip address 144.254.100.5 255.255.255.0
 atm pvc 151 0 151 aal5snap
 atm pvc 152 0 152 aal5snap
 atm pvc 153 0 153 aal5snap
 atm pvc 154 0 154 aal5snap
 atm pvc 156 0 156 aal5snap
 atm pvc 157 0 157 aal5snap
 atm pvc 158 0 158 aal5snap
 atm pvc 159 0 159 aal5snap
 map-group ipPvc
 map-group ipxPvc
 ipx network 100
```

continues

Example C-26 *Router 5 Configuration for Lab 9-3 (Continued)*

```
!
interface ATM0.2 multipoint
 ip address 144.254.200.5 255.255.255.0
 atm nsap-address 55.55550000000000000000000.000000000000.00
 map-group ipSvc
 map-group ipxSvc
 ipx network 200
!
interface FastEthernet0
 no ip address
 shutdown
!
router igrp 100
 network 144.254.0.0
!
no ip classless
!
map-list ipPvc
 ip 144.254.100.1 atm-vc 151 broadcast
 ip 144.254.100.2 atm-vc 152 broadcast
 ip 144.254.100.3 atm-vc 153 broadcast
 ip 144.254.100.4 atm-vc 154 broadcast
 ip 144.254.100.6 atm-vc 156 broadcast
 ip 144.254.100.7 atm-vc 157 broadcast
 ip 144.254.100.8 atm-vc 158 broadcast
 ip 144.254.100.9 atm-vc 159 broadcast
!
map-list ipxPvc
 ipx 100.0000.0000.0001 atm-vc 151 broadcast
 ipx 100.0000.0000.0002 atm-vc 152 broadcast
 ipx 100.0000.0000.0003 atm-vc 153 broadcast
 ipx 100.0000.0000.0004 atm-vc 154 broadcast
 ipx 100.0000.0000.0006 atm-vc 156 broadcast
 ipx 100.0000.0000.0007 atm-vc 157 broadcast
 ipx 100.0000.0000.0008 atm-vc 158 broadcast
 ipx 100.0000.0000.0009 atm-vc 159 broadcast
!
map-list ipSvc
 ip 144.254.200.1 atm-nsap 11.11110000000000000000000.000000000000.00 broadcast
 ip 144.254.200.2 atm-nsap 22.22220000000000000000000.000000000000.00 broadcast
 ip 144.254.200.3 atm-nsap 33.33330000000000000000000.000000000000.00 broadcast
 ip 144.254.200.4 atm-nsap 44.44440000000000000000000.000000000000.00 broadcast
 ip 144.254.200.5 atm-nsap 55.55550000000000000000000.000000000000.00 broadcast
 ip 144.254.200.6 atm-nsap 66.66660000000000000000000.000000000000.00 broadcast
 ip 144.254.200.7 atm-nsap 77.77770000000000000000000.000000000000.00 broadcast
 ip 144.254.200.8 atm-nsap 88.88880000000000000000000.000000000000.00 broadcast
 ip 144.254.200.9 atm-nsap 99.99990000000000000000000.000000000000.00 broadcast
!
map-list ipxSvc
 ipx 200.0000.0000.0001 atm-nsap 11.11110000000000000000000.000000000000.00
```

Example C-26 *Router 5 Configuration for Lab 9-3 (Continued)*

```
 broadcast
 ipx 200.0000.0000.0002 atm-nsap 22.22220000000000000000000000.000000000000.00
 broadcast
 ipx 200.0000.0000.0003 atm-nsap 33.33330000000000000000000000.000000000000.00
 broadcast
 ipx 200.0000.0000.0004 atm-nsap 44.44440000000000000000000000.000000000000.00
 broadcast
 ipx 200.0000.0000.0005 atm-nsap 55.55550000000000000000000000.000000000000.00
 broadcast
 ipx 200.0000.0000.0006 atm-nsap 66.66660000000000000000000000.000000000000.00
 broadcast
 ipx 200.0000.0000.0007 atm-nsap 77.77770000000000000000000000.000000000000.00
 broadcast
 ipx 200.0000.0000.0008 atm-nsap 88.88880000000000000000000000.000000000000.00
 broadcast
 ipx 200.0000.0000.0009 atm-nsap 99.99990000000000000000000000.000000000000.00
 broadcast
!
!
line con 0
 exec-timeout 0 0
line aux 0
line vty 0 4
 exec-timeout 0 0
 password cisco
 login
!
end
```

Example C-27 *Router 6 Configuration for Lab 9-3*

```
!
version 11.2
no service password-encryption
no service udp-small-servers
no service tcp-small-servers
!
hostname R6
!
enable password sanfran
!
no ip domain-lookup
ipx routing 0000.0000.0006
ipx maximum-paths 2
!
!
interface Ethernet0
 ip address 144.254.6.6 255.255.255.0
 ipx network 60
!
```

continues

Lab 9-3 Solution

Example C-27 *Router 6 Configuration for Lab 9-3 (Continued)*

```
interface Ethernet1
 ip address 10.0.0.6 255.0.0.0
 media-type 10BaseT
!
interface ATM0
 no ip address
 atm pvc 5 0 5 qsaal
!
interface ATM0.1 multipoint
 ip address 144.254.100.6 255.255.255.0
 atm pvc 161 0 161 aal5snap
 atm pvc 162 0 162 aal5snap
 atm pvc 163 0 163 aal5snap
 atm pvc 164 0 164 aal5snap
 atm pvc 165 0 165 aal5snap
 atm pvc 167 0 167 aal5snap
 atm pvc 168 0 168 aal5snap
 atm pvc 169 0 169 aal5snap
 map-group ipPvc
 map-group ipxPvc
 ipx network 100
!
interface ATM0.2 multipoint
 ip address 144.254.200.6 255.255.255.0
 atm nsap-address 66.6666000000000000000000000.000000000000.00
 map-group ipSvc
 map-group ipxSvc
 ipx network 200
!
interface FastEthernet0
 no ip address
 shutdown
!
router igrp 100
 network 144.254.0.0
!
no ip classless
!
map-list ipPvc
 ip 144.254.100.1 atm-vc 161 broadcast
 ip 144.254.100.2 atm-vc 162 broadcast
 ip 144.254.100.3 atm-vc 163 broadcast
 ip 144.254.100.4 atm-vc 164 broadcast
 ip 144.254.100.5 atm-vc 165 broadcast
 ip 144.254.100.7 atm-vc 167 broadcast
 ip 144.254.100.8 atm-vc 168 broadcast
 ip 144.254.100.9 atm-vc 169 broadcast
!
map-list ipxPvc
 ipx 100.0000.0000.0001 atm-vc 161 broadcast
```

Example C-27 *Router 6 Configuration for Lab 9-3 (Continued)*

```
 ipx 100.0000.0000.0002 atm-vc 162 broadcast
 ipx 100.0000.0000.0003 atm-vc 163 broadcast
 ipx 100.0000.0000.0004 atm-vc 164 broadcast
 ipx 100.0000.0000.0005 atm-vc 165 broadcast
 ipx 100.0000.0000.0007 atm-vc 167 broadcast
 ipx 100.0000.0000.0008 atm-vc 168 broadcast
 ipx 100.0000.0000.0009 atm-vc 169 broadcast
!
map-list ipSvc
 ip 144.254.200.1 atm-nsap 11.11110000000000000000000.000000000000.00 broadcast
 ip 144.254.200.2 atm-nsap 22.22220000000000000000000.000000000000.00 broadcast
 ip 144.254.200.3 atm-nsap 33.33330000000000000000000.000000000000.00 broadcast
 ip 144.254.200.4 atm-nsap 44.44440000000000000000000.000000000000.00 broadcast
 ip 144.254.200.5 atm-nsap 55.55550000000000000000000.000000000000.00 broadcast
 ip 144.254.200.6 atm-nsap 66.66660000000000000000000.000000000000.00 broadcast
 ip 144.254.200.7 atm-nsap 77.77770000000000000000000.000000000000.00 broadcast
 ip 144.254.200.8 atm-nsap 88.88880000000000000000000.000000000000.00 broadcast
 ip 144.254.200.9 atm-nsap 99.99990000000000000000000.000000000000.00 broadcast
!
map-list ipxSvc
 ipx 200.0000.0000.0001 atm-nsap 11.11110000000000000000000.000000000000.00
  broadcast
 ipx 200.0000.0000.0002 atm-nsap 22.22220000000000000000000.000000000000.00
  broadcast
 ipx 200.0000.0000.0003 atm-nsap 33.33330000000000000000000.000000000000.00
  broadcast
 ipx 200.0000.0000.0004 atm-nsap 44.44440000000000000000000.000000000000.00
  broadcast
 ipx 200.0000.0000.0005 atm-nsap 55.55550000000000000000000.000000000000.00
  broadcast
 ipx 200.0000.0000.0006 atm-nsap 66.66660000000000000000000.000000000000.00
  broadcast
 ipx 200.0000.0000.0007 atm-nsap 77.77770000000000000000000.000000000000.00
  broadcast
 ipx 200.0000.0000.0008 atm-nsap 88.88880000000000000000000.000000000000.00
  broadcast
 ipx 200.0000.0000.0009 atm-nsap 99.99990000000000000000000.000000000000.00
  broadcast
!
!
line con 0
 exec-timeout 0 0
line aux 0
line vty 0 4
 exec-timeout 0 0
 password cisco
 login
!
end
```

Lab 9-3 Solution

continues

Example C-28 *Router 7 Configuration for Lab 9-3*

```
!
version 11.2
no service password-encryption
no service udp-small-servers
no service tcp-small-servers
!
hostname R7
!
enable password sanfran
!
no ip domain-lookup
ipx routing 0000.0000.0007
ipx maximum-paths 2
!
!
interface Ethernet0
 ip address 144.254.7.7 255.255.255.0
 ipx network 70
!
interface Ethernet1
 ip address 10.0.0.7 255.0.0.0
 media-type 10BaseT
!
interface ATM0
 no ip address
 atm pvc 5 0 5 qsaal
!
interface ATM0.1 multipoint
 ip address 144.254.100.7 255.255.255.0
 atm pvc 171 0 171 aal5snap
 atm pvc 172 0 172 aal5snap
 atm pvc 173 0 173 aal5snap
 atm pvc 174 0 174 aal5snap
 atm pvc 175 0 175 aal5snap
 atm pvc 176 0 176 aal5snap
 atm pvc 178 0 178 aal5snap
 atm pvc 179 0 179 aal5snap
 map-group ipPvc
 map-group ipxPvc
 ipx network 100
!
interface ATM0.2 multipoint
 ip address 144.254.200.7 255.255.255.0
 atm nsap-address 77.7777000000000000000000000.000000000000.00
 map-group ipSvc
 map-group ipxSvc
 ipx network 200
!
interface FastEthernet0
 no ip address
```

Example C-28 *Router 7 Configuration for Lab 9-3 (Continued)*

```
 shutdown
!
router igrp 100
 network 144.254.0.0
!
no ip classless
!
map-list ipPvc
 ip 144.254.100.1 atm-vc 171 broadcast
 ip 144.254.100.2 atm-vc 172 broadcast
 ip 144.254.100.3 atm-vc 173 broadcast
 ip 144.254.100.4 atm-vc 174 broadcast
 ip 144.254.100.5 atm-vc 175 broadcast
 ip 144.254.100.6 atm-vc 176 broadcast
 ip 144.254.100.8 atm-vc 178 broadcast
 ip 144.254.100.9 atm-vc 179 broadcast
!
map-list ipxPvc
 ipx 100.0000.0000.0001 atm-vc 171 broadcast
 ipx 100.0000.0000.0002 atm-vc 172 broadcast
 ipx 100.0000.0000.0003 atm-vc 173 broadcast
 ipx 100.0000.0000.0004 atm-vc 174 broadcast
 ipx 100.0000.0000.0005 atm-vc 175 broadcast
 ipx 100.0000.0000.0006 atm-vc 176 broadcast
 ipx 100.0000.0000.0008 atm-vc 178 broadcast
 ipx 100.0000.0000.0009 atm-vc 179 broadcast
!
map-list ipSvc
 ip 144.254.200.1 atm-nsap 11.11110000000000000000000.000000000000.00 broadcast
 ip 144.254.200.2 atm-nsap 22.22220000000000000000000.000000000000.00 broadcast
 ip 144.254.200.3 atm-nsap 33.33330000000000000000000.000000000000.00 broadcast
 ip 144.254.200.4 atm-nsap 44.44440000000000000000000.000000000000.00 broadcast
 ip 144.254.200.5 atm-nsap 55.55550000000000000000000.000000000000.00 broadcast
 ip 144.254.200.6 atm-nsap 66.66660000000000000000000.000000000000.00 broadcast
 ip 144.254.200.7 atm-nsap 77.77770000000000000000000.000000000000.00 broadcast
 ip 144.254.200.8 atm-nsap 88.88880000000000000000000.000000000000.00 broadcast
 ip 144.254.200.9 atm-nsap 99.99990000000000000000000.000000000000.00 broadcast
!
map-list ipxSvc
 ipx 200.0000.0000.0001 atm-nsap 11.11110000000000000000000.000000000000.00
  broadcast
 ipx 200.0000.0000.0002 atm-nsap 22.22220000000000000000000.000000000000.00
  broadcast
 ipx 200.0000.0000.0003 atm-nsap 33.33330000000000000000000.000000000000.00
  broadcast
 ipx 200.0000.0000.0004 atm-nsap 44.44440000000000000000000.000000000000.00
  broadcast
 ipx 200.0000.0000.0005 atm-nsap 55.55550000000000000000000.000000000000.00
  broadcast
 ipx 200.0000.0000.0006 atm-nsap 66.66660000000000000000000.000000000000.00
```

continues

Example C-28 *Router 7 Configuration for Lab 9-3 (Continued)*

```
 broadcast
ipx 200.0000.0000.0007 atm-nsap 77.7777000000000000000000000.000000000000.00
 broadcast
ipx 200.0000.0000.0008 atm-nsap 88.8888000000000000000000000.000000000000.00
 broadcast
ipx 200.0000.0000.0009 atm-nsap 99.9999000000000000000000000.000000000000.00
 broadcast
!
line con 0
 exec-timeout 0 0
line aux 0
line vty 0 4
 exec-timeout 0 0
 password cisco
 login
!
end
```

Example C-29 *Router 8 Configuration for Lab 9-3*

```
!
version 11.2
no service password-encryption
no service udp-small-servers
no service tcp-small-servers
!
hostname R8
!
enable password sanfran
!
no ip domain-lookup
ipx routing 0000.0000.0008
ipx maximum-paths 2
!
!
interface Ethernet0
 ip address 144.254.8.8 255.255.255.0
 ipx network 80
!
interface Ethernet1
 ip address 10.0.0.8 255.0.0.0
 media-type 10BaseT
!
interface ATM0
 no ip address
 atm pvc 5 0 5 qsaal
!
interface ATM0.1 multipoint
 ip address 144.254.100.8 255.255.255.0
 atm pvc 181 0 181 aal5snap
```

Example C-29 *Router 8 Configuration for Lab 9-3 (Continued)*

```
atm pvc 182 0 182 aal5snap
atm pvc 183 0 183 aal5snap
atm pvc 184 0 184 aal5snap
atm pvc 185 0 185 aal5snap
atm pvc 186 0 186 aal5snap
atm pvc 187 0 187 aal5snap
atm pvc 189 0 189 aal5snap
map-group ipPvc
map-group ipxPvc
ipx network 100
!
interface ATM0.2 multipoint
 ip address 144.254.200.8 255.255.255.0
 atm nsap-address 88.888800000000000000000000.000000000000.00
 map-group ipSvc
 map-group ipxSvc
 ipx network 200
!
interface FastEthernet0
 no ip address
 shutdown
!
router igrp 100
 network 144.254.0.0
!
no ip classless
!
map-list ipPvc
 ip 144.254.100.1 atm-vc 181 broadcast
 ip 144.254.100.2 atm-vc 182 broadcast
 ip 144.254.100.3 atm-vc 183 broadcast
 ip 144.254.100.4 atm-vc 184 broadcast
 ip 144.254.100.5 atm-vc 185 broadcast
 ip 144.254.100.6 atm-vc 186 broadcast
 ip 144.254.100.7 atm-vc 187 broadcast
 ip 144.254.100.9 atm-vc 189 broadcast
!
map-list ipxPvc
 ipx 100.0000.0000.0001 atm-vc 181 broadcast
 ipx 100.0000.0000.0002 atm-vc 182 broadcast
 ipx 100.0000.0000.0003 atm-vc 183 broadcast
 ipx 100.0000.0000.0004 atm-vc 184 broadcast
 ipx 100.0000.0000.0005 atm-vc 185 broadcast
 ipx 100.0000.0000.0006 atm-vc 186 broadcast
 ipx 100.0000.0000.0007 atm-vc 187 broadcast
 ipx 100.0000.0000.0009 atm-vc 189 broadcast
!
map-list ipSvc
 ip 144.254.200.1 atm-nsap 11.111100000000000000000000.000000000000.00 broadcast
 ip 144.254.200.2 atm-nsap 22.222200000000000000000000.000000000000.00 broadcast
```

continues

Lab 9-3 Solution

Example C-29 *Router 8 Configuration for Lab 9-3 (Continued)*

```
 ip 144.254.200.3 atm-nsap 33.33330000000000000000000.000000000000.00 broadcast
 ip 144.254.200.4 atm-nsap 44.44440000000000000000000.000000000000.00 broadcast
 ip 144.254.200.5 atm-nsap 55.55550000000000000000000.000000000000.00 broadcast
 ip 144.254.200.6 atm-nsap 66.66660000000000000000000.000000000000.00 broadcast
 ip 144.254.200.7 atm-nsap 77.77770000000000000000000.000000000000.00 broadcast
 ip 144.254.200.8 atm-nsap 88.88880000000000000000000.000000000000.00 broadcast
 ip 144.254.200.9 atm-nsap 99.99990000000000000000000.000000000000.00 broadcast
!
map-list ipxSvc
 ipx 200.0000.0000.0001 atm-nsap 11.11110000000000000000000.000000000000.00
  broadcast
 ipx 200.0000.0000.0002 atm-nsap 22.22220000000000000000000.000000000000.00
  broadcast
 ipx 200.0000.0000.0003 atm-nsap 33.33330000000000000000000.000000000000.00
  broadcast
 ipx 200.0000.0000.0004 atm-nsap 44.44440000000000000000000.000000000000.00
  broadcast
 ipx 200.0000.0000.0005 atm-nsap 55.55550000000000000000000.000000000000.00
  broadcast
 ipx 200.0000.0000.0006 atm-nsap 66.66660000000000000000000.000000000000.00
  broadcast
 ipx 200.0000.0000.0007 atm-nsap 77.77770000000000000000000.000000000000.00
  broadcast
 ipx 200.0000.0000.0008 atm-nsap 88.88880000000000000000000.000000000000.00
  broadcast
 ipx 200.0000.0000.0009 atm-nsap 99.99990000000000000000000.000000000000.00
  broadcast
!
line con 0
 exec-timeout 0 0
line aux 0
line vty 0 4
 exec-timeout 0 0
 password cisco
 login
!
end
```

Example C-30 *Router 9 Configuration for Lab 9-3*

```
!
version 11.2
no service password-encryption
no service udp-small-servers
no service tcp-small-servers
!
hostname R9
!
enable password sanfran
!
```

Example C-30 *Router 9 Configuration for Lab 9-3 (Continued)*

```
no ip domain-lookup
ipx routing 0000.0000.0009
ipx maximum-paths 2
!
!
interface Ethernet0
 ip address 144.254.9.9 255.255.255.0
 ipx network 90
!
interface Ethernet1
 ip address 10.0.0.9 255.0.0.0
 media-type 10BaseT
!
interface ATM0
 no ip address
 atm pvc 5 0 5 qsaal
!
interface ATM0.1 multipoint
 ip address 144.254.100.9 255.255.255.0
 atm pvc 191 0 191 aal5snap
 atm pvc 192 0 192 aal5snap
 atm pvc 193 0 193 aal5snap
 atm pvc 194 0 194 aal5snap
 atm pvc 195 0 195 aal5snap
 atm pvc 196 0 196 aal5snap
 atm pvc 197 0 197 aal5snap
 atm pvc 198 0 198 aal5snap
 map-group ipPvc
 map-group ipxPvc
 ipx network 100
!
interface ATM0.2 multipoint
 ip address 144.254.200.9 255.255.255.0
 atm nsap-address 99.999900000000000000000000.000000000000.00
 map-group ipSvc
 map-group ipxSvc
 ipx network 200
!
interface FastEthernet0
 no ip address
 shutdown
!
router igrp 100
 network 144.254.0.0
!
no ip classless
!
map-list ipPvc
 ip 144.254.100.1 atm-vc 191 broadcast
 ip 144.254.100.2 atm-vc 192 broadcast
```

continues

Example C-30 *Router 9 Configuration for Lab 9-3 (Continued)*

```
 ip 144.254.100.3 atm-vc 193 broadcast
 ip 144.254.100.4 atm-vc 194 broadcast
 ip 144.254.100.5 atm-vc 195 broadcast
 ip 144.254.100.6 atm-vc 196 broadcast
 ip 144.254.100.7 atm-vc 197 broadcast
 ip 144.254.100.8 atm-vc 198 broadcast
!
map-list ipxPvc
 ipx 100.0000.0000.0001 atm-vc 191 broadcast
 ipx 100.0000.0000.0002 atm-vc 192 broadcast
 ipx 100.0000.0000.0003 atm-vc 193 broadcast
 ipx 100.0000.0000.0004 atm-vc 194 broadcast
 ipx 100.0000.0000.0005 atm-vc 195 broadcast
 ipx 100.0000.0000.0006 atm-vc 196 broadcast
 ipx 100.0000.0000.0007 atm-vc 197 broadcast
 ipx 100.0000.0000.0008 atm-vc 198 broadcast
!
map-list ipSvc
 ip 144.254.200.1 atm-nsap 11.11110000000000000000000.000000000000.00 broadcast
 ip 144.254.200.2 atm-nsap 22.22220000000000000000000.000000000000.00 broadcast
 ip 144.254.200.3 atm-nsap 33.33330000000000000000000.000000000000.00 broadcast
 ip 144.254.200.4 atm-nsap 44.44440000000000000000000.000000000000.00 broadcast
 ip 144.254.200.5 atm-nsap 55.55550000000000000000000.000000000000.00 broadcast
 ip 144.254.200.6 atm-nsap 66.66660000000000000000000.000000000000.00 broadcast
 ip 144.254.200.7 atm-nsap 77.77770000000000000000000.000000000000.00 broadcast
 ip 144.254.200.8 atm-nsap 88.88880000000000000000000.000000000000.00 broadcast
 ip 144.254.200.9 atm-nsap 99.99990000000000000000000.000000000000.00 broadcast
!
map-list ipxSvc
 ipx 200.0000.0000.0001 atm-nsap 11.11110000000000000000000.000000000000.00
  broadcast
 ipx 200.0000.0000.0002 atm-nsap 22.22220000000000000000000.000000000000.00
  broadcast
 ipx 200.0000.0000.0003 atm-nsap 33.33330000000000000000000.000000000000.00
  broadcast
 ipx 200.0000.0000.0004 atm-nsap 44.44440000000000000000000.000000000000.00
  broadcast
 ipx 200.0000.0000.0005 atm-nsap 55.55550000000000000000000.000000000000.00
  broadcast
 ipx 200.0000.0000.0006 atm-nsap 66.66660000000000000000000.000000000000.00
  broadcast
 ipx 200.0000.0000.0007 atm-nsap 77.77770000000000000000000.000000000000.00
  broadcast
 ipx 200.0000.0000.0008 atm-nsap 88.88880000000000000000000.000000000000.00
  broadcast
 ipx 200.0000.0000.0009 atm-nsap 99.99990000000000000000000.000000000000.00
  broadcast
!
!
line con 0
```

Example C-30 *Router 9 Configuration for Lab 9-3 (Continued)*

```
 exec-timeout 0 0
line aux 0
line vty 0 4
 exec-timeout 0 0
 password cisco
 login
 !
end
```

Solutions to Lab 9-4: Configuring RFC 2225 (Classical IP) on the Router

Examples C-31 through C-39 provide the configuration solutions that satisfy all the exercises for Lab 9-4. Specifically, the exercises asked for the following:

1 Remove the **ip map-group** statement from ATM 0.2 to allow for dynamic mapping to occur.

2 Initially, R3 is the only ARP server for the network, with all other routers set up as clients pointing themselves to R3.

3 Test your configuration and IP connectivity. Also, ensure that IPX connectivity is working as expected.

4 Implement a second redundant ARP server, R6, using Cisco's proprietary solution.

5 Verify your configuration, and test the failover capability.

Example C-31 *Router 1 Configuration for Lab 9-4*

```
!
version 11.2
no service password-encryption
no service udp-small-servers
no service tcp-small-servers
!
hostname R1
!
enable password sanfran
!
no ip domain-lookup
ipx routing 0000.0000.0001
ipx maximum-paths 2
!
!
interface Ethernet0
 ip address 144.254.1.1 255.255.255.0
 ipx network 10
!
```

continues

Lab 9-4 Solution

Example C-31 *Router 1 Configuration for Lab 9-4 (Continued)*

```
interface Ethernet1
 ip address 10.0.0.1 255.0.0.0
 media-type 10BaseT
!
interface ATM0
 no ip address
 atm pvc 5 0 5 qsaal
 atm pvc 16 0 16 ilmi
!
interface ATM0.1 multipoint
 ip address 144.254.100.1 255.255.255.0
 atm pvc 112 0 112 aal5snap inarp
 atm pvc 113 0 113 aal5snap inarp
 atm pvc 114 0 114 aal5snap inarp
 atm pvc 115 0 115 aal5snap inarp
 atm pvc 116 0 116 aal5snap inarp
 atm pvc 117 0 117 aal5snap inarp
 atm pvc 118 0 118 aal5snap inarp
 atm pvc 119 0 119 aal5snap inarp
 map-group ipxPvc
 ipx network 100
!
interface ATM0.2 multipoint
 ip address 144.254.200.1 255.255.255.0
 atm nsap-address 11.111100000000000000000000.000000000000.00
 atm classic-ip-extensions BFI
 atm arp-server nsap 66.666600000000000000000000.000000000000.00
 atm arp-server nsap 33.333300000000000000000000.000000000000.00
 map-group ipxSvc
 ipx network 200
!
interface FastEthernet0
 no ip address
 shutdown
!
router igrp 100
 network 144.254.0.0
!
no ip classless
!
!
map-list ipxPvc
 ipx 100.0000.0000.0002 atm-vc 112 broadcast
 ipx 100.0000.0000.0003 atm-vc 113 broadcast
 ipx 100.0000.0000.0004 atm-vc 114 broadcast
 ipx 100.0000.0000.0005 atm-vc 115 broadcast
 ipx 100.0000.0000.0006 atm-vc 116 broadcast
 ipx 100.0000.0000.0007 atm-vc 117 broadcast
 ipx 100.0000.0000.0008 atm-vc 118 broadcast
 ipx 100.0000.0000.0009 atm-vc 119 broadcast
```

Example C-31 *Router 1 Configuration for Lab 9-4 (Continued)*

```
!
!
map-list ipxSvc
 ipx 200.0000.0000.0001 atm-nsap 11.11110000000000000000000000.000000000000.00
  broadcast
 ipx 200.0000.0000.0002 atm-nsap 22.22220000000000000000000000.000000000000.00
  broadcast
 ipx 200.0000.0000.0003 atm-nsap 33.33330000000000000000000000.000000000000.00
  broadcast
 ipx 200.0000.0000.0004 atm-nsap 44.44440000000000000000000000.000000000000.00
  broadcast
 ipx 200.0000.0000.0005 atm-nsap 55.55550000000000000000000000.000000000000.00
  broadcast
 ipx 200.0000.0000.0006 atm-nsap 66.66660000000000000000000000.000000000000.00
  broadcast
 ipx 200.0000.0000.0007 atm-nsap 77.77770000000000000000000000.000000000000.00
  broadcast
 ipx 200.0000.0000.0008 atm-nsap 88.88880000000000000000000000.000000000000.00
  broadcast
 ipx 200.0000.0000.0009 atm-nsap 99.99990000000000000000000000.000000000000.00
  broadcast
!
!
!
!
!
line con 0
 exec-timeout 0 0
line aux 0
line vty 0 4
 exec-timeout 0 0
 password cisco
 login
!
end
```

Example C-32 *Router 2 Configuration for Lab 9-4*

```
!
version 11.2
no service password-encryption
no service udp-small-servers
no service tcp-small-servers
!
hostname R2
!
enable password sanfran
!
no ip domain-lookup
ipx routing 0000.0000.0002
```

continues

Lab 9-4 Solution

Example C-32 *Router 2 Configuration for Lab 9-4 (Continued)*

```
ipx maximum-paths 2
!
!
interface Ethernet0
 ip address 144.254.2.2 255.255.255.0
 ipx network 20
!
interface Ethernet1
 ip address 10.0.0.2 255.0.0.0
 media-type 10BaseT
!
interface ATM0
 no ip address
 atm pvc 5 0 5 qsaal
 atm pvc 16 0 16 ilmi
!
interface ATM0.1 multipoint
 ip address 144.254.100.2 255.255.255.0
 atm pvc 121 0 121 aal5snap inarp
 atm pvc 123 0 123 aal5snap inarp
 atm pvc 124 0 124 aal5snap inarp
 atm pvc 125 0 125 aal5snap inarp
 atm pvc 126 0 126 aal5snap inarp
 atm pvc 127 0 127 aal5snap inarp
 atm pvc 128 0 128 aal5snap inarp
 atm pvc 129 0 129 aal5snap inarp
 map-group ipxPvc
 ipx network 100
!
interface ATM0.2 multipoint
 ip address 144.254.200.2 255.255.255.0
 atm nsap-address 22.222200000000000000000000.000000000000.00
 atm classic-ip-extensions BFI
 atm arp-server nsap 33.333300000000000000000000.000000000000.00
 atm arp-server nsap 66.666600000000000000000000.000000000000.00
 map-group ipxSvc
 ipx network 200
!
interface FastEthernet0
 no ip address
 shutdown
!
router igrp 100
 network 144.254.0.0
!
no ip classless
!
map-list ipxPvc
 ipx 100.0000.0000.0001 atm-vc 121 broadcast
 ipx 100.0000.0000.0003 atm-vc 123 broadcast
```

Example C-32 *Router 2 Configuration for Lab 9-4 (Continued)*

```
 ipx 100.0000.0000.0004 atm-vc 124 broadcast
 ipx 100.0000.0000.0005 atm-vc 125 broadcast
 ipx 100.0000.0000.0006 atm-vc 126 broadcast
 ipx 100.0000.0000.0007 atm-vc 127 broadcast
 ipx 100.0000.0000.0008 atm-vc 128 broadcast
 ipx 100.0000.0000.0009 atm-vc 129 broadcast
 !
 !
map-list ipxSvc
 ipx 200.0000.0000.0001 atm-nsap 11.11110000000000000000000.000000000000.00
  broadcast
 ipx 200.0000.0000.0002 atm-nsap 22.22220000000000000000000.000000000000.00
  broadcast
 ipx 200.0000.0000.0003 atm-nsap 33.33330000000000000000000.000000000000.00
  broadcast
 ipx 200.0000.0000.0004 atm-nsap 44.44440000000000000000000.000000000000.00
  broadcast
 ipx 200.0000.0000.0005 atm-nsap 55.55550000000000000000000.000000000000.00
  broadcast
 ipx 200.0000.0000.0006 atm-nsap 66.66660000000000000000000.000000000000.00
  broadcast
 ipx 200.0000.0000.0007 atm-nsap 77.77770000000000000000000.000000000000.00
  broadcast
 ipx 200.0000.0000.0008 atm-nsap 88.88880000000000000000000.000000000000.00
  broadcast
 ipx 200.0000.0000.0009 atm-nsap 99.99990000000000000000000.000000000000.00
  broadcast
 !
line con 0
 exec-timeout 0 0
line aux 0
line vty 0 4
 exec-timeout 0 0
 password cisco
 login
 !
end
```

Example C-33 *Router 3 Configuration for Lab 9-4*

```
 !
version 11.2
no service password-encryption
no service udp-small-servers
no service tcp-small-servers
 !
hostname R3
 !
enable password sanfran
 !
```

continues

Example C-33 *Router 3 Configuration for Lab 9-4 (Continued)*

```
no ip domain-lookup
ipx routing 0000.0000.0003
ipx maximum-paths 2
!
!
interface Ethernet0
 ip address 144.254.3.3 255.255.255.0
 ipx network 30
!
interface Ethernet1
 ip address 10.0.0.3 255.0.0.0
 media-type 10BaseT
!
interface ATM0
 no ip address
 atm pvc 5 0 5 qsaal
 atm pvc 16 0 16 ilmi
!
interface ATM0.1 multipoint
 ip address 144.254.100.3 255.255.255.0
 atm pvc 131 0 131 aal5snap inarp
 atm pvc 132 0 132 aal5snap inarp
 atm pvc 133 0 133 aal5snap inarp
 atm pvc 134 0 134 aal5snap inarp
 atm pvc 135 0 135 aal5snap inarp
 atm pvc 136 0 136 aal5snap inarp
 atm pvc 137 0 137 aal5snap inarp
 atm pvc 138 0 138 aal5snap inarp
 atm pvc 139 0 139 aal5snap inarp
 map-group ipxPvc
 ipx network 100
!
interface ATM0.2 multipoint
 ip address 144.254.200.3 255.255.255.0
 atm nsap-address 33.33330000000000000000000.000000000000.00
 atm classic-ip-extensions BFI
 atm arp-server self
 atm arp-server nsap 66.66660000000000000000000.000000000000.00
 map-group ipxSvc
 ipx network 200
!
interface FastEthernet0
 no ip address
 shutdown
!
router igrp 100
 network 144.254.0.0
!
no ip classless
!
```

Example C-33 *Router 3 Configuration for Lab 9-4 (Continued)*

```
map-list ipxPvc
 ipx 100.0000.0000.0001 atm-vc 131 broadcast
 ipx 100.0000.0000.0002 atm-vc 132 broadcast
 ipx 100.0000.0000.0004 atm-vc 134 broadcast
 ipx 100.0000.0000.0005 atm-vc 135 broadcast
 ipx 100.0000.0000.0006 atm-vc 136 broadcast
 ipx 100.0000.0000.0007 atm-vc 137 broadcast
 ipx 100.0000.0000.0008 atm-vc 138 broadcast
 ipx 100.0000.0000.0009 atm-vc 139 broadcast
!
map-list ipxSvc
 ipx 200.0000.0000.0001 atm-nsap 11.11110000000000000000000.000000000000.00
  broadcast
 ipx 200.0000.0000.0002 atm-nsap 22.22220000000000000000000.000000000000.00
  broadcast
 ipx 200.0000.0000.0003 atm-nsap 33.33330000000000000000000.000000000000.00
  broadcast
 ipx 200.0000.0000.0004 atm-nsap 44.44440000000000000000000.000000000000.00
  broadcast
 ipx 200.0000.0000.0005 atm-nsap 55.55550000000000000000000.000000000000.00
  broadcast
 ipx 200.0000.0000.0006 atm-nsap 66.66660000000000000000000.000000000000.00
  broadcast
 ipx 200.0000.0000.0007 atm-nsap 77.77770000000000000000000.000000000000.00
  broadcast
 ipx 200.0000.0000.0008 atm-nsap 88.88880000000000000000000.000000000000.00
  broadcast
 ipx 200.0000.0000.0009 atm-nsap 99.99990000000000000000000.000000000000.00
  broadcast
!
line con 0
 exec-timeout 0 0
line aux 0
line vty 0 4
 password cisco
 login
!
end
```

Example C-34 *Router 4 Configuration for Lab 9-4*

```
!
version 11.2
no service password-encryption
no service udp-small-servers
no service tcp-small-servers
!
hostname R4
!
enable password sanfran
```

continues

Example C-34 *Router 4 Configuration for Lab 9-4 (Continued)*

```
!
no ip domain-lookup
ipx routing 0000.0000.0004
ipx maximum-paths 2
!
!
interface Ethernet0
 ip address 144.254.4.4 255.255.255.0
 ipx network 40
!
interface Ethernet1
 ip address 10.0.0.4 255.0.0.0
 media-type 10BaseT
!
interface ATM0
 no ip address
 atm pvc 5 0 5 qsaal
 atm pvc 16 0 16 ilmi
!
interface ATM0.1 multipoint
 ip address 144.254.100.4 255.255.255.0
 atm pvc 141 0 141 aal5snap inarp
 atm pvc 142 0 142 aal5snap inarp
 atm pvc 143 0 143 aal5snap inarp
 atm pvc 145 0 145 aal5snap inarp
 atm pvc 146 0 146 aal5snap inarp
 atm pvc 147 0 147 aal5snap inarp
 atm pvc 148 0 148 aal5snap inarp
 atm pvc 149 0 149 aal5snap inarp
 map-group ipxPvc
 ipx network 100
!
interface ATM0.2 multipoint
 ip address 144.254.200.4 255.255.255.0
 atm nsap-address 44.44440000000000000000000.000000000000.00
 atm classic-ip-extensions BFI
 atm arp-server nsap 33.33330000000000000000000.000000000000.00
 atm arp-server nsap 66.66660000000000000000000.000000000000.00
 map-group ipxSvc
 ipx network 200
!
interface FastEthernet0
 no ip address
 shutdown
!
router igrp 100
 network 144.254.0.0
!
no ip classless
!
```

Example C-34 *Router 4 Configuration for Lab 9-4 (Continued)*

```
map-list ipxPvc
 ipx 100.0000.0000.0001 atm-vc 141 broadcast
 ipx 100.0000.0000.0002 atm-vc 142 broadcast
 ipx 100.0000.0000.0003 atm-vc 143 broadcast
 ipx 100.0000.0000.0005 atm-vc 145 broadcast
 ipx 100.0000.0000.0006 atm-vc 146 broadcast
 ipx 100.0000.0000.0007 atm-vc 147 broadcast
 ipx 100.0000.0000.0008 atm-vc 148 broadcast
 ipx 100.0000.0000.0009 atm-vc 149 broadcast
!
map-list ipxSvc
 ipx 200.0000.0000.0001 atm-nsap 11.11110000000000000000000000.000000000000.00
  broadcast
 ipx 200.0000.0000.0002 atm-nsap 22.22220000000000000000000000.000000000000.00
  broadcast
 ipx 200.0000.0000.0003 atm-nsap 33.33330000000000000000000000.000000000000.00
  broadcast
 ipx 200.0000.0000.0004 atm-nsap 44.44440000000000000000000000.000000000000.00
  broadcast
 ipx 200.0000.0000.0005 atm-nsap 55.55550000000000000000000000.000000000000.00
  broadcast
 ipx 200.0000.0000.0006 atm-nsap 66.66660000000000000000000000.000000000000.00
  broadcast
 ipx 200.0000.0000.0007 atm-nsap 77.77770000000000000000000000.000000000000.00
  broadcast
 ipx 200.0000.0000.0008 atm-nsap 88.88880000000000000000000000.000000000000.00
  broadcast
 ipx 200.0000.0000.0009 atm-nsap 99.99990000000000000000000000.000000000000.00
  broadcast
!
!
line con 0
 exec-timeout 0 0
line aux 0
line vty 0 4
 exec-timeout 0 0
 password cisco
 login
!
end
```

Example C-35 *Router 5 Configuration for Lab 9-4*

```
!
version 11.2
no service password-encryption
no service udp-small-servers
no service tcp-small-servers
!
hostname R5
```

continues

Example C-35 *Router 5 Configuration for Lab 9-4 (Continued)*

```
!
enable password sanfran
!
no ip domain-lookup
ipx routing 0000.0000.0005
ipx maximum-paths 2
!
!
interface Ethernet0
 ip address 144.254.5.5 255.255.255.0
 ipx network 50
!
interface Ethernet1
 ip address 10.0.0.5 255.0.0.0
 media-type 10BaseT
!
interface ATM0
 no ip address
 atm pvc 5 0 5 qsaal
 atm pvc 16 0 16 ilmi
!
interface ATM0.1 multipoint
 ip address 144.254.100.5 255.255.255.0
 atm pvc 151 0 151 aal5snap inarp
 atm pvc 152 0 152 aal5snap inarp
 atm pvc 153 0 153 aal5snap inarp
 atm pvc 154 0 154 aal5snap inarp
 atm pvc 156 0 156 aal5snap inarp
 atm pvc 157 0 157 aal5snap inarp
 atm pvc 158 0 158 aal5snap inarp
 atm pvc 159 0 159 aal5snap inarp
 map-group ipxPvc
 ipx network 100
!
interface ATM0.2 multipoint
 ip address 144.254.200.5 255.255.255.0
 atm nsap-address 55.5555000000000000000000.000000000000.00
 atm classic-ip-extensions BFI
 atm arp-server nsap 33.3333000000000000000000.000000000000.00
 atm arp-server nsap 66.6666000000000000000000.000000000000.00
 map-group ipxSvc
 ipx network 200
!
interface FastEthernet0
 no ip address
 shutdown
!
router igrp 100
 network 144.254.0.0
!
```

Example C-35 *Router 5 Configuration for Lab 9-4 (Continued)*

```
no ip classless
!
map-list ipxPvc
 ipx 100.0000.0000.0001 atm-vc 151 broadcast
 ipx 100.0000.0000.0002 atm-vc 152 broadcast
 ipx 100.0000.0000.0003 atm-vc 153 broadcast
 ipx 100.0000.0000.0004 atm-vc 154 broadcast
 ipx 100.0000.0000.0006 atm-vc 156 broadcast
 ipx 100.0000.0000.0007 atm-vc 157 broadcast
 ipx 100.0000.0000.0008 atm-vc 158 broadcast
 ipx 100.0000.0000.0009 atm-vc 159 broadcast
!
map-list ipxSvc
 ipx 200.0000.0000.0001 atm-nsap 11.11110000000000000000000.000000000000.00
  broadcast
 ipx 200.0000.0000.0002 atm-nsap 22.22220000000000000000000.000000000000.00
  broadcast
 ipx 200.0000.0000.0003 atm-nsap 33.33330000000000000000000.000000000000.00
  broadcast
 ipx 200.0000.0000.0004 atm-nsap 44.44440000000000000000000.000000000000.00
  broadcast
 ipx 200.0000.0000.0005 atm-nsap 55.55550000000000000000000.000000000000.00
  broadcast
 ipx 200.0000.0000.0006 atm-nsap 66.66660000000000000000000.000000000000.00
  broadcast
 ipx 200.0000.0000.0007 atm-nsap 77.77770000000000000000000.000000000000.00
  broadcast
 ipx 200.0000.0000.0008 atm-nsap 88.88880000000000000000000.000000000000.00
  broadcast
 ipx 200.0000.0000.0009 atm-nsap 99.99990000000000000000000.000000000000.00
  broadcast
!
!
line con 0
 exec-timeout 0 0
line aux 0
line vty 0 4
 exec-timeout 0 0
 password cisco
 login
!
end
```

Example C-36 *Router 6 Configuration for Lab 9-4*

```
!
version 11.2
no service password-encryption
no service udp-small-servers
no service tcp-small-servers
```

Lab 9-4 Solution

Example C-36 *Router 6 Configuration for Lab 9-4 (Continued)*

```
!
hostname R6
!
enable password sanfran
!
no ip domain-lookup
ipx routing 0000.0000.0006
ipx maximum-paths 2
!
!
interface Ethernet0
 ip address 144.254.6.6 255.255.255.0
 ipx network 60
!
interface Ethernet1
 ip address 10.0.0.6 255.0.0.0
 media-type 10BaseT
!
interface ATM0
 no ip address
 atm pvc 5 0 5 qsaal
 atm pvc 16 0 16 ilmi
!
interface ATM0.1 multipoint
 ip address 144.254.100.6 255.255.255.0
 atm pvc 161 0 161 aal5snap inarp
 atm pvc 162 0 162 aal5snap inarp
 atm pvc 163 0 163 aal5snap inarp
 atm pvc 164 0 164 aal5snap inarp
 atm pvc 165 0 165 aal5snap inarp
 atm pvc 167 0 167 aal5snap inarp
 atm pvc 168 0 168 aal5snap inarp
 atm pvc 169 0 169 aal5snap inarp
 map-group ipxPvc
 ipx network 100
!
interface ATM0.2 multipoint
 ip address 144.254.200.6 255.255.255.0
 atm nsap-address 66.6666000000000000000000000.000000000000.00
 atm classic-ip-extensions BFI
 atm arp-server self
 atm arp-server nsap 33.3333000000000000000000000.000000000000.00
 map-group ipxSvc
 ipx network 200
!
interface FastEthernet0
 no ip address
 shutdown
!
router igrp 100
```

Example C-36 *Router 6 Configuration for Lab 9-4 (Continued)*

```
 network 144.254.0.0
!
no ip classless
!
map-list ipxPvc
 ipx 100.0000.0000.0001 atm-vc 161 broadcast
 ipx 100.0000.0000.0002 atm-vc 162 broadcast
 ipx 100.0000.0000.0003 atm-vc 163 broadcast
 ipx 100.0000.0000.0004 atm-vc 164 broadcast
 ipx 100.0000.0000.0005 atm-vc 165 broadcast
 ipx 100.0000.0000.0007 atm-vc 167 broadcast
 ipx 100.0000.0000.0008 atm-vc 168 broadcast
 ipx 100.0000.0000.0009 atm-vc 169 broadcast
!
map-list ipxSvc
 ipx 200.0000.0000.0001 atm-nsap 11.11110000000000000000000.000000000000.00
  broadcast
 ipx 200.0000.0000.0002 atm-nsap 22.22220000000000000000000.000000000000.00
  broadcast
 ipx 200.0000.0000.0003 atm-nsap 33.33330000000000000000000.000000000000.00
  broadcast
 ipx 200.0000.0000.0004 atm-nsap 44.44440000000000000000000.000000000000.00
  broadcast
 ipx 200.0000.0000.0005 atm-nsap 55.55550000000000000000000.000000000000.00
  broadcast
 ipx 200.0000.0000.0006 atm-nsap 66.66660000000000000000000.000000000000.00
  broadcast
 ipx 200.0000.0000.0007 atm-nsap 77.77770000000000000000000.000000000000.00
  broadcast
 ipx 200.0000.0000.0008 atm-nsap 88.88880000000000000000000.000000000000.00
  broadcast
 ipx 200.0000.0000.0009 atm-nsap 99.99990000000000000000000.000000000000.00
  broadcast
!
line con 0
 exec-timeout 0 0
line aux 0
line vty 0 4
 exec-timeout 0 0
 password cisco
 login
!
end
```

Example C-37 *Router 7 Configuration for Lab 9-4*

```
!
version 11.2
no service password-encryption
no service udp-small-servers
```

Example C-37 *Router 7 Configuration for Lab 9-4 (Continued)*

```
no service tcp-small-servers
!
hostname R7
!
enable password sanfran
!
no ip domain-lookup
ipx routing 0000.0000.0007
ipx maximum-paths 2
!
!
interface Ethernet0
 ip address 144.254.7.7 255.255.255.0
 ipx network 70
!
interface Ethernet1
 ip address 10.0.0.7 255.0.0.0
 media-type 10BaseT
!
interface ATM0
 no ip address
 atm pvc 5 0 5 qsaal
 atm pvc 16 0 16 ilmi
!
interface ATM0.1 multipoint
 ip address 144.254.100.7 255.255.255.0
 atm pvc 171 0 171 aal5snap inarp
 atm pvc 172 0 172 aal5snap inarp
 atm pvc 173 0 173 aal5snap inarp
 atm pvc 174 0 174 aal5snap inarp
 atm pvc 175 0 175 aal5snap inarp
 atm pvc 176 0 176 aal5snap inarp
 atm pvc 178 0 178 aal5snap inarp
 atm pvc 179 0 179 aal5snap inarp
 map-group ipxPvc
 ipx network 100
!
interface ATM0.2 multipoint
 ip address 144.254.200.7 255.255.255.0
 atm nsap-address 77.7777000000000000000000000.000000000000.00
 atm classic-ip-extensions BFI
 atm arp-server nsap 33.3333000000000000000000000.000000000000.00
 atm arp-server nsap 66.6666000000000000000000000.000000000000.00
 map-group ipxSvc
 ipx network 200
!
interface FastEthernet0
 no ip address
 shutdown
!
```

Example C-37 *Router 7 Configuration for Lab 9-4 (Continued)*

```
router igrp 100
 network 144.254.0.0
!
no ip classless
!
!
map-list ipxPvc
 ipx 100.0000.0000.0001 atm-vc 171 broadcast
 ipx 100.0000.0000.0002 atm-vc 172 broadcast
 ipx 100.0000.0000.0003 atm-vc 173 broadcast
 ipx 100.0000.0000.0004 atm-vc 174 broadcast
 ipx 100.0000.0000.0005 atm-vc 175 broadcast
 ipx 100.0000.0000.0006 atm-vc 176 broadcast
 ipx 100.0000.0000.0008 atm-vc 178 broadcast
 ipx 100.0000.0000.0009 atm-vc 179 broadcast
!
map-list ipxSvc
 ipx 200.0000.0000.0001 atm-nsap 11.11110000000000000000000.000000000000.00
  broadcast
 ipx 200.0000.0000.0002 atm-nsap 22.22220000000000000000000.000000000000.00
  broadcast
 ipx 200.0000.0000.0003 atm-nsap 33.33330000000000000000000.000000000000.00
  broadcast
 ipx 200.0000.0000.0004 atm-nsap 44.44440000000000000000000.000000000000.00
  broadcast
 ipx 200.0000.0000.0005 atm-nsap 55.55550000000000000000000.000000000000.00
  broadcast
 ipx 200.0000.0000.0006 atm-nsap 66.66660000000000000000000.000000000000.00
  broadcast
 ipx 200.0000.0000.0007 atm-nsap 77.77770000000000000000000.000000000000.00
  broadcast
 ipx 200.0000.0000.0008 atm-nsap 88.88880000000000000000000.000000000000.00
  broadcast
 ipx 200.0000.0000.0009 atm-nsap 99.99990000000000000000000.000000000000.00
  broadcast
!
!
line con 0
 exec-timeout 0 0
line aux 0
line vty 0 4
 exec-timeout 0 0
 password cisco
 login
!
end
```

Example C-38 *Router 8 Configuration for Lab 9-4*

```
!
```

continues

Example C-38 *Router 8 Configuration for Lab 9-4 (Continued)*

```
version 11.2
no service password-encryption
no service udp-small-servers
no service tcp-small-servers
!
hostname R8
!
enable password sanfran
!
no ip domain-lookup
ipx routing 0000.0000.0008
ipx maximum-paths 2
!
!
interface Ethernet0
 ip address 144.254.8.8 255.255.255.0
 ipx network 80
!
interface Ethernet1
 ip address 10.0.0.8 255.0.0.0
 media-type 10BaseT
!
interface ATM0
 no ip address
 atm pvc 5 0 5 qsaal
 atm pvc 16 0 16 ilmi
!
interface ATM0.1 multipoint
 ip address 144.254.100.8 255.255.255.0
 atm pvc 181 0 181 aal5snap inarp
 atm pvc 182 0 182 aal5snap inarp
 atm pvc 183 0 183 aal5snap inarp
 atm pvc 184 0 184 aal5snap inarp
 atm pvc 185 0 185 aal5snap inarp
 atm pvc 186 0 186 aal5snap inarp
 atm pvc 187 0 187 aal5snap inarp
 atm pvc 189 0 189 aal5snap inarp
 map-group ipxPvc
 ipx network 100
!
interface ATM0.2 multipoint
 ip address 144.254.200.8 255.255.255.0
 atm nsap-address 88.888800000000000000000000.000000000000.00
 atm classic-ip-extensions BFI
 atm arp-server nsap 33.333300000000000000000000.000000000000.00
 atm arp-server nsap 66.666600000000000000000000.000000000000.00
 map-group ipxSvc
 ipx network 200
!
interface FastEthernet0
```

Example C-38 *Router 8 Configuration for Lab 9-4 (Continued)*

```
 no ip address
 shutdown
!
router igrp 100
 network 144.254.0.0
!
no ip classless
!
map-list ipxPvc
 ipx 100.0000.0000.0001 atm-vc 181 broadcast
 ipx 100.0000.0000.0002 atm-vc 182 broadcast
 ipx 100.0000.0000.0003 atm-vc 183 broadcast
 ipx 100.0000.0000.0004 atm-vc 184 broadcast
 ipx 100.0000.0000.0005 atm-vc 185 broadcast
 ipx 100.0000.0000.0006 atm-vc 186 broadcast
 ipx 100.0000.0000.0007 atm-vc 187 broadcast
 ipx 100.0000.0000.0009 atm-vc 189 broadcast
!
map-list ipxSvc
 ipx 200.0000.0000.0001 atm-nsap 11.11110000000000000000000.000000000000.00
  broadcast
 ipx 200.0000.0000.0002 atm-nsap 22.22220000000000000000000.000000000000.00
  broadcast
 ipx 200.0000.0000.0003 atm-nsap 33.33330000000000000000000.000000000000.00
  broadcast
 ipx 200.0000.0000.0004 atm-nsap 44.44440000000000000000000.000000000000.00
  broadcast
 ipx 200.0000.0000.0005 atm-nsap 55.55550000000000000000000.000000000000.00
  broadcast
 ipx 200.0000.0000.0006 atm-nsap 66.66660000000000000000000.000000000000.00
  broadcast
 ipx 200.0000.0000.0007 atm-nsap 77.77770000000000000000000.000000000000.00
  broadcast
 ipx 200.0000.0000.0008 atm-nsap 88.88880000000000000000000.000000000000.00
  broadcast
 ipx 200.0000.0000.0009 atm-nsap 99.99990000000000000000000.000000000000.00
  broadcast
!
!
line con 0
 exec-timeout 0 0
line aux 0
line vty 0 4
 exec-timeout 0 0
 password cisco
 login
!
end
```

Lab 9-4 Solution

Example C-39 *Router 9 Configuration for Lab 9-4*

```
!
version 11.2
no service password-encryption
no service udp-small-servers
no service tcp-small-servers
!
hostname R9
!
enable password sanfran
!
no ip domain-lookup
ipx routing 0000.0000.0009
ipx maximum-paths 2
!
!
interface Ethernet0
 ip address 144.254.9.9 255.255.255.0
 ipx network 90
!
interface Ethernet1
 ip address 10.0.0.9 255.0.0.0
 media-type 10BaseT
!
interface ATM0
 no ip address
 atm pvc 5 0 5 qsaal
 atm pvc 16 0 16 ilmi
!
interface ATM0.1 multipoint
 ip address 144.254.100.9 255.255.255.0
 atm pvc 191 0 191 aal5snap inarp
 atm pvc 192 0 192 aal5snap inarp
 atm pvc 193 0 193 aal5snap inarp
 atm pvc 194 0 194 aal5snap inarp
 atm pvc 195 0 195 aal5snap inarp
 atm pvc 196 0 196 aal5snap inarp
 atm pvc 197 0 197 aal5snap inarp
 atm pvc 198 0 198 aal5snap inarp
 map-group ipxPvc
 ipx network 100
!
interface ATM0.2 multipoint
 ip address 144.254.200.9 255.255.255.0
 atm nsap-address 99.99990000000000000000000000.000000000000.00
 atm classic-ip-extensions BFI
 atm arp-server nsap 33.33330000000000000000000000.000000000000.00
 atm arp-server nsap 66.66660000000000000000000000.000000000000.00
 map-group ipxSvc
 ipx network 200
!
```

Example C-39 *Router 9 Configuration for Lab 9-4 (Continued)*

```
interface FastEthernet0
 no ip address
 shutdown
!
router igrp 100
 network 144.254.0.0
!
no ip classless
!
map-list ipxPvc
 ipx 100.0000.0000.0001 atm-vc 191 broadcast
 ipx 100.0000.0000.0002 atm-vc 192 broadcast
 ipx 100.0000.0000.0003 atm-vc 193 broadcast
 ipx 100.0000.0000.0004 atm-vc 194 broadcast
 ipx 100.0000.0000.0005 atm-vc 195 broadcast
 ipx 100.0000.0000.0006 atm-vc 196 broadcast
 ipx 100.0000.0000.0007 atm-vc 197 broadcast
 ipx 100.0000.0000.0008 atm-vc 198 broadcast
!
map-list ipxSvc
 ipx 200.0000.0000.0001 atm-nsap 11.11110000000000000000000.000000000000.00
  broadcast
 ipx 200.0000.0000.0002 atm-nsap 22.22220000000000000000000.000000000000.00
  broadcast
 ipx 200.0000.0000.0003 atm-nsap 33.33330000000000000000000.000000000000.00
  broadcast
 ipx 200.0000.0000.0004 atm-nsap 44.44440000000000000000000.000000000000.00
  broadcast
 ipx 200.0000.0000.0005 atm-nsap 55.55550000000000000000000.000000000000.00
  broadcast
 ipx 200.0000.0000.0006 atm-nsap 66.66660000000000000000000.000000000000.00
  broadcast
 ipx 200.0000.0000.0007 atm-nsap 77.77770000000000000000000.000000000000.00
  broadcast
 ipx 200.0000.0000.0008 atm-nsap 88.88880000000000000000000.000000000000.00
  broadcast
 ipx 200.0000.0000.0009 atm-nsap 99.99990000000000000000000.000000000000.00
  broadcast
!
!
line con 0
 exec-timeout 0 0
line aux 0
line vty 0 4
 exec-timeout 0 0
 password cisco
 login
!
end
```

Lab 9-4 Solution

Solutions to Lab 9-5: Configuring Next Hop Resolution Protocol on Routers

Examples C-40 through C-48 provide the configuration solutions that satisfy all the exercises for Lab 9-5. Specifically, the exercises asked for the following:

1 You are to use new subinterfaces—ATM 0.3 and, on some routers, ATM 0.4—to implement this lab solution. Migrate your router NSAP (AESA) address from ATM 0.2 to subinterface ATM 0.3, and shut down your ATM 0.2 subinterface.

2 RFC 2225 is deployed in the lab within an LIS. This implies that you require a separate ARP server (because you are using SVCs) within a single LIS. Have R3 be the ARP server in LIS1, R8 be the ARP Server in LIS2, and R5 be the ARP Server in LIS3.

3 As per the lab schematic in Figure 9-15 on page 359, R9 and R6 both are associated logically with two logical IP subnets. They require a second NSAP address and a second IP address to support the second subnet, associated with subinterface ATM 0.4. Note that you are still using the same Layer 3 IP routing protocol, IGRP.

4 Configure your ATM 0.3 (and ATM 0.4) subinterfaces and ensure that you are associating the correct ARP servers to the correct subinterfaces.

5 Verify that you have full IP connectivity between all routers. Using pings and the **show ip route** command, ensure that the IGRP routing strategy is working as expected. You have not yet turned on or activated NHRP.

6 Use the **trace** command to demonstrate the path taken when you forward packets to remote IP destinations from you router—for example, from R2, **trace 144.254.7.7**, **trace 144.254.4.4**.

7 Configure NHRP at the subinterface level with the **ip nhrp network-id 1** command.

8 Use the **trace** command on your router to demonstrate that IP, as per the IP routing table information, can take an extra hop to go to 144.254.4.X and 144.254.5.X destinations. For example, from R2 or R3, trace IP address 144.254.4.4.

9 Now that all routers participate in the NHRP, verify that you no longer have to go via extra hop to reach destinations 144.254.4.X and 144.254.5.X, as before. For example, on R3 or R2, repeat the **trace** test to IP destinations used previously. You see the cut-through routing event.

Example C-40   *Router 1 Configuration for Lab 9-5*

```
!
version 11.2
no service password-encryption
no service udp-small-servers
no service tcp-small-servers
!
hostname R1
```

Example C-40 *Router 1 Configuration for Lab 9-5 (Continued)*

```
!
enable password sanfran
!
no ip domain-lookup
ipx routing 0000.0000.0001
!
!
interface Ethernet0
 ip address 144.254.1.1 255.255.255.0
 ipx network 10
!
interface Ethernet1
 ip address 10.0.0.1 255.0.0.0
 media-type 10BaseT
!
interface ATM0
 no ip address
 atm pvc 5 0 5 qsaal
!
interface ATM0.1 multipoint
 ip address 144.254.100.1 255.255.255.0
 shutdown
 atm pvc 112 0 112 aal5snap
 atm pvc 113 0 113 aal5snap
 atm pvc 114 0 114 aal5snap
 atm pvc 115 0 115 aal5snap
 atm pvc 116 0 116 aal5snap
 atm pvc 117 0 117 aal5snap
 atm pvc 118 0 118 aal5snap
 atm pvc 119 0 119 aal5snap
 map-group ipPvc
 map-group ipxPvc
 ipx network 100
!
interface ATM0.2 multipoint
 ip address 144.254.200.1 255.255.255.0
 shutdown
 ipx network 200
!
interface ATM0.3 multipoint
 ip address 144.254.10.1 255.255.255.0
 ip nhrp network-id 1
 atm nsap-address 11.11110000000000000000000000.000000000000.00
 atm arp-server nsap 33.33330000000000000000000000.000000000000.00
!
interface FastEthernet0
 no ip address
 shutdown
!
router igrp 100
```

continues

Example C-40 *Router 1 Configuration for Lab 9-5 (Continued)*

```
 network 144.254.0.0
!
no ip classless
!
map-list ipPvc
 ip 144.254.100.2 atm-vc 112 broadcast
 ip 144.254.100.3 atm-vc 113 broadcast
 ip 144.254.100.4 atm-vc 114 broadcast
 ip 144.254.100.5 atm-vc 115 broadcast
 ip 144.254.100.6 atm-vc 116 broadcast
 ip 144.254.100.7 atm-vc 117 broadcast
 ip 144.254.100.8 atm-vc 118 broadcast
 ip 144.254.100.9 atm-vc 119 broadcast
!
map-list ipxPvc
 ipx 100.0000.0000.0002 atm-vc 112 broadcast
 ipx 100.0000.0000.0003 atm-vc 113 broadcast
 ipx 100.0000.0000.0004 atm-vc 114 broadcast
 ipx 100.0000.0000.0005 atm-vc 115 broadcast
 ipx 100.0000.0000.0006 atm-vc 116 broadcast
 ipx 100.0000.0000.0007 atm-vc 117 broadcast
 ipx 100.0000.0000.0008 atm-vc 118 broadcast
 ipx 100.0000.0000.0009 atm-vc 119 broadcast
!
!
line con 0
 exec-timeout 0 0
line aux 0
line vty 0 4
 exec-timeout 0 0
 password cisco
 login
!
end
```

Example C-41 *Router 2 Configuration for Lab 9-5*

```
!
version 11.2
no service password-encryption
no service udp-small-servers
no service tcp-small-servers
!
hostname R2
!
enable password sanfran
!
no ip domain-lookup
ipx routing 0000.0000.0002
!
```

Example C-41 *Router 2 Configuration for Lab 9-5 (Continued)*

```
!
interface Ethernet0
 ip address 144.254.2.2 255.255.255.0
 ipx network 20
!
interface Ethernet1
 ip address 10.0.0.2 255.0.0.0
 media-type 10BaseT
!
interface ATM0
 no ip address
 atm pvc 5 0 5 qsaal
!
interface ATM0.1 multipoint
 ip address 144.254.100.2 255.255.255.0
 shutdown
 atm pvc 121 0 121 aal5snap
 atm pvc 123 0 123 aal5snap
 atm pvc 124 0 124 aal5snap
 atm pvc 125 0 125 aal5snap
 atm pvc 126 0 126 aal5snap
 atm pvc 127 0 127 aal5snap
 atm pvc 128 0 128 aal5snap
 atm pvc 129 0 129 aal5snap
 map-group ipPvc
 map-group ipxPvc
 ipx network 100
!
interface ATM0.2 multipoint
 ip address 144.254.200.2 255.255.255.0
 shutdown
 ipx network 200
!
interface ATM0.3 multipoint
 ip address 144.254.10.2 255.255.255.0
 ip nhrp network-id 1
 atm nsap-address 22.222200000000000000000000.000000000000.00
 atm arp-server nsap 33.333300000000000000000000.000000000000.00

!
interface FastEthernet0
 no ip address
 shutdown
!
router igrp 100
 network 144.254.0.0
!
no ip classless
!
map-list ipPvc
```

continues

Example C-41 *Router 2 Configuration for Lab 9-5 (Continued)*

```
 ip 144.254.100.1 atm-vc 121 broadcast
 ip 144.254.100.3 atm-vc 123 broadcast
 ip 144.254.100.4 atm-vc 124 broadcast
 ip 144.254.100.5 atm-vc 125 broadcast
 ip 144.254.100.6 atm-vc 126 broadcast
 ip 144.254.100.7 atm-vc 127 broadcast
 ip 144.254.100.8 atm-vc 128 broadcast
 ip 144.254.100.9 atm-vc 129 broadcast
!
map-list ipxPvc
 ipx 100.0000.0000.0001 atm-vc 121 broadcast
 ipx 100.0000.0000.0003 atm-vc 123 broadcast
 ipx 100.0000.0000.0004 atm-vc 124 broadcast
 ipx 100.0000.0000.0005 atm-vc 125 broadcast
 ipx 100.0000.0000.0006 atm-vc 126 broadcast
 ipx 100.0000.0000.0007 atm-vc 127 broadcast
 ipx 100.0000.0000.0008 atm-vc 128 broadcast
 ipx 100.0000.0000.0009 atm-vc 129 broadcast
!
!
line con 0
 exec-timeout 0 0
line aux 0
line vty 0 4
 exec-timeout 0 0
 password cisco
 login
!
end
```

Example C-42 *Router 3 Configuration for Lab 9-5*

```
!
version 11.2
no service password-encryption
no service udp-small-servers
no service tcp-small-servers
!
hostname R3
!
enable password sanfran
!
no ip domain-lookup
ipx routing 0000.0000.0003
!
!
interface Ethernet0
 ip address 144.254.3.3 255.255.255.0
 ipx network 30
!
```

Example C-42 *Router 3 Configuration for Lab 9-5 (Continued)*

```
interface Ethernet1
 ip address 10.0.0.3 255.0.0.0
 media-type 10BaseT
!
interface ATM0
 no ip address
 atm pvc 5 0 5 qsaal
!
interface ATM0.1 multipoint
 ip address 144.254.100.3 255.255.255.0
 shutdown
 atm pvc 131 0 131 aal5snap
 atm pvc 132 0 132 aal5snap
 atm pvc 133 0 133 aal5snap
 atm pvc 134 0 134 aal5snap
 atm pvc 135 0 135 aal5snap
 atm pvc 136 0 136 aal5snap
 atm pvc 137 0 137 aal5snap
 atm pvc 138 0 138 aal5snap
 atm pvc 139 0 139 aal5snap
 map-group ipPvc
 map-group ipxPvc
 ipx network 100
!
interface ATM0.2 multipoint
 ip address 144.254.200.3 255.255.255.0
 shutdown
 map-group ipSvc
!
interface ATM0.3 multipoint
 ip address 144.254.10.3 255.255.255.0
 ip nhrp network-id 1
 atm nsap-address 33.333300000000000000000000.000000000000.00
 atm arp-server self
!
interface FastEthernet0
 no ip address
 shutdown
!
router igrp 100
 network 144.254.0.0
!
no ip classless
!
map-list ipPvc
 ip 144.254.100.1 atm-vc 131 broadcast
 ip 144.254.100.2 atm-vc 132 broadcast
 ip 144.254.100.4 atm-vc 134 broadcast
 ip 144.254.100.5 atm-vc 135 broadcast
 ip 144.254.100.6 atm-vc 136 broadcast
```

continues

Example C-42 *Router 3 Configuration for Lab 9-5 (Continued)*

```
ip 144.254.100.7 atm-vc 137 broadcast
ip 144.254.100.8 atm-vc 138 broadcast
ip 144.254.100.9 atm-vc 139 broadcast
!
map-list ipxPvc
 ipx 100.0000.0000.0001 atm-vc 131 broadcast
 ipx 100.0000.0000.0002 atm-vc 132 broadcast
 ipx 100.0000.0000.0004 atm-vc 134 broadcast
 ipx 100.0000.0000.0005 atm-vc 135 broadcast
 ipx 100.0000.0000.0006 atm-vc 136 broadcast
 ipx 100.0000.0000.0007 atm-vc 137 broadcast
 ipx 100.0000.0000.0008 atm-vc 138 broadcast
 ipx 100.0000.0000.0009 atm-vc 139 broadcast
!
!
line con 0
 exec-timeout 0 0
line aux 0
line vty 0 4
 password cisco
 login
!
end
```

Example C-43 *Router 4 Configuration for Lab 9-5*

```
!
version 11.2
no service password-encryption
no service udp-small-servers
no service tcp-small-servers
!
hostname R4
!
enable password sanfran
!
no ip domain-lookup
ipx routing 0000.0000.0004
!
!
interface Ethernet0
 ip address 144.254.4.4 255.255.255.0
 ipx network 40
!
interface Ethernet1
 ip address 10.0.0.4 255.0.0.0
 media-type 10BaseT
!
interface ATM0
 no ip address
```

Example C-43   *Router 4 Configuration for Lab 9-5 (Continued)*

```
atm pvc 5 0 5 qsaal
!
interface ATM0.1 multipoint
 ip address 144.254.100.4 255.255.255.0
 shutdown
 atm pvc 141 0 141 aal5snap
 atm pvc 142 0 142 aal5snap
 atm pvc 143 0 143 aal5snap
 atm pvc 145 0 145 aal5snap
 atm pvc 146 0 146 aal5snap
 atm pvc 147 0 147 aal5snap
 atm pvc 148 0 148 aal5snap
 atm pvc 149 0 149 aal5snap
 map-group ipPvc
 map-group ipxPvc
 ipx network 100
!
interface ATM0.2 multipoint
 ip address 144.254.200.4 255.255.255.0
 shutdown
 map-group ipSvc
!
interface ATM0.3 multipoint
 ip address 144.254.30.4 255.255.255.0
 ip nhrp network-id 1
 atm nsap-address 44.444400000000000000000000.000000000000.00
 atm arp-server nsap 55.555500000000000000000000.000000000000.00
!
interface FastEthernet0
 no ip address
 shutdown
!
router igrp 100
 network 144.254.0.0
!
no ip classless
!
map-list ipPvc
 ip 144.254.100.1 atm-vc 141 broadcast
 ip 144.254.100.2 atm-vc 142 broadcast
 ip 144.254.100.3 atm-vc 143 broadcast
 ip 144.254.100.5 atm-vc 145 broadcast
 ip 144.254.100.6 atm-vc 146 broadcast
 ip 144.254.100.7 atm-vc 147 broadcast
 ip 144.254.100.8 atm-vc 148 broadcast
 ip 144.254.100.9 atm-vc 149 broadcast
!
map-list ipxPvc
 ipx 100.0000.0000.0001 atm-vc 141 broadcast
 ipx 100.0000.0000.0002 atm-vc 142 broadcast
```

continues

Lab 9-5 Solution

Example C-43 *Router 4 Configuration for Lab 9-5 (Continued)*

```
ipx 100.0000.0000.0003 atm-vc 143 broadcast
ipx 100.0000.0000.0005 atm-vc 145 broadcast
ipx 100.0000.0000.0006 atm-vc 146 broadcast
ipx 100.0000.0000.0007 atm-vc 147 broadcast
ipx 100.0000.0000.0008 atm-vc 148 broadcast
ipx 100.0000.0000.0009 atm-vc 149 broadcast
!
!
line con 0
 exec-timeout 0 0
line aux 0
line vty 0 4
 exec-timeout 0 0
 password cisco
 login
!
end
```

Example C-44 *Router 5 Configuration for Lab 9-5*

```
!
version 11.2
no service password-encryption
no service udp-small-servers
no service tcp-small-servers
!
hostname R5
!
enable password sanfran
!
no ip domain-lookup
ipx routing 0000.0000.0005
!
!
interface Ethernet0
 ip address 144.254.5.5 255.255.255.0
 ipx network 50
!
interface Ethernet1
 ip address 10.0.0.5 255.0.0.0
 media-type 10BaseT
!
interface ATM0
 no ip address
 atm pvc 5 0 5 qsaal
!
interface ATM0.1 multipoint
 ip address 144.254.100.5 255.255.255.0
 shutdown
 atm pvc 151 0 151 aal5snap
```

Example C-44 *Router 5 Configuration for Lab 9-5 (Continued)*

```
atm pvc 152 0 152 aal5snap
atm pvc 153 0 153 aal5snap
atm pvc 154 0 154 aal5snap
atm pvc 156 0 156 aal5snap
atm pvc 157 0 157 aal5snap
atm pvc 158 0 158 aal5snap
atm pvc 159 0 159 aal5snap
map-group ipPvc
map-group ipxPvc
ipx network 100
!
interface ATM0.2 multipoint
 ip address 144.254.200.5 255.255.255.0
 shutdown
 map-group ipSvc
!
interface ATM0.3 multipoint
 ip address 144.254.30.5 255.255.255.0
 ip nhrp network-id 1
 atm nsap-address 55.555500000000000000000000.000000000000.00
 atm arp-server self
!
interface FastEthernet0
 no ip address
 shutdown
!
router igrp 100
 network 144.254.0.0
!
no ip classless
!
map-list ipPvc
 ip 144.254.100.1 atm-vc 151 broadcast
 ip 144.254.100.2 atm-vc 152 broadcast
 ip 144.254.100.3 atm-vc 153 broadcast
 ip 144.254.100.4 atm-vc 154 broadcast
 ip 144.254.100.6 atm-vc 156 broadcast
 ip 144.254.100.7 atm-vc 157 broadcast
 ip 144.254.100.8 atm-vc 158 broadcast
 ip 144.254.100.9 atm-vc 159 broadcast
!
map-list ipxPvc
 ipx 100.0000.0000.0001 atm-vc 151 broadcast
 ipx 100.0000.0000.0002 atm-vc 152 broadcast
 ipx 100.0000.0000.0003 atm-vc 153 broadcast
 ipx 100.0000.0000.0004 atm-vc 154 broadcast
 ipx 100.0000.0000.0006 atm-vc 156 broadcast
 ipx 100.0000.0000.0007 atm-vc 157 broadcast
 ipx 100.0000.0000.0008 atm-vc 158 broadcast
 ipx 100.0000.0000.0009 atm-vc 159 broadcast
```

Lab 9-5 Solution

continues

Example C-44 *Router 5 Configuration for Lab 9-5 (Continued)*

```
!
!
line con 0
 exec-timeout 0 0
line aux 0
line vty 0 4
 exec-timeout 0 0
 password cisco
 login
!
end
```

Example C-45 *Router 6 Configuration for Lab 9-5*

```
!
version 11.2
no service password-encryption
no service udp-small-servers
no service tcp-small-servers
!
hostname R6
!
enable password sanfran
!
no ip domain-lookup
ipx routing 0000.0000.0006
!
!
interface Ethernet0
 ip address 144.254.6.6 255.255.255.0
 ipx network 60
!
interface Ethernet1
 ip address 10.0.0.6 255.0.0.0
 media-type 10BaseT
!
interface ATM0
 no ip address
 atm pvc 5 0 5 qsaal
!
interface ATM0.1 multipoint
 ip address 144.254.100.6 255.255.255.0
 shutdown
 atm pvc 161 0 161 aal5snap
 atm pvc 162 0 162 aal5snap
 atm pvc 163 0 163 aal5snap
 atm pvc 164 0 164 aal5snap
 atm pvc 165 0 165 aal5snap
 atm pvc 167 0 167 aal5snap
 atm pvc 168 0 168 aal5snap
```

Example C-45 *Router 6 Configuration for Lab 9-5 (Continued)*

```
atm pvc 169 0 169 aal5snap
map-group ipPvc
map-group ipxPvc
ipx network 100
!
interface ATM0.2 multipoint
 ip address 144.254.200.6 255.255.255.0
 shutdown
 map-group ipSvc
!
interface ATM0.3 multipoint
 ip address 144.254.30.6 255.255.255.0
 ip nhrp network-id 1
 atm nsap-address 66.66660000000000000000000.000000000000.00
 atm arp-server nsap 55.55550000000000000000000.000000000000.00
!
interface ATM0.4 multipoint
 ip address 144.254.20.6 255.255.255.0
 ip nhrp network-id 1
 atm nsap-address 66.66640000000000000000000.000000000000.00
 atm arp-server 88.88880000000000000000000.000000000000.00
!
interface FastEthernet0
 no ip address
 shutdown
!
router igrp 100
 network 144.254.0.0
!
no ip classless
!
map-list ipPvc
 ip 144.254.100.1 atm-vc 161 broadcast
 ip 144.254.100.2 atm-vc 162 broadcast
 ip 144.254.100.3 atm-vc 163 broadcast
 ip 144.254.100.4 atm-vc 164 broadcast
 ip 144.254.100.5 atm-vc 165 broadcast
 ip 144.254.100.7 atm-vc 167 broadcast
 ip 144.254.100.8 atm-vc 168 broadcast
 ip 144.254.100.9 atm-vc 169 broadcast
!
map-list ipxPvc
 ipx 100.0000.0000.0001 atm-vc 161 broadcast
 ipx 100.0000.0000.0002 atm-vc 162 broadcast
 ipx 100.0000.0000.0003 atm-vc 163 broadcast
 ipx 100.0000.0000.0004 atm-vc 164 broadcast
 ipx 100.0000.0000.0005 atm-vc 165 broadcast
 ipx 100.0000.0000.0007 atm-vc 167 broadcast
 ipx 100.0000.0000.0008 atm-vc 168 broadcast
 ipx 100.0000.0000.0009 atm-vc 169 broadcast
```

Lab 9-5 Solution

continues

Example C-45 *Router 6 Configuration for Lab 9-5 (Continued)*

```
!
!
!
line con 0
 exec-timeout 0 0
line aux 0
line vty 0 4
 exec-timeout 0 0
 password cisco
 login
!
end
```

Example C-46 *Router 7 Configuration for Lab 9-5*

```
!
version 11.2
no service password-encryption
no service udp-small-servers
no service tcp-small-servers
!
hostname R7
!
enable password sanfran
!
no ip domain-lookup
ipx routing 0000.0000.0007
!
!
interface Ethernet0
 ip address 144.254.7.7 255.255.255.0
 ipx network 70
!
interface Ethernet1
 ip address 10.0.0.7 255.0.0.0
 media-type 10BaseT
!
interface ATM0
 no ip address
 atm pvc 5 0 5 qsaal
!
interface ATM0.1 multipoint
 ip address 144.254.100.7 255.255.255.0
 shutdown
 atm pvc 171 0 171 aal5snap
 atm pvc 172 0 172 aal5snap
 atm pvc 173 0 173 aal5snap
 atm pvc 174 0 174 aal5snap
 atm pvc 175 0 175 aal5snap
 atm pvc 176 0 176 aal5snap
```

Example C-46 *Router 7 Configuration for Lab 9-5 (Continued)*

```
 atm pvc 178 0 178 aal5snap
 atm pvc 179 0 179 aal5snap
 map-group ipPvc
 map-group ipxPvc
 ipx network 100
!
interface ATM0.2 multipoint
 ip address 144.254.200.7 255.255.255.0
 shutdown
 map-group ipSvc
!
interface ATM0.3 multipoint
 ip address 144.254.20.7 255.255.255.0
 ip nhrp network-id 1
 atm nsap-address 77.77770000000000000000000000.000000000000.00
 atm arp-server nsap 88.88880000000000000000000000.000000000000.00
!
interface FastEthernet0
 no ip address
 shutdown
!
router igrp 100
 network 144.254.0.0
!
no ip classless
!
map-list ipPvc
 ip 144.254.100.1 atm-vc 171 broadcast
 ip 144.254.100.2 atm-vc 172 broadcast
 ip 144.254.100.3 atm-vc 173 broadcast
 ip 144.254.100.4 atm-vc 174 broadcast
 ip 144.254.100.5 atm-vc 175 broadcast
 ip 144.254.100.6 atm-vc 176 broadcast
 ip 144.254.100.8 atm-vc 178 broadcast
 ip 144.254.100.9 atm-vc 179 broadcast
!
map-list ipxPvc
 ipx 100.0000.0000.0001 atm-vc 171 broadcast
 ipx 100.0000.0000.0002 atm-vc 172 broadcast
 ipx 100.0000.0000.0003 atm-vc 173 broadcast
 ipx 100.0000.0000.0004 atm-vc 174 broadcast
 ipx 100.0000.0000.0005 atm-vc 175 broadcast
 ipx 100.0000.0000.0006 atm-vc 176 broadcast
 ipx 100.0000.0000.0008 atm-vc 178 broadcast
 ipx 100.0000.0000.0009 atm-vc 179 broadcast
!
!
line con 0
 exec-timeout 0 0
line aux 0
```

Lab 9-5 Solution

continues

Example C-46 *Router 7 Configuration for Lab 9-5 (Continued)*

```
line vty 0 4
 exec-timeout 0 0
 password cisco
 login
!
end
```

Example C-47 *Router 8 Configuration for Lab 9-5*

```
!
version 11.2
no service password-encryption
no service udp-small-servers
no service tcp-small-servers
!
hostname R8
!
enable password sanfran
!
no ip domain-lookup
ipx routing 0000.0000.0008
!
!
interface Ethernet0
 ip address 144.254.8.8 255.255.255.0
 ipx network 80
!
interface Ethernet1
 ip address 10.0.0.8 255.0.0.0
 media-type 10BaseT
!
interface ATM0
 no ip address
 atm pvc 5 0 5 qsaal
!
interface ATM0.1 multipoint
 ip address 144.254.100.8 255.255.255.0
 shutdown
 atm pvc 181 0 181 aal5snap
 atm pvc 182 0 182 aal5snap
 atm pvc 183 0 183 aal5snap
 atm pvc 184 0 184 aal5snap
 atm pvc 185 0 185 aal5snap
 atm pvc 186 0 186 aal5snap
 atm pvc 187 0 187 aal5snap
 atm pvc 189 0 189 aal5snap
 map-group ipPvc
 map-group ipxPvc
 ipx network 100
!
```

Example C-47 *Router 8 Configuration for Lab 9-5 (Continued)*

```
interface ATM0.2 multipoint
 ip address 144.254.200.8 255.255.255.0
 shutdown
 map-group ipSvc
!
interface ATM0.3 multipoint
 ip address 144.254.20.8 255.255.255.0
 ip nhrp network-id 1
 atm nsap-address 88.888800000000000000000000.000000000000.00
 atm arp-server self
!
interface FastEthernet0
 no ip address
 shutdown
!
router igrp 100
 network 144.254.0.0
!
no ip classless
!
map-list ipPvc
 ip 144.254.100.1 atm-vc 181 broadcast
 ip 144.254.100.2 atm-vc 182 broadcast
 ip 144.254.100.3 atm-vc 183 broadcast
 ip 144.254.100.4 atm-vc 184 broadcast
 ip 144.254.100.5 atm-vc 185 broadcast
 ip 144.254.100.6 atm-vc 186 broadcast
 ip 144.254.100.7 atm-vc 187 broadcast
 ip 144.254.100.9 atm-vc 189 broadcast
!
map-list ipxPvc
 ipx 100.0000.0000.0001 atm-vc 181 broadcast
 ipx 100.0000.0000.0002 atm-vc 182 broadcast
 ipx 100.0000.0000.0003 atm-vc 183 broadcast
 ipx 100.0000.0000.0004 atm-vc 184 broadcast
 ipx 100.0000.0000.0005 atm-vc 185 broadcast
 ipx 100.0000.0000.0006 atm-vc 186 broadcast
 ipx 100.0000.0000.0007 atm-vc 187 broadcast
 ipx 100.0000.0000.0009 atm-vc 189 broadcast
!
!
line con 0
 exec-timeout 0 0
line aux 0
line vty 0 4
 exec-timeout 0 0
 password cisco
 login
!
end
```

Lab 9-5 Solution

Example C-48 *Router 9 Configuration for Lab 9-5*

```
!
version 11.2
no service password-encryption
no service udp-small-servers
no service tcp-small-servers
!
hostname R9
!
enable password sanfran
!
no ip domain-lookup
ipx routing 0000.0000.0009
!
!
interface Ethernet0
 ip address 144.254.9.9 255.255.255.0
 ipx network 90
!
interface Ethernet1
 ip address 10.0.0.9 255.0.0.0
 media-type 10BaseT
!
interface ATM0
 no ip address
 atm pvc 5 0 5 qsaal
!
interface ATM0.1 multipoint
 ip address 144.254.100.9 255.255.255.0
 shutdown
 atm pvc 191 0 191 aal5snap
 atm pvc 192 0 192 aal5snap
 atm pvc 193 0 193 aal5snap
 atm pvc 194 0 194 aal5snap
 atm pvc 195 0 195 aal5snap
 atm pvc 196 0 196 aal5snap
 atm pvc 197 0 197 aal5snap
 atm pvc 198 0 198 aal5snap
 map-group ipPvc
 map-group ipxPvc
 ipx network 100
!
interface ATM0.2 multipoint
 ip address 144.254.200.9 255.255.255.0
 shutdown
 map-group ipSvc
!
interface ATM0.3 multipoint
 ip address 144.254.20.9 255.255.255.0
 ip nhrp network-id 1
 atm nsap-address 99.999900000000000000000000.000000000000.00
```

Example C-48 *Router 9 Configuration for Lab 9-5 (Continued)*

```
 atm arp-server nsap 88.8888000000000000000000000.000000000000.00
 !
interface ATM0.4 multipoint
 ip address 144.254.10.9 255.255.255.0
 ip nhrp network-id 1
 atm nsap-address 99.9994000000000000000000000.000000000000.00
 atm arp-server nsap 33.3333000000000000000000000.000000000000.00
 !
interface FastEthernet0
 no ip address
 shutdown
 !
router igrp 100
 network 144.254.0.0
 !
no ip classless
 !
map-list ipPvc
 ip 144.254.100.1 atm-vc 191 broadcast
 ip 144.254.100.2 atm-vc 192 broadcast
 ip 144.254.100.3 atm-vc 193 broadcast
 ip 144.254.100.4 atm-vc 194 broadcast
 ip 144.254.100.5 atm-vc 195 broadcast
 ip 144.254.100.6 atm-vc 196 broadcast
 ip 144.254.100.7 atm-vc 197 broadcast
 ip 144.254.100.8 atm-vc 198 broadcast
 !
map-list ipxPvc
 ipx 100.0000.0000.0001 atm-vc 191 broadcast
 ipx 100.0000.0000.0002 atm-vc 192 broadcast
 ipx 100.0000.0000.0003 atm-vc 193 broadcast
 ipx 100.0000.0000.0004 atm-vc 194 broadcast
 ipx 100.0000.0000.0005 atm-vc 195 broadcast
 ipx 100.0000.0000.0006 atm-vc 196 broadcast
 ipx 100.0000.0000.0007 atm-vc 197 broadcast
 ipx 100.0000.0000.0008 atm-vc 198 broadcast
 !
 !
line con 0
 exec-timeout 0 0
line aux 0
line vty 0 4
 exec-timeout 0 0
 password cisco
 login
 !
end
```

Lab 9-5 Solution

Solutions to Lab 9-6: ATM NPM-to-ATM NPM Configuration

Examples C-49 and C-50 provide the configuration solutions that satisfy all the exercises for Lab 9-6. Specifically, the exercises asked for the following:

1   Using Figure 9-16 on page 361 for configuration, assign the IP address to the subinterface.

2   Associate your list of mapped addresses to this subinterface.

3   Change the clocking to rely on the internal clock of the router—routers 1, 2, 3, and 4 *only!*

4   Create your PVC segment using the addresses shown in Figure 9-16 on page 361.

5   Create your list of mapped addresses.

6   Check for connectivity of the 144.254.7.x cloud.

7   Examples C-49 and C-50 illustrate configurations for only one pair of routers, Router 1 and Router 5. The configuration for other pairs of routers is very similar.

Example C-49   *Router 1 Configuration for Lab 9-6*

```
!
version 11.2
no service password-encryption
no service udp-small-servers
no service tcp-small-servers
!
hostname R1
!
enable password sanfran
!
no ip domain-lookup

!
interface Ethernet0
 ip address 144.254.1.1 255.255.255.0
!
interface Ethernet1
 ip address 10.0.0.1 255.0.0.0
 media-type 10BaseT
!
interface ATM0
 no ip address
 atm clock internal
!
interface ATM0.7 multipoint
 ip address 144.254.7.1 255.255.255.0
 atm pvc 212 0 112 aal5snap
 map-group ipPvc
!
```

Example C-49 *Router 1 Configuration for Lab 9-6 (Continued)*

```
interface FastEthernet0
 no ip address
 shutdown
!
router igrp 100
 network 144.254.0.0
!
no ip classless
!
map-list ipPvc
 ip 144.254.7.5 atm-vc 212 broadcast
!
!
line con 0
 exec-timeout 0 0
line aux 0
line vty 0 4
 exec-timeout 0 0
 password cisco
 login
!
end
```

Example C-50 *Router 5 Configuration for Lab 9-6*

```
!
version 11.2
no service password-encryption
no service udp-small-servers
no service tcp-small-servers
!
hostname R5
!
enable password sanfran
!
no ip domain-lookup

!
interface Ethernet0
 ip address 144.254.5.5 255.255.255.0
!
interface Ethernet1
 ip address 10.0.0.5 255.0.0.0
 media-type 10BaseT
!
interface ATM0
 no ip address
!
interface ATM0.7 multipoint
 ip address 144.254.7.5 255.255.255.0
```

continues

Example C-50 *Router 5 Configuration for Lab 9-6 (Continued)*

```
atm pvc 221 0 121 aal5snap
 map-group ipPvc
!
interface FastEthernet0
 no ip address
 shutdown
!
router igrp 100
 network 144.254.0.0
!
no ip classless
!
map-list ipPvc
 ip 144.254.7.1 atm-vc 221 broadcast
!
!
line con 0
 exec-timeout 0 0
line aux 0
line vty 0 4
 exec-timeout 0 0
 password cisco
 login
!
end
```

Solutions for Lab 10-1: Configuring LANE for a Single ELAN

Examples C-51 through C-62 provide the configuration solutions that satisfy all the exercises for Lab 10-1. Specifically, the exercises asked for the following:

1 Telnet to R6. Record the ESI portion of the address of R6.

LECS ESI for R6: **00e0.1455.02c3.00**

2 Telnet to Switch 2. R6 is directly connected to Switch 2. Therefore, the prefix portion of the LECS' AESA is Switch 2's prefix. What is the prefix?

Switch 2 prefix: 47.0091.8100.0000.0010.0739.c301

3 What is the LECS AESA?

LECS Address: 47.0091.8100.0000.0010.0739.c301.00e0.1455.02c3.00

4 What is the R6 LES address for this ELAN? Note that the port selector field of the LES must be changed from ** to the interface number where you are putting the LES. You are putting this functionality on subinterface 16. Remember that the subinterface must be expressed in hexadecimal notation when associated as a part of the ATM address.

R6 LES ESI Address: **00E0.1455.02C1.10**

R6 LES NSAP Address: 47.0091.8100.0000.0010.0739.C301.00E0.1455.02C1.10

5 R6 also must create the database. Call the database **cisco**.

6 Add the ELAN called **easy** to the database. Use the AESA found in Task 4.

7 R6 also must enter the default ELAN for this domain. The default is the ELAN named **easy**.

8 On the major ATM interface, each client must enter some basic information. This includes the MTU size, the ilmi PVC, and the capability to learn where the LECS is located.

9 R6 on the major ATM interface also must enter the command to start up the LECS software and associate with database **cisco**.

10 All LECs (clients) must declare themselves as such. Therefore, on **subinterface 16**, enter the IP address from the range 144.254.16.x, as shown in Figure 10-8 on page 390, and declare your subinterface as a client joining the **easy** ELAN.

11 R6, on subinterface 16, also must declare itself to be the LES and the BUS.

12 Verify that your clients are seeing the correct LECS.

13 Verify that your clients are operational.

14 Check your LANE cache to see which destinations you have addresses for.

15 Check for connectivity of the 144.254.16.x cloud.

16 Telnet to R6 and check to see if your router is in R6's server cache.

Example C-51 *Router 1 Configuration for Lab 10-1*

```
Current configuration:
!
version 12.0
service timestamps debug uptime
service timestamps log uptime
no service password-encryption
!
hostname R1
!
enable password sanfran
!
ip subnet-zero
no ip domain-lookup
!
!
ipx routing 0000.0000.0001
!
cns event-service server
!
!
```

continues

Example C-51 *Router 1 Configuration for Lab 10-1 (Continued)*

```
process-max-time 200
!
interface Ethernet0
 ip address 144.254.1.1 255.255.255.0
 no ip directed-broadcast
!
interface Ethernet1
 ip address 10.0.0.1 255.0.0.0
 no ip directed-broadcast
 media-type 10BaseT
!
interface ATM0
 mtu 1500
 no ip address
 no ip directed-broadcast

 atm uni-version 4.0
 atm pvc 1 0 5 qsaal
 atm pvc 3 0 16 ilmi
 no atm ilmi-keepalive
lane auto-config-atm-address
!
interface ATM0.16 multipoint
 ip address 144.254.16.1 255.255.255.0
 no ip directed-broadcast
 lane client ethernet easy
 ipx network 16
!
interface FastEthernet0
 no ip address
 no ip directed-broadcast
 shutdown
!
router igrp 100
 network 144.254.0.0
!
no ip classless
no ip http server
!
!
line con 0
 password sanfran
 transport input none
line aux 0
line vty 0 4
 password sanfran
 login
!
end
```

Example C-52 *Router 2 Configuration for Lab 10-1*

```
Current configuration:
!
version 12.0
service timestamps debug uptime
service timestamps log uptime
no service password-encryption
!
hostname R2
!
enable password sanfran
!
ip subnet-zero
no ip domain-lookup
!
ipx routing 0000.0000.0002
!
cns event-service server
!
!
process-max-time 200
!
interface Ethernet0
 ip address 144.254.2.2 255.255.255.0
 no ip directed-broadcast
!
interface Ethernet1
 ip address 10.0.0.2 255.0.0.0
 no ip directed-broadcast
 media-type 10BaseT
!
interface ATM0
 mtu 1500
 no ip address
 no ip directed-broadcast

 atm uni-version 4.0
 atm pvc 1 0 5 qsaal
 atm pvc 3 0 16 ilmi
 no atm ilmi-keepalive
 lane auto-config-atm-address
!
interface ATM0.16 multipoint
 ip address 144.254.16.2 255.255.255.0
 no ip directed-broadcast
 lane client ethernet easy
 ipx network 16
!
interface FastEthernet0
 no ip address
 no ip directed-broadcast
```

continues

Example C-52 *Router 2 Configuration for Lab 10-1 (Continued)*

```
shutdown
!
router igrp 100
 network 144.254.0.0
!
no ip classless
no ip http server
!
!
line con 0
 password sanfran
 transport input none
line aux 0
line vty 0 4
 password sanfran
 login
!
end
```

Example C-53 *Router 3 Configuration for Lab 10-1*

```
Current configuration:
!
version 12.0
service timestamps debug uptime
service timestamps log uptime
no service password-encryption
!
hostname r3
!
enable secret 5 $1$gjkI$WbGgotlrksCglA7aTCH6B1
enable password sanfran
!
!
!
ip subnet-zero
no ip domain-lookup
!
ipx routing 0000.0000.0003
!
cns event-service server
!
!
process-max-time 200
!
interface Ethernet0
 ip address 144.254.3.3 255.255.255.0
 no ip directed-broadcast
 no ip mroute-cache
 ipx network 30
```

Example C-53 *Router 3 Configuration for Lab 10-1 (Continued)*

```
 no mop enabled
!
interface Ethernet1
 ip address 10.0.0.3 255.0.0.0
 no ip directed-broadcast
 no ip mroute-cache
 media-type 10BaseT
 no mop enabled
!
interface TokenRing0
 no ip address
 no ip directed-broadcast
 no ip mroute-cache
 shutdown
!
interface ATM0
 mtu 1500
 no ip address
 no ip directed-broadcast
 no ip mroute-cache

 atn uni-version 4.0
 atm pvc 2 0 16 ilmi
 atm pvc 5 0 5 qsaal
 no atm ilmi-keepalive
 lane auto-config-atm-address
!
interface ATM0.16 multipoint
 ip address 144.254.16.3 255.255.255.0
 no ip directed-broadcast
 lane client ethernet easy
 ipx network 16
!
router igrp 100
 network 144.254.0.0
!
no ip classless
no ip http server
!
!
!
line con 0
 transport input none
line aux 0
line vty 0 4
 password sanfran
 login
!
end
```

Example C-54 *Router 4 Configuration for Lab 10-1*

```
Current configuration:
!
version 12.0
service timestamps debug uptime
service timestamps log uptime
no service password-encryption
!
hostname R4
!
enable secret 5 $1$c4x5$EhhlcLP/.mCgg4bs6bZZx0
enable password sanfran
!
!
ip subnet-zero
no ip domain-lookup
!
ipx routing 0000.0000.0004
!
cns event-service server
!
!
process-max-time 200
!
interface Ethernet0
 ip address 144.254.4.4 255.255.255.0
 no ip directed-broadcast
 ipx network 40
 no mop enabled
!
interface Ethernet1
 ip address 10.0.0.4 255.0.0.0
 no ip directed-broadcast
 media-type 10BaseT
!
interface Serial0
 no ip address
 no ip directed-broadcast
 shutdown
!
interface Serial1
 no ip address
 no ip directed-broadcast
 shutdown
!
interface ATM0
 no ip address
 no ip directed-broadcast

 atm uni-version 4.0
 atm pvc 1 0 16 ilmi
```

Example C-54 *Router 4 Configuration for Lab 10-1 (Continued)*

```
 atm pvc 10 0 5 qsaal
 atm ilmi-keepalive
 lane auto-config-atm-address
!
interface ATM0.16 multipoint
 ip address 144.254.16.4 255.255.255.0
 no ip directed-broadcast
 lane client ethernet easy
 ipx network 16
!
router igrp 100
 network 144.254.0.0
!
no ip classless
no ip http server
!
!
line con 0
 transport input none
line aux 0
line vty 0 4
 password cisco
 login
!
end
```

Example C-55 *Router 5 Configuration for Lab 10-1*

```
Current configuration:
!
version 12.0
service timestamps debug uptime
service timestamps log uptime
no service password-encryption
!
hostname R5
!
enable secret 5 $1$LOME$zd59yCi.wNaeSPPV1Cz9I0
enable password sanfran
!
!
!
ip subnet-zero
no ip domain-lookup
!
ipx routing 0000.0000.0005
!
cns event-service server
!
!
```

continues

Example C-55 *Router 5 Configuration for Lab 10-1 (Continued)*

```
process-max-time 200
!
interface Ethernet0
 ip address 144.254.5.5 255.255.255.0
 no ip directed-broadcast
 ipx network 50
 no mop enabled
!
interface Ethernet1
 ip address 10.0.0.5 255.0.0.0
 no ip directed-broadcast
 media-type 10BaseT
!
interface ATM0
 no ip address
 no ip directed-broadcast

 atm uni-version 4.0
 atm pvc 1 0 16 ilmi
 atm pvc 5 0 5 qsaal
 no atm ilmi-keepalive
 lane auto-config-atm-address
!
interface ATM0.16 multipoint
 ip address 144.254.16.5 255.255.255.0
 no ip directed-broadcast
 lane client ethernet easy
 ipx network 16
!
interface FastEthernet0
 no ip address
 no ip directed-broadcast
 shutdown
!
router igrp 100
 network 144.254.0.0
!
no ip classless
no ip http server
!
!
!
line con 0
 transport input none
line aux 0
line vty 0 4
 password cisco
 login
!
end
```

Example C-56   *Router 6 Configuration for Lab 10-1*

```
Current configuration:
!
version 12.0
service timestamps debug uptime
service timestamps log uptime
no service password-encryption
!
hostname R6
!
enable secret 5 $1$/pVo$QkJYB4ad/.E4mCL62xYfe1
enable password cisco!
!
!
ip subnet-zero
no ip domain-lookup
!
!
lane database cisco
  name easy server-atm-address 47.00918100000000100739C301.00E0145502C1.10
  default-name easy
!
ipx routing 0000.0000.0006
!
cns event-service server
!
!
process-max-time 200
!
interface Ethernet0
 ip address 144.254.6.6 255.255.255.0
 no ip directed-broadcast
 ipx network 66
 no mop enabled
!
interface Ethernet1
 ip address 10.0.0.6 255.0.0.0
 no ip directed-broadcast
 media-type 10BaseT
!
interface ATM0
 no ip address
 no ip directed-broadcast

 atm uni-version 4.0
 atm pvc 1 0 16 ilmi
 atm pvc 10 0 5 qsaal
 no atm ilmi-keepalive
 lane config auto-config-atm-address
 lane config database cisco
 lane auto-config-atm-address
```

continues

Example C-56 *Router 6 Configuration for Lab 10-1 (Continued)*

```
!
interface ATM0.16 multipoint
 ip address 144.254.16.6 255.255.255.0
 no ip directed-broadcast
 lane server-bus ethernet easy
 lane client ethernet easy
 ipx network 16
!
router igrp 100
 redistribute connected
 network 144.254.0.0
!
no ip classless
no ip http server
!
!
line con 0
 transport input none
line aux 0
line vty 0 4
 password cisco
 login
!
end
```

Example C-57 *Router 7 Configuration for Lab 10-1*

```
Current configuration:
!
version 12.0
service timestamps debug uptime
service timestamps log uptime
no service password-encryption
!
hostname r7
!
enable password sanfran
!
!
!
ip subnet-zero
!
ipx routing 0000.0000.0007
!
cns event-service server
!
!
process-max-time 200
!
interface Ethernet0
```

Example C-57 *Router 7 Configuration for Lab 10-1 (Continued)*

```
 ip address 144.254.7.7 255.255.255.0
 no ip directed-broadcast
 ipx network 77
 no mop enabled
!
interface Ethernet1
 ip address 10.0.0.7 255.0.0.0
 no ip directed-broadcast
 media-type 10BaseT
!
interface ATM0
 no ip address
 no ip directed-broadcast

 atm uni-version 4.0
 atm pvc 5 0 5 qsaal
 atm pvc 16 0 16 ilmi
 no atm ilmi-keepalive
 lane auto-config-atm-address
!
interface ATM0.16 multipoint
 ip address 144.254.16.7 255.255.255.0
 no ip directed-broadcast
 lane client ethernet easy
 ipx network 16
!
interface FastEthernet0
 no ip address
 no ip directed-broadcast
 shutdown
!
router igrp 100
 network 144.254.0.0
!
no ip classless
no ip http server
!
!
line con 0
 transport input none
line aux 0
line vty 0 4
 password sanfran
 login
!
end
```

Example C-58 *Router 8 Configuration for Lab 10-1*

```
Current configuration:
```

Example C-58 *Router 8 Configuration for Lab 10-1 (Continued)*

```
!
version 12.0
service timestamps debug uptime
service timestamps log uptime
no service password-encryption
!
hostname r8
!
enable password sanfran
!
!
!
ip subnet-zero
!
ipx routing 0000.0000.0008
!
cns event-service server
!
!
process-max-time 200
!
interface Ethernet0
 ip address 144.254.8.8 255.255.255.0
 no ip directed-broadcast
 ipx network 88
 no mop enabled
!
interface Ethernet1
 ip address 10.0.0.8 255.0.0.0
 no ip directed-broadcast
 media-type 10BaseT
!
interface ATM0
 no ip address
 no ip directed-broadcast

 atm uni-version 4.0
 atm pvc 5 0 5 qsaal
 atm pvc 16 0 16 ilmi
 no atm ilmi-keepalive
 lane auto-config-atm-address
!
interface ATM0.16 multipoint
 ip address 144.254.16.8 255.255.255.0
 no ip directed-broadcast
lane client ethernet easy
 ipx network 16
!
interface FastEthernet0
 no ip address
```

Example C-58 *Router 8 Configuration for Lab 10-1 (Continued)*

```
 no ip directed-broadcast
 shutdown
!
router igrp 100
 network 144.254.0.0
!
no ip classless
no ip http server
!
!
line con 0
 transport input none
line aux 0
line vty 0 4
 password sanfran
 login
!
end
```

Example C-59 *Router 9 Configuration for Lab 10-1*

```
Current configuration:
!
version 12.0
service timestamps debug uptime
service timestamps log uptime
no service password-encryption
!
hostname r9
!
enable password sanfran
!
!
!
ip subnet-zero
!
ipx routing 0000.0000.0009
!
cns event-service server
!
!
process-max-time 200
!
interface Ethernet0
 ip address 144.254.9.9 255.255.255.0
 no ip directed-broadcast
 ipx network 99
 no mop enabled
!
interface Ethernet1
```

continues

Example C-59 *Router 9 Configuration for Lab 10-1 (Continued)*

```
 ip address 10.0.0.9 255.0.0.0
 no ip directed-broadcast
 media-type 10BaseT
!
interface TokenRing0
 no ip address
 no ip directed-broadcast
 shutdown
!
interface ATM0
 no ip address
 no ip directed-broadcast

 atm uni-version 4.0
 atm pvc 5 0 5 qsaal
 atm pvc 16 0 16 ilmi
 no atm ilmi-keepalive
 lane auto-config-atm-address
!
interface ATM0.16 multipoint
 ip address 144.254.16.9 255.255.255.0
 no ip directed-broadcast
 lane client ethernet easy
 ipx network 16
!
router igrp 100
 network 144.254.0.0
!
no ip classless
no ip http server
!
!
!
!
!
line con 0
 transport input none
line aux 0
line vty 0 4
 password sanfran
 login
!
end
```

Example C-60 *Switch 1 Configuration for Lab 10-1*

```
!
version 11.3
no service pad
no service udp-small-servers
```

Example C-60 *Switch 1 Configuration for Lab 10-1 (Continued)*

```
no service tcp-small-servers
!
hostname Switch_1
!
enable password sanfran
!
no ip domain-lookup
!
atm address 47.0091.8100.0000.0010.0739.9e01.0010.0739.9e01.00
atm lecs-address-default 47.0091.8100.0000.0010.0739.c301.00e0.1455.02c3.00 01
!
atm router pnni
 node 1 level 56 lowest
  redistribute atm-static
!
!
interface ATM0/0/0
 shutdown
 no ip address
!
interface ATM0/0/1
 no ip address
!
interface ATM0/0/2
 no ip address
!
interface ATM0/0/3
 no ip address
 shutdown
!
interface ATM0/1/0
 no ip address
 no atm auto-configuration
 atm uni version 3.1
 atm maxvpi-bits 3
 atm maxvci-bits 10
 atm pvc 0 114  interface  ATM0/0/1 0 114
 atm pvc 0 115  interface  ATM0/0/1 0 115
 atm pvc 0 116  interface  ATM0/0/1 0 116
 atm pvc 0 117  interface  ATM0/0/2 0 117
 atm pvc 0 118  interface  ATM0/0/2 0 118
 atm pvc 0 119  interface  ATM0/0/2 0 119
!
interface ATM0/1/1
 no ip address
 no atm auto-configuration
 atm uni version 3.1
 atm maxvpi-bits 3
 atm maxvci-bits 10
 atm pvc 0 121  interface  ATM0/1/0 0 112
```

continues

Example C-60 *Switch 1 Configuration for Lab 10-1 (Continued)*

```
atm pvc 0 124   interface  ATM0/0/1 0 124
atm pvc 0 125   interface  ATM0/0/1 0 125
atm pvc 0 126   interface  ATM0/0/1 0 126
atm pvc 0 127   interface  ATM0/0/2 0 127
atm pvc 0 128   interface  ATM0/0/2 0 128
atm pvc 0 129   interface  ATM0/0/2 0 129
!
interface ATM0/1/2
 no ip address
 no atm auto-configuration
 atm uni version 3.1
 atm maxvpi-bits 3
 atm maxvci-bits 10
 atm pvc 0 120   interface  ATM0/1/0 0 120
 atm pvc 0 131   interface  ATM0/1/0 0 113
 atm pvc 0 132   interface  ATM0/1/1 0 123
 atm pvc 0 134   interface  ATM0/0/1 0 134
 atm pvc 0 135   interface  ATM0/0/1 0 135
 atm pvc 0 136   interface  ATM0/0/1 0 136
 atm pvc 0 137   interface  ATM0/0/2 0 137
 atm pvc 0 138   interface  ATM0/0/2 0 138
 atm pvc 0 139   interface  ATM0/0/2 0 139
!
interface ATM0/1/3
 no ip address
!
interface ATM2/0/0
 no ip address
 atm maxvp-number 0
!
interface Ethernet2/0/0
 ip address 10.0.0.11 255.0.0.0
!
ip classless
!
line con 0
 exec-timeout 0 0
 password cisco
 login
line aux 0
line vty 0 4
 exec-timeout 0 0
 password cisco
 login
!
end
```

Example C-61 *Switch 2 Configuration for Lab 10-1*

```
!
```

Example C-61 *Switch 2 Configuration for Lab 10-1 (Continued)*

```
version 11.3
no service pad
no service udp-small-servers
no service tcp-small-servers
!
hostname Switch_2
!
enable password sanfran
!
no ip domain-lookup
!
atm address 47.0091.8100.0000.0010.0739.a101.0010.0739.a101.00
atm lecs-address-default 47.0091.8100.0000.0010.0739.c301.00e0.1455.02c3.00 01
!
atm router pnni
 node 1 level 56 lowest
  redistribute atm-static
!
!
interface ATM0/0/0
 shutdown
 no ip address
!
interface ATM0/0/1
 no ip address
!
interface ATM0/0/2
 shutdown
 no ip address
!
interface ATM0/0/3
 no ip address
!
interface ATM0/1/0
 no ip address
 no atm auto-configuration
 atm uni version 3.1
 atm maxvpi-bits 3
 atm maxvci-bits 10
 atm pvc 0 141   interface   ATM0/0/1 0 114
 atm pvc 0 142   interface   ATM0/0/1 0 124
 atm pvc 0 143   interface   ATM0/0/1 0 134
 atm pvc 0 147   interface   ATM0/0/3 0 147
 atm pvc 0 148   interface   ATM0/0/3 0 148
 atm pvc 0 149   interface   ATM0/0/3 0 149
!
interface ATM0/1/1
 no ip address
 no atm auto-configuration
 atm uni version 3.1
```

continues

Example C-61   *Switch 2 Configuration for Lab 10-1 (Continued)*

```
atm maxvpi-bits 3
atm maxvci-bits 10
atm pvc 0 151   interface  ATM0/0/1 0 115
atm pvc 0 152   interface  ATM0/0/1 0 125
atm pvc 0 153   interface  ATM0/0/1 0 135
atm pvc 0 154   interface  ATM0/1/0 0 145
atm pvc 0 157   interface  ATM0/0/3 0 157
atm pvc 0 158   interface  ATM0/0/3 0 158
atm pvc 0 159   interface  ATM0/0/3 0 159
!
interface ATM0/1/2
 no ip address
 no atm auto-configuration
 atm uni version 3.1
 atm maxvpi-bits 3
 atm maxvci-bits 10
 atm pvc 0 161   interface  ATM0/0/1 0 116
 atm pvc 0 162   interface  ATM0/0/1 0 126
 atm pvc 0 163   interface  ATM0/0/1 0 136
 atm pvc 0 164   interface  ATM0/1/0 0 146
 atm pvc 0 165   interface  ATM0/1/1 0 156
 atm pvc 0 167   interface  ATM0/0/3 0 167
 atm pvc 0 168   interface  ATM0/0/3 0 168
 atm pvc 0 169   interface  ATM0/0/3 0 169
!
interface ATM0/1/3
 no ip address
!
interface ATM2/0/0
 no ip address
 atm maxvp-number 0
!
interface Ethernet2/0/0
 ip address 10.0.0.12 255.0.0.0
!
ip classless
!
line con 0
 exec-timeout 0 0
 password cisco
 login
line aux 0
line vty 0 4
 exec-timeout 0 0
 password cisco
 login
!
end
```

Example C-62 *Switch 3 Configuration for Lab 10-1*

```
!
version 11.3
no service pad
no service udp-small-servers
no service tcp-small-servers
!
hostname Switch_3
!
boot system flash bootflash:ls1010-wp-mz.113-0.8.TWA4.2.bin
enable password sanfran
!
no ip domain-lookup
!
atm address 47.0091.8100.0000.0010.0739.c301.0010.0739.c301.00
atm lecs-address-default 47.0091.8100.0000.0010.0739.c301.00e0.1455.02c3.00 01
!
atm router pnni
 node 1 level 56 lowest
  redistribute atm-static
!
!
interface ATM0/0/0
 shutdown
 no ip address
!
interface ATM0/0/1
 shutdown
 no ip address
!
interface ATM0/0/2
 no ip address
!
interface ATM0/0/3
 no ip address
!
interface ATM0/1/0
 no ip address
 no atm auto-configuration
 atm uni version 3.1
 atm maxvpi-bits 3
 atm maxvci-bits 10
 atm pvc 0 171  interface  ATM0/0/2 0 117
 atm pvc 0 172  interface  ATM0/0/2 0 127
 atm pvc 0 173  interface  ATM0/0/2 0 137
 atm pvc 0 174  interface  ATM0/0/3 0 147
 atm pvc 0 175  interface  ATM0/0/3 0 157
 atm pvc 0 176  interface  ATM0/0/3 0 167
!
interface ATM0/1/1
 no ip address
```

continues

Example C-62 *Switch 3 Configuration for Lab 10-1 (Continued)*

```
no atm auto-configuration
atm uni version 3.1
atm maxvpi-bits 3
atm maxvci-bits 10
atm pvc 0 181   interface   ATM0/0/2 0 118
atm pvc 0 182   interface   ATM0/0/2 0 128
atm pvc 0 183   interface   ATM0/0/2 0 138
atm pvc 0 184   interface   ATM0/0/3 0 148
atm pvc 0 185   interface   ATM0/0/3 0 158
atm pvc 0 186   interface   ATM0/0/3 0 168
atm pvc 0 187   interface   ATM0/1/0 0 178
!
interface ATM0/1/2
 no ip address
 no atm auto-configuration
 atm uni version 3.1
 atm maxvpi-bits 3
 atm maxvci-bits 10
 atm pvc 0 191   interface   ATM0/0/2 0 119
 atm pvc 0 192   interface   ATM0/0/2 0 129
 atm pvc 0 193   interface   ATM0/0/2 0 139
 atm pvc 0 194   interface   ATM0/0/3 0 149
 atm pvc 0 195   interface   ATM0/0/3 0 159
 atm pvc 0 196   interface   ATM0/0/3 0 169
 atm pvc 0 197   interface   ATM0/1/0 0 179
 atm pvc 0 198   interface   ATM0/1/1 0 189
!
interface ATM0/1/3
 no ip address
!
interface ATM1/0/0
 no ip address
!
interface ATM1/0/1
 no ip address
!
interface ATM1/0/2
 no ip address
!
interface ATM1/0/3
 no ip address
!
interface ATM2/0/0
 no ip address
 atm maxvp-number 0
!
interface Ethernet2/0/0
 ip address 10.0.0.13 255.0.0.0
!
ip classless
```

Example C-62 *Switch 3 Configuration for Lab 10-1 (Continued)*

```
!
line con 0
 exec-timeout 0 0
 password cisco
 login
line aux 0
line vty 0 4
 exec-timeout 0 0
 password cisco
 login
!
end
```

Solutions for Lab 10-2: Configuring LANE for a Single ELAN with SSRP

Examples C-63 through C-74 provide the configuration solutions that satisfy all the exercises for Lab 10-2. Specifically, the exercises asked for the following:

1 Copy the LECS database from R6 exactly.

2 Add R1's AESA to the LECS list.

3 Set up R8 as an LES/BUS.

4 Change the LECS database of R1 to reflect R8 as a secondary LES/BUS.

5 Change the LECS database of R6 to reflect R8 as a secondary LES/BUS.

Example C-63 *Router 1 Configuration for Lab 10-2*

```
Current configuration:
!
version 12.0
service timestamps debug uptime
service timestamps log uptime
no service password-encryption
!
hostname R1
!
enable password sanfran
!
ip subnet-zero
no ip domain-lookup
!
lane database cisco
  name easy server-atm-address 47.00918100000000100739C301.00E0145502C1.10
  name easy server-atm-address 47.00918100000000100739A101.00E01454DCE1.10
  default-name easy
```

continues

Example C-63   *Router 1 Configuration for Lab 10-2 (Continued)*

```
!
ipx routing 0000.0000.0001
!
cns event-service server
!
!
process-max-time 200
!
interface Ethernet0
 ip address 144.254.1.1 255.255.255.0
 no ip directed-broadcast
!
interface Ethernet1
 ip address 10.0.0.1 255.0.0.0
 no ip directed-broadcast
 media-type 10BaseT
!
interface ATM0
 mtu 1500
 no ip address
 no ip directed-broadcast
 atm uni-version 4.0
 atm pvc 1 0 5 qsaal
 atm pvc 3 0 16 ilmi
 no atm ilmi-keepalive
 lane config auto-config-atm-address
 lane config database cisco
 lane auto-config-atm-address
!
interface ATM0.16 multipoint
 ip address 144.254.16.1 255.255.255.0
 no ip directed-broadcast
 lane client ethernet easy
 ipx network 16
!
interface FastEthernet0
 no ip address
 no ip directed-broadcast
 shutdown
!
router igrp 100
 network 144.254.0.0
!
no ip classless
no ip http server
!
!
line con 0
 password sanfran
 transport input none
```

Example C-63 *Router 1 Configuration for Lab 10-2 (Continued)*

```
line aux 0
line vty 0 4
 password sanfran
 login
!
end
```

Example C-64 *Router 2 Configuration for Lab 10-2*

```
Current configuration:
!
version 12.0
service timestamps debug uptime
service timestamps log uptime
no service password-encryption
!
hostname R2
!
enable password sanfran
!
ip subnet-zero
no ip domain-lookup
!
ipx routing 0000.0000.0002
!
cns event-service server
!
!
process-max-time 200
!
interface Ethernet0
 ip address 144.254.2.2 255.255.255.0
 no ip directed-broadcast
!
interface Ethernet1
 ip address 10.0.0.2 255.0.0.0
 no ip directed-broadcast
 media-type 10BaseT
!
interface ATM0
 mtu 1500
 no ip address
 no ip directed-broadcast
 atm uni-version 4.0
 atm pvc 1 0 5 qsaal
 atm pvc 3 0 16 ilmi
 no atm ilmi-keepalive
 lane auto-config-atm-address
!
interface ATM0.16 multipoint
```

continues

Example C-64 *Router 2 Configuration for Lab 10-2 (Continued)*

```
 ip address 144.254.16.2 255.255.255.0
 no ip directed-broadcast
 lane client ethernet easy
 ipx network 16
!
interface FastEthernet0
 no ip address
 no ip directed-broadcast
 shutdown
!
router igrp 100
 network 144.254.0.0
!
no ip classless
no ip http server
!
!
line con 0
 password sanfran
 transport input none
line aux 0
line vty 0 4
 password sanfran
 login
!
end
```

Example C-65 *Router 3 Configuration for Lab 10-2*

```
Current configuration:
!
version 12.0
service timestamps debug uptime
service timestamps log uptime
no service password-encryption
!
hostname r3
!
enable secret 5 $1$gjkI$WbGgotlrksCglA7aTCH6B1
enable password sanfran
!
!
!
ip subnet-zero
no ip domain-lookup
!
ipx routing 0000.0000.0003
!
cns event-service server
!
```

Example C-65 *Router 3 Configuration for Lab 10-2 (Continued)*

```
!
process-max-time 200
!
interface Ethernet0
 ip address 144.254.3.3 255.255.255.0
 no ip directed-broadcast
 no ip mroute-cache
 ipx network 30
 no mop enabled
!
interface Ethernet1
 ip address 10.0.0.3 255.0.0.0
 no ip directed-broadcast
 no ip mroute-cache
 media-type 10BaseT
 no mop enabled
!
interface TokenRing0
 no ip address
 no ip directed-broadcast
 no ip mroute-cache
 shutdown
!
interface ATM0
 mtu 1500
 no ip address
 no ip directed-broadcast
 no ip mroute-cache
 atm uni-version 4.0
 atm pvc 2 0 16 ilmi
 atm pvc 5 0 5 qsaal
 no atm ilmi-keepalive
 lane auto-config-atm-address
!
interface ATM0.16 multipoint
 ip address 144.254.16.3 255.255.255.0
 no ip directed-broadcast
 lane client ethernet easy
 ipx network 16
!
router igrp 100
 network 144.254.0.0
!
no ip classless
no ip http server
!
!
!
line con 0
 transport input none
```

continues

Example C-65 *Router 3 Configuration for Lab 10-2 (Continued)*

```
line aux 0
line vty 0 4
 password sanfran
 login
!
end
```

Example C-66 *Router 4 Configuration for Lab 10-2*

```
Current configuration:
!
version 12.0
service timestamps debug uptime
service timestamps log uptime
no service password-encryption
!
hostname R4
!
enable secret 5 $1$c4x5$EhhlcLP/.mCgg4bs6bZZx0
enable password sanfran
!
!
ip subnet-zero
no ip domain-lookup
!
ipx routing 0000.0000.0004
!
cns event-service server
!
!
process-max-time 200
!
interface Ethernet0
 ip address 144.254.4.4 255.255.255.0
 no ip directed-broadcast
 ipx network 40
 no mop enabled
!
interface Ethernet1
 ip address 10.0.0.4 255.0.0.0
 no ip directed-broadcast
 media-type 10BaseT
!
interface Serial0
 no ip address
 no ip directed-broadcast
 shutdown
!
interface Serial1
 no ip address
```

Example C-66 *Router 4 Configuration for Lab 10-2 (Continued)*

```
 no ip directed-broadcast
 shutdown
!
interface ATM0
 no ip address
 no ip directed-broadcast
 atm uni-version 4.0
 atm pvc 1 0 16 ilmi
 atm pvc 10 0 5 qsaal
 atm ilmi-keepalive
 lane auto-config-atm-address
!
interface ATM0.16 multipoint
 ip address 144.254.16.4 255.255.255.0
 no ip directed-broadcast
 lane client ethernet easy
 ipx network 16
!
router igrp 100
 network 144.254.0.0
!
no ip classless
no ip http server
!
!
line con 0
 transport input none
line aux 0
line vty 0 4
 password cisco
 login
!
end
```

Example C-67 *Router 5 Configuration for Lab 10-2*

```
Current configuration:
!
version 12.0
service timestamps debug uptime
service timestamps log uptime
no service password-encryption
!
hostname R5
!
enable secret 5 $1$LOME$zd59yCi.wNaeSPPV1Cz9I0
enable password sanfran
!
!
!
```

continues

Example C-67 *Router 5 Configuration for Lab 10-2 (Continued)*

```
ip subnet-zero
no ip domain-lookup
!
ipx routing 0000.0000.0005
!
cns event-service server
!
!
process-max-time 200
!
interface Ethernet0
 ip address 144.254.5.5 255.255.255.0
 no ip directed-broadcast
 ipx network 50
 no mop enabled
!
interface Ethernet1
 ip address 10.0.0.5 255.0.0.0
 no ip directed-broadcast
 media-type 10BaseT
!
interface ATM0
 no ip address
 no ip directed-broadcast
 atm uni-version 4.0
 atm pvc 1 0 16 ilmi
 atm pvc 5 0 5 qsaal
 no atm ilmi-keepalive
 lane auto-config-atm-address
!
interface ATM0.16 multipoint
 ip address 144.254.16.5 255.255.255.0
 no ip directed-broadcast
 lane client ethernet easy
 ipx network 16
!
interface FastEthernet0
 no ip address
 no ip directed-broadcast
 shutdown
!
router igrp 100
 network 144.254.0.0
!
no ip classless
no ip http server
!
!
!
line con 0
```

Example C-67 *Router 5 Configuration for Lab 10-2 (Continued)*

```
 transport input none
line aux 0
line vty 0 4
 password cisco
 login
!
end
```

Example C-68 *Router 6 Configuration for Lab 10-2*

```
Current configuration:
!
version 12.0
service timestamps debug uptime
service timestamps log uptime
no service password-encryption
!
hostname R6
!
enable secret 5 $1$/pVo$QkJYB4ad/.E4mCL62xYfe1
enable password cisco!
!
!
ip subnet-zero
no ip domain-lookup
!
!
lane database cisco
  name easy server-atm-address 47.00918100000000100739C301.00E0145502C1.10
  name easy server-atm-address 47.00918100000000100739A101.00E01454DCE1.10
  default-name easy
!
ipx routing 0000.0000.0006
!
cns event-service server
!
!
process-max-time 200
!
interface Ethernet0
 ip address 144.254.6.6 255.255.255.0
 no ip directed-broadcast
 ipx network 66
 no mop enabled
!
interface Ethernet1
 ip address 10.0.0.6 255.0.0.0
 no ip directed-broadcast
 media-type 10BaseT
!
```

continues

Example C-68 *Router 6 Configuration for Lab 10-2 (Continued)*

```
interface ATM0
 no ip address
 no ip directed-broadcast
 atm uni-version 4.0
 atm pvc 1 0 16 ilmi
 atm pvc 10 0 5 qsaal
 no atm ilmi-keepalive
 lane config auto-config-atm-address
 lane config database cisco
 lane auto-config-atm-address
!
interface ATM0.16 multipoint
 ip address 144.254.16.6 255.255.255.0
 no ip directed-broadcast
 lane server-bus ethernet easy
 lane client ethernet easy
 ipx network 16
!
router igrp 100
 redistribute connected
 network 144.254.0.0
!
no ip classless
no ip http server
!
!
line con 0
 transport input none
line aux 0
line vty 0 4
 password cisco
 login
!
end
```

Example C-69 *Router 7 Configuration for Lab 10-2*

```
Current configuration:
!
version 12.0
service timestamps debug uptime
service timestamps log uptime
no service password-encryption
!
hostname r7
!
enable password sanfran
!
!
!
```

Example C-69 *Router 7 Configuration for Lab 10-2 (Continued)*

```
ip subnet-zero
!
ipx routing 0000.0000.0007
!
cns event-service server
!
!
process-max-time 200
!
interface Ethernet0
 ip address 144.254.7.7 255.255.255.0
 no ip directed-broadcast
 ipx network 77
 no mop enabled
!
interface Ethernet1
 ip address 10.0.0.7 255.0.0.0
 no ip directed-broadcast
 media-type 10BaseT
!
interface ATM0
 no ip address
 no ip directed-broadcast
 atm uni-version 4.0
 atm pvc 5 0 5 qsaal
 atm pvc 16 0 16 ilmi
 no atm ilmi-keepalive
 lane auto-config-atm-address
!
interface ATM0.16 multipoint
 ip address 144.254.16.7 255.255.255.0
 no ip directed-broadcast
 lane client ethernet easy
 ipx network 16
!
interface FastEthernet0
 no ip address
 no ip directed-broadcast
 shutdown
!
router igrp 100
 network 144.254.0.0
!
no ip classless
no ip http server
!
!
line con 0
 transport input none
line aux 0
```

continues

Example C-69 *Router 7 Configuration for Lab 10-2 (Continued)*

```
line vty 0 4
 password sanfran
 login
!
end
```

Example C-70 *Router 8 Configuration for Lab 10-2*

```
Current configuration:
!
version 12.0
service timestamps debug uptime
service timestamps log uptime
no service password-encryption
!
hostname r8
!
enable password sanfran
!
!
!
ip subnet-zero
!
ipx routing 0000.0000.0008
!
cns event-service server
!
!
process-max-time 200
!
interface Ethernet0
 ip address 144.254.8.8 255.255.255.0
 no ip directed-broadcast
 ipx network 88
 no mop enabled
!
interface Ethernet1
 ip address 10.0.0.8 255.0.0.0
 no ip directed-broadcast
 media-type 10BaseT
!
interface ATM0
 no ip address
 no ip directed-broadcast
 atm uni-version 4.0
 atm pvc 5 0 5 qsaal
 atm pvc 16 0 16 ilmi
 no atm ilmi-keepalive
 lane auto-config-atm-address
!
```

Example C-70 *Router 8 Configuration for Lab 10-2 (Continued)*

```
interface ATM0.16 multipoint
 ip address 144.254.16.8 255.255.255.0
 no ip directed-broadcast
 lane server-bus ethernet easy
 lane client ethernet easy
 ipx network 16
!
interface FastEthernet0
 no ip address
 no ip directed-broadcast
 shutdown
!
router igrp 100
 network 144.254.0.0
!
no ip classless
no ip http server
!
!
line con 0
 transport input none
line aux 0
line vty 0 4
 password sanfran
 login
!
end
```

Example C-71 *Router 9 Configuration for Lab 10-2*

```
Current configuration:
!
version 12.0
service timestamps debug uptime
service timestamps log uptime
no service password-encryption
!
hostname r9
!
enable password sanfran
!
!
!
ip subnet-zero
!
ipx routing 0000.0000.0009
!
cns event-service server
!
!
```

continues

Example C-71   *Router 9 Configuration for Lab 10-2 (Continued)*

```
process-max-time 200
!
interface Ethernet0
 ip address 144.254.9.9 255.255.255.0
 no ip directed-broadcast
 ipx network 99
 no mop enabled
!
interface Ethernet1
 ip address 10.0.0.9 255.0.0.0
 no ip directed-broadcast
 media-type 10BaseT
!
interface TokenRing0
 no ip address
 no ip directed-broadcast
 shutdown
!
interface ATM0
 no ip address
 no ip directed-broadcast
 atm uni-version 4.0
 atm pvc 5 0 5 qsaal
 atm pvc 16 0 16 ilmi
 no atm ilmi-keepalive
 lane auto-config-atm-address
!
interface ATM0.16 multipoint
 ip address 144.254.16.9 255.255.255.0
 no ip directed-broadcast
 lane client ethernet easy
 ipx network 16
!
router igrp 100
 network 144.254.0.0
!
no ip classless
no ip http server
!
!
!
!
!
line con 0
 transport input none
line aux 0
line vty 0 4
 password sanfran
 login
!
```

Example C-71 *Router 9 Configuration for Lab 10-2 (Continued)*

```
end
```

Example C-72 *Switch 1 Configuration for Lab 10-2*

```
!
version 11.3
no service pad
no service udp-small-servers
no service tcp-small-servers
!
hostname Switch_1
!
enable password sanfran
!
no ip domain-lookup
!
atm address 47.0091.8100.0000.0010.0739.9e01.0010.0739.9e01.00
atm lecs-address-default 47.0091.8100.0000.0010.0739.c301.00e0.1455.02c3.00 01
atm lecs-address-default 47.0091.8100.0000.0010.0739.a101.00e0.1a56.54c1.00 02
!
atm router pnni
 node 1 level 56 lowest
  redistribute atm-static
!
!
interface ATM0/0/0
 shutdown
 no ip address
!
interface ATM0/0/1
 no ip address
!
interface ATM0/0/2
 no ip address
!
interface ATM0/0/3
 no ip address
 shutdown
!
interface ATM0/1/0
 no ip address
 no atm auto-configuration
 atm uni version 3.1
 atm maxvpi-bits 3
 atm maxvci-bits 10
 atm pvc 0 114  interface  ATM0/0/1 0 114
 atm pvc 0 115  interface  ATM0/0/1 0 115
 atm pvc 0 116  interface  ATM0/0/1 0 116
 atm pvc 0 117  interface  ATM0/0/2 0 117
 atm pvc 0 118  interface  ATM0/0/2 0 118
```

continues

Example C-72 *Switch 1 Configuration for Lab 10-2 (Continued)*

```
 atm pvc 0 119  interface  ATM0/0/2 0 119
!
interface ATM0/1/1
 no ip address
 no atm auto-configuration
 atm uni version 3.1
 atm maxvpi-bits 3
 atm maxvci-bits 10
 atm pvc 0 121  interface  ATM0/1/0 0 112
 atm pvc 0 124  interface  ATM0/0/1 0 124
 atm pvc 0 125  interface  ATM0/0/1 0 125
 atm pvc 0 126  interface  ATM0/0/1 0 126
 atm pvc 0 127  interface  ATM0/0/2 0 127
 atm pvc 0 128  interface  ATM0/0/2 0 128
 atm pvc 0 129  interface  ATM0/0/2 0 129
!
interface ATM0/1/2
 no ip address
 no atm auto-configuration
 atm uni version 3.1
 atm maxvpi-bits 3
 atm maxvci-bits 10
 atm pvc 0 120  interface  ATM0/1/0 0 120
 atm pvc 0 131  interface  ATM0/1/0 0 113
 atm pvc 0 132  interface  ATM0/1/1 0 123
 atm pvc 0 134  interface  ATM0/0/1 0 134
 atm pvc 0 135  interface  ATM0/0/1 0 135
 atm pvc 0 136  interface  ATM0/0/1 0 136
 atm pvc 0 137  interface  ATM0/0/2 0 137
 atm pvc 0 138  interface  ATM0/0/2 0 138
 atm pvc 0 139  interface  ATM0/0/2 0 139
!
interface ATM0/1/3
 no ip address
!
interface ATM2/0/0
 no ip address
 atm maxvp-number 0
!
interface Ethernet2/0/0
 ip address 10.0.0.11 255.0.0.0
!
ip classless
!
line con 0
 exec-timeout 0 0
 password cisco
 login
line aux 0
line vty 0 4
```

Example C-72 *Switch 1 Configuration for Lab 10-2 (Continued)*

```
exec-timeout 0 0
password cisco
login
!
end
```

Example C-73 *Switch 2 Configuration for Lab 10-2*

```
!
version 11.3
no service pad
no service udp-small-servers
no service tcp-small-servers
!
hostname Switch_2
!
enable password sanfran
!
no ip domain-lookup
!
atm address 47.0091.8100.0000.0010.0739.a101.0010.0739.a101.00
atm lecs-address-default 47.0091.8100.0000.0010.0739.c301.00e0.1455.02c3.00 01
atm lecs-address-default 47.0091.8100.0000.0010.0739.a101.00e0.1a56.54c1.00 02
!
atm router pnni
 node 1 level 56 lowest
   redistribute atm-static
!
!
interface ATM0/0/0
 shutdown
 no ip address
!
interface ATM0/0/1
 no ip address
!
interface ATM0/0/2
 shutdown
 no ip address
!
interface ATM0/0/3
 no ip address
!
interface ATM0/1/0
 no ip address
 no atm auto-configuration
 atm uni version 3.1
 atm maxvpi-bits 3
 atm maxvci-bits 10
 atm pvc 0 141  interface  ATM0/0/1 0 114
```

continues

Example C-73 *Switch 2 Configuration for Lab 10-2 (Continued)*

```
atm pvc 0 142   interface   ATM0/0/1 0 124
atm pvc 0 143   interface   ATM0/0/1 0 134
atm pvc 0 147   interface   ATM0/0/3 0 147
atm pvc 0 148   interface   ATM0/0/3 0 148
atm pvc 0 149   interface   ATM0/0/3 0 149
!
interface ATM0/1/1
 no ip address
 no atm auto-configuration
 atm uni version 3.1
 atm maxvpi-bits 3
 atm maxvci-bits 10
 atm pvc 0 151   interface   ATM0/0/1 0 115
 atm pvc 0 152   interface   ATM0/0/1 0 125
 atm pvc 0 153   interface   ATM0/0/1 0 135
 atm pvc 0 154   interface   ATM0/1/0 0 145
 atm pvc 0 157   interface   ATM0/0/3 0 157
 atm pvc 0 158   interface   ATM0/0/3 0 158
 atm pvc 0 159   interface   ATM0/0/3 0 159
!
interface ATM0/1/2
 no ip address
 no atm auto-configuration
 atm uni version 3.1
 atm maxvpi-bits 3
 atm maxvci-bits 10
 atm pvc 0 161   interface   ATM0/0/1 0 116
 atm pvc 0 162   interface   ATM0/0/1 0 126
 atm pvc 0 163   interface   ATM0/0/1 0 136
 atm pvc 0 164   interface   ATM0/1/0 0 146
 atm pvc 0 165   interface   ATM0/1/1 0 156
 atm pvc 0 167   interface   ATM0/0/3 0 167
 atm pvc 0 168   interface   ATM0/0/3 0 168
 atm pvc 0 169   interface   ATM0/0/3 0 169
!
interface ATM0/1/3
 no ip address
!
interface ATM2/0/0
 no ip address
 atm maxvp-number 0
!
interface Ethernet2/0/0
 ip address 10.0.0.12 255.0.0.0
!
ip classless
!
line con 0
 exec-timeout 0 0
 password cisco
```

Example C-73 *Switch 2 Configuration for Lab 10-2 (Continued)*

```
 login
line aux 0
line vty 0 4
 exec-timeout 0 0
 password cisco
 login
!
end
```

Example C-74 *Switch 3 Configuration for Lab 10-2*

```
!
version 11.3
no service pad
no service udp-small-servers
no service tcp-small-servers
!
hostname Switch_3
!
boot system flash bootflash:ls1010-wp-mz.113-0.8.TWA4.2.bin
enable password sanfran
!
no ip domain-lookup
!
atm address 47.0091.8100.0000.0010.0739.c301.0010.0739.c301.00
atm lecs-address-default 47.0091.8100.0000.0010.0739.c301.00e0.1455.02c3.00 01
atm lecs-address-default 47.0091.8100.0000.0010.0739.a101.00e0.1a56.54c1.00 02
!
atm router pnni
 node 1 level 56 lowest
   redistribute atm-static
!
!
interface ATM0/0/0
 shutdown
 no ip address
!
interface ATM0/0/1
 shutdown
 no ip address
!
interface ATM0/0/2
 no ip address
!
interface ATM0/0/3
 no ip address
!
interface ATM0/1/0
 no ip address
 no atm auto-configuration
```

continues

Example C-74 *Switch 3 Configuration for Lab 10-2 (Continued)*

```
 atm uni version 3.1
 atm maxvpi-bits 3
 atm maxvci-bits 10
 atm pvc 0 171  interface  ATM0/0/2 0 117
 atm pvc 0 172  interface  ATM0/0/2 0 127
 atm pvc 0 173  interface  ATM0/0/2 0 137
 atm pvc 0 174  interface  ATM0/0/3 0 147
 atm pvc 0 175  interface  ATM0/0/3 0 157
 atm pvc 0 176  interface  ATM0/0/3 0 167
!
interface ATM0/1/1
 no ip address
 no atm auto-configuration
 atm uni version 3.1
 atm maxvpi-bits 3
 atm maxvci-bits 10
 atm pvc 0 181  interface  ATM0/0/2 0 118
 atm pvc 0 182  interface  ATM0/0/2 0 128
 atm pvc 0 183  interface  ATM0/0/2 0 138
 atm pvc 0 184  interface  ATM0/0/3 0 148
 atm pvc 0 185  interface  ATM0/0/3 0 158
 atm pvc 0 186  interface  ATM0/0/3 0 168
 atm pvc 0 187  interface  ATM0/1/0 0 178
!
interface ATM0/1/2
 no ip address
 no atm auto-configuration
 atm uni version 3.1
 atm maxvpi-bits 3
 atm maxvci-bits 10
 atm pvc 0 191  interface  ATM0/0/2 0 119
 atm pvc 0 192  interface  ATM0/0/2 0 129
 atm pvc 0 193  interface  ATM0/0/2 0 139
 atm pvc 0 194  interface  ATM0/0/3 0 149
 atm pvc 0 195  interface  ATM0/0/3 0 159
 atm pvc 0 196  interface  ATM0/0/3 0 169
 atm pvc 0 197  interface  ATM0/1/0 0 179
 atm pvc 0 198  interface  ATM0/1/1 0 189
!
interface ATM0/1/3
 no ip address
!
interface ATM1/0/0
 no ip address
!
interface ATM1/0/1
 no ip address
!
interface ATM1/0/2
 no ip address
```

Example C-74 *Switch 3 Configuration for Lab 10-2 (Continued)*

```
!
interface ATM1/0/3
 no ip address
!
interface ATM2/0/0
 no ip address
 atm maxvp-number 0
!
interface Ethernet2/0/0
 ip address 10.0.0.13 255.0.0.0
!
ip classless
!
line con 0
 exec-timeout 0 0
 password cisco
 login
line aux 0
line vty 0 4
 exec-timeout 0 0
 password cisco
 login
!
end
```

Solutions for Lab 10-3: Configuring LANE for Multiple ELANs

Examples C-75 through C-86 provide the configuration solutions that satisfy all the exercises for Lab 10-3. Specifically, the exercises asked for the following:

1 What is the LES AESA for every router (remember that the port selector is in hex)?

Here is the LES AESA for every router:

Router #	ELAN Name	LES AESA
R1	eng	47.0091.81000000001007399E01.00FE5432D213.0B
R2	mkt	47.0091.81000000001007399e01.00C01344AC23.0C
R3	sales	47.0091.81000000001007399e01.012C544A2355.0D
R4	devtest	47.00918100000000100739C301.00F123345C11.0E
R5	training	47.00918100000000100739C301.01EF44CA21B1.0F
Router #	**ELAN Name**	**LES AESA**
R6	easy	47.00918100000000100739C301.00E0145502C1.10

continues

R7	R&d	47.00918100000000100739A101.0345EC11336A.11
R8	admin	47.00918100000000100739A101. 00E01454DCE1.12
R9	hr	47.00918100000000100739A101.0354CA123265.12

2 Telnet to R6. Enter all ELANs into the **cisco** database.

3 Using the Boardwork Illustration in Figure 10-10 on page 395, on the correct subinterfaces, configure your LES, BUS, and LEC of the ELANs assigned to every router. Also, configure all routers to be part of each other's broadcast domains by assigning the addresses 144.254.*y*.*x* to the *y* subinterfaces. *x* is the destination router number, as depicted in Figure 10-10. Note that R6 has already been configured for this in Lab 10-2.

4 On the other subinterfaces listed, declare yourself as a client only.

5 Verify that every LEC is operational.

6 Check your LANE cache to see which destinations you have AESAs for.

7 Check for connectivity of the 144.254.*y*.*x* cloud, where *y* is the subinterface and *x* is the destination router.

8 Telnet to R6 and check to see if your server is in the database.

9 Check to see if you have all the clients registered in your server's database. How many connections do you currently have?

Example C-75 *Router 1 Configuration for Lab 10-3*

```
Current configuration:
!
version 12.0
service timestamps debug uptime
service timestamps log uptime
no service password-encryption
!
hostname R1
!
enable password sanfran
!
ip subnet-zero
no ip domain-lookup
!
lane database cisco
  name easy server-atm-address 47.00918100000000100739C301.00E0145502C1.10
  name eng server-atm-address  47.0091.81000000001007399E01.00FE5432D213.0B
  name mkt server-atm-address  47.0091.81000000001007399e01.00C01344AC23.0C
  name sales server-atm-address 47.0091.81000000001007399e01.012C544A2355.0D
  name devtest server-atm-address 47.00918100000000100739C301.00F123345C11.0E
  name training server-atm-address 47.00918100000000100739C301.01EF44CA21B1.0F
  name r&d server-atm-address 47.00918100000000100739A101.0345EC11336A.11
  name admin server-atm-address 47.00918100000000100739A101. 00E01454DCE1.12
```

Example C-75   *Router 1 Configuration for Lab 10-3 (Continued)*

```
    name hr server-atm-address 47.00918100000000100739A101.0354CA123265.12
    default-name easy
!
ipx routing 0000.0000.0001
!
cns event-service server
!
!b
process-max-time 200
!
interface Ethernet0
 ip address 144.254.1.1 255.255.255.0
 no ip directed-broadcast
!
interface Ethernet1
 ip address 10.0.0.1 255.0.0.0
 no ip directed-broadcast
 media-type 10BaseT
!
interface ATM0
 mtu 1500
 no ip address
 no ip directed-broadcast
 atm uni-version 4.0
 atm pvc 1 0 5 qsaal
 atm pvc 3 0 16 ilmi
 no atm ilmi-keepalive
 lane config auto-config-atm-address
 lane config database cisco
 lane auto-config-atm-address
!
interface ATM0.11 multipoint
 ip address 144.254.11.1 255.255.255.0
 no ip directed-broadcast
 lane server-bus ethernet eng
 lane client ethernet eng
 ipx network 11
!
interface ATM0.12 multipoint
 ip address 144.254.12.1 255.255.255.0
 no ip directed-broadcast
 lane client ethernet mkt
 ipx network 12
!
interface ATM0.13 multipoint
 ip address 144.254.13.1 255.255.255.0
 no ip directed-broadcast
 lane client ethernet sales
 ipx network 13
!
```

continues

Example C-75 *Router 1 Configuration for Lab 10-3 (Continued)*

```
interface ATM0.14 multipoint
 ip address 144.254.14.1 255.255.255.0
 no ip directed-broadcast
 lane client ethernet devtest
 ipx network 14
!
interface ATM 0.15 multipoint
 ip address 144.254.15.1 255.255.255.0
 no ip directed-broadcast
 lane client ethernet training
 ipx network 15
!
interface ATM0.16 multipoint
 ip address 144.254.16.1 255.255.255.0
 no ip directed-broadcast
 lane client ethernet easy
 ipx network 16
!
interface ATM0.17 multipoint
 ip address 144.254.17.1 255.255.255.0
 no ip directed-broadcast
 lane client ethernet r&d
 ipx network 17
!
interface ATM0.18 multipoint
 ip address 144.254.18.1 255.255.255.0
 no ip directed-broadcast
 lane client ethernet admin
 ipx network 18
!
interface ATM0.19 multipoint
 ip address 144.254.19.1 255.255.255.0
 no ip directed-broadcast
 lane client ethernet hr
 ipx network 19
!
interface FastEthernet0
 no ip address
 no ip directed-broadcast
 shutdown
!
router igrp 100
 network 144.254.0.0
!
no ip classless
no ip http server
!
!
line con 0
 password sanfran
```

Example C-75 *Router 1 Configuration for Lab 10-3 (Continued)*

```
 transport input none
line aux 0
line vty 0 4
 password sanfran
 login
!
end
```

Example C-76 *Router 2 Configuration for Lab 10-3*

```
Current configuration:
!
version 12.0
service timestamps debug uptime
service timestamps log uptime
no service password-encryption
!
hostname R2
!
enable password sanfran
!
ip subnet-zero
no ip domain-lookup
!
ipx routing 0000.0000.0002
!
cns event-service server
!
!
process-max-time 200
!
interface Ethernet0
 ip address 144.254.2.2 255.255.255.0
 no ip directed-broadcast
!
interface Ethernet1
 ip address 10.0.0.2 255.0.0.0
 no ip directed-broadcast
 media-type 10BaseT
!
interface ATM0
 mtu 1500
 no ip address
 no ip directed-broadcast
 atm uni-version 4.0
 atm pvc 1 0 5 qsaal
 atm pvc 3 0 16 ilmi
 no atm ilmi-keepalive
 lane auto-config-atm-address
!
```

continues

Example C-76 *Router 2 Configuration for Lab 10-3 (Continued)*

```
interface ATM0.11 multipoint
 ip address 144.254.11.1 255.255.255.0
 no ip directed-broadcast
 lane client ethernet eng
 ipx network 11
!
interface ATM0.12 multipoint
 ip address 144.254.12.1 255.255.255.0
 no ip directed-broadcast
 lane server-bus ethernet mkt
 lane client ethernet mkt
 ipx network 12
!
interface ATM0.13 multipoint
 ip address 144.254.13.1 255.255.255.0
 no ip directed-broadcast
 lane client ethernet sales
 ipx network 13
!
interface ATM0.14 multipoint
 ip address 144.254.14.1 255.255.255.0
 no ip directed-broadcast
 lane client ethernet devtest
 ipx network 14
!
interface ATM 0.15 multipoint
 ip address 144.254.15.1 255.255.255.0
 no ip directed-broadcast
 lane client ethernet training
 ipx network 15
!
interface ATM0.16 multipoint
 ip address 144.254.16.2 255.255.255.0
 no ip directed-broadcast
 lane client ethernet easy
 ipx network 16
!
interface ATM0.17 multipoint
 ip address 144.254.17.1 255.255.255.0
 no ip directed-broadcast
 lane client ethernet r&d
 ipx network 17
!
interface ATM0.18 multipoint
 ip address 144.254.18.1 255.255.255.0
 no ip directed-broadcast
 lane client ethernet admin
 ipx network 18
!
interface ATM0.19 multipoint
```

Example C-76 *Router 2 Configuration for Lab 10-3 (Continued)*

```
 ip address 144.254.19.1 255.255.255.0
 no ip directed-broadcast
 lane client ethernet hr
 ipx network 19
!
interface FastEthernet0
 no ip address
 no ip directed-broadcast
 shutdown
!
router igrp 100
 network 144.254.0.0
!
no ip classless
no ip http server
!
!
line con 0
 password sanfran
 transport input none
line aux 0
line vty 0 4
 password sanfran
 login
!
end
```

Example C-77 *Router 3 Configuration for Lab 10-3*

```
Current configuration:
!
version 12.0
service timestamps debug uptime
service timestamps log uptime
no service password-encryption
!
hostname r3
!
enable secret 5 $1$gjkI$WbGgotlrksCglA7aTCH6B1
enable password sanfran
!
!
!
ip subnet-zero
no ip domain-lookup
!
ipx routing 0000.0000.0003
!
cns event-service server
!
```

continues

Example C-77 *Router 3 Configuration for Lab 10-3 (Continued)*

```
!
process-max-time 200
!
interface Ethernet0
 ip address 144.254.3.3 255.255.255.0
 no ip directed-broadcast
 no ip mroute-cache
 ipx network 30
 no mop enabled
!
interface Ethernet1
 ip address 10.0.0.3 255.0.0.0
 no ip directed-broadcast
 no ip mroute-cache
 media-type 10BaseT
 no mop enabled
!
interface TokenRing0
 no ip address
 no ip directed-broadcast
 no ip mroute-cache
 shutdown
!
interface ATM0
 mtu 1500
 no ip address
 no ip directed-broadcast
 no ip mroute-cache
 atm uni-version 4.0
 atm pvc 2 0 16 ilmi
 atm pvc 5 0 5 qsaal
 no atm ilmi-keepalive
 lane auto-config-atm-address
!
interface ATM0.11 multipoint
 ip address 144.254.11.1 255.255.255.0
 no ip directed-broadcast
lane client ethernet eng
 ipx network 11
!
interface ATM0.12 multipoint
 ip address 144.254.12.1 255.255.255.0
 no ip directed-broadcast
 lane client ethernet mkt
 ipx network 12
!
interface ATM0.13 multipoint
 ip address 144.254.13.1 255.255.255.0
 no ip directed-broadcast
 lane server-bus ethernet sales
```

Example C-77 *Router 3 Configuration for Lab 10-3 (Continued)*

```
 lane client ethernet sales
 ipx network 13
!
interface ATM0.14 multipoint
 ip address 144.254.14.1 255.255.255.0
 no ip directed-broadcast
 lane client ethernet devtest
 ipx network 14
!
interface ATM 0.15 multipoint
 ip address 144.254.15.1 255.255.255.0
 no ip directed-broadcast
 lane client ethernet training
 ipx network 15
!
interface ATM0.16 multipoint
 ip address 144.254.16.3 255.255.255.0
 no ip directed-broadcast
 lane client ethernet easy
 ipx network 16
!
interface ATM0.17 multipoint
 ip address 144.254.17.1 255.255.255.0
 no ip directed-broadcast
 lane client ethernet r&d
 ipx network 17
!
interface ATM0.18 multipoint
 ip address 144.254.18.1 255.255.255.0
 no ip directed-broadcast
 lane client ethernet admin
 ipx network 18
!
interface ATM0.19 multipoint
 ip address 144.254.19.1 255.255.255.0
 no ip directed-broadcast
 lane client ethernet hr
 ipx network 19
!
router igrp 100
 network 144.254.0.0
!
no ip classless
no ip http server
!
!
!
line con 0
 transport input none
line aux 0
```

continues

Example C-77 *Router 3 Configuration for Lab 10-3 (Continued)*

```
line vty 0 4
 password sanfran
 login
!
end
```

Example C-78 *Router 4 Configuration for Lab 10-3*

```
Current configuration:
!
version 12.0
service timestamps debug uptime
service timestamps log uptime
no service password-encryption
!
hostname R4
!
enable secret 5 $1$c4x5$EhhlcLP/.mCgg4bs6bZZx0
enable password sanfran
!
!
ip subnet-zero
no ip domain-lookup
!
ipx routing 0000.0000.0004
!
cns event-service server
!
!
process-max-time 200
!
interface Ethernet0
 ip address 144.254.4.4 255.255.255.0
 no ip directed-broadcast
 ipx network 40
 no mop enabled
!
interface Ethernet1
 ip address 10.0.0.4 255.0.0.0
 no ip directed-broadcast
 media-type 10BaseT
!
interface Serial0
 no ip address
 no ip directed-broadcast
 shutdown
!
interface Serial1
 no ip address
 no ip directed-broadcast
```

Example C-78 *Router 4 Configuration for Lab 10-3 (Continued)*

```
shutdown
!
interface ATM0
 no ip address
 no ip directed-broadcast
 atm uni-version 4.0
 atm pvc 1 0 16 ilmi
 atm pvc 10 0 5 qsaal
 atm ilmi-keepalive
 lane auto-config-atm-address
!
int interface ATM0.11 multipoint
 ip address 144.254.11.1 255.255.255.0
 no ip directed-broadcast
 lane client ethernet eng
 ipx network 11
!
interface ATM0.12 multipoint
 ip address 144.254.12.1 255.255.255.0
 no ip directed-broadcast
 lane client ethernet mkt
 ipx network 12
!
interface ATM0.13 multipoint
 ip address 144.254.13.1 255.255.255.0
 no ip directed-broadcast
 lane client ethernet sales
 ipx network 13
!
interface ATM0.14 multipoint
 ip address 144.254.14.1 255.255.255.0
 no ip directed-broadcast
 lane server-bus ethernet devtest
 lane client ethernet devtest
 ipx network 14
!
interface ATM 0.15 multipoint
 ip address 144.254.15.1 255.255.255.0
 no ip directed-broadcast
 lane client ethernet training
 ipx network 15
!
interface ATM0.16 multipoint
 ip address 144.254.16.4 255.255.255.0
 no ip directed-broadcast
 lane client ethernet easy
 ipx network 16
!
interface ATM0.17 multipoint
 ip address 144.254.17.1 255.255.255.0
```

continues

Example C-78 *Router 4 Configuration for Lab 10-3 (Continued)*

```
 no ip directed-broadcast
 lane client ethernet r&d
 ipx network 17
!
interface ATM0.18 multipoint
 ip address 144.254.18.1 255.255.255.0
 no ip directed-broadcast
 lane client ethernet admin
 ipx network 18
!
interface ATM0.19 multipoint
 ip address 144.254.19.1 255.255.255.0
 no ip directed-broadcast
 lane client ethernet hr
 ipx network 19
!
router igrp 100
 network 144.254.0.0
!
no ip classless
no ip http server
!
!
line con 0
 transport input none
line aux 0
line vty 0 4
 password cisco
 login
!
end
```

Example C-79 *Router 5 Configuration for Lab 10-3*

```
Current configuration:
!
version 12.0
service timestamps debug uptime
service timestamps log uptime
no service password-encryption
!
hostname R5
!
enable secret 5 $1$LOME$zd59yCi.wNaeSPPV1Cz9I0
enable password sanfran
!
!
!
ip subnet-zero
no ip domain-lookup
```

Example C-79 *Router 5 Configuration for Lab 10-3 (Continued)*

```
!
ipx routing 0000.0000.0005
!
cns event-service server
!
!
process-max-time 200
!
interface Ethernet0
 ip address 144.254.5.5 255.255.255.0
 no ip directed-broadcast
 ipx network 50
 no mop enabled
!
interface Ethernet1
 ip address 10.0.0.5 255.0.0.0
 no ip directed-broadcast
 media-type 10BaseT
!
interface ATM0
 no ip address
 no ip directed-broadcast
 atm uni-version 4.0
 atm pvc 1 0 16 ilmi
 atm pvc 5 0 5 qsaal
 no atm ilmi-keepalive
 lane auto-config-atm-address
!
interface ATM0.11 multipoint
 ip address 144.254.11.1 255.255.255.0
 no ip directed-broadcast
 lane client ethernet eng
 ipx network 11
!
interface ATM0.12 multipoint
 ip address 144.254.12.1 255.255.255.0
 no ip directed-broadcast
 lane client ethernet mkt
 ipx network 12
!
interface ATM0.13 multipoint
 ip address 144.254.13.1 255.255.255.0
 no ip directed-broadcast
 lane client ethernet sales
 ipx network 13
!
interface ATM0.14 multipoint
 ip address 144.254.14.1 255.255.255.0
 no ip directed-broadcast
 lane client ethernet devtest
```

continues

Lab 10-3 Solution

Example C-79 *Router 5 Configuration for Lab 10-3 (Continued)*

```
 ipx network 14
!
interface ATM 0.15 multipoint
 ip address 144.254.15.1 255.255.255.0
 no ip directed-broadcast
 lane server-bus ethernet training
 lane client ethernet training
 ipx network 15
!
interface ATM0.16 multipoint
 ip address 144.254.16.5 255.255.255.0
 no ip directed-broadcast
 lane client ethernet easy
 ipx network 16
!
interface ATM0.17 multipoint
 ip address 144.254.17.1 255.255.255.0
 no ip directed-broadcast
 lane client ethernet r&d
 ipx network 17
!
interface ATM0.18 multipoint
 ip address 144.254.18.1 255.255.255.0
 no ip directed-broadcast
 lane client ethernet admin
 ipx network 18
!
interface ATM0.19 multipoint
 ip address 144.254.19.1 255.255.255.0
 no ip directed-broadcast
 lane client ethernet hr
 ipx network 19
!
interface FastEthernet0
 no ip address
 no ip directed-broadcast
 shutdown
!
router igrp 100
 network 144.254.0.0
!
no ip classless
no ip http server
!
!
!
line con 0
 transport input none
line aux 0
line vty 0 4
```

Example C-79 *Router 5 Configuration for Lab 10-3 (Continued)*

```
 password cisco
 login
!
end
```

Example C-80 *Router 6 Configuration for Lab 10-3*

```
Current configuration:
!
version 12.0
service timestamps debug uptime
service timestamps log uptime
no service password-encryption
!
hostname R6
!
enable secret 5 $1$/pVo$QkJYB4ad/.E4mCL62xYfe1
enable password cisco!
!
!
ip subnet-zero
no ip domain-lookup
!
!
lane database cisco
  name easy server-atm-address 47.00918100000000100739C301.00E0145502C1.10
  name eng server-atm-address  47.0091.81000000001007399E01.00FE5432D213.0B
  name mkt server-atm-address  47.0091.81000000001007399e01.00C01344AC23.0C
  name sales server-atm-address 47.0091.81000000001007399e01.012C544A2355.0D
  name devtest server-atm-address 47.00918100000000100739C301.00F123345C11.0E
  name training server-atm-address 47.00918100000000100739C301.01EF44CA21B1.0F
  name r&d server-atm-address 47.00918100000000100739A101.0345EC11336A.11
  name admin server-atm-address 47.00918100000000100739A101. 00E01454DCE1.12
  name hr server-atm-address 47.00918100000000100739A101.0354CA123265.12
  default-name easy
!
ipx routing 0000.0000.0006
!
cns event-service server
!
!
process-max-time 200
!
interface Ethernet0
 ip address 144.254.6.6 255.255.255.0
 no ip directed-broadcast
 ipx network 66
 no mop enabled
!
interface Ethernet1
```

continues

Example C-80 *Router 6 Configuration for Lab 10-3 (Continued)*

```
 ip address 10.0.0.6 255.0.0.0
 no ip directed-broadcast
 media-type 10BaseT
!
interface ATM0
 no ip address
 no ip directed-broadcast
 atm uni-version 4.0
 atm pvc 1 0 16 ilmi
 atm pvc 10 0 5 qsaal
 no atm ilmi-keepalive
 lane config auto-config-atm-address
 lane config database cisco
 lane auto-config-atm-address
!
interface ATM0.11 multipoint
 ip address 144.254.11.1 255.255.255.0
 no ip directed-broadcast
 lane client ethernet eng
 ipx network 11
!
interface ATM0.12 multipoint
 ip address 144.254.12.1 255.255.255.0
 no ip directed-broadcast
 lane client ethernet mkt
 ipx network 12
!
interface ATM0.13 multipoint
 ip address 144.254.13.1 255.255.255.0
 no ip directed-broadcast
 lane client ethernet sales
 ipx network 13
!
interface ATM0.14 multipoint
 ip address 144.254.14.1 255.255.255.0
 no ip directed-broadcast
 lane client ethernet devtest
 ipx network 14
!
interface ATM 0.15 multipoint
 ip address 144.254.15.1 255.255.255.0
 no ip directed-broadcast
 lane client ethernet training
 ipx network 15
!
interface ATM0.16 multipoint
 ip address 144.254.16.6 255.255.255.0
 no ip directed-broadcast
 lane server-bus ethernet easy
 lane client ethernet easy
```

Example C-80 *Router 6 Configuration for Lab 10-3 (Continued)*

```
 ipx network 16
!
interface ATM0.17 multipoint
 ip address 144.254.17.1 255.255.255.0
 no ip directed-broadcast
 lane client ethernet r&d
 ipx network 17
!
interface ATM0.18 multipoint
 ip address 144.254.18.1 255.255.255.0
 no ip directed-broadcast
 lane client ethernet admin
 ipx network 18
!
interface ATM0.19 multipoint
 ip address 144.254.19.1 255.255.255.0
 no ip directed-broadcast
 lane client ethernet hr
 ipx network 19
!
router igrp 100
 redistribute connected
 network 144.254.0.0
!
no ip classless
no ip http server
!
!
line con 0
 transport input none
line aux 0
line vty 0 4
 password cisco
 login
!
end
```

Example C-81 *Router 7 Configuration for Lab 10-3*

```
Current configuration:
!
version 12.0
service timestamps debug uptime
service timestamps log uptime
no service password-encryption
!
hostname r7
!
enable password sanfran
!
```

continues

Example C-81 *Router 7 Configuration for Lab 10-3 (Continued)*

```
!
!
ip subnet-zero
!
ipx routing 0000.0000.0007
!
cns event-service server
!
!
process-max-time 200
!
interface Ethernet0
 ip address 144.254.7.7 255.255.255.0
 no ip directed-broadcast
 ipx network 77
 no mop enabled
!
interface Ethernet1
 ip address 10.0.0.7 255.0.0.0
 no ip directed-broadcast
 media-type 10BaseT
!
interface ATM0
 no ip address
 no ip directed-broadcast
 atm uni-version 4.0
 atm pvc 5 0 5 qsaal
 atm pvc 16 0 16 ilmi
 no atm ilmi-keepalive
 lane auto-config-atm-address
!
interface ATM0.11 multipoint
 ip address 144.254.11.1 255.255.255.0
 no ip directed-broadcast
 lane client ethernet eng
 ipx network 11
!
interface ATM0.12 multipoint
 ip address 144.254.12.1 255.255.255.0
 no ip directed-broadcast
 lane client ethernet mkt
 ipx network 12
!
interface ATM0.13 multipoint
 ip address 144.254.13.1 255.255.255.0
 no ip directed-broadcast
 lane client ethernet sales
 ipx network 13
!
interface ATM0.14 multipoint
```

Example C-81 *Router 7 Configuration for Lab 10-3 (Continued)*

```
 ip address 144.254.14.1 255.255.255.0
 no ip directed-broadcast
 lane client ethernet devtest
 ipx network 14
!
interface ATM 0.15 multipoint
 ip address 144.254.15.1 255.255.255.0
 no ip directed-broadcast
 lane client ethernet training
 ipx network 15
!
interface ATM0.16 multipoint
 ip address 144.254.16.7 255.255.255.0
 no ip directed-broadcast
 lane client ethernet easy
 ipx network 16
!
interface ATM0.17 multipoint
 ip address 144.254.17.1 255.255.255.0
 no ip directed-broadcast
 lane server-bus ethernet r&d
 lane client ethernet r&d
 ipx network 17
!
interface ATM0.18 multipoint
 ip address 144.254.18.1 255.255.255.0
 no ip directed-broadcast
 lane client ethernet admin
 ipx network 18
!
interface ATM0.19 multipoint
 ip address 144.254.19.1 255.255.255.0
 no ip directed-broadcast
 lane client ethernet hr
 ipx network 19
!
interface FastEthernet0
 no ip address
 no ip directed-broadcast
 shutdown
!
router igrp 100
 network 144.254.0.0
!
no ip classless
no ip http server
!
!                                                          continues
line con 0
 transport input none
```

Example C-81 *Router 7 Configuration for Lab 10-3 (Continued)*

```
line aux 0
line vty 0 4
 password sanfran
 login
!
end
```

Example C-82 *Router 8 Configuration for Lab 10-3*

```
Current configuration:
!
version 12.0
service timestamps debug uptime
service timestamps log uptime
no service password-encryption
!
hostname r8
!
enable password sanfran
!
!
!
ip subnet-zero
!
ipx routing 0000.0000.0008
!
cns event-service server
!
!
process-max-time 200
!
interface Ethernet0
 ip address 144.254.8.8 255.255.255.0
 no ip directed-broadcast
 ipx network 88
 no mop enabled
!
interface Ethernet1
 ip address 10.0.0.8 255.0.0.0
 no ip directed-broadcast
 media-type 10BaseT
!
interface ATM0
 no ip address
 no ip directed-broadcast
 atm uni-version 4.0
 atm pvc 5 0 5 qsaal
 atm pvc 16 0 16 ilmi
 no atm ilmi-keepalive
 lane auto-config-atm-address
```

Example C-82 *Router 8 Configuration for Lab 10-3 (Continued)*

```
!
interface ATM0.11 multipoint
 ip address 144.254.11.1 255.255.255.0
 no ip directed-broadcast
 lane client ethernet eng
 ipx network 11
!
interface ATM0.12 multipoint
 ip address 144.254.12.1 255.255.255.0
 no ip directed-broadcast
 lane client ethernet mkt
 ipx network 12
!
interface ATM0.13 multipoint
 ip address 144.254.13.1 255.255.255.0
 no ip directed-broadcast
 lane client ethernet sales
 ipx network 13
!
interface ATM0.14 multipoint
 ip address 144.254.14.1 255.255.255.0
 no ip directed-broadcast
 lane client ethernet devtest
 ipx network 14
!
interface ATM 0.15 multipoint
 ip address 144.254.15.1 255.255.255.0
 no ip directed-broadcast
 lane client ethernet training
 ipx network 15
!
interface ATM0.16 multipoint
 ip address 144.254.16.8 255.255.255.0
 no ip directed-broadcast
 lane client ethernet easy
 ipx network 16
!
interface ATM0.17 multipoint
 ip address 144.254.17.1 255.255.255.0
 no ip directed-broadcast
 lane client ethernet r&d
 ipx network 17
!
interface ATM0.18 multipoint
 ip address 144.254.18.1 255.255.255.0
 no ip directed-broadcast
 lane server-bus ethernet admin
 lane client ethernet admin
 ipx network 18
!
```

continues

Lab 10-3 Solution

Example C-82   *Router 8 Configuration for Lab 10-3 (Continued)*

```
interface ATM0.19 multipoint
 ip address 144.254.19.1 255.255.255.0
 no ip directed-broadcast
 lane client ethernet hr
 ipx network 19
!
interface FastEthernet0
 no ip address
 no ip directed-broadcast
 shutdown
!
router igrp 100
 network 144.254.0.0
!
no ip classless
no ip http server
!
!
line con 0
 transport input none
line aux 0
line vty 0 4
 password sanfran
 login
!
end
```

Example C-83   *Router 9 Configuration for Lab 10-3*

```
Current configuration:
!
version 12.0
service timestamps debug uptime
service timestamps log uptime
no service password-encryption
!
hostname r9
!
enable password sanfran
!
!
!
ip subnet-zero
!
ipx routing 0000.0000.0009
!
cns event-service server
!
!
process-max-time 200
```

Example C-83 *Router 9 Configuration for Lab 10-3 (Continued)*

```
!
interface Ethernet0
 ip address 144.254.9.9 255.255.255.0
 no ip directed-broadcast
 ipx network 99
 no mop enabled
!
interface Ethernet1
 ip address 10.0.0.9 255.0.0.0
 no ip directed-broadcast
 media-type 10BaseT
!
interface TokenRing0
 no ip address
 no ip directed-broadcast
 shutdown
!
interface ATM0
 no ip address
 no ip directed-broadcast
 atm uni-version 4.0
 atm pvc 5 0 5 qsaal
 atm pvc 16 0 16 ilmi
 no atm ilmi-keepalive
 lane auto-config-atm-address
!
interface ATM0.11 multipoint
 ip address 144.254.11.1 255.255.255.0
 no ip directed-broadcast
 lane client ethernet eng
 ipx network 11
!
interface ATM0.12 multipoint
 ip address 144.254.12.1 255.255.255.0
 no ip directed-broadcast
 lane client ethernet mkt
 ipx network 12
!
interface ATM0.13 multipoint
 ip address 144.254.13.1 255.255.255.0
 no ip directed-broadcast
 lane client ethernet sales
 ipx network 13
!
interface ATM0.14 multipoint
 ip address 144.254.14.1 255.255.255.0
 no ip directed-broadcast
 lane client ethernet devtest
 ipx network 14
!
```

Lab 10-3 Solution

continues

Example C-83 *Router 9 Configuration for Lab 10-3 (Continued)*

```
interface ATM 0.15 multipoint
 ip address 144.254.15.1 255.255.255.0
 no ip directed-broadcast
 lane client ethernet training
 ipx network 15
!
interface ATM0.16 multipoint
 ip address 144.254.16.9 255.255.255.0
 no ip directed-broadcast
 lane client ethernet easy
 ipx network 16
!
interface ATM0.17 multipoint
 ip address 144.254.17.1 255.255.255.0
 no ip directed-broadcast
 lane client ethernet r&d
 ipx network 17
!
interface ATM0.18 multipoint
 ip address 144.254.18.1 255.255.255.0
 no ip directed-broadcast
 lane client ethernet admin
 ipx network 18
!
interface ATM0.19 multipoint
 ip address 144.254.19.1 255.255.255.0
 no ip directed-broadcast
 lane server-bus ethernet hr
 lane client ethernet hr
 ipx network 19
!
router igrp 100
 network 144.254.0.0
!
no ip classless
no ip http server
!
!
!
!
!
line con 0
 transport input none
line aux 0
line vty 0 4
 password sanfran
 login
!
end
```

Example C-84 *Switch 1 Configuration for Lab 10-3*

```
!
version 11.3
no service pad
no service udp-small-servers
no service tcp-small-servers
!
hostname Switch_1
!
enable password sanfran
!
no ip domain-lookup
!
atm address 47.0091.8100.0000.0010.0739.9e01.0010.0739.9e01.00
atm lecs-address-default 47.0091.8100.0000.0010.0739.c301.00e0.1455.02c3.00 01
atm lecs-address-default 47.0091.8100.0000.0010.0739.a101.00e0.1a56.54c1.00 02
!
atm router pnni
 node 1 level 56 lowest
  redistribute atm-static
!
!
interface ATM0/0/0
 shutdown
 no ip address
!
interface ATM0/0/1
 no ip address
!
interface ATM0/0/2
 no ip address
!
interface ATM0/0/3
 no ip address
 shutdown
!
interface ATM0/1/0
 no ip address
 no atm auto-configuration
 atm uni version 3.1
 atm maxvpi-bits 3
 atm maxvci-bits 10
 atm pvc 0 114  interface  ATM0/0/1 0 114
 atm pvc 0 115  interface  ATM0/0/1 0 115
 atm pvc 0 116  interface  ATM0/0/1 0 116
 atm pvc 0 117  interface  ATM0/0/2 0 117
 atm pvc 0 118  interface  ATM0/0/2 0 118
 atm pvc 0 119  interface  ATM0/0/2 0 119
!
interface ATM0/1/1
 no ip address
```

continues

Lab 10-3 Solution

Example C-84 *Switch 1 Configuration for Lab 10-3 (Continued)*

```
 no atm auto-configuration
 atm uni version 3.1
 atm maxvpi-bits 3
 atm maxvci-bits 10
 atm pvc 0 121  interface  ATM0/1/0 0 112
 atm pvc 0 124  interface  ATM0/0/1 0 124
 atm pvc 0 125  interface  ATM0/0/1 0 125
 atm pvc 0 126  interface  ATM0/0/1 0 126
 atm pvc 0 127  interface  ATM0/0/2 0 127
 atm pvc 0 128  interface  ATM0/0/2 0 128
 atm pvc 0 129  interface  ATM0/0/2 0 129
!
interface ATM0/1/2
 no ip address
 no atm auto-configuration
 atm uni version 3.1
 atm maxvpi-bits 3
 atm maxvci-bits 10
 atm pvc 0 120  interface  ATM0/1/0 0 120
 atm pvc 0 131  interface  ATM0/1/0 0 113
 atm pvc 0 132  interface  ATM0/1/1 0 123
 atm pvc 0 134  interface  ATM0/0/1 0 134
 atm pvc 0 135  interface  ATM0/0/1 0 135
 atm pvc 0 136  interface  ATM0/0/1 0 136
 atm pvc 0 137  interface  ATM0/0/2 0 137
 atm pvc 0 138  interface  ATM0/0/2 0 138
 atm pvc 0 139  interface  ATM0/0/2 0 139
!
interface ATM0/1/3
 no ip address
!
interface ATM2/0/0
 no ip address
 atm maxvp-number 0
!
interface Ethernet2/0/0
 ip address 10.0.0.11 255.0.0.0
!
ip classless
!
line con 0
 exec-timeout 0 0
 password cisco
 login
line aux 0
line vty 0 4
 exec-timeout 0 0
 password cisco
 login
!
```

Example C-84 *Switch 1 Configuration for Lab 10-3 (Continued)*

```
end
```

Example C-85 *Switch 2 Configuration for Lab 10-3*

```
!
version 11.3
no service pad
no service udp-small-servers
no service tcp-small-servers
!
hostname Switch_2
!
enable password sanfran
!
no ip domain-lookup
!
atm address 47.0091.8100.0000.0010.0739.a101.0010.0739.a101.00
atm lecs-address-default 47.0091.8100.0000.0010.0739.c301.00e0.1455.02c3.00 01
atm lecs-address-default 47.0091.8100.0000.0010.0739.a101.00e0.1a56.54c1.00 02
!
atm router pnni
 node 1 level 56 lowest
   redistribute atm-static
!
!
interface ATM0/0/0
 shutdown
 no ip address
!
interface ATM0/0/1
 no ip address
!
interface ATM0/0/2
 shutdown
 no ip address
!
interface ATM0/0/3
 no ip address
!
interface ATM0/1/0
 no ip address
 no atm auto-configuration
 atm uni version 3.1
 atm maxvpi-bits 3
 atm maxvci-bits 10
 atm pvc 0 141   interface  ATM0/0/1 0 114
 atm pvc 0 142   interface  ATM0/0/1 0 124
 atm pvc 0 143   interface  ATM0/0/1 0 134
 atm pvc 0 147   interface  ATM0/0/3 0 147
 atm pvc 0 148   interface  ATM0/0/3 0 148
```

continues

Example C-85   *Switch 2 Configuration for Lab 10-3 (Continued)*

```
atm pvc 0 149  interface  ATM0/0/3 0 149
!
interface ATM0/1/1
 no ip address
 no atm auto-configuration
 atm uni version 3.1
 atm maxvpi-bits 3
 atm maxvci-bits 10
 atm pvc 0 151  interface  ATM0/0/1 0 115
 atm pvc 0 152  interface  ATM0/0/1 0 125
 atm pvc 0 153  interface  ATM0/0/1 0 135
 atm pvc 0 154  interface  ATM0/1/0 0 145
 atm pvc 0 157  interface  ATM0/0/3 0 157
 atm pvc 0 158  interface  ATM0/0/3 0 158
 atm pvc 0 159  interface  ATM0/0/3 0 159
!
interface ATM0/1/2
 no ip address
 no atm auto-configuration
 atm uni version 3.1
 atm maxvpi-bits 3
 atm maxvci-bits 10
 atm pvc 0 161  interface  ATM0/0/1 0 116
 atm pvc 0 162  interface  ATM0/0/1 0 126
 atm pvc 0 163  interface  ATM0/0/1 0 136
 atm pvc 0 164  interface  ATM0/1/0 0 146
 atm pvc 0 165  interface  ATM0/1/1 0 156
 atm pvc 0 167  interface  ATM0/0/3 0 167
 atm pvc 0 168  interface  ATM0/0/3 0 168
 atm pvc 0 169  interface  ATM0/0/3 0 169
!
interface ATM0/1/3
 no ip address
!
interface ATM2/0/0
 no ip address
 atm maxvp-number 0
!
interface Ethernet2/0/0
 ip address 10.0.0.12 255.0.0.0
!
ip classless
!
line con 0
 exec-timeout 0 0
 password cisco
 login
line aux 0
line vty 0 4
 exec-timeout 0 0
```

Example C-85 *Switch 2 Configuration for Lab 10-3 (Continued)*

```
 password cisco
 login
!
end
```

Example C-86 *Switch 3 Configuration for Lab 10-3*

```
!
version 11.3
no service pad
no service udp-small-servers
no service tcp-small-servers
!
hostname Switch_3
!
boot system flash bootflash:ls1010-wp-mz.113-0.8.TWA4.2.bin
enable password sanfran
!
no ip domain-lookup
!
atm address 47.0091.8100.0000.0010.0739.c301.0010.0739.c301.00
atm lecs-address-default 47.0091.8100.0000.0010.0739.c301.00e0.1455.02c3.00 01
atm lecs-address-default 47.0091.8100.0000.0010.0739.a101.00e0.1a56.54c1.00 02
!
atm router pnni
 node 1 level 56 lowest
   redistribute atm-static
!
!
interface ATM0/0/0
 shutdown
 no ip address
!
interface ATM0/0/1
 shutdown
 no ip address
!
interface ATM0/0/2
 no ip address
!
interface ATM0/0/3
 no ip address
!
interface ATM0/1/0
 no ip address
 no atm auto-configuration
 atm uni version 3.1
 atm maxvpi-bits 3
 atm maxvci-bits 10
 atm pvc 0 171  interface  ATM0/0/2 0 117
```

continues

Example C-86 *Switch 3 Configuration for Lab 10-3 (Continued)*

```
atm pvc 0 172  interface  ATM0/0/2 0 127
atm pvc 0 173  interface  ATM0/0/2 0 137
atm pvc 0 174  interface  ATM0/0/3 0 147
atm pvc 0 175  interface  ATM0/0/3 0 157
atm pvc 0 176  interface  ATM0/0/3 0 167
!
interface ATM0/1/1
 no ip address
 no atm auto-configuration
 atm uni version 3.1
 atm maxvpi-bits 3
 atm maxvci-bits 10
 atm pvc 0 181  interface  ATM0/0/2 0 118
 atm pvc 0 182  interface  ATM0/0/2 0 128
 atm pvc 0 183  interface  ATM0/0/2 0 138
 atm pvc 0 184  interface  ATM0/0/3 0 148
 atm pvc 0 185  interface  ATM0/0/3 0 158
 atm pvc 0 186  interface  ATM0/0/3 0 168
 atm pvc 0 187  interface  ATM0/1/0 0 178
!
interface ATM0/1/2
 no ip address
 no atm auto-configuration
 atm uni version 3.1
 atm maxvpi-bits 3
 atm maxvci-bits 10
 atm pvc 0 191  interface  ATM0/0/2 0 119
 atm pvc 0 192  interface  ATM0/0/2 0 129
 atm pvc 0 193  interface  ATM0/0/2 0 139
 atm pvc 0 194  interface  ATM0/0/3 0 149
 atm pvc 0 195  interface  ATM0/0/3 0 159
 atm pvc 0 196  interface  ATM0/0/3 0 169
 atm pvc 0 197  interface  ATM0/1/0 0 179
 atm pvc 0 198  interface  ATM0/1/1 0 189
!
interface ATM0/1/3
 no ip address
!
interface ATM1/0/0
 no ip address
!
interface ATM1/0/1
 no ip address
!
interface ATM1/0/2
 no ip address
!
interface ATM1/0/3
 no ip address
!
```

Example C-86   *Switch 3 Configuration for Lab 10-3 (Continued)*

```
interface ATM2/0/0
 no ip address
 atm maxvp-number 0
!
interface Ethernet2/0/0
 ip address 10.0.0.13 255.0.0.0
!
ip classless
!
line con 0
 exec-timeout 0 0
 password cisco
 login
line aux 0
line vty 0 4
 exec-timeout 0 0
 password cisco
 login
!
end
```

Solutions for Lab 10-4: Configuring LANE for Dual-Homed Catalyst Switches with Redundancy

Examples C-87 through C-100 provide the configuration solutions that satisfy all the exercises for Lab 10-4. Specifically, the exercises asked for the following:

1 Configure the 5000 switches. Ensure that physical and IP connectivity are established to the 5000 switches.

2 Configure two Catalyst 5000s to interconnect their VLAN 2 to ELAN **easy**.

3 On the 5000 switches, configure the ATM interface with the appropriate terminating PVCs (signaling PVC and ILMI PVC) and the MTU size.

4 Identify the appropriate LECS addresses for CAT1 and CAT2 based on the associated ATM switch prefix to be used, depending on the appropriate LANE port A or port B to be active at one time.

CAT1 LECS address: 47.0091.8100.0000.0061.705B.8301.0040.0BFF.0015.00

CAT1 LECS address: 47.0091.8100.0000.0010.0739.A101.0040.0BFF.0015.00

CAT2 LECS address: 47.0091.8100.0000.0010.0739.C301.0040.0BFF.0013.00

CAT2 LECS address: 47.0091.8100.0000.0010.0739.A101.0040.0BFF.0013.00

5 Configure the LS1010 switches with the appropriate LECS addresses to be used, CAT1 being identified as the primary LECS and CAT2 identified as the secondary LECS. Ensure that all appropriate LECS addresses being used take physical redundancy into consideration.

6 As per Lab 10-1, where you implemented ELAN **easy**, you can use subinterface ATM0.16 on the Catalyst 5000 to enable the LANE client and LES/BUS services. Map VLAN2 with ELAN **easy**.

7 As done in the previous labs for this chapter, identify the AESA LES addresses pertaining to CAT1 and CAT2. Configure the appropriate LANE databases on CAT1 and CAT2, identifying all required LES AESA address entries to provide full physical redundancy, as per the design. Activate the LECS service with the appropriate database on both CAT 5000 switches.

8 Ensure that ELAN **easy** is up and working with full membership, with CAT1 as the primary LECS, LES/BUS. Verify the design's reliability by disabling the appropriate ATM interface on the ATM switch that currently provides connectivity to CAT1. Verify that CAT1 still remains active in support of the ELAN services using the second physical port on the LANE module.

9 Shut down the appropriate LS1010 ATM interface port to isolate CAT1 and provided LANE services, and verify that CAT2 indeed provides the required LANE services redundancy. Ensure that full ELAN **easy** membership is reestablished.

10 Similar to Task 7, ensure that CAT2 can provide LANE services, after connectivity to its default LANE module port A is terminated. Again, verify full ELAN **easy** membership.

This lab illustrates the quadruple redundancy. If CAT1 becomes disabled (the primary LECS, LES/BUS), CAT2 becomes the primary LECS and LES/BUS. Furthermore, each CAT is attached dually to the ATM cloud. If the preferred link of the primary CAT1 becomes unavailable, the secondary link is used. Dual-attachment provisions for redundancy within the ATM network itself as well. That is, if the S3 becomes unavailable (thus bringing the preferred link A down), S2 provides the ATM connectivity using link B.

Example C-87 *Router 1 Configuration for Lab 10-4*

```
Current configuration:
!
version 12.0
service timestamps debug uptime
service timestamps log uptime
no service password-encryption
!
hostname R1
!
enable password sanfran
!
ip subnet-zero
```

Example C-87   *Router 1 Configuration for Lab 10-4 (Continued)*

```
!
no ip domain-lookup
!
!
ipx routing 0000.0000.0001
!
cns event-service server
!
!
process-max-time 200
!
interface Ethernet0
 ip address 144.254.1.1 255.255.255.0
 no ip directed-broadcast
!
interface Ethernet1
 ip address 10.0.0.1 255.0.0.0
 no ip directed-broadcast
 media-type 10BaseT
!
interface ATM0
 mtu 1500
 no ip address
 no ip directed-broadcast
 atm uni-version 4.0
 atm pvc 1 0 5 qsaal
 atm pvc 3 0 16 ilmi
 no atm ilmi-keepalive
 lane auto-config-atm-address
!
interface ATM0.16 multipoint
 ip address 144.254.16.1 255.255.255.0
 no ip directed-broadcast
 lane client ethernet easy
 ipx network 16
!
interface FastEthernet0
 no ip address
 no ip directed-broadcast
 shutdown
!
router igrp 100
 network 144.254.0.0
!
no ip classless
no ip http server
!
!
line con 0
 password sanfran
```

continues

Example C-87 *Router 1 Configuration for Lab 10-4 (Continued)*

```
 transport input none
line aux 0
line vty 0 4
 password sanfran
 login
!
end
```

Example C-88 *Router 2 Configuration for Lab 10-4*

```
Current configuration:
!
version 12.0
service timestamps debug uptime
service timestamps log uptime
no service password-encryption
!
hostname R2
!
enable password sanfran
!
ip subnet-zero
no ip domain-lookup
!
ipx routing 0000.0000.0002
!
cns event-service server
!
!
process-max-time 200
!
interface Ethernet0
 ip address 144.254.2.2 255.255.255.0
 no ip directed-broadcast
!
interface Ethernet1
 ip address 10.0.0.2 255.0.0.0
 no ip directed-broadcast
 media-type 10BaseT
!
interface ATM0
 mtu 1500
 no ip address
 no ip directed-broadcast
 atm uni-version 4.0
 atm pvc 1 0 5 qsaal
 atm pvc 3 0 16 ilmi
 no atm ilmi-keepalive
 lane auto-config-atm-address
 !
```

Example C-88 *Router 2 Configuration for Lab 10-4 (Continued)*

```
interface ATM0.16 multipoint
 ip address 144.254.16.2 255.255.255.0
 no ip directed-broadcast
 lane client ethernet easy
 ipx network 16
!
interface FastEthernet0
 no ip address
 no ip directed-broadcast
 shutdown
!
router igrp 100
 network 144.254.0.0
!
no ip classless
no ip http server
!
!
line con 0
 password sanfran
 transport input none
line aux 0
line vty 0 4
 password sanfran
 login
!
end
```

Example C-89 *Router 3 Configuration for Lab 10-4*

```
Current configuration:
!
version 12.0
service timestamps debug uptime
service timestamps log uptime
no service password-encryption
!
hostname r3
!
enable secret 5 $1$gjkI$WbGgotlrksCglA7aTCH6B1
enable password sanfran
!
!
!
ip subnet-zero
no ip domain-lookup
!
ipx routing 0000.0000.0003
!
cns event-service server
```

continues

Example C-89 *Router 3 Configuration for Lab 10-4 (Continued)*

```
!
!
process-max-time 200
!
interface Ethernet0
 ip address 144.254.3.3 255.255.255.0
 no ip directed-broadcast
 no ip mroute-cache
 ipx network 30
 no mop enabled
!
interface Ethernet1
 ip address 10.0.0.3 255.0.0.0
 no ip directed-broadcast
 no ip mroute-cache
 media-type 10BaseT
 no mop enabled
!
interface TokenRing0
 no ip address
 no ip directed-broadcast
 no ip mroute-cache
 shutdown
!
interface ATM0
 mtu 1500
 no ip address
 no ip directed-broadcast
 no ip mroute-cache
 atm uni-version 4.0
 atm pvc 2 0 16 ilmi
 atm pvc 5 0 5 qsaal
 no atm ilmi-keepalive
 lane auto-config-atm-address
!
interface ATM0.16 multipoint
 ip address 144.254.16.3 255.255.255.0
 no ip directed-broadcast
 lane client ethernet easy
 ipx network 16
!
router igrp 100
 network 144.254.0.0
!
no ip classless
no ip http server
!
!
!
line con 0
```

Example C-89   *Router 3 Configuration for Lab 10-4 (Continued)*

```
 transport input none
line aux 0
line vty 0 4
 password sanfran
 login
!
end
```

Example C-90   *Router 4 Configuration for Lab 10-4*

```
Current configuration:
!
version 12.0
service timestamps debug uptime
service timestamps log uptime
no service password-encryption
!
hostname R4
!
enable secret 5 $1$c4x5$EhhlcLP/.mCgg4bs6bZZx0
enable password sanfran
!
!
ip subnet-zero
no ip domain-lookup
!
ipx routing 0000.0000.0004
!
cns event-service server
!
!
process-max-time 200
!
interface Ethernet0
 ip address 144.254.4.4 255.255.255.0
 no ip directed-broadcast
 ipx network 40
 no mop enabled
!
interface Ethernet1
 ip address 10.0.0.4 255.0.0.0
 no ip directed-broadcast
 media-type 10BaseT
!
interface Serial0
 no ip address
 no ip directed-broadcast
 shutdown
!
interface Serial1
```

continues

Lab 10-4 Solution

Example C-90 *Router 4 Configuration for Lab 10-4 (Continued)*

```
 no ip address
 no ip directed-broadcast
 shutdown
!
interface ATM0
 no ip address
 no ip directed-broadcast
 atm uni-version 4.0
 atm pvc 1 0 16 ilmi
 atm pvc 10 0 5 qsaal
 atm ilmi-keepalive
 lane auto-config-atm-address
!
interface ATM0.16 multipoint
 ip address 144.254.16.4 255.255.255.0
 no ip directed-broadcast
 lane client ethernet easy
 ipx network 16
!
router igrp 100
 network 144.254.0.0
!
no ip classless
no ip http server
!
!
line con 0
 transport input none
line aux 0
line vty 0 4
 password cisco
 login
!
end
```

Example C-91 *Router 5 Configuration for Lab 10-4*

```
Current configuration:
!
version 12.0
service timestamps debug uptime
service timestamps log uptime
no service password-encryption
!
hostname R5
!
enable secret 5 $1$LOME$zd59yCi.wNaeSPPV1Cz9I0
enable password sanfran
!
!
```

Example C-91 *Router 5 Configuration for Lab 10-4 (Continued)*

```
!
ip subnet-zero
no ip domain-lookup
!
ipx routing 0000.0000.0005
!
cns event-service server
!
!
process-max-time 200
!
interface Ethernet0
 ip address 144.254.5.5 255.255.255.0
 no ip directed-broadcast
 ipx network 50
 no mop enabled
!
interface Ethernet1
 ip address 10.0.0.5 255.0.0.0
 no ip directed-broadcast
 media-type 10BaseT
!
interface ATM0
 no ip address
 no ip directed-broadcast
 atm uni-version 4.0
 atm pvc 1 0 16 ilmi
 atm pvc 5 0 5 qsaal
 no atm ilmi-keepalive
 lane auto-config-atm-address
!
interface ATM0.16 multipoint
 ip address 144.254.16.5 255.255.255.0
 no ip directed-broadcast
 lane client ethernet easy
 ipx network 16
!
interface FastEthernet0
 no ip address
 no ip directed-broadcast
 shutdown
!
router igrp 100
 network 144.254.0.0
!
no ip classless
no ip http server
!
!
!
```

Lab 10-4 Solution

continues

Example C-91 *Router 5 Configuration for Lab 10-4 (Continued)*

```
line con 0
 transport input none
line aux 0
line vty 0 4
 password cisco
 login
!
end
```

Example C-92 *Router 6 Configuration for Lab 10-4*

```
Current configuration:
!
version 12.0
service timestamps debug uptime
service timestamps log uptime
no service password-encryption
!
hostname R6
!
enable secret 5 $1$/pVo$QkJYB4ad/.E4mCL62xYfe1
enable password cisco!
!
!
ip subnet-zero
no ip domain-lookup
!
!
ipx routing 0000.0000.0006
!
cns event-service server
!
!
process-max-time 200
!
interface Ethernet0
 ip address 144.254.6.6 255.255.255.0
 no ip directed-broadcast
 ipx network 66
 no mop enabled
!
interface Ethernet1
 ip address 10.0.0.6 255.0.0.0
 no ip directed-broadcast
 media-type 10BaseT
!
interface ATM0
 no ip address
 no ip directed-broadcast
 atm uni-version 4.0
```

Example C-92 *Router 6 Configuration for Lab 10-4 (Continued)*

```
atm pvc 1 0 16 ilmi
atm pvc 10 0 5 qsaal
no atm ilmi-keepalive
lane auto-config-atm-address
!
interface ATM0.16 multipoint
 ip address 144.254.16.6 255.255.255.0
 no ip directed-broadcast
 lane client ethernet easy
 ipx network 16
!
router igrp 100
 redistribute connected
 network 144.254.0.0
!
no ip classless
no ip http server
!
!
line con 0
 transport input none
line aux 0
line vty 0 4
 password cisco
 login
!
end
```

Example C-93 *Router 7 Configuration for Lab 10-4*

```
Current configuration:
!
version 12.0
service timestamps debug uptime
service timestamps log uptime
no service password-encryption
!
hostname r7
!
enable password sanfran
!
!
!
ip subnet-zero
!
ipx routing 0000.0000.0007
!
cns event-service server
!
!
```

continues

Example C-93 *Router 7 Configuration for Lab 10-4 (Continued)*

```
process-max-time 200
!
interface Ethernet0
 ip address 144.254.7.7 255.255.255.0
 no ip directed-broadcast
 ipx network 77
 no mop enabled
!
interface Ethernet1
 ip address 10.0.0.7 255.0.0.0
 no ip directed-broadcast
 media-type 10BaseT
!
interface ATM0
 no ip address
 no ip directed-broadcast
 atm uni-version 4.0
 atm pvc 5 0 5 qsaal
 atm pvc 16 0 16 ilmi
 no atm ilmi-keepalive
 lane auto-config-atm-address
!
interface ATM0.16 multipoint
 ip address 144.254.16.7 255.255.255.0
 no ip directed-broadcast
 lane client ethernet easy
 ipx network 16
!
interface FastEthernet0
 no ip address
 no ip directed-broadcast
 shutdown
!
router igrp 100
 network 144.254.0.0
!
no ip classless
no ip http server
!
!
line con 0
 transport input none
line aux 0
line vty 0 4
 password sanfran
 login
!
end
```

Example C-94 *Router 8 Configuration for Lab 10-4*

```
Current configuration:
!
version 12.0
service timestamps debug uptime
service timestamps log uptime
no service password-encryption
!
hostname r8
!
enable password sanfran
!
!
!
ip subnet-zero
!
ipx routing 0000.0000.0008
!
cns event-service server
!
!
process-max-time 200
!
interface Ethernet0
 ip address 144.254.8.8 255.255.255.0
 no ip directed-broadcast
 ipx network 88
 no mop enabled
!
interface Ethernet1
 ip address 10.0.0.8 255.0.0.0
 no ip directed-broadcast
 media-type 10BaseT
!
interface ATM0
 no ip address
 no ip directed-broadcast
 atm uni-version 4.0
 atm pvc 5 0 5 qsaal
 atm pvc 16 0 16 ilmi
 no atm ilmi-keepalive
 lane auto-config-atm-address
!
interface ATM0.16 multipoint
 ip address 144.254.16.8 255.255.255.0
 no ip directed-broadcast
 lane client ethernet easy
 ipx network 16
!
interface FastEthernet0
 no ip address
```

continues

Example C-94 *Router 8 Configuration for Lab 10-4 (Continued)*

```
 no ip directed-broadcast
 shutdown
!
router igrp 100
 network 144.254.0.0
!
no ip classless
no ip http server
!
!
line con 0
 transport input none
line aux 0
line vty 0 4
 password sanfran
 login
!
end
```

Example C-95 *Router 9 Configuration for Lab 10-4*

```
Current configuration:
!
version 12.0
service timestamps debug uptime
service timestamps log uptime
no service password-encryption
!
hostname r9
!
enable password sanfran
!
!
!
ip subnet-zero
!
ipx routing 0000.0000.0009
!
cns event-service server
!
!
process-max-time 200
!
interface Ethernet0
 ip address 144.254.9.9 255.255.255.0
 no ip directed-broadcast
 ipx network 99
 no mop enabled
!
interface Ethernet1
```

Example C-95 *Router 9 Configuration for Lab 10-4 (Continued)*

```
 ip address 10.0.0.9 255.0.0.0
 no ip directed-broadcast
 media-type 10BaseT
!
interface TokenRing0
 no ip address
 no ip directed-broadcast
 shutdown
!
interface ATM0
 no ip address
 no ip directed-broadcast
 atm uni-version 4.0
 atm pvc 5 0 5 qsaal
 atm pvc 16 0 16 ilmi
 no atm ilmi-keepalive
 lane auto-config-atm-address
!
interface ATM0.16 multipoint
 ip address 144.254.16.9 255.255.255.0
 no ip directed-broadcast
 lane client ethernet easy
 ipx network 16
!
router igrp 100
 network 144.254.0.0
!
no ip classless
no ip http server
!
!
!
!
!
line con 0
 transport input none
line aux 0
line vty 0 4
 password sanfran
 login
!
end
```

Example C-96 *Catalyst Switch 1 Configuration for Lab 10-4*

```
lane database cisco
    name easy server-atm-address 47.00918100000000100739C301. 00400BFF0011.10
    name easy server-atm-address 47.00918100000000100739A101. 00400BFF0011.10
    name easy server-atm-address 47.0091810000000061705B8301. 00400BFF0013.10
    name easy server-atm-address 47.00918100000000100739A101. 00400BFF0013.10
```

continues

Example C-96 *Catalyst Switch 1 Configuration for Lab 10-4 (Continued)*

```
default-name easy
!
interface ATM0
 atm preferred phy A
 atm pvc 1 0 5 qsaal
 atm pvc 2 0 16 ilmi
 lane config auto-config-atm-address
 lane auto-config-atm-address
 lane config database cisco
!
 interface atm 0.16
    lane server-bus ethernet easy
  lane client ethernet 2 easy
```

Example C-97 *Catalyst Switch 2 Configuration for Lab 10-4*

```
lane database cisco
   name easy server-atm-address 47.00918100000000100739C301. 00400BFF0011.10
   name easy server-atm-address 47.00918100000000100739A101. 00400BFF0011.10
   name easy server-atm-address 47.0091810000000061705B8301. 00400BFF0013.10
   name easy server-atm-address 47.00918100000000100739A101. 00400BFF0013.10
 default-name easy
!
interface ATM0
 atm preferred phy A
 atm pvc 1 0 5 qsaal
 atm pvc 2 0 16 ilmi
 lane config auto-config-atm-address
 lane auto-config-atm-address
 lane config database cisco
!
 interface atm 0.16
    lane server-bus ethernet easy
  lane client ethernet 2 easy
```

Example C-98 *Switch 1 Configuration for Lab 10-4*

```
!
version 11.3
no service pad
no service udp-small-servers
no service tcp-small-servers
!
hostname Switch_1
!
enable password sanfran
!
no ip domain-lookup
!
atm address 47.0091.8100.0000.0010.0739.9e01.0010.0739.9e01.00
```

Example C-98 *Switch 1 Configuration for Lab 10-4 (Continued)*

```
atm lecs-address-default 47.0091.8100.0000.0010.0739.C301.0040.0BFF.0013.00 01
atm lecs-address-default 47.0091.8100.0000.0010.0739.A101.0040.0BFF.0013.00 02
atm lecs-address-default 47.0091.8100.0000.0061.705B.8301.0040.0BFF.0015.00 03
atm lecs-address-default 47.0091.8100.0000.0010.0739.A101.0040.0BFF.0015.00 04
!
atm router pnni
 node 1 level 56 lowest
  redistribute atm-static
 !
!
interface ATM0/0/0
 shutdown
 no ip address
!
interface ATM0/0/1
 no ip address
!
interface ATM0/0/2
 no ip address
!
interface ATM0/0/3
 no ip address
 shutdown
!
interface ATM0/1/0
 no ip address
 no atm auto-configuration
 atm uni version 3.1
 atm maxvpi-bits 3
 atm maxvci-bits 10
 atm pvc 0 114  interface  ATM0/0/1 0 114
 atm pvc 0 115  interface  ATM0/0/1 0 115
 atm pvc 0 116  interface  ATM0/0/1 0 116
 atm pvc 0 117  interface  ATM0/0/2 0 117
 atm pvc 0 118  interface  ATM0/0/2 0 118
 atm pvc 0 119  interface  ATM0/0/2 0 119
!
interface ATM0/1/1
 no ip address
 no atm auto-configuration
 atm uni version 3.1
 atm maxvpi-bits 3
 atm maxvci-bits 10
 atm pvc 0 121  interface  ATM0/1/0 0 112
 atm pvc 0 124  interface  ATM0/0/1 0 124
 atm pvc 0 125  interface  ATM0/0/1 0 125
 atm pvc 0 126  interface  ATM0/0/1 0 126
 atm pvc 0 127  interface  ATM0/0/2 0 127
 atm pvc 0 128  interface  ATM0/0/2 0 128
 atm pvc 0 129  interface  ATM0/0/2 0 129
```

Lab 10-4 Solution

continues

Example C-98 *Switch 1 Configuration for Lab 10-4 (Continued)*

```
!
interface ATM0/1/2
 no ip address
 no atm auto-configuration
 atm uni version 3.1
 atm maxvpi-bits 3
 atm maxvci-bits 10
 atm pvc 0 120  interface  ATM0/1/0 0 120
 atm pvc 0 131  interface  ATM0/1/0 0 113
 atm pvc 0 132  interface  ATM0/1/1 0 123
 atm pvc 0 134  interface  ATM0/0/1 0 134
 atm pvc 0 135  interface  ATM0/0/1 0 135
 atm pvc 0 136  interface  ATM0/0/1 0 136
 atm pvc 0 137  interface  ATM0/0/2 0 137
 atm pvc 0 138  interface  ATM0/0/2 0 138
 atm pvc 0 139  interface  ATM0/0/2 0 139
!
interface ATM0/1/3
 no ip address
!
interface ATM2/0/0
 no ip address
 atm maxvp-number 0
!
interface Ethernet2/0/0
 ip address 10.0.0.11 255.0.0.0
!
ip classless
!
line con 0
 exec-timeout 0 0
 password cisco
 login
line aux 0
line vty 0 4
 exec-timeout 0 0
 password cisco
 login
!
end
```

Example C-99 *Switch 2 Configuration for Lab 10-4*

```
!
version 11.3
no service pad
no service udp-small-servers
no service tcp-small-servers
!
hostname Switch_2
```

Example C-99 *Switch 2 Configuration for Lab 10-4 (Continued)*

```
!
enable password sanfran
!
no ip domain-lookup
!
atm address 47.0091.8100.0000.0010.0739.a101.0010.0739.a101.00
atm lecs-address-default 47.0091.8100.0000.0010.0739.C301.0040.0BFF.0013.00 01
atm lecs-address-default 47.0091.8100.0000.0010.0739.A101.0040.0BFF.0013.00 02
atm lecs-address-default 47.0091.8100.0000.0061.705B.8301.0040.0BFF.0015.00 03
atm lecs-address-default 47.0091.8100.0000.0010.0739.A101.0040.0BFF.0015.00 04
!
atm router pnni
 node 1 level 56 lowest
  redistribute atm-static
!
!
interface ATM0/0/0
 shutdown
 no ip address
!
interface ATM0/0/1
 no ip address
!
interface ATM0/0/2
 shutdown
 no ip address
!
interface ATM0/0/3
 no ip address
!
interface ATM0/1/0
 no ip address
 no atm auto-configuration
 atm uni version 3.1
 atm maxvpi-bits 3
 atm maxvci-bits 10
 atm pvc 0 141   interface   ATM0/0/1 0 114
 atm pvc 0 142   interface   ATM0/0/1 0 124
 atm pvc 0 143   interface   ATM0/0/1 0 134
 atm pvc 0 147   interface   ATM0/0/3 0 147
 atm pvc 0 148   interface   ATM0/0/3 0 148
 atm pvc 0 149   interface   ATM0/0/3 0 149
!
interface ATM0/1/1
 no ip address
 no atm auto-configuration
 atm uni version 3.1
 atm maxvpi-bits 3
 atm maxvci-bits 10
 atm pvc 0 151   interface   ATM0/0/1 0 115
```

continues

Example C-99 *Switch 2 Configuration for Lab 10-4 (Continued)*

```
atm pvc 0 152   interface   ATM0/0/1 0 125
atm pvc 0 153   interface   ATM0/0/1 0 135
atm pvc 0 154   interface   ATM0/1/0 0 145
atm pvc 0 157   interface   ATM0/0/3 0 157
atm pvc 0 158   interface   ATM0/0/3 0 158
atm pvc 0 159   interface   ATM0/0/3 0 159
!
interface ATM0/1/2
 no ip address
 no atm auto-configuration
 atm uni version 3.1
 atm maxvpi-bits 3
 atm maxvci-bits 10
 atm pvc 0 161   interface   ATM0/0/1 0 116
 atm pvc 0 162   interface   ATM0/0/1 0 126
 atm pvc 0 163   interface   ATM0/0/1 0 136
 atm pvc 0 164   interface   ATM0/1/0 0 146
 atm pvc 0 165   interface   ATM0/1/1 0 156
 atm pvc 0 167   interface   ATM0/0/3 0 167
 atm pvc 0 168   interface   ATM0/0/3 0 168
 atm pvc 0 169   interface   ATM0/0/3 0 169
!
interface ATM0/1/3
 no ip address
!
interface ATM2/0/0
 no ip address
 atm maxvp-number 0
!
interface Ethernet2/0/0
 ip address 10.0.0.12 255.0.0.0
!
ip classless
!
line con 0
 exec-timeout 0 0
 password cisco
 login
line aux 0
line vty 0 4
 exec-timeout 0 0
 password cisco
 login
!
end
```

Example C-100 *Switch 3 Configuration for Lab 10-4*

```
!
version 11.3
```

Example C-100 *Switch 3 Configuration for Lab 10-4 (Continued)*

```
no service pad
no service udp-small-servers
no service tcp-small-servers
!
hostname Switch_3
!
boot system flash bootflash:ls1010-wp-mz.113-0.8.TWA4.2.bin
enable password sanfran
!
no ip domain-lookup
!
atm address 47.0091.8100.0000.0010.0739.c301.0010.0739.c301.00
atm lecs-address-default 47.0091.8100.0000.0010.0739.C301.0040.0BFF.0013.00 01
atm lecs-address-default 47.0091.8100.0000.0010.0739.A101.0040.0BFF.0013.00 02
atm lecs-address-default 47.0091.8100.0000.0061.705B.8301.0040.0BFF.0015.00 03
atm lecs-address-default 47.0091.8100.0000.0010.0739.A101.0040.0BFF.0015.00 04
!
atm router pnni
 node 1 level 56 lowest
  redistribute atm-static
!
!
interface ATM0/0/0
 shutdown
 no ip address
!
interface ATM0/0/1
 shutdown
 no ip address
!
interface ATM0/0/2
 no ip address
!
interface ATM0/0/3
 no ip address
!
interface ATM0/1/0
 no ip address
 no atm auto-configuration
 atm uni version 3.1
 atm maxvpi-bits 3
 atm maxvci-bits 10
 atm pvc 0 171   interface  ATM0/0/2 0 117
 atm pvc 0 172   interface  ATM0/0/2 0 127
 atm pvc 0 173   interface  ATM0/0/2 0 137
 atm pvc 0 174   interface  ATM0/0/3 0 147
 atm pvc 0 175   interface  ATM0/0/3 0 157
 atm pvc 0 176   interface  ATM0/0/3 0 167
!
interface ATM0/1/1
```

continues

Lab 10-4 Solution

Example C-100 *Switch 3 Configuration for Lab 10-4 (Continued)*

```
 no ip address
 no atm auto-configuration
 atm uni version 3.1
 atm maxvpi-bits 3
 atm maxvci-bits 10
 atm pvc 0 181   interface   ATM0/0/2 0 118
 atm pvc 0 182   interface   ATM0/0/2 0 128
 atm pvc 0 183   interface   ATM0/0/2 0 138
 atm pvc 0 184   interface   ATM0/0/3 0 148
 atm pvc 0 185   interface   ATM0/0/3 0 158
 atm pvc 0 186   interface   ATM0/0/3 0 168
 atm pvc 0 187   interface   ATM0/1/0 0 178
!
interface ATM0/1/2
 no ip address
 no atm auto-configuration
 atm uni version 3.1
 atm maxvpi-bits 3
 atm maxvci-bits 10
 atm pvc 0 191   interface   ATM0/0/2 0 119
 atm pvc 0 192   interface   ATM0/0/2 0 129
 atm pvc 0 193   interface   ATM0/0/2 0 139
 atm pvc 0 194   interface   ATM0/0/3 0 149
 atm pvc 0 195   interface   ATM0/0/3 0 159
 atm pvc 0 196   interface   ATM0/0/3 0 169
 atm pvc 0 197   interface   ATM0/1/0 0 179
 atm pvc 0 198   interface   ATM0/1/1 0 189
!
interface ATM0/1/3
 no ip address
!
interface ATM1/0/0
 no ip address
!
interface ATM1/0/1
 no ip address
!
interface ATM1/0/2
 no ip address
!
interface ATM1/0/3
 no ip address
!
interface ATM2/0/0
 no ip address
 atm maxvp-number 0
!
interface Ethernet2/0/0
 ip address 10.0.0.13 255.0.0.0
!
```

Example C-100 *Switch 3 Configuration for Lab 10-4 (Continued)*

```
ip classless
!
line con 0
 exec-timeout 0 0
 password cisco
 login
line aux 0
line vty 0 4
 exec-timeout 0 0
 password cisco
 login
!
end
```

Solutions for Lab 11-1: Configuring MPOA

Examples C-101 through C-112 provide the configuration solutions that satisfy all of the exercises for Lab 11-1. Specifically, the exercises asked for the following:

1 You are to use new subinterfaces ATM 0.50, ATM 0.60, and ATM 0.70 to implement this lab solution. Notice, that because MPOA is based on LANE, you will rely on the dynamic AESA address registration. Configure the subinterfaces according to the Table 11-4 on page 419.

2 LANE is deployed in the lab within an LIS. This implies that you require a separate LES-BUS server within a single broadcast domain. Configure R2 as the LES-BUS server in the LIS1, R8 as the LES-BUS Server in the LIS2, and R5 as the LES-BUS Server in the LIS3.

3 As per the lab schematic, R3 and R4 are both logically associated with two logical IP subnets. They require a second AESA address, which they obtain dynamically and a second IP address to support the second subnet, associated with another subinterface, as depicted in the Table 11-4. Note that you are still using the same Layer 3 IP routing protocol, IGRP.

4 Configure LECs on all the routers, identifying ELANs according to the Figure 11-4.

5 Configure R6 as the LECS, as you did for the LANE labs in Chapter 10.

6 Configure MPC and MPS binding to LANE clients, as indicated in the Figure 11-4.

7 Verify that you have full IP connectivity between all routers. Using ping and the show ip route command to ensure that the IGRP routing strategy is working as expected.

8 Use the trace command to demonstrate the path taken when you forward packets to remote IP destinations from your router. For example, from R2, trace 144.254.7.7, trace 144.254.4.4. Make sure that this the first trace you are performing so that you can witness the first "passage" of packets. You will see that the packets will be entering and exiting ATM network more than ones. This only happens when the packet traverses the ATM network very first time.

9 Use another trace command on your router to demonstrate that ATM "fools" IP, by providing cut-through routing. For example, on R3 or R2, repeat the trace test to IP destinations used previously. You will see the cut-through routing event.

Example C-101 *Router 1 Configuration for Lab 11-1*

```
Current configuration:
!
version 12.0
service timestamps debug uptime
service timestamps log uptime
no service password-encryption
!
hostname R1
!
enable password sanfran
!
ip subnet-zero
no ip domain-lookup
!
ipx routing 0000.0000.0001
!
mpoa client config name r1
    shortcut-frame-time 60
!
cns event-service server
!
!
process-max-time 200
!
interface Ethernet0
 ip address 144.254.1.1 255.255.255.0
 no ip directed-broadcast
!
interface Ethernet1
 ip address 10.0.0.1 255.0.0.0
 no ip directed-broadcast
 media-type 10BaseT
!
interface ATM0
 mtu 1500
 no ip address
 no ip directed-broadcast
 atm uni-version 4.0
 atm pvc 1 0 5 qsaal
 atm pvc 3 0 16 ilmi
 no atm ilmi-keepalive
```

Example C-101 *Router 1 Configuration for Lab 11-1*

```
 lane auto-config-atm-address
 mpoa client name r1
!
interface ATM0.50 multipoint
 ip address 144.254.50.1 255.255.255.0
 no ip directed-broadcast
 lane client mpoa client name r1
 lane client ethernet mkt
 ipx network 50
!
interface FastEthernet0
 no ip address
 no ip directed-broadcast
 shutdown
!
router igrp 100
 network 144.254.0.0
!
no ip classless
no ip http server
!
!
line con 0
 password sanfran
 transport input none
line aux 0
line vty 0 4
 password sanfran
 login
!
end
```

Example C-102 *Router 2 Configuration for Lab 11-1*

```
Current configuration:
!
version 12.0
service timestamps debug uptime
service timestamps log uptime
no service password-encryption
!
hostname R2
!
enable password sanfran
!
ip subnet-zero
no ip domain-lookup
!
ipx routing 0000.0000.0002
!
```

continues

Example C-102 *Router 2 Configuration for Lab 11-1 (Continued)*

```
mpoa client config name r2
    shortcut-frame-time 60
!
cns event-service server
!
!
process-max-time 200
!
interface Ethernet0
 ip address 144.254.2.2 255.255.255.0
 no ip directed-broadcast
!
interface Ethernet1
 ip address 10.0.0.2 255.0.0.0
 no ip directed-broadcast
 media-type 10BaseT
!
interface ATM0
 mtu 1500
 no ip address
 no ip directed-broadcast
 atm uni-version 4.0
 atm pvc 1 0 5 qsaal
 atm pvc 3 0 16 ilmi
 no atm ilmi-keepalive
 lane auto-config-atm-address
 mpoa client name r2
!
interface ATM0.50 multipoint
 ip address 144.254.50.2 255.255.255.0
 no ip directed-broadcast
 lane server-bus ethernet mkt elan-id 50
 lane client mpoa client name r2
 lane client ethernet mkt
 ipx network 50
!
interface FastEthernet0
 no ip address
 no ip directed-broadcast
 shutdown
!
router igrp 100
 network 144.254.0.0
!
no ip classless
no ip http server
!
!
line con 0
 password sanfran
```

Example C-102 *Router 2 Configuration for Lab 11-1 (Continued)*

```
 transport input none
line aux 0
line vty 0 4
 password sanfran
 login
 !
end
```

Example C-103 *Router 3 Configuration for Lab 11-1*

```
Current configuration:
!
version 12.0
service timestamps debug uptime
service timestamps log uptime
no service password-encryption
!
hostname r3
!
enable password sanfran
!
!
!
ip subnet-zero
no ip domain-lookup
!
ipx routing 0000.0000.0003
!
mpoa server config name r3
  holding-time 7200
!
cns event-service server
!
!
process-max-time 200
!
interface Ethernet0
 ip address 144.254.3.3 255.255.255.0
 no ip directed-broadcast
 no ip mroute-cache
 ipx network 30
 no mop enabled
!
interface Ethernet1
 ip address 10.0.0.3 255.0.0.0
 no ip directed-broadcast
 no ip mroute-cache
 media-type 10BaseT
 no mop enabled
!
```

continues

Lab 11-1 Solution

Example C-103   *Router 3 Configuration for Lab 11-1 (Continued)*

```
interface TokenRing0
 no ip address
 no ip directed-broadcast
 no ip mroute-cache
 shutdown
!
interface ATM0
 mtu 1500
 no ip address
 no ip directed-broadcast
 no ip mroute-cache
 atm uni-version 4.0
 atm pvc 2 0 16 ilmi
 atm pvc 5 0 5 qsaal
 no atm ilmi-keepalive
 lane auto-config-atm-address
 mpoa server name r3
!
interface ATM0.50 multipoint
 ip address 144.254.50.3 255.255.255.0
 no ip directed-broadcast
 lane client mpoa server name r3
 lane client ethernet mkt
 ipx network 50
!
interface ATM0.60 multipoint
 ip address 144.254.60.3 255.255.255.0
 no ip directed-broadcast
 lane client mpoa server name r3
 lane client ethernet sales
 ipx network 60
!
router igrp 100
 network 144.254.0.0
!
no ip classless
no ip http server
!
!
!
line con 0
 password sanfran
 transport input none
line aux 0
line vty 0 4
 password sanfran
 login
!
end
```

Example C-104 *Router 4 Configuration for Lab 11-1*

```
Current configuration:
!
version 12.0
service timestamps debug uptime
service timestamps log uptime
no service password-encryption
!
hostname R4
!
enable password sanfran
!
!
!
!
!
ip subnet-zero
no ip domain-lookup
!
ipx routing 0000.0000.0004
!
mpoa server config name r4
  holding-time 7200
!
cns event-service server
!
!
process-max-time 200
!
interface Ethernet0
 ip address 144.254.4.4 255.255.255.0
 no ip directed-broadcast
 ipx network 40
 no mop enabled
!
interface Ethernet1
 ip address 10.0.0.4 255.0.0.0
 no ip directed-broadcast
 media-type 10BaseT
!
interface Serial0
 no ip address
 no ip directed-broadcast
 shutdown
!
interface Serial1
 no ip address
 no ip directed-broadcast
 shutdown
!
interface ATM0
```

continues

Lab 11-1 Solution

Example C-104 *Router 4 Configuration for Lab 11-1 (Continued)*

```
 no ip address
 no ip directed-broadcast
 atm uni-version 4.0
 atm pvc 1 0 16 ilmi
 atm pvc 10 0 5 qsaal
 atm ilmi-keepalive
 lane auto-config-atm-address
 mpoa server name r4
!
interface ATM0.60 multipoint
 ip address 144.254.60.4 255.255.255.0
 no ip directed-broadcast
 lane client mpoa server name r4
 lane client ethernet sales
 ipx network 60
!
interface ATM0.70 multipoint
 ip address 144.254.70.4 255.255.255.0
 no ip directed-broadcast
 lane client mpoa server name r4
 lane client ethernet engineering
 ipx network 70
!
router igrp 100
 network 144.254.0.0
!
no ip classless
no ip http server
!
!
line con 0
 password sanfran
 transport input none
line aux 0
line vty 0 4
 password sanfran
 login
!
end
```

Example C-105 *Router 5 Configuration for Lab 11-1*

```
Current configuration:
!
version 12.0
service timestamps debug uptime
service timestamps log uptime
no service password-encryption
!
hostname R5
```

Example C-105 *Router 5 Configuration for Lab 11-1 (Continued)*

```
!
enable password sanfran
!
!
!
ip subnet-zero
no ip domain-lookup
!
ipx routing 0000.0000.0005
!
mpoa client config name r5
!
cns event-service server
!
!
process-max-time 200
!
interface Ethernet0
 ip address 144.254.5.5 255.255.255.0
 no ip directed-broadcast
 ipx network 50
 no mop enabled
!
interface Ethernet1
 ip address 10.0.0.5 255.0.0.0
 no ip directed-broadcast
 media-type 10BaseT
!
interface ATM0
 no ip address
 no ip directed-broadcast
 atm uni-version 4.0
 atm pvc 1 0 16 ilmi
 atm pvc 5 0 5 qsaal
 no atm ilmi-keepalive
 lane auto-config-atm-address
 mpoa client name r5
!
interface ATM0.70 multipoint
 ip address 144.254.70.5 255.255.255.0
 no ip directed-broadcast
 lane server-bus ethernet engineering elan-id 70
 lane client mpoa client name r5
 lane client ethernet engineering
 ipx network 70
!
interface FastEthernet0
 no ip address
 no ip directed-broadcast
 shutdown
```

continues

Lab 11-1 Solution

Example C-105 *Router 5 Configuration for Lab 11-1 (Continued)*

```
!
router igrp 100
 redistribute connected
 network 144.254.0.0
!
no ip classless
no ip http server
!
!
!
line con 0
 password sanfran
 transport input none
line aux 0
line vty 0 4
 password sanfran
 login
!
end
```

Example C-106 *Router 6 Configuration for Lab 11-1*

```
Current configuration:
!
version 12.0
service timestamps debug uptime
service timestamps log uptime
no service password-encryption
!
hostname R6
!
enable password cisco!
!
!
ip subnet-zero
no ip domain-lookup
!
!
lane database galina
  name mkt server-atm-address 47.009181000000001007399E01.00E0145505C1.32
  name mkt elan-id 50
  name sales server-atm-address 47.00918100000000100739C301.00E0145502C1.3C
  name sales elan-id 60
  name engineering server-atm-address 47.00918100000000100739A101.00E01454DCE1.4
6
  name engineering elan-id 70
ipx routing 0000.0000.0006
!
mpoa client config name r6
    shortcut-frame-time 60
```

Example C-106 *Router 6 Configuration for Lab 11-1 (Continued)*

```
!
cns event-service server
!
!
process-max-time 200
!
interface Ethernet0
 ip address 144.254.6.6 255.255.255.0
 no ip directed-broadcast
 ipx network 66
 no mop enabled
!
interface Ethernet1
 ip address 10.0.0.6 255.0.0.0
 no ip directed-broadcast
 media-type 10BaseT
!
interface ATM0
 no ip address
 no ip directed-broadcast
 atm uni-version 4.0
 atm pvc 1 0 16 ilmi
 atm pvc 10 0 5 qsaal
 no atm ilmi-keepalive
 lane config auto-config-atm-address
 lane config database galina
 lane auto-config-atm-address
 mpoa client name r6
!
interface ATM0.70 multipoint
 ip address 144.254.70.6 255.255.255.0
 no ip directed-broadcast
 lane client mpoa client name r6
 lane client ethernet engineering
 ipx network 70
!
router igrp 100
 redistribute connected
 network 144.254.0.0
!
no ip classless
no ip http server
!
!
line con 0
 password sanfran
 transport input none
line aux 0
line vty 0 4
 password sanfran
```

continues

Lab 11-1 Solution

Example C-106 *Router 6 Configuration for Lab 11-1 (Continued)*

```
 login
!
end
```

Example C-107 *Router 7 Configuration for Lab 11-1*

```
Current configuration:
!
version 12.0
service timestamps debug uptime
service timestamps log uptime
no service password-encryption
!
hostname r7
!
enable password sanfran
!
!
!
ip subnet-zero
!
ipx routing 0000.0000.0007
!
mpoa client config name r7
     shortcut-frame-time 60
!
cns event-service server
!
!
process-max-time 200
!
interface Ethernet0
 ip address 144.254.7.7 255.255.255.0
 no ip directed-broadcast
 ipx network 77
 no mop enabled
!
interface Ethernet1
 ip address 10.0.0.7 255.0.0.0
 no ip directed-broadcast
 media-type 10BaseT
!
interface ATM0
 no ip address
 no ip directed-broadcast
 atm uni-version 4.0
 atm pvc 5 0 5 qsaal
 atm pvc 16 0 16 ilmi
 no atm ilmi-keepalive
 lane auto-config-atm-address
```

Example C-107 *Router 7 Configuration for Lab 11-1 (Continued)*

```
 mpoa client name r7
!
interface ATM0.60 multipoint
 ip address 144.254.60.7 255.255.255.0
 no ip directed-broadcast
 lane client mpoa client name r7
 lane client ethernet sales
 ipx network 60
!
interface FastEthernet0
 no ip address
 no ip directed-broadcast
 shutdown
!
router igrp 100
 network 144.254.0.0
!
no ip classless
no ip http server
!
!
line con 0
 password sanfran
 transport input none
line aux 0
line vty 0 4
 password sanfran
 login
!
end
```

Example C-108 *Router 8 Configuration for Lab 11-1*

```
Current configuration:
!
version 12.0
service timestamps debug uptime
service timestamps log uptime
no service password-encryption
!
hostname r8
!
enable password sanfran
!
!
!
ip subnet-zero
!
ipx routing 0000.0000.0008
!
```

continues

Example C-108 *Router 8 Configuration for Lab 11-1 (Continued)*

```
mpoa client config name r8
    shortcut-frame-time 60
!
cns event-service server
!
!
process-max-time 200
!
interface Ethernet0
 ip address 144.254.8.8 255.255.255.0
 no ip directed-broadcast
 ipx network 88
 no mop enabled
!
interface Ethernet1
 ip address 10.0.0.8 255.0.0.0
 no ip directed-broadcast
 media-type 10BaseT
!
interface ATM0
 no ip address
 no ip directed-broadcast
 atm uni-version 4.0
 atm pvc 5 0 5 qsaal
 atm pvc 16 0 16 ilmi
 no atm ilmi-keepalive
 lane auto-config-atm-address
 mpoa client name r8
!
interface ATM0.60 multipoint
 ip address 144.254.60.8 255.255.255.0
 no ip directed-broadcast
 lane server-bus ethernet sales elan-id 60
 lane client mpoa client name r8
 lane client ethernet sales
 ipx network 60
!
interface FastEthernet0
 no ip address
 no ip directed-broadcast
 shutdown
!
router igrp 100
 network 144.254.0.0
!
no ip classless
no ip http server
!
!
line con 0
```

Example C-108 *Router 8 Configuration for Lab 11-1 (Continued)*

```
 password sanfran
 transport input none
line aux 0
line vty 0 4
 password sanfran
 login
!
end
```

Example C-109 *Router 9 Configuration for Lab 11-1*

```
Current configuration:
!
version 12.0
service timestamps debug uptime
service timestamps log uptime
no service password-encryption
!
hostname r9
!
enable password sanfran
!
!
!
ip subnet-zero
!
ipx routing 0000.0000.0009
!
mpoa client config name r9
!
cns event-service server
!
!
process-max-time 200
!
interface Ethernet0
 ip address 144.254.9.9 255.255.255.0
 no ip directed-broadcast
 ipx network 99
 no mop enabled
!
interface Ethernet1
 ip address 10.0.0.9 255.0.0.0
 no ip directed-broadcast
 media-type 10BaseT
!
interface TokenRing0
 no ip address
 no ip directed-broadcast
 shutdown
```

continues

Lab 11-1 Solution

Example C-109 *Router 9 Configuration for Lab 11-1 (Continued)*

```
!
interface ATM0
 no ip address
 no ip directed-broadcast
 atm uni-version 4.0
 atm pvc 5 0 5 qsaal
 atm pvc 16 0 16 ilmi
 no atm ilmi-keepalive
 lane auto-config-atm-address
 mpoa client name r9
!
interface ATM0.60 multipoint
 ip address 144.254.60.9 255.255.255.0
 no ip directed-broadcast
 lane client mpoa client name r9
 lane client ethernet sales
 ipx network 60
!
router igrp 100
 network 144.254.0.0
!
no ip classless
no ip http server
!
!
!
!
!
line con 0
 password sanfran
 transport input none
line aux 0
line vty 0 4
 password sanfran
 login
!
end
```

Example C-110 *Switch 1 Configuration for Lab 11-1*

```
!
version 11.3
no service pad
no service udp-small-servers
no service tcp-small-servers
!
hostname Switch_1
!
enable password sanfran
!
```

Example C-110 *Switch 1 Configuration for Lab 11-1 (Continued)*

```
no ip domain-lookup
!
atm address 47.0091.8100.0000.0010.0739.9e01.0010.0739.9e01.00
atm lecs-address-default 47.0091.8100.0000.0010.0739.c301.00e0.1455.02c3.00 01
!
atm router pnni
 node 1 level 56 lowest
  redistribute atm-static
!
!
interface ATM0/0/0
 shutdown
 no ip address
!
interface ATM0/0/1
 no ip address
!
interface ATM0/0/2
 no ip address
!
interface ATM0/0/3
 no ip address
 shutdown
!
interface ATM0/1/0
 no ip address
 no atm auto-configuration
 atm uni version 4.0
 atm maxvpi-bits 3
 atm maxvci-bits 10
 atm pvc 0 114  interface  ATM0/0/1 0 114
 atm pvc 0 115  interface  ATM0/0/1 0 115
 atm pvc 0 116  interface  ATM0/0/1 0 116
 atm pvc 0 117  interface  ATM0/0/2 0 117
 atm pvc 0 118  interface  ATM0/0/2 0 118
 atm pvc 0 119  interface  ATM0/0/2 0 119
!
interface ATM0/1/1
 no ip address
 no atm auto-configuration
 atm uni version 4.0
 atm maxvpi-bits 3
 atm maxvci-bits 10
 atm pvc 0 121  interface  ATM0/1/0 0 112
 atm pvc 0 124  interface  ATM0/0/1 0 124
 atm pvc 0 125  interface  ATM0/0/1 0 125
 atm pvc 0 126  interface  ATM0/0/1 0 126
 atm pvc 0 127  interface  ATM0/0/2 0 127
 atm pvc 0 128  interface  ATM0/0/2 0 128
 atm pvc 0 129  interface  ATM0/0/2 0 129
```

Lab 11-1 Solution

Example C-110 *Switch 1 Configuration for Lab 11-1 (Continued)*

```
!
interface ATM0/1/2
 no ip address
 no atm auto-configuration
 atm uni version 4.0
 atm maxvpi-bits 3
 atm maxvci-bits 10
 atm pvc 0 120  interface  ATM0/1/0 0 120
 atm pvc 0 131  interface  ATM0/1/0 0 113
 atm pvc 0 132  interface  ATM0/1/1 0 123
 atm pvc 0 134  interface  ATM0/0/1 0 134
 atm pvc 0 135  interface  ATM0/0/1 0 135
 atm pvc 0 136  interface  ATM0/0/1 0 136
 atm pvc 0 137  interface  ATM0/0/2 0 137
 atm pvc 0 138  interface  ATM0/0/2 0 138
 atm pvc 0 139  interface  ATM0/0/2 0 139
!
interface ATM0/1/3
 no ip address
!
interface ATM2/0/0
 no ip address
 atm maxvp-number 0
!
interface Ethernet2/0/0
 ip address 10.0.0.11 255.0.0.0
!
ip classless
!
line con 0
 exec-timeout 0 0
 password cisco
 login
line aux 0
line vty 0 4
 exec-timeout 0 0
 password cisco
 login
!
end
```

Example C-111 *Switch 2 Configuration for Lab 11-1*

```
!
version 11.3
no service pad
no service udp-small-servers
no service tcp-small-servers
!
hostname Switch_2
```

Example C-111 *Switch 2 Configuration for Lab 11-1 (Continued)*

```
!
enable password sanfran
!
no ip domain-lookup
!
atm address 47.0091.8100.0000.0010.0739.a101.0010.0739.a101.00
atm lecs-address-default 47.0091.8100.0000.0010.0739.c301.00e0.1455.02c3.00 01
!
atm router pnni
 node 1 level 56 lowest
  redistribute atm-static
 !
 !
interface ATM0/0/0
 shutdown
 no ip address
!
interface ATM0/0/1
 no ip address
!
interface ATM0/0/2
 shutdown
 no ip address
!
interface ATM0/0/3
 no ip address
!
interface ATM0/1/0
 no ip address
 no atm auto-configuration
 atm uni version 4.0
 atm maxvpi-bits 3
 atm maxvci-bits 10
 atm pvc 0 141  interface  ATM0/0/1 0 114
 atm pvc 0 142  interface  ATM0/0/1 0 124
 atm pvc 0 143  interface  ATM0/0/1 0 134
 atm pvc 0 147  interface  ATM0/0/3 0 147
 atm pvc 0 148  interface  ATM0/0/3 0 148
 atm pvc 0 149  interface  ATM0/0/3 0 149
!
interface ATM0/1/1
 no ip address
 no atm auto-configuration
 atm uni version 4.0
 atm maxvpi-bits 3
 atm maxvci-bits 10
 atm pvc 0 151  interface  ATM0/0/1 0 115
 atm pvc 0 152  interface  ATM0/0/1 0 125
 atm pvc 0 153  interface  ATM0/0/1 0 135
 atm pvc 0 154  interface  ATM0/1/0 0 145
```

continues

Lab 11-1 Solution

Example C-111 *Switch 2 Configuration for Lab 11-1 (Continued)*

```
 atm pvc 0 157  interface  ATM0/0/3 0 157
 atm pvc 0 158  interface  ATM0/0/3 0 158
 atm pvc 0 159  interface  ATM0/0/3 0 159
!
interface ATM0/1/2
 no ip address
 no atm auto-configuration
 atm uni version 4.0
 atm maxvpi-bits 3
 atm maxvci-bits 10
 atm pvc 0 161  interface  ATM0/0/1 0 116
 atm pvc 0 162  interface  ATM0/0/1 0 126
 atm pvc 0 163  interface  ATM0/0/1 0 136
 atm pvc 0 164  interface  ATM0/1/0 0 146
 atm pvc 0 165  interface  ATM0/1/1 0 156
 atm pvc 0 167  interface  ATM0/0/3 0 167
 atm pvc 0 168  interface  ATM0/0/3 0 168
 atm pvc 0 169  interface  ATM0/0/3 0 169
!
interface ATM0/1/3
 no ip address
!
interface ATM2/0/0
 no ip address
 atm maxvp-number 0
!
interface Ethernet2/0/0
 ip address 10.0.0.12 255.0.0.0
!
ip classless
!
line con 0
 exec-timeout 0 0
 password cisco
 login
line aux 0
line vty 0 4
 exec-timeout 0 0
 password cisco
 login
!
end
```

Example C-112 *Switch 3 Configuration for Lab 11-1*

```
!
version 11.3
no service pad
no service udp-small-servers
no service tcp-small-servers
```

Example C-112 *Switch 3 Configuration for Lab 11-1 (Continued)*

```
!
hostname Switch_3
!
boot system flash bootflash:ls1010-wp-mz.113-0.8.TWA4.2.bin
enable password sanfran
!
no ip domain-lookup
!
atm address 47.0091.8100.0000.0010.0739.c301.0010.0739.c301.00
atm lecs-address-default 47.0091.8100.0000.0010.0739.c301.00e0.1455.02c3.00 01
!
atm router pnni
 node 1 level 56 lowest
  redistribute atm-static
!
!
interface ATM0/0/0
 shutdown
 no ip address
!
interface ATM0/0/1
 shutdown
 no ip address
!
interface ATM0/0/2
 no ip address
!
interface ATM0/0/3
 no ip address
!
interface ATM0/1/0
 no ip address
 no atm auto-configuration
 atm uni version 4.0
 atm maxvpi-bits 3
 atm maxvci-bits 10
 atm pvc 0 171   interface  ATM0/0/2 0 117
 atm pvc 0 172   interface  ATM0/0/2 0 127
 atm pvc 0 173   interface  ATM0/0/2 0 137
 atm pvc 0 174   interface  ATM0/0/3 0 147
 atm pvc 0 175   interface  ATM0/0/3 0 157
 atm pvc 0 176   interface  ATM0/0/3 0 167
!
interface ATM0/1/1
 no ip address
 no atm auto-configuration
 atm uni version 4.0
 atm maxvpi-bits 3
 atm maxvci-bits 10
 atm pvc 0 181   interface  ATM0/0/2 0 118
```

continues

Lab 11-1 Solution

Example C-112 *Switch 3 Configuration for Lab 11-1 (Continued)*

```
atm pvc 0 182  interface  ATM0/0/2 0 128
atm pvc 0 183  interface  ATM0/0/2 0 138
atm pvc 0 184  interface  ATM0/0/3 0 148
atm pvc 0 185  interface  ATM0/0/3 0 158
atm pvc 0 186  interface  ATM0/0/3 0 168
atm pvc 0 187  interface  ATM0/1/0 0 178
!
interface ATM0/1/2
 no ip address
 no atm auto-configuration
 atm uni version 4.0
 atm maxvpi-bits 3
 atm maxvci-bits 10
 atm pvc 0 191  interface  ATM0/0/2 0 119
 atm pvc 0 192  interface  ATM0/0/2 0 129
 atm pvc 0 193  interface  ATM0/0/2 0 139
 atm pvc 0 194  interface  ATM0/0/3 0 149
 atm pvc 0 195  interface  ATM0/0/3 0 159
 atm pvc 0 196  interface  ATM0/0/3 0 169
 atm pvc 0 197  interface  ATM0/1/0 0 179
 atm pvc 0 198  interface  ATM0/1/1 0 189
!
interface ATM0/1/3
 no ip address
!
interface ATM1/0/0
 no ip address
!
interface ATM1/0/1
 no ip address
!
interface ATM1/0/2
 no ip address
!
interface ATM1/0/3
 no ip address
!
interface ATM2/0/0
 no ip address
 atm maxvp-number 0
!
interface Ethernet2/0/0
 ip address 10.0.0.13 255.0.0.0
!
ip classless
!
line con 0
 exec-timeout 0 0
 password cisco
 login
```

Example C-112 *Switch 3 Configuration for Lab 11-1 (Continued)*

```
line aux 0
line vty 0 4
 exec-timeout 0 0
 password cisco
 login
!
end
```

Solutions for Lab 13-1: PVC Segment Setup on the LS1010

Examples C-113 through C-115 provide the configuration solutions that satisfy all the exercises for Lab 13-1. Specifically, the exercises ask for the following:

1 Complete the charts in Table 13-15 through Table 13-20 on pages 502–504.

Table C–1 *Lab 13-1 PVC Mapping Charts: Switch 1 Local PVC Mapping (Table 13-15)*

From	In	In	In	Out	Out	Out	To
Router #	Port	VPI	VCI	Port	VPI	VCI	Router #
R1	0/1/0	0	112	0/1/1	0	121	R2
R2	0/1/1	0	123	0/1/2	0	132	R3
R3	0/1/2	0	131	0/1/0	0	113	R1

Table C–2 *Lab 13-1 PVC Mapping Charts: Switch 2 Local PVC Mapping (Table 13-16)*

From	In	In	In	Out	Out	Out	To
Router #	Port	VPI	VCI	Port	VPI	VCI	Router #
R4	0/1/0	0	145	0/1/1	0	154	R5
R5	0/1/1	0	156	0/1/2	0	165	R6
R6	0/1/2	0	164	0/1/0	0	146	R4

Table C–3 *Lab 13-1 PVC Mapping Charts: Switch 3 Local PVC Mapping (Table 13-17)*

From	In	In	In	Out	Out	Out	To
Router #	Port	VPI	VCI	Port	VPI	VCI	Router #
R7	0/1/0	0	178	0/1/1	0	187	R8
R8	0/1/1	0	189	0/1/2	0	198	R9
R9	0/1/2	0	197	0/1/0	0	179	R7

Table C–4   *Lab 13-1 PVC Mapping Charts: Interswitch Mapping from Switch 1's Perspective (Table 13-18)*

| Switch 1 | | | | | | | | Switch 2 or Switch 3 | | | | | | |
From Router	In Port	In VPI	In VCI	Out Port	Out VPI	Out VCI	NNI	In Port	In VPI	In VCI	Out Port	Out VPI	Out VCI	To Router
R1	0/1/0	0	114	0/0/1	0	114	0/0/1	0/0/1	0	114	0/1/0	0	141	R4
R1	0/1/0	0	115	0/0/1	0	115	0/0/1	0/0/1	0	115	0/1/1	0	151	R5
R1	0/1/0	0	116	0/0/1	0	116	0/0/1	0/0/1	0	116	0/1/2	0	161	R6
R1	0/1/0	0	117	0/0/2	0	117	0/0/2	0/0/2	0	117	0/1/0	0	171	R7
R1	0/1/0	0	118	0/0/2	0	118	0/0/2	0/0/2	0	118	0/1/1	0	181	R8
R1	0/1/0	0	119	0/0/2	0	119	0/0/2	0/0/2	0	119	0/1/2	0	191	R9
R2	0/1/1	0	124	0/0/1	0	124	0/0/1	0/0/1	0	124	0/1/0	0	142	R4
R2	0/1/1	0	125	0/0/1	0	125	0/0/1	0/0/1	0	125	0/1/1	0	152	R5
R2	0/1/1	0	126	0/0/1	0	126	0/0/1	0/0/1	0	126	0/1/2	0	162	R6
R2	0/1/1	0	127	0/0/2	0	127	0/0/2	0/0/2	0	127	0/1/0	0	172	R7
R2	0/1/1	0	128	0/0/2	0	128	0/0/2	0/0/2	0	128	0/1/1	0	182	R8
R2	0/1/1	0	129	0/0/2	0	129	0/0/2	0/0/2	0	129	0/1/2	0	192	R9
R3	0/1/2	0	134	0/0/1	0	134	0/0/1	0/0/1	0	134	0/1/0	0	143	R4

| Switch 1 | | | | | | | | Switch 2 or Switch 3 | | | | | | |
From Router	In Port	In VPI	In VCI	Out Port	Out VPI	Out VCI	NNI	In Port	In VPI	In VCI	Out Port	Out VPI	Out VCI	To Router
R3	0/1/2	0	135	0/0/1	0	135	0/0/1	0/0/1	0	135	0/1/1	0	153	R5
R3	0/1/2	0	136	0/0/1	0	136	0/0/1	0/0/1	0	136	0/1/2	0	163	R6
R3	0/1/2	0	137	0/0/2	0	137	0/0/2	0/0/2	0	137	0/1/0	0	173	R7
R3	0/1/2	0	138	0/0/2	0	138	0/0/2	0/0/2	0	138	0/1/1	0	183	R8
R3	0/1/2	0	139	0/0/2	0	139	0/0/2	0/0/2	0	139	0/1/2	0	193	R9

Table C–5   *Lab 13-1 PVC Mapping Charts: Inter-Switch Mapping from Switch 2's Perspective (Table 13-19)*

| Switch 2 | | | | | | | | Switch 1 or Switch 3 | | | | | | |
From Router	In Port	In VPI	In VCI	Out Port	Out VPI	Out VCI	NNI	In Port	In VPI	In VCI	Out Port	Out VPI	Out VCI	To Router
R4	0/1/0	0	141	0/0/1	0	114	0/0/1	0/0/1	0	114	0/1/0	0	114	R1
R4	0/1/0	0	142	0/0/1	0	124	0/0/1	0/0/1	0	124	0/1/1	0	124	R2

Table C–5 *Lab 13-1 PVC Mapping Charts: Inter-Switch Mapping from Switch 2's Perspective (Table 13-19)*

Switch 2							Switch 1 or Switch 3						
From Router	In Port	In VPI	In VCI	Out Port	Out VPI	Out VCI	NNI	In Port	In VPI	In VCI	Out Port	Out VPI	Out VCI	To Router
R4	0/1/0	0	143	0/0/1	0	134	0/0/1	0/0/1	0	134	0/1/2	0	134	R3
R4	0/1/0	0	147	0/0/3	0	147	0/0/3	0/0/3	0	147	0/1/0	0	174	R7
R4	0/1/0	0	148	0/0/3	0	148	0/0/3	0/0/3	0	148	0/1/1	0	184	R8
R4	0/1/0	0	149	0/0/3	0	149	0/0/3	0/0/3	0	149	0/1/2	0	194	R9
R5	0/1/1	0	151	0/0/1	0	115	0/0/1	0/0/1	0	115	0/1/0	0	115	R1
R5	0/1/1	0	152	0/0/1	0	125	0/0/1	0/0/1	0	125	0/1/1	0	125	R2
R5	0/1/1	0	153	0/0/1	0	135	0/0/1	0/0/1	0	135	0/1/2	0	135	R3
R5	0/1/1	0	157	0/0/3	0	157	0/0/3	0/0/3	0	157	0/1/0	0	175	R7
R5	0/1/1	0	158	0/0/3	0	158	0/0/3	0/0/3	0	158	0/1/1	0	185	R8
R5	0/1/1	0	159	0/0/3	0	159	0/0/3	0/0/3	0	159	0/1/2	0	195	R9
R6	0/1/2	0	161	0/0/1	0	116	0/0/1	0/0/1	0	116	0/1/0	0	116	R1
R6	0/1/2	0	162	0/0/1	0	126	0/0/1	0/0/1	0	126	0/1/1	0	126	R2
R6	0/1/2	0	163	0/0/1	0	136	0/0/1	0/0/1	0	136	0/1/2	0	136	R3
R6	0/1/2	0	167	0/0/3	0	167	0/0/3	0/0/3	0	167	0/1/0	0	176	R7
R6	0/1/2	0	168	0/0/3	0	168	0/0/3	0/0/3	0	168	0/1/1	0	186	R8
R6	0/1/2	0	169	0/0/3	0	169	0/0/3	0/0/3	0	169	0/1/2	0	196	R9

Table C–6 *Lab 13-1 PVC Mapping Charts: Inter-Switch Mapping from Switch 3's Perspective (Table 13-20)*

Switch 3							Switch 1 or Switch 2						
From Router	In Port	In VPI	In VCI	Out Port	Out VPI	Out VCI	NNI	In Port	In VPI	In VCI	Out Port	Out VPI	Out VCI	To Router
R7	0/1/0	0	171	0/0/2	0	117	0/0/2	0/0/2	0	117	0/1/0	0	117	R1
R7	0/1/0	0	172	0/0/2	0	127	0/0/2	0/0/2	0	127	0/1/1	0	127	R2
R7	0/1/0	0	173	0/0/2	0	137	0/0/2	0/0/2	0	137	0/1/2	0	137	R3
R7	0/1/0	0	174	0/0/3	0	147	0/0/3	0/0/3	0	147	0/1/0	0	147	R4
R7	0/1/0	0	175	0/0/3	0	157	0/0/3	0/0/3	0	157	0/1/1	0	157	R5
R7	0/1/0	0	176	0/0/3	0	167	0/0/3	0/0/3	0	167	0/1/2	0	167	R6

continues

Table C–6 *Lab 13-1 PVC Mapping Charts: Inter-Switch Mapping from Switch 3's Perspective (Table 13-20)*

Switch 3								Switch 1 or Switch 2						
From Router	In Port	In VPI	In VCI	Out Port	Out VPI	Out VCI	NNI	In Port	In VPI	In VCI	Out Port	Out VPI	Out VCI	To Router
R8	0/1/1	0	181	0/0/2	0	118	0/0/2	0/0/2	0	118	0/1/0	0	118	R1
R8	0/1/1	0	182	0/0/2	0	128	0/0/2	0/0/2	0	128	0/1/1	0	128	R2
R8	0/1/1	0	183	0/0/2	0	138	0/0/2	0/0/2	0	138	0/1/2	0	138	R3
R8	0/1/1	0	184	0/0/3	0	148	0/0/3	0/0/3	0	148	0/1/0	0	148	R4
R8	0/1/1	0	185	0/0/3	0	158	0/0/3	0/0/3	0	158	0/1/1	0	158	R5
R8	0/1/1	0	186	0/0/3	0	168	0/0/3	0/0/3	0	168	0/1/2	0	168	R6
R9	0/1/2	0	191	0/0/2	0	119	0/0/2	0/0/2	0	119	0/1/0	0	119	R1
R9	0/1/2	0	192	0/0/2	0	129	0/0/2	0/0/2	0	129	0/1/1	0	129	R2
R9	0/1/2	0	193	0/0/2	0	139	0/0/2	0/0/2	0	139	0/1/2	0	139	R3
R9	0/1/2	0	194	0/0/3	0	149	0/0/3	0/0/3	0	149	0/1/0	0	149	R4
R9	0/1/2	0	195	0/0/3	0	159	0/0/3	0/0/3	0	159	0/1/1	0	159	R5
R9	0/1/2	0	196	0/0/3	0	169	0/0/3	0/0/3	0	169	0/1/2	0	169	R6

2 Set up the E1 interface as shown in Figure 13-15 on page 501.

3 Add all the PVC segments in all LS1010s.

4 Check for full connectivity between your router and every other router attached to the IP 144.254.100.X cloud.

Example C-113 *Switch 1 Configuration for Lab 13-1*

```
!
version 11.3
no service pad
no service udp-small-servers
no service tcp-small-servers
!
hostname Switch_1
!
enable password sanfran
!
no ip domain-lookup
!
atm address 47.0091.8100.0000.0010.0739.9e01.0010.0739.9e01.00
atm router pnni
 node 1 level 56 lowest
  redistribute atm-static
```

Example C-113 *Switch 1 Configuration for Lab 13-1 (Continued)*

```
!
!
interface ATM0/0/0
 no ip address
!
interface ATM0/0/1
 no ip address
!
interface ATM0/0/2
 no ip address
!
interface ATM0/0/3
 no ip address
!
interface ATM0/1/0
 no ip address
 atm pvc 0 114  interface  ATM0/0/1 0 114
 atm pvc 0 115  interface  ATM0/0/1 0 115
 atm pvc 0 116  interface  ATM0/0/1 0 116
 atm pvc 0 117  interface  ATM0/0/2 0 117
 atm pvc 0 118  interface  ATM0/0/2 0 118
 atm pvc 0 119  interface  ATM0/0/2 0 119
!
interface ATM0/1/1
 no ip address
 atm pvc 0 121  interface  ATM0/1/0 0 112
 atm pvc 0 124  interface  ATM0/0/1 0 124
 atm pvc 0 125  interface  ATM0/0/1 0 125
 atm pvc 0 126  interface  ATM0/0/1 0 126
 atm pvc 0 127  interface  ATM0/0/2 0 127
 atm pvc 0 128  interface  ATM0/0/2 0 128
 atm pvc 0 129  interface  ATM0/0/2 0 129
!
interface ATM0/1/2
 no ip address
 atm pvc 0 120  interface  ATM0/1/0 0 120
 atm pvc 0 131  interface  ATM0/1/0 0 113
 atm pvc 0 132  interface  ATM0/1/1 0 123
 atm pvc 0 134  interface  ATM0/0/1 0 134
 atm pvc 0 135  interface  ATM0/0/1 0 135
 atm pvc 0 136  interface  ATM0/0/1 0 136
 atm pvc 0 137  interface  ATM0/0/2 0 137
 atm pvc 0 138  interface  ATM0/0/2 0 138
 atm pvc 0 139  interface  ATM0/0/2 0 139
!
interface ATM0/1/3
 no ip address
!
interface ATM2/0/0
 no ip address
```

Lab 13-1 Solution

continues

Example C-113 *Switch 1 Configuration for Lab 13-1 (Continued)*

```
 atm maxvp-number 0
!
interface Ethernet2/0/0
 ip address 10.0.0.11 255.0.0.0
!
ip classless
!
line con 0
 exec-timeout 0 0
 password cisco
 login
 logging synchronous
line aux 0
line vty 0 4
 exec-timeout 0 0
 password cisco
 login
!
end
```

Example C-114 *Switch 2 Configuration for Lab 13-1*

```
!
version 11.3
no service pad
no service udp-small-servers
no service tcp-small-servers
!
hostname Switch_2
!
enable password sanfran
!
no ip domain-lookup
!
atm address 47.0091.8100.0000.0010.0739.a101.0010.0739.a101.00
atm router pnni
 node 1 level 56 lowest
   redistribute atm-static
!
!
interface ATM0/0/0
 no ip address
!
interface ATM0/0/1
 no ip address
!
interface ATM0/0/2
 no ip address
!
interface ATM0/0/3
```

Example C-114 *Switch 2 Configuration for Lab 13-1 (Continued)*

```
 no ip address
!
interface ATM0/1/0
 no ip address
 atm pvc 0 141   interface  ATM0/0/1 0 114
 atm pvc 0 142   interface  ATM0/0/1 0 124
 atm pvc 0 143   interface  ATM0/0/1 0 134
 atm pvc 0 147   interface  ATM0/0/3 0 147
 atm pvc 0 148   interface  ATM0/0/3 0 148
 atm pvc 0 149   interface  ATM0/0/3 0 149
!
interface ATM0/1/1
 no ip address
 atm pvc 0 151   interface  ATM0/0/1 0 115
 atm pvc 0 152   interface  ATM0/0/1 0 125
 atm pvc 0 153   interface  ATM0/0/1 0 135
 atm pvc 0 154   interface  ATM0/1/0 0 145
 atm pvc 0 157   interface  ATM0/0/3 0 157
 atm pvc 0 158   interface  ATM0/0/3 0 158
 atm pvc 0 159   interface  ATM0/0/3 0 159
!
interface ATM0/1/2
 no ip address
 atm pvc 0 161   interface  ATM0/0/1 0 116
 atm pvc 0 162   interface  ATM0/0/1 0 126
 atm pvc 0 163   interface  ATM0/0/1 0 136
 atm pvc 0 164   interface  ATM0/1/0 0 146
 atm pvc 0 165   interface  ATM0/1/1 0 156
 atm pvc 0 167   interface  ATM0/0/3 0 167
 atm pvc 0 168   interface  ATM0/0/3 0 168
 atm pvc 0 169   interface  ATM0/0/3 0 169
!
interface ATM0/1/3
 no ip address
!
interface ATM2/0/0
 no ip address
 atm maxvp-number 0
!
interface Ethernet2/0/0
 ip address 10.0.0.12 255.0.0.0
!
ip classless
!
line con 0
 exec-timeout 0 0
 password cisco
 login
 logging synchronous
line aux 0
```

Lab 13-1 Solution

continues

Example C-114 *Switch 2 Configuration for Lab 13-1 (Continued)*

```
line vty 0 4
 exec-timeout 0 0
 password cisco
 login
!
end
```

Example C-115 *Switch 3 Configuration for Lab 13-1*

```
!
version 11.3
no service pad
no service udp-small-servers
no service tcp-small-servers
!
hostname Switch_3
!
boot system flash bootflash:ls1010-wp-mz.113-0.8.TWA4.2.bin
enable password sanfran
!
no ip domain-lookup
!
atm address 47.0091.8100.0000.0010.0739.c301.0010.0739.c301.00
atm router pnni
 node 1 level 56 lowest
   redistribute atm-static
!
!
interface ATM0/0/0
 no ip address
!
interface ATM0/0/1
 no ip address
!
interface ATM0/0/2
 no ip address
!
interface ATM0/0/3
 no ip address
!
interface ATM0/1/0
 no ip address
 atm pvc 0 171  interface  ATM0/0/2 0 117
 atm pvc 0 172  interface  ATM0/0/2 0 127
 atm pvc 0 173  interface  ATM0/0/2 0 137
 atm pvc 0 174  interface  ATM0/0/3 0 147
 atm pvc 0 175  interface  ATM0/0/3 0 157
 atm pvc 0 176  interface  ATM0/0/3 0 167
!
interface ATM0/1/1
```

Example C-115 *Switch 3 Configuration for Lab 13-1 (Continued)*

```
 no ip address
 atm pvc 0 181   interface   ATM0/0/2 0 118
 atm pvc 0 182   interface   ATM0/0/2 0 128
 atm pvc 0 183   interface   ATM0/0/2 0 138
 atm pvc 0 184   interface   ATM0/0/3 0 148
 atm pvc 0 185   interface   ATM0/0/3 0 158
 atm pvc 0 186   interface   ATM0/0/3 0 168
 atm pvc 0 187   interface   ATM0/1/0 0 178
!
interface ATM0/1/2
 no ip address
 atm pvc 0 191   interface   ATM0/0/2 0 119
 atm pvc 0 192   interface   ATM0/0/2 0 129
 atm pvc 0 193   interface   ATM0/0/2 0 139
 atm pvc 0 194   interface   ATM0/0/3 0 149
 atm pvc 0 195   interface   ATM0/0/3 0 159
 atm pvc 0 196   interface   ATM0/0/3 0 169
 atm pvc 0 197   interface   ATM0/1/0 0 179
 atm pvc 0 198   interface   ATM0/1/1 0 189
!
interface ATM0/1/3
 no ip address
!
interface ATM1/0/0
 no ip address
!
interface ATM1/0/1
 no ip address
!
interface ATM1/0/2
 no ip address
!
interface ATM1/0/3
 no ip address
!
interface ATM2/0/0
 no ip address
 atm maxvp-number 0
!
interface Ethernet2/0/0
 ip address 10.0.0.13 255.0.0.0
!
ip classless
!
line con 0
 exec-timeout 0 0
 password cisco
 login
 logging synchronous
line aux 0
```

continues

Lab 13-1 Solution

Example C-115 *Switch 3 Configuration for Lab 13-1 (Continued)*

```
line vty 0 4
 exec-timeout 0 0
 password cisco
 login
!
end
```

Solutions for Lab 13-2: Configuring Static Routes Using IISP

Examples C-116 through C-118 provide the configuration solutions that satisfy all the exercises for Lab 13-2. Specifically, the exercises ask for the following:

1 Configure the two ATM route statements into the switch as designated here:

- On Switch 1:

  —Routes for Routers 1, 4, and 7

  —Routes for Routers 2, 5, and 8

  —Routes for Routers 3, 6, and 9

- On Switch 2:

  —Routes for Router 1, 4, and 7

  —Routes for Router 2, 5, and 8

  —Routes for Router 3, 6, and 9

- On Switch 3:

  —Routes for Router 1, 4, and 7

  —Routes for Router 2, 5, and 8

  —Routes for Router 3, 6, and 9

2 Check for full connectivity between your router and every other router attached to the IP 144.254.200.x cloud.

3 Try the various **atm ping** commands to show connectivity at the switch level.

Example C-116 *Switch 1 Configuration for Lab 13-2*

```
!
version 11.3
no service pad
no service udp-small-servers
no service tcp-small-servers
```

Example C-116 *Switch 1 Configuration for Lab 13-2*

```
!
hostname Switch_1
!
enable password sanfran
!
no ip domain-lookup
!
atm address 47.0091.8100.0000.0010.0739.9e01.0010.0739.9e01.00
atm router pnni
 node 1 level 56 lowest
   redistribute atm-static
 !
 !
interface ATM0/0/0
 no ip address
 shutdown
!
interface ATM0/0/1
 no ip address
 no atm auto-configuration
 atm iisp
!
interface ATM0/0/2
 no ip address
 no atm auto-configuration
 atm iisp side user
!
interface ATM0/0/3
 no ip address
 shutdown
!
interface ATM0/1/0
 no ip address
 no atm auto
 atm pvc 0 114   interface   ATM0/0/1 0 114
 atm pvc 0 115   interface   ATM0/0/1 0 115
 atm pvc 0 116   interface   ATM0/0/1 0 116
 atm pvc 0 117   interface   ATM0/0/2 0 117
 atm pvc 0 118   interface   ATM0/0/2 0 118
 atm pvc 0 119   interface   ATM0/0/2 0 119
!
interface ATM0/1/1
 no ip address
 no atm auto
 atm pvc 0 121   interface   ATM0/1/0 0 112
 atm pvc 0 124   interface   ATM0/0/1 0 124
 atm pvc 0 125   interface   ATM0/0/1 0 125
 atm pvc 0 126   interface   ATM0/0/1 0 126
 atm pvc 0 127   interface   ATM0/0/2 0 127
 atm pvc 0 128   interface   ATM0/0/2 0 128
```

continues

Example C-116 *Switch 1 Configuration for Lab 13-2*

```
 atm pvc 0 129  interface  ATM0/0/2 0 129
!
interface ATM0/1/2
 no ip address
 no atm auto
 atm pvc 0 120  interface  ATM0/1/0 0 120
 atm pvc 0 131  interface  ATM0/1/0 0 113
 atm pvc 0 132  interface  ATM0/1/1 0 123
 atm pvc 0 134  interface  ATM0/0/1 0 134
 atm pvc 0 135  interface  ATM0/0/1 0 135
 atm pvc 0 136  interface  ATM0/0/1 0 136
 atm pvc 0 137  interface  ATM0/0/2 0 137
 atm pvc 0 138  interface  ATM0/0/2 0 138
 atm pvc 0 139  interface  ATM0/0/2 0 139
!
interface ATM0/1/3
 no ip address
!
interface ATM2/0/0
 no ip address
 atm maxvp-number 0
!
interface Ethernet2/0/0
 ip address 10.0.0.11 255.0.0.0
!
ip classless
atm route 1... ATM0/1/0
atm route 2... ATM0/1/1
atm route 3... ATM0/1/2
atm route 4... ATM0/0/1
atm route 5... ATM0/0/1
atm route 6... ATM0/0/1
atm route 7... ATM0/0/2
atm route 8... ATM0/0/2
atm route 9... ATM0/0/2
!
line con 0
 exec-timeout 0 0
 password cisco
 login
 logging synchronous
line aux 0
line vty 0 4
 exec-timeout 0 0
 password cisco
 login
!
end
```

Example C-117 *Switch 2 Configuration for Lab 13-2*

```
!
version 11.3
no service pad
no service udp-small-servers
no service tcp-small-servers
!
hostname Switch_2
!
enable password sanfran
!
no ip domain-lookup
!
atm address 47.0091.8100.0000.0010.0739.a101.0010.0739.a101.00
atm router pnni
 node 1 level 56 lowest
  redistribute atm-static
!
!
interface ATM0/0/0
 no ip address
 shutdown
!
interface ATM0/0/1
 no ip address
 no atm auto-configuration
 atm iisp side user
!
interface ATM0/0/2
 no ip address
 shutdown
!
interface ATM0/0/3
 no ip address
 no atm auto-configuration
 atm iisp
!
interface ATM0/1/0
 no ip address
 no atm auto
 atm pvc 0 141   interface   ATM0/0/1 0 114
 atm pvc 0 142   interface   ATM0/0/1 0 124
 atm pvc 0 143   interface   ATM0/0/1 0 134
 atm pvc 0 147   interface   ATM0/0/3 0 147
 atm pvc 0 148   interface   ATM0/0/3 0 148
 atm pvc 0 149   interface   ATM0/0/3 0 149
!
interface ATM0/1/1
 no ip address
 no atm auto
 atm pvc 0 151   interface   ATM0/0/1 0 115
```

continues

Example C-117 *Switch 2 Configuration for Lab 13-2 (Continued)*

```
atm pvc 0 152  interface  ATM0/0/1 0 125
atm pvc 0 153  interface  ATM0/0/1 0 135
atm pvc 0 154  interface  ATM0/1/0 0 145
atm pvc 0 157  interface  ATM0/0/3 0 157
atm pvc 0 158  interface  ATM0/0/3 0 158
atm pvc 0 159  interface  ATM0/0/3 0 159
!
interface ATM0/1/2
 no ip address
 no atm auto
 atm pvc 0 161  interface  ATM0/0/1 0 116
 atm pvc 0 162  interface  ATM0/0/1 0 126
 atm pvc 0 163  interface  ATM0/0/1 0 136
 atm pvc 0 164  interface  ATM0/1/0 0 146
 atm pvc 0 165  interface  ATM0/1/1 0 156
 atm pvc 0 167  interface  ATM0/0/3 0 167
 atm pvc 0 168  interface  ATM0/0/3 0 168
 atm pvc 0 169  interface  ATM0/0/3 0 169
!
interface ATM0/1/3
 no ip address
!
interface ATM2/0/0
 no ip address
 atm maxvp-number 0
!
interface Ethernet2/0/0
 ip address 10.0.0.12 255.0.0.0
!
ip classless
atm route 4... ATM0/1/0
atm route 5... ATM0/1/1
atm route 6... ATM0/1/2
atm route 1... ATM0/0/1
atm route 2... ATM0/0/1
atm route 3... ATM0/0/1
atm route 7... ATM0/0/3
atm route 8... ATM0/0/3
atm route 9... ATM0/0/3
!
line con 0
 exec-timeout 0 0
 password cisco
 login
 logging synchronous
line aux 0
line vty 0 4
 exec-timeout 0 0
 password cisco
 login
```

Example C-117 *Switch 2 Configuration for Lab 13-2 (Continued)*

```
!
end
```

Example C-118 *Switch 3 Configuration for Lab 13-2*

```
!
version 11.3
no service pad
no service udp-small-servers
no service tcp-small-servers
!
hostname Switch_3
!
boot system flash bootflash:ls1010-wp-mz.113-0.8.TWA4.2.bin
enable password sanfran
!
no ip domain-lookup
!
atm address 47.0091.8100.0000.0010.0739.c301.0010.0739.c301.00
atm router pnni
 node 1 level 56 lowest
   redistribute atm-static
!
!
interface ATM0/0/0
 no ip address
 shutdown
!
interface ATM0/0/1
 no ip address
 shutdown
!
interface ATM0/0/2
 no ip address
 no atm auto-configuration
 atm iisp
!
interface ATM0/0/3
 no ip address
 no atm auto-configuration
 atm iisp side user
!
interface ATM0/1/0
 no ip address
 no atm auto
 atm pvc 0 171   interface  ATM0/0/2 0 117
 atm pvc 0 172   interface  ATM0/0/2 0 127
 atm pvc 0 173   interface  ATM0/0/2 0 137
 atm pvc 0 174   interface  ATM0/0/3 0 147
 atm pvc 0 175   interface  ATM0/0/3 0 157
```

continues

Example C-118   *Switch 3 Configuration for Lab 13-2 (Continued)*

```
 atm pvc 0 176   interface   ATM0/0/3 0 167
!
interface ATM0/1/1
 no ip address
 no atm auto
 atm pvc 0 181   interface   ATM0/0/2 0 118
 atm pvc 0 182   interface   ATM0/0/2 0 128
 atm pvc 0 183   interface   ATM0/0/2 0 138
 atm pvc 0 184   interface   ATM0/0/3 0 148
 atm pvc 0 185   interface   ATM0/0/3 0 158
 atm pvc 0 186   interface   ATM0/0/3 0 168
 atm pvc 0 187   interface   ATM0/1/0 0 178
!
interface ATM0/1/2
 no ip address
 no atm auto
 atm pvc 0 191   interface   ATM0/0/2 0 119
 atm pvc 0 192   interface   ATM0/0/2 0 129
 atm pvc 0 193   interface   ATM0/0/2 0 139
 atm pvc 0 194   interface   ATM0/0/3 0 149
 atm pvc 0 195   interface   ATM0/0/3 0 159
 atm pvc 0 196   interface   ATM0/0/3 0 169
 atm pvc 0 197   interface   ATM0/1/0 0 179
 atm pvc 0 198   interface   ATM0/1/1 0 189
!
interface ATM0/1/3
 no ip address
!
interface ATM1/0/0
 no ip address
!
interface ATM1/0/1
 no ip address
!
interface ATM1/0/2
 no ip address
!
interface ATM1/0/3
 no ip address
!
interface ATM2/0/0
 no ip address
 atm maxvp-number 0
!
interface Ethernet2/0/0
 ip address 10.0.0.13 255.0.0.0
!
ip classless
atm route 7... ATM0/1/0
atm route 8... ATM0/1/1
```

Example C-118 *Switch 3 Configuration for Lab 13-2 (Continued)*

```
atm route 9... ATM0/1/2
atm route 1... ATM0/0/2
atm route 2... ATM0/0/2
atm route 3... ATM0/0/2
atm route 4... ATM0/0/3
atm route 5... ATM0/0/3
atm route 6... ATM0/0/3
!
line con 0
 exec-timeout 0 0
 password cisco
 login
 logging synchronous
line aux 0
line vty 0
 exec-timeout 0 0
 password cisco
 login
!
end
```

Solutions for Lab 13-3: Configuring VP Tunnels on LS1010

Examples C-119 through C-121 provide the configuration solutions that satisfy all the exercises for Lab 13-3. Specifically, the exercises ask for the following:

1   Configure the primary ATM interswitch links as IISP links and ensure that the secondary inter-switch links are shut down. The routers make use of their SVC-based solution with their ATM0.2 subinterface and appropriate AESA address—the ATM 0.1 subinterface is shut down.

2   Ensure that switch S1 has only the appropriate static routes to reach AESA address prefixes 1..., 2..., 3.... Remove any additional static routes and verify with the **show atm route** command.

3   Similarly, ensure that switch S2 has only the appropriate static routes to reach AESA address prefixes 4..., 5..., and 6.... Remove any additional static routes and verify with the **show atm route** command.

4   Similarly, ensure that switch S3 has only the appropriate static routes to reach AESA address prefixes 4..., 5..., and 6.... Remove any additional static routes and verify with the **show atm route** command.

5   Verify that routers locally attached to the same switch can set up SVCs successfully between themselves and can provide Layer 3 connectivity. Currently, connectivity cannot be established between remote routers. Verify with the appropriate **show** commands.

6   Set up VP tunnels 14, 47, and 17 to allow connectivity between R1, R4, and R7.

7   Set up VP tunnels 25, 58, and 28 to allow connectivity between R2, R5, and R8.

8   Set up VP tunnels 36, 69, and 39 to allow connectivity between R3, R6, and R9.

9   Set up IISP through the tunnels. Make sure the IISP sides are "user" to "network," or vice versa.

10 Verify that the ATM switches are discovering the additional required AESA address via IISP through the tunnels. Also, verify that SVCs between remote routers (routers not connected to the same ATM switch) are being supported via the VP tunnels. Verify that from the router's perspective, you now have full Layer 3 connectivity.

Example C-119 *Switch 1 Configuration for Lab 13-3*

```
!
version 11.3
no service pad
no service udp-small-servers
no service tcp-small-servers
!
hostname Switch_1
!
enable password sanfran
!
no ip domain-lookup
!
atm address 47.0091.8100.0000.0010.0739.9e01.0010.0739.9e01.00
atm router pnni
 node 1 level 56 lowest
   redistribute atm-static
!
!
interface ATM0/0/0
 no ip address
 shutdown
!
interface ATM0/0/1
 no ip address
 no atm auto-configuration
 atm iisp
 atm pvp 17
 atm pvp 28
 atm pvp 39
!
interface ATM0/0/1.17 point-to-point
 no atm auto-configuration
```

Example C-119 *Switch 1 Configuration for Lab 13-3 (Continued)*

```
 atm iisp
!
interface ATM0/0/1.28 point-to-point
 no atm auto-configuration
 atm iisp
!
interface ATM0/0/1.39 point-to-point
 no atm auto-configuration
 atm iisp
!
interface ATM0/0/2
 no ip address
 no atm auto-configuration
 atm iisp side user
 atm pvp 14
 atm pvp 25
 atm pvp 36
 atm pvp 47   interface  ATM0/0/1 47
 atm pvp 58   interface  ATM0/0/1 58
 atm pvp 69   interface  ATM0/0/1 69
!
interface ATM0/0/2.14 point-to-point
 no atm auto-configuration
 atm iisp side user
!
interface ATM0/0/2.25 point-to-point
 no atm auto-configuration
 atm iisp side user
!
interface ATM0/0/2.36 point-to-point
 no atm auto-configuration
 atm iisp side user
!
interface ATM0/0/3
 no ip address
 shutdown
!
interface ATM0/1/0
 no ip address
 atm pvc 0 114   interface  ATM0/0/1 0 114
 atm pvc 0 115   interface  ATM0/0/1 0 115
 atm pvc 0 116   interface  ATM0/0/1 0 116
 atm pvc 0 117   interface  ATM0/0/2 0 117
 atm pvc 0 118   interface  ATM0/0/2 0 118
 atm pvc 0 119   interface  ATM0/0/2 0 119
!
interface ATM0/1/1
 no ip address
 atm pvc 0 121   interface  ATM0/1/0 0 112
 atm pvc 0 124   interface  ATM0/0/1 0 124
```

continues

Example C-119 *Switch 1 Configuration for Lab 13-3 (Continued)*

```
 atm pvc 0 125  interface  ATM0/0/1 0 125
 atm pvc 0 126  interface  ATM0/0/1 0 126
 atm pvc 0 127  interface  ATM0/0/2 0 127
 atm pvc 0 128  interface  ATM0/0/2 0 128
 atm pvc 0 129  interface  ATM0/0/2 0 129
!
interface ATM0/1/2
 no ip address
 atm pvc 0 120  interface  ATM0/1/0 0 120
 atm pvc 0 131  interface  ATM0/1/0 0 113
 atm pvc 0 132  interface  ATM0/1/1 0 123
 atm pvc 0 134  interface  ATM0/0/1 0 134
 atm pvc 0 135  interface  ATM0/0/1 0 135
 atm pvc 0 136  interface  ATM0/0/1 0 136
 atm pvc 0 137  interface  ATM0/0/2 0 137
 atm pvc 0 138  interface  ATM0/0/2 0 138
 atm pvc 0 139  interface  ATM0/0/2 0 139
!
interface ATM0/1/3
 no ip address
!
interface ATM2/0/0
 no ip address
 atm maxvp-number 0
!
interface Ethernet2/0/0
 ip address 10.0.0.11 255.0.0.0
!
ip classless
atm route 1... ATM0/1/0
atm route 2... ATM0/1/1
atm route 3... ATM0/1/2
atm route 4... ATM0/0/2.14
atm route 5... ATM0/0/2.25
atm route 6... ATM0/0/2.36
atm route 9... ATM0/0/1.39
atm route 8... ATM0/0/1.28
atm route 7... ATM0/0/1.17
!
line con 0
 exec-timeout 0 0
 password cisco
 logging synchronous
 login
line aux 0
line vty 0 4
 exec-timeout 0 0
 password cisco
 login
```

Example C-119 *Switch 1 Configuration for Lab 13-3 (Continued)*

```
!
end
```

Example C-120 *Switch 2 Configuration for Lab 13-3*

```
!
version 11.3
no service pad
no service udp-small-servers
no service tcp-small-servers
!
hostname Switch_2
!
enable password sanfran
!
no ip domain-lookup
!
atm address 47.0091.8100.0000.0010.0739.a101.0010.0739.a101.00
atm router pnni
 node 1 level 56 lowest
  redistribute atm-static
!
!
interface ATM0/0/0
 no ip address
 shutdown
!
interface ATM0/0/1
 no ip address
 no atm auto-configuration
 atm iisp side user
 atm pvp 47
 atm pvp 58
 atm pvp 69
!
interface ATM0/0/1.47 point-to-point
 no atm auto-configuration
 atm iisp side user
!
interface ATM0/0/1.58 point-to-point
 no atm auto-configuration
 atm iisp side user
!
interface ATM0/0/1.69 point-to-point
 no atm auto-configuration
 atm iisp side user
!
interface ATM0/0/2
 no ip address
 shutdown
```

continues

Example C-120 *Switch 2 Configuration for Lab 13-3 (Continued)*

```
!
interface ATM0/0/3
 no ip address
 no atm auto-configuration
 atm iisp
 atm pvp 14
 atm pvp 17   interface  ATM0/0/1 17
 atm pvp 25
 atm pvp 28   interface  ATM0/0/1 28
 atm pvp 36
 atm pvp 39   interface  ATM0/0/1 39
!
interface ATM0/0/3.14 point-to-point
 no atm auto-configuration
 atm iisp
!
interface ATM0/0/3.25 point-to-point
 no atm auto-configuration
 atm iisp
!
interface ATM0/0/3.36 point-to-point
 no atm auto-configuration
 atm iisp
!
interface ATM0/1/0
 no ip address
 atm pvc 0 141   interface  ATM0/0/1 0 114
 atm pvc 0 142   interface  ATM0/0/1 0 124
 atm pvc 0 143   interface  ATM0/0/1 0 134
 atm pvc 0 147   interface  ATM0/0/3 0 147
 atm pvc 0 148   interface  ATM0/0/3 0 148
 atm pvc 0 149   interface  ATM0/0/3 0 149
!
interface ATM0/1/1
 no ip address
 atm pvc 0 151   interface  ATM0/0/1 0 115
 atm pvc 0 152   interface  ATM0/0/1 0 125
 atm pvc 0 153   interface  ATM0/0/1 0 135
 atm pvc 0 154   interface  ATM0/1/0 0 145
 atm pvc 0 157   interface  ATM0/0/3 0 157
 atm pvc 0 158   interface  ATM0/0/3 0 158
 atm pvc 0 159   interface  ATM0/0/3 0 159
!
interface ATM0/1/2
 no ip address
 atm pvc 0 161   interface  ATM0/0/1 0 116
 atm pvc 0 162   interface  ATM0/0/1 0 126
 atm pvc 0 163   interface  ATM0/0/1 0 136
 atm pvc 0 164   interface  ATM0/1/0 0 146
 atm pvc 0 165   interface  ATM0/1/1 0 156
```

Example C-120 *Switch 2 Configuration for Lab 13-3 (Continued)*

```
atm pvc 0 167   interface  ATM0/0/3 0 167
atm pvc 0 168   interface  ATM0/0/3 0 168
atm pvc 0 169   interface  ATM0/0/3 0 169
!
interface ATM0/1/3
 no ip address
!
interface ATM2/0/0
 no ip address
 atm maxvp-number 0
!
interface Ethernet2/0/0
 ip address 10.0.0.12 255.0.0.0
!
ip classless
atm route 5... ATM0/1/1
atm route 6... ATM0/1/2
atm route 4... ATM0/1/0
atm route 1... ATM0/0/3.14
atm route 2... ATM0/0/3.25
atm route 3... ATM0/0/3.36
atm route 7... ATM0/0/1.47
atm route 8... ATM0/0/1.58
atm route 9... ATM0/0/1.69
!
line con 0
 exec-timeout 0 0
 password cisco
 logging synchronous
 login
line aux 0
line vty 0 4
 exec-timeout 0 0
 password cisco
 login
!
end
```

Example C-121 *Switch 3 Configuration for Lab 13-3*

```
!
version 11.3
no service pad
no service udp-small-servers
no service tcp-small-servers
!
hostname Switch_3
!
boot system flash bootflash:ls1010-wp-mz.113-0.8.TWA4.2.bin
enable password sanfran
```

continues

Example C-121 *Switch 3 Configuration for Lab 13-3*

```
!
no ip domain-lookup
!
atm address 47.0091.8100.0000.0010.0739.c301.0010.0739.c301.00
atm router pnni
 node 1 level 56 lowest
  redistribute atm-static
!
!
interface ATM0/0/0
 no ip address
 shutdown
!
interface ATM0/0/1
 no ip address
 shutdown
!
interface ATM0/0/2
 no ip address
 no atm auto-configuration
 atm iisp
 atm pvp 47
 atm pvp 58
 atm pvp 69
!
interface ATM0/0/2.47 point-to-point
 no atm auto-configuration
 atm iisp
!
interface ATM0/0/2.58 point-to-point
 no atm auto-configuration
 atm iisp
!
interface ATM0/0/2.69 point-to-point
 no atm auto-configuration
 atm iisp
!
interface ATM0/0/3
 no ip address
 no atm auto-configuration
 atm iisp side user
 atm pvp 14   interface   ATM0/0/2 14
 atm pvp 17
 atm pvp 25   interface   ATM0/0/2 25
 atm pvp 28
 atm pvp 36   interface   ATM0/0/2 36
 atm pvp 39
!
interface ATM0/0/3.17 point-to-point
 no atm auto-configuration
```

Example C-121 *Switch 3 Configuration for Lab 13-3*

```
 atm iisp side user
!
interface ATM0/0/3.28 point-to-point
 no atm auto-configuration
 atm iisp side user
!
interface ATM0/0/3.39 point-to-point
 no atm auto-configuration
 atm iisp side user
!
interface ATM0/1/0
 no ip address
 atm pvc 0 171   interface   ATM0/0/2 0 117
 atm pvc 0 172   interface   ATM0/0/2 0 127
 atm pvc 0 173   interface   ATM0/0/2 0 137
 atm pvc 0 174   interface   ATM0/0/3 0 147
 atm pvc 0 175   interface   ATM0/0/3 0 157
 atm pvc 0 176   interface   ATM0/0/3 0 167
!
interface ATM0/1/1
 no ip address
 atm pvc 0 181   interface   ATM0/0/2 0 118
 atm pvc 0 182   interface   ATM0/0/2 0 128
 atm pvc 0 183   interface   ATM0/0/2 0 138
 atm pvc 0 184   interface   ATM0/0/3 0 148
 atm pvc 0 185   interface   ATM0/0/3 0 158
 atm pvc 0 186   interface   ATM0/0/3 0 168
 atm pvc 0 187   interface   ATM0/1/0 0 178
!
interface ATM0/1/2
 no ip address
 atm pvc 0 191   interface   ATM0/0/2 0 119
 atm pvc 0 192   interface   ATM0/0/2 0 129
 atm pvc 0 193   interface   ATM0/0/2 0 139
 atm pvc 0 194   interface   ATM0/0/3 0 149
 atm pvc 0 195   interface   ATM0/0/3 0 159
 atm pvc 0 196   interface   ATM0/0/3 0 169
 atm pvc 0 197   interface   ATM0/1/0 0 179
 atm pvc 0 198   interface   ATM0/1/1 0 189
!
interface ATM0/1/3
 no ip address
!
interface ATM1/0/0
 no ip address
!
interface ATM1/0/1
 no ip address
!
interface ATM1/0/2
```

continues

Lab 13-3 Solution

Example C-121 *Switch 3 Configuration for Lab 13-3*

```
no ip address
!
interface ATM1/0/3
 no ip address
!
interface ATM2/0/0
 no ip address
 atm maxvp-number 0
!
interface Ethernet2/0/0
 ip address 10.0.0.13 255.0.0.0
!
ip classless
atm route 7... ATM0/1/0
atm route 8... ATM0/1/1
atm route 9... ATM0/1/2
atm route 1... ATM0/0/3.17
atm route 2... ATM0/0/3.28
atm route 3... ATM0/0/3.39
atm route 4... ATM0/0/2.47
atm route 5... ATM0/0/2.58
atm route 6... ATM0/0/2.69
!
line con 0
 exec-timeout 0 0
 password cisco
 login
 logging synchronous
line aux 0
line vty 0 4
 exec-timeout 0 0
 password cisco
 login
!
end
```

Solutions for Lab 13-4: Private Network-to-Network Interface (PNNI)

Examples C-122 through C-133 provide the configuration solutions that satisfy all the exercises for Lab 13-4. Specifically, the exercises ask for the following:

1 Configure a signaling PVC on your router.

2 Configure ILMI on your router.

3 Create a subinterface ATM 0.32 on your router. Assign the IP address of 144.254.32.#, where # is your router number. For example, for Router 8, the address is 144.254.32.8.

4   On the ATM0.32 subinterface (on the router), configure your 7-byte End Station Identifier. The ESI is <RRRRRRRRRRRR.20>. For example, for Router 8, the ESI is 888888888888.20.

5   Configure every switch with a new ATM address, which consists of the following prefixes:

Switch 1: 11.1111.1111.1111.1111.1111.1111

Switch 2: 22.2222.2222.2222.2222.2222.2222

Switch 3: 33.3333.3333.3333.3333.3333.3333

To complete the ATM addresses, copy the ESIs from the existing ATM addresses in the switches. These are not used by routers, because each router has its own preconfigured ESI (as per previous exercise 4).

6   Ensure that the prefix of your switch has been downloaded via **show atm ilmi**.

7   To test the connectivity, implement RFC 2684 between the routers. The implementation steps of RFC 2684 are described in Lab 9-3, "Configuring SVCs on Cisco 4500 Routers, RFC 2684." Remember, static mappings must be done between the NSAP addresses and the IP addresses of the edge devices (in this case, routers). Log into your respective switch and show the routing table via **show atm route**. Ensure that your port in the switch has a routing entry.

Example C-122 *Router 1 Configuration for Lab 13-4*

```
!
version 11.2
no service password-encryption
no service udp-small-servers
no service tcp-small-servers
!
hostname R1
!
enable password sanfran
!
no ip domain-lookup
ipx routing 0000.0000.0001
ipx maximum-paths 2
!
!
interface Ethernet0
 ip address 144.254.1.1 255.255.255.0
 ipx network 10
!
interface Ethernet1
 ip address 10.0.0.1 255.0.0.0
 media-type 10BaseT
!
interface Serial0
 no ip address
```

continues

Example C-122 *Router 1 Configuration for Lab 13-4 (Continued)*

```
 shutdown
!
interface Serial1
 no ip address
 shutdown
!
interface ATM0
 no ip address
 atm pvc 5 0 5 qsaal
 atm pvc 16 0 16 ilmi
!
interface ATM0.1 multipoint
 ip address 144.254.100.1 255.255.255.0
 atm pvc 112 0 112 aal5snap
 atm pvc 113 0 113 aal5snap
 atm pvc 114 0 114 aal5snap
 atm pvc 115 0 115 aal5snap
 atm pvc 116 0 116 aal5snap
 atm pvc 117 0 117 aal5snap
 atm pvc 118 0 118 aal5snap
 atm pvc 119 0 119 aal5snap
 map-group ipPvc
 map-group ipxPvc
 ipx network 100
!
interface ATM0.2 multipoint
 ip address 144.254.200.1 255.255.255.0
 atm nsap-address 11.11110000000000000000000000.000000000000.00
 map-group ipSvc
 map-group ipxSvc
 ipx network 200
!
interface ATM0.32 multipoint
 ip address 144.254.32.1 255.255.255.0
 atm esi-address 111111111111.20
 map-group newNsaps
!
router igrp 100
 network 144.254.0.0
!
no ip classless
!
map-list ipPvc
 ip 144.254.100.2 atm-vc 112 broadcast
 ip 144.254.100.3 atm-vc 113 broadcast
 ip 144.254.100.4 atm-vc 114 broadcast
 ip 144.254.100.5 atm-vc 115 broadcast
 ip 144.254.100.6 atm-vc 116 broadcast
 ip 144.254.100.7 atm-vc 117 broadcast
 ip 144.254.100.8 atm-vc 118 broadcast
```

Example C-122   *Router 1 Configuration for Lab 13-4 (Continued)*

```
 ip 144.254.100.9 atm-vc 119 broadcast
!
map-list ipxPvc
 ipx 100.0000.0000.0002 atm-vc 112 broadcast
 ipx 100.0000.0000.0003 atm-vc 113 broadcast
 ipx 100.0000.0000.0004 atm-vc 114 broadcast
 ipx 100.0000.0000.0005 atm-vc 115 broadcast
 ipx 100.0000.0000.0006 atm-vc 116 broadcast
 ipx 100.0000.0000.0007 atm-vc 117 broadcast
 ipx 100.0000.0000.0008 atm-vc 118 broadcast
 ipx 100.0000.0000.0009 atm-vc 119 broadcast
!
map-list ipSvc
 ip 144.254.200.1 atm-nsap 11.11110000000000000000000.000000000000.00 broadcast
 ip 144.254.200.2 atm-nsap 22.22220000000000000000000.000000000000.00 broadcast
 ip 144.254.200.3 atm-nsap 33.33330000000000000000000.000000000000.00 broadcast
 ip 144.254.200.4 atm-nsap 44.44440000000000000000000.000000000000.00 broadcast
 ip 144.254.200.5 atm-nsap 55.55550000000000000000000.000000000000.00 broadcast
 ip 144.254.200.6 atm-nsap 66.66660000000000000000000.000000000000.00 broadcast
 ip 144.254.200.7 atm-nsap 77.77770000000000000000000.000000000000.00 broadcast
 ip 144.254.200.8 atm-nsap 88.88880000000000000000000.000000000000.00 broadcast
 ip 144.254.200.9 atm-nsap 99.99990000000000000000000.000000000000.00 broadcast
!
map-list ipxSvc
 ipx 200.0000.0000.0001 atm-nsap 11.11110000000000000000000.000000000000.00
  broadcast
 ipx 200.0000.0000.0002 atm-nsap 22.22220000000000000000000.000000000000.00
  broadcast
 ipx 200.0000.0000.0003 atm-nsap 33.33330000000000000000000.000000000000.00
  broadcast
 ipx 200.0000.0000.0004 atm-nsap 44.44440000000000000000000.000000000000.00
  broadcast
 ipx 200.0000.0000.0005 atm-nsap 55.55550000000000000000000.000000000000.00
  broadcast
 ipx 200.0000.0000.0006 atm-nsap 66.66660000000000000000000.000000000000.00
  broadcast
 ipx 200.0000.0000.0007 atm-nsap 77.77770000000000000000000.000000000000.00
  broadcast
 ipx 200.0000.0000.0008 atm-nsap 88.88880000000000000000000.000000000000.00
  broadcast
 ipx 200.0000.0000.0009 atm-nsap 99.99990000000000000000000.000000000000.00
  broadcast
!
map-list newNsaps
 ip 144.254.32.1 atm-nsap 11.11111111111111111111111.111111111111.20 broadcast
 ip 144.254.32.2 atm-nsap 11.11111111111111111111111.222222222222.20 broadcast
 ip 144.254.32.3 atm-nsap 11.11111111111111111111111.333333333333.20 broadcast
 ip 144.254.32.4 atm-nsap 22.22222222222222222222222.444444444444.20 broadcast
 ip 144.254.32.5 atm-nsap 22.22222222222222222222222.555555555555.20 broadcast
 ip 144.254.32.6 atm-nsap 22.22222222222222222222222.666666666666.20 broadcast
```

continues

Example C-122 *Router 1 Configuration for Lab 13-4 (Continued)*

```
ip 144.254.32.7 atm-nsap 33.3333333333333333333333333.777777777777.20 broadcast
ip 144.254.32.8 atm-nsap 33.3333333333333333333333333.888888888888.20 broadcast
ip 144.254.32.9 atm-nsap 33.3333333333333333333333333.999999999999.20 broadcast
!
line con 0
 exec-timeout 0 0
line aux 0
line vty 0 4
 exec-timeout 0 0
 password cisco
 login
!
end
```

Example C-123 *Router 2 Configuration for Lab 13-4*

```
!
version 11.2
no service password-encryption
no service udp-small-servers
no service tcp-small-servers
!
hostname R2
!
enable password sanfran
!
no ip domain-lookup
ipx routing 0000.0000.0002
ipx maximum-paths 2
!
!
interface Ethernet0
 ip address 144.254.2.2 255.255.255.0
 ipx network 20
!
interface Ethernet1
 ip address 10.0.0.2 255.0.0.0
 media-type 10BaseT
!
interface ATM0
 no ip address
 atm pvc 5 0 5 qsaal
 atm pvc 16 0 16 ilmi
!
interface ATM0.1 multipoint
 ip address 144.254.100.2 255.255.255.0
 atm pvc 121 0 121 aal5snap
 atm pvc 123 0 123 aal5snap
 atm pvc 124 0 124 aal5snap
 atm pvc 125 0 125 aal5snap
```

Example C-123 *Router 2 Configuration for Lab 13-4 (Continued)*

```
atm pvc 126 0 126 aal5snap
atm pvc 127 0 127 aal5snap
atm pvc 128 0 128 aal5snap
atm pvc 129 0 129 aal5snap
map-group ipPvc
map-group ipxPvc
ipx network 100
!
interface ATM0.2 multipoint
 ip address 144.254.200.2 255.255.255.0
 atm nsap-address 22.222200000000000000000000.000000000000.00
 map-group ipSvc
 map-group ipxSvc
 ipx network 200
!
interface ATM0.32 multipoint
 ip address 144.254.32.2 255.255.255.0
 atm esi-address 222222222222.20
 map-group newNsaps
!
interface FastEthernet0
 no ip address
 shutdown
!
router igrp 100
 network 144.254.0.0
!
no ip classless
!
map-list ipPvc
 ip 144.254.100.1 atm-vc 121 broadcast
 ip 144.254.100.3 atm-vc 123 broadcast
 ip 144.254.100.4 atm-vc 124 broadcast
 ip 144.254.100.5 atm-vc 125 broadcast
 ip 144.254.100.6 atm-vc 126 broadcast
 ip 144.254.100.7 atm-vc 127 broadcast
 ip 144.254.100.8 atm-vc 128 broadcast
 ip 144.254.100.9 atm-vc 129 broadcast
!
map-list ipxPvc
 ipx 100.0000.0000.0001 atm-vc 121 broadcast
 ipx 100.0000.0000.0003 atm-vc 123 broadcast
 ipx 100.0000.0000.0004 atm-vc 124 broadcast
 ipx 100.0000.0000.0005 atm-vc 125 broadcast
 ipx 100.0000.0000.0006 atm-vc 126 broadcast
 ipx 100.0000.0000.0007 atm-vc 127 broadcast
 ipx 100.0000.0000.0008 atm-vc 128 broadcast
 ipx 100.0000.0000.0009 atm-vc 129 broadcast
!
map-list ipSvc
```

Lab 13-4 Solution

continues

Example C-123 *Router 2 Configuration for Lab 13-4 (Continued)*

```
 ip 144.254.200.1 atm-nsap 11.11110000000000000000000.000000000000.00 broadcast
 ip 144.254.200.2 atm-nsap 22.22220000000000000000000.000000000000.00 broadcast
 ip 144.254.200.3 atm-nsap 33.33330000000000000000000.000000000000.00 broadcast
 ip 144.254.200.4 atm-nsap 44.44440000000000000000000.000000000000.00 broadcast
 ip 144.254.200.5 atm-nsap 55.55550000000000000000000.000000000000.00 broadcast
 ip 144.254.200.6 atm-nsap 66.66660000000000000000000.000000000000.00 broadcast
 ip 144.254.200.7 atm-nsap 77.77770000000000000000000.000000000000.00 broadcast
 ip 144.254.200.8 atm-nsap 88.88880000000000000000000.000000000000.00 broadcast
 ip 144.254.200.9 atm-nsap 99.99990000000000000000000.000000000000.00 broadcast
!
map-list ipxSvc
 ipx 200.0000.0000.0001 atm-nsap 11.11110000000000000000000.000000000000.00
  broadcast
 ipx 200.0000.0000.0002 atm-nsap 22.22220000000000000000000.000000000000.00
  broadcast
 ipx 200.0000.0000.0003 atm-nsap 33.33330000000000000000000.000000000000.00
  broadcast
 ipx 200.0000.0000.0004 atm-nsap 44.44440000000000000000000.000000000000.00
  broadcast
 ipx 200.0000.0000.0005 atm-nsap 55.55550000000000000000000.000000000000.00
  broadcast
 ipx 200.0000.0000.0006 atm-nsap 66.66660000000000000000000.000000000000.00
  broadcast
 ipx 200.0000.0000.0007 atm-nsap 77.77770000000000000000000.000000000000.00
  broadcast
 ipx 200.0000.0000.0008 atm-nsap 88.88880000000000000000000.000000000000.00
  broadcast
 ipx 200.0000.0000.0009 atm-nsap 99.99990000000000000000000.000000000000.00
  broadcast
!
map-list newNsaps
 ip 144.254.32.1 atm-nsap 11.11111111111111111111111.111111111111.20 broadcast
 ip 144.254.32.2 atm-nsap 11.11111111111111111111111.222222222222.20 broadcast
 ip 144.254.32.3 atm-nsap 11.11111111111111111111111.333333333333.20 broadcast
 ip 144.254.32.4 atm-nsap 22.22222222222222222222222.444444444444.20 broadcast
 ip 144.254.32.5 atm-nsap 22.22222222222222222222222.555555555555.20 broadcast
 ip 144.254.32.6 atm-nsap 22.22222222222222222222222.666666666666.20 broadcast
 ip 144.254.32.7 atm-nsap 33.33333333333333333333333.777777777777.20 broadcast
 ip 144.254.32.8 atm-nsap 33.33333333333333333333333.888888888888.20 broadcast
 ip 144.254.32.9 atm-nsap 33.33333333333333333333333.999999999999.20 broadcast
!
!
line con 0
 exec-timeout 0 0
line aux 0
line vty 0 4
 exec-timeout 0 0
 password cisco
```

Example C-123 *Router 2 Configuration for Lab 13-4 (Continued)*

```
 login
 !
 end
```

Example C-124 *Router 3 Configuration for Lab 13-4*

```
 !
 version 11.3
 service timestamps debug uptime
 service timestamps log uptime
 no service password-encryption
 !
 hostname R3
 !
 enable password sanfran
 !
 no ip domain-lookup
 ipx routing 0000.0000.0003
 ipx maximum-paths 2
 !
 !
 interface Ethernet0
  ip address 144.254.3.3 255.255.255.0
  ipx network 30
 !
 interface Ethernet1
  ip address 10.0.0.3 255.0.0.0
  media-type 10BaseT
 !
 interface TokenRing0
  no ip address
  shutdown
 !
 interface ATM0
  no ip address
  atm pvc 5 0 5 qsaal
  atm pvc 16 0 16 ilmi
 !
 interface ATM0.1 multipoint
  ip address 144.254.100.3 255.255.255.0
  atm pvc 131 0 131 aal5snap
  atm pvc 132 0 132 aal5snap
  atm pvc 133 0 133 aal5snap
  atm pvc 134 0 134 aal5snap
  atm pvc 135 0 135 aal5snap
  atm pvc 136 0 136 aal5snap
  atm pvc 137 0 137 aal5snap
  atm pvc 138 0 138 aal5snap
  atm pvc 139 0 139 aal5snap
  map-group ipPvc
```

continues

Example C-124 *Router 3 Configuration for Lab 13-4 (Continued)*

```
 map-group ipxPvc
 ipx network 100
!
interface ATM0.2 multipoint
 ip address 144.254.200.3 255.255.255.0
 atm nsap-address 33.333300000000000000000000.000000000000.00
 map-group ipSvc
 map-group ipxSvc
 ipx network 200
!
interface ATM0.32 multipoint
 ip address 144.254.32.3 255.255.255.0
 atm esi-address 333333333333.20
 map-group newNsaps
!
router igrp 100
 network 144.254.0.0
!
no ip classless
!
!
map-list ipPvc
 ip 144.254.100.1 atm-vc 131 broadcast
 ip 144.254.100.2 atm-vc 132 broadcast
 ip 144.254.100.4 atm-vc 134 broadcast
 ip 144.254.100.5 atm-vc 135 broadcast
 ip 144.254.100.6 atm-vc 136 broadcast
 ip 144.254.100.7 atm-vc 137 broadcast
 ip 144.254.100.8 atm-vc 138 broadcast
 ip 144.254.100.9 atm-vc 139 broadcast
!
map-list ipxPvc
 ipx 100.0000.0000.0001 atm-vc 131 broadcast
 ipx 100.0000.0000.0002 atm-vc 132 broadcast
 ipx 100.0000.0000.0004 atm-vc 134 broadcast
 ipx 100.0000.0000.0005 atm-vc 135 broadcast
 ipx 100.0000.0000.0006 atm-vc 136 broadcast
 ipx 100.0000.0000.0007 atm-vc 137 broadcast
 ipx 100.0000.0000.0008 atm-vc 138 broadcast
 ipx 100.0000.0000.0009 atm-vc 139 broadcast
!
map-list ipSvc
 ip 144.254.200.1 atm-nsap 11.111100000000000000000000.000000000000.00 broadcast
 ip 144.254.200.2 atm-nsap 22.222200000000000000000000.000000000000.00 broadcast
 ip 144.254.200.3 atm-nsap 33.333300000000000000000000.000000000000.00 broadcast
 ip 144.254.200.4 atm-nsap 44.444400000000000000000000.000000000000.00 broadcast
 ip 144.254.200.5 atm-nsap 55.555500000000000000000000.000000000000.00 broadcast
 ip 144.254.200.6 atm-nsap 66.666600000000000000000000.000000000000.00 broadcast
 ip 144.254.200.7 atm-nsap 77.777700000000000000000000.000000000000.00 broadcast
 ip 144.254.200.8 atm-nsap 88.888800000000000000000000.000000000000.00 broadcast
```

Example C-124 *Router 3 Configuration for Lab 13-4 (Continued)*

```
    ip 144.254.200.9 atm-nsap 99.99990000000000000000000.000000000000.00 broadcast
 !
map-list ipxSvc
 ipx 200.0000.0000.0001 atm-nsap 11.11110000000000000000000.000000000000.00
   broadcast
 ipx 200.0000.0000.0002 atm-nsap 22.22220000000000000000000.000000000000.00
   broadcast
 ipx 200.0000.0000.0003 atm-nsap 33.33330000000000000000000.000000000000.00
   broadcast
 ipx 200.0000.0000.0004 atm-nsap 44.44440000000000000000000.000000000000.00
   broadcast
 ipx 200.0000.0000.0005 atm-nsap 55.55550000000000000000000.000000000000.00
   broadcast
 ipx 200.0000.0000.0006 atm-nsap 66.66660000000000000000000.000000000000.00
   broadcast
 ipx 200.0000.0000.0007 atm-nsap 77.77770000000000000000000.000000000000.00
   broadcast
 ipx 200.0000.0000.0008 atm-nsap 88.88880000000000000000000.000000000000.00
   broadcast
 ipx 200.0000.0000.0009 atm-nsap 99.99990000000000000000000.000000000000.00
   broadcast
 !
map-list newNsaps
 ip 144.254.32.1 atm-nsap 11.1111111111111111111111111.11111111111.20 broadcast
 ip 144.254.32.2 atm-nsap 11.1111111111111111111111111.222222222222.20 broadcast
 ip 144.254.32.3 atm-nsap 11.1111111111111111111111111.333333333333.20 broadcast
 ip 144.254.32.4 atm-nsap 22.2222222222222222222222222.444444444444.20 broadcast
 ip 144.254.32.5 atm-nsap 22.2222222222222222222222222.555555555555.20 broadcast
 ip 144.254.32.6 atm-nsap 22.2222222222222222222222222.666666666666.20 broadcast
 ip 144.254.32.7 atm-nsap 33.3333333333333333333333333.777777777777.20 broadcast
 ip 144.254.32.8 atm-nsap 33.3333333333333333333333333.888888888888.20 broadcast
 ip 144.254.32.9 atm-nsap 33.3333333333333333333333333.999999999999.20 broadcast
 !
 !
line con 0
 exec-timeout 0 0
line aux 0
line vty 0 4
 password cisco
 login
 !
end
```

Example C-125 *Router 4 Configuration for Lab 13-4*

```
 !
version 11.2
no service password-encryption
no service udp-small-servers
no service tcp-small-servers
```

continues

Example C-125 *Router 4 Configuration for Lab 13-4 (Continued)*

```
!
hostname R4
!
enable password sanfran
!
no ip domain-lookup
ipx routing 0000.0000.0004
ipx maximum-paths 2
!
!
interface Ethernet0
 ip address 144.254.4.4 255.255.255.0
 ipx network 40
!
interface Ethernet1
 ip address 10.0.0.4 255.0.0.0
 media-type 10BaseT
!
interface Serial0
 no ip address
 shutdown
!
interface Serial1
 no ip address
 shutdown
!
interface ATM0
 no ip address
 atm pvc 5 0 5 qsaal
 atm pvc 16 0 16 ilmi
!
interface ATM0.1 multipoint
 ip address 144.254.100.4 255.255.255.0
 atm pvc 141 0 141 aal5snap
 atm pvc 142 0 142 aal5snap
 atm pvc 143 0 143 aal5snap
 atm pvc 145 0 145 aal5snap
 atm pvc 146 0 146 aal5snap
 atm pvc 147 0 147 aal5snap
 atm pvc 148 0 148 aal5snap
 atm pvc 149 0 149 aal5snap
 map-group ipPvc
 map-group ipxPvc
 ipx network 100
!
interface ATM0.2 multipoint
 ip address 144.254.200.4 255.255.255.0
 atm nsap-address 44.44440000000000000000000000.000000000000.00
 map-group ipSvc
 map-group ipxSvc
```

Example C-125 *Router 4 Configuration for Lab 13-4 (Continued)*

```
 ipx network 200
 !
 interface ATM0.32 multipoint
  ip address 144.254.32.4 255.255.255.0
  atm esi-address 444444444444.20
  map-group newNsaps
 !
 router igrp 100
  network 144.254.0.0
 !
 no ip classless
 !
 map-list ipPvc
  ip 144.254.100.1 atm-vc 141 broadcast
  ip 144.254.100.2 atm-vc 142 broadcast
  ip 144.254.100.3 atm-vc 143 broadcast
  ip 144.254.100.5 atm-vc 145 broadcast
  ip 144.254.100.6 atm-vc 146 broadcast
  ip 144.254.100.7 atm-vc 147 broadcast
  ip 144.254.100.8 atm-vc 148 broadcast
  ip 144.254.100.9 atm-vc 149 broadcast
 !
 map-list ipxPvc
  ipx 100.0000.0000.0001 atm-vc 141 broadcast
  ipx 100.0000.0000.0002 atm-vc 142 broadcast
  ipx 100.0000.0000.0003 atm-vc 143 broadcast
  ipx 100.0000.0000.0005 atm-vc 145 broadcast
  ipx 100.0000.0000.0006 atm-vc 146 broadcast
  ipx 100.0000.0000.0007 atm-vc 147 broadcast
  ipx 100.0000.0000.0008 atm-vc 148 broadcast
  ipx 100.0000.0000.0009 atm-vc 149 broadcast
 !
 map-list ipSvc
  ip 144.254.200.1 atm-nsap 11.1111000000000000000000000.000000000000.00 broadcast
  ip 144.254.200.2 atm-nsap 22.2222000000000000000000000.000000000000.00 broadcast
  ip 144.254.200.3 atm-nsap 33.3333000000000000000000000.000000000000.00 broadcast
  ip 144.254.200.4 atm-nsap 44.4444000000000000000000000.000000000000.00 broadcast
  ip 144.254.200.5 atm-nsap 55.5555000000000000000000000.000000000000.00 broadcast
  ip 144.254.200.6 atm-nsap 66.6666000000000000000000000.000000000000.00 broadcast
  ip 144.254.200.7 atm-nsap 77.7777000000000000000000000.000000000000.00 broadcast
  ip 144.254.200.8 atm-nsap 88.8888000000000000000000000.000000000000.00 broadcast
  ip 144.254.200.9 atm-nsap 99.9999000000000000000000000.000000000000.00 broadcast
 !
 map-list ipxSvc
  ipx 200.0000.0000.0001 atm-nsap 11.1111000000000000000000000.000000000000.00
   broadcast
  ipx 200.0000.0000.0002 atm-nsap 22.2222000000000000000000000.000000000000.00
   broadcast
  ipx 200.0000.0000.0003 atm-nsap 33.3333000000000000000000000.000000000000.00
   broadcast
```

continues

Example C-125 *Router 4 Configuration for Lab 13-4 (Continued)*

```
ipx 200.0000.0000.0004 atm-nsap 44.444400000000000000000000.000000000000.00
  broadcast
ipx 200.0000.0000.0005 atm-nsap 55.555500000000000000000000.000000000000.00
  broadcast
ipx 200.0000.0000.0006 atm-nsap 66.666600000000000000000000.000000000000.00
  broadcast
ipx 200.0000.0000.0007 atm-nsap 77.777700000000000000000000.000000000000.00
  broadcast
ipx 200.0000.0000.0008 atm-nsap 88.888800000000000000000000.000000000000.00
  broadcast
ipx 200.0000.0000.0009 atm-nsap 99.999900000000000000000000.000000000000.00
  broadcast
!
map-list newNsaps
 ip 144.254.32.1 atm-nsap 11.111111111111111111111111.111111111111.20 broadcast
 ip 144.254.32.2 atm-nsap 11.111111111111111111111111.222222222222.20 broadcast
 ip 144.254.32.3 atm-nsap 11.111111111111111111111111.333333333333.20 broadcast
 ip 144.254.32.4 atm-nsap 22.222222222222222222222222.444444444444.20 broadcast
 ip 144.254.32.5 atm-nsap 22.222222222222222222222222.555555555555.20 broadcast
 ip 144.254.32.6 atm-nsap 22.222222222222222222222222.666666666666.20 broadcast
 ip 144.254.32.7 atm-nsap 33.333333333333333333333333.777777777777.20 broadcast
 ip 144.254.32.8 atm-nsap 33.333333333333333333333333.888888888888.20 broadcast
 ip 144.254.32.9 atm-nsap 33.333333333333333333333333.999999999999.20 broadcast
!
!
line con 0
 exec-timeout 0 0
line aux 0
line vty 0 4
 exec-timeout 0 0
 password cisco
 login
!
end
```

Example C-126 *Router 5 Configuration for Lab 13-4*

```
!
version 11.2
no service password-encryption
no service udp-small-servers
no service tcp-small-servers
!
hostname R5
!
enable password sanfran
!
no ip domain-lookup
ipx routing 0000.0000.0005
ipx maximum-paths 2
```

Example C-126   *Router 5 Configuration for Lab 13-4 (Continued)*

```
!
!
interface Ethernet0
 ip address 144.254.5.5 255.255.255.0
 ipx network 50
!
interface Ethernet1
 ip address 10.0.0.5 255.0.0.0
 media-type 10BaseT
!
interface ATM0
 no ip address
 atm pvc 5 0 5 qsaal
 atm pvc 666 0 16 ilmi
!
interface ATM0.1 multipoint
 ip address 144.254.100.5 255.255.255.0
 atm pvc 151 0 151 aal5snap
 atm pvc 152 0 152 aal5snap
 atm pvc 153 0 153 aal5snap
 atm pvc 154 0 154 aal5snap
 atm pvc 156 0 156 aal5snap
 atm pvc 157 0 157 aal5snap
 atm pvc 158 0 158 aal5snap
 atm pvc 159 0 159 aal5snap
 map-group ipPvc
 map-group ipxPvc
 ipx network 100
!
interface ATM0.2 multipoint
 ip address 144.254.200.5 255.255.255.0
 atm nsap-address 55.5555000000000000000000000.000000000000.00
 map-group ipSvc
 map-group ipxSvc
 ipx network 200
!
interface ATM0.32 multipoint
 ip address 144.254.32.5 255.255.255.0
 atm esi-address 555555555555.20
 map-group newNsaps
!
interface FastEthernet0
 no ip address
 shutdown
!
router igrp 100
 network 144.254.0.0
!
no ip classless
!
```

continues

Example C-126 *Router 5 Configuration for Lab 13-4 (Continued)*

```
map-list ipPvc
 ip 144.254.100.1 atm-vc 151 broadcast
 ip 144.254.100.2 atm-vc 152 broadcast
 ip 144.254.100.3 atm-vc 153 broadcast
 ip 144.254.100.4 atm-vc 154 broadcast
 ip 144.254.100.6 atm-vc 156 broadcast
 ip 144.254.100.7 atm-vc 157 broadcast
 ip 144.254.100.8 atm-vc 158 broadcast
 ip 144.254.100.9 atm-vc 159 broadcast
!
map-list ipxPvc
 ipx 100.0000.0000.0001 atm-vc 151 broadcast
 ipx 100.0000.0000.0002 atm-vc 152 broadcast
 ipx 100.0000.0000.0003 atm-vc 153 broadcast
 ipx 100.0000.0000.0004 atm-vc 154 broadcast
 ipx 100.0000.0000.0006 atm-vc 156 broadcast
 ipx 100.0000.0000.0007 atm-vc 157 broadcast
 ipx 100.0000.0000.0008 atm-vc 158 broadcast
 ipx 100.0000.0000.0009 atm-vc 159 broadcast
!
map-list ipSvc
 ip 144.254.200.1 atm-nsap 11.11110000000000000000000.000000000000.00 broadcast
 ip 144.254.200.2 atm-nsap 22.22220000000000000000000.000000000000.00 broadcast
 ip 144.254.200.3 atm-nsap 33.33330000000000000000000.000000000000.00 broadcast
 ip 144.254.200.4 atm-nsap 44.44440000000000000000000.000000000000.00 broadcast
 ip 144.254.200.5 atm-nsap 55.55550000000000000000000.000000000000.00 broadcast
 ip 144.254.200.6 atm-nsap 66.66660000000000000000000.000000000000.00 broadcast
 ip 144.254.200.7 atm-nsap 77.77770000000000000000000.000000000000.00 broadcast
 ip 144.254.200.8 atm-nsap 88.88880000000000000000000.000000000000.00 broadcast
 ip 144.254.200.9 atm-nsap 99.99990000000000000000000.000000000000.00 broadcast
!
map-list ipxSvc
 ipx 200.0000.0000.0001 atm-nsap 11.11110000000000000000000.000000000000.00
  broadcast
 ipx 200.0000.0000.0002 atm-nsap 22.22220000000000000000000.000000000000.00
  broadcast
 ipx 200.0000.0000.0003 atm-nsap 33.33330000000000000000000.000000000000.00
  broadcast
 ipx 200.0000.0000.0004 atm-nsap 44.44440000000000000000000.000000000000.00
  broadcast
 ipx 200.0000.0000.0005 atm-nsap 55.55550000000000000000000.000000000000.00
  broadcast
 ipx 200.0000.0000.0006 atm-nsap 66.66660000000000000000000.000000000000.00
  broadcast
 ipx 200.0000.0000.0007 atm-nsap 77.77770000000000000000000.000000000000.00
  broadcast
 ipx 200.0000.0000.0008 atm-nsap 88.88880000000000000000000.000000000000.00
  broadcast
 ipx 200.0000.0000.0009 atm-nsap 99.99990000000000000000000.000000000000.00
  broadcast
```

Example C-126   *Router 5 Configuration for Lab 13-4 (Continued)*

```
!
map-list newNsaps
 ip 144.254.32.1 atm-nsap 11.111111111111111111111111.111111111111.20 broadcast
 ip 144.254.32.2 atm-nsap 11.111111111111111111111111.222222222222.20 broadcast
 ip 144.254.32.3 atm-nsap 11.111111111111111111111111.333333333333.20 broadcast
 ip 144.254.32.4 atm-nsap 22.222222222222222222222222.444444444444.20 broadcast
 ip 144.254.32.5 atm-nsap 22.222222222222222222222222.555555555555.20 broadcast
 ip 144.254.32.6 atm-nsap 22.222222222222222222222222.666666666666.20 broadcast
 ip 144.254.32.7 atm-nsap 33.333333333333333333333333.777777777777.20 broadcast
 ip 144.254.32.8 atm-nsap 33.333333333333333333333333.888888888888.20 broadcast
 ip 144.254.32.9 atm-nsap 33.333333333333333333333333.999999999999.20 broadcast
!
!
line con 0
 exec-timeout 0 0
line aux 0
line vty 0 4
 exec-timeout 0 0
 password cisco
 login
!
end
```

Example C-127   *Router 6 Configuration for Lab 13-4*

```
!
version 11.2
no service password-encryption
no service udp-small-servers
no service tcp-small-servers
!
hostname R6
!
enable password sanfran
!
no ip domain-lookup
ipx routing 0000.0000.0006
ipx maximum-paths 2
!
!
interface Ethernet0
 ip address 144.254.6.6 255.255.255.0
 ipx network 60
!
interface Ethernet1
 ip address 10.0.0.6 255.0.0.0
 media-type 10BaseT
!
interface ATM0
 no ip address
```

continues

Lab 13-4 Solution

Example C-127 *Router 6 Configuration for Lab 13-4 (Continued)*

```
 atm pvc 5 0 5 qsaal
 atm pvc 16 0 16 ilmi
!
interface ATM0.1 multipoint
 ip address 144.254.100.6 255.255.255.0
 atm pvc 161 0 161 aal5snap
 atm pvc 162 0 162 aal5snap
 atm pvc 163 0 163 aal5snap
 atm pvc 164 0 164 aal5snap
 atm pvc 165 0 165 aal5snap
 atm pvc 167 0 167 aal5snap
 atm pvc 168 0 168 aal5snap
 atm pvc 169 0 169 aal5snap
 map-group ipPvc
 map-group ipxPvc
 ipx network 100
!
interface ATM0.2 multipoint
 ip address 144.254.200.6 255.255.255.0
 atm nsap-address 66.66660000000000000000000000.000000000000.00
 map-group ipSvc
 map-group ipxSvc
 ipx network 200
!
interface ATM0.32 multipoint
 ip address 144.254.32.6 255.255.255.0
 atm esi-address 666666666666.20
 map-group newNsaps
!
router igrp 100
 network 144.254.0.0
!
no ip classless
!
map-list ipPvc
 ip 144.254.100.1 atm-vc 161 broadcast
 ip 144.254.100.2 atm-vc 162 broadcast
 ip 144.254.100.3 atm-vc 163 broadcast
 ip 144.254.100.4 atm-vc 164 broadcast
 ip 144.254.100.5 atm-vc 165 broadcast
 ip 144.254.100.7 atm-vc 167 broadcast
 ip 144.254.100.8 atm-vc 168 broadcast
 ip 144.254.100.9 atm-vc 169 broadcast
!
map-list ipxPvc
 ipx 100.0000.0000.0001 atm-vc 161 broadcast
 ipx 100.0000.0000.0002 atm-vc 162 broadcast
 ipx 100.0000.0000.0003 atm-vc 163 broadcast
 ipx 100.0000.0000.0004 atm-vc 164 broadcast
 ipx 100.0000.0000.0005 atm-vc 165 broadcast
```

Example C-127 *Router 6 Configuration for Lab 13-4 (Continued)*

```
 ipx 100.0000.0000.0007 atm-vc 167 broadcast
 ipx 100.0000.0000.0008 atm-vc 168 broadcast
 ipx 100.0000.0000.0009 atm-vc 169 broadcast
!
map-list ipSvc
 ip 144.254.200.1 atm-nsap 11.11110000000000000000000.000000000000.00 broadcast
 ip 144.254.200.2 atm-nsap 22.22220000000000000000000.000000000000.00 broadcast
 ip 144.254.200.3 atm-nsap 33.33330000000000000000000.000000000000.00 broadcast
 ip 144.254.200.4 atm-nsap 44.44440000000000000000000.000000000000.00 broadcast
 ip 144.254.200.5 atm-nsap 55.55550000000000000000000.000000000000.00 broadcast
 ip 144.254.200.6 atm-nsap 66.66660000000000000000000.000000000000.00 broadcast
 ip 144.254.200.7 atm-nsap 77.77770000000000000000000.000000000000.00 broadcast
 ip 144.254.200.8 atm-nsap 88.88880000000000000000000.000000000000.00 broadcast
 ip 144.254.200.9 atm-nsap 99.99990000000000000000000.000000000000.00 broadcast
!
map-list ipxSvc
 ipx 200.0000.0000.0001 atm-nsap 11.11110000000000000000000.000000000000.00
  broadcast
 ipx 200.0000.0000.0002 atm-nsap 22.22220000000000000000000.000000000000.00
  broadcast
 ipx 200.0000.0000.0003 atm-nsap 33.33330000000000000000000.000000000000.00
  broadcast
 ipx 200.0000.0000.0004 atm-nsap 44.44440000000000000000000.000000000000.00
  broadcast
 ipx 200.0000.0000.0005 atm-nsap 55.55550000000000000000000.000000000000.00
  broadcast
 ipx 200.0000.0000.0006 atm-nsap 66.66660000000000000000000.000000000000.00
  broadcast
 ipx 200.0000.0000.0007 atm-nsap 77.77770000000000000000000.000000000000.00
  broadcast
 ipx 200.0000.0000.0008 atm-nsap 88.88880000000000000000000.000000000000.00
  broadcast
 ipx 200.0000.0000.0009 atm-nsap 99.99990000000000000000000.000000000000.00
  broadcast
!
map-list newNsaps
 ip 144.254.32.1 atm-nsap 11.11111111111111111111111.111111111111.20 broadcast
 ip 144.254.32.2 atm-nsap 11.11111111111111111111111.222222222222.20 broadcast
 ip 144.254.32.3 atm-nsap 11.11111111111111111111111.333333333333.20 broadcast
 ip 144.254.32.4 atm-nsap 22.22222222222222222222222.444444444444.20 broadcast
 ip 144.254.32.5 atm-nsap 22.22222222222222222222222.555555555555.20 broadcast
 ip 144.254.32.6 atm-nsap 22.22222222222222222222222.666666666666.20 broadcast
 ip 144.254.32.7 atm-nsap 33.33333333333333333333333.777777777777.20 broadcast
 ip 144.254.32.8 atm-nsap 33.33333333333333333333333.888888888888.20 broadcast
 ip 144.254.32.9 atm-nsap 33.33333333333333333333333.999999999999.20 broadcast
!
!
line con 0
 exec-timeout 0 0
line aux 0
```

Lab 13-4 Solution

continues

Example C-127 *Router 6 Configuration for Lab 13-4 (Continued)*

```
line vty 0 4
 exec-timeout 0 0
 password cisco
 login
!
end
```

Example C-128 *Router 7 Configuration for Lab 13-4*

```
!
version 11.2
no service password-encryption
no service udp-small-servers
no service tcp-small-servers
!
hostname R7
!
enable password sanfran
!
no ip domain-lookup
ipx routing 0000.0000.0007
ipx maximum-paths 2
!
!
interface Ethernet0
 ip address 144.254.7.7 255.255.255.0
 ipx network 70
!
interface Ethernet1
 ip address 10.0.0.7 255.0.0.0
 media-type 10BaseT
!
interface Serial0
 no ip address
 shutdown
!
interface Serial1
 no ip address
 shutdown
!
interface ATM0
 no ip address
 atm pvc 5 0 5 qsaal
 atm pvc 16 0 16 ilmi
!
interface ATM0.1 multipoint
 ip address 144.254.100.7 255.255.255.0
 atm pvc 171 0 171 aal5snap
 atm pvc 172 0 172 aal5snap
 atm pvc 173 0 173 aal5snap
```

Example C-128   *Router 7 Configuration for Lab 13-4 (Continued)*

```
 atm pvc 174 0 174 aal5snap
 atm pvc 175 0 175 aal5snap
 atm pvc 176 0 176 aal5snap
 atm pvc 178 0 178 aal5snap
 atm pvc 179 0 179 aal5snap
 map-group ipPvc
 map-group ipxPvc
 ipx network 100
!
interface ATM0.2 multipoint
 ip address 144.254.200.7 255.255.255.0
 atm nsap-address 77.77770000000000000000000000.000000000000.00
 map-group ipSvc
 map-group ipxSvc
 ipx network 200
!
interface ATM0.32 multipoint
 ip address 144.254.32.7 255.255.255.0
 atm esi-address 777777777777.20
 map-group newNsaps
!
router igrp 100
 network 144.254.0.0
!
no ip classless
!
map-list ipPvc
 ip 144.254.100.1 atm-vc 171 broadcast
 ip 144.254.100.2 atm-vc 172 broadcast
 ip 144.254.100.3 atm-vc 173 broadcast
 ip 144.254.100.4 atm-vc 174 broadcast
 ip 144.254.100.5 atm-vc 175 broadcast
 ip 144.254.100.6 atm-vc 176 broadcast
 ip 144.254.100.8 atm-vc 178 broadcast
 ip 144.254.100.9 atm-vc 179 broadcast
!
map-list ipxPvc
 ipx 100.0000.0000.0001 atm-vc 171 broadcast
 ipx 100.0000.0000.0002 atm-vc 172 broadcast
 ipx 100.0000.0000.0003 atm-vc 173 broadcast
 ipx 100.0000.0000.0004 atm-vc 174 broadcast
 ipx 100.0000.0000.0005 atm-vc 175 broadcast
 ipx 100.0000.0000.0006 atm-vc 176 broadcast
 ipx 100.0000.0000.0008 atm-vc 178 broadcast
 ipx 100.0000.0000.0009 atm-vc 179 broadcast
!
map-list ipSvc
 ip 144.254.200.1 atm-nsap 11.11110000000000000000000000.000000000000.00 broadcast
 ip 144.254.200.2 atm-nsap 22.22220000000000000000000000.000000000000.00 broadcast
 ip 144.254.200.3 atm-nsap 33.33330000000000000000000000.000000000000.00 broadcast
```

continues

Example C-128 *Router 7 Configuration for Lab 13-4 (Continued)*

```
 ip 144.254.200.4 atm-nsap 44.44440000000000000000000.000000000000.00 broadcast
 ip 144.254.200.5 atm-nsap 55.55550000000000000000000.000000000000.00 broadcast
 ip 144.254.200.6 atm-nsap 66.66660000000000000000000.000000000000.00 broadcast
 ip 144.254.200.7 atm-nsap 77.77770000000000000000000.000000000000.00 broadcast
 ip 144.254.200.8 atm-nsap 88.88880000000000000000000.000000000000.00 broadcast
 ip 144.254.200.9 atm-nsap 99.99990000000000000000000.000000000000.00 broadcast
!
map-list ipxSvc
 ipx 200.0000.0000.0001 atm-nsap 11.11110000000000000000000.000000000000.00
  broadcast
 ipx 200.0000.0000.0002 atm-nsap 22.22220000000000000000000.000000000000.00
  broadcast
 ipx 200.0000.0000.0003 atm-nsap 33.33330000000000000000000.000000000000.00
  broadcast
 ipx 200.0000.0000.0004 atm-nsap 44.44440000000000000000000.000000000000.00
  broadcast
 ipx 200.0000.0000.0005 atm-nsap 55.55550000000000000000000.000000000000.00
  broadcast
 ipx 200.0000.0000.0006 atm-nsap 66.66660000000000000000000.000000000000.00
  broadcast
 ipx 200.0000.0000.0007 atm-nsap 77.77770000000000000000000.000000000000.00
  broadcast
 ipx 200.0000.0000.0008 atm-nsap 88.88880000000000000000000.000000000000.00
  broadcast
 ipx 200.0000.0000.0009 atm-nsap 99.99990000000000000000000.000000000000.00
  broadcast
!
map-list newNsaps
 ip 144.254.32.1 atm-nsap 11.11111111111111111111111.111111111111.20 broadcast
 ip 144.254.32.2 atm-nsap 11.11111111111111111111111.222222222222.20 broadcast
 ip 144.254.32.3 atm-nsap 11.11111111111111111111111.333333333333.20 broadcast
 ip 144.254.32.4 atm-nsap 22.22222222222222222222222.444444444444.20 broadcast
 ip 144.254.32.5 atm-nsap 22.22222222222222222222222.555555555555.20 broadcast
 ip 144.254.32.6 atm-nsap 22.22222222222222222222222.666666666666.20 broadcast
 ip 144.254.32.7 atm-nsap 33.33333333333333333333333.777777777777.20 broadcast
 ip 144.254.32.8 atm-nsap 33.33333333333333333333333.888888888888.20 broadcast
 ip 144.254.32.9 atm-nsap 33.33333333333333333333333.999999999999.20 broadcast
!
line con 0
 exec-timeout 0 0
line aux 0
line vty 0 4
 exec-timeout 0 0
 password cisco
 login
!
end
```

Example C-129 *Router 8 Configuration for Lab 13-4*

```
!
version 11.2
no service password-encryption
no service udp-small-servers
no service tcp-small-servers
!
hostname R8
!
enable password sanfran
!
no ip domain-lookup
ipx routing 0000.0000.0008
ipx maximum-paths 2
!
!
interface Ethernet0
 ip address 144.254.8.8 255.255.255.0
 ipx network 80
!
interface Ethernet1
 ip address 10.0.0.8 255.0.0.0
 media-type 10BaseT
!
interface ATM0
 no ip address
 atm pvc 5 0 5 qsaal
 atm pvc 16 0 16 ilmi
!
interface ATM0.1 multipoint
 ip address 144.254.100.8 255.255.255.0
 atm pvc 181 0 181 aal5snap
 atm pvc 182 0 182 aal5snap
 atm pvc 183 0 183 aal5snap
 atm pvc 184 0 184 aal5snap
 atm pvc 185 0 185 aal5snap
 atm pvc 186 0 186 aal5snap
 atm pvc 187 0 187 aal5snap
 atm pvc 189 0 189 aal5snap
 map-group ipPvc
 map-group ipxPvc
 ipx network 100
!
interface ATM0.2 multipoint
 ip address 144.254.200.8 255.255.255.0
 atm nsap-address 88.888800000000000000000000.000000000000.00
 map-group ipSvc
 map-group ipxSvc
 ipx network 200
!
interface ATM0.32 multipoint
```

continues

Lab 13-4 Solution

Example C-129 *Router 8 Configuration for Lab 13-4 (Continued)*

```
ip address 144.254.32.8 255.255.255.0
atm esi-address 888888888888.20
map-group newNsaps
!
interface FastEthernet0
 no ip address
 shutdown
!
router igrp 100
 network 144.254.0.0
!
no ip classless
!
map-list ipPvc
 ip 144.254.100.1 atm-vc 181 broadcast
 ip 144.254.100.2 atm-vc 182 broadcast
 ip 144.254.100.3 atm-vc 183 broadcast
 ip 144.254.100.4 atm-vc 184 broadcast
 ip 144.254.100.5 atm-vc 185 broadcast
 ip 144.254.100.6 atm-vc 186 broadcast
 ip 144.254.100.7 atm-vc 187 broadcast
 ip 144.254.100.9 atm-vc 189 broadcast
!
map-list ipxPvc
 ipx 100.0000.0000.0001 atm-vc 181 broadcast
 ipx 100.0000.0000.0002 atm-vc 182 broadcast
 ipx 100.0000.0000.0003 atm-vc 183 broadcast
 ipx 100.0000.0000.0004 atm-vc 184 broadcast
 ipx 100.0000.0000.0005 atm-vc 185 broadcast
 ipx 100.0000.0000.0006 atm-vc 186 broadcast
 ipx 100.0000.0000.0007 atm-vc 187 broadcast
 ipx 100.0000.0000.0009 atm-vc 189 broadcast
!
map-list ipSvc
 ip 144.254.200.1 atm-nsap 11.1111000000000000000000.000000000000.00 broadcast
 ip 144.254.200.2 atm-nsap 22.2222000000000000000000.000000000000.00 broadcast
 ip 144.254.200.3 atm-nsap 33.3333000000000000000000.000000000000.00 broadcast
 ip 144.254.200.4 atm-nsap 44.4444000000000000000000.000000000000.00 broadcast
 ip 144.254.200.5 atm-nsap 55.5555000000000000000000.000000000000.00 broadcast
 ip 144.254.200.6 atm-nsap 66.6666000000000000000000.000000000000.00 broadcast
 ip 144.254.200.7 atm-nsap 77.7777000000000000000000.000000000000.00 broadcast
 ip 144.254.200.8 atm-nsap 88.8888000000000000000000.000000000000.00 broadcast
 ip 144.254.200.9 atm-nsap 99.9999000000000000000000.000000000000.00 broadcast
!
map-list ipxSvc
 ipx 200.0000.0000.0001 atm-nsap 11.1111000000000000000000.000000000000.00
  broadcast
 ipx 200.0000.0000.0002 atm-nsap 22.2222000000000000000000.000000000000.00
  broadcast
 ipx 200.0000.0000.0003 atm-nsap 33.3333000000000000000000.000000000000.00
```

Example C-129 *Router 8 Configuration for Lab 13-4 (Continued)*

```
   broadcast
  ipx 200.0000.0000.0004 atm-nsap 44.4444000000000000000000000.000000000000.00
   broadcast
  ipx 200.0000.0000.0005 atm-nsap 55.5555000000000000000000000.000000000000.00
   broadcast
  ipx 200.0000.0000.0006 atm-nsap 66.6666000000000000000000000.000000000000.00
   broadcast
  ipx 200.0000.0000.0007 atm-nsap 77.7777000000000000000000000.000000000000.00
   broadcast
  ipx 200.0000.0000.0008 atm-nsap 88.8888000000000000000000000.000000000000.00
   broadcast
  ipx 200.0000.0000.0009 atm-nsap 99.9999000000000000000000000.000000000000.00
   broadcast
 !
 map-list newNsaps
  ip 144.254.32.1 atm-nsap 11.1111111111111111111111111.111111111111.20 broadcast
  ip 144.254.32.2 atm-nsap 11.1111111111111111111111111.222222222222.20 broadcast
  ip 144.254.32.3 atm-nsap 11.1111111111111111111111111.333333333333.20 broadcast
  ip 144.254.32.4 atm-nsap 22.2222222222222222222222222.444444444444.20 broadcast
  ip 144.254.32.5 atm-nsap 22.2222222222222222222222222.555555555555.20 broadcast
  ip 144.254.32.6 atm-nsap 22.2222222222222222222222222.666666666666.20 broadcast
  ip 144.254.32.7 atm-nsap 33.3333333333333333333333333.777777777777.20 broadcast
  ip 144.254.32.8 atm-nsap 33.3333333333333333333333333.888888888888.20 broadcast
  ip 144.254.32.9 atm-nsap 33.3333333333333333333333333.999999999999.20 broadcast
 !
 !
 line con 0
  exec-timeout 0 0
 line aux 0
 line vty 0 4
  exec-timeout 0 0
  password cisco
  login
 !
 end
```

Example C-130 *Router 9 Configuration for Lab 13-4*

```
 !
 version 11.2
 no service password-encryption
 no service udp-small-servers
 no service tcp-small-servers
 !
 hostname R9
 !
 enable password sanfran
 !
 no ip domain-lookup
 ipx routing 0000.0000.0009
```

continues

Example C-130 *Router 9 Configuration for Lab 13-4 (Continued)*

```
ipx maximum-paths 2
!
!
interface Ethernet0
 ip address 144.254.9.9 255.255.255.0
 ipx network 90
!
interface Ethernet1
 ip address 10.0.0.9 255.0.0.0
 media-type 10BaseT
!
interface TokenRing0
 no ip address
 shutdown
!
interface ATM0
 no ip address
 atm pvc 5 0 5 qsaal
 atm pvc 16 0 16 ilmi
!
interface ATM0.1 multipoint
 ip address 144.254.100.9 255.255.255.0
 atm pvc 191 0 191 aal5snap
 atm pvc 192 0 192 aal5snap
 atm pvc 193 0 193 aal5snap
 atm pvc 194 0 194 aal5snap
 atm pvc 195 0 195 aal5snap
 atm pvc 196 0 196 aal5snap
 atm pvc 197 0 197 aal5snap
 atm pvc 198 0 198 aal5snap
 map-group ipPvc
 map-group ipxPvc
 ipx network 100
!
interface ATM0.2 multipoint
 ip address 144.254.200.9 255.255.255.0
 atm nsap-address 99.9999000000000000000000000.000000000000.00
 map-group ipSvc
 map-group ipxSvc
 ipx network 200
!
interface ATM0.32 multipoint
 ip address 144.254.32.9 255.255.255.0
 atm esi-address 999999999999.20
 map-group newNsaps
!
router igrp 100
 network 144.254.0.0
!
no ip classless
```

Example C-130 *Router 9 Configuration for Lab 13-4 (Continued)*

```
!
map-list ipPvc
 ip 144.254.100.1 atm-vc 191 broadcast
 ip 144.254.100.2 atm-vc 192 broadcast
 ip 144.254.100.3 atm-vc 193 broadcast
 ip 144.254.100.4 atm-vc 194 broadcast
 ip 144.254.100.5 atm-vc 195 broadcast
 ip 144.254.100.6 atm-vc 196 broadcast
 ip 144.254.100.7 atm-vc 197 broadcast
 ip 144.254.100.8 atm-vc 198 broadcast
!
map-list ipxPvc
 ipx 100.0000.0000.0001 atm-vc 191 broadcast
 ipx 100.0000.0000.0002 atm-vc 192 broadcast
 ipx 100.0000.0000.0003 atm-vc 193 broadcast
 ipx 100.0000.0000.0004 atm-vc 194 broadcast
 ipx 100.0000.0000.0005 atm-vc 195 broadcast
 ipx 100.0000.0000.0006 atm-vc 196 broadcast
 ipx 100.0000.0000.0007 atm-vc 197 broadcast
 ipx 100.0000.0000.0008 atm-vc 198 broadcast
!
map-list ipSvc
 ip 144.254.200.1 atm-nsap 11.11110000000000000000000.000000000000.00 broadcast
 ip 144.254.200.2 atm-nsap 22.22220000000000000000000.000000000000.00 broadcast
 ip 144.254.200.3 atm-nsap 33.33330000000000000000000.000000000000.00 broadcast
 ip 144.254.200.4 atm-nsap 44.44440000000000000000000.000000000000.00 broadcast
 ip 144.254.200.5 atm-nsap 55.55550000000000000000000.000000000000.00 broadcast
 ip 144.254.200.6 atm-nsap 66.66660000000000000000000.000000000000.00 broadcast
 ip 144.254.200.7 atm-nsap 77.77770000000000000000000.000000000000.00 broadcast
 ip 144.254.200.8 atm-nsap 88.88880000000000000000000.000000000000.00 broadcast
 ip 144.254.200.9 atm-nsap 99.99990000000000000000000.000000000000.00 broadcast
!
map-list ipxSvc
 ipx 200.0000.0000.0001 atm-nsap 11.11110000000000000000000.000000000000.00
broadcast
 ipx 200.0000.0000.0002 atm-nsap 22.22220000000000000000000.000000000000.00
broadcast
 ipx 200.0000.0000.0003 atm-nsap 33.33330000000000000000000.000000000000.00
broadcast
 ipx 200.0000.0000.0004 atm-nsap 44.44440000000000000000000.000000000000.00
broadcast
 ipx 200.0000.0000.0005 atm-nsap 55.55550000000000000000000.000000000000.00
broadcast
 ipx 200.0000.0000.0006 atm-nsap 66.66660000000000000000000.000000000000.00
broadcast
 ipx 200.0000.0000.0007 atm-nsap 77.77770000000000000000000.000000000000.00
broadcast
 ipx 200.0000.0000.0008 atm-nsap 88.88880000000000000000000.000000000000.00
broadcast
```

continues

Lab 13-4 Solution

Example C-130 *Router 9 Configuration for Lab 13-4 (Continued)*

```
 ipx 200.0000.0000.0009 atm-nsap 99.99990000000000000000000000.000000000000.00
broadcast
!
map-list newNsaps
 ip 144.254.32.1 atm-nsap 11.11111111111111111111111111.111111111111.20 broadcast
 ip 144.254.32.2 atm-nsap 11.11111111111111111111111111.222222222222.20 broadcast
 ip 144.254.32.3 atm-nsap 11.11111111111111111111111111.333333333333.20 broadcast
 ip 144.254.32.4 atm-nsap 22.22222222222222222222222222.444444444444.20 broadcast
 ip 144.254.32.5 atm-nsap 22.22222222222222222222222222.555555555555.20 broadcast
 ip 144.254.32.6 atm-nsap 22.22222222222222222222222222.666666666666.20 broadcast
 ip 144.254.32.7 atm-nsap 33.33333333333333333333333333.777777777777.20 broadcast
 ip 144.254.32.8 atm-nsap 33.33333333333333333333333333.888888888888.20 broadcast
 ip 144.254.32.9 atm-nsap 33.33333333333333333333333333.999999999999.20 broadcast
!
!
line con 0
 exec-timeout 0 0
line aux 0
line vty 0 4
 exec-timeout 0 0
 password cisco
 login
!
end
```

Example C-131 *Switch 1 Configuration for Lab 13-4*

```
!
version 11.3
no service pad
no service udp-small-servers
no service tcp-small-servers
!
hostname Switch_1
!
enable password sanfran
!
no ip domain-lookup
!
atm address 47.0091.8100.0000.0010.0739.9e01.0010.0739.9e01.00
atm address 11.1111.1111.1111.1111.1111.1111.0010.0739.9e01.00
atm router pnni
 node 1 level 56 lowest
  redistribute atm-static
!
!
interface ATM0/0/0
 no ip address
!
interface ATM0/0/1
```

Example C-131 *Switch 1 Configuration for Lab 13-4 (Continued)*

```
 no ip address
!
interface ATM0/0/2
 no ip address
!
interface ATM0/0/3
 no ip address
!
interface ATM0/1/0
 no ip address
 atm pvc 0 114   interface   ATM0/0/1 0 114
 atm pvc 0 115   interface   ATM0/0/1 0 115
 atm pvc 0 116   interface   ATM0/0/1 0 116
 atm pvc 0 117   interface   ATM0/0/2 0 117
 atm pvc 0 118   interface   ATM0/0/2 0 118
 atm pvc 0 119   interface   ATM0/0/2 0 119
!
interface ATM0/1/1
 no ip address
 atm pvc 0 121   interface   ATM0/1/0 0 112
 atm pvc 0 124   interface   ATM0/0/1 0 124
 atm pvc 0 125   interface   ATM0/0/1 0 125
 atm pvc 0 126   interface   ATM0/0/1 0 126
 atm pvc 0 127   interface   ATM0/0/2 0 127
 atm pvc 0 128   interface   ATM0/0/2 0 128
 atm pvc 0 129   interface   ATM0/0/2 0 129
!
interface ATM0/1/2
 no ip address
 atm pvc 0 120   interface   ATM0/1/0 0 120
 atm pvc 0 131   interface   ATM0/1/0 0 113
 atm pvc 0 132   interface   ATM0/1/1 0 123
 atm pvc 0 134   interface   ATM0/0/1 0 134
 atm pvc 0 135   interface   ATM0/0/1 0 135
 atm pvc 0 136   interface   ATM0/0/1 0 136
 atm pvc 0 137   interface   ATM0/0/2 0 137
 atm pvc 0 138   interface   ATM0/0/2 0 138
 atm pvc 0 139   interface   ATM0/0/2 0 139
!
interface ATM0/1/3
 no ip address
!
interface ATM2/0/0
 no ip address
 atm maxvp-number 0
!
interface Ethernet2/0/0
 ip address 10.0.0.11 255.0.0.0
!
ip classless
```

Lab 13-4 Solution

continues

Example C-131 *Switch 1 Configuration for Lab 13-4 (Continued)*

```
atm route 1... ATM0/1/0
atm route 2... ATM0/1/1
atm route 3... ATM0/1/2
!
line con 0
 exec-timeout 0 0
 password cisco
 logging synchronous
 login
line aux 0
line vty 0 4
 exec-timeout 0 0
 password cisco
 login
!
end
```

Example C-132 *Switch 2 Configuration for Lab 13-4*

```
!
version 11.3
no service pad
no service udp-small-servers
no service tcp-small-servers
!
hostname Switch_2
!
enable password sanfran
!
no ip domain-lookup
!
atm address 47.0091.8100.0000.0010.0739.a101.0010.0739.a101.00
atm address 22.2222.2222.2222.2222.2222.2222.0010.0739.a101.00
atm router pnni
 node 1 level 56 lowest
  redistribute atm-static
!
!
interface ATM0/0/0
 no ip address
!
interface ATM0/0/1
 no ip address
!
interface ATM0/0/2
 no ip address
!
interface ATM0/0/3
 no ip address
!
```

Example C-132 *Switch 2 Configuration for Lab 13-4 (Continued)*

```
interface ATM0/1/0
 no ip address
 atm pvc 0 141   interface   ATM0/0/1 0 114
 atm pvc 0 142   interface   ATM0/0/1 0 124
 atm pvc 0 143   interface   ATM0/0/1 0 134
 atm pvc 0 147   interface   ATM0/0/3 0 147
 atm pvc 0 148   interface   ATM0/0/3 0 148
 atm pvc 0 149   interface   ATM0/0/3 0 149
!
interface ATM0/1/1
 no ip address
 atm pvc 0 151   interface   ATM0/0/1 0 115
 atm pvc 0 152   interface   ATM0/0/1 0 125
 atm pvc 0 153   interface   ATM0/0/1 0 135
 atm pvc 0 154   interface   ATM0/1/0 0 145
 atm pvc 0 157   interface   ATM0/0/3 0 157
 atm pvc 0 158   interface   ATM0/0/3 0 158
 atm pvc 0 159   interface   ATM0/0/3 0 159
!
interface ATM0/1/2
 no ip address
 atm pvc 0 161   interface   ATM0/0/1 0 116
 atm pvc 0 162   interface   ATM0/0/1 0 126
 atm pvc 0 163   interface   ATM0/0/1 0 136
 atm pvc 0 164   interface   ATM0/1/0 0 146
 atm pvc 0 165   interface   ATM0/1/1 0 156
 atm pvc 0 167   interface   ATM0/0/3 0 167
 atm pvc 0 168   interface   ATM0/0/3 0 168
 atm pvc 0 169   interface   ATM0/0/3 0 169
!
interface ATM0/1/3
 no ip address
!
interface ATM2/0/0
 no ip address
 atm maxvp-number 0
!
interface Ethernet2/0/0
 ip address 10.0.0.12 255.0.0.0
!
ip classless
atm route 5... ATM0/1/1
atm route 6... ATM0/1/2
atm route 4... ATM0/1/0
!
line con 0
 exec-timeout 0 0
 password cisco
 logging synchronous
 login
```

continues

Example C-132   *Switch 2 Configuration for Lab 13-4 (Continued)*

```
line aux 0
line vty 0 4
 exec-timeout 0 0
 password cisco
 login
!
end
```

Example C-133   *Switch 3 Configuration for Lab 13-4*

```
!
version 11.3
no service pad
no service udp-small-servers
no service tcp-small-servers
!
hostname Switch_3
!
boot system flash bootflash:ls1010-wp-mz.113-0.8.TWA4.2.bin
enable password sanfran
!
no ip domain-lookup
!
atm address 47.0091.8100.0000.0010.0739.c301.0010.0739.c301.00
atm address 33.3333.3333.3333.3333.3333.3333.0010.0739.c301.00
atm router pnni
 node 1 level 56 lowest
   redistribute atm-static
!
!
interface ATM0/0/0
 no ip address
!
interface ATM0/0/1
 no ip address
!
interface ATM0/0/2
 no ip address
!
interface ATM0/0/3
 no ip address
!
interface ATM0/1/0
 no ip address
 atm pvc 0 171  interface  ATM0/0/2 0 117
 atm pvc 0 172  interface  ATM0/0/2 0 127
 atm pvc 0 173  interface  ATM0/0/2 0 137
 atm pvc 0 174  interface  ATM0/0/3 0 147
 atm pvc 0 175  interface  ATM0/0/3 0 157
 atm pvc 0 176  interface  ATM0/0/3 0 167
```

Example C-133   *Switch 3 Configuration for Lab 13-4 (Continued)*

```
!
interface ATM0/1/1
 no ip address
 atm pvc 0 181   interface   ATM0/0/2 0 118
 atm pvc 0 182   interface   ATM0/0/2 0 128
 atm pvc 0 183   interface   ATM0/0/2 0 138
 atm pvc 0 184   interface   ATM0/0/3 0 148
 atm pvc 0 185   interface   ATM0/0/3 0 158
 atm pvc 0 186   interface   ATM0/0/3 0 168
 atm pvc 0 187   interface   ATM0/1/0 0 178
!
interface ATM0/1/2
 no ip address
 atm pvc 0 191   interface   ATM0/0/2 0 119
 atm pvc 0 192   interface   ATM0/0/2 0 129
 atm pvc 0 193   interface   ATM0/0/2 0 139
 atm pvc 0 194   interface   ATM0/0/3 0 149
 atm pvc 0 195   interface   ATM0/0/3 0 159
 atm pvc 0 196   interface   ATM0/0/3 0 169
 atm pvc 0 197   interface   ATM0/1/0 0 179
 atm pvc 0 198   interface   ATM0/1/1 0 189
!
interface ATM0/1/3
 no ip address
!
interface ATM1/0/0
 no ip address
!
interface ATM1/0/1
 no ip address
!
interface ATM1/0/2
 no ip address
!
interface ATM1/0/3
 no ip address
!
interface ATM2/0/0
 no ip address
 atm maxvp-number 0
!
interface Ethernet2/0/0
 ip address 10.0.0.13 255.0.0.0
!
ip classless
atm route 7... ATM0/1/0
atm route 8... ATM0/1/1
atm route 9... ATM0/1/2
!
line con 0
```

continues

Lab 13-4 Solution

Example C-133 *Switch 3 Configuration for Lab 13-4 (Continued)*

```
 exec-timeout 0 0
 password cisco
 logging synchronous
 login
line aux 0
line vty 0 4
 exec-timeout 0 0
 password cisco
 login
!
end
```

Solutions for Lab 13-5: Configuring Soft PVCs on LS1010

Examples C-134 through C-136 provide the configuration solutions that satisfy all the exercises for Lab 13-5. Specifically, the exercises ask for the following:

1 Restore router configurations to the PVC lab solution using ATM 0.1 subinterface. Ensure that subinterface ATM 0.2 is shut down. Restore the ATM switch configurations, if required, to ensure that the PVC mapping support is still provided. Verify from the routers' viewpoint that full Layer 3 connectivity is present for IP and IPX.

2 Ensure that the ATM interswitch links are configured currently for PNNI.

3 On ATM switch S1, eliminate the PVC mappings that support connectivity between R1 and R4, R1 and R5, and R1 and R6 only—three PVC mappings need to be eliminated on S1. Verify from the routers' Layer 3 perspective that connectivity is no longer working between these routers.

4 Introduce a Soft PVC on the S1 switch to reestablish connectivity between R1 and R4. First, on S2, you need to identify the appropriate Soft VC address that pertains to R4's ATM switch port.

S2 Soft VC address: 47.0091.8100.0000.0010.0739.a101.4000.0c80.1000.00

Make use of this Soft VC address to set up Soft PVC on S1 with the following command:

atm soft-vc *vpi vci* **dest-address** *soft-vc nsap address vpi vci*

Make use of the **show atm vc conn-type soft-vc** command to verify the status of the VC. Make the necessary changes on S2 to eliminate the local PVC mapping that supports the R1 to R4 connectivity. Make the necessary configuration changes on S1's ATM interface 0/1/0 to ensure that the Soft VC works properly. Use the **show atm vc conn-type soft-vc** switch command.

5 Verify from S1 and S2's perspective that the Soft PVC is operational. From R1 and R4's Layer 3 perspective, verify that IP connectivity is reestablished and the IGRP routing strategy is working as expected.

6 Introduce a Soft PVC on the S1 switch to reestablish connectivity between R1 and R5. First, on S2, you need to identify the appropriate Soft VC address that pertains to R5's ATM switch port:

S2 Soft VC address: 47.0091.8100.0000.0010.0739.a101.4000.0c80.1010.00

Make use of this Soft VC address to set up the Soft PVC on S1 with the following command:

```
atm soft-vc vpi vci dest-address soft-vc nsap address vpi vci
```

Make the necessary changes on S1 to eliminate the local PVC mapping that supports the R1 to R5 connectivity. Make use of the **show atm vc conn-type soft-vc** command to verify the status of VC. Make any necessary configuration changes on S1's ATM interface 0/1/0 to ensure the Soft VC works properly.

7 Verify from S1 and S2's perspective that the Soft PVC is operational. From R1 and R5's Layer 3 perspective, verify that IP connectivity is reestablished and the IGRP routing strategy is working as expected.

8 Introduce a Soft PVC on the S1 switch to reestablish connectivity between R1 and R6. First, on S2, you need to identify the appropriate Soft VC address that pertains to R6's ATM switch port.

S2 Soft VC address: 47.0091.8100.0000.0010.0739.a101.4000.0c80.1020.00

Make use of this Soft VC address to set up the Soft PVC on S1 with the following command:

```
atm soft-vc vpi vci dest-address soft-vc nsap address vpi vci
```

Make use of the **show atm vc conn-type soft-vc** command to verify the status of the VC. Make the necessary changes on S2 to eliminate the local PVC mapping that supports the R1 to R6 connectivity. Make the necessary configuration changes on S1's ATM interface 0/1/0 to ensure the Soft VC works properly. Use the **show atm vc conn-type soft-vc** switch command.

9 Verify from S1 and S2's perspective that the two Soft PVCs are operational now. From R1 and R6's Layer 3 perspective, verify that IP connectivity is reestablished and the IGRP routing strategy is working as expected.

10 Verify from S1 and S2's perspective that the three Soft PVCs are now operational and that full IP connectivity has been reestablished between the routers. Verify that all is okay from IGRP's viewpoint.

11 Verify that the three Soft PVCs introduced are using interswitch link(s) between S1 and S2. Disable physical connectivity between S1 and S2 to verify that the Soft PVC automatically re-routes around the failure and sets up again via ATM switch S3.

Lab 13-5 Solution

12 Notice the impact to the Soft PVCs when physical connectivity is reestablished between S1 and S2.

Example C-134 *Switch 1 Configuration for Lab 13-5*

```
!
version 11.3
no service pad
no service udp-small-servers
no service tcp-small-servers
!
hostname Switch_1
!
enable password sanfran
!
no ip domain-lookup
!
atm address 47.0091.8100.0000.0010.0739.9e01.0010.0739.9e01.00
atm router pnni
 node 1 level 56 lowest
  redistribute atm-static
!
!
interface ATM0/0/0
 no ip address
!
interface ATM0/0/1
 no ip address
!
interface ATM0/0/2
 no ip address
!
interface ATM0/0/3
 no ip address
!
interface ATM0/1/0
 no ip address
 atm pvc 0 117  interface  ATM0/0/2 0 117
 atm pvc 0 118  interface  ATM0/0/2 0 118
 atm pvc 0 119  interface  ATM0/0/2 0 119
 atm soft-vc 0 114 dest-address 47.0091.8100.0000.0010.0739.a101.4000.0c80.1000.
  00  0 141 slow 60 rx-cttr 1 tx-cttr 1
 atm soft-vc 0 115 dest-address 47.0091.8100.0000.0010.0739.a101.4000.0c80.1010.
  00  0 151 slow 60 rx-cttr 1 tx-cttr 1
 atm soft-vc 0 116 dest-address 47.0091.8100.0000.0010.0739.a101.4000.0c80.1020.
  00  0 161 slow 60 rx-cttr 1 tx-cttr 1
!
interface ATM0/1/1
 no ip address
 atm pvc 0 121  interface  ATM0/1/0 0 112
 atm pvc 0 124  interface  ATM0/0/1 0 124
 atm pvc 0 125  interface  ATM0/0/1 0 125
```

Example C-134   *Switch 1 Configuration for Lab 13-5 (Continued)*

```
atm pvc 0 126   interface  ATM0/0/1 0 126
atm pvc 0 127   interface  ATM0/0/2 0 127
atm pvc 0 128   interface  ATM0/0/2 0 128
atm pvc 0 129   interface  ATM0/0/2 0 129
!
interface ATM0/1/2
 no ip address
 atm pvc 0 131   interface  ATM0/1/0 0 113
 atm pvc 0 132   interface  ATM0/1/1 0 123
 atm pvc 0 134   interface  ATM0/0/1 0 134
 atm pvc 0 135   interface  ATM0/0/1 0 135
 atm pvc 0 136   interface  ATM0/0/1 0 136
 atm pvc 0 137   interface  ATM0/0/2 0 137
 atm pvc 0 138   interface  ATM0/0/2 0 138
 atm pvc 0 139   interface  ATM0/0/2 0 139
!
interface ATM0/1/3
 no ip address
!
interface ATM2/0/0
 no ip address
 atm maxvp-number 0
!
interface Ethernet2/0/0
 ip address 10.0.0.11 255.0.0.0
!
ip classless
atm route 1... ATM0/1/0
atm route 2... ATM0/1/1
atm route 3... ATM0/1/2
!
line con 0
 exec-timeout 0 0
 password cisco
 login
line aux 0
line vty 0 4
 exec-timeout 0 0
 password cisco
 login
!
end
```

Example C-135   *Switch 2 Configuration for Lab 13-5*

```
!
version 11.3
no service pad
no service udp-small-servers
no service tcp-small-servers
```

continues

Lab 13-5 Solution

Example C-135 *Switch 2 Configuration for Lab 13-5 (Continued)*

```
!
hostname Switch_2
!
enable password sanfran
!
no ip domain-lookup
!
atm address 47.0091.8100.0000.0010.0739.a101.0010.0739.a101.00
atm router pnni
 node 1 level 56 lowest
  redistribute atm-static
 !
 !
interface ATM0/0/0
 no ip address
 !
interface ATM0/0/1
 no ip address
 !
interface ATM0/0/2
 no ip address
 !
interface ATM0/0/3
 no ip address
 !
interface ATM0/1/0
 no ip address
 atm pvc 0 142   interface   ATM0/0/1 0 124
 atm pvc 0 143   interface   ATM0/0/1 0 134
 atm pvc 0 147   interface   ATM0/0/3 0 147
 atm pvc 0 148   interface   ATM0/0/3 0 148
 atm pvc 0 149   interface   ATM0/0/3 0 149
 !
interface ATM0/1/1
 no ip address
 atm pvc 0 152   interface   ATM0/0/1 0 125
 atm pvc 0 153   interface   ATM0/0/1 0 135
 atm pvc 0 154   interface   ATM0/1/0 0 145
 atm pvc 0 157   interface   ATM0/0/3 0 157
 atm pvc 0 158   interface   ATM0/0/3 0 158
 atm pvc 0 159   interface   ATM0/0/3 0 159
 !
interface ATM0/1/2
 no ip address
 atm pvc 0 162   interface   ATM0/0/1 0 126
 atm pvc 0 163   interface   ATM0/0/1 0 136
 atm pvc 0 164   interface   ATM0/1/0 0 146
 atm pvc 0 165   interface   ATM0/1/1 0 156
 atm pvc 0 167   interface   ATM0/0/3 0 167
 atm pvc 0 168   interface   ATM0/0/3 0 168
```

Example C-135 *Switch 2 Configuration for Lab 13-5 (Continued)*

```
 atm pvc 0 169  interface  ATM0/0/3 0 169
!
interface ATM0/1/3
 no ip address
!
interface ATM2/0/0
 no ip address
 atm maxvp-number 0
!
interface Ethernet2/0/0
 ip address 10.0.0.12 255.0.0.0
!
ip classless
atm route 5... ATM0/1/1
atm route 6... ATM0/1/2
atm route 4... ATM0/1/0
!
line con 0
 exec-timeout 0 0
 password cisco
 login
line aux 0
line vty 0 4
 exec-timeout 0 0
 password cisco
 login
!
end
```

Example C-136 *Switch 3 Configuration for Lab 13-5*

```
!
version 11.3
no service pad
no service udp-small-servers
no service tcp-small-servers
!
hostname Switch_3
!
boot system flash bootflash:ls1010-wp-mz.113-0.8.TWA4.2.bin
enable password sanfran
!
no ip domain-lookup
!
atm address 47.0091.8100.0000.0010.0739.c301.0010.0739.c301.00
atm router pnni
 node 1 level 56 lowest
   redistribute atm-static
!
!
```

Lab 13-5 Solution

Example C-136 *Switch 3 Configuration for Lab 13-5 (Continued)*

```
interface ATM0/0/0
 no ip address
!
interface ATM0/0/1
 no ip address
!
interface ATM0/0/2
 no ip address
!
interface ATM0/0/3
 no ip address
!
interface ATM0/1/0
 no ip address
 atm pvc 0 171  interface  ATM0/0/2 0 117
 atm pvc 0 172  interface  ATM0/0/2 0 127
 atm pvc 0 173  interface  ATM0/0/2 0 137
 atm pvc 0 174  interface  ATM0/0/3 0 147
 atm pvc 0 175  interface  ATM0/0/3 0 157
 atm pvc 0 176  interface  ATM0/0/3 0 167
!
interface ATM0/1/1
 no ip address
 atm pvc 0 181  interface  ATM0/0/2 0 118
 atm pvc 0 182  interface  ATM0/0/2 0 128
 atm pvc 0 183  interface  ATM0/0/2 0 138
 atm pvc 0 184  interface  ATM0/0/3 0 148
 atm pvc 0 185  interface  ATM0/0/3 0 158
 atm pvc 0 186  interface  ATM0/0/3 0 168
 atm pvc 0 187  interface  ATM0/1/0 0 178
!
interface ATM0/1/2
 no ip address
 atm pvc 0 191  interface  ATM0/0/2 0 119
 atm pvc 0 192  interface  ATM0/0/2 0 129
 atm pvc 0 193  interface  ATM0/0/2 0 139
 atm pvc 0 194  interface  ATM0/0/3 0 149
 atm pvc 0 195  interface  ATM0/0/3 0 159
 atm pvc 0 196  interface  ATM0/0/3 0 169
 atm pvc 0 197  interface  ATM0/1/0 0 179
 atm pvc 0 198  interface  ATM0/1/1 0 189
!
interface ATM0/1/3
 no ip address
!
interface ATM1/0/0
 no ip address
!
interface ATM1/0/1
 no ip address
```

Example C-136 *Switch 3 Configuration for Lab 13-5 (Continued)*

```
!
interface ATM1/0/2
 no ip address
!
interface ATM1/0/3
 no ip address
!
interface ATM2/0/0
 no ip address
 atm maxvp-number 0
!
interface Ethernet2/0/0
 ip address 10.0.0.13 255.0.0.0
!
ip classless
atm route 7... ATM0/1/0
atm route 8... ATM0/1/1
atm route 9... ATM0/1/2
!
line con 0
 exec-timeout 0 0
 password cisco
 login
line aux 0
line vty 0 4
 exec-timeout 0 0
 password cisco
 login
!
end
```

Answers to Review Questions

Answers to Chapter 1 Review Questions

1 What is ATM?

Answer: ATM (Asynchronous Transfer Mode) is a high-bandwidth, low-delay, connection-oriented cell switching and multiplexing technology that uses fixed-size cells.

2 Why would you choose ATM?

Answer: A primary reason for establishing ATM networks is the requirement to handle multimedia applications that include voice, video, and/or data. ATM provides QoS based on different types of traffic. Another reason is the flexibility of the virtual networks—ATM is based on the virtual circuit (VC) concept, be it permanent or switched.

3 What is POS?

Answer: Packet over Sonet (POS) provides PPP encapsulation of Layer 3 packets over SONET frames.

4 Are there advantages to using POS or Gigabit Ethernet versus ATM?

Answer: The answer to this question is…it depends. If you carry only data, POS or Gigabit Ethernet is the solution. Be aware that Gigabit Ethernet has limitations. ATM provides much higher speeds than Gigabit Ethernet. If you need to carry voice and video applications as well, ATM is the way to go. After all, you still end up with similar overhead in POS when voice is put on top of IP.

5 How can you categorize various ATM switches?

Answer: You can categorize ATM switches into workgroup, campus, and enterprise/multiservice. The differences are based largely on the scalability of the equipment.

6 What is DWDM?

Answer: Dense Wavelength Division Multiplexing (DWDM) allows multiple wavelengths or colors to be multiplexed onto the same strand of fiber. This results in much higher bandwidth availability.

7 What standards bodies are responsible for ATM standardization?

Answer: Two major organizations are responsible: the ITU-T and the ATM Forum. The ITU-T and the ATM Forum are both international standards. The ATM Forum's responsibility is to speed up the process of standardization.

Answers to Chapter 2 Review Questions

1   What are the sublayers of the Physical Layer of ATM?

Answer: The ATM physical layer is divided into two sublayers: Transmission Convergence (TC) and Physical Media Dependent (PMD).

2   What is cell delineation?

Answer: The purpose behind cell delineation is to maintain cell boundaries. A switch counts the first seven cells and ignores them.

3   What is rate decoupling?

Answer: Because ATM is asynchronous, and physical media are synchronous, ATM must inject empty cells into the stream, should there be no traffic. This process is called rate decoupling.

4   What is the difference between SONET and STS?

Answer: SONET refers to the synchronous optical signal hierarchy, whereas STS refers to the synchronous electrical signal hierarchy in North America.

5   At what layer is the HEC performed?

Answer: HEC is performed at the top sublayer of the Physical Layer—Transmission Convergence.

6   What is the purpose of the ATM Layer?

Answer: The ATM Layer is responsible for cell switching and multiplexing through the ATM network. The ATM Layer is the highest layer within the ATM cloud that the switches deploy when switching payload traffic.

7   What is the purpose of PTI and CLP bits?

Answer: The CLP bit denotes the priority of a cell—high or low. The PTI field consists of three bits. The first bit specifies whether the cell is the management cell or regular data; the second bit specifies whether there is congestion in the network; the third bit specifies whether this is the last cell of a frame/packet.

8   How many bits are used for VPI and VCI at UNI and NNI?

Answer: At the UNI level, VPI uses 8 bits. At the NNI level, VPI uses 12 bits. VCI uses 16 bits in both UNI and NNI cases.

9   How many sublayers does AAL consist of, and what are they?

Answer: AAL consists of two sublayers—the Convergence Sublayer (CS) and the Segmentation and Reassembly Sublayer (SAR).

10 What is the purpose of AAL2?

Answer: AAL2 handles compressed voice up to 5.3 kbps, silence detection/suppression/removal, CCS, and echo cancellation, thus providing bandwidth efficiency. AAL2 also provides the functionality of packaging small packets into one or more ATM cells. This results in much higher bandwidth utilization.

11 Which AAL is more bandwidth-efficient, AAL3/4 or AAL5? Why?

Answer: AAL5 utilizes bandwidth much more efficiently than AAL3/4, because it uses all 48 bytes for the payload. AAL3/4 uses the 4 bits from the payload portion, leaving only 44 bytes for the payload.

12 What is the purpose of the PAD field?

Answer: The PAD field adds extra bytes as necessary to the frame/packet so that the frame/packet can be divided into whole 48 bytes, not fractions.

13 How can you categorize various types of traffic?

Answer: Types of traffic can be categorized as follows:

— *CBR* is used by connections that require a constant amount of bandwidth that is continuously available during the connection.

— *rt-VBR* is intended for real-time applications, requiring tight constraints with cell delay and delay variation. Sources of this service category transmit at a rate that varies in time.

— *nrt-VBR* is used by non–real-time applications with bursty behavior.

— *UBR* is intended for non–real-time applications, meaning that cell delay is not an issue. UBR service does not provide any guarantees.

— *ABR* is not intended to support real-time applications. The ABR service allows end-systems to adapt their traffic in accordance with the feedback that they receive from the network. Therefore, the number of lost cells should be minimal.

Answers to Chapter 3 Review Questions

1 What steps are involved in ATM call setup?

Answer: ATM is a connection-oriented protocol. It consists of three steps: setup, talk, and tear-down. During the call setup phase (in the SVC's case), a signaling frame "drills a hole through the ATM network," establishing the call dynamically with the specified QoS parameters.

2 What types of virtual connections does ATM have? What are the differences between them?

Answer: The types of connections are PVC, SVC, and Soft PVC. A PVC is permanently set up by the network administrator, whereas an SVC is established dynamically. A Soft PVC is interconnected through an SVC ATM network, using PVCs to access the network.

3 How do you set up an SVC connection?

Answer: Using the signaling protocol, which is Q.2931. The edge devices must have a PVC defined for the signaling protocol to use, the VCI of which equals 5.

4 What form of addressing is used by a PVC? By an SVC?

Answer: PVCs use locally significant addresses, expressed by the pair VPI/VCI. SVCs use globally significant addresses to set up the VC dynamically. After the completion of the setup, the SVCs are using VPI/VCI.

5 What forms of ATM global addresses exist? What are the differences?

Answer: There are two forms of ATM addresses: E.164 and NSAP. E.164 is used for public domains; whereas, NSAP addressing is used for private ATM networks.

6 How long is an NSAP prefix?

Answer: It is 13 bytes long.

7 What is ANS?

Answer: ANS is ATM Name System, which provides a function similar to DNS (Domain Name System) in TCP/IP networks.

8 What is ILMI?

Answer: Integrated Local Management Interface, one of the functions of which is to enable automatic ATM address registration.

9 What is SAAL? What does it consist of?

Answer: Signaling uses the services of the Signaling AAL (SAAL). SAAL uses AAL5, which consists of Common Part Convergence Sublayer (CPCS) and Service-Specific Convergence Sublayer (SSCS).

10 What is Q.2931?

Answer: Q.2931 is the ATM signaling protocol. It is an application of ATM.

11 What types of connections does ATM support?

Answer: ATM supports point-to-point, point-to-multipoint, and anycast connections. Point-to-point connections are bidirectional, whereas point-to-multipoint and anycast are unidirectional.

12 What is ATM anycast?

Answer: The ATM anycast capability is available only with UNI 4.0. It allows a user to request a point-to-point connection to a single ATM end system that is part of an ATM group.

13 What is FUNI?

Answer: Frame Relay UNI (FUNI) offers the benefit of a new encapsulation method with the capability to support ATM signaling, QoS, and ATM management.

14 What is the difference between FRF.5 and FRF.8?

Answer: The FRF.8 specification is responsible for converting—call it translating—between Frame Relay and ATM. The FRF.5 specification performs transparent tunneling of Frame Relay user traffic and PVCs over ATM.

15 What is SMDS? How do you interwork ATM with SMDS?

Answer: Switched Multimegabit Data Service (SMDS) has been defined as a three-level stack with a level 3 PDU that contains the variable-length packet, and E.164 source and destination addressing. It is based on a 53-byte cell. These cells have a different format from an ATM cell. AAL 3/4 and a Connectionless Server Function (CLSF) handle the SMDS- to-ATM interworking.

16 What is CES?

Answer: The Circuit Emulation Service (CES) allows traffic from legacy systems not supporting ATM, such as PBXs, to be transported over an ATM infrastructure.

17 What is CAS?

Answer: Channel Associated Signaling (CAS) is a dynamic method of detecting "on/off" hook situations. This allows for dynamic bandwidth allocation for non-real-time traffic in the "on-hook" case.

18 What is RFC 2684?

Answer: RFC 2684 is an encapsulation method for Layer 3 and Layer 2 protocols over ATM. RFC 2684 provides provisions for VPNs and security.

19 What is the difference between mux and LLC encapsulation?

Answer: LLC encapsulation allows multiple protocols to be carried over a single VC, whereas mux encapsulation allows for a single protocol per VC.

20 What is LANE?

Answer: LAN Emulation (LANE) extends a Layer 2 broadcast domain over ATM.

21 What are the advantages of RFC 2225?

Answer: RFC 2225—Classical IP—allows dynamic address resolution to take place. The resolution is between ATM and IP addresses.

22 What is the disadvantage of using RFC 2225 in multi-LIS networks?

Answer: RFC 2225 does not specify cut-through routing, which has been rectified by NHRP.

23 What is MPOA, and how does it compare with MPLS?

Answer: MPOA is based on LANE version 2 and NHRP. It relies on the dynamics of LANE with provisions for QoS and dynamic VC setup, based on required QoS, using PNNI. The whole process of MPOA is handled at the ATM layer.

MPLS uses Layer 3 protocols and Layer 3 routing protocols to allocate labels that reflect the required QoS. MPLS does not require LANE or PNNI. When positioned over ATM, the dynamically generated labels translate into an ATM VPI/VCI.

Answers to Chapter 4 Review Questions

1 What is the role of traffic management? How can you subdivide the ATM traffic management responsibilities?

Answer: The role of traffic management is to protect the network and end systems from congestion. The ATM traffic management responsibilities can be subdivided into connection establishment and data flow processes.

2 When is the traffic contract specified? What does it consist of?

Answer: The traffic contract is specified at the time of a connection establishment. It consists of traffic parameters and QoS. Various classes of service have different requirements regarding the traffic parameters and QoS.

3 What is ATM QoS?

Answer: ATM QoS consists of two values: cell loss ratio and cell transfer delay.

4 What is CAC? Do switches have to have compatible CAC algorithms?

Answer: The ATM Forum does not specify the Connection Admission Control (CAC) algorithm. The main purpose of the CAC algorithm is to check the memory, the bandwidth allocation, and so on—the resources within a switch itself. Hence, the CAC of one switch does not have to be compatible with the CAC of another switch. The generic CAC (GCAC) performs the correspondence between the switches concerning the successful versus unsuccessful outcome of CAC.

5 What kind of information is sent within a UNI signal's information element field?

Answer: The information element field of the UNI signal carries the destination and the source NSAP addresses, the QoS parameters, the AAL type, and the source route information (if PNNI1 is used).

6 What type of connections can be established in ATM, and what are their directions?

Answer: Point-to-point and point-to-multipoint connections can be established. Point-to-point is bidirectional, and point-to-multipoint is unidirectional.

7 What are the ATM routing protocols used for? Name them.

Answer: ATM routing protocols are used for routing the signaling request when the SVC is established. There are two types: IISP and PNNI.

8 What type of protocol is IISP? What are its advantages and disadvantages?

Answer: IISP is a static routing protocol. Its only advantage is that it is simple. Disadvantages include that it is labor-intensive and not loop-free.

9 What are the responsibilities of traffic control function during data flow traffic management?

Answer: Traffic control functions include traffic shaping and traffic policing. Traffic shaping smoothes out the rough edges and burstiness. Traffic policing is a method of marking non-conforming cells with low priority by setting CLP=1.

10 What is the main problem with congested ATM networks?

Answer: Network congestion is a very devastating experience for ATM, because it is a recursive problem. A loss of one cell could imply a resend of hundreds of other cells.

11 What techniques are used to reduce ATM traffic when congestion occurs?

Answer: The techniques include Early Packet Discard and Tail Packet Discard.

12 How does an ATM node "know" that there is congestion?

Answer: By the EFCI or RRM method. The RRM method is much more effective because the edge devices are notified faster.

13 What is PNNI?

Answer: The formula for the characteristics of the Private Network-to-Network Interface (PNNI) is as follows: link-state routing + allows partitioned areas + source routing + 104 layers of hierarchy + QoS routing + autosummarization and flexible summarization + multiple routing metrics and attributes.

14 What is a PNNI node?

Answer: A PNNI node can be physical or logical. A group of switches forms a logical PNNI node.

15 What is a peer group?

Answer: A peer group is a collection of switches within the same hierarchical level.

16 What is PTSE?

Answer: PNNI Topology State Elements (PTSE) are link updates from all the nodes within a PNNI network that form a topological database, which must be identical in all the nodes.

17 How many layers of hierarchy does PNNI have?

Answer: PNNI has 104 layers of hierarchy.

18 How does a switch establish the SVC connection using PNNI?

Answer: PNNI signaling is used with the mechanisms of source routing and crankback. At the ingress switch, the signaling packet obtains the source route of the entire path. Then, following the source route and deploying the Designated Transit Lists (DTLs) data structure, the signaling starts drilling through the cloud. When the source route information and the network availability are inconsistent, the crankback mechanism allows the signal to come back to the border node, where a new source route is provided.

19   What is the difference between F4 and F5 OAM cells?

Answer: F4 monitors the VPC, whereas F5 monitors the VCC.

Answers to Chapter 5 Review Questions

1   What is an ELAN? How does it compare to a VLAN?

Answer: An ELAN is Emulated LAN. It is similar logically to a VLAN. Like a VLAN, it extends a single broadcast domain over longer distances. The difference between a VLAN and an ELAN is that the VLAN extends the broadcast domain over native Ethernet or Token Ring switches, whereas ELAN extends the broadcast domain over ATM, thus requiring some sort of adaptation between the Ethernet/Token Ring protocols and the ATM protocols.

2   What processing architecture does a LANE implementation use?

Answer: LANE uses a client/server architecture.

3   What is the purpose of the LECS, LES, BUS, SMS, and LEC?

Answer: The LECS is like directory assistance for LANE. It provides the addresses of LESs to an LEC for the broadcast domain to which the LEC belongs.

The LES is the server that helps a client resolve MAC-to-ATM addresses. The LES also provides the address of a BUS, which must reside within the same platform as the LES.

The BUS is a server that sends broadcast frames to all the registered clients, the SMS, and the other BUSs. It also handles the very first frame of a unicast message.

The SMS is a multicast server that handles Layer 2 multicast frames.

The LEC is a LANE client. Legacy workstations, which do not know anything about ATM, connect to an LEC.

4   How can you divide various LANE VCs?

Answer: LANE v2 VCs are divided into Control, Synchronization, and Data VCs. LANE v1 VCs are divided into Control and Data VCs only, because LANE v1 does not allow redundancy.

5   What VCs are generated in LANE?

Answer:

- Control VCs:
    —Configuration Direct
    —Control Coordinate

—Control Direct

—Control Distribute

- Synchronization VCs:

    — LECS Synchronization

    — Cache Synchronization

- Data VCs:

    — Multicast Forward

    — Default Multicast Send

    — Selective Multicast Send

    — Data Direct

6 What are the differences between LANE v1 and LANE v2?

Answer:

——LANE v2 has redundancy in services, whereas LANE v1 does not.

——LANE v2 handles multicasts, whereas LANE v1 cannot distinguish between multicasts and broadcasts.

——LANE v2 can use LLC/SNAP encapsulation, thus saving on the number of VCs; whereas, LANE v1 uses mux encapsulation.

——LANE v2 can handle QoS and ABR traffic, but LANE v1 cannot.

7 What is the Cache Synchronization VC used for?

Answer: The Cache Synchronization VC is used to synchronize the databases between the LESs and LESs/SMSs. This VC enables the dynamic updating of databases between redundant servers.

8 How does LANE ensure that the cells are received in order at the destination?

Answer: When the Data Direct VC is set, a source LEC uses the Flush protocol. The source LEC sends out the last message to the destination LEC via the old path. The Flush protocol frames are marked so that the destination LEC understands it. When the destination LEC receives the Flush Request message, it must reply to the source LEC. The source LEC can start using the Data Direct VC to the destination client only after it receives the Flush Response message.

9 How many BUSs and LESs can your LANE have?

Answer: It depends. LANE v1 allows only a single LES/BUS per broadcast domain or ELAN. LANE v2 allows for redundancy, meaning you can have any number of LESs/BUSs.

10 How many LECSs does your LANE have?

Answer: It depends. LANE v1 allows only a single LECS per ATM domain, whereas LANE v2 allows you to have as many as you want.

Answers to Chapter 6 Review Questions

1 What is MPOA?

Answer: Multiprotocol over ATM (MPOA) is a dynamic method of interconnecting various hosts across an ATM domain through the deployment of cut-through routing and QoS.

2 How do LANE and MPOA compare?

Answer: There is only one commonality between LANE and MPOA—dynamic establishment of VCs. LANE is a Layer 2 method of interconnection, while MPOA is a Layer 3 technology. Hence, MAC addressing is a point of reference in LANE, whereas Layer 3 logical addressing is a point of reference in MPOA. Also, MPOA is based on LANE v2.

3 What is MPOA based on?

Answer: MPOA is based on the following three main blocks: LANE v2, NHRP, and MARS.

4 What is MARS?

Answer: MARS (Multicast Address Resolution Server) enables Layer 3 multicast communication across an ATM network.

5 What does MPOA architecture consist of, and what are the functions of its components?

Answer: MPOA architecture consists of MPOA Clients (MPCs) and MPOA Servers (MPSs). The MPC must have a knowledge of internetwork shortcuts. The MPS provides Layer 3 forwarding information to MPCs.

6 Name and describe the MPOA connection types.

Answer: The MPOA VCs are divided into Control and Data VCs. The Control VCs include MPC-MPS, MPC-MPC, MPS-MPS, and Configuration VCs to the LECS. The Data VCs include MPC-MPC and MPC-NHS.

7 What happens when an MPC receives a packet with no TTL (for IP) or maximum TC value (for IPX)?

Answer: The MPC must discard the packet and send an ICMP message.

8 What types of interVLAN data transfer flows does MPOA have? Which one is the most scalable?

Answer: MPOA has two types of interVLAN transfer flows—the default type and the shortcut flow. The shortcut flow scales much better because it involves less processing and fewer hops.

9 How does intraVLAN data transfer flow over MPOA occur?

Answer: IntraVLAN data transfer flow over MPOA uses LANE VCs.

Answers to Chapter 7 Review Questions

1 What is an ATM "native" interface?

Answer: An ATM "native" interface performs encapsulation segmentation/reassembly of frames into cells, without the help of any external devices.

2 What types of interfaces do 7000 series routers support? What are the differences between them?

Answer: 7000 series support AIP, ATM PA-A1, and ATM PA-A3 type interface cards. AIP is the first-generation ATM card. Its advantage, when compared to PA-A3, is that it supports AAL3/4. When compared to PA-A1, it has more advantages, including support of traffic shaping and DS3/ E3 connections.

3 What types of connections do the Cisco 4000 and 7000 series routers support?

Answer: They support PVC-based and SVC-based connections. The supported internetworking protocols include RFC 2684, RFC 2225, and LANE.

4 What are all the encapsulations that ATM edge routers (4000 and 7000 series) support?

Answer: The supported encapsulations are aal5snap, aal5mux, aal5nplid, aal34smds, qsaal, and ilmi.

5 What is traffic shaping?

Answer: Traffic shaping smoothes down the traffic that needs to be sent through the ATM network to reduce the chances of ATM network congestion.

6 Why is traffic shaping recommended?

Answer: Traffic shaping is a means to avoid the occurrence of congestion on the network. When traffic is smoothed out, it is much easier to predict the required bandwidth in the core.

7 What technique does the 7000 series router use to shape traffic?

Answer: Depending on the ATM card being used, the technique varies. The AIP card uses eight rate queues and the Leaky Bucket algorithm, whereas the ATM PA-A3 uses a wheel-based calendar scheduling algorithm.

8 What PCR values should be assigned to VCs?

Answer: The sum of all PCR values for all the VCs should not exceed the total bandwidth of the ATM connection.

Answers to Chapter 8 Review Questions

1 What is the main disadvantage of having separate networks for voice and data?

Answer: You can think of many disadvantages: cost of staff, different equipment, and various network management tools. However, it all boils down to one thing—cost. The bottom line drives it all!

2 What is the advantage of CES?

Answer: CES enables PBXs to connect to ATM networks natively using DS-1/E1 circuits, which reduces the cost of such equipment as DSUs and MUXs.

3 What four key functions does a CES module provide?

Answer: CES-IWF, unstructured DS-1/E1, structured DS-1/E1, and CAS.

4 How does structured DS-1/E1 differ from unstructured DS-1/E1?

Answer: Structured DS-1/E1, also called channelized DS-1, allows the mapping of one or multiple DS0 channels across the ATM network, whereas the unstructured DS-1/E1, also called clear channel, allows the entire DS-1/E1 to be emulated across the ATM network.

5 What is CAS?

Answer: Channel-Associated Signaling (CAS) is an in-band signaling function that enables the efficient and dynamic use of bandwidth. It allows CES to detect on-hook situations, which results in allocating CBR bandwidth to the ABR/UBR traffic.

6 Why is CAS called *robbed bit signaling*?

Answer: CAS is called *robbed bit signaling* only in DS-1 framing. The reason why is that CAS uses 8 kbps out of each 64-kbps channel to carry signaling information, leaving 56 kbps for the voice channel. E1 CAS uses two whole time slots—slot 1 for framing information and slot 16 for signaling for all the other time slots.

7 What clocking modes does CES use?

Answer: CES uses one of the following clocking modes: synchronous, SRTS, or adaptive.

8 What is the limitation of the SRTS clocking mode?

Answer: The SRTS clocking mode supports only unstructured CBR traffic.

Answers to Chapter 9 Review Questions

1 What steps are necessary to implement RFC 2684 using PVCs?

Answer:

Step 1 Create a PVC. Assign an identifier and a VPI/VCI to PVC.

Step 2 Define the encapsulation technique. Will this VC carry a single protocol or multiple protocols? Is this an ILMI VC, and so on.

Step 3 Optionally, identify the rate queue(s).

Step 4 Map the protocol address to a VC identifier that represents this VC.

2 What is VCD? Is it locally significant?

Answer: Virtual circuit descriptor (VCD) is used to define a PVC using a single-number identifier. It is locally significant only and must be unique within a router.

3 What does "aal5mux" stand for?

Answer: "aal5mux" specifies the encapsulation type of ATM adaptation layer 5, with a single VC per protocol for a specific PVC.

4 How do you configure RFC 2225 using PVCs?

Answer: The configuration is very similar to RFC 2684 with the following exceptions: Put **inarp** at the end of the **pvc** command and omit the **map-group** statement.

5 How does the RFC 2684 implementation vary for SVCs when compared to its use with a PVC?

Answer: The only difference is the reference to addressing. In the PVC case, the reference is to the VPI/VCI numbers (using VCDs). In the SVC case, the reference is to the NSAP addresses, which are globally significant.

6 What does RFC 2225 SVC implementation use as a model?

Answer: RFC 2225 SVC implementation uses a client/server architecture as its model. You must define an ATMARP server, which keeps a reference table of IP and ATM addresses.

7 What is the major difference between RFC 2225 and RFC 1577?

Answer: The prime difference between RFC 2225 and RFC 1577 is the fact that RFC 2225 allows for ATMARP server redundancy.

8 What types of NHRP implementations do Cisco routers support?

Answer: Cisco routers support NHRP in fabric mode or server mode. The fabric mode results in every router running NHRP, whereas the server mode calls for the existence of an NHS.

9 What should you be careful of when implementing NHRP?

Answer: The prime caution is the compatibility of NHRP versions. IOS Release 12.0 and prior releases support different, incompatible versions of NHRP. Another caution applies to the memory and CPU utilization.

Answers to Chapter 10 Review Questions

1 What are the differences between LANE, ELAN, and VLAN?

Answer: A single ELAN is a single broadcast domain over ATM. It is the same as a VLAN, except that it is implemented over ATM instead of over a real LAN. LANE is the supporting architecture for ELANs.

2 What are the main design considerations that you should be aware of when planning for LANE?

Answer: Things to watch for are the capacity of the edge device and the ATM switch, and selecting the right platform for the performing servers' functionality and redundancy.

3 What are the advantages and disadvantages of PVC-based LANE?

Answer: The disadvantages are that PVC-based LANE requires very heavy administration, is fixed in its configuration, and does not provide any VC redundancy. The only thing that potentially could be called an advantage is that the VCs are all predefined; thus, no time is required for their setup.

4 Which LANE server is most heavily utilized? Why?

Answer: The most heavily utilized server is the BUS, which is in charge of handling all broadcast, multicast, and unknown-destination-type traffic.

5 How is Spanning Tree convergence improved over LANE?

Answer: To speed up the Spanning Tree convergence over LANE, two types of messages—LE-Topology-Request and LE-NARP—are used. Clients send LE-Topology-Request and LE-NARP messages to the LES when they detect a network topology change. When the LES distributes this request to all other clients, the clients update their ARP caches.

6 How does a LANE client learn the address of the LECS in LANE v1?

Answer: There are three methods of obtaining an LECS address:

— Using ILMI and obtaining the LECS address from the ingress ATM switch

— Using a well-known NSAP address, reserved for LECS

— Using the well-known PVC (0,17) to locate the LECS address

7 What is SSRP?

Answer: SSRP (Simple Server Redundancy Protocol) is Cisco's method to overcome the limitations of LANE v1. It provides LECS, LES, and BUS redundancy.

8 How does SSRP determine which LECS is the primary one?

Answer: To determine the primary LECS, SSRP uses the rank number that is assigned by the ATM switches when LECS addresses are programmed in. The lower the number, the higher the rank. The highest-ranking LECS does not have any other LECS connecting to it from above.

9 What is the difference between SSRP and FSSRP?

Answer: FSSRP ensures that all LANE clients have VCs pre-established to all servers, up to a maximum of four at any given time. This guarantees that an instantaneous switch to a backup server will occur if the primary server fails.

10 What are the important rules for proper SSRP operation?

Answer: Each LECS must maintain the same database of ELANs. Each ATM switch must have an identical LECS address table, defined in the same order.

11 How can you obtain the LANE component NSAP addresses?

Answer: Each Cisco device has a predefined set of ESI numbers for all LANE components if the device is to be one of them. Each edge device obtains the prefix from the ingress ATM switch, using ILMI to complete the full 40 hex NSAP address.

12 What is the value of the Selector byte in the LANE NSAP address?

Answer: If it is the LECS NSAP address, the Selector byte value is 0x00. If the NSAP address represents an LES, BUS, or LEC, its Selector byte value must be equal to the subinterface number, expressed in hex.

13 What is the main difference between configuring LECS and other LANE components?

Answer: The main difference is that you configure LECS only on the major interface, whereas you can configure the other components at the subinterface level.

Answers to Chapter 11 Review Questions

1 What is MPOA?

Answer: MPOA is a method of handling Layer 3 protocols over ATM, where multihop routing is replaced by a direct connection between the ingress and egress edge devices across an ATM network, bypassing multiple LIS domains.

2 What are the advantages of MPOA?

Answer: MPOA results in increased performance and lower latencies of communications between the edge devices due to "shortcut" VCs.

3 What is the implementation of MPOA based on?

Answer: MPOA is based on LANE v2 and NHRP.

4 What are the components of the MPOA architecture, and what are their functions?

Answer: MPOA consists of two components: MPS and MPC. MPC establishes a shortcut between two MPCs with the help of the NHRP-based MPS. Also, MPCs initiate the call to an MPS. The MPS fulfills its duty of resolving the address of the egress MPC with help from NHRP.

5 What is the relationship between MPOA and the LANE components?

Answer: An MPC or an MPS can function as an LEC and can serve one or more LECs. Also, an LEC can be associated with any MPS/MPC function in the router and can be attached to both an MPC and an MPS simultaneously.

6   What are the MPC's functions?

Answer: MPC functions include ingress/egress cache management, MPOA frame processing, MPOA flow detection, shortcut VC establishment and management, and LEC connectivity to Layer 3.

7   What are the MPS's functions?

Answer: MPS supplies forwarding information to MPCs. MPS uses NHRP to support query and response functions issued by MPC. MPS uses MPOA frames that are identical to NHRP frames with a few modifications.

8   What are the general steps involved in configuring an MPC and an MPS?

Answer:

> **Step 1**   Define the ELAN ID.
>
> **Step 2**   Define a name for the MPC/MPS.
>
> **Step 3**   Attach the MPC/MPS to an interface.
>
> **Step 4**   Assign an ATM address to the MPC/MPS.
>
> **Step 5**   Bind the MPC/MPS to multiple LANE clients.
>
> **Step 6**   Define MPC/MPS variables.

9   What could be one of the possible reasons for MPOA failure?

Answer: One of the reasons that MPOA might fail would be the configuration of different ELAN IDs for the associated LECs and MPCs. LECs and MPCs must have the same ELAN IDs.

Answers to Chapter 12 Review Questions

1   What is the application of the LS1010?

Answer: The LS1010 is a campus switch designed to provide the high-speed campus backbone interconnecting your voice, data, and video traffic using ATM technology.

2   What kind of switching architecture does the LS1010 use?

Answer: The LS1010 uses shared memory architecture.

3   What two types of switching architectures exist, and what are the differences?

Answer: There are two types of switching architectures: shared memory and shared medium. A shared memory switch is totally nonblocking and achieves the optimal delay-throughput performance for unicast or point-to-point traffic. The shared medium fabric is based on a time-division multiplexing (TDM) bus or ring. The shared memory switch, when compared to the shared medium switch, has the advantages of more efficient hardware utilization and higher buffering efficiency that reduces the total buffer and memory requirements.

4 What is the difference between "hot-swappable" and "OIR"? Which one applies to LS1010 components?

Answer: Hot-swappable means that you can remove ports and parts with total transparency—users do not have any downtime. OIR means that you can move ports around without powering down a device. LS1010 power supplies are hot-swappable; the rest of the components are OIR.

5 What kinds of ports are available on an LS1010 switch?

Answer: The ports that are available on LS1010 switches are physical and logical. Physical ports include the actual physical interfaces, whereas the logical ports include tunnels and CPU port.

6 How would you refer to the interface associated with the CAM located in the second slot, the first PAM, and the third port in the PAM?

Answer: ATM 1/0/2.

7 When you see traffic terminating in port 2/0/0, what does it mean?

Answer: The only traffic terminating in port 2/0/0, which is the CPU port, is the type that is destined for the switch itself. For example, ILMI, signaling, and OAM terminate in port 2/0/0.

8 How does the LS1010 handle multicast and broadcast traffic?

Answer: The LS1010 stores only a single copy of a multicast cell in the common cell memory. This results in buffer requirement reduction for multicast traffic. Also, the LS1010 uses a specialized Fast Multicast Engine (FME), which replicates only pointers to the buffer location for each leaf of the point-to-multipoint connection.

9 What clocking sources does the LS1010 use when connecting via the T1/E1 CES interface?

Answer: The LS1010 T1/E1 CES PAM supports four modes of clocking: adaptive clocking, SRTS clocking, synchronous timing, and global network clock synchronization.

10 What connection types does the LS1010 support?

Answer: The LS1010 supports PVC, SVC, Soft PVC, and PVP.

11 What are the LS1010 responsibilities during the connection setup phase?

Answer: During the connection setup phase, the LS1010 tries to prevent congestion. The switch must guarantee what it is asked to reserve, if it can. If the connection is impossible to establish, the ingress LS1010 must reject the connection request. The steps involved in the connection setup are negotiating traffic contract, using traffic parameters and QoS, executing CAC, and doing PNNI QoS routing.

12 What is the difference between CAC and GCAC?

Answer: CAC is an internal LS1010 algorithm that is proprietary. The GCAC algorithm tries to predict a typical node's CAC algorithm results. You can use it to determine whether a potential route has sufficient resources to support a connection.

13 How does PNNI contribute to QoS?

Answer: PNNI performs QoS routing. In fact, "hop"-wise, the path might not be optimal at all. The prime concern of PNNI is to provide the requested QoS—hence, QoS routing.

14 What is the purpose of UPC?

Answer: ATM Forum traffic policing is called Usage Parameter Control (UPC). UPC is a set of actions taken by an LS1010 to monitor and control traffic at the UNI. UPC is applied at the edges of the ATM network, strictly at the UNI side, be it private or public. The objective of the UPC is to protect the network from the misbehavior of another network user.

15 How does the LS1010 react to the full buffer condition?

Answer: When the LS1010 experiences the full buffer condition, it evokes EPD. The only cells that are not dropped during that period are the last cells of the packets.

16 How does the LS1010 react when it sees low-priority cells?

Answer: It depends. If it receives the congestion notification, the LS1010 switch drops low-priority cells and evokes ITPD. If no congestion exists, the switch passes all the cells through. The last cells of the packets are always sent.

17 What kind of management capabilities does the LS1010 provide?

Answer: The LS1010 supports full autoconfiguration with the help of the ILMI, PNNI, and BOOTP functions. The configurations can be obtained dynamically. The ATM addresses are configured dynamically. PNNI is configured dynamically and sets up the SVCs.

Answers to Chapter 13 Review Questions

1 What type of UNIs does the LightStream 1010 support?

Answer: LightStream 1010s support UNIs 3.0, 3.1, and 4.0.

2 What are the VPI/VCI space management rules?

Answer:

— VCIs ranging from 0 to 31 (inclusive) are reserved by the ITU-T and the ATM Forum, so you cannot assign those values.

— For logical ports, the VPI for all VCs must equal the VPI of the tunneling VP.

— For the CPU port, the VPI must be 0.

— For PVCs, it is highly recommended that you use high VCI numbers.

— For SVCs, the LS1010 chooses the first available VCI when the LS1010 is not on the network side of the UNI; the LS1010 is on the network side of the IISP; the LS1010 is NNI and has the higher node ID.

3 What are the restrictions of the CPU port?

Answer: UNI/NNI/IISP cannot be configured on the CPU port. The virtual path cannot be configured on the CPU port. The VP tunnel cannot be configured on the CPU port. The CPU port cannot be shut down. The CPU port cannot be deleted.

4 What types of VCs does the LS1010 support?

Answer: The LS1010 supports PVC, PVP, Soft VC, PVP Tunneling, and SVC.

5 What must you do prior to using the **rx-cttr** or **tx-cttr** options in the **pvc** command?

Answer: You must configure the CTT row with the value(s) specified in the **rx-cttr** or **tx-cttr** parameters.

6 Can you configure virtual paths within a VP tunnel? Within virtual channels?

Answer: Virtual paths cannot be configured within a tunnel; however, virtual channels can.

7 Can you delete all logical ports on the LS1010?

Answer: All logical ports, with the exception of the CPU port, can be deleted.

8 When configuring a Soft VC, how many switches have to be involved in the configuration?

Answer: Only one, because the VC is bidirectional.

9 What configuration steps are required to configure PNNI without hierarchy?

Answer: None.

10 What is the meaning of PNNI address scope?

Answer: PNNI address scope allows the constraint of advertised reachability information within configurable bounds. The higher the value of the scope, the larger the network reachability.

11 What are the rules of PGL election?

Answer: A node with the highest election leadership priority is elected PGL. If two nodes share the same election priority, the node with the higher node identifier becomes the PGL. To kill the chances of a node becoming a PGL, its priority must be set to 0.

12 In what cases does it make sense to deploy the background routes mode?

Answer: The background routes mode should be enabled in large networks where better scalability is required.

13 What role does precedence play in the PNNI algorithm?

Answer: Precedence is used as one of the PNNI attributes. When multiple longest match reachable address prefixes are known to the switch, the route selection algorithm first attempts to find routes to reachable addresses with the greatest precedence values. Next, among multiple longest match reachable address prefixes of the same precedence value, routes with the least total AW are chosen first.

14 Why is configuring the significant change threshold an important feature to have for PNNI?

Answer: The significant change threshold is a very important feature of PNNI because it allows it to scale better. It provides flexibility for defining which changes for which parameters are significant enough to issue PTSEs and flood the network.

GLOSSARY

A

AAL. ATM adaptation layer: The standards layer that allows multiple applications to have data converted to and from the ATM cell. A protocol used to translate higher-layer services into the size and the format of an ATM cell.

AAL Connection. An association established by the AAL between two or more next higher layer entities.

AAL1. ATM adaptation layer Type 1: AAL functions in support of constant bit rate, time-dependent traffic, such as voice and video.

AAL2. ATM adaptation layer Type 2: The International Standards bodies have not defined this AAL although the ATM Forum has. It is a placeholder for variable bit rate video transmission and compressed voice.

AAL3/4. ATM adaptation layer Type 3/4: AAL functions in support of variable bit rate, delay-tolerant data traffic requiring some sequencing, and/or error detection support. Originally, there were two AAL types, that is, connection-oriented and connectionless, which have been combined.

AAL5. ATM adaptation layer Type 5: AAL functions in support of variable bit rate, delay-tolerant connection-oriented data traffic requiring minimal sequencing or error detection support.

ABR. Available bit rate: ABR is an ATM layer service category for which the limiting ATM layer transfer characteristics provided by the network might change subsequent to connection establishment. A flow control mechanism is specified that supports several types of feedback to control the source rate in response to changing ATM layer transfer characteristics. It is expected that an end-system that adapts its traffic in accordance with the feedback will experience a low cell loss ratio and will obtain a fair share of the available bandwidth according to a network specific allocation policy. Cell delay variation is not controlled in this service, although admitted cells are not delayed unnecessarily.

ACR. Attenuation to Crosstalk Ratio: One of the factors that limits the distance a signal can be sent through a given media. ACR is the ratio of the power of the received signal, attenuated by the media, over the power of the NEXT crosstalk from the local transmitter, usually expressed in decibels (db). To achieve a desired bit error rate, the received signal power usually must be several times larger than the NEXT power or plus several db. Increasing a marginal ACR can decrease the bit error rate.

ACR. Available cell rate: An ABR service parameter, ACR is the current rate in cells/sec at which a source is allowed to send.

Address Prefix. A string of 0 or more bits up to a maximum of 152 bits that is the lead portion of one or more ATM addresses.

Address Resolution. Address resolution is the procedure by which a client associates a LAN destination with the ATM address of another client or the BUS.

Adjacency. The relationship between two communicating neighboring peer nodes.

Administrative Domain. A collection of managed entities grouped for administrative reasons.

ADPCM. Adaptive differential pulse code modulation: A reduced bit rate variant of PCM audio encoding (see also PCM). This algorithm encodes the difference between an actual audio sample amplitude and a predicted amplitude and adapts the resolution based on recent differential values.

ADTF. ACR Decrease Time Factor: This is the time permitted between sending RM-cells before the rate is decreased to Initial Cell Rate (ICR). The ADTF range is .01 to 10.23 sec. with granularity of 10 ms.

AFI. Authority and Format Identifier: This identifier is part of the network-level address header.

Aggregation Token. A number assigned to an outside link by the border nodes at the ends of the outside link. The same number is associated with all uplinks and induced uplinks associated with the outside link. In the parent and all higher-level peer groups, all uplinks with the same aggregation token are aggregated.

AHFG. ATM-attached Host Functional Group: The group of functions performed by an ATM-attached host that is participating in the MPOA service.

Ai. Signaling ID assigned by Exchange A.

AIMUX. ATM Inverse Multiplexing: A device that allows multiple T1 or E1 communications facilities to be combined into a single broadband facility for the transmission of ATM cells.

AIR. Additive Increase Rate: An ABR service parameter, AIR controls the rate at which the cell transmission rate increases. It is signaled as AIRF, where AIRF = AIR×Nrm÷PCR.

AIRF. Additive Increase Rate Factor: Refer to AIR.

AIS. Alarm Indication Signal: An all-ones signal sent down stream or upstream by a device when it detects an error condition, receives an error condition, or receives an error notification from another unit in the transmission path.

Alternate Routing. A mechanism that supports the use of a new path after an attempt to set up a connection along a previously selected path fails.

AMI. Alternate Mark Inversion: A line coding format used on T1 facilities that transmits ones by alternate positive and negative pulses.

Ancestor Node. A logical group node that has a direct parent relationship to a given node (that is, it is the parent of that node, or the parent's parent, and so on).

ANI. Automatic Number Identification: A charge number parameter that normally is included in the Initial Address Message to the succeeding carrier for billing purposes.

ANM. Answer Message: A BISUP call control message from the receiving exchange to the sending exchange indicating an answer and that a through connection should be completed in both directions.

ANSI. American National Standards Institute: A U.S. standards body.

API. Application Program Interface: API is a programmatic interface used for interprogram communications or for interfacing between protocol layers.

API_connection. Native ATM Application Program Interface Connection: API_connection is a relationship between an API_endpoint and other ATM devices.

ARE. All Routes Explorer: A specific frame initiated by a source that is sent on all possible routes in Source Route Bridging.

ARP. Address Resolution Protocol: The procedures and messages in a communications protocol that determine which physical network address (MAC) corresponds to the IP address in the packet.

ASP. Abstract Service Primitive: An implementation-independent description of an interaction between a service-user and a service-provider at a particular service boundary, as defined by the Open Systems Interconnection (OSI).

Assigned Cell. A cell that provides a service to an upper layer entity or an ATM Layer Management entity (ATMM-entity).

Asynchronous Time Division Multiplexing. A multiplexing technique in which a transmission capability is organized in *a priori* unassigned time slots. The time slots are assigned to cells upon request of each application's instantaneous real need.

ATM. Asynchronous Transfer Mode: A transfer mode in which the information is organized into cells. It is asynchronous in the sense that the recurrence of cells containing information from an individual user is not necessarily periodic.

ATM Address. Defined in the UNI Specification as three formats, each being 20 bytes in length, including country, area, and end-system identifiers.

ATM Anycast Capability. The capability to allow an application to request a point-to-point connection to a single ATM end-system that is part of an ATM group.

ATM Layer Link. A section of an ATM Layer connection between two adjacent active ATM Layer entities (ATM-entities).

ATM Link. A virtual path link (VPL) or a virtual channel link (VCL).

ATM Peer-to-Peer Connection. A virtual channel connection (VCC) or a virtual path connection (VPC).

ATM Traffic Descriptor. A generic list of traffic parameters that can be used to capture the intrinsic traffic characteristics of a requested ATM connection.

ATM User-User Connection. An association established by the ATM Layer to support communication between two or more ATM service users (that is, between two or more next higher entities or between two or more ATM-entities). The communications over an ATM Layer connection can be either bidirectional or unidirectional. The same Virtual Channel Identifier (VCI) is issued for both directions of a connection at an interface.

Attenuation. The process of the reduction of the power of a signal as it passes through most media. Usually proportional to distance, attenuation is sometimes the factor that limits the distance a signal can be transmitted through a media before it can no longer be received.

B

B-ICI. B-ISDN Inter Carrier Interface: An ATM Forum–defined specification for the interface between public ATM networks to support user services across multiple public carriers.

B-ICI SAAL. B-ICI Signaling ATM Adaptation Layer: A signaling layer that permits the transfer of connection control signaling and ensures reliable delivery of the protocol message. The SAAL is divided into a service-specific part and a common part (AAL5).

B-ISDN. Broadband Integrated Services Digital Network: A high-speed network standard (more than 1.544 Mbps) that evolved from Narrowband ISDN with existing and new services with voice, data, and video in the same network.

B-LLI. Broadband low-layer information: This is a Q.2931 information element that identifies a Layer 2 and a Layer 3 protocol used by the application.

B-TE. Broadband Terminal Equipment: An equipment category for B-ISDN that includes terminal adapters and terminals.

BBC. Broadband Bearer Capability: A bearer class field that is part of the initial address message.

BCD. Binary Coded Decimal: A form of coding of each octet within a cell where each bit has one of two allowable states, 1 or 0.

BCOB. Broadband Connection-Oriented Bearer: Information in the SETUP message that indicates the type of service requested by the calling user.

BCOB-A. Bearer Class A: Indicated by the ATM end user in the SETUP message for connection-oriented, constant bit rate service. The network can perform internetworking based on the AAL information element (IE).

BCOB-C. Bearer Class C: Indicated by the ATM end user in the SETUP message for connection-oriented, variable bit rate service. The network can perform internetworking based on the AAL information element (IE).

BCOB-X. Bearer Class X: Indicated by the ATM end user in the SETUP message for ATM transport service where AAL, traffic type, and timing requirements are transparent to the network.

BECN. Backward Explicit Congestion Notification: A Resource Management (RM) cell type generated by the network or the destination, indicating congestion or approaching congestion for traffic flowing in the direction opposite that of the BECN cell.

BER. Bit Error Rate: A measure of transmission quality. It is generally shown as a negative exponent, (for example, 10-7, which means 1 out of 107 bits are in error or 1 out of 10,000,000 bits are in error).

BHLI. Broadband high-layer information: This is a Q.2931 information element that identifies an application (or the session layer protocol of an application).

Bi. Signaling ID assigned by Exchange B.

BIP. Bit Interleaved Parity: A method used at the PHY layer to monitor the error performance of the link. A check bit or word is sent in the link overhead covering the previous block or frame. Bit errors in the payload are detected and reported as maintenance information.

BIS. Border Intermediate System.

BISUP. Broadband ISDN User's Part: A SS7 protocol that defines the signaling messages to control connections and services.

BN. Bridge Number: A locally administered bridge ID used in Source Route Bridging to uniquely identify a route between two LANs.

BN. BECN cell: A Resource Management (RM) cell type indicator. The network or the destination can generate a Backward Explicit Congestion Notification (BECN) RM-cell. To do so, BN=1 is set to indicate the cell is not source-generated, and DIR=1 to indicate the backward flow. Source generated RM-cells are initialized with BN=0.

BOM. Beginning of Message: An indicator contained in the first cell of an ATM segmented packet.

Border Node. A logical node that is in a specified peer group, and has at least one link that crosses the peer group boundary.

BPDU. Bridge Protocol Data Unit: A message type used by bridges to exchange management and control information.

BPP. Bridge Port Pair (Source Routing Descriptor): Frame header information identifying a bridge/LAN pair of a source route segment.

Broadband. A service or system requiring transmission channels capable of supporting rates greater than the Integrated Services Digital Network (ISDN) primary rate.

Broadband Access. An ISDN access capable of supporting one or more broadband services.

Broadcast. Data transmission to all addresses or functions.

BT. Burst tolerance: BT applies to ATM connections supporting VBR services and is the limit parameter of the GCRA.

Btag. Beginning Tag: A one-octet field of the CPCS_PDU used in conjunction with the Etag octet to form an association between the beginning of the message and the end of the message.

BUS. Broadcast and Unknown Server: This server handles data sent by an LE Client to the broadcast MAC address ('FFFFFFFFFFFF'), all multicast traffic, and the initial unicast frames that are sent by a LAN Emulation Client.

BW. Bandwidth: A numerical measurement of throughput of a system or network.

Bypass. A bypass represents the connectivity between two ports in the complex node representation. A bypass is always an exception.

C

CAC. Connection Admission Control: Connection Admission Control is defined as the set of actions taken by the network during the call setup phase (or during the call re-negotiation phase) to determine whether a connection request can be accepted or should be rejected (or whether a request for re-allocation can be accommodated).

Call. A call is an association between two or more users or between a user and a network entity that is established by the use of network capabilities. This association can have zero or more connections.

CAS. Channel Associated Signaling: A form of circuit state signaling in which the circuit state is indicated by one or more bits of signaling status sent repetitively and associated with that specific circuit.

CBDS. Connectionless Broadband Data Service: A connectionless service similar to Bellcore's SMDS that is defined by the European Telecommunications Standards Institute (ETSI).

CBR. Constant Bit Rate: An ATM service category that supports a constant or guaranteed rate to transport services, such as video or voice, as well as circuit emulation, which requires rigorous timing control and performance parameters.

CCR. Current Cell Rate: The CCR is an RM-cell field set by the source to its current ACR when it generates a forward RM-cell. This field can be used to facilitate the calculation of ER, and cannot be changed by network elements. CCR is formatted as a rate.

CCS. Common Channel Signaling: A form signaling which group of circuits share a signaling channel. See also SS7.

CD-ROM. Compact Disk-Read Only Memory: Used by a computer to store large amounts of data. Commonly used for interactive video games.

CDF. Cutoff Decrease Factor: CDF controls the decrease in ACR (Allowed Cell Rate) associated with CRM.

CDV. Cell Delay Variation: CDV is a component of cell transfer delay, induced by buffering and cell scheduling. Peak-to-peak CDV is a QoS delay parameter associated with CBR and VBR services. The peak-to-peak CDV is the (1-a) quantile of the CTD minus the fixed CTD that could be experienced by any delivered cell on a connection during the entire connection holding time. The parameter "a" is the probability of a cell arriving late. See also CDVT.

CDVT. Cell Delay Variation Tolerance: ATM layer functions can alter the traffic characteristics of ATM connections by introducing cell delay variation. When cells from two or more ATM connections are multiplexed, cells of a given ATM connection can be delayed while cells of another ATM connection are inserted at the output of the multiplexer. Similarly, some cells can be delayed while physical layer overhead or OAM cells are inserted. Consequently, some randomness might affect the inter-arrival time between consecutive cells of a connection as monitored at the UNI. The upper bound on the "clumping" measure is the CDVT.

CE. Connection Endpoint: A terminator at one end of a layer connection within a SAP.

CEI. Connection Endpoint Identifier: The identifier of a CE that can be used to identify the connection at an SAP.

Cell. A unit of transmission in ATM. A fixed-size frame consisting of a 5-octet header and a 48-octet payload.

Cell Header. ATM Layer protocol control information.

Cells in Frames. Cells in Frames is a protocol established by the CIF Alliance that specifies how to transport ATM protocol over Ethernet, Token Ring, and other frame protocols. CIF uses software at the workstation instead of a new hardware Network Interface Card to do QOS scheduling and ABR flow control.

CER. Cell Error Ratio: The ratio of errored cells in a transmission in relation to the total cells sent in a transmission. The measurement is taken over a time interval and is desirable to be measured on an in-service circuit.

CES. Circuit Emulation Service: The ATM Forum circuit emulation service interoperability specification specifies interoperability agreements for supporting constant bit rate (CBR) traffic over ATM networks that comply with the other ATM Forum interoperability agreements. Specifically, this specification supports the emulation of existing TDM circuits over ATM networks.

Child Node. A node at the next lower level of the hierarchy that is contained in the peer group represented by the logical group node currently referenced. This could be a logical group node or a physical node.

Child Peer Group. A child peer group of a peer group is any one containing a child node of a logical group node in that peer group. A child peer group of a logical group node is the one containing the child node of that logical group node.

CI. Congestion Indicator: This is a field in a RM-cell, and is used to cause the source to decrease its ACR. The source sets CI=0 when it sends an RM-cell. Setting CI=1 is typically how destinations indicate that EFCI has been received on a previous data cell.

CIP. Carrier Identification Parameter: A 3- or 4-digit code in the initial address message identifying the carrier to be used for the connection.

CIR. Committed Information Rate: CIR is the information transfer rate that a network offering Frame Relay Services (FRSs) is committed to transfer under normal conditions. The rate is averaged over a minimum increment of time.

CL. Connectionless Service: A service that allows the transfer of information among service subscribers without the need for end-to-end establishment procedures.

CLP. Cell Loss Priority: This bit in the ATM cell header indicates two levels of priority for ATM cells. CLP=0 cells are higher priority than CLP=1 cells. CLP=1 cells can be discarded during periods of congestion to preserve the CLR of CLP=0 cells.

CLR. Cell Loss Ratio: CLR is a negotiated QoS parameter and acceptable values are network specific. The objective is to minimize CLR provided the end-system adapts the traffic to the changing ATM layer transfer characteristics. The CLR is defined for a connection as: Lost Cells/Total Transmitted Cells. The CLR parameter is the value of CLR that the network agrees to offer as an objective over the lifetime of the connection. It is expressed as an order of magnitude, having a range of 10-1 to 10-15 and unspecified.

CMIP. Common Management Interface Protocol: An ITU-TSS standard for the message formats and procedures used to exchange management information to operate, administer, maintain, and provision a network.

CMR. Cell Misinsertion Rate: The ratio of cells received at an endpoint that were not transmitted originally by the source end in relation to the total number of cells properly transmitted.

CNR. Complex Node Representation: A collection of nodal state parameters that provide detailed state information associated with a logical node.

COD. Connection Oriented Data: Data requiring the sequential delivery of its component PDUs to ensure correct functioning of its supported application (for example, voice or video).

COM. Continuation of Message: An indicator used by the ATM Adaptation Layer to indicate that a particular ATM cell is a continuation of a higher layer information packet that has been segmented.

Common Peer Group. The lowest level peer group in which a set of nodes is represented. A node is represented in a peer group either directly or through one of its ancestors.

Communication Endpoint. An object associated with a set of attributes that are specified at the communication creation time.

Complex Node Represenation. See CNR.

Configuration. The phase in which the LE client discovers the LE service.

Connection. 1. An ATM connection consists of concatenation of ATM Layer links to provide an end-to-end information transfer capability to access points.

2. In switched virtual connection (SVC) environments, the LAN Emulation Management entities set up connections between each other using UNI signaling.

Connection-Oriented. A type of communication in which a connection must be established between senders and receivers before data transmission can occur.

Connection Scope. The level of routing hierarchy within which a given connection request to a group address is constrained.

Connectionless. Refers to the capability of existing LANs to send data without previously establishing connections.

Control Connections. A Control VCC links the LEC to the LECS. Control VCCs also link the LEC to the LES and carry LE_ARP traffic and control frames. The Control VCCs never carry data frames.

Corresponding Entities. Peer entities with a lower layer connection among them.

CPCS. Common Part Convergence Sublayer: The portion of the convergence sublayer of an AAL that remains the same regardless of the traffic type.

CPCS-SDU. Common Part Convergence Sublayer-Service Data Unit: The protocol data unit to be delivered to the receiving AAL layer by the destination CP convergence sublayer.

CPE. Customer Premises Equipment: The end user equipment that resides on the customer's premise that cannot be owned by the local exchange carrier.

CPN. Calling Party Number: A parameter of the initial address message that identifies the calling number and is sent to the destination carrier.

Crankback. A mechanism for partially releasing a connection setup in progress that has encountered a failure. This mechanism allows PNNI to perform alternate routing.

CRC. Cyclic Redundancy Check: A mathematical algorithm that computes a numerical value based on the bits in a block of data. This number is transmitted with the data and the receiver uses this information and the same algorithm to ensure the accurate delivery of data by comparing the results of the algorithm and the number received. If a mismatch occurs, an error in transmission is presumed.

CRF. Cell Relay Function: This is the basic function that an ATM network performs to provide a cell relay service to ATM end-stations.

CRF. Connection Related Function: A term used by Traffic Management to reference a point in a network or a network element where per connection functions are occurring. This is the point where policing at the VCC or VPC level can occur.

CRM. Missing RM-cell Count: CRM limits the number of forward RM-cells that can be sent in the absence of received backward RM-cells.

CRM. Cell Rate Margin: This is a measure of the difference between the effective bandwidth allocation and the allocation for sustainable rate in cells per second.

CRS. Cell Relay Service: A carrier service that supports the receipt and the transmission of ATM cells between end users in compliance with ATM standards and implementation specifications.

CS. Convergence Sublayer: The general procedures and functions that convert between ATM and non-ATM formats. This describes the functions of the upper half of the AAL layer. This also is used to describe the conversion functions between non-ATM protocols, such as frame relay or SMDS, and ATM protocols above the AAL layer.

CSU. Channel Service Unit: An interface for digitally leased lines that performs loopback testing and line conditioning.

CT. Conformance Test: Testing to determine whether an implementation complies with the specifications of a standard and exhibits the behaviors mandated by that standard.

CTD. Cell Transfer Delay: This is defined as the elapsed time between a cell exit event at measurement point 1 (for example, at the source UNI) and the corresponding cell entry event at measurement point 2 (for example, the destination UNI) for a particular connection. The cell transfer delay between two measurement points is the sum of the total inter-ATM node transmission delay and the total ATM node processing delay.

D

DA. Destination Address: Information sent in the forward direction indicating the address of the called station or customer.

DA. Destination MAC Address: A six-octet value uniquely identifying an endpoint that is sent in IEEE LAN frame headers to indicate frame destination.

Data Connections. Data VCCs connect the LECs to each other and to the Broadcast and Unknown Server. These carry Ethernet/IEEE 802.3 or IEEE 802.5 data frames as well as flush messages.

DCC. Data Country Code: This specifies the country in which an address is registered. The codes are given in ISO 3166. The length of this field is two octets. The digits of the data country code are encoded in Binary Coded Decimal (BCD) syntax. The codes are left justified and are padded on the right with the hexadecimal value "F" to fill the two octets.

DCE. Data Communication Equipment: A generic definition of computing equipment that attaches to a network via a DTE.

Default Node Representation. A single value for each nodal state parameter giving the presumed value between any entry or exit to the logical node and the nucleus.

Demultiplexing. A function performed by a layer entity that identifies and separates SDUs from a single connection to more than one connection.

DES. Destination End Station: An ATM termination point that is the destination for ATM messages of a connection and is used as a reference point for ABR services. See also SES.

Dijkstra's Algorithm. An algorithm that is sometimes used to calculate routes given a link and nodal state topology database.

DIR. This is a field in an RM-cell that indicates the direction of the RM-cell with respect to the data flow with which it is associated. The source sets DIR=0 and the destination sets DIR=1.

Direct Set. A set of host interfaces that can establish direct Layer 2 communications for unicast (not needed in MPOA).

DLPI. UNIX International, Data Link Provider Interface (DLPI) Specification: Revision 2.0.0, OSI Work Group, August 1991.

Domain. See Administrative Domain.

DS-0. Digital Signal, Level 0: The 64-kbps rate that is the basic building block for both the North American and European digital hierarchies.

DS-1. Digital Signal, Level 1: The North American Digital Hierarchy signaling standard for transmission at 1.544 Mbps. This standard supports 24 simultaneous DS-0 signals. The term often is used interchangeably with T1 carriers although DS-1 signals can be exchanged over other transmission systems.

DS-2. Digital Signal, Level 2: The North American Digital Hierarchy signaling standard for transmission of 6.312 Mbps that is used by T2 carrier that supports 96 calls.

DS-3. Digital Signal, Level 3: The North American Digital Hierarchy signaling standard for transmission at 44.736 Mbps that is used by T3 carrier. DS-3 supports 28 DS-1s plus overhead.

DS3 PLCP. Physical Layer Convergence Protocol: An alternate method used by older T carrier equipment to locate ATM cell boundaries. This method recently has been moved to an informative appendix of the ATM DS3 specification and has been replaced by the HEC method.

DSS1. Digital Subscriber Signalling System #1: N-ISDN UNI Signalling.

DSS2 Setup. DSS2 Digital Subscriber Signalling System #2: B-ISDN UNI Signalling.

DSU. Data Service Unit: Equipment used to attach users' computing equipment to a public network.

DTE. Data Terminal Equipment: A generic definition of external networking interface equipment, such as a modem.

DTL. Designated Transit List: A list of nodes and optional link IDs that completely specify a path across a single PNNI peer group.

DTL Originator. The first switching system within the entire PNNI routing domain to build the initial DTL stack for a given connection.

DTL Terminator. The last switching system within the entire PNNI routing domain to process the connection and thus the connection's DTL.

DXI. Data Exchange Interface: A variable length frame-based ATM interface between a DTE and a special ATM CSU/DSU. The ATM CSU/DSU converts between the variable-length DXI frames and the fixed-length ATM cells.

E

E.164. A public network addressing standard utilizing up to a maximum of 15 digits. ATM uses E.164 addressing for public network addressing.

E1. Also known as CEPT1, the 2.048 Mbps rate used by European CEPT carrier to transmit 30 64-kbps digital channels for voice or data calls, plus a 64-kbps signaling channel and a 64-kbps channel for framing and maintenance.

E3. Also known as CEPT3, the 34.368 Mbps rate used by the European CEPT carrier to transmit 16 CEPT1s plus overhead.

Edge Device. A physical device that is capable of forwarding packets between legacy interworking interfaces (for example, Ethernet, Token Ring, and so on) and ATM interfaces based on data-link and network layer information but that does not participate in the running of any network layer routing protocols. An edge device obtains forwarding descriptions using the route distribution protocol.

EFCI. Explicit Forward Congestion Indication: EFCI is an indication in the ATM cell header. A network element in an impending-congested state or a congested state can set EFCI so that this indication can be examined by the destination end-system. For example, the end system might use this indication to implement a protocol that adaptively lowers the cell rate of the connection during congestion or impending congestion. A network element that is not in a congestion state or an impending congestion state cannot modify the value of this indication. Impending congestion is the state when network equipment is operating around its engineered capacity level.

EFS. Error Free Seconds: A unit used to specify the error performance of T carrier systems, usually expressed as EFS per hour, day, or week. This method gives a better indication of the distribution of bit errors than a simple bit error rate (BER). See also SES.

ELAN. Emulated Local Area Network: A logical network initiated by using the mechanisms defined by LAN Emulation. This could include ATM and legacy attached end-system.

EMI. Electromagnetic Interference: Equipment used in high speed data systems, including ATM, that generate and transmit many signals in the radio frequency portion of the electromagnetic spectrum. Interference to other equipment or radio services might result if sufficient power from these signals escapes the equipment enclosures or transmission media. National and international regulatory agencies (FCC, CISPR, and so on) set limits for these emissions. Class A is for industrial use and Class B is for residential use.

EML. Element Management Layer: An abstraction of the functions provided by systems that manage each network element on an individual basis.

EMS. Element Management System: A management system that provides functions at the element Management Layer.

End Station. These devices (for example, hosts or PCs) enable the communication between ATM end stations and end stations on "legacy" LANs or among ATM end stations.

Entry Border Node. The node that receives a call over an outside link. This is the first node within a peer group to see this call.

EOM. End of Message: An indicator used in the AAL that identifies the last ATM cell containing information from a data packet that has been segmented.

EPD. Early Packet Discard: A mechanism employed by some ATM switches that allows a complete AAL 5 frame to be discarded when a threshold condition is met, such as one indicating that congestion is imminent. Useful for avoiding unwanted congestion situations that might jeopardize the switch's capability to support the existing connections properly, with a guaranteed service.

ER. Explicit Rate: The Explicit Rate is an RM-cell field used to limit the source ACR to a specific value. It is set initially by the source to a requested rate (such as PCR). It subsequently can be reduced by any network element in the path to a value that the element can sustain. ER is formatted as a rate.

ES. End-System: A system where an ATM connection is terminated or initiated. An originating end-system initiates the ATM connection, and the terminating end-system terminates the ATM connection. OAM cells can be generated and received.

ESF. Extended Superframe: A DS-1 framing format in which 24 DS-0 times lots plus a coded framing bit are organized into a frame that is repeated 24 times to form a superframe.

ESI. End-System Identifier: This identifier distinguishes multiple nodes at the same level in case the lower level peer group is partitioned.

ETSI. European Telecommunications Standards Institute: The primary telecommunications standards organization.

Exception. A connectivity advertisement in a PNNI complex node representation that represents something other than the default node representation.

Exit Border Node. The node that progresses a call over an outside link. This is the last node within a peer group to see this call.

Exterior. Denotes that an item (for example, link, node, or reachable address) is outside a PNNI routing domain.

Exterior Link. A link that crosses the boundary of the PNNI routing domain. The PNNI protocol does not run over an exterior link.

Exterior Reachable Address. An address that can be reached through a PNNI routing domain but is not located in that PNNI routing domain.

Exterior Route. A route that traverses an exterior link.

F

Fairness. As related to Generic Flow Control (GFC), fairness is defined as meeting all the agreed quality of service (QOS) requirements, by controlling the order of service for all active connections.

FC. Feedback Control: Feedback controls are defined as the set of actions taken by the network and by the end-systems to regulate the traffic submitted on ATM connections according to the state of network elements.

FCS. Frame Check Sequence: Any mathematical formula that derives a numeric value based on the bit pattern of a transmitted block of information and uses that value at the receiving end to determine the existence of any transmission errors.

FDDI. Fiber Distributed Data Interface: A 100-Mbps local-area network standard that was developed by ANSI that is designed to work on fiber-optic cables, using techniques similar to Token Ring.

FEBE. Far End Block Error: A maintenance signal transmitted in the PHY overhead that a bit error(s) has been detected at the PHY layer at the far end of the link. This is used to monitor bit error performance of the link.

FEC. Forward Error Correction: A technique for detection and correction of errors in a digital data stream.

FG. Functional Group: A collection of functions related in such a way that they are provided by a single logical component. Examples include the Route Server Functional Group (RSFG), the Internetwork Address Sub-Group (IASG), the

Coordination Functional Group (ICFG), the Edge Device Functional Group (EDFG), and the ATM-attached Host Behavior Functional Group (AHFG).

Flush Protocol. The flush protocol is provided to ensure the correct order of delivery of unicast data frames.

Foreign Address. An address that does not match any of a given node's summary addresses.

Forwarding Description. The resolved mapping of an MPOA Target to a set of parameters used to set up an ATM connection on which to forward packets.

FRS. Frame Relay Service: A connection-oriented service that is capable of carrying up to 4096 bytes per frame.

FRTT. Fixed Round-Trip Time: This is the sum of the fixed and propagation delays from the source to the furthest destination and back.

G

G.703. ITU-T Recommendation G.703, "Physical/Electrical Characteristics of Hierarchical Digital Interfaces."

G.704. ITU-T Recommendation G.704, "Synchronous Frame Structures Used at Primary and Secondary Hierarchy Levels."

G.804. ITU-T Recommendation G.804, "ATM Cell Mapping into Plesiochronous Digital Hierarchy (PDH)."

GCAC. Generic Connection Admission Control: This is a process to determine whether a link has potentially enough resources to support a connection.

GCRA. Generic Cell Rate Algorithm: The GCRA is used to define conformance with respect to the traffic contract of the connection. For each cell arrival, the GCRA determines whether the cell conforms to the traffic contract. The UPC function can implement the GCRA, or one or more equivalent algorithms to enforce conformance. The GCRA is defined with two parameters: the Increment (I) and the Limit (L).

GFC. Generic Flow Control: GFC is a field in the ATM header that can be used to provide local functions (for example, flow control). It has local significance only and the value encoded in the field is not carried end-to-end.

H

H-Channel. H-Channels are ISDN bearer services that have pre-defined speeds, have starting and stopping locations on a PRI, and are contiguously transported from one PRI site through networks to another PRI site.

H0 Channel. A 384-kbps channel that consists of six contiguous DS-0s (64 kbps) of a T1 line.

H10 Channel. The North American 1472-kbps channel from a T1 or a primary rate carrier. This is equivalent to twenty-three 64-kbps channels.

H11 Channel. The North American primary rate used as a single 1536-kbps channel. This channel uses 24 contiguous DS-0s or the entire T1 line except for the 8-kbps framing pattern.

H12. The European primary rate used as a single 1920-kbps channel (thirty 64-kbps channels) or the entire E1 line except for the 64 kbps framing and maintenance channel.

HBFG. Host Behavior Functional Group: The group of functions performed by an ATM-attached host that is participating in the MPOA service.

HDLC. High Level Data Link Control: An ITU-TSS link layer protocol standard for point-to-point and point-to-multipoint communications.

Header. Protocol control information located at the beginning of a protocol data unit.

HEC. Header Error Check: Using the fifth octet in the ATM cell header, ATM equipment can check for an error and correct the contents of the header. The check character is calculated using a CRC algorithm allowing a single bit error in the header to be corrected or multiple errors to be detected.

Hello Packet. A type of PNNI Routing packet that is exchanged between neighboring logical nodes.

Hierarchically Complete Source Route. A stack of DTLs representing a route across a PNNI routing domain such that a DTL is included for each hierarchical level between and including the current level and the lowest visible level in which the source and the destination are reachable.

Hop-by-Hop Route. A route that is created by having each switch along the path use its own routing knowledge to determine the next hop of the route, with the expectation that all switches choose consistent hops such that the call can reach the desired destination. PNNI does not use hop-by-hop routing.

Horizontal Link. A link between two logical nodes that belong to the same peer group.

Host Apparent Address. A set of internetwork layer addresses that a host can resolve directly to lower layer addresses.

I

I.356. ITU-T Specifications for Traffic Measurement.

I.361. B-ISDN ATM Layer Specification.

I.362. B-ISDN ATM Layer (AAL) Functional Description.

I.363. B-ISDN ATM Layer (AAL) Specification.

I.432. ITU-T Recommendation for B-ISDN User-network Interface.

IASG. Internetwork Address Sub-Group: A range of internetwork layer addresses summarized in an internetwork layer routing protocol.

ICD. International Code Designator: This identifies an international organization. The registration authority for the International Code Designator is maintained by the British Standards Institute. The length of this field is two octets.

ICR. Initial Cell Rate: An ABR service parameter, in cells/sec, that is the rate at which a source should send initially and after an idle period.

IDU. Interface Data Unit: The unit of information transferred to and from the upper layer in a single interaction across the SAP. Each IDU contains interface control information and also can contain the whole or part of the SDU.

IEC. Inter-exchange Carrier: A long distance telephone company.

IEEE. Institute of Electrical and Electronics Engineers: A worldwide engineering publishing and standards-making body for the electronics industry.

IEEE 802.3. A local-area network protocol suite commonly known as Ethernet. Ethernet has either a 10 Mbps or 100 Mbps throughput and uses carrier sense multiple access/ collision detect (CSMA/CD). This method allows users to share the network cable. However, only one station can use the cable at a time. A variety of physical medium– dependent protocols are supported.

IEEE 802.5. A local-area network protocol suite commonly known as Token Ring. A standard originated by IBM for a token passing ring network that can be configured in a star topology. Versions supported are 4 Mbps and 16 Mbps.

IETF. Internet Engineering Task Force: The organization that provides the coordination of standards and specification development for TCP/IP networking.

IISP. Interim-Interswitch Signaling Protocol: Formerly known as PNNI Phase 0, IISP is a basic call routing scheme agreed to while waiting for PNNI Phase 1 completion (PNNI 1.0). IISP relies on static routing tables established by the network administrator.

ILMI. Integrated Local Management Interface: An ATM Forum--defined interim specification for network management functions between an end user and a public or private network and between a public network and a private network. This is based on a limited subset of SNMP capabilities.

Induced Uplink. An uplink A that is created due to the existence of an uplink B in the child peer group represented by the node that created uplink A. Both A and B share the same upnode, which is higher in the PNNI hierarchy than the peer group in which uplink A is seen.

Inside Link. Synonymous with horizontal link.

Instance ID. A subset of an object's attributes that serve to uniquely identify a MIB instance.

Interior. Denotes that an item (for example, link, node, or reachable address) is inside a PNNI routing domain.

Internal Reachable Address. An address of a destination that is attached directly to the logical node advertising the address.

IOP. Interoperability: The capability of equipment from different manufacturers (or different implementation) to operate together.

IP. Internet Protocol: Originally developed by the Department of Defense to support interworking of dissimilar computers across a network. This protocol works in conjunction with TCP and usually is identified as TCP/IP. A connectionless protocol that operates at the network layer (Layer 3) of the OSI model.

IPX. Internetwork Packet Exchange: A built-in networking protocol for Novell NetWare. It was derived from the Xerox Network System protocol and operates at the network layer of the OSI protocol model.

IS. Intermediate System: A system that provides forwarding functions or relaying functions, or both, for a specific ATM connection. OAM cells can be generated and received.

ISO. International Organization for Standardization: An international organization for standardization, based in Geneva, Switzerland, that establishes voluntary standards and promotes global trade of 90 member countries.

Isochronous. Signals that are dependent on some uniform timing or carry their own timing information embedded as part of the signal.

ITU-T. International Telecommunications Union Telecommunications: ITU-T is an international body of member countries whose task is to define recommendations and standards relating to the international telecommunications industry. The fundamental standards for ATM have been defined and published by the ITU-T (previously the CCITT).

ITU H.222. An ITU-T Study Group 15 standard that addresses the multiplexing of multimedia data on an ATM network.

ITU Q.2100. B-ISDN Signaling ATM Adapation Layer Overview.

ITU Q.2110. B-ISDN Adapation Layer—Service Specific Connection Oriented Protocol.

ITU Q.2130. B-ISDN Adapation Layer—Service Specific Connection-Oriented Function for Support of Signaling at the UNI.

ITU Q.2931. The signaling standard for ATM to support Switched Virtual Connections (SVCs). This is based on the signaling standard for ISDN.

ITU Q.931. The signaling standard for ISDN to support SVCs. The basis for the signaling standard developed for Frame Relay and ATM.

ITU Q.933. The signaling standard for Frame Relay to support SVCs. This is based on the signaling standard for ISDN.

IUT. Implementation Under Test: The particular portion of equipment that is to be studied for testing. The implementation can include one or more protocols.

IWF. Interworking Function.

J–K–L

Joining. The phase in which the LE Client establishes its control connections to the LE Server.

JPEG. Joint Photographic Experts Group: An ISO Standards group that defines how to compress still pictures.

LAN. Local-area network: A network designed to move data between stations within a campus.

LANE. LAN Emulation: The set of services, functional groups, and protocols that provide for the emulation of LANS utilizing ATM as a backbone to allow connectivity among LAN- and ATM-attached end stations.

LAPD. Link Access Procedure D: A Layer 2 protocol defined by CCITT (original name of ITU-T). This protocol reliably transfers blocks of information across a single Layer 1 link and supports the multiplexing of different connections at Layer 2.

Layer Entity. An active element within a layer.

Layer Function. A part of the activity of the layer entities.

Layer Service. A capability of a layer and the layers beneath it that is provided to the upper layer entities at the boundary between that layer and the next higher layer.

Layer User Data. Data transferred between corresponding entities on behalf of the upper layer or layer management entities for which they are providing services.

LB. Leaky Bucket: Leaky Bucket is the term used as an analogous description of the algorithm used for conformance checking of cell flows from a user or network (see Leaky Bucket). See also GCRA, UPC, and NPC. The "leaking hole in the bucket" applies to the sustained rate at which cells can be accommodated, whereas the "bucket depth" applies to the tolerance to cell bursting over a given time period.

LE. LAN Emulation. See LANE.

LE_ARP. LAN Emulation Address Resolution Protocol: A message issued by an LE client to solicit the ATM address of another function.

Leadership Priority. The priority with which a logical node wants to be elected peer group leader of its peer group. Generally, of all nodes in a peer group, the one with the highest leadership priority is elected as the peer group leader.

Leaky Bucket. An informal term for the Generic Cell Rate Algorithm. See LB.

LEC. LAN Emulation Client: The entity in end-systems that performs data forwarding, address resolution, and other control functions.

LEC. Local Exchange Carrier: A telephone company affiliate of a Regional Bell Operating Company or an Independent Telephone Company.

LECID. LAN Emulation Client Identifier: This identifier, contained in the LAN Emulation header, indicates the ID of the ATM host or the ATM-LAN bridge. It is unique for every ATM Client.

LECS. LAN Emulation Configuration Server: This implements the policy-controlled assignment of individual LE clients to different emulated LANs by providing the LES ATM addresses.

LES. LAN Emulation Server: This implements the control coordination function for the Emulated LAN, examples are enabling a LEC to join an ELAN or resolving MAC to ATM addresses.

Level. The level is the position in the PNNI hierarchy at which a particular node or peer group exists. A level that has a smaller numerical value implies greater topology aggregation, and thus is called a "higher level" in the PNNI hierarchy. Conversely, a level that has a larger numerical value implies less topology aggregation, and is called a "lower level" in the PNNI hierarchy.

LGN. Logical Group Node: LGN is a single node that represents the lowest-level peer groups in the respective higher-level peer group.

LIJP. Leaf Initiated Joint Parameter: Root screening options and Information Element (IE) instructions carried in SETUP messages.

Link. An entity that defines a topological relationship (including available transport capacity) between two nodes in different subnetworks. Multiple links can exist between a pair of subnetworks. Synonymous with logical link.

Link Aggregation Token. See Aggregation Token.

Link Attribute. A link state parameter that is considered individually to determine whether a given link is acceptable and/or desirable for carrying a given connection.

Link Connection. A link connection (for example, at the VP-level) is a connection capable of transferring information transparently across a link without adding any overhead, such as cells for purposes for monitoring. It is delineated by connection points at the boundary of the subnetwork.

Link Constraint. A restriction on the use of links for path selection for a specific connection.

Link Metric. A link parameter that requires the values of the parameter for all links along a given path to be combined to determine whether the path is acceptable and/or desirable for carrying a given connection.

Link State Parameter. Information that captures an aspect or a property of a link.

LNNI. LANE NNI: The standardized interface between two LAN servers (LES-LES, BUS-BUS, LECS-LECS, and LECS-LES).

LOC. Loss of Cell Delineation: A condition at the receiver or a maintenance signal transmitted in the PHY overhead indicating that the receiving equipment has lost cell delineation. Used to monitor the performance of the PHY layer.

LOF. Loss of Frame: A condition at the receiver or a maintenance signal transmitted in the PHY overhead indicating that the receiving equipment has lost frame delineation. This is used to monitor the performance of the PHY layer.

Logical Group Node. A logical node that represents a lower level peer group as a single point for purposes of operating at one level of the PNNI routing hierarchy.

Logical Link. An abstract representation of the connectivity between two logical nodes. This includes individual physical links,

individual virtual path connections, and parallel physical links and/or virtual path connections.

Logical Node. An abstract representation of a peer group or a switching system as a single point.

Logical Node ID. A string of bits that unambiguously identifies a logical node within a routing domain.

LOP. Loss of Pointer: A condition at the receiver or a maintenance signal transmitted in the PHY overhead indicating that the receiving equipment has lost the pointer to the start of a cell in the payload. This is used to monitor the performance of the PHY layer.

LOS. Loss of Signal: A condition at the receiver or a maintenance signal transmitted in the PHY overhead indicating that the receiving equipment has lost the received signal. This is used to monitor the performance of the PHY layer.

Lowest Level Node. A leaf in the PNNI routing hierarchy; an abstraction representing a single instance of the PNNI routing protocol. Lowest-level nodes are created in a switching system via configuration. They are not created dynamically.

LPF. Low Pass Filter: In an MPEG-2 clock recovery circuit, it is a technique for smoothing or averaging changes to the system clock.

LSAP. Link Service Access Point: Logical address of boundary between Layer 3 and LLC sublayer 2.

LSB. Least Significant Bit: The lowest order bit in the binary representation of a numerical value.

LSR. Leaf Setup Request: A setup message type used when a leaf node requests connection to existing point-to-multipoint connection or requests creation of a new multipoint connection.

LT. Lower Tester: The representation in ISO/IEC 9646 of the means of providing, during test execution, indirect control, and observation of the lower service boundary of the IUT using the underlying service provider.

LTE. SONET Lite Terminating Equipment: ATM equipment terminating a communications facility using a SONET Lite Transmission Convergence (TC) layer. This usually is reserved for end user or LAN equipment. The SONET Lite TC does not implement some of the maintenance functions used in long haul networks, such as termination of path, line, and section overhead.

LUNI. LANE UNI: The standardized interface between an LE client and an LE Server (LES, LECS, and BUS).

M

M1. Management Interface 1: The management of ATM end devices.

M2. Management Interface 2: The management of private ATM networks or switches.

M3. Management Interface 3: The management of links between public and private networks.

M4. Management Interface 4: The management of public ATM networks.

M5. Management Interface 5: The management of links between two public networks.

MAC. Media Access Control: IEEE specifications for the lower half of the data link layer (Layer 2) that defines topology dependent access control protocols for IEEE LAN specifications.

MAN. Metropolitan-area network: A network designed to carry data over an area larger than a campus, such as an entire city and its outlying area.

Managed System. An entity that is managed by one or more management systems, which can be either Element Management Systems, Subnetwork, or Network Management Systems, or any other management systems.

Management Domain. An entity used here to define the scope of naming.

Management System. An entity that manages a set of managed systems, which can be either NEs, subnetworks, or other management systems.

MaxCR. Maximum Cell Rate: This is the maximum capacity usable by connections belonging to the specified service category.

MBS. Maximum Burst Size: In the signaling message, the Burst Tolerance (BT) is conveyed through the MBS, which is coded as a number of cells. The BT together with the SCR and the GCRA determine the MBS that can be transmitted at the peak rate and still be in conformance with the GCRA.

MCDV. Maximum Cell Delay Variance: This is the maximum two-point CDV objective across a link or a node for the specified service category.

MCLR. Maximum Cell Loss Ratio: This is the maximum ratio of the number of cells that do not make it across the link or the node to the total number of cells arriving at the link or the node.

MCR. Minimum Cell Rate: An ABR service traffic descriptor, in cells/sec, that is the rate at which the source always is allowed to send.

MCTD. Maximum Cell Transfer Delay: This is the sum of the fixed delay component across the link or the node and the MCDV.

Membership Scope. The level of routing hierarchy within which advertisement of a given address is contained.

Metasignaling. ATM Layer Management (LM) process that manages different types of signaling and possibly semipermanent virtual channels (VCs), including the assignment, the removal, and the checking of VCs.

Metasignaling VCs. The standardized VCs that convey metasignaling information across a User-Network Interface (UNI).

MIB. Management Information Base: A definition of management items for some network component that can be accessed by a network manager. A MIB includes the names of objects it contains and the type of information retained.

MIB Attribute. A single piece of configuration, management, or statistical information that pertains to a specific part of the PNNI protocol operation.

MIB Instance. An incarnation of a MIB object that applies to a specific part, piece, or aspect of the PNNI protocol's operation.

MIB Object. A collection of attributes that can be used to configure, manage, or analyze an aspect of the PNNI protocol's operation.

MID. Message Identifier: The message identifier is used to associate ATM cells that carry segments from the same higher layer packet.

MIR. Maximum Information Rate: See PCR.

MMF. Multimode Fiberoptic Cable: Fiberoptic cable in which the signal or light propagates in multiple modes or paths. Because these paths can have varying lengths, a transmitted pulse of light can be received at different times and smeared to the point that pulses might interfere with surrounding pulses. This can cause the signal to be difficult or impossible to receive. This pulse dispersion sometimes limits the distance over which an MMF link can operate.

MPEG. Motion Picture Experts Group: An ISO Standards group dealing with video and audio compression techniques and mechanisms for multiplexing and synchronizing various media streams.

MPOA. Multiprotocol over ATM: An effort taking place in the ATM Forum to standardize protocols for the purpose of running multiple network layer protocols over ATM.

MPOA Client. A device that implements the client side of one or more of the MPOA protocols (that is, an SCP client and/or an RDP client). An MPOA Client is either an Edge Device Functional Group (EDFG) or a Host Behavior Functional Group (HBFG).

MPOA Server. An MPOA Server is an ICFG or an RSFG.

MPOA Service Area. The collection of server functions and their clients. A collection of physical devices consisting of an MPOA server plus the set of clients served by that server.

MPOA Target. A set of protocol addresses and path attributes (for example, internetwork layer QoS and other information derivable from received packet) describing the intended destination and its path attributes that MPOA devices can use as lookup keys.

Mrm. An ABR service parameter that controls the allocation of bandwidth between forward RM-cells, backward RM-cells, and data cells.

MSB. Most Significant Bit: The highest order bit in the binary representation of a numerical value.

MT. Message type: Message type is the field containing the bit flags of an RM-cell. These flags are as follows: DIR = 0 for forward; RM-cells = 1 for backward; RM-cells BN = 1 for Non-Source Generated (BECN), RM-cells = 0 for Source Generated RM-cells; CI = 1 to indicate congestion = 0; otherwise NI = 1 to indicate no additive increase allowed = 0 otherwise RA—Not used for ATM Forum ABR.

MTP. Message Transfer Part: Levels 1 through 3 protocols of the SS7 protocol stack. MTP 3 (Level 3) is used to support BISUP.

Multicasting. The transmit operation of a single PDU by a source interface where the PDU reaches a group of one or more destinations.

Multiplexing. A function within a layer that interleaves the information from multiple connections into one connection.

Multipoint Access. User access in which more than one terminal equipment (TE) is supported by a single network termination.

Multipoint-to-Multipoint Connection. A multipoint-to-multipoint Connection is a collection of associated ATM VC or VP links and their associated nodes, with the following properties:

1. All nodes in the connection, called endpoints, serve as a root node in a point-to-multipoint connection to all of the (N-1) remaining endpoints.

2. Each of the endpoints on the connection can send information directly to any other endpoint, but the receiving endpoint cannot distinguish which of the endpoints is sending information without additional (for example, higher layer) information.

Multipoint-to-Point Connection. A point-to-multipoint connection can have zero bandwidth from the root node to the leaf nodes, and non-zero return bandwidth from the leaf nodes to the root node. Such a connection also is known as a multipoint-to-point connection. Note that UNI 4.0 does not support this connection type.

N

N-ISDN. Narrowband Integrated Services Digital Network: Services include basic rate interface (2B+D or BRI) and primary rate interface (30B+D in Europe and 23B+D in North America or PRI). Supports narrowband speeds at or below 1.5 Mbps.

Native Address. An address that matches one of a given node's summary addresses.

NDIS. Network Driver Interface Specification: Refer to 3COM/Microsoft, LAN Manager: Network Driver Interface Specification, October 8, 1990.

NE. Network Element: A system that supports at least NEFs and also can support Operation System Functions/Mediation Functions. An ATM NE can be realized as either a standalone device or a geographically distributed system. It cannot be further decomposed into managed elements in the context of a given management function.

NEF. Network Element Function: A function within an ATM entity that supports the ATM-based network transport services (for example, multiplexing and cross-connection).

Neighbor Node. A node that is connected directly to a particular node via a logical link.

NEL. Network Element Layer: An abstraction of functions related specifically to the technology, the vendor, and the network resources or network elements that provide basic communications services.

NEXT. Near End Crosstalk: Equipment that must receive on one wire pair and transmit on another wire pair concurrently. The same cable bundle must accommodate NEXT interference. NEXT is the portion of the transmitted signal that leaks into the receive pair. At this point on the link, because the transmitted signal is at maximum and the receive signal has been attenuated, it can be difficult to maintain an acceptable ACR with the received signal if the cable media allows large amounts of crosstalk leakage to occur. Foiled or shielded cables generally have less crosstalk than unshielded varieties.

NM. Network Management Entity: The body of software in a switching system that provides the capability to manage the PNNI protocol. NM interacts with the PNNI protocol through the MIB.

NML. Network Management Layer: An abstraction of the functions provided by systems that manage network elements on a collective basis, so as to monitor and control the network end-to-end.

NMS. Network Management System: An entity that implements functions at the Network Management Layer. It also can include Element Management Layer functions. A Network Management System can manage one or more other Network Management Systems.

NMS Environment. A set of NMSs that cooperate to manage one or more subnetworks.

NNI. Network Node Interface: An interface between ATM switches defined as the interface between two network nodes.

Nodal Attribute. A nodal state parameter that is considered individually to determine whether a given node is acceptable and/or desirable for carrying a given connection.

Nodal Constraint. A restriction on the use of nodes for path selection for a specific connection.

Nodal Metric. A nodal parameter that requires the values of the parameter for all nodes along a given path to be combined to determine whether the path is acceptable and/or desirable for carrying a given connection.

Nodal State Parameter. Information that captures an aspect or a property of a node.

Node. Synonymous with logical node.

Non-Branching Node. A node that cannot currently support additional branching points for point-to-multipoint calls.

NPC. Network Parameter Control: Network Parameter Control is defined as the set of actions taken by the network to monitor and control traffic from the NNI. Its main purpose is to protect network resources from malicious as well as unintentional misbehavior, which can affect the QoS of other already established connections by detecting violations of negotiated parameters and taking appropriate actions. See also UPC.

Nrm. An ABR service parameter, Nrm is the maximum number of cells a source can send for each forward RM-cell.

NSAP. Network Service Access Point: OSI generic standard for a network address consisting of 20 octets. ATM has specified E.164 for public network addressing and the NSAP address structure for private network addresses.

NSR. Non-Source Routed: Frame forwarding through a mechanism other than Source Route Bridging.

NT. Network Termination: Network Termination represents the termination point of a Virtual Channel, Virtual Path, or Virtual Path/Virtual Channel at the UNI.

NTSC. National Television System Committee: An industry group that defines how television signals are encoded and transmitted in the U.S.

Nucleus. The interior reference point of a logical node in the PNNI complex node representation.

Null. A value of all zeros.

nx64K. This refers to a circuit bandwidth or speed provided by the aggregation of nx64 kbps channels (where n = integer > 1). The 64K or DS-0 channel is the basic rate provided by the T Carrier systems.

O

OAM. Operations, Administration, and Maintenance: A group of network management functions that provide network fault indication, performance information, and data and diagnosis functions.

Octet. A term for eight (8) bits that is sometimes used interchangeably with *byte* to mean the same thing.

ODI. Open Data-Link Interface: This refers to Novell Incorporated, Open Data-Link Interface Developer's Guide, March 20, 1992.

One Hop Set. A set of hosts that are one hop apart in terms of internetwork protocols TTLs (TTL = 0 -on the wire+).

OOF. Out of Frame. Refer to LOF.

OSI. Open Systems Interconnection: A seven-layer architecture model for communications systems developed by the ISO for the interconnection of data communications systems. Each layer uses and builds on the services provided by those below it.

OSPF. Open Shortest Path First: A link-state routing algorithm that is used to calculate routes based on the number of routers, transmission speeds, delays, and route costs.

OUI. Organizationally Unique Identifier: The OUI is a three-octet field in the IEEE 802.1a defined SubNetwork Attachment Point (SNAP) header, identifying an organization that administers the meaning of the following two-octet Protocol Identifier

(PID) field in the SNAP header. Together, they identify a distinct routed or bridged protocol.

Outlier. A node whose exclusion from its containing peer group significantly improves the accuracy and the simplicity of the aggregation of the remainder of the peer group topology.

Outside Link. A link to an outside node.

Outside Node. A node that is participating in PNNI routing, but is not a member of a particular peer group.

P

PAD. Packet Assembler and Disassembler: A PAD assembles packets of asynchronous data and emits these buffers in a burst to a packet switch network. The PAD also disassembles packets from the network and emits the data to the non-packet device.

Parent Node. The logical group node that represents the containing peer group of a specific node at the next higher level of the hierarchy.

Parent Peer Group. The parent peer group of a peer group is the one containing the logical group node representing that peer group. The parent peer group of a node is the one containing the parent node of that node.

Path Constraint. A bound on the combined value of a topology metric along a path for a specific connection.

Path Scope. The highest level of PNNI hierarchy used by a path.

PBX. Private Branch eXchange: PBX is the term given to a device that provides private local voice switching and voice-related services within the private network. A PBX could have an ATM API to utilize ATM services, for example, Circuit Emulation Service.

PC. Protocol Control: Protocol control is a mechanism that a given application protocol can employ to determine or control the performance and the health of the application. For example, protocol liveness might require that protocol control information be sent at some minimum rate; some applications might become intolerable to users if they cannot send at least at some minimum rate. For such applications, the concept of MCR is defined. See also MCR.

PCM. Pulse Code Modulation: An audio encoding algorithm that encodes the amplitude of a repetitive series of audio samples. This encoding algorithm converts analog voice samples into a digital bit stream.

PCO. Point of Control and Observation: A place (point) within a testing environment where the occurrence of test events is to be controlled and observed as defined by the particular abstract test method used.

PCR. Program Clock Reference: A timestamp that is inserted by the MPEG-2 encoder into the Transport Stream to aid the decoder in recovering and tracking the encoder clock.

PCR. Peak Cell Rate: The peak cell rate, in cells/sec, is the cell rate that the source can never exceed.

PDH. Plesiochronous Digital Hierarchy: PDH (plesiochronous means nearly synchronous) was developed to carry digitized voice over twisted pair cabling more efficiently. This evolved into North American, European, and Japanese digital hierarchies where only a discrete set of fixed rates is available, namely, nxDS0 (DS-0 is a 64-kbps rate), and then the next levels in the respective multiplex hierarchies.

PDU. Protocol Data Unit: A PDU is a message of a given protocol comprising payload and protocol-specific control information, typically contained in a header. PDUs pass over the protocol interfaces, which exist between the layers of protocols (per OSI model).

Peer Entities. Entities within the same layer.

Peer Group. A set of logical nodes that are grouped for the purposes of creating a routing hierarchy. PTSEs are exchanged among all members of the group.

Peer Group Identifier. A string of bits that is used to identify a peer group unambiguously.

Peer Group Leader. A node that has been elected to perform some of the functions associated with a logical group node.

Peer Group Level. The number of significant bits in the peer group identifier of a particular peer group.

Peer Node. A node that is a member of the same peer group as a given node.

PES. Packetized Elementary Stream: In MPEG-2, after the media stream has been digitized and compressed, it is formatted into packets before it is multiplexed into either a Program Stream or a Transport Stream.

PG. Peer Group: A set of logical nodes that are grouped for the purposes of creating a routing hierarchy. PTSEs are exchanged among all members of the group.

PGL. Peer Group Leader: A single real physical system that has been elected to perform some of the functions associated with a logical group node.

PHY. OSI Physical Layer: The physical layer provides for the transmission of cells over a physical medium connecting two ATM devices. This physical layer is comprised of two sublayers: the Physical Medium Dependent (PMD) sublayer, and the Transmission Convergence (TC) sublayer. See also PMD and TC.

Physical Layer (PHY) Connection. An association established by the PHY between two or more ATM entities. A PHY connection consists of the concatenation of PHY links to provide an end-to-end transfer capability to PHY SAPs.

Physical Link. A real link that attaches two switching systems.

PICS. Protocol Implementation Conformance Statement: A statement made by the supplier of an implementation or system stating which capabilities have been implemented for a given protocol.

PID. Protocol Identification. See OUI.

Plastic Fiber Optics. An optical fiber where the core transmission media is plastic in contrast to glass or silica cores. Proposed plastic fibers generally have larger attenuation and dispersion than glass fiber but might have applications where the distance is limited. Plastic systems also can offer lower cost connectors that can be installed with simple tools and a limited amount of training.

PLCP. Physical Layer Convergence Protocol: The IEEE 802.6 defines the PLCP. It is used for DS-3 transmission of ATM. ATM cells are encapsulated in a 125-microsecond frame defined by the PLCP, which is defined inside the DS-3 M-frame.

PLL. Phase Lock Loop: Phase Lock Loop is a mechanism whereby timing information is transferred within a data stream and the receiver derives the signal element timing by locking its local clock source to the received timing information.

PM. Physical Medium: Physical medium refers to the actual physical interfaces. Several interfaces are defined, including STS-1, STS-3c, STS-12c, STM-1, STM-4, DS-1, E1, DS-2, E3, DS-3, E4, FDDI-based, Fiber Channel-based, and STP. These range in speeds from 1.544 Mbps through 622.08 Mbps.

PMD. Physical Media Dependent: This sublayer defines the parameters at the lowest level, such as the speed of the bits on the media.

PNI. Permit Next Increase: An ABR service parameter, PNI is a flag controlling the increase of ACR upon reception of the next backward RM-cell. PNI = 0 inhibits increase. The range is 0 to 1.

PNNI. Private Network-to-Network Interface: A routing information protocol that enables extremely scalable, full function, dynamic, multi-vendor ATM switches to be integrated in the same network.

PNNI Protocol Entity. The body of software in a switching system that executes the PNNI protocol and provides the routing service.

PNNI Routing Control Channel. VCCs used for the exchange of PNNI routing protocol messages.

PNNI Routing Domain. A group of topologically contiguous systems that run one instance of the PNNI routing.

PNNI Routing Hierarchy. The hierarchy of peer groups used for PNNI routing.

PNNI Topology State Element. A collection of PNNI information that is flooded among all logical nodes within a peer group.

PNNI Topology State Packet. A type of PNNI routing packet that is used for flooding PTSEs among logical nodes within a peer group.

POH. Path Overhead: A maintenance channel transmitted in the SONET overhead following the path from the beginning multiplexer to the ending demultiplexer. This is not implemented in SONET Lite.

Point-to-Multipoint Connection. A point-to-multipoint connection is a collection of associated ATM VC or VP links, with associated endpoint nodes, with the following properties:

1. One ATM link, called the Root Link, serves as the root in a simple tree topology. When the Root Node sends information, all the remaining nodes on the connection, called leaf nodes, receive copies of the information.

2. Each of the Leaf Nodes on the connection can send information directly to the Root Node. The root node cannot distinguish which leaf is sending information without additional (higher layer) information. (See the note following this list for UNI 4.0 support.)

3. The Leaf Nodes cannot communicate directly to each other with this connection type.

   UNI 4.0 does not support traffic sent from a leaf to the root.

Point-to-Point Connection. A connection with only two endpoints.

Port Identifier. The identifier assigned by a logical node to represent the point of attachment of a link to that node.

Port Snooping. A mechanism that some ATM switches can employ to eavesdrop on a selected ATM port and copy all those cells to another port where an ATM analyzer is attached.

PRI. Primary Rate Interface: An ISDN standard for provisioning of 1.544 Mbps (DS-1 in North America, Japan, and all) or

2.048 Mbps (E1 in Europe) ISDN services. DS-1 is 23 B channels of 64 kbps each and one signalling D channel of 64 kbps. E1 is 30 B channels of 64 kbps each and one signalling D channel of 64 kbps.

PRS. Primary Reference Source.

Primitive. An abstract, implementation-independent interaction between a layer service user and a layer service provider.

Private ATM Address. A 20-byte address used to identify an ATM connection termination point.

Protocol. A set of rules and formats (semantic and syntactic) that determines the communication behavior of layer entities in the performance of the layer functions.

Protocol Control Information. Information exchanged between corresponding entities, using a lower layer connection, to coordinate their joint operation.

PT. Payload Type: Payload Type is a 3-bit field in the ATM cell header that discriminates between a cell carrying management information and one carrying user information.

PTI. Payload Type Indicator: Payload Type Indicator is the Payload Type field value distinguishing the various management cells and user cells. Example: Resource Management cell has PTI = 110, end-to-end OAM, F5 flow cell has PTI = 101.

PTMPT. Point-to-multipoint: A main source to many destination connections.

PTS. Presentation Time Stamp: A timestamp that is inserted by the MPEG-2 encoder into the packetized elementary stream to allow the decoder to synchronize different elementary streams (that is, lip sync).

PTSE. PNNI Topology State Element: A collection of PNNI information that is flooded among all logical nodes within a peer group.

PTSP. PNNI Topology State Packet: A type of PNNI routing packet that is used for flooding PTSEs among logical nodes within a peer group.

PVC. Permanent Virtual Circuit: This is a link with static route defined in advance, usually by manual setup.

PVCC. Permanent Virtual Channel Connection: A Virtual Channel Connection (VCC) is an ATM connection where switching is performed on the VPI/VCI fields of each cell. A Permanent VCC is one that is provisioned through some network management function and left up indefinitely.

PVPC. Permanent Virtual Path Connection: A Virtual Path Connection (VPC) is an ATM connection where switching is performed on the VPI field only of each cell. A Permanent VPC is one that is provisioned through some network management function and left up indefinitely.

Q–R

QD. Queuing Delay: Queuing Delay refers to the delay imposed on a cell by its having to be buffered because of unavailability of resources to pass the cell onto the next network function or element. This buffering could be a result of oversubscription of a physical link, or due to a connection of higher priority or tighter service constraints getting the resource of the physical link.

QoS. Quality of Service: Quality of Service is defined on an end-to-end basis in terms of the following attributes of the end-to-end ATM connection:

- Cell Loss Ratio
- Cell Transfer Delay
- Cell Delay Variation

Q.SIG. A symmetrical adaptation of N-ISDN signalling (DSS1) for inter-PBX signalling.

RBOC. Regional Bell Operating Company: Seven companies formed to manage the local exchanges originally owned by AT&T. These companies were created as a result of an agreement between AT&T and the United States Department of Justice.

RD. Routing Domain: A group of topologically contiguous systems that are running one instance of routing.

RDF. Rate Decrease Factor: An ABR service parameter, RDF controls the decrease in the cell transmission rate. RDF is a power of 2 from 1/32,768 to 1.

RO. Read-Only: Attributes that are read-only cannot be written by Network Management. Only the PNNI Protocol entity can change the value of a read-only attribute. Network Management entities are restricted to reading only such read-only attributes. Read-only attributes are typically for statistical information, including reporting the result of actions taken by auto-configuration.

RRM. Relative Rate Marking: One of the congestion feedback modes allowed in Available Bit Rate (ABR) service. In the Relative Rate Marking mode, switches can set a bit within either forward or backward Resource Management cells (RM-cells) or both to indicate congestion.

RW. Read-Write: Attributes that are read-write cannot be written by the PNNI protocol entity. Only the Network Management Entity can change the value of a read-write attribute. The PNNI Protocol Entity is restricted to reading only such read-write attributes. Read-write attributes typically are used to provide the capability for Network Management to configure, control, and manage a PNNI Protocol Entity's behavior.

Reachable Address Prefix. A prefix on a 20-byte ATM address indicating that all addresses beginning with this prefix are reachable.

Registration. The address registration function is the mechanism by which clients provide address information to the LAN Emulation server.

Relaying. The function of a layer by which means a layer entity receives data from a corresponding entity and transmits it to another corresponding entity.

Restricted Transit Node. A node that is to be used for transit by a call only in restricted ciscumstances. It is free from such restriction when it is used to originate or terminate a call.

RFC. Request for Comment: The development of TCP/IP standards, procedures, and specifications is done via this mechanism. RFCs are documents that progress through several development stages, under the control of IETF, until they are finalized or discarded.

RFC1695. Definitions of Managed Objects for ATM Management or AToM MIB.

RFI. Radio Frequency Interface: See EMI.

RIF. Rate Increase Factor: This controls the amount by which the cell transmission rate can increase upon the receipt of an RM-cell. The additive increase rate AIR = PCR × RIF. RIF is a power of 2, ranging from 1/32,768 to 1.

RISC. Reduced Instruction Set Computing: A computer processing technology in which a microprocessor understands a few simple instructions, thereby providing fast, predictable instruction flow.

RM. Resource Management: Resource Management is the management of critical resources in an ATM network. Two critical resources are buffer space and trunk bandwidth. Provisioning can be used to allocate network resources to separate traffic flows according to service characteristics. VPCs play a key role in resource management. By reserving capacity on VPCs, the processing required to establish individual VCCs is reduced. See also RM-cell.

RM-Cell. Resource Management Cell: Information about the state of the network, such as bandwidth availability, state of congestion, and impending congestion, is conveyed to the source through special control cells called Resource Management cells (RM-cells).

Route Server. A physical device that runs one or more network layer routing protocols, and that uses a route query protocol to provide network layer routing forwarding descriptions to clients.

Router. A physical device that is capable of forwarding packets based on network layer information and that participates in running one or more network layer routing protocols.

Routing Computation. The process of applying a mathematical algorithm to a topology database to compute routes. There are many types of routing computations that can be used. The Djikstra algorithm is one particular example of a possible routing computation.

Routing Constraint. A generic term that refers to either a topology constraint or a path constraint.

Routing Protocol. A general term indicating a protocol run between routers and/or route servers to exchange information used to allow the computation of routes. The result of the routing computation is one or more forwarding descriptions.

RS. Remote single-layer (Test Method): An abstract test method in which the upper tester is within the system under test and there is a point of control and observation at the upper service boundary of the Implementation Under Test (IUT) for testing one protocol layer. Test events are specified in terms of the abstract service primitives (ASPs) and/or protocol data units at the lower tester PCO.

RSE. Remote Single-layer Embedded (Test Method): An abstract test method in which the upper tester is within the system under test and there is a point of control and observation at the upper service boundary of the Implementation Under Test (IUT) for testing a protocol layer or sublayer that is part of a multi-protocol IUT.

RSFG. Route Server Functional Group: The group of functions performed to provide internetworking level functions in an MPOA System. This includes running conventional interworking Routing Protocols and providing inter-IASG destination resolution.

S

SA. Source Address: The address from which the message or the data originated.

SA. Source MAC Address: A six-octet value uniquely identifying an end point and that is sent in an IEEE LAN frame header to indicate source of frame.

SAAL. Signaling ATM Adaptation Layer: This resides between the ATM Layer and the Q.2931 function. The SAAL provides the reliable transport of Q.2931 messages between Q.2931 entities (for example, the ATM switch and the host) over the ATM Layer. It has two sublayers: common part and service specific part.

SAP. Service Access Point: A SAP is used for the following purposes:

1. When the application initiates an outgoing call to a remote ATM device, a destination_SAP specifies the ATM address of the remote device, plus further addressing

that identifies the target software entity within the remote device.

2. When the application prepares to respond to incoming calls from remote ATM devices, a local_SAP specifies the ATM address of the device housing the application, plus further addressing that identifies the application within the local device.

There are several groups of SAPs that are specified as valid for Native ATM Services.

SAR. Segmentation and Reassembly: Method of breaking up arbitrarily sized packets.

Scope. A scope defines the level of advertisement for an address. The level is a level of a peer group in the PNNI routing hierarchy.

SCCP. Signaling Connection and Control Part: An SS7 protocol that provides additional functions to the Message Transfer Part (MTP). It typically supports the Transaction Capabilities Application Part (TCAP).

SCP. Service Control Point: A computer and database system that executes service logic programs to provide customer services through a switching system. Messages are exchanged with the SSP through the SS7 network.

SCR. Sustainable Cell Rate: The SCR is an upper bound on the conforming average rate of an ATM connection over time scales, which are long relative to those for which the PCR is defined. Enforcement of this bound by the UPC could allow the network to allocate sufficient resources, but less than those based on the PCR, and still ensure that the performance objectives (for example, for cell loss ratio) can be achieved.

SDH. Synchronous Digital Hierarchy: The ITU-TSS International Standard for transmitting information over optical fiber.

SDT. Structured Data Transfer: An AAL1 data transfer mode in which data is structured into blocks that are then segmented into cells for transfer.

SDU. Service Data Unit: A unit of interface information whose identity is preserved from one end of a layer connection to the other.

SE. Switching Element: Switching element refers to the device or network node that performs the ATM switching functions based on the VPI or VPI/VCI pair.

SEAL. Simple and Efficient Adapation Layer: An earlier name for AAL5.

Segment. A single ATM link or group of interconnected ATM links of an ATM connection.

SEL. Selector: A subfield carried in the SETUP message part of the ATM endpoint address Domain Specific Part (DSP) defined by ISO 10589. Not used for ATM network routing; used by ATM end systems only.

Semipermanent Connection. A connection established via a service order or via network management.

SES. Severely Errored Seconds: A unit used to specify the error performance of T carrier systems. This indicates a second containing 10 or more errors, usually expressed as SES per hour, day, or week. This method gives a better indication of the distribution of bit errors than a simple Bit Error Rate (BER). See also EFS.

SES. Source End Station: An ATM termination point, which is the source of ATM messages of a connection, and is used as a reference point for ABR services. See also DES.

SF. SuperFrame: A DS-1 framing format in which 24 DS-0 timeslots plus a coded framing bit are organized into a frame that is repeated 12 times to form the superframe.

Shaping Descriptor. N ordered pairs of GCRA parameters (I,L) used to define the negotiated traffic shape of a connection.

SIPP. SMDS Interface Protocol: Protocol where Layer 2 is based on ATM, AAL, and DQDB. Layer 1 is DS-1 and DS-3.

SMDS. Switched Multi-Megabit Data Service: A connectionless service used to connect LANs, MANs, and WANs to exchange data.

SMF. Single Mode Fiber: Fiber optic cable in which the signal or light propagates in a single mode or path. Because all light follows the same path or travels the same distance, a transmitted pulse is not dispersed and does not interfere with adjacent pulses. SMF fibers can support longer distances and are limited mainly by the amount of attenuation. See also MMF.

SN. Sequence Number: SN is a 4-octet field in a Resource Management cell defined by the ITU-T in recommendation I.371 to sequence such cells. It is not used for ATM Forum ABR. An ATM switch either preserves this field or sets it in accordance with I.371.

SN Cell. Sequence Number Cell: A cell sent periodically on each link of an AIMUX to indicate how many cells have been transmitted since the previous SN cell. These cells are used to verify the sequence of payload cells reassembled at the receiver.

SNA. Systems Network Architecture: IBM's seven layer, vendor-specific architecture for data communications.

SNC. Subnetwork Connection: In the context of ATM, an entity that passes ATM cells transparently, (that is, without adding any overhead). A SNC can be either a stand-alone SNC, or a concatenation of SNCs and link connections.

SNMP. Simple Network Management Protocol: Originally designed for the Department of Defense network to support TCP/IP Network Management. It has been implemented widely to support the management of a broad range of network products and functions. SNMP is the IETF standard management protocol for TCP/IP networks.

SONET. Synchronous Optical Network: An ANSI standard for transmitting information over optical fiber. This standard is used or accepted in the United States and Canada and is a variation of the SDH International Standard.

Source Route. As used in this book, a hierarchically complete source route.

Source Traffic. A set of traffic parameters belonging to the ATM Traffic Descriptor that is used during the connection setup to capture the intrinsic traffic characteristics of the connection requested by the source.

SPE. SONET Synchronous Payload Envelope.

Split System. A switching system that implements the functions of more than one logical node.

Spoke. In the complex node representation, the spoke represents the connectivity between the nucleus and a specific port.

SPTS. Single Program Transport Stream: An MPEG-2 Transport Stream that consists of only one program.

SR. Source Routing: A bridged method whereby the source at a data exchange determines the route that subsequent frames will use.

SRF. Specifically Routed Frame: A Source Routing Bridging Frame that uses a specific route between the source and the destination.

SRT. Source Routing Transparent: An IETF Bridging Standard combining Transparent Bridging and Source Route Bridging.

SRTS. Synchronous Residual Time Stamp: A clock recovery technique in which different signals between source timing and a network reference timing signal are transmitted to allow reconstruction of the source timing at the destination.

SSCF. Service Specific Coordination Function: SSCF is a function defined in Q.2130, B-ISDN Signaling ATM Adaptation

Layer-Service Specific Coordination Function for Support of Signaling at the User-Network Interface.

SSCOP. Service Specific Connection Oriented Protocol: An adaptation layer protocol defined in ITU-T Specification: Q.2110.

SSCS. Service Specific Convergence Sublayer: The portion of the convergence sublayer that is dependent upon the type of traffic that is being converted.

SS7. Signal System Number 7: A family of signaling protocols originating from narrowband telephony. They are used to set up, manage, and tear down connections as well as to exchange non-connection associated information. Refer to BISUP, MTP, SCCP, and TCAP.

STC. System Time Clock: The master clock in an MPEG-2 encoder or decoder system.

STE. Spanning Tree Explorer: A Source Route Bridging frame that uses the Spanning Tree algorithm in determining a route.

STE. SONET Section Terminating Equipment: SONET equipment that terminates a section of a link between a transmitter and a repeater, a repeater and a repeater, or a repeater and a receiver. This usually is implemented in wide-area facilities and not implemented by SONET Lite.

STM. Synchronous Transfer Module: STM is a basic building block used for a synchronous multiplexing hierarchy defined by the CCITT/ITU-T. STM-1 operates at a rate of 155.52 Mbps (same as STS-3).

STM-1. Synchronous Transport Module 1: SDH standard for transmission over OC-3 optical fiber at 155.52 Mbps.

STM-n. Synchronous Transport Module n (where n is an integer): SDH standards for transmission over optical fiber (OC-'n x 3) by multiplexing n STM-1 frames,(for example, STM-4 at 622.08 Mbps and STM-16 at 2.488 Gbps).

STM-nc. Synchronous Transport Module n concatenated (where n is an integer): SDH standards for transmission over optical fiber (OC-'n x 3) by multiplexing n STM-1 frames, (for example, STM-4 at 622.08 Mbps and STM-16 at 2.488 Gbps, but treating the information fields as a single concatenated payload).

STP. Signaling Transfer Point: A high-speed, reliable, special purpose packet switch for signaling messages in the SS7 network.

STP. Shielded Twisted Pair: A cable containing one or more twisted pair wires with each pair having a shield of foil wrap.

STS-1. Synchronous Transport Signal 1: SONET standard for transmission over OC-1 optical fiber at 51.84 Mbps.

STS-n. Synchronous Transport Signal n (where n is an integer): SONET standards for transmission over OC-n optical fiber by multiplexing n STS-1 frames (for example, STS-3 at 155.52 Mbps, STS-12 at 622.08 Mbps, and STS-48 at 2.488 Gbps).

STS-nc. Synchronous Transport Signal n concatenated (where n is an integer): SONET standards for transmission over OC-n optical fiber by multiplexing n STS-1 frames (for example, STS-3 at 155.52 Mbps, STS-12 at

622.08 Mbps, and STS-48 at 2.488 Gbps, but treating the information fields as a single concatenated payload).

Sublayer. A logical sub-division of a layer.

Subnet. The use of the term *subnet* to mean a LAN technology is a historical use and is not specific enough in the MPOA work. See also Internetwork Address Sub-Group, Direct Set, Host Apparent Address Sub-Group, and One Hop Set for more specific definitions.

Subnetwork. A collection of managed entities grouped together from a connectivity perspective, according to their capability to transport ATM cells.

subNMS. Subnetwork Management System: A Network Management system that is manages one or more subnetworks and that is managed by one or more Network Management systems.

Summary Address. An address prefix that tells a node how to summarize reachability information.

SUT. System Under Test: The real open system in which the Implementation Under Test (IUT) resides.

SVC. Switched Virtual Circuit: A connection established via signaling. The user defines the endpoints when the call is initiated.

SVCC. Switched Virtual Channel Connection: A Switched VCC is one that is established and taken down dynamically through control signaling. A Virtual Channel Connection (VCC) is an ATM connection where switching is performed on the VPI/VCI fields of each cell.

SVPC. Switched Virtual Path Connection: A Switched Virtual Path Connection is one that is established and taken down dynamically through control signaling. A Virtual Path Connection (VPC) is an ATM connection where switching is performed on the VPI field only of each cell.

Switched Connection. A connection established via signaling.

Switching System. A set of one or more systems that act together and appear as a single switch for the purposes of PNNI routing.

Symmetric Connection. A connection with the same bandwidth value specified for both directions.

Synchronous. Signals that are sourced from the same timing reference and have the same frequency.

T

T1E1. An ANSI standards sub-committee dealing with network interfaces.

T1M1. An ANSI standards sub-committee dealing with Inter-Network Operations, Administration, and Maintenance.

T1Q1. An ANSI standards sub-committee dealing with performance.

T1S1. An ANSI standards sub-committee dealing with services, architecture, and signaling.

T1X1. An ANSI standards sub-committee dealing with digital hierarchy and synchronization.

TB. Transparent Bridging: An IETF bridging standard where bridge behavior is transparent to the data traffic. To avoid ambiguous routes or loops, a Spanning Tree algorithm is utilized.

TBE. Transient Buffer Exposure: This is a negotiated number of cells that the network wants to limit the source to sending during startup periods, before the first RM-cell returns.

TC. Transaction Capabilities: TCAP plus supporting Presentation, Session, and Transport protocol layers. See also TCAP.

TC. Transmission Convergence: The TC sublayer transforms the flow of cells into a steady flow of bits and bytes for transmission over the physical medium. On transmit, the TC sublayer maps the cells to the frame format, generates the Header Error Check (HEC), and sends idle cells when the ATM layer has none to send. On reception, the TC sublayer delineates individual cells in the received bit stream, and uses the HEC to detect and correct received errors.

TCAP. Transaction Capabilities Applications Part: A connectionless SS7 protocol for the exchange of information outside the context of a call or connection. It typically runs over SCCP and MTP 3.

TCP. Test Coordination Procedure: A set of rules to coordinate the test process between the lower tester and the upper tester. The purpose is to enable the lower tester to control the operation of the upper tester. An abstract test suite might or might not specify these procedures.

TCP. Transmission Control Protocol: Originally developed by the Department of Defense to support interworking of dissimilar computers across a network. A protocol that provides end-to-end, connection-oriented, reliable transport layer (Layer 4) functions over IP-controlled networks. TCP performs the following functions: flow control between two systems, acknowledgements of packets received, and end-to-end sequencing of packets.

TCR. Tagged Cell Rate: An ABR service parameter, TCR limits the rate at which a source can send out-of-rate forward RM-cells. TCR is a constant fixed at 10 cells/second.

TCS. Transmission Convergence Sublayer: This is part of the ATM physical layer that defines how cells are transmitted by the actual physical layer.

TDF. An ABR service parameter, TDF controls the decrease in ACR associated with TOF. TDF is signaled as TDFF, where TDF = TDFF/RDF times the smallest power of 2 greater or equal to PCR. TDF is in units of 1/seconds.

TDFF. See TDF. TDFF is either zero or a power of 2 in the range 1/64 to 1 in units of 1/cells.

TDM. Time Division Multiplexing: A method in which a transmission facility is multiplexed among a number of channels by allocating the facility to the channels on the basis of time slots.

TE. Terminal Equipment: Terminal equipment represents the endpoint of ATM connection(s) and the termination of the various protocols within the connection(s).

TLV. Type / Length / Value: A coding methodology that provides a flexible and extensible means of coding parameters within a frame. Type indicates the parameter type. Length indicates the parameter's value length. Value indicates the actual parameter value.

TM. Traffic Management: Traffic Management is the aspect of the traffic control and congestion control procedures for ATM. ATM layer traffic control refers to the set of actions taken by the network to avoid congestion conditions. ATM layer congestion control refers to the set of actions taken by the network to minimize the intensity, the spread, and the duration of congestion. The following functions form a framework for managing and controlling traffic and congestion in ATM networks and can be used in appropriate combinations:

- Connection Admission Control
- Feedback Control
- Usage Parameter Control
- Priority Control
- Traffic Shaping
- Network Resource Management
- Frame Discard
- ABR Flow Control

TMP. Test Management Protocol: A protocol that is used in the test coordination procedures for a particular test suite.

TNS. Transit Network Selection: A signaling element that identifies a public carrier to which a connection setup should be routed.

TOF. Time Out Factor: An ABR service parameter, TOF controls the maximum time permitted between sending forward RM-cells before a rate decrease is required. It is signaled as TOFF where TOF=TOFF+1. TOFF is a power of 2 in the range 1/8 to 4,096.

TOFF. Time Out Factor: See TOF.

Topology Aggregation. The process of summarizing and compressing topology information at a hierarchical level to be advertised at the level above.

Topology Attribute. A generic term that refers to either a link attribute or a nodal attribute.

Topology Constraint. A topology constraint is a generic term that refers to either a link constraint or a nodal constraint.

Topology Database. The database that describes the topology of the entire PNNI routing domain as seen by a node.

Topology Metric. A generic term that refers to either a link metric or a nodal metric.

Topology State Parameter. A generic term that refers to either a link parameter or a nodal parameter.

TP-MIC. Twisted-Pair Media Interface Connector: This refers to the connector jack at the end user or the network equipment that receives the twisted pair plug.

TPCC. Third Party Call Control: A connection setup and management function that is executed from a third party that is not involved in the data flow.

TPD. Tail Packet Discard: A mechanism employed by some ATM switches that allows the remaining cells supporting an AAL5 frame to be discarded when one or more cells of that AAL5 frame have been dropped/lost. This avoids the unwanted waste associated with sending partial AAL5 frames through the ATM network when they likely are to be retransmitted by the sender.

Traffic Policing. A mechanism used to detect and discard or modify cells/traffic that violate the traffic contract agreed to at connection setup. Although applicable to both public and private networks, traffic policing most likely is used by public ATM service providers where tariffing can be based on guaranteed service.

Trail. An entity that transfers information provided by a client layer network between access points in a server layer network. The transported information is monitored at the termination points.

Trailer. Protocol control information located at the end of a PDU.

Transit Delay. The time difference between the instant at which the first bit of a PDU crosses one designated boundary and the instant at which the last bit of the same PDU crosses a second designated boundary.

Trm. An ABR service parameter that provides an upper bound on the time between forward RM-cells for an active source. It is 100 times a power of 2 with a range of $100 \times 2-7$ to 100×20.

TS. Time Stamp: Time stamping is used on OAM cells to compare the time of entry of a cell to the time of exit of a cell, which determines the cell transfer delay of the connection.

TS. Traffic Shaping: Traffic shaping is a mechanism that alters the traffic characteristics of a stream of cells on a connection to achieve better network efficiency, while meeting the QoS objectives, or to ensure conformance at a subsequent interface. Traffic shaping must maintain cell sequence integrity on a connection. Shaping modifies traffic characteristics of a cell flow with the consequence of increasing the mean Cell Transfer Delay.

TS. Transport Stream: One of two types of streams produced by the MPEG-2 Systems layer. The Transport Stream consists of 188-byte packets and can contain multiple programs.

TTCN. Tree and Tabular Combined Notation: The internationally standardized test script notation for specifying abstract test suites. TTCN provides a notation that is independent of test methods, layers, and protocol.

U

UBR. Unspecified Bit Rate: UBR is an ATM service category that does not specify traffic-related service guarantees. Specifically, UBR does not include the notion of a per-connection negotiated bandwidth. No numerical commitments are made with respect to the cell loss ratio experienced by a UBR connection, or as to the cell transfer delay experienced by cells on the connection.

UDP. User Datagram Protocol: This protocol is part of the TCP/IP protocol suite and provides a means for applications to access the connectionless features of IP. UDP operates at Layer 4 of the OSI reference model and provides for the exchange of datagrams without acknowledgements or guaranteed delivery.

UME. UNI Management Entity: The software residing in the ATM devices at each end of the UNI circuit that implements the management interface to the ATM network.

Unassigned Cells. A cell identified by a standardized virtual path identifier (VPI) and a virtual channel identifier (VCI) value, which has been generated and does not carry information from an application using the ATM Layer service.

UNI. User-Network Interface: An interface point between ATM end users and a private ATM switch, or between a private ATM switch and the public carrier ATM network; defined by physical and protocol specifications per the ATM Forum UNI documents. The standard adopted by the ATM Forum to define connections between users or end stations and a local switch.

Unicasting. The transmit operation of a single PDU by a source interface where the PDU reaches a single destination.

UPC. Usage Parameter Control: Usage Parameter Control is defined as the set of actions taken by the network to monitor and control traffic, in terms of traffic offered and validity of the ATM connection, at the end-system access. Its main purpose is to protect network resources from malicious as well as unintentional misbehavior, which can affect

the QoS of other, already established connections by detecting violations of negotiated parameters and taking appropriate actions.

Uplink. Represents the connectivity from a border node to an upnode.

Upnode. The node that represents a border node's outside neighbor in the common peer group. The upnode must be a neighboring peer of one of the border node's ancestors.

UT. Upper Tester: The representation in ISO/IEC 9646 of the means of providing, during test execution, control and observation of the upper service boundary of the IUT, as defined by the chosen Abstract Test Method.

UTOPIA. Universal Test and Operations Interface for ATM: Refers to an electrical interface between the TC and PMD sublayers of the PHY layer.

UTP. Unshielded Twisted Pair: A cable having one or more twisted pairs, but with no shield per pair.

V

VBR. Variable bit rate: An ATM Forum–defined service category that supports variable bit rate data traffic with average and peak traffic parameters.

VC. A communications channel that provides for the sequential unidirectional transport of ATM cells.

VCC. Virtual Channel Connection: A concatenation of VCLs that extends between the points where the ATM service users access the ATM layer. The points at which the

ATM cell payload is passed to, or received from, the users of the ATM Layer (that is, a higher layer or an ATM-entity) for processing signify the endpoints of a VCC. VCCs are unidirectional.

VCI. Virtual Channel Identifier: A unique numerical tag as defined by a 16-bit field in the ATM cell header that identifies a virtual channel, over which the cell is to travel.

VCL. Virtual Channel Link: A means of unidirectional transport of ATM cells between the point where a VCI value is assigned and the point where that value is translated or removed.

VCO. Voltage Controlled Oscillator: An oscillator whose clock frequency is determined by the magnitude of the voltage presented at its input. The frequency changes when the voltage changes.

VD. Virtual Destination. See VS/VD.

VF. Variance Factor: VF is a relative measure of a cell rate margin normalized by the variance of the aggregate cell rate on the link.

Virtual Channel Switch. A network element that connects VCLs. It terminates VPCs and translates VCI values. It is directed by Control Plane functions and relays the cells of a VC.

Virtual Path Switch. A network element that connects VPLs. It translates VPI (not VCI) values and is directed by Control Plane functions. It relays the cell of the VP.

VLAN. Virtual local-area network: Work stations connected to an intelligent device that provides the capabilities to define LAN membership.

VP. Virtual Path: A unidirectional logical association or bundle of VCs.

VPC. Virtual Path Connection: A concatenation of VPLs between Virtual Path Terminators (VPTs). VPCs are unidirectional.

VPI. Virtual Path Identifier: An 8-bit field in the ATM cell header that indicates the virtual path over which the cell should be routed.

VPL. Virtual Path Link: A means of unidirectional transport of ATM cells between the point where a VPI value is assigned and the point where that value is translated or removed.

VPT. Virtual Path Terminator: A system that unbundles the VCs of a VP for the independent processing of each VC.

VS. Virtual Scheduling: Virtual scheduling is a method to determine the conformance of an arriving cell. The virtual scheduling algorithm updates a Theoretical Arrival Time (TAT), which is the "nominal" arrival time of the cell assuming that the active source sends equally spaced cells. If the actual arrival time of a cell is not "too" early relative to the TAT, then the cell is conforming. Otherwise, the cell is non-conforming.

VS. Virtual Source. See VS/VD.

VS/VD. Virtual Source/Virtual Destination: An ABR connection can be divided into two or more separately controlled ABR segments. Each ABR control segment, except the first, is sourced by a virtual source. A virtual source implements the behavior of an ABR source endpoint. Backward RM-cells received by a virtual source are removed from the connection. Each ABR control segment, except the last, is terminated by a virtual destination. A virtual destination assumes the behavior of an ABR destination endpoint. Forward RM-cells received by a virtual destination are turned around and not forwarded to the next segment of the connection.

VTOA. Voice and Telephony Over ATM: The ATM Forum voice and telephony over ATM service interoperability specifications address three applications for carrying voice over ATM networks: desktop (or LAN services), trunking (or WAN services), and mobile services.

W–Z

WAN. Wide-area network: This is a network that spans a large geographic area relative to the office and campus environment of a LAN (local-area network). WAN is characterized by having much greater transfer delays due to the laws of physics.

XDF. Xrm Decrease Factor: An ABR service parameter, XDF controls the decrease in ACR associated with Xrm. It is a power of 2 in the range [0, 1].

Xrm. An ABR service parameter, Xrm limits the number of forward RM-cells that can be sent in the absence of received backward RM-cells. The range is 0 to 255.

M